INTERNATIONAL NEGOTIATION IN THE TWENTY-FIRST CENTURY

France, argues Alain Plantey, owes its survival as much to its skills in diplomacy as to its force of arms. Relations between States are more complex and diverse than ever – especially with the emergence of new actors on the international stage. Traditional bilateral diplomacy must coexist with multilateral conferences and multipartite institutions. International negotiation addresses an unprecedented range of subjects, and the stakes grow ever higher. The maintenance of peace and the avoidance of conflict, by deterrence or otherwise, still depend on international negotiation – but so does, now, the struggle to regulate the future uses of the planet's resources and to ensure that the world's response to increasingly potent and widespread threats such as nuclear destruction and terrorism is based on order, equity and cooperation.

More than ever, it is vital that those engaged in international negotiation understand how it works. This magisterial work, written by a former Justice of the Conseil d'Etat, a former ambassador, a former President of the French Academy and one of the co-authors of General de Gaulle's Constitution of 1958, offers a complete analysis of its principles, techniques and practice, explaining its historical perspective and the role it plays in the present international context, and arguing passionately for its continued adaptation in the future.

Alain Plantey is Doyen de la section Législation, Droit public et Jurisprudence at the French Academie des Sciences Morales et Politiques.

The University of Texas at Austin Studies in Foreign and Transnational Law

General Editors: Professor Sir Basil Markesinis and Dr Jörg Fedtke

INTERNATIONAL NEGOTIATION IN THE TWENTY-FIRST CENTURY

Alain Plantey

Translation by Frances Meadows

Routledge·Cavendish
Taylor & Francis Group

First published 2007 by Cavendish Publishing

Transferred to digital printing 2007
by Routledge-Cavendish
2 Park Square, Milton Park, Abingdon, Oxon, OX14 4RN

Simultaneously published in the USA and Canada
by Routledge-Cavendish
270 Madison Ave, New York NY 10016

Routledge-Cavendish is an imprint of the Taylor & Francis Group, an informa business

© 2007 Alain Plantey

Typeset in Sabon by Newgen Imaging Systems (P) Ltd, Chennai, India

British Library Cataloguing in Publication Data
A catalogue record for this book is available from the British Library

Library of Congress Cataloging in Publication Data
A catalog record for this book has been requested

ISBN10: 1–84472–049–7 (hbk)
ISBN10: 0–415–44347–4 (pbk)

ISBN13: 978–1–84472–049–1 (hbk)
ISBN13: 978–0–415–44347–0 (pbk)

Contents

Foreword |

Any publishing house anywhere in the world would be honoured to secure the publication rights on a book written by Ambassador Alain Plantey. The University of Texas at Austin is thus, understandably, both honoured and delighted that the author of this book has allowed us to include it in its new series *Studies in Foreign and Transnational Law*. For, as the summary of his life and work (given on the book flaps) suggests, his has been a rich and varied life at the centre of French politics, diplomacy, judicial and intellectual life. For Alain Plantey has served his country as a judge in France's most senior Administrative Court, an Ambassador-at-large, representing General de Gaulle (with whom he started working soon after they met at the end of the War), as an author (with more than twenty books and scores of legal articles on varied topics to his name), as a draftsman of France's famous 1958 Constitution, as a Member (Fellow as we would say in Anglo-American parlance) of the Academy of the Moral and Political Sciences, subsequently its President and, eventually, President of the entire *Institute of France* (the umbrella organisation of the Five Academies). The variety of his interests is breathtaking, equalled only by the excellence achieved while cultivating them and the honours he has received from many countries and varied quarters of social life. All come together in this highly original book on international negotiation.

There is no law of any kind without negotiation and this is especially true of public international law. This is why, in a series of books on international law, there is place for a work devoted to negotiation – understood, as its distinguished author said in the preface to the first edition, as a method, a style and an art, and studied from the perspective of the lessons of history and experience. This then is a book about means rather than ends, process rather than content.

Negotiation is sometimes taken for granted – wrongly so because without it there would be no international relations, trade or cooperation, no *détente*, no alliances, no international law, no machinery for dispute resolution and no peace and stability. Countries that flourish – the history of the author's own country offers an excellent illustration – owe their survival and much of their prestige as much to the skills of their diplomacy as to the force of arms. So this book takes us to the borderland between law and political science. The history, philosophy and techniques of international negotiation make for fascinating, and important, study – to my knowledge a task rarely, if ever, undertaken until Ambassador Plantey addressed the subject and brought to it the breadth of his historical scholarship, legal expertise, broader culture and insight.

This book first saw the light of day in 1994. By 2002 successive reprints had run out and the accelerated pace of international change was such that a new edition was launched. Four years later, the pace of change has remained as rapid as it ever was and this has called for substantive rewriting of parts of the French edition and not just a well-overdue translation of this book so as to make it available to an English-speaking public. This pace throws into sharp focus the need for international relations to adapt by negotiating. It also prompts a second observation: very many of the trends predicted by the author when this book first appeared in 1994 – for instance, concerning terrorism, ideological confrontation and global environmental issues – have (alas) been borne out, sometimes with alarming accuracy. His underlying analysis of the factors and considerations that influence negotiation, however, has not changed.

At the beginning, the author reminds us, the methods of diplomacy were fashioned out of those of trade. Even now, the links between commerce and political power remain strong and, as the author illustrates, some of the most critical and controversial negotiations of modern times take place within the framework of the World Trade Organisation (WTO). On a more general level, every negotiation is an exchange, the subject of which has a different value to each party.

The classic model of bilateral negotiations between plenipotentiaries has to some degree been overtaken. The challenges facing international society in the new century are of a radically different order: they are global, urgent and potentially devastating. The international community must organise and negotiate collective responses to the threat posed by weapons of mass destruction, and collective regulation of the use of the planet's scarce resources. There is no time to lose. The focus in future will be on prevention, limitation and security. Solidarity, not only between nations but other parties with a stake, must be negotiated, whether in summits or international conferences or organisations, official or otherwise. From the United Nations down, the primary function of international organisations is to serve as fora for negotiation, in which States can execute their manoeuvres, and, as the author shows, the traditional model is proving adaptable.

It is a curious paradox that, in parallel with the spread of democracy, State sovereignty – the traditional framework of diplomatic negotiation – is being eroded by the expansion of multinational corporations, the Internet, the mass media and the increasing role of civil society and non-governmental organisations. Also, an increasing proportion of what might be described as traditional diplomatic negotiation takes the form of participation in multilateral conferences and institutions rather than bilateral 'single-issue' diplomacy. That said, as the author shows, the nation-state has retained its character as the primary actor in international relations. 'Summit' negotiations are ever more frequent, and the author suggests that the increasing rigidity of international organisational procedures may even prompt a revival of bilateral diplomacy.

Change has been particularly dramatic within the European Union, both in terms of its expansion and internal functioning. The author has thus substantially revised the chapter on the European Union to take account of developments, including the referenda held on the draft 'Constitution', which took place as the laborious task of the translation of his book was in mid-stream. Some of the patterns and structures of negotiation emerging within Europe are highly innovative.

The history of traditional diplomacy, and therefore of diplomatic negotiation, began in Europe. This, coupled with the fact that the book was originally written in French and aimed at a French readership – inevitably one would suggest – gave it a certain Eurocentric flavour. Some (but not all) of this has survived the process of translation and updating. But the universality of the message of the book has not, thereby, been diminished. References to European history have been retained, and sometimes expanded, wherever they seemed to offer powerful illustrations of phenomena still relevant today, both in Europe and elsewhere. Others sections or references, more obscure or more appropriate to a purely French audience, have been eliminated. This has been true of many older French language footnotes, despite their intrinsic value to pure researchers, and this has been done so in order to make the book more approachable to a much wider readership. Thus, students of international relations, diplomats, lawyers, politicians and, indeed, anyone engaged in international business should find a wealth of material for reflection in its pages.

The book is divided into four main sections. Part I deals with 'Diplomatic Negotiation'. Part II covers 'Institutional Negotiation'. Part III looks at 'Prospective Negotiation' while Part IV looks at 'Negotiation as A Political Art'. The traditional presentation of French academic textbooks is that of numbered paragraphs, with key ideas in italics and cross-references to paragraphs rather than pages, as well as the usual index. In order to preserve the essential integrity of Ambassador Plantey's book, and simplify the already complex task of translation of such a highly nuanced work, we have chosen to retain this formula. There is also a substantial bibliography, which the author has kindly updated for this edition. Together, these should help researchers, young or not so young, to build on this innovative work.

A work of such size, breadth, complexity and style does not lend itself easily to translation. In addition, the author of this Foreword has had the privilege of working with the author of this book for many years now and has developed a healthy respect for Ambassador Plantey's linguistic abilities, attention to nuances and fastidiousness. For a long time finding a translator that could rise to such a challenge felt like an unrealisable dream, and finding the funds to back such an operation remained for long a near impossibility.

Happily, the School of Law of The University of Texas at Austin, thanks to the cosmopolitan interests of its then Dean (and now President of the entire University) Professor William Powers Jr., decided to launch its new law series, and my recommendation that this opus magnum be included in the series was accepted. With Professor Powers 'on board', the financial support of the M. D. Anderson Foundation of Houston soon followed, which was given with the imagination and grace which so often characterises the gestures of selfless benefactors. No doubt, the most effective advocate for this gesture was my good friend Mr. Gibson Gayle, formerly Managing Partner of the great American law firm of Fulbright and Jaworski. It is most appropriate that his interest in strengthening American–French relations should be recorded by us as it has already been acknowledged by the

French State which made him a *Chevalier de la Legion d'honneur* for his part in setting up the website of translated cases of the three French Supreme Courts and, most recently, an imaginative programme of Judicial Fellowships that will allow young French judges to spend some time in the United States familiarising themselves with some of the best achievements of American law.

Ambassadors, deans, institutional benefactors and senior attorneys thus came together in order to ensure the appearance of this book in the English language. And what brought them all together was, first and foremost, the open-mindedness one finds in persons of culture and intellectual curiosity quick and able to recognise something good when they see it. But their efforts were also supported by the belief they all share in strengthening American–European relations in general, and American–French relations in particular. For, despite occasional ups and downs in their international relations, the cultural and political links between France and the United States are not only old but also valuable to both and must therefore be kept in good repair. This book fits in this wider effort, and for its author – committed as he is to the idea of give and take, so implicit in the notion itself of negotiation – it must be seen as a living embodiment of a life's beliefs.

Yet all these good intentions, great scholarship and wish to innovate would still not have sufficed to bring this project to fruition if it were not for Frances Meadows. She may be here thanked last but never did the expression 'last but by no means least' have more significance than in this instance. For her unique background, scholarly as well as practical, has made her 'sensitive' to the culture and language of two great nations. Above all, her success has not deprived her of her 'humanity'. For though an acclaimed professional translator, she immediately recognised the intellectual merits of this project and agreed to undertake the extremely onerous task of translating this work on terms which almost amounted to a gift of her valuable time.

To Ambassador Plantey we thus owe a great, indeed unique, work, and to Frances Meadows we are grateful for a most readable rendition of a text written in a language which for many has come to be the embodiment of elegance and style.

Sir Basil Markesinis QC, FBA,
Corresponding Member of the Institut de France

Abbreviations

1 – International institutions

ADI	Haye Academy of International Law
CJEC	Court of Justice of the European Community
CSCE	Commission on Security and Cooperation in Europe
ECSC	European Coal and Steel Community
EEC	European Economic Community
EHRC	European Human Rights Commission
EU	European Union
GATT	General Agreement on Tariffs and Trade
ICJ	International Court of Justice
ILO	International Labour Organisation
LN	League of Nations
OECD	Organisation for Economic Cooperation and Development
OPEC	Organisation of the Petroleum Exporting Countries
OSCE	Organisation for Security and Cooperation in Europe
UN	United Nations
UNCTAD	United Nations Conference on Trade and Development
UNESCO	United Nations Educations, Scientific and Cultural Organisation
UNGA	United Nations General Assembly
UNITAR	United Nations Institute for Training and Research
WEN	Western European Union
WTO	World Trade Organisation

2 – Bibliography

AEAP	*Annuaire européen d'administration publique*
AFDI	*Annuaire français de droit international*
AJNU	*Annuaire juridique des Nations Unies*
CDE	*Cahiers de droit européen*
CMLR	*Common Market Law Review*
CNRS	*Centre national de la recherche scientifique*
ELR	*European Law Reviews*
JCMS	*Journal of Common Market Studies*
OJEC	*Official Journal of the European Community*
RCADI	*Recueil des cours de l'Académie de droit international*

Rec.	*Recueil officiel des jugements*
RGDIP	*Revue générale de droit international public*
RMC	*Revue du Marché commun*
RTDE	*Revue trimestrielle de droit européen*
SFDI	*Société française de droit international*

1 – For every nation, history is an adventure. Each one confronts a succession of uncertainties, dramas and sometimes grave risks, the worst of which for mankind is that, to this day, the survival of whole populations, especially in the developing world, remains threatened. The forces that unite nations and set them against each other have been rooted for centuries in basic needs or religious ideals. National sentiment is now giving them fresh impetus. From the time nations first came into existence as stable and organised entities, their relations have often been marked by distrust, fear and sometimes hostility, with no people willing to sacrifice its interests to those of the others, unless constrained to do so by threat, force or necessity.

2 – This holds true especially for States founded on the model fashioned in Europe five centuries ago out of the principles of Roman law, of *the State as the legal and organisational embodiment of a group of people with stable and lasting control over a territory. The model is still valid in an international society made up of a juxtaposition of States, showing ever-increasing fragmentation because their numbers are not limited by any rule or proportion.*

3 – In this sense at least, there is nothing immutable about the way the world is divided. Numerous ideologies and religions have aspired to outgrow the phenomenon of the nation, and some of them have, up to a point, succeeded. The pressures weighing upon the State structure, both internally and externally, are heavy.[1] Nor is their growth at an end, judging, for example, by the problems contemporary States must face either because they are too small or too large, or because they are multi-ethnic.

Alongside the power of States, if not in opposition to it, are the private interest or pressure groups whose strength and dynamism have launched them onto the international stage.

4 – No matter how much more organised international life becomes, and irrespective of the strengthening of relations between peoples, the global expansion of trade and the effects of universalist ideologies, the phenomenon of the State remains an absolute contemporary reality. Even the most recent political developments and diplomatic negotiations among the nations of Europe have this as their legal frame of reference. Leaders of revolutionary movements, too, clothe their strivings in the banner of a patriotism or 'separatism' inherited from a

---

1 W. FRIEDMANN: *Théorie générale du droit*, Paris, LGDJ, 1965.

tradition that is foreign, if not contrary, to their ideals. Nations that have recently won their freedom not only adopt all the usual signs of sovereignty – flag, anthem, currency and embassies – but, before they have even defined their policies and secured the foundations of their independence, they also practise a form of nationalism that today seems excessive, aggressive and outmoded. (see *1866*)

The past century confirmed the sometimes explosive strength of ethnic ties: the dissolution of the Soviet Union gave place to the Russian nation, which reappeared in its original form and with its traditional symbols. (see *339*)

5 – The newer the nation-state, the more easily it appears to take offence: this is because it derives its legitimacy from the struggle for emancipation, especially in the eyes of the people who had previously been dominated. The difficulties of mere existence are no obstacle: countries must assert their nationalism in order to survive, in the words of Luis Etcheverria, and also in order to grow. Léopold Senghor observed that, to have the strength to assimilate European culture, they must first be true to their own.

6 – The division of territories, artificial though it is, and the attachments of populations, even when contested, are fundamental to international life just as they are to animal biology. Law and practice will usually question these divisions only as a last resort, but instead extend their limits outwards even over air and sea.[2] (see *652*)

In spite of all the problems posed by European State frontiers, the principle of maintaining the status quo was established without any real difficulty at the start of the Helsinki Conference on Security and Cooperation in Europe in 1973, after which some frontier modifications were agreed upon (in 1995, 1996 and 1997). (see *76, 2273*)

The Balkan area of Europe, Central Asia and Central Africa are examples of areas where it is becoming increasingly clear that border disputes have huge potential to explode and to jeopardise the normal diplomatic process.

7 – Boundary delimitation provides a legal frame of reference for States engaged in dividing populations, resources, the means of production, authority and influence, even where there are disputes going back for centuries. The Europe of the Treaties of Westphalia (1648) is still so much alive that the liberating effects of the euro are limited to those States of the European Union that decided to choose it as their common currency. There are many zones whose status is indeterminate, like the Caspian Sea, that are the subject of acrimonious negotiations over their rich resources. (see *76, 637*)

8 – The fate of the nation-state is far from being sealed, as it rests on the living feelings, fears, pride, ambitions and hatreds that embody the power of popular imagination even within the confined area of the old Europe. In spite of a Council of Europe resolution in 1974 and attempts on the part of the Community, no

---

2 H. RUIZ-FABRI: 'Maîtrise du territoire et rôle international de l'Etat', *Revue des sciences morales et politiques*, 2000. D. BARBERIS: 'Les liens juridiques entre l'Etat et son territoire', *AFDI*, 1999, p. 132.

European government has yet judged the time right to allow diplomatic negotiation between neighbouring regions or to go as far as functional integration. (see *614, 2310, 2321*)

The European Union itself makes reference to 'national identities' in the Amsterdam Treaty of 1997, while at the same time its territory has been implicitly enlarged, notably as a result of the reunification of Germany in 1990.[3]

Notwithstanding this, modern civilisation has a tendency to underestimate the strength of tribal or religious attachments. Spread across the territories of several States and without regard for their frontiers, there are some dependent peoples that have preserved their culture, refusing any political subservience and sometimes living in a state of permanent revolt.

For many years to come, citizens will continue to look to the State to reconcile freedom with security and to make and enforce the law. (see *2301*)

9 – In an environment still so poorly organised and so unfamiliar with ethics as international society, *no entity will obtain the respect of others unless it is in a position to demand it* – that is, unless it fulfils its conditions, both legal and factual. This is why a common legal denominator has come to exist, based on a kind of reciprocal acquiescence, that expresses not only a nation's capacity to be recognised by others as organised and autonomous, but also the capacity of its authorities to assume the defence of its interests and responsibility for its conduct. That denominator is sovereignty, defined in both diplomatic practice and international law.[4] (see *606*)

10 – A territory with resources, a population with strength in numbers and a constituted authority with policies:[5] these are the three components of the legal and political entity that today we call the State, which faces both inwards towards its own government and outwards towards other States. From this derives the principle that it is through the State that the interests of nations and their ideals can be given due consideration at an international level, even including universal ideals such as respect for mankind and its environment, solidarity between nations and peace. (see *2318*)

Private sector companies, even the powerful ones, do not operate at the same level, except where their activities are bound up with national strategy, usually in investment or energy production.

11 – Even between those ethnic and tribal groups whose traditions and aspirations bind them together into nations and thereby set them apart from other nations, there has always been fear and prejudice, jealousy and resentment. *Men are brought closer or driven asunder by contradictory forces that change down the ages, depending on their interests and sentiments.* (see *2304*)

12 – Any State that follows its own course must expect reaction from others, since there is no reason, a priori, why their policies should coincide with its own in all

---

3 *Institutions européennes et identités nationales*, Brussels, Bruylant, 1998.
4 C. de VISSCHER: *Théories et réalités en droit international public*, Paris, Pedone, 1960.
5 R. ARON: *Paix et guerre entre les nations*, Paris, Calmann-Lévy, 1962.

respects and over long periods. Faced with an uncertain future, therefore, and having made an assessment of its capabilities, a State must marshal and maintain all the means at its disposal to achieve the objectives it has decided upon. As General de Gaulle proclaimed, to play an international role it is necessary to exist by oneself, in oneself and on one's own land.[6]

The disintegration of certain countries following ethnic, political, cultural or religious conflicts has led to the questioning of the traditional foundations of the State: a delimited territory, a defined population and a real authority. This has introduced a new element of unpredictability into diplomacy: territorial dislocation, uncontrolled populations and disputed governments, all of them traps for the negotiator. (see *1616*)

13 – Establishing order and harmony among peoples is a magnificent enterprise in which no wartime or peacetime leader has ever succeeded: nations have either dominated or been dominated. Only very late, shortly before its own break-up, did the Roman Empire start to practise the assimilation or unification of races and individuals on a basis of equality and yet it is still held up as the most advanced legal form of political supremacy. Later, Rome in its turn faced submission and ruin.

14 – A nation that enjoys self-determination does so not only through internal politics; it can only succeed by asserting its independence in its dealings with others. If a people fails to invest the effort required to be worthy of national sovereignty, if it does not assume the responsibility of exercising its freedom of choice and defending its positions, its interests and its ideals, another will soon appear and impose its will. Mere possession of means, resources or even power does not guarantee they will be used: there must also be the will to use them.

Independence is not so much a position as an assertion of will; to invoke a right is to exercise it. (see *616*)

15 – The life of any nation cannot be frozen at a given point in time. Its relations with others follow their course, develop and change. The result is an unending series of actions and reactions, some of them imposed and some of them voluntary, all of which have to be accommodated and coordinated in arriving at a foreign policy. The means deployed and the actions taken in the service of that policy are the ingredients of diplomacy, understood as both the art and the science of relations between Sovereign States.[7]

16 – The modern era is characterised by the proliferation and complexity of relations and communications between nations, in other words by the development of diplomacy. Contrary to what is generally thought, diplomacy plays an increasingly important part in the future of each State: diplomatic decisions are usually taken, and sometimes also carried out, at the highest levels. (see *2325*)

---

6 C. de GAULLE: 'Discours de Dakar, 13 déc. 1959', in *Discours et messages*, III, p. 151: 'l'essentiel, pour jouer un rôle international, c'est d'exister par soi-même, en soi-même, chez soi'.

7 H. NICOLSON: *Diplomacy*, Oxford University Press, 1945.

Networks of influence, communication, cooperation and business create a virtual space expanding in line with the growth in the number and importance of dealings and exchanges they generate. Some of these networks are used for transferring funds, spreading slogans or disseminating ideologies that may be violent and contagious. Some of them, too, have substantial logistical underpinnings.[8] (see *3, 30, 1688, 1690, 1834, 1866*)

Many private enterprises and various other groups have also become fully fledged actors on the international scene, forming their own networks in a market where everything can be bought and sold, and almost anything can be negotiated. (see *397, 1821, 1995*)

17 – In the international arena as well as within the State, political ends are achieved by decisions and acts which, when combined together and directed towards an objective, constitute a manoeuvre.[9] Manoeuvres become more difficult, more fraught with risk, and sometimes more advantageous, as the rivalry between men and nations, interests and ideals, is stepped up.

Negotiation is one of the forms these relations between peoples and nations can take.

18 – It is advisable to refrain from value judgements about the principle of diplomatic action: it is a fact of political, economic and cultural life. Even a global government, if one existed, could not avoid the need to manoeuvre, albeit internally. Conflict does not always break out into open combat: it may also take the form of emulation, competition or dispute. It finds expression, too, in policies designed to ensure that a given interest will prevail, to avoid a danger, to achieve domination and even to establish a new and stable order.

There can be no solution to the problem of legitimacy in an environment where there is no common scale of values.

19 – In his *Nichomachean Ethics*, Aristotle identified the notion of the common good as the ultimate aim of life in any society. Man still shows the same obvious, and normal, desire to project his wishes, his concerns and his ambitions beyond himself and into the future. All living creatures manoeuvre in order to feed themselves, protect themselves and reproduce: the same is true for peoples.

20 – The collective existence of a nation, of society in general, expresses itself through its relations with others – relations which, while adapting to circumstances, are ordered around the constant themes of affirming its existence, expressing the need to protect itself against danger or threat and sometimes also conveying its willingness to resort to aggression in order to claim its rights. Human sciences can, or should, shed light on these dominant themes and explain how they function.

---

8 M. BONNEFOUS: 'Logique des réseaux, logique des territoires', *Défense nationale*, July 2001, p. 134. M. CASTELLS: *La Société en réseaux*, Paris, Fayard, 1998.

9 A. PLANTEY: *De la politique entre les Etats. Principes de diplomatie*, Paris, Pedone, 1992, p. 29.

21 – This is what is meant by diplomatic manoeuvre. It should not be understood in a pejorative sense, as it is an essential element in the political game, setting out to achieve objectives external to its author, using factors over which he has no control. Manoeuvre is an expression of will and shares the same characteristics: it might be free, purposeful and broad in its ambitions, or on the contrary constrained, indecisive and feeble. (see *1870*)

22 – There is no place for illusions here. International competition grows relentlessly as civilisation becomes more technically adept, and no nation can exist in isolation from it: a State that does not manoeuvre will be dominated by one that does. All one can reasonably hope is that their policies will be aimed at conciliating rivalries rather than aggravating antagonisms.

Not to act is to subordinate oneself to the chosen objectives of another. (see *198*)

23 – Domestic opinion is generally not much interested in diplomacy. Civil servants operate within an administrative system that remains, along with sport, one of the refuges of nationalism. In almost all countries, something dramatic has to happen before foreign events have an effect on domestic politics. (see *2626*)

24 – Likewise, the diplomatic apparatus and its workings are misunderstood and undervalued. This is the case with Ministries of Foreign Affairs, their structures and officials, and the same applies to the methods they use to obtain intelligence and do their work. And, naturally, it is also the case with negotiation – how it is prepared, how it is conducted, the background to it and the consequences it can have.

25 – A wealth of original literature has been devoted to these subjects, particularly in French, from the time of the monarchy. Today, though, many studies limit themselves to the legal aspects of treaties and international agreements. As to the study of international relations, not much space is devoted to international negotiation in the pure sense, in isolation from the underlying politics. At the same time, there has been a veritable flowering of research on international issues, especially in collectively authored works.[10]

26 – Alongside the study of the workings of the law of nations and the unfolding of the great conflicts of history, there is place for the study of the major strands in relations between States: competition and hostility, affinity and alliance, organisation and anticipation. This is a subject of great importance. The geopolitical significance of major diplomatic manoeuvres has far-reaching implications both for the history of nations and their future. France and other European nations owe their existence as much to skill in diplomacy as to military force; this is true of the majority of modern States in their present form.[11]

---

10 S. HOFFMANN: *Contemporary Theory in International Relations*, Englewood Cliffs, Prentice Hall, 1960. F. MOUSSA: *Diplomatie contemporaine*, Geneva, Carnegie Endowment, 1966. J.-B. DUROSELLE: 'L'évolution des formes de la diplomatie et son effet sur la politique des Etats', in *La Politique étrangère et ses fondements*, Paris, Colin, 1954, p. 325.

11 M. MERLE: *Bilan des relations internationales contemporaines*, Paris, Economica, 1966.

27 – Some of the most important events of our own time can also be attributed to negotiation. As an example, despite some exaggerated criticism, it must be recognised that the results of the Yalta Conference – the wiping out of several old nations and the lasting division of Europe into two zones of influence controlled from outside – have had a deep and lasting impact not only on Europe but on the whole world. Until 1989, the results of that negotiation had withstood the severest tests of the Cold War as well as of the *Détente* which began in 1966. It produced, simultaneously, a state of potential rivalry, permanent liaison and – viewed objectively – solidarity between the United States and the former USSR, which shared a common interest in keeping the continent divided. More recently, on the political level, the reunification of Germany resulted from a diplomatic agreement in 1990 between Bonn and Moscow.

Namibia, too, owes its independence to a process organised by the United Nations that produced the Brazzaville Protocol of 13 December 1988.

28 – The existence of spheres of influence arouses hostile reactions on the part of all peoples concerned for their independence. For them, diplomacy is more important now than ever before. The progress towards European unification is due to the sustained negotiations undertaken by the countries of the West. True, these bargaining processes do not always bring rapid success, as can be seen from the unfolding of events in the Near East. But an understanding of their principles and methods is a necessary precondition if they are to succeed. (see *625, 2250*)

29 – As with private enterprise, a State's government is open to the opportunities as well as the constraints of outside influence. This can be seen particularly clearly in the growing pattern of continuous and wide-ranging negotiation within the European Union. The same is true, to a lesser extent, for all continents.

Much of the interplay of investments, networks, trade, services and influence is carried on without regard for frontiers, and this contributes to the spread of the process of international negotiation, while at the same time putting State power in a different perspective. (see *1680, 1815, 1968, 2202, 2302*)

30 – With the welfare of nations depending more and more on their relations and exchanges with each other, no political leader, civil servant or businessman can afford to ignore the external dimension of the issues he deals with. *The quality of a State's diplomacy is a major factor in its competitiveness.*

31 – The study of diplomacy is thus interesting on both scientific and educational grounds, to permit the relationship between the forces at play to be analysed, as well as their combined effects, and also to educate political leaders, diplomats, soldiers and anyone else in a high position of responsibility in the public and private domains.

32 – It is not enough to explain history. Lessons must be learned from it for the future, in an age when, more than at any other time, international relations resemble a mass of intersecting manoeuvres, meetings and dealings with no readily identifiable guiding principles. This is the approach Western countries take to the very severe challenges presented by the problems of emerging and developing

countries, the persistent crises in the planet's many areas of high tension, the disorder in monetary systems and the rise in piracy and terrorism. (see *334, 1678, 1706, 1873*)

33 – The right path is not always easy to find, and initiatives may cost both time and effort. Attempts to assess the situation may prove more or less haphazard as the picture changes and unexpected delays occur. One thing is certain: *diplomacy is not best served by improvisation. Even when they are motivated by generosity and enthusiasm, relations between princes and peoples must be conceived and carried out with due regard to passions and interests, enmities and calculations.*[12]

34 – The best statesman has the ability, based on both instinct and reason, to manage forces that are beyond his control while at the same time keeping his objective in view, and the capacity to define, carry out and even to impose a policy until it achieves its goal, in spite of the sometimes inextricable complexities of the diplomatic configuration of the time. (see *2327*)

35 – Cardinal de Richelieu, Prime Minister under Louis XIII of France, was one of the first to understand the advantage to States of carrying on continuing negotiations, provided these were conducted with prudence:[13] each partner becomes aware of the intentions of the others, and finds the right moment and the right means to assert its own interests. No one has anything to lose from such contacts, if they are pursued with discretion and dignity.

36 – Subject to exceptions (mainly war), diplomatic relations between modern nations follow their course uninterrupted: wide-ranging and continuous, they allow a fabric of exchanges to be woven that creates solid and stable ties. The institution of permanent diplomatic representation enables certain envoys to be entrusted with a mission to communicate in the name of a Head of State, to represent him and in some cases enter into binding commitments with another State on his behalf.

37 – Diplomacy is not to be confused with the actions of ambassadors: *international dealings today are carried on at every level and in every sphere of activity, sometimes unhurriedly and without ostentation, at other times in the heat of tension and anxiety, as when major legal disputes are about to be decided, or when conflict threatens to break out.* The role of ambassadors remains important, however, in providing the framework for foreign relations, even those involving private business.[14]

38 – States alone have the capacity to act at international level, for the time being at least. The traditional principle is that, except in cases of coercion, a State is bound only by those obligations it has accepted and by those rules it has recognised. (see *598*)

---

12 N. MACHIAVELLI: *Il principe*, 1513.
13 Cardinal de RICHELIEU: *Testament politique*, 6, Paris, Laffont, 1947, p. 28.
14 K. HAMILTON and R. LANGHORNE: *The Practice of Diplomacy*, New York, Routledge, 1998.

Nationhood still underlies all international negotiation. In reality, however, among the major actors on the diplomatic stage, neither the United States nor Russia, both of which have a vibrant tradition of patriotism, is in reality a 'nation-state'. (see *16, 76*)

39 – Neither the fact that sovereignty is not absolute, nor the respect for humanitarian ideals hostile to the cynicism of certain leaders, prohibits a State from devising its own foreign policy and applying it in its negotiations with the outside world. Military, economic or other disasters however reveal the unwisdom of allowing each nation to conduct its business in an arbitrary, unilateral manner; dialogue thus appears as the most suitable and equitable means of adapting the divergent or even contradictory forces in national policies.

40 – No people can be obliged to give up their independence, and yet the very progress of civilisation requires that they do.[15] To borrow a well-known axiom, it could be said that one country's sovereignty stops where another's begins. (see *605*)

41 – At the international level, in the absence of a legislature, government, judiciary or any system of collective organisation other than those that have been agreed, and in the absence even of the necessary willingness to sacrifice the national interest to the common interests of mankind, people and leaders must look to diplomacy to bring peace – or at least to ensure that the ends and means of different national policies are compatible with it. In the commercial world, people look to the negotiation of contracts to get business done. (see *1968*)

42 – Between two or more partners, diplomatic manoeuvre can lead to consultation and dialogue. This, for example, was the purpose ascribed to national foreign policy by the Conference on International Economic Cooperation (the 'North–South Conference'), whose final communiqué in December 1975 did not hide the risks created by the global economic situation, but sought to resolve them by the pursuit of international discussion on energy, raw materials, finance and other development-related problems.

43 – Negotiation transcends simple dialogue: it is the best way of leading parties towards an agreement. It embraces all the practices that permit the peaceful accommodation of the antagonistic or divergent interests of independent social groups or entities.[16] Where diplomatic manoeuvres are in logical and chronological conjunction they can have an exceptionally broad and vital effect on international society. [17]

44 – Knowledge of the customs, rules and spirit of diplomacy can serve the interests not only of a State, but also of the peaceful society of nations, in more than one way. Facts and know-how must be kept constantly up to date: *each international crisis changes the hierarchy among nations, the nature of their*

---

15 P. J. PROUDHON: *La Guerre et la Paix*, Paris, Rivière, 1927.
16 L. CONSTANTIN: *Psychologie de la négociation: économie privée*, Paris, PUF, 1971, p. 35.
17 H. RAIFFA: *The Art and Science of Negotiation*, Cambridge, Harvard University Press, 1982.

relations and the circuits in which they negotiate. The same holds true for banking, trade and the media.

45 – The history of diplomacy shows how the participants in, and the foundations of, international dialogue have altered over time, and how this has resulted in changes to its methods: International Dialogue has progressed from the policy of princes to that of peoples and nations, from the secrets and ceremonial of the chanceries to the frequent public sessions of numerous conferences and from compromises over borders to the establishment of powerful and lasting companies and institutions.

46 – When there are major interests at stake and difficult issues to be tackled, the consequences of agreement or conflict between States are more far reaching and more serious for their people. Negotiation is the means of turning these new trends to their best advantage, and preparing the way for a new world with its sights set on development and cooperation. (see *2192*)

47 – Preservation of the status quo is a reflex of the rich. Expansionist doctrines view the State as an entity in constant evolution, and the international community as a grouping undergoing radical transformation. Within thirty years, the United Nations has seen the number of its members almost quadruple, with many of these countries representing populations for whom present world conditions are intolerable.

48 – On a planet that has now been fully explored, and whose limited resources are fought over, the challenges for diplomacy in the traditional sense are only just beginning. The principles of order, balance and cohesion the world has aspired to since the classical era are being rejected, along with the rejection of Western ideologies. This calls into question aspects of modern civilisation in a way that affects the content of international relations as well as its practices. It elevates to a universal level debates and quarrels that used to be the domestic preserve of States. (see *2192*)

49 – The development of international negotiations shows how well State institutions can adapt, by sheer vitality and combativeness, to the evolving context in which they find themselves. But if scarcity of resources is not to lead to violence, all available means will have to be exploited to achieve voluntary agreement between nations, even on the simplest issues.

50 – Many States of course do not have the means to be truly independent. Some only manifest a deceptive outward appearance of it. Even so, they are starting to take part in the collective life of nations, where they derive additional strength from being in competition with the Great Powers. *The enlargement of the field of play brings with it an increase in contacts, relations and therefore confrontations.* (see *1965*)

51 – The opening up of international relations to newcomers has not only increased the complexity of diplomatic life and multiplied the chances of confrontation but also assumes that the methods of traditional European diplomacy, which used to be legal and formalistic in nature, will undergo a real regeneration. In an age of multipolarity, each country must exercise more and more vigilance over what the others are doing. (see *2190*)

52 – It so happens that this phenomenon is taking place under the threat of nuclear havoc. *The effect of this is not only to heighten the climate of psychological tension; it also raises the threshold above which the major powers might prefer war to negotiation and their neutralisation helps to give the others greater freedom of action.* To expand on one of Clausewitz's ideas, when force of arms is equal, what matters is the exercise of power, the political and diplomatic environment and the methods used for forecasting and negotiation.[18]

53 – For reasons that are not only technical,[19] the fabric of human societies is weaving itself more tightly, one of the consequences being that State sovereignty is increasingly restricted by bilateral or multilateral commitments. Negotiation thus becomes more useful as international relations become more complex: their increasing intensity carries the risk that contrasts will be thrown into sharper focus, divergences will multiply and confrontations deteriorate.

54 – Technical progress has multiplied communications and contacts between States, and with them the opportunity for conflict, not only on earth, in the air and on the seas but now, too, in the ocean depths and outer space. Population growth and the needs of societies to ensure their survival and development are opening up ever wider areas to competition: economy, culture, technology and the media – all sectors in which overindustrialised societies are acquiring the means to dominate and experiencing the need for cooperation. Businesses and private associations thus conclude contracts among themselves, from one country to another, often on matters that are of great interest to governments. (see *1500*)

Increasingly, the mass of international society depends on practices, regulations and contracts that governments often have no part in creating but are bound to respect. (see *1519, 2199, 2205*)

55 – Not a day goes by without problems arising that transcend national boundaries, or without more exchanges of all kinds between nations and across continents, or multinational or global forces intervening. The tide of anxiety rises still further in the face of uncertainties about the future, the discontent of those in poverty that sometimes turns to violence and the inadequacy of the existing system of regulation. For governments faced with the threat of anarchy and chaos, negotiation becomes an instrument for controlling hazards and crises. (see *2249, 2262*)

With the biggest, most profitable and dynamic markets having freed themselves from the constraints of borders, private business now comes within the ambit of international negotiation. The largest companies are permanently engaged in

18 C. von CLAUSEWITZ: *On War*, I, chapter 3.
19 A. SOREL: 'La diplomatie et le progrès', in *Essais d'histoire et de critique*, 1883, p. 281.

mutual dealings, even where these are carried on through their worldwide communications and financial networks. At this point the distinctions between diplomacy and trading become thoroughly blurred: the economy, too, is subject to the rules governing the exercise of power. (see *405, 1680*)

56 – As for the steadily growing number of international institutions, their true role is to provide a framework within which States can conduct their reciprocal exchanges of information, consultations, concerted actions and cooperation, using both technical and administrative means. This has prompted the development of an increasingly diversified intergovernmental administration within which multilateral negotiations take place, using new methods, still in a spirit of willingness and perseverance. State manoeuvres can therefore now extend further, taking on new forms and becoming institutionalised as public services, especially in Europe.

57 – Diplomacy is progressively extending into fields such as future planning, crisis prevention and development aid. The foreseeable needs of international society loom large in national policies, however uncertain these may be: governments are obliged to devote increasing attention to cooperating with each other, now and in the future. Within nations, as well as between them, *the art of negotiation is becoming more essential than ever to the exercise of power*. (see *2265*)

One major phenomenon, characteristic of the modern age, will have to be acknowledged: the appearance on the international scene of large private groups (banks, insurance companies, service providers, sellers of basic products, media and communications companies) whose flourishing trading activities become intertwined with those of States, especially in emerging and developing countries. *In a world of hard bargaining where national preferences count for less, the mutual influence of public and business dealings will force a reappraisal of international negotiation, both in terms of its principles and its methods*. (see *1806*)

58 – The extension of the scope of international negotiation means that its methods and objectives will vary. Diplomatic negotiation exists to regulate the respective relations of States, institutional negotiation offers ways for them to cooperate, and prospective negotiation sets the further objectives of order, fairness and cooperation among nations.

Thus begins the gradual process of diluting the cold rigour and cynical aims of that school of diplomatic realism usually known as *realpolitik*. (see *2305*)

Today's technological civilisation, sometimes called post-industrial, is built on the development of services that enhance and extend the activities of direct production. It will afford an increasing role for negotiation, seeing it as a means of maximising national, economic, technical and cultural benefits and keeping them in harmony, and a way of administering and governing international society as it advances. (see *1502, 2167, 2248*)

Part I:
Diplomatic Negotiation

59 – In the great encounters of history, it is difficult to know how much was due to art and how much to chance. Certainly, many victories can be put down to luck, but the essence of skill must surely be the ability to seize each opportunity and turn events to one's advantage. In a social order where any balance is relatively unstable, no one system can determine policy in the long term.

60 – In the course of any nation's existence, and of the coexistence of nations with each other, every day brings its share of events, and international life refashions itself into new and different configurations on an almost daily basis. In relations between nations, nothing is settled, no position can be taken for granted and no judgement is set in stone. It is unsafe to rely on any declaration that is not supported, or to treat any long-held claim as justified, or any undefended space as secure, or any non-combatant authority as legitimate. The art of politics and negotiation requires those who practise it to adapt constantly to changing circumstances. (see *219, 2248*)

The negotiator must be both willing and able. He must seek to explore fresh possibilities, renew the methods he uses and project strategies into the future. Diplomacy is all about new beginnings and the unending business of adapting to new realities: it is a never-ending struggle. (see *2398*)

The unpredictability of the international environment means that many negotiations produce precarious results. Gains are only made by behaving with moderation. Exaggerated demands are not consonant with good faith. (see *81*)

61 – Negotiation will obviously not have the same value or importance each time and everywhere. Defence and diplomacy will not mean the same for a country protected by its geographical situation as they will for one that is not so favoured. Insularity encourages isolationism and often xenophobia.

There is no diplomatic innovation without calculation and risk. Nor can there be any meaningful negotiation with a partner that lacks the means to put it into effect.

62 – As a form of relations between sovereign States, negotiation can encompass issues of the greatest magnitude as well as matters of detail. It ranges over war, business and science as well as diplomatic representation and consular protection. It implements the strategies of political leaders and can also be used to defend private interests. (see *1674*)

63 – For *the historian, the great peace conferences are as important as the great battles.* These conferences have a great impact, not only because they decide the fate of nations, sometimes against their will, but also because they are almost

invariably followed by more bloodshed. Within modern times, the Peace of Westphalia, the Congress of Vienna, the Treaty of Versailles and its ancillary agreements, and also the Yalta and Potsdam Conferences successively reassembled the pieces of the map of central Europe that had been torn apart by the adventures of leaders and the clash of nations, and, each time a new order was set up, it degenerated into fresh conflict. *The quality of the negotiations on such occasions may quite simply be measured by the length of the truce that followed.* (see **999**)

64 – Competition and rivalry do not exclude compromise and *entente*, which is itself only one of the factors at play in political manoeuvre. This is amply demonstrated by the nature of the relations between the two great powers for over forty years: the antagonists came together as partners as soon as the need arose to stabilise a world threatened by risks without precedent in history. (see *1761*)

In the early days, diplomacy was often only a matter of accommodating the pretensions and the sometimes sordid interests of a few sovereigns. Things are undoubtedly very different now.

Chapter I:
Diplomatic Negotiation and
the Themes of War

65 – *Trials are part of life, for States as well as people.* Birth is the first trauma. After that, every change causes apprehension, and every encounter carries an implied risk of opposition, competition or sometimes violence, even gratuitous violence. For Darwin, Nietzsche, Marx and even Freud, the *tao* of nature, history and mankind is struggle.[1]

66 – Competition between individuals and groups is the driving force behind the advance of humanity. It is neither possible nor desirable to reduce this diversity to uniformity. Experience has taught that groups wishing to be seen as unique or unitary, as is the case with certain dominant political parties, are not in fact homogeneous, and that the sorts of conflict they prevent in the outside world surface within their own internal workings. *Conflict permits society to remain in a state of constant evolution.*[2] (see *1879*)

67 – Peoples have been in confrontation from the beginning of time in their pursuit of incompatible goals,[3] whether over the search for the means of survival, the acquisition of territory or out of a need for political, religious or economic domination. They all, however, share the desire to steer clear of any venture which might endanger their own security.

68 – Some have viewed the age-old use of force for the resolution of disputes not just as an expression of human ambition but as a fundamental biological reality. Far from being a means for man to pursue his aims, they say, war in fact makes an instrument of him, because it plays a major role in regulating society and moving it forward. It does so, allegedly, by eliminating surplus populations and excesses of wealth, reinforcing group cohesion, satisfying the need to indulge in quarrels and the impulse to self-sacrifice, and acting as a spur to creation and to man's need to excel himself in all fields of human endeavour.[4]

69 – The truth of these observations can be seen more clearly at the international level than within State structures themselves. Throughout its entire existence,[5] the society of nations has been made up of the juxtaposition of entities whose mutual relations have been lively, changing and sometimes marked by conflict or anarchy. The delicate

1 A. MALRAUX: *La Tête d'obsidienne*, Paris, Gallimard, 1976, p. 194.
2 I. M. HAAS: *International conflict*, New York, Bobbs-Merrill, 1974.
3 R. ARON: *Paix et guerre entre les nations*, Paris, Calmann-Lévy, 1962.
4 G. BOUTHOUL: *Les guerres, éléments de polémologie*, Paris, Payot, 1951.
5 C. de VISSCHER: *Théories et réalités en droit international*, Paris, Pedone, 1960, p. 11.

features of this environment, which is not subject to any higher normative power, have evolved considerably in recent times, but at bottom they remain the same as they were when Machiavelli devised his first formula for contemporary diplomacy.

The more ancient the antagonisms, and the deeper and wider they extend, the more difficult it is to prevent and resolve disputes.

70 – *In an unregulated environment, the mere existence of others can constitute a danger if concern for security is ignored.* Wars arise out of exactly the same difficult environment in which normal relations are formed and normal exchanges take place between countries. Unless regulated by negotiation, it takes very little for it to be shaken by conflict.

Since the post-war illusion of the 1920s, security has reasserted itself over peace as the overriding concern.[6]

71 – King Frederick II of Prussia took the view that war was so profound a source of misery and so uncertain in outcome that no amount of reflection was too much before committing one's forces.[7] This did not prevent him, any more than other princes, from straying beyond the paths of peace in seeking solutions to his problems. Harmony between nations will not be achieved overnight, however much the survivors of each conflict hope that it will prove to be the last.

72 – The diplomat lives in hope that evolution will follow its inevitable course without overt violence between nations. He offers his contribution without excessive illusions, in the knowledge that *peace is more the result of the balance of power than of treaties and that this balance must constantly be readjusted.*

But he knows, too, that there will never be a finer opportunity to practise his art, nor a greater reason to succeed, than in times of confrontation.

Section 1: The confrontation of forces

73 – The place each nation occupies in relation to others, starting with its neighbours, is the product of a combination of strengths and weaknesses.[8] Surrounded as it is by rivals, each State will seek to impose its will and its glorious superiority and to avoid having to bow to the choices and interests of its adversaries. Competition favours change, while fears for security make the status quo seem preferable. The will to survive, whether by combat or negotiation, is influenced as much by national temperament as it is by circumstances.

74 – Serious disputes between human groupings have been decided by force, most often physical force, from time immemorial. Everyone's inclination is to take the law into his own hands, if he can. Kant said that the natural state was a state of war, always threatened if not actually declared.[9]

---

6 P. RENOUVIN and J. B. DUROSELLE: *Introduction à l'histoire des relations internationales*, Paris, Colin, 1964, p. 340.
7 FREDERICK II of PRUSSIA: *L'Anti-Machiavel*, Chapter 26.
8 H. MORGENTHAU: *Politics among Nations*, New York, Knopf, 1967.
9 E. KANT: *Essay on perpetual peace*, 1795.

Today more than ever, money and trade are factors of strength, often in the hands of private sector companies more active than many States.

Even now, wealth and power are the subject of sometimes fierce rivalries between nations.

75 – Social peace does not come about by itself; man instinctively desires it, but he also harbours the instinct to fight. It is not without significance that no one has yet succeeded in defining peace, except as a lasting period of absence of war, and that, bound up as it is with considerations both of reason and passion, the very concept generates huge controversy. *Some have sought to justify violence and war on grounds of religion, the quest for freedom and justice or as the instruments of law or humanitarian aid.*[10] (see *218, 1677*)

76 – *A nation's freedom depends on the relationships of power it establishes with others.* But at the same time, its identity and autonomy of will, and its ability to minimise the constraints imposed by others will also be factors in assessing these relationships.

The delimitation of a Sovereign State's territory and jurisdiction shows what it aspires to achieve by defence and negotiation, while at the same time leaving scope for others to exercise initiative. (see *609*)

Following the European Stability Pact (OSCE, Paris, 1995) and the measures adopted to give it effect, and also with a view to their subsequent adhesion to the European Union, Hungary, Poland, Romania, Slovakia and the Czech Republic entered into agreements in 1995, 1996 and 1997 on the respective limits of their territories.[11] (see *1330, 1417, 1692, 1833, 1884*)

Maritime and air boundaries have also been negotiated, in the Montego Bay Convention of 1982 and the Paris and Chicago Conventions of 1919 and 1944 respectively.

77 – It is because they have power, and exercise it, that States are the principal actors in international life. They unite when faced with a threat to this monopoly, such as nuclear terrorism. (see *372, 618*)

But with more and more actors on the world stage, the balance of power becomes more complex and changeable, as the play of antagonisms comes to depend on the internal affairs of a growing number of countries. (see *1676*)

The early part of the twenty-first century has been characterised by the simultaneous appearance of various competing power relationships. (see *1677, 1686, 1807*)

78 – All possible means have been used, down to plotting and revolution, to weaken a foreign government feared because of its weight or effectiveness. (see *637, 2250, 2312*)

If power is accepted as the prime mover in relations between nations, the first aim of diplomatic negotiation is to discipline its use and mitigate its effects: *society*

---

10 E. de VATTEL: *Le Droit des gens ou principes du droit naturel*, 1758, III, I.
11 G. HERCZEGH: 'Les accords récents conclu entre la Hongrie et ses voisins', *AFDI*, 1996, p. 255.

cannot exist if the different forces at play within it cannot be reconciled.[12] (see *605, 2253*)

§1. The temptation of force

79 – Some States may find that they possess the means to bend others to their will, or to compel partners and adversaries alike to submit to their manoeuvre. These means will take a different form, however, depending on the era and the society in question. *The technical advances of civilisation have altered the traditional criteria for the use of force, but they have not stopped it being used.*

In the era of globalisation, competition and conflict between international corporations are fiercer than rivalries between States.

Successive hegemonies have used external supremacy to express the dynamism that is still, first and foremost, a function of each partner's internal potential. (see *628, 1690, 2311*)

80 – *In contrast to war, where the decision depends on the outcome of battle, diplomacy works by presenting power under different guises*; the same is true in private business. The physical, psychological and political aspects of confrontation are becoming more complex, variable and subtle.[13]

Brute force is a crude weapon, the very act of negotiating about whether to use it is a step in the direction of compromise. Combat can decide which party will prevail; only negotiation can say which is right. (see *1694*)

81 – The diplomat knows that political action turns out to be motivated by factors going beyond tradition, custom, history and treaties – factors that are unknown but often decisive. The diplomat knows, too, that relations between nations must never be assessed simply in terms of ethics, law and ideals, and that neither friendship nor trust will stand the test of time or withstand the sacred ego of the group. He will therefore resist the temptation to consider that relations between peoples are naturally inclined towards stability, peace and happiness.

Force is one of the prerequisites of effectiveness, the foundation stone of international relations.[14] (see *2230*)

82 – Power is constantly taking new and sometimes unexpected forms. It is unwise to hold to a fixed or mechanical idea of the relations it creates between nations, or to take them for granted, especially at a time when it is tempting to interfere in other States' domestic affairs. (see *387, 1683*)

Peace itself provides a favourable climate which nurtures the very tensions that threaten it. Neither ethics nor law can contain overt force for any length of time, negotiation has a purpose precisely because it recognises this. (see *1788*)

83 – In diplomacy as sometimes in war and business, strength can be its own enemy, whether because it gives rise to a false sense of security, a slackening of will,

---

12 J. FRANKEL: *International Politics: Conflict and Harmony*, London, Penguin, 1973.
13 J. B. DUROSELLE: *Le Conflit de Trieste*, Brussels, Free University, 1966.
14 C. CHAUMONT: *Cours général de droit international public*, RCADI, 1970, I, p. 430.

the suspicion of friends or the coalition of adversaries. A good negotiator prefers a strong adversary to an indecisive partner. (see *413*)

It is a natural and universal tendency to claim, or pretend to have, more power or merit than is really the case.

84 – Strength does not necessarily bring security, nor can it offer protection from all forms of danger; it is wrong to believe the contrary. As early as 1919, France, though victorious, was aware of the threat that neighbouring Germany, still a large and unified country, was destined to become powerful once more and exact revenge.

Power cannot be measured in terms of legal classifications or material assessments. The inequality of resources and territory between States does not automatically determine the real, deeply rooted relationship of force between them. Besides, in the words of the French philosopher Montesquieu, all greatness, all might and all power is relative.[15] (see *415, 1686*)

85 – Strength and weakness are not always to be found where one might expect them. What a State lacks in power or wealth may be made up for in intelligence and character. In his *Mémoires de guerre*, General de Gaulle told how he negotiated the Franco-Russian Pact of 1944 with Stalin. In spite of the disproportion in terms of strength, and notwithstanding threats, persuasion and blackmail, he held out, refusing to trade that treaty (which he needed to consolidate France's international position) for recognition by the Committee for Polish Liberation, which had the backing, at the time, of the USSR under Stalin. He knew that his interlocutor wished to bring the discussions to an end and thus, at the last minute, he got what he wanted.

Coercion

86 – To take another of Montesquieu's ideas, it could be said that *every sovereign and every people with power at their disposal are inclined to abuse it*. The distinguishing feature of diplomacy is that it holds this tendency in check, while combat, on the other hand, gives it free rein. But it cannot be expected to make the inequalities of means and of will between nations simply disappear.

87 – The means used to exert pressure at the international level are more or less characteristic, and they can be discreet, violent or prudent. New methods are used now, such as the media, intelligence, communications and culture. But in the final analysis, the foreign relations of States will always ultimately depend on their political will and military might.

Because it offers a means of response, as well as of attack, the holding of sophisticated weapons acts as an incentive to, and contributes to, peaceful negotiation and balance between the powers. (see *1093, 1686*)

88 – When excessive superiority comes into play in negotiation it tends to skew the discussions and derail them. No one believes in being bound for any length of time

---

15 C. de MONTESQUIEU: *De l'esprit des lois*, Geneva, 1748, IX, 9: 'Toute grandeur, toute force, toute puissance est relative'.

by commitments exacted under duress or by violence, hence the reaction of France to the annexation of Alsace-Lorraine by Germany in 1871. As the philosopher Jean-Jacques Rousseau wrote, giving in to force is an act of necessity, not of will.[16]

History nonetheless offers well-known examples of pressure brought to bear on States, as well as on their emissaries in person. (see *747*)

89 – The methods of coercion are varied: when their object is tactical, the interlocutor must be left no time to escape or to parry. This is the case with an ultimatum. (see *98, 144*)

To the vanquished, the conditions of peace are always dictated by force. (see *750*)

90 – Some constraints are direct, open and constant, when they are the product of too great an inequality between partners in an alliance. Especially today, States that live and sometimes indeed prosper under the military protection of another State enjoy the same sort of autonomy in their foreign policy that the Greek republics had under Roman control. (see *748, 894*)

The interdependence of nations brings diversification in the methods of coercion, and this sometimes works in favour of the less powerful. *Preparation for negotiation involves assessing what level of pressure one's adversary might be able to apply.*

91 – Even when conducted under the guise of an international organisation, international coercion implies relations between States. For each protagonist, it represents a way of imposing views that it knows the other would not subscribe to freely. But coercion can also be the subject of negotiation, for example, when several governments join forces to use coercion in order to bring about the execution of a treaty or a collective decision, as was the case in the Gulf War of 1991, and, at least in part, at the time of the disintegration of the former Yugoslavia. (see *1661*)

92 – Since the function of diplomacy is to mitigate the effects of changes in the relative strength of States, and prevent or moderate the exercise of unilateral pressure or interference, the determined conqueror resists being bound by its procedures and discipline. *It is difficult to negotiate with those who derive their legitimacy from military success, economic expansion or ideological conquest.* (see *1867*)

93 – When placed at the disposal of an even moderately aggressive will, even relative strength is always effective.

The negotiator must bear in mind the temptation of unilateral manoeuvre, whether on the part of his interlocutors, in his own camp or coming from third parties; failure to consider the wishes of others increases the chances of misunderstandings or even discord. (see *271, 445, 2502*)

94 – This is why it is said that no negotiation, however welcome or sincere, can prevent interference or circumvention; the diplomat must always be on the alert, even though it may not help him at the time to know who is right and who is wrong. (see *637, 2359*)

---

16 J.-J. ROUSSEAU: *Du contrat social*, I, 3: 'Céder à la force est un acte de nécessité, non de volonté', Amsterdam, 1762.

Peace itself has no absolute value, since it can serve to harbour the worst kinds of oppression. (see *1592, 1622*)

95 – This also explains the manoeuvre whereby one of the factors in a possible settlement is placed beyond the scope of all discussion or bargaining. *The politics of the fait accompli is exploited at every opportunity.* Today it even extends to the use of State terrorism.

One good response to the *fait accompli* is to seek an implicit negotiation with the support of all those who are threatened by it. (see *512*)

Threat

96 – When an act of force is predicted or imminent this has a profound impact on freedom of action and thus freedom to negotiate. Reactions may be short-lived terror or lasting fear; they might be instinctive and irrational, or based on reasoned analysis. Such reactions could either be the result of a specific and immediate danger or of a general climate of insecurity, and, as such, they will not respond to the same diplomatic treatment.

A party wishing to negotiate does so in the hope of averting the worst consequences of its opponent's manoeuvres, and containing the reaction of panic; it wishes to be seen as reassuring. (see *955*)

97 – Even when it takes the form of diplomacy, intimidation is a type of resort to force, because it relies on the use of fear as a means of exerting pressure. Gunboat diplomacy goes back further than the deployment of modern naval fleets, and today the same purpose is served by satellites.

For governments as well as the private sector, the modern international environment presents threats that are both unpredictable and highly dangerous.

98 – Fear is not, in reality, a strategic weapon. Its effect must be swift and tactical, otherwise it works against the interests of those using it by causing their opponents to unite. Any great danger will produce agreement between those whom it threatens. It was when he sought to prevent French rearmament in 1875 that Bismarck handed France its first diplomatic success since 1871: support from Britain and Russia.[17] (see *89*)

99 – It is easy to see why, for a State aiming to intimidate, the power and mobility of the navy is, thanks to the freedom of the high seas, a classic instrument of diplomatic manoeuvre and negotiation. Russia's policy in the Balkans was dictated by its need to control the Bosphorus.

100 – The effect of a threat will depend on the relative positions of the protagonists, and, principally, on the strength and determination of the party issuing it. Its success depends not only on the means that State has at its disposal, but on the probability that it will use them.[18] The wise negotiator will verify the

---

17 M. BAUMONT: *L'Essor industriel et l'impérialisme colonial*, Paris, PUF, 1949.
18 T. C. SCHELLING: *The Strategy of Conflict*, Harvard University Press, 1960, p. 35.

position before factoring the risk into his assessment or, as the case may be, seeking a compromise. (see *1709, 1711, 2615*)

Often, if one party is credible, the other will react by believing it.

101 – Some threats may present themselves in a disguised form, but they are no less real. This is the case, for instance, with threats that are formulated within an international organisation whose role is to regulate relations between States in a manner supposedly decided by common consent.

102 – When manoeuvres are discreetly and efficiently combined, this can leave the impression that the party taking a decision has freedom of action, whereas in fact it is giving way to them. It was under such conditions that France was led to end its occupation of the Rühr in 1925.[19]

103 – The will to convince an opponent is one of the preconditions of success; arguing one's case does not amount to coercion, but when powerfully framed and forcefully presented, an argument will carry conviction by virtue of its moral and psychological impact.

The expression of determination always commands respect.

104 – A warning derives its force from logic – from the normal course of dealings, from the international context and the assessment of outside events. As a negotiating procedure it differs from an order, a summons or an ultimatum in that it is an appeal for moderation.

105 – A State in a position to issue threats will be tempted to use them against its opponent or even against a third party. Threats in fact help the weak and will generally provoke the other to react by hardening its position, or engaging in avoidance or cover-up, none of which is conducive to good negotiation.[20] American pressure in 1954 did not have the desired effect of facilitating the ratification of the European Defence Community Treaty when France refused to do so. (see *750*)

106 – Threats sour relations and push weaker States to extremes that might have been avoided if the issues had been put to them more reasonably.[21] As a means of exerting pressure, threats often appear too direct and too specific. The diplomat moderates how he expresses his opinions, his positions and his warnings in order to avoid being criticised for threatening behaviour. (see *2438*)

107 – *The more powerful a protagonist is, the less tempted it will be to put its pressure into words; the visible disparity in strength will be enough.* The negotiator in a delicate position, with limited means at his disposal, is the most likely to be tempted to issue an overt threat, while he is the very one at risk of not being able to carry it out. Even in trade and in the private sector, a negotiator who is sure of

---

19 M. BAUMONT: *La Faillite de la paix*, Paris, PUF, 1960, I, p. 274.
20 M. DEUTSCH and R. KRAUSS: 'The Effects of Threat upon Interpersonal Bargaining', *Journal of Abnormal Soc. Psychol.*, 1960, p. 181.
21 F. de CALLIERES: *De la manière de négocier avec les souverains*, Paris, 1716, XVI.

himself takes the risks seriously; the more uncertain his own ground, the less he is inclined to view his opponent's strength as real and substantial.[22]

108 – Threats are not always carried out. Where this would have been impossible, which fact might come to light only after the event, it is commonly referred to as bluffing. Such a tactic can backfire if the opponent holds out, in which case the issuer of the threat will be weakened and left without credibility.[23] *Any threat must be in proportion to what is at stake.* (see *305*)

109 – Except where he knows in advance that matters must be taken to their limits, the wise negotiator will eschew intimidation as a method and will beware of pushing a weak State into positions or alliances it would otherwise have avoided. Once expressed, a threat must be maintained, and this is not always either possible or desirable. (see *852*)

110 – If threats are to be avoided, what of force itself? Throughout the last century, relations between the States of Central Europe were characterised by sudden offensives that went as far as the annexation of territories or foreign countries. Both the annexation of Bosnia-Herzegovina in 1908 and German expansionism from 1936 onwards triggered crises that degenerated into world wars. The notion that attack brings immediate success, when played out against a dramatic background, had so distorted the practice of diplomacy that, by the time the declaration of war came, it was accepted, even welcomed, by public opinion. (see *749*)

111 – *The role of deterrence is to seek to discourage direct action for fear of a riposte out of all proportion to what would be gained by the manoeuvre*; at this level, threat can lead to negotiation. A variety of preventive measures can be taken or announced to bring this about. The purpose of diplomacy is to clothe them in reasons, to explain their scope and exploit their effects: England, Austria and Prussia managed to prevent the creation of a Franco-Belgian customs union in 1842 by announcing that it could lead them into war. (see *1705, 1717*)

112 – Resort to force does not have to involve acts of open warfare; military measures such as a naval exercise or deployment of troops can sometimes have the same impact on a negotiation as the outbreak of the hostilities they herald. The same effect can be produced by economic measures such as a naval blockade or an embargo on the production or sale of certain essential goods.

113 – Nuclear deterrence is also a means of demonstrating strength. Its novel characteristics impart both prospective and systematic content to contemporary negotiation. The uncertainty surrounding its use only serves to increase the pressure it exerts. (see *1695*)

---

22 S. LINDSKOLD and J. TEDESCHI: *Self-Esteem and Reaction to Threats and Promises*, Miami, 1969.

23 F. C. IKLE: *How Nations Negotiate*, New York, Harper Row, 1964, p. 77.

Aggression

114 – Whether it is based on national or religious impulses, or fuelled by interests or by direct or indirect provocation, and whether it is opportunistic or the product of long-term planning by certain leaders, *aggression is a basic fact of international life even though, according to the United Nations, it can never be justified in relations between States*. Whether it is used in the service of some grand political design, or is the product of general ill-feeling or a specific dispute, it is a daily reality of proximity and coexistence.[24]

115 – The reality of this risk provides the driving force behind an entire branch of diplomatic negotiation, that of non-aggression pacts, defence agreements and regional security treaties.[25] (see *853, 1691, 1694*)

Since, for any State, the gravest danger lies in the possible disruption of the equilibrium on which its strategy is based, all forms of aggression call for a response from third parties, even when they are not themselves directly involved. (see *147*)

116 – When he invaded Silesia in 1740, Frederick II of Prussia acknowledged that he was guilty of aggression, even while finding a variety of reasons to justify it.[26] But such an attitude is rare.[27] Most of the time the identification of the aggressor – not necessarily the same as the attacker – gives rise to numerous controversies which are important in the formation of alliances between States.

Some revealing examples can be cited. In August 1914, on the eve of war, the French government decided to pull back its troops by 10 km behind the frontier. Again, at Pearl Harbour, the American losses were attributed to the surprise effect of the Japanese attack, but it has been argued, with some credibility, that F. D. Roosevelt had in fact been warned and was expecting to use this provocation to mobilise public opinion.

117 – Half a century of efforts, first by the League of Nations and later by the United Nations, have produced a legal definition of aggression as the use of armed force by a State against the sovereignty, territorial integrity or political independence of another State, or in any other manner inconsistent with the Charter of the United Nations (UNGA Resolution 3314 of 14 December 1974).

118 – That definition is however too recent to have been applied in a comprehensive and consistent manner. Furthermore, the identification of the attacker in any given case is difficult and requires a rapid and effective reaction on the part of those institutions whose responsibility it is to keep the peace, such as the Security Council. The resulting interventions often meet with reactions of distrust, scepticism and cynicism. (see *1132*)

24 L. BERKOWITZ: *Aggression: a Social Psychological Analysis*, New York, McGraw Hill, 1962. A. H. BUSS: *The Psychology of Aggression*, New York, Wiley, 1961.
25 C. de VISSCHER: *Théories et réalités en droit international public*, Paris, Pedone, 1960, p. 152.
26 P. RAIN: *La diplomatie française d'Henri IV à Vergennes*, Paris, Plon, 1945, p. 185.
27 G. BOUTHOUL and R. GARRERE: *Le Défi de la guerre*, Paris, PUF, 1976.

119 – There are many ways of committing aggression. Some, such as military invasion, the bombardment of a territory, the blockade of ports or coasts, attacking the country's armed forces, use of troops against the country where they are stationed or sending in bands of irregulars, have been chronicled in negotiations. But there are countless others, such as the issue of warnings and press campaigns. The terrorist attacks of 11 September 2001 on New York and Washington confirmed the readiness of certain fundamentalist groups to make war. (see *1678, 1872*)

120 – The risk of aggression should never be ignored. Those who know their enemy but neither engage him in open and direct combat, nor have any dealings with him, adopt an ambivalent stance which, according to Machiavelli, can be the least desirable of all. If they are thereby reduced to the point where they can 'neither accept a peace nor sustain a war', their submission becomes inevitable. *It is vital to know when to manoeuvre and when the time has come to negotiate.* (see *189, 864*)

In diplomacy, fear can serve a useful purpose; it is conducive to respect, prudence and negotiation.

121 – As long as a country has the choice of fighting if it can no longer attain its objectives by negotiation, aggression will remain a fact of international life. Indeed, it will become an ever-growing menace because of progress in weaponry and the increase in the number of actors on the international scene. At the same time, nations cannot be blamed for the quarrels, however trivial, which form part of their history. (see *146*)

122 – Often, a manoeuvre is aggressive because it amounts to provocation. History is replete with examples of positions taken with the deliberate intention of provoking conflict. The outbreak of the Franco-German War of 1870 illustrates this well: knowing that France was unfavourable to the northern German Confederation, and wishing to overcome its opposition, Bismarck used the proposal of a Hohenzollern candidate to the Spanish throne to provoke Napoleon III into declaring war.

More recently, the occupation of Kuwait by Iraqi troops in August 1990 bore all the hallmarks of an audacious provocation.

123 – An attitude of provocation is deliberately contrary to negotiation, especially when it seeks to attach conditions that are unacceptable or offensive, but it is not always direct. A well-orchestrated press campaign can lend an almost official air of authenticity to a piece of disinformation which of course will only be reinforced by denials. *By controlling the media, a government can arouse public sentiments to the point of passion and deliberately generate a political crisis.* Hitler's tactics consisted of keeping his opponents in a state of exhaustion by oscillating between attack and offers of negotiation.[28]

124 – Internal destabilisation is a disguised form of provocation even when it is not an act of force, and it adds to the climate of diplomatic uncertainty. Powers interested in maintaining the status quo are tempted to intervene at the level of the

---

28 L. NOEL: *L'Agression allemande contre la Pologne*, Paris, Flammarion, 1946.

underlying cause of the dispute. But those who stand to gain by upsetting the established order – States in the course of expansion, oppressed minorities, pressure groups and ideological movements – will tend to do what they can to bring that about. For them, negotiation is synonymous with compromise. (see *637, 2312*)

125 – At a time when each power is constantly monitoring the others and thwarting their manoeuvres on all fronts, *negotiation is the favoured means of understanding and preventing aggression, and contributing to enhanced international peace and security.*[29] (see *388, 2033, 2251*)

§2. The balance of power

126 – In spite of all the theories, in negotiation as elsewhere, and now more than ever before, power makes for inequality. Inequality must be accepted as a basic fact of international life, as its influence does not always favour the same parties.[30] Similarly, the diplomat will seek to use it to his advantage, for example when jockeying for a better position before or during the battle, in much the same way as does the soldier.

Every astute tactician has to exploit and maximise inequality and make it work to his advantage.

127 – In these circumstances, it comes as no surprise that differences exist between States, according to their respective material or ideological strength and their military or diplomatic potential. However, their influence remains entirely relative where negotiation is concerned, since external circumstances play such a dominant role.

For the weaker party as well as the stronger, negotiation remains an essential means of demonstrating political will in all fields of social activity. It provides the tools for realising hopes while setting limits on what hope might achieve. At the same time, it points up the respective size and rank of nations. (see *2322*)

128 – In the contemporary world, where change is rapid and many diverse players are involved in diplomacy, the balance of power is subject to extreme variations. Negotiation must adapt to these with realism and flexibility. If the Locarno Treaties appeared to succeed in bringing about a sort of diplomatic equilibrium in Western Europe, their effects were merely transitory.[31] (see *82, 1686*)

Negotiations must be conducted on the basis of the balance of power and interests, taking minimal account of the domestic régimes of the States involved.

Predominance

129 – Certain States, possessing the exceptional power that derives from exceptional means, use it in their interactions to misrepresent responsibilities as

---

29 L. M. GOODRICH: 'The Maintenance of Peace and Security', in *The Theory and Practice of International Relations*, Englewood Cliffs, Prentice Hall, 1966, p. 393.
30 R. P. ANAND: 'On the Equality of States', ibid., p. 23.
31 C. de VISSCHER: *Théories et réalités en droit international public*, Paris, Pedone, 1960, p. 78.

prerogatives, which they exercise without consulting those whom they are committing. This is the classic posture of dominant nations, which as history shows will be different ones over time. (see *1733*)

Nations are moreover instinctively inclined to turn towards more powerful States, whose strength and resolve give them reassurance that the commitments they have negotiated will be respected.

130 – Experience shows that, little by little, a negotiation will always find its way through the manoeuvres of the parties. New and healthier power balances will be preceded and accompanied by discussions, which continue to take place within alliances to give them life and keep them flexible and effective. (see *957, 970*)

131 – Differences between the traditional roles of States will sometimes be confirmed by negotiations. During the preparations for the Treaty of Versailles, in 1919, States such as the United States, France, Great Britain, Italy and Japan could be identified among those present at the Paris Conference as being those of the belligerent powers with 'general interests'. (see *915*)

The notion of a '*Directoire*' has for decades underlain international negotiation and international organisations, and has found expression in the financial and economic summits held since 1973, originally known as the Group of 7, then G8, with the addition of Russia, and now G9, with China. (see *1113, 1537, 2489*)

The periodic meetings of this informal group are devoted to a variety of political issues, including Europe, the Middle East and East–West relations. (see *1950, 2495*)

132 – In the nineteenth century, the horizons of British politics were worldwide;[32] almost all colonial powers of the period were in that position, but they did not always have the means to back their pretensions. Negotiation allowed them to defend widespread interests ranging over a broad field of diplomatic activity, only confronting each given problem as the need arose and solving them locally, one after the other. Europe's fratricidal wars put an end to that supple and pragmatic approach, with the entry onto the scene of heavyweight and cohesive States whose role in world affairs has been characterised by dreadful conflict, hard bargaining and the accumulation of power. (see *1691*)

133 – When States have dominant power they are obliged, whether they like it or not, to play a predominant diplomatic role. This has been the case with the United States since the First World War, even during the periods when they reverted to isolation or isolationism. Moreover, experience shows the extent to which men can be seduced by power, especially the ones who wield it.[33] *Failure to use predominant force paves the way for another to achieve a predominant position.* (see *911, 1247, 1932*)

Predominance is made up of several elements, and is enough in itself to produce results. In 1990–1991, during the Yugoslav crisis, the Federal Republic of Germany practically dictated to the other western European States how they should behave with regard to Slovenia and Croatia.

---

32 P. RENOUVIN: *Historie des relations internationales. Le XIXe siècle*, Paris, Hachette, II, 1955.

33 R. ARON: *République impériale. Les Etats-Unis dans le monde (1945–1972)*, Paris, Calmann-Lévy, 1973, p. 322.

134 – Nations cannot ignore or avoid the disadvantages or the responsibilities of greatness, which according to Montesquieu should always be kept in mind. As an example, the United States was wrong to refuse to ratify the League of Nations Pact and to withdraw from the negotiations which were, in 1920, to decide the fate of the Ottoman Empire. The resulting Treaty of Sèvres left Britain a great deal of room to manoeuvre, and this was ultimately to lead to the present-day American commitment in the Near East.[34]

135 – The more unequal the balance of power, the more difficult will be the negotiation, despite the fact that for the weaker party it is a matter of necessity. The more the balance evens out, the more inevitable negotiation becomes as a means of resolving issues. In both such cases, the avoidance of conflict would seem to be the wise course. One of the characteristics of the system created by international political organisations is that it produces complex effects on the balance of power, with the result that predominance tends to become blurred to the point of dissolving altogether. (see *1536*)

However, this observation should be tempered by prudence, as is shown by the behaviour of the members of the European Union when faced with the Yugoslav crisis.

136 – The predominance of some players weighs heavily on the negotiations of lower-ranking powers. The tension between the hegemonies is felt throughout the whole field of diplomatic activity: sometimes it puts a high price on certain stakes, as was the case with the city of Berlin after the last world war; sometimes, on the other hand, it makes them dependent upon foreign strategies, as has happened in the Near East.

Generosity in negotiation might sometimes makes hegemony tolerable, but it does not make it agreeable.[35]

137 – While seeking to limit the impact of inequalities of power, diplomacy takes realistic account of it in treaties. Examples are peace treaties and those that lay down spheres of competence within a wide variety of international organisations, sometimes granting more powers to those countries with a higher burden of responsibility than to others. (see *89, 750, 1116, 1650, 1653*)

The most unequal treaties are those where one power is not only predominant but also interfering in the other's affairs.

138 – The fact that a State does not have sufficient power to counterbalance that of its adversary does not mean that it cannot use its diplomatic prerogative. On the contrary, negotiation will serve it extremely well: it is better to win over stronger parties by persuasion than offer them opposition.[36] Mao learned the lesson in his youth that if the weak give in the strong will strike harder and that on the other hand, the strong will yield if the weak risk everything to defend their rights before the world.[37] (see *908*)

---

34 J.-B. DUROSELLE: *Histoire diplomatique de 1919 à nos jours*, Paris, Dalloz, 1978, p. 31.
35 H. A. KISSINGER: *White House Years*, Boston, Little, Brown & Co., 1979.
36 C. de GAULLE: *Mémoires de guerre*, Paris, Plon, 1954–1959, 3.
37 A. PEYREFITTE: *Quand la Chine s'éveillera*, Paris, Fayard, 1973, p. 10.

Negotiation can only exist if it is backed by the will to refuse: refusal is an expression of freedom.

139 – One thing is certain: opening and pursuing negotiations requires a greater effort from a weak party than a strong one – it will have to show a large part, if not all, of its hand. The more limited its means, the more modest must be its objective. (see *2358*)

The relative position of the negotiating partners changes the normal interplay of factors: a debt that might cause loss to a weaker party can also strengthen its hand if it restricts the freedom of its creditor. (see *990*)

140 – It is a law of nature that the weak will seek the protection of the strong.[38] In the practice of diplomacy, there are those who are quick to seek the support or arbitration of stronger powers in order to avoid having to deal with their peers. This can be a fatal mistake. Instead of resolving their disputes, the Eastern European States, born out of the defeat of the central Empires in 1918, waited in vain for the support they needed from their French protector, when the crisis came it found them weakened and divided. La Fontaine gave the moral of the story: *'Princelings, end your own disputes and be glad. To call on kings for help you would truly be mad. In your wars you must never let them take a hand, nor ever invite them onto your land'*.[39] (see *908*)

141 – For a nation to place its security and its interests in another's hands amounts to losing the independence and dignity that are fundamental to its ability to deal. Often, interdependence is nothing more than dependence for the weakest and domination for the strongest. This is the real meaning of doctrines like the Monroe Doctrine, used to disguise a predominant position. It was equally true of the so-called theory of limited sovereignty in the time of Brezhnev. (see *159, 905, 1891*)

142 – In politics, the road from inequality to dependence is short. A State that allows itself to be disarmed, physically or morally, by its adversary will be left with no choice but to accede to its conditions, however tough these may be.[40] *In the absence of the strength and the skill to enforce the agreement, there can be no negotiation.*

In the shrinking world of international business competition, large corporations use their strength and strategic influence to operate and manoeuvre between States.

143 – Like war, negotiation can be used in the service of a policy of domination or expansion; not all aggression is armed. Even the most overt imperialism can count

38 P. J. PROUDHON: *La Guerre et la Paix*, Paris, Rivière, 1927, p. 137: 'C'est une loi de la nature, que la faiblesse se place sous la protection de la force'.

39 J. de la FONTAINE: *Le Jardinier et son Seigneur*, Fables, Book IV, Fable 4, 1668–1693. (*'Petits princes, videz vos débats entre vous. De recourir aux rois vous seriez de grands fous. Il ne les faut jamais engager dans vos guerres, ni les faire entrer sur vos terres'*. Translation by Norman B. Spector, *The Complete Works of Jean de la Fontaine*, Northwestern University Press.)

40 M. BAUMONT: *La Faillite de la paix*, Paris, PUF, 1960, I, p. 67. P. RENOUVIN: *Le Traité de Versailles*, Paris, Flammarion, 1969.

on support from well-primed public opinion provided it was initially successful. The negotiator must therefore exercise the greatest care before agreeing to the conditions of a stronger partner: acceding to its demands, whatever their nature, not only takes it outside the negotiating framework which, legally at least, is one of equality, but most of all it means giving up its sovereign freedom of choice.

144 – The ultimatum aims at coercion: it gives the last word in a negotiation, setting out the maximum possible concession, coupled with specific threats and deadlines intended to influence the outcome of the dispute. If this meets with a refusal or with silence, discussions are broken off and the conflict spills into the open, unless a third party intervenes on the side of the victim. (see *556*)

145 – As with blackmail, an ultimatum is the first step in a spiral of deterioration which, once set in motion, is difficult to break. In France in 1801, the freedom of the Catholic church was in issue. Rather than agreeing to sign the Concordat on the unfavourable terms offered by Napoleon, but still within the deadline given, Pope Pius VII sent his Secretary of State to see the Emperor in person. In so doing, he was able to keep the discussion going without giving in to force or losing face.

146 – Negotiations about collective security established by a treaty have proved too unpredictable for small nations to give up seeking support from those powers that are, if not the most friendly, then the least dangerous. This, at least, is what China, attacked in Manchuria by Japan in 1931, and Ethiopia, invaded by Italian troops in 1935, learned from the League of Nations experience. The way the UN Charter has been implemented would suggest the same conclusions. (see *1781, 1794*)

Balance

147 – Even where it is not total or general, imbalance between forces is a factor to be taken into account in negotiation. The prospect of crushing victories, disproportion in resources and overwhelming alliances – and, today, the potential for nuclear war – have provided certain States with instruments of coercion that they have not failed to use. (see *115*)

148 – No person can order if he does not have the moral or physical power to compel, but the mere ability to issue commands naturally induces people on occasion to demand or forbid things that would not normally be permissible. Napoleon's diplomacy is replete with examples of this. It was the Emperor's sheer virtuosity that proved his ultimate undoing: his domination owed more to his tactical skills in warfare and diplomacy than to actually having forces at his disposal greater than those of the enemies ranged against him. His victories were no more than short lived.

In war as in negotiation, it is superiority that concerns each of the protagonists; balance matters more to third parties. (see *171*)

149 – Since ancient times, too, prudence, good sense and a certain instinct have led diplomats to devote attention to the balance between countries, a balance that means no one of them is able to impose its laws, its will and its interests on the others. The Treaty of Utrecht (1713) referred to the true equilibrium between powers as a condition for peace and tranquillity in the small world of Europe.

Peace does not rest upon the illusion of disarmament, which can never be achieved, but on a balance of power that gives reason to hope that force of arms will never be put to the test. (see *719, 1613, 1703, 1787*)

150 – It was by applying the principle of the balance of power that, in the eighteenth century, Prussia turned itself into a power capable of taking on France, Austria and Russia; King Frederick II revealed his genius in understanding this and in adjusting his military and diplomatic actions to follow where it led him.

Today, the search for balance in Europe has given way to the search for global balance as the goal of international politics, with the help of organisational negotiation. (see *1002, 1692*)

151 – Once established, imbalance will tend to increase: *nothing feeds success like success itself.* The hasty acceptance of the breach in the balance of power in Central Europe, already compromised by the annexation of Austria in 1936, by the Western negotiators of the Munich agreements offered up to Germany in 1938 the sacrifice of the whole League of Nations system, and with it, of peace.[41]

152 – Excessive weakness is no less dangerous for peace than excess of strength.[42] A negotiator who fails to act at once to reestablish the balance between the protagonists will have to work harder to achieve the same result later on – assuming he still can.

Any party that is too weak either to carry out a commitment or breach it, loses all capacity to negotiate freely.

153 – To weigh up objectively what is required to neutralise the forces of aggression requires assessments that are often very delicate: *without resolve and courage, strength is useless.* Negotiation has fostered the search for and exchange of the information needed for the play of changing configurations of checks, balances and alliances on the international scene. (see *2028*)

154 – Parity is relative, and it fluctuates: *the balance of power and influence can only be empirically measured, and has to be constantly adjusted.* The quest for it has been used to justify numerous abandonments and betrayals, as it leads to resistance to any form of domination, whether by a country or a coalition, and it renders any alliance or commitment unpredictable. A good example of this is the consistent British practice of never regarding any pact with a continental European country as desirable or definitive, in order to preserve intact the freedom necessary for manoeuvre. (see *718, 884, 895*)

155 – Superiority in wealth or intelligence is difficult to forgive: as with people, States experience jealousy and rancour towards each other, and hold each other responsible for the injustices of fate or nature. Great powers when they negotiate

---

41 J.-B. DUROSELLE: *La Décadence, 1932–1939*, Paris, Imp. Nationale, 1979, p. 351.
    L. NOEL: *La guerre de 1939 a commencé quatre ans plus tôt*, Paris, France-Empire, 1979.
·42 R. ARON: *Paix et guerre entre les nations*, Paris, Calmann-Lévy, 1962, p. 20.

rarely prove capable of persuading lesser nations to put aside their inferiority complex and react on the merits of what is proposed.

156 – Weaker States, for their part, like to think of themselves as united in the face of a more powerful one, in the hope that this unity will serve to reestablish a certain balance of power, or give them back some freedom of choice. They tend to prefer procedures and institutions in which the will to dominate is undermined, even at the expense of effectiveness. (see *1031*)

157 – A State must avoid imposing unacceptable conditions for peace if it does not wish to be forced into conflict. Britain made this mistake after the Treaty of Amiens in 1802, but quickly rectified it by reopening hostilities and rebuilding the coalition against Napoleon.
  Attempting to secure a balance of power requires vigilance and, sometimes, suspicion.[43]

158 – Negotiation offers several ways in which some equality of strength can be reestablished, without which the fight will be lost before it has begun. One such possibility is diplomatic multipolarity, in which the balance is spread over several pillars so that rules are respected and vulnerabilities shared. The formation of alliances is another, and also the creation of international organisations. Each State is in fact seeking security in the diplomatic system that it cannot attain by its own means. (see *1028, 1724*)

159 – It is not uncommon for one power to come to the aid of another, sometimes quite spontaneously, in order to restore the balance, without necessarily expecting anything in return except not to be threatened.
  A negotiation that succeeds beyond the bounds of what is tolerable opens itself up to challenge. It is unwise, and presumptuous, to expect voluntary compliance with an agreement from a party that no longer has anything to gain from it.

160 – A State which agrees to the reinforcement of another is acting against its own interests, even if it derives some immediate gain.
  Anything that harms a State serves the cause of its rivals; anything that cuts the powerful down to size is to be desired. Such has been the constant aim of Britain with regard to the countries that have successively dominated continental Europe, even after as severe an ordeal as the First World War; since 1919, the whole thrust of its European diplomacy has been to weaken France, to the point that in 1925 it gave Germany a guarantee of stability on the Rhine while at the same time maintaining its position on reparations to France.

161 – The dearest wish of the strategist is to prevent a State viewed as an actual or potential adversary from achieving a predominant position. In order to do this, one must either weaken the other by provoking some domestic or external problem, as Britain did all the time with Louis XIV, or isolate it, as Bismarck did when he succeeded in driving a wedge between France and the other States in Europe, or

---

43 C. de VISSCHER: *Théories et réalités en droit international public*, Paris, Pedone, 1960, p. 38.

promote its natural enemies following the model of Bonaparte, who as part of his Germanic policy consistently strengthened certain States such as Bavaria against Austria.

162 – Given the choice, a weak neighbour is preferable to a strong one. Austria and Britain installed Prussia on the Rhine on the basis of this principle, thus definitively thwarting the policy France had been cultivating for many centuries. The great fear of the Central European powers has always been having to fight on two fronts as, each time, France negotiated a rearguard alliance with one of the Eastern States, Poland, Turkey or Russia, in order to undermine its immediate neighbour.

163 – There is no shortage of examples illustrating the rivalry between great neighbours: the competition between Austria and Prussia in Germany lasted for more than a century, and in modern times one need only look at the frontiers of Siberia.

Montesquieu advised that it was as important to avoid the ruin of a neighbouring State in decline as it was to avoid conquering it.[44]

164 – Faced with a dangerous power, a weak State will always find supporters: ever since 1919, one of the dominant themes of United States policy towards Europe has been to help Germany back on its feet each time it suffered defeat, military or otherwise.

165 – The defensive response to a specific threat is to adapt and conclude alliances, particularly in the form of coalitions that can be dissolved once the danger is past. From 1813 onwards, Austria and Britain were disturbed by Russia's intrusion into Central Europe and they considered allowing their main adversary, Napoleon, to retain some of his power. Right up to his death, Hitler hoped for a separate peace with the West, and Stalin feared it. (see *861*)

166 – *Similar vulnerabilities are often more conducive to agreement than similar interests.* This is why Bonaparte set up a system of secondary States in Germany, for whom Austria and Prussia presented such a threat that they required the backing of France. (see *109*)

167 – Following the example of Bonaparte, who signed a separate peace treaty with each country he conquered, the better to impose his conditions, the ambitious State must negotiate to divide the forces that thwart its plans. On the other hand, it also helps to bring together those that might be of assistance: it was the incessant quarrelling between the Danube nations that made it easier for Germany to pursue its 1941 offensive across Europe and against the USSR.

168 – Opponents of a State with hegemonic ambitions would do better to agree on the best way to contain it rather than to have to use force against it. (see *853*)

This is how, in diplomacy as in war, fronts are formed and manoeuvres develop. Bilateral negotiations are like limited engagements: they are a way of weakening the position of the other side while strengthening one's own.

---

44 C. de MONTESQUIEU: *De l'esprit des lois*, IX, 10.

169 – Finally, the loser can rely on victory to divide its opponents, given that all alliances are the products of circumstance and will last only as long as circumstances favour or require them. (see *859*)

170 – The laws of equilibrium operate against any expansion of power: the closer it is, the more fear or envy it will incite. All things considered, both influence and protection are more acceptable if exercised from a distance.

The domination of one power will, as with that of an individual, be tolerated only as long as it continues to be successful. At the first lapse or sign of failure its authority will be challenged and rejected. (see *916*)

171 – Political cynicism distinguishes between the acknowledgement of the need for international equilibrium and each State's interpretation of this with respect to its own behaviour. It was King Frederick II who said that peace in Europe was founded on the maintenance of that wise mechanism whereby the superior strength of one monarchy was counterbalanced by the combined power of a number of other sovereigns.[45]

Each State's strategy will generally tend to tilt the balance of power in its favour: negotiation is one way it can do this, particularly if it makes use of alliances. Any margin of superiority, however slight, brings reassurance.

§3. *Force versus negotiation*

172 – In international relations, the risk of conflict and the propensity to combat are so great that at a given time, opposition between particular States can come to dominate the entire diplomatic scene. Such was the case with Franco-German relations between the 1870 and 1914 wars.

The competition between the two great nuclear powers lasted for a quarter of a century, until the downfall of communism. But, at the same time, the fact that nuclear weapons were neutralised gave the middle-ranking powers greater freedom to commit aggression than the superpowers had. (see *1757, 1760*)

173 – However worthy the ideals and however skilled the diplomats, the force of confrontation may be strong enough to carry all before it. When France was forced into war in 1914, because of the interplay of its alliances and against the tide of popular feeling, it went forward with a high heart.

174 – Diplomacy based on a consistent policy of conciliation is therefore an illusion. Even when it is disguised as ideology, competition from partners will remain fierce. Staying out of other States' quarrels and showing neutrality with regard to the great powers and their ventures does not mean that a State has given up the defence of its own interests. (see *1870*)

The purpose of negotiation, like war, is to acquire, conquer and preserve. Like other states, the United States grew by force of arms as well as money.[46]

---

45 FREDERICK II of PRUSSIA: *L'Anti-Machiavel*, XXVI.
46 R. ARON: *République impériale, Les Etats-Unis dans le monde*, Paris, Calmann-Lévy, 1973, p. 20.

Aggressivity

175 – Every living entity, whether individual or collective, has to struggle endlessly to stay alive. One component of this combative attitude is aggressivity, in other words, a tendency to attack, sometimes prompted by instincts or passions, and sometimes driven by the hope of glory or possession.

176 – This behaviour, which is probably both innate and learned – the question has never been answered – is most often the product of a reaction to one's surroundings, of frustration, refusal or conquest.[47] It is a propensity that sometimes finds an outlet in games, celebrations or disasters, but also reveals itself in sentiment and passion – animosity, jealousy or hatred, which translate into dislikes, quarrels, confrontations and the many and varied forms of violence between groups or individuals.

177 – It seems that some nations are more inclined to moderation and wisdom than others. This might sometimes be due to their geographical situation, which places them beyond the reach of any direct threat, or to their economic activities, which lead them to maintain foreign trading outposts and commercial fleets, sometimes very far away, or even to a level of civilisation which teaches them to place a high value on the arts, literature and justice. Thus we have come to credit the cities of ancient Phoenicia and Greece with the earliest forms of international law – alliances, treaties and the rules of war and peace. After them came Byzantium where artifice was elevated into an art, and Venice, where they first practised diplomacy.

178 – By contrast, some nations, at least at certain periods in their history, have seemed to show a predisposition for war. Looking no further than antiquity and taking Sparta or Rome, they could even be said to have cultivated these traits, preferring domination over negotiation as a way to achieve their ambitions.

179 – From that point on, two opposing concepts of international relations have existed. The mercantile model allegedly seeks to forge lasting understanding between nations, based on mutual concessions and respect for each other's interests: its objective is the maintenance of good relations through eliminating the desire for greatness and fostering the settlement of rival claims. The second strand is characterised by a striving for outright victory over adversaries with only the minimum of concessions. When negotiation is used to secure a victory, there is no limit to the means that can be used to weaken or dominate – surprise, intimidation, intransigence, even threats and brutality.[48]

180 – This is too simple an analysis: the distinctions between the methods and practices of international negotiation and those of war are not nearly so clear-cut as those between maritime and continental societies. The drive for conquest has occurred in cities built on trade, while on the other hand, there are plenty of warlike nations who have nonetheless entered into relationships with others based

---

47 K. LORENZ: *Das sogenannte Böse, zur Naturgeschichte der Agression*, Vienna, Borotha-Schoeler, 1964. *L'Agression, une histoire naturelle du mal*, Paris, Flammarion, 1969.
48 N. NICOLSON: *Diplomacy*, Oxford, Oxford University Press, 1945, II, 5.

on the practice of diplomacy. In building its federation, Rome constantly alternated between combat and negotiation, first in Italy, and then beyond. Closer to our own time, countries very different from one another have adopted first one approach and then the other, depending their strength and the nature of their adversary. Between 1740 and 1974, there were over 350 cases of armed conflict, and both France and Britain were involved in some forty wars.[49]

181 – Many tyrants owed their salvation to attacks carried out abroad. But aggression is no longer the sign of power alone, whether personal or autocratic, as history might lead one to believe. After 1792, in the name of the sovereignty of the people, the French Revolution overturned all pre-existing conventions in its unscrupulous advance. Acting swiftly and without restraint, it unleashed destruction unparalleled at the time and forced changes on Europe that its peoples had neither foreseen nor wanted. Bonaparte had no difficulty in pursuing his course by both negotiation and war.

182 – *No one can choose not to have enemies.* The most peace loving of populations can provoke aggressive impulses in others: it is for their leaders to take timely preventive measures. Civilisation can only exist by having procedures in place to control the spontaneous expression of collective impulses. Negotiation is among the most widely used of these, and has become the most essential now that nuclear weapons, in desperate hands, present a threat of blind and total destruction. (see *77, 119, 1701*)

183 – The inherent tendency to competition in trade could be viewed in the same light: it frequently degenerates into rivalry, antagonism and conflict. The same sort of dynamic is at work in the natural world: all beings need space and have a tendency to seek more. Human society is no exception to this. The demographic pressures and tensions that result from developmental inequality magnify its effects in the modern world.

A predominant position can incite aggressive tendencies on the part of those who feel its weight upon them. (see *1933*)

184 – Leaders harness this dynamism when they impose a new order in place of the old – as Bonaparte did, by provoking a quarrel. Bismarck did the same in creating the new Germany. This dynamism is what mostly keeps negotiation moving forward. (see *2345*)

185 – Sometimes aggressivity results from instability or tensions within a State, quarrels between political and military factions, or a government's desire to distract the attention of the population from unresolved issues, or destabilise its neighbours as a way of reducing their competitiveness.

186 – So widespread is the problem that every nation, unless it is confined to a far-flung island territory, will in the end be obliged to put security above all other considerations.

---

49 G. BOUTHOUL and R. CARRERE: *Le Défi de la guerre*, Paris, PUF, 1976.

In politics at least, all that counts is what is feared. This is exactly what makes terrorism so disturbing as a form of aggressivity: those responsible are often difficult to identify, which undermines the ability of governments to negotiate.

187 – It would be wrong to believe that conflict can only arise in a situation that has become intolerable: aggressivity can also be prompted by any interesting objective that is accessible and easy to attain. The potential for explosion thus depends more on the actors and their political manoeuvres than on their rights. (see *119*)

The wealth and energy spent on conflict could be put to better use in negotiating, but this alone would generally not avert violence. (see *1758, 1867*)

188 – These findings are very important in diplomacy. Not only do States generally miss no opportunity to enhance their importance compared to others, but they are obliged to do so: to paraphrase the great Florentine, Machiavelli, a State that makes another powerful does so at its peril.

189 – In order to realise their projects, many nations or leaders have to choose between open force and negotiation. While it is useless for them to fight in order to obtain something that does not require such effort, it is equally certain that peace and justice are not their only foreign policy objectives.

A party wishing to attack will often use negotiation to limit the scope of the dispute to subjects that will not provoke third party intervention, or to present itself as the victim. Such manoeuvres serve as useful warnings to the statesman.

190 – No matter how sophisticated and extensive are international relations, strategists or negotiators who underestimate the risks of conflict are guilty of an error all the more serious because *war, as the open and often prestigious expression of the spirit of domination, arouses more approval, interest and sometimes passion than diplomacy, which flourishes in a climate of moderation, prudence and discretion.* (see *1758, 1760*)

Neutrality

191 – Some States have a policy of steering clear of conflict in general or of certain conflicts in particular. The reason for this neutrality is that they do not consider themselves bound to either of the opposing parties and do not wish to contribute to the victory of either by force of arms or otherwise.

192 – Neutrality must be distinguished from non-engagement, which is essentially a response to political circumstances, does not involve any specific obligations and has all the appeal of a game of seesaw.[50]

As to non-alignment, born out of the 1961 Belgrade Conference, this is not neutrality either. First of all it was hostility to colonial imperialism (from the time of the Bandung Conference in 1955), then a refusal to see the world divided into

---

50 J. W. BURTON: *International Relations, a General Theory*, Cambridge University Press, 1965, p. 163.

two antagonistic hegemonic blocs and, later, the search for a lasting grouping of countries that were in practice hostile to the United States. More than a hundred countries were grouped under this banner, though the collapse of the system of two nuclear blocs has now forced it to look for a new source of legitimacy. The aggravation of North–South tensions has arrested its decline. This doctrine implies an active diplomatic approach which imposes its own *sui generis* strategy on negotiations.[51]

193 – Neutrality can quite simply be a decision not to intervene in a given conflict. It therefore implies abstention – which must be respected by the parties to the conflict – from participation of any kind, even indirect, in the fighting and the operations surrounding it. However, it does not exclude the negotiation of concessions from the protagonists themselves. (see *582*)

194 – Neutrality can also be the product of a permanent diplomatic policy, such as Switzerland has successfully maintained for almost two centuries while European wars have been waged all around it. In the present state of international society, no neutrality should be regarded as sacred; it not only limits the country's freedom to enter into agreements, but it also requires active diplomacy to keep it alive.

195 – It can happen that neutrality is imposed on a country by powers that find it convenient to refrain from conflict in a region where they fear adverse reactions, and demand guarantees that these injunctions will be respected. This creates a diplomatic relationship of subordination that reduces the negotiating freedom of the State concerned. It will seek to escape from such constraints, as can be seen from the evolution in Austria's diplomacy since 1899.

196 – Neutralisation means that a State is not allowed any military or even diplomatic choices between the opposing parties. This, for example, was the position in which Luxemburg found itself as a result of the Treaty of London in 1867.

Demilitarisation, which forbids the maintenance or deployment of armed forces, weapons and sometimes even military installations, can also have the effect of reducing or removing the capacity to negotiate.

197 – The obligations of neutrality are often ill defined and always difficult to comply with. There is no shortage of examples of breach: commercial and financial transactions, supplies and transportation, telecommunications, information and espionage continue to flourish either because of this protection or in spite of it.

Implicit negotiation can sometimes lead the protagonists to accept derogations such as these,[52] in other cases, by contrast, it reinforces their vigilance.

198 – Neutrality is not a strategy. Rather, it is the very opposite of one, which means that it is conditioned by the strategies of others. It was not declarations or

51 H. LAURENS: 'Les Afro-asiatiques, acteurs ou enjeux de la scène politique internationale', *Politique étrangère*, Paris, 2000, 3, p. 887.
52 M. F. FURET, J. C. MARTINEZ and H. DORANDEU: *La Guerre et le Droit*, Paris, Pedone, 1979, p. 52.

treaties that saved Belgium from being invaded on two successive occasions, and the same could be said of several other countries. (see *24*)

199 – Abstention is always a deliberate attitude, adopted in full knowledge of the risks. It is founded on strength and favourable to diplomatic manoeuvres. (see *582*)

Those who believe that reaffirming their neutrality in the face of another State's manoeuvres can justify passivity are guilty of presumption: they are preparing themselves as victims for the first aggressor to appear. There can be no neutrality without weapons to defend it, and negotiation is one of them.

200 – Neither non-belligerence, neutrality nor neutralisation prohibit a country from taking care of its interests, especially from taking part – as long as it does so impartially – in diplomatic negotiations, if only to facilitate them. It was the assistance of the Swedish Consul General in Paris, enabling negotiations to take place between the German military authorities and the leaders of the French Resistance, that saved the city from destruction.

201 – In truth, all nations are interested to a greater or lesser degree in the way major international military or diplomatic manoeuvres develop, even if they declare themselves indifferent to the quarrels and rivalries of others.[53] Naturally, they will continue to trade and expand their influence, and to sell arms to whoever is willing to buy. But, above all, they cannot afford to deliberately ignore the outcome of conflicts or negotiations, at the risk of having their own interests compromised or of becoming the next victim of the winning side.

The global interdependency of economies and cultures has made neutrality ever more uncertain and relative. Impartiality can never be the refuge of indifference or irresponsibility.

Conflict

202 – Some researchers have attempted to define and map out a model profile of a conflict, from outbreak to conclusion. Such an analysis would be of real interest for diplomats, as, provided it was sufficiently broad in scope and detailed in content, it could serve to guide their initiatives.[54] In reality, each civilisation has its own type of war. (see *1677, 2144*)

203 – It is clear that the study of the *casus belli*, meaning the act to which a State claims the only response is war, might permit a schematic model to be devised whereby negotiation could be substituted for conflict. Case by case knowledge of the limits of unilateral action could be used to set the threshold above which organised processes of conciliation and settlement must be triggered in order to avoid condemnation. (see *93, 2157*)

53 H. LAUTERPACHT: *Disputes, War and Neutrality*, London, Longmans Green, 1952.
54 M. HAAS: *International Conflict*, Indianapolis, New York, Bobbs-Merrill, 1974.
   T. C. SCHELLING: *The Strategy of Conflict*, Harvard University Press, 1960.
   M. SCHERIF: *Group Conflict and Cooperation, their Social Psychology*, London, Routledge, 1967.

204 – In his justification of war, a notion which seemed to him to dominate history, law, politics and ethics, the French philosopher Proudhon saw it as a factor inherent in humanity, 'divinely' inspired, meaning that it proceeded directly from the creative power without question or doubt: according to him, war decided between peoples on the basis of physical and moral strength, and in so doing, gave rise to law, because law is first and foremost the result of force, of which the rule of the majority is one expression.[55]

205 – If negotiations and treaties have partly succeeded in imposing certain rules on the conduct of belligerent activities, this is because war has become accepted as a way of resolving international conflicts and bringing about the great upheavals of history. *In part at least, the law of nations derives from the laws of war: the former has developed in line with the latter.*

206 – Peace was first of all the outcome of a treaty, settlement or pact: negotiation was therefore an inherent part of it. Since then, negotiation has been influential in preventing the proliferation of conflicts and avoiding widespread recourse to force and violence. It has succeeded in limiting the ways of striking at an enemy.

207 – As the supreme expression of sovereignty, the right to make war does not easily wear procedures and restrictions. A declaration of war avoids the effect of surprise, but is used less and less for exactly that reason. Breaking off diplomatic relations serves as a warning, and does not in fact prohibit negotiation from being carried on through intermediaries, or even directly. In the future, international procedures for inquiry and conciliation could limit the outbreak of hostilities. (see *603, 2332*)

208 – Negotiation also aims to give combat a human face and limit its effects. Several congresses throughout the nineteenth and twentieth centuries were devoted to the regulation of war.

Conventions exist that regulate and provide guarantees for enemy personnel and assets, and the conditions of combatants, the wounded and prisoners; others outlaw certain types of conduct or certain weapons. Negotiations are going on with a view to limiting the number and power of weapons of mass destruction. But the moral decline of international society reduces the chances that humanitarian initiatives will succeed, though States cannot rely on open warfare as an excuse. (see *237*)

209 – Today, the creeping menace of insecurity, terrorism and subversion gives particular importance to diplomatic processes geared towards the collective prevention of certain risks, and here, there is great solidarity between governments. Organisational and prospective negotiation play their part, especially in the economy, trade and development, where the danger of conflicts continues to increase. (see *1676*)

210 – In Washington, at the start of the American engagement in Vietnam, and for reasons which are easy to understand, a document appeared that purported

---

55 P. J. PROUDHON: *La Guerre et la Paix*, Paris, Rivière, 1927. D. BRODIE: 'Changing attitudes towards war', in *The Theory and Practice of International Relations*, p. 173.

to emanate from a high-level study group, containing a discreet analysis of the non-military functions of war. Its conclusions created a major scandal, because they suggested that war gives humanity objectives, and therefore motivations, the strength of which has never been equalled, even today.[56]

211 – Some take the view that the absence of war frustrates whole generations of young men by depriving them of the privilege of an epic adventure, the ability to make a historic gesture, and deflects their aggressivity into internal disorder, organised crime, terrorism and violence in all its forms.

In spite of the growth in international negotiation and technical progress, people today still live in fear of bloody confrontation.

212 – *Conflict, internal or external, remains a daily reality for many nations.* It is a matter of concern, because it happens so frequently, that nations accept a so-called Cold War as a more or less uneasy truce without making any attempt to remedy it. While undoubtedly preferable to the horrors of war, this state of indecision is symptomatic of a weak will to negotiate.

213 – Peace has to be assiduously nurtured. It is less difficult to open and conduct hostilities than to end them: instability is self-renewing, particularly in those areas where conflicts have a habit of breaking out.

The precarious nature of *détente*, a process which began with the official visit of General de Gaulle to the USSR in 1966, has shown how deep and lasting are suspicions and incomprehension between nations and ideologies. (see *1692*)

Each time it is put to the test, national motivation finds renewed strength, in combat as well as in negotiation. Newly independent States manifest this sentiment to an even greater degree.

214 – Many attempts have been made to create order, calm and conciliation, but none of pressure, faith, reason or even fear have been able to sustain *entente* between nations in the long term. A world said to be peaceful often only has the appearance of peace. Under the cloak of high principles, this appearance of peace enables dominations and even antagonisms to develop. (see *94*)

215 – It was thought that the progress of civilisations would lead naturally to their harmony: in fact it has today produced increasing tensions and crises, and these are spreading into new areas. *The difficulty of instituting an indispensable world order stems largely from the suspicions of trickery and insincerity that dominate the minds of many protagonists, prompting precautions, fear and reticence.* (see *1970, 1973*)

The appearance – or reappearance – of entities claiming to have the competence of States without either the legitimacy or the means, has triggered an exaggerated appeal to national sentiment, making negotiation more difficult in countries with powerful ethnic, linguistic or religious minorities.

216 – As to making war illegal, diplomacy was doomed to fail. After the creation of the League of Nations, the most celebrated initiative in that direction was the Briand-Kellogg Pact (signed in Paris on 28 August 1928), to which some sixty

56 *Report from Iron Mountain on the Possibility and Desirability of Peace*, Washington, 1967.

States had adhered by 1939: the sequel to that solemn renunciation of war, which provided no sanction other than moral, nor any concrete procedures for preventing aggression, is well known.[57] (see *1779*)

217 – Until today, the procedures for the peaceful settlement of disputes laid down first under the League of Nations, then in the UN Charter (see Article 2 (3) on the obligation to settle disputes peacefully), have proved disappointing, as have the Security Council and, latterly, the General Assembly.

Since 1975, the Conference on Security and Cooperation in Europe (now the OSCE) has provided a negotiating framework designed to structure and calm diplomatic relations in Europe: it has, however, proved unable to prevent or reduce certain severe confrontations. It has, on the other hand, provided some directions for the future (the 1990 Paris Charter for a New Europe), though even these are not free from a certain amount of equivocation. (see *76, 928, 1123, 1190, 1241*)

Conflict prevention remains one of the objectives of prospective and organisational negotiation. (see *2093*)

218 – Security is a classic and inexhaustible theme of international debate. It is not an abstract goal, nor can it be achieved by treaties, because relations between nations can never be set in stone. The preservation of peace requires the law to be constantly adapted to changing realities, crises to be predicted and resolved in good time, national expectations to be reset and forces kept in constant readiness.

To live in peace, it is necessary to know how to combine the forces and interests that divide societies – in other words, nations, since the entire world today is divided. This, internally as well as between nations, is the purpose of negotiation. (see *150*)

219 – Relations between nations that proceed by exchange instead of by taking, avoid conflict and safeguard balance and security, deserve to be studied carefully and encouraged. Diplomacy and its underlying attitudes, the methods it teaches and the agreements it can produce, adapt to the balance of power and have the advantage of producing a certain kind of social order, which is not always fair but is at least accepted and less vulnerable. (see *335*)

§4. Negotiation and war

220 – Napoleon deemed war to be the natural state of mankind. Nothing in history, ancient or modern, gives grounds for contradicting him. But negotiation, too, is a natural state of affairs: even among the most primitive peoples, it has always preceded, accompanied and followed hostilities.

Negotiation is often presented as the antithesis of combat, because it tends to head off bloody confrontations and promote agreement between the parties by means of mutual concessions. This is wrong, because, like war, negotiation fulfils the essential needs of the group – survival, improvement in its conditions, protection against external dangers and the organisation of its security.

---

57 J.-B. DUROSELLE: *Histoire diplomatique de 1919 à nos jours*, Paris, Dalloz, 1978, p. 93.

221 – It is not possible to treat war and peace as opposites when history shows us countless examples of undeclared belligerence and countless examples of physical or psychological violence between nations, and while, in the words of General de Gaulle, the story of every war begins in peacetime. (see *1761*)

The modern era prefers to think of war in terms of form rather than function, or more precisely in terms of its forms, since many of these are new: as well as traditional warfare we now have conflicts that are delocalised, deterritorialised, demilitarised, destructured and denationalised, but that still involve the deaths of people, many of whom are non-belligerents. (see *1692*)

222 – *Combat is a sanction for negotiation, as negotiation is for combat.* In relations between States, temporal power depends on the strength of armies: Stalin's question, 'How many divisions has the Pope?' was not without relevance.

Each State must therefore limit its efforts and its strategic engagements to match its military capabilities.

223 – Negotiation can enhance military power, but is no substitute for it.[58] Negotiation works better if the risk of war is acknowledged so decisions can be taken about what is at stake and what means to deploy. But, at the same time, it is only meaningful if it carries a sanction, providing an overriding reason for reaching agreement, in other words if the price of failure might be open hostility. (see *1749*)

224 – Once the principles are settled and the strategy established, each of these different activities comes into its own. The art of negotiating is distinct from the art of government, but respects its choices. War sets itself against diplomacy as confrontation does against compromise, command against discussion and the rigours of discipline against the flavours of subtlety. (see *928*)

225 – Open combat and negotiation are concomitant and sometimes competing types of relations between human societies; each of them provides the means for any nation to express the same historic destiny, and the same political will. Neither statesmen nor military chiefs can afford to ignore or underestimate either one without risking severe disappointment. (see *1699, 1750, 1175, 2325*)

226 – Experience shows, moreover, that it is vain to try to solve political problems by military expedients or expeditions: provided they are begun in time, discussions stand a better chance of limiting the scope of a conflict. And, even the greatest victory can be precarious. (see *1721*)

Sooner or later, States come round to negotiating; sooner or later, they will negotiate about real issues.

227 – Great political enterprises often go hand in hand with events of extreme gravity in the life of nations: diplomatic manoeuvres are governed and explained by their historical, even chronological, context. The characteristic of decisive negotiations is that they normally take place against a background of conflict.

The more war loses its decisive role, the more negotiation takes its place as a form of combat, at the deciding phase of the conflict. (see *1775*)

---

58 H. A. KISSINGER, *White House Years*, Boston, Little, Brown & Co., 1979.

228 – Crises are also favourable to the diplomatic approach, as they induce each party to establish its priorities and find out those of its partners. A party that gives ground under pressure from another will often be clearing the way for a new equilibrium to be agreed upon that proves a good solution. *Negotiations begin in a climate of tension, not of indifference.* (see **555, 2158**)

229 – A further effect of conflict is the solidarity between the protagonists, a solidarity which finds expression in negotiation. In practice this brings out changes in behaviour and in reactions, and the balancing of arguments and concessions that create bonds – often very powerful – between the opposing parties. Often, the more intense the antagonism, the more solid the result of the negotiation. *The most stable solutions are often those that have been most strongly debated.* (see **1761, 2051**)

230 – A spirit of conciliation is often the result of prosperity or weariness. But no power will ever compromise over the essential underpinnings of its existence: Poland exposed itself to the risk of war in order to protect the status given to the city of Danzig by the Treaty of Versailles, which gave it access to the sea. (see **2304**)

231 – Where it is inevitable that a given event will provoke a confrontation, it is as well to give one's adversary timely warning. Ways can probably be found of avoiding conflict. This is how Britain succeeded, in 1830, in ensuring that King Louis Philippe did not accept the crown offered to him by the Belgians.

232 – Certain doctrines have served as the legal basis for war: a just cause, just behaviour or a just result have frequently been invoked by belligerents. (see **733**)

The point was made with great force by Proudhon, who insisted that diplomacy was nothing more than the official mouthpiece of war.

233 – It always helps the cause of combat if the negotiator can give it a plausible justification, such as legitimate defence, the prevention of crime, the means of fighting injustice or the fulfilment of an obligation.[59] Austria's intervention in Italy, and that of France in Spain in 1822 and 1823, gained from having the support of the Holy Alliance. The United States embarked on the Korean War in 1950 in the name of the United Nations, and used the cover of the United Nations for the Gulf campaign of 1990–1991 – a diplomatic tactic which, in the latter case, had the effect of reining in the reaction of the Arab world.

234 – *Combat proves the sincerity of an alliance.* Conventions without the sword are mere words.[60] The negotiator should be as concerned about how the treaty will be put into effect as by his own commitment to do so, should it enter into force: France should have been able to take military initiatives to prevent Germany from breaching the essential provisions of the Treaty of Versailles.[61] Diplomacy therefore undoubtedly has a military dimension.[62] (see **864**)

---

59 C. de VISSCHER: *Théories et réalités en droit international public*, Paris, Pedone, 1960, p. 152.
60 T. HOBBES: *Leviathan*, London, 1651, Chapter 16.
61 R. ARON: *Paix et guerre entre les nations*, Paris, Calmann-Lévy, 1962, p. 53.
62 F. SONDERMAN, etc.: *The Theory and Practice of International Relations*, Englewood Cliffs, Prentice Hall, 1970, p. 167.

235 – If the diplomat for his part prefers negotiation, he often counts on the soldier to ensure the most favourable conditions. It can even happen that a rapidly executed military operation will overtake a diplomatic one. This was the case with Napoleon's Italian campaign, the consequences of which for European diplomacy from the Rhine to the Mediterranean were appreciated by his contemporaries only after the event, when Austria fell from predominance in Europe. (see *1752*)

The victor in combat becomes a negotiating partner who must be reckoned with: Russia's entry onto the European diplomatic scene dates from the appearance of its armies on the Danube and later in the Alps, at the end of the eighteenth century.

236 – War and negotiation often go together. Leaders negotiate, or order negotiations to be conducted, in secret, while their soldiers are fighting each other.[63] Military operations go ahead even while official talks are taking place: in Munster, in 1648, work on the Treaties of Westphalia changed direction several times, depending on the successes or failures of the armies of the King of France; and at Luneville, in 1801, Austria's diplomats gave ground each time their armies suffered defeat at the hands of Bonaparte.

The good military chief uses negotiation to undermine the strength, the numbers or the determination of his enemies.

237 – The link is even more vital today: with the appearance of atomic weapons, the traditional hope for victory has given way to an overriding concern for collective survival. When nuclear conflict threatens, its prevention is no longer a game: it becomes a necessity. (see *1731*)

Confrontations, even virtual confrontations, give rise to intense negotiating activity, secret or official, as soon as governments realise that their problems are not capable of being solved by force.[64] (see *854, 1722, 1749*)

Total technological warfare risks leaving no more place for negotiation: its implacable and overwhelming logic would stifle all peaceable humanitarian initiatives.

238 – In any political enterprise, up to the point of victory and even after, negotiation and combat complement and reflect each other. This is true even beforehand: prevention must start not at the moment when the quarrel erupts, but before that, wherever it is that the risk arises, before antagonisms are allowed to develop that may be inevitable but should not necessarily lead to war. The negotiation of alliances serves to deter aggression. (see *853*)

239 – The role of diplomacy is to enable nations to bring about change without blood being shed. It therefore looks with disfavour on personal hostility and verbal abuse, as these are the first signs of open aggression.

240 – The tendency to treat frontiers as sacred has increased the temptation to interfere: war takes the form of subversion, terrorism or revolution, and

---

63 G. PEDRONCINI: *Les Négociations secrètes pendant la Grande Guerre*, Paris, Flammarion, 1969.

64 P. JESSUP: 'Should International Law Recognise an Intermediate Status between Peace and War?', *AJIL*, 1954, p. 58.

non-belligerence can serve as a cover for indirect intervention. National defence systems are disorganised and prone to challenge, a situation which is aggravated by economic and cultural tensions. Negotiation thus appears one of the most effective ways of expressing, and safeguarding, sovereignty, as long as it maintains the levels of communication necessary not only for social cohesion, but also for an assessment of the risks. (see *636, 876, 2250*)

241 – When conducted in an attentive, well-informed and consistent manner, negotiation fulfils the fundamental need for security felt by all human societies: it allows for external dangers to be guarded against and kept at bay, at least to the greatest extent possible. Indeed, no nation can be protected completely and for all time against events which might imperil its peace, its independence or even its very existence, in other words, all the elements on which its security depends.

The preventive function of military diplomacy continues to grow in importance. (see *1689, 2093*)

242 – Military defeat always ends by forcing parties to deal with each other, but the shrewd statesman will learn this lesson from victory well before his opponent is reduced to ruin. History shows, however, that the victor is often more interested in pursuing his adversary than in achieving his rational objectives.

Those who are reluctant to negotiate in good time, end up doing so too late. (see *521*)

243 – An armistice allows a temporary halt to hostilities so that negotiations can take place. In reality a truce often serves as an opportunity for the belligerent forces to regroup: in 1813, after Lutzen and Bautzen, Napoleon used the chance to bring in more troops, and his opponents doubled their own.

244 – The ending of a state of war can result in the normalisation of relations between the belligerent States and, above all, in the reestablishment of diplomatic relations. But the fabric of the legal relationship will have been torn, and negotiations must be resumed across all areas in order to reconcile the interests of the former enemies: the treaty entered into in August 1978 between China and Japan represents an effort of this type.

Nowadays the peace treaty has tended to become an instrument of collective bargaining between nations, thus compounding the difficulties involved in negotiating.

245 – If negotiation can put an end to wars, its primary function is to exploit the conflict, by imparting stability and approval to gains made by combat. For Montesquieu, the purpose of victory is conquest, and the purpose of conquest is preservation: one should take only what one can keep.[65] Put another way, not everything gained by war is necessarily later sanctioned by negotiation.

To the losing party, timely negotiation offers the chance to limit the losses sustained, mitigate or halt its collapse and stifle other sources of potential conflict.

246 – The evolution in military concepts has itself been shaped by the diplomatic context. The notion of victory is a case in point. Where this is achieved by the

---

65 C. de MONTESQUIEU: *De l'esprit des lois*, X, 3.

vanquished submitting to the will of the victor, the latter can no longer hope for total domination: it must seek not so much to annihilate its enemy's forces as to weaken them to the point where they no longer stand in its way, while preserving their capacity to safeguard internal order and guarantee external commitments.

247 – The context and objective of a battle will therefore be dominated by the strategic concept of preserving the elements needed to reestablish a peaceful balance of power after the event. All *'après-guerre'* experiences point in the same direction, despite certain atrocities that have been greeted with horror. Britain under Lord Castlereagh opposed the dismemberment of France after the Hundred Days War, in order to leave open the possibility of reestablishing the balance of power in Europe; Britain under Lloyd George opposed the breaking up of Germany in 1919 as a way of avoiding French domination of the continent.

248 – If victory is the reason and purpose of combat, its only strategic value lies in the benefit it can produce in political terms. During the last world war, as soon as the danger of Communism became real for them, the Western Allies lost no time in declaring that their intention was to wipe out Germany's militarism and totalitarianism, but not to destroy Germany.

Negotiation puts the final touches to what has been achieved by combat, and ensures, to the extent possible, that the results are lasting and conclusive. It is through negotiation that the vanquished can moderate the victor.

249 – Strategy must therefore look beyond the war itself, to make sure that its very excesses do not give rise to fresh instability. Demanding the unconditional surrender of one's enemy can prove to be a mistake if capitulation creates a vacuum and thus a serious diplomatic imbalance. It is not uncommon for rivalry between two parties to have left a third, sometimes less favoured, in control of the situation. (see *452*)

250 – Even though the inclination to negotiate is undoubtedly in conflict with the impulse for domination, whether ideological or military, negotiation remains a means whereby strong nations may gain the upper hand and weaker ones can defend themselves against subjugation.

251 – A statesman will choose whichever solution suits him, usually the best, but sometimes the only one available given the limitations of time and place. Given the power to do so, experience shows that he will not hesitate to impose an unequal bargain, even if he does not always do this by means of threats or physical coercion. Peace under the Roman Empire was maintained by war as well as negotiation, but neither heeded the wishes of peoples incapable of any resistance. A much later example was President Woodrow Wilson: however generous he may have been in his statements, he was intractable when it came to curbing the ambitions of France and Italy in 1919. (see *656*)

252 – In this respect, the attitude of leaders is of the utmost importance. When this is driven by a wish to dominate or by a dogmatic fixation, it does not sit well with the spirit of negotiation, even if some of the motions are gone through. When they fail to respect principles such as non-interference in the affairs of another nation,

respect for its dignity and its freedom to make decisions, diplomats open up the way to the soldiers.

Section 2: Thought and action

253 – *Negotiation is to diplomacy what battle is to war, the principal means by which it is carried on.*

Clausewitz saw the opening of battle as the real purpose of war, because its object is to subdue and defeat one's opponent. The diplomat, like the warrior, enjoys a succession of combats, varying in scale, each of which helps to put the parties in a new situation either of attack or defence. There are many similarities in the approach each of these requires. From his first Italian campaign, Bonaparte showed his talent for dividing the forces of the enemy: one after the other, he neutralised Sardinia, Parma, Modena, Naples and the Holy See, in order to deprive Austria of its allies on the front, but he did so more by negotiation than by fighting.

254 – Despite the rich body of theory devoted to it, however, the traditional battle remains an activity with a stunningly simple objective. What is at stake on the field of battle is a matter of life and death, and, especially for the commander, the survival of his men. A confrontation of two hostile forces produces a more clear-cut situation than is often the case in negotiation, where the goal is not necessarily to crush one's opponent, and which can equally well involve discussions between several participants.

255 – It is easy to see, then, why the simplified view soldiers take of the practice of their main activity, as well as of its value, will not work for diplomacy: the human factor is the same, but the stakes are much more subtle. Victory for a diplomat does not mean routing one's opponent, but will often involve signing a settlement or postponing discussion of a particular issue. In 1813, Metternich contributed to Napoleon's defeat without having to face him on the battlefield: as talks went on, he moved from alliance to hostility. The transition took place over several months, starting with a declaration of benevolent neutrality and proceeding to an offer of mediation that was bound to be refused.

256 – The qualities of the strategist may be deployed in negotiation as well as in war:[66] the principles that dictate the means to be used are effective only because their choice and implementation adapt to changing circumstances. The particular character of the people concerned will also come into play. Sooner or later, every nation has had to perfect the art which will enable it to dominate, be it warfare, trade or negotiation. (see *2325*)

§1. Negotiation as a tactic

257 – Negotiation is a means of settling disputes, in other words a type of combat carried on by means which, while falling short of outright hostility, are not

---

66 G. ALLISON: *Essence of Decision: Explaining the Cuban Missile Crisis*, Boston, Little Brown, 1971.

always peaceful.[67] *Diplomatic tactics are based as much, if not more, on the analysis of differences and conflicts as on the desire for conciliation, settlement and accord: national policies will inevitably diverge.* So opposed were the strategies of Austria and Russia in the Balkans in 1914 that the compromise proposed by Britain with regard to Serbia was not enough to prevent war.

258 – The very nature of a negotiation can render it spurious. Sometimes, as with the Romans, it is seen as a means of imposing domination without a fight, and sometimes it offers a good opportunity for a battle, as was the case with the fall of Napoleon. What were the three Great Powers hoping for when they sowed the seeds of discord in agreeing to the status of Berlin after the last world war?

259 – Diplomatic manoeuvre is not always the instrument of peace. Such is the inevitable conclusion from the behaviour of almost all the great statesmen of old Europe, whether sovereigns, cardinals or ministers.

Negotiation is thus one of the expressions of conflict: when skilfully practised, it can reveal the weaknesses in an opponent's armoury, or lead one of the protagonists to commit the error by which the other will in the long term be weakened.

260 – By contrast with war, where feelings of hostility reach levels of frenzy that permit no restraint and sometimes exceed even the wishes of the belligerents, and where, as Clausewitz observed, each of the opposing parties tends to escalating extremes of violence and even cruelty, diplomacy is dependent on reason, and usually follows a pattern the participants accept. (see *2332*)

261 – In negotiation as in war, each protagonist seeks to impose its will and does its utmost not to be subjected to the will of the other. It comes as no surprise, then, that the methods of diplomacy are not always directed towards achieving agreement between the partners. Sometimes the weaker party will get what it wants by challenging the stronger.

262 – Diplomacy can also be the scene of the most brutal and coercive of undertakings: in 1938 and 1939, in the space of a few months and with no apparent difficulty, Germany succeeded, by using every form of verbal and psychological coercion, in annexing Austria and dividing up Czechoslovakia. In deliberately triggering a crisis whose violence reached the level of collective hysteria, and in total disregard for the law, Hitler got what he wanted before the eyes of all, by issuing promises, taunts and threats irrespective of borders and authorities. Nor is this the only example of what might be described as diplomatic war.

263 – Negotiation broadly depends on psychological factors. Uncertainty, like surprise, has long been used to make an impression on the opponent, and reduce his physical and mental resistance. Fear is aggravated by fatigue. This tactic brings into play two key elements in negotiation, determination and tenacity, which are also two characteristics of the fighter.[68] (see *1709*)

---

67 A. PLANTEY: 'La négociation, quelques considérations sur l'art de la diplomatie comparé à celui de la guerre', *Revue de défense nationale*, June 1974, p. 15.
68 R. ARON: *Penser la guerre, Clausewitz*, Paris, Gallimard, 1976.

264 – As with all fields of human activity, especially combat, negotiation involves a subject that is alive and will react. It takes account of the balance of power, which can be extremely complex and fluctuating: the outcome of congresses has often been decided by the outcome of fighting. *Negotiators not only adapt to the imponderable and the unforeseeable, but also take account of new facts and outcomes as they happen, whether these are part of the discussion or external to it.* (see *2146*)

Initiative

265 – Diplomatic initiative gives the negotiator a considerable advantage: it allows him to choose the moment, the conditions and the subject matter of the discussions. But it can only be gained by those with highly developed qualities of imagination, intuition and calculation, and then, only if there is no coercion or threat to limit their independence of action. After Napoleon's retreat from Russia in 1812, Metternich pursued his negotiations as the Emperor progressively weakened. (see *522*)

266 – Dialogue can sometimes serve to break a process which appears to be headed for inevitable conflict. The more serious and sudden the attack, the more radical the response will tend to be, and the speedier and simpler must be the negotiation. Even where it involves a concession, a unilateral manoeuvre can create a situation that makes it difficult to reach agreement, where there is no appropriate tactical response. This is all the more true of the sort of ultimatum to which the other might respond with a peace-making overture, as happened when Germany sent a gunboat to Agadir in 1911.[69] (see *104, 112*)

267 – Once lost, the diplomatic initiative is difficult to recapture, especially for a government whose position is deteriorating, even temporarily. During the 1813 campaigns, Napoleon was wrong to wait for his most severe reversals before agreeing to negotiate with his enemies: it must be said, however, that Metternich did everything in his power to ensure the Emperor had been defeated. After Napoleon's second abdication, Louis XVIII of France, despite all his prudence and the aid of Talleyrand, encountered the greatest difficulty in putting France back in an acceptable diplomatic position. (see *522*)

268 – Anyone who sees it is in his interests will begin a negotiation, sometimes simply because he senses danger. This does not mean, however, that the process will work to his advantage. *No one ever regretted approaching a negotiation as if it were a fight, by weighing up the possible consequences of defeat.*

269 – No one should open a negotiation if their aim is to win at any price, whether because of weakness, vanity or the pursuit of glory. As the French philosopher La Rochefoucauld remarked, such a negotiator will lose sight of the interests he is supposed to be defending: he will no longer fight but give way, to the great disappointment of those instructing him. (see *2406*)

---

69 G. BONNEFOUS: *Histoire politique de la Troisième République*, I, Paris, PUF, 1956, p. 256.

270 – The stakes in a negotiation might not always be as dramatic as those in battle, but they can nonetheless be high. Many statesmen have accepted the risks of war, driven by their own aggressive instincts, and pushed the bounds of diplomatic blackmail to its very limits. In the face of defeat or emergency, the freedom of a nation has sometimes depended on the quality of its diplomatic envoys: Florence was saved more than once by the skills of Machiavelli. (see *2400*)

271 – In order to keep nations at the negotiating table, there must not be too great a disparity between what is at stake for each of them. If there is no such balance, the severity of the risks will lead each of the parties to take unilateral action in the form of preventive or protective measures, and possibly provoke armed conflict. It thus becomes ever more important to be able to predict how events will turn out, and to take timely steps to limit confrontation, ward off threats and open up a dialogue. (see *93, 2076*)

272 – On the whole, negotiation will only be meaningful or have sufficient impact to modify the course of events, let alone succeed in accomplishing its objectives, if those planning and conducting it assume the risk of failure. Then, they will use every means they can to succeed, with the fighter's determination and tenacity. Talleyrand and Metternich were never such fine negotiators or such effective fighters as when their backs were to the wall: when everything depended on it, their talents could be displayed to the full. (see *2446*)

273 – From the moment a negotiation opens, it will always settle something, whether expressly or by implication. Negotiation presupposes that a party intends to affect the course of events in order to achieve a specific objective, and to do so by acting with or against one or more other parties. (see *2328*)

It is as instructive to examine the circumstances in which negotiations are not opened as those where they are.

274 – The mere possibility of negotiation is enough to assess the balance of power and guess at the intentions of the countries concerned. It therefore has implications for the way events unfold, sometimes because it enables the parties to foresee and prepare for a confrontation, and sometimes because the failure of initial approaches will allow them to construct working hypotheses about the attitude of the other parties. In this respect, the months that preceded the Second World War are a rich source of information.[70]

275 – *A decision not to resolve an issue, or not to enter into a negotiation, is already a decision in itself, even if only to accept the authority of the most powerful. In war, too, the less confident will avoid open hostilities.* (see *526*)

The negotiator can also use the tactics of attrition.

Engagement

276 – Negotiation must get off to a good start if it is to succeed. In 1800, France wanted peace and Bonaparte set about giving it to her by using a strategy aimed at

---

70 J.-B. DUROSELLE: *Histoire diplomatique de 1919 à nos jours*, Paris, Dalloz, 1978, p. 244.

consolidating the conquests of the Revolution. He therefore needed to maintain the divisions in the camp of those who he sensed would still be ranged against him. Thus he made it his business to enter into separate discussions with each of them, all the time ensuring that circumstances favoured his achieving what he wanted against each one. In the space of a few months, he had held talks in Madrid with Spain, in Luneville with Austria, in Paris with the Turks and the Russians and then with the British at Amiens. All of them were successful.

In diplomacy, as in war, it is better to deal separately with powers which, if they were united, would prove stronger.

277 – Once a major error has been committed, nothing can be done to correct it:[71] a position, once disarmed, can no longer be defended. The same is true for a party that agrees to, or is compelled to negotiate from, a gratuitous concession, or a position which is too unfavourable. It would need all the skill of Talleyrand to be the exception to the rule.

278 – Rivalries between leaders, ethnic divisions and competition between States are responsible for many negotiations getting off to a bad start: this has been evident in the Near East since 1919, and there are daily examples of it in contemporary diplomacy. Like the soldier, the negotiator must prepare painstakingly before committing, by assembling information, choosing the ground on which he will fight and constructing his arguments. (see *2116*)

279 – The negotiator often hesitates to venture into unknown territory, and the slow progress of a negotiation is often a sign of its importance. This was true of the process of rapprochement between China under Mao and the United States under Nixon. Any major change of direction is more productive if taken at a cautious pace, as it is often only by stages that the real issues come to light. There also has to be a real willingness and need for dialogue, as the progress of the proceedings will show. (see *2008, 2148*)

280 – *It is unwise to give up a favourable position, a guarantee or an advantage, without getting something in return.* Anyone doing so will soon regret not being able to use it to facilitate the transaction, especially when faced with a calculating and determined partner. The retreat of American forces in 1945 from the line they had reached in fighting – as far as Saxony and Bohemia – gave such satisfaction to Stalin, even before the Potsdam Conference, that he could have given something in return. (see *579*)

281 – No statesman will undertake any move from a position of weakness, on pain of being coerced or outbid, and of exposing himself to the risks of tactics founded on irritation and excess. If his aim is to impose his will on a powerful adversary, he must first either convince, isolate or disarm him, and also reinforce his own position, decide what he can offer in return, or find allies. (see *142, 1702*)

282 – The diplomat is better off playing for time than accepting another's predominant position. If he cannot do this, he should limit the subject of the

---

71 A. SIEGFRIED: *La Fontaine, Machiavel français*, Paris, Ventadour, 1955, p. 24.

discussions and of any agreement, breaking down the problem until the point is reached where there is an advantage on which he can rely.

The one who can wait will emerge the stronger: he has time on his side.

283 – If victory cannot be obtained, it is often enough not to lose, to preserve the opportunity to carry on the fight in the hope of an acceptable outcome. Many young nations have found their way to independence by carrying an unequal combat from the military into the political arena.

284 – From the beginning, the negotiator must pay attention to every factor that prejudges the outcome of the discussions, even if it is of secondary importance, such as the choice of venue, who takes the chair and the terms of reference of the meeting. This is all the more true for points that will be decisive of the overall issues, and when the central core of the negotiation is reached. He should choose the ground with care, in anticipation of the answers he will receive.

Every line of argument contains within it the logic of its own contradiction: an argument can be turned so that it can be used later. (see **2441**)

Confrontation

285 – The will must be strong to do what has been decided upon, Richelieu wrote. Like the warrior, the diplomat must determine his line before engaging in any kind of combat. Thereafter, he must follow it, and make sure his subordinates and allies follow it too. He must decide not only on his strategic objective – the grand design – but also the methods he will use to reach it, in other words his tactics. If he needs to negotiate in order to do this, he should not be prevented from undertaking other manoeuvres, even in the event of disagreement. (see **2325**)

286 – Firmness of purpose in no way inhibits flexibility of approach, provided there is no wavering, contradiction or lack of commitment. The negotiator should beware, though, of believing that diplomacy is designed to solve everything, or capable of doing so: the more direct the line a diplomat wishes to pursue, the firmer he must be.

287 – Nothing is more difficult than to hold to the line of measure and impartiality in a world where these are unknown. *There is no moderation without firmness, in negotiation as elsewhere.* (see **2327**)

288 – The primary function of strategic judgment is to decide where is the heart of the matter, or the centre of gravity of the forces in play. This is also true in diplomacy. The solution must address these issues, if it is to be fully effective. Anyone who undertakes or leads a negotiation must set his main objective on the basis not only of his own long-term interests, but also of a careful evaluation of the weaknesses of his opponent. (see **2340**)

289 – Here, too, the means deployed must be in line with the intended objective. A grand design will be executed over a long period of time, even if achieving it sometimes involves detours from the chosen path. This can be seen from the building of the great European States, which came about mostly through

negotiation rather than war. The Soviet strategy for Poland was the same with regard to the Allies as it was with regard to Germany: to ensure that the USSR had a protective zone around it, but this disappeared with the fall of the Communist bloc and the loss of Moscow's supremacy.[72] (see *2326*)

290 – Success depends less on means than on how they are used. Any plan too ambitious for the means available to implement it is bound to fail. The same is true of any negotiation which goes against the order of things: Austria, left weakened and isolated by the treaties of 1919, could not hold out against Pan-Germanism without an effective guarantee from some of the great powers. Likewise, the Franco-Russian pact was a dead letter by 1936 in the face of German aggression, since neither Poland nor Romania intended to allow the deployment of Soviet forces.

291 – The principles governing the means to be used only work when adapted to the circumstances.[73] The negotiator who remains indifferent to major changes in the situation is doomed to fail: if he does not rethink his strategy he should at least review his tactics, in other words, how the engagement is conducted.

292 – Fate accounts for half our actions and leaves the other half more or less under our control:[74] those who persist in a certain course of action without heed to the fact that their own position is slipping in relation to the others should not be surprised to find themselves disarmed when the critical point is reached in the negotiation.

293 – By watching the situation attentively, the diplomat can understand what to do, preferably before the party who might derive an advantage. He will show perspicacity and tenacity in his efforts, adapting his moves to vulnerabilities in his opponent's position or his own, and also to the overall context. When in discussions with Germany in 1939, Stalin could see that war was inevitable and took that danger into account in his strategy, but he made the tactical error of allowing himself to be taken by surprise by his accomplice's swift about-turn in 1941 and almost fell victim to aggression.

294 – According to the French diplomat de Callières, the statesman should keep the situation under constant review. He does not hesitate to take advantage of the slightest error on the part of his adversary, or even of his success if this destabilises the overall position. But he will not consent to be led into a confrontation in which he will be forced to make concessions. Such is the lesson to be learned from Talleyrand's masterly tactics after the defeat of Napoleon, though admittedly this was at a time when the need for patience was understood. (see *519, 539*)

295 – Normally, the negotiator deals with whoever is designated as his official interlocutor, but he might have to fight on other fronts as well. He should take care to deal with the smallest possible number of people, while still following every

72 J. LALOY: *Entre guerres et paix*, Pzris, Plon, 1966.
73 C. de GAULLE: *Le Fil de l'épée (de la doctrine)*, Editions Bergres-Levrault, 1932, I.
74 N. MACHIAVELLI: *Il Principe*, Florence, 1513, Chapter 25.

point made and every comment, not only in the hope of obtaining information that should not have been divulged, but because there will be useful information on which to base his judgements. And, like a soldier, he should be mindful of the security of his own camp and ensure his secrets are safe. (see *690*)

296 – De Callières explained that the two main duties of a negotiator were to do his government's business and find out the business of the other side. Like the art of war, the art of negotiation sets great store by uncovering the secrets of one's opponent. (see *2011*)

Sun Tse taught that one should have spies everywhere and neither neglect any intelligence coming to hand, nor indiscreetly pass any on. As for enemy spies, they might prove very useful if they could be easily induced to convey disinformation to those who sent them.[75]

297 – The negotiator will not gather intelligence himself, but will entrust this to a discreet member of his team. He should not forget, however, that others will be doing the same to him. (see *2465*)

La Fontaine, the French moralist, said that those who make no noise are as dangerous as the rest, if not more so.

298 – By definition, a manoeuvre is something one can have carried out by others: so is negotiation, which is often conducted at different times and on several levels. The strategist must secure the collaboration of all those whose participation is essential for success, and of them alone. It is up to him to decide how much to reveal to them of his objectives and tactics, so as to allow each one to play an effective part in the enterprise without running the risk of confusion or indiscretion. (see *451*)

299 – An effective manoeuvre, especially in times of difficulty, is one based on the simple precepts of good sense, experience and history. By contrast with the sometimes rough or heavy-handed approach to diplomacy, there also exist elaborate and complex negotiations played out in several places at once, by successive stages, leading in a number of different directions, on subjects that can be interrelated or contradictory. At one time the Papacy excelled at just such exercises as these, which involved them in little risk. (see *2337*)

300 – The reasoned logic of negotiation presupposes that each of the protagonists is capable of controlling his behaviour to the very end, and of remaining faithful to his line of action. However, this should not necessarily be disclosed at the outset, unless it is to make a definitive commitment that might have an effect on the other party's resolve. (see *2053*)

301 – There seems no reason not to reveal one's precise objective, if the intention is to reject any counter proposal. This is not a wise posture, however, for a party ready to make concessions in order to succeed at any price. According to Balzac, respect is won by holding steadfastly to one's latest resolutions.

---

75 SUN TSE: *The Thirteen Articles*, Fifth century BC.

302 – It is rare for a negotiation not to present a way of overcoming opposition and arriving at a compromise acceptable to all interested parties, sometimes including those who were not represented at the negotiating table.

303 – As the negotiations progress, deadlines become more urgent, the terms of the exchange more defined and motives clearer. Incidental issues fall by the wayside. In war, too, up to the moment when the final outcome is decided by force of arms, tactics are adapted and forces adjusted in a balance each party seeks to unsettle or reestablish to its own advantage. Only after the negotiation has ended can it be seen how the different factors weighed in the balance.

304 – Many negotiators have observed that intransigence is more profitable than conciliation:[76] *diplomatic engagement is still a combat, in which it may be necessary to use force in order to win.* In a serious negotiation, an expression of goodwill or magnanimity will be interpreted as a sign of weakness or vulnerability, or as a ruse: it will not lead the other party to do something similar. No attitude is worse when negotiating than to appear uninterested in what is at stake. (see *2152*)

305 – Taken to their logical conclusion, some declarations or developments can lead to absurd results. This happens when a party adopts a posture of intransigence it does not have the means to defend, or is forced to carry out a threat which is against its obvious interests. The clear-headed statesman will therefore refrain from becoming embroiled in any diplomatic or military process that might one day turn out to his disadvantage. (see *108*)

306 – The experienced negotiator thus avoids making boastful claims, or any declarations that are not backed by power. For he will be put to the test: when the French minister Thiers was abandoned by King Louis Philippe in the face of Palmerston's threatened military intervention, he found himself, in 1840, unable to offer the Egyptian Pacha Mohammed Ali the support he had promised him against Turkey. After that, he lost face and had to relinquish power.[77] (see *2438*)

307 – Having a special relationship with a State is no guarantee that it will not exert pressure. On the contrary: a friend or ally may find it easy to ask for a concession, a change of direction or collusion from a party for whom refusal would be difficult.
Striking first at a party that offers no threat can mask real aggressive intent.

308 – Diplomatic tactics, like military tactics, are replete with negative manoeuvres. Obstruction works both ways. It can derail or suspend a discussion that is going in the wrong direction, or on the other hand it can be used to prevent an opponent from delaying a desired outcome. It can be used to consolidate a position that would otherwise have had to change, or on the other hand to block undesired developments. It allows one party to wait until the other is no longer there, or is in a better frame of mind, or even to discredit it. (see *542*)

---

76 J. C. FAUVET: *Pour comprendre les conflits sociaux*, Paris, Editions d'organisation, 1973, p. 68.
77 P. RENOUVIN: *Histoire des relations internationales. Le XIXe siècle*, I, Paris, Hachette, 1954, p. 120.

309 – Proposing something that cannot be accepted amounts to obstructing a solution: when, in 1814, Austria in the person of Metternich, and Britain in the person of Castelreagh wanted to guarantee the borders of Turkey, Tsar Alexander forced them to abandon the idea by imposing the condition that territorial disputes were resolved first. (see *593*)

Scope for manoeuvre

310 – Negotiation does not restrict the scope for diplomatic manoeuvre. True, its effects are limited, in the legal sense, to the parties around the table and the terms of the agreement. But negotiation forms part of a complex and changing pattern of international relations in which a balance establishes itself, and must thus contribute to that balance. (see *2259*)

311 – It is sometimes recommended to break down one negotiation into as many specific negotiations as possible: this way, each party retains a greater freedom to manoeuvre and will tend to concentrate its forces where its most important interests are at stake. This method can prove effective where there are a varying or indefinite number of parties. Otherwise, there is a natural tendency for generalised bargaining to take place, or at least an exchange of concessions, resulting in a package deal. (see *276*)

312 – Some methods of diplomacy tend to divide up negotiations in order to preserve as much freedom of action and superiority as possible: Britain has long been careful to deal with separate interlocutors on matters concerning Europe, as well as on maritime issues. Nowadays it is difficult for powers with extensive interests to separate world politics into isolated compartments: the balance ultimately establishes itself at a global level.

Negotiating on several fronts allows one to select the most promising partner. (see *2335*)

313 – The diplomatic resolution to the First World War was brought about in separate, successive phases, involving different parties depending on what the situation required. It began with President Wilson asking the Allies and the Germans to accept as 'preliminaries' his fourteen points of 18 January 1918. For a time, Marshal Foch was given authority to hold discussions with his opponents to regulate the consequences of the Armistice. The provisions of the treaty to be signed with Germany were negotiated only between the Allies.[78]

314 – Taking a broad view of the balance between nations, it is normal for the impact of any one negotiation to extend beyond the parties themselves: their agreement becomes a new factor in manoeuvres by other States. (see *935*)

315 – Obviously, then, the statesman cannot limit his attention merely to the negotiations immediately in hand. Agreements between third parties can have a major impact, direct or indirect, on his diplomatic position. In 1807, Napoleon

---

78 P. RENOUVIN: *Le Traité de Versailles*, Paris, Flammarion, 1969.

and Tsar Alexander made peace at Tilsit and forged a friendship that did not last, but produced a secret pact of offensive and defensive alliance. Their agreement also governed the conditions France imposed on Prussia, that Prussia had to accept, in a treaty that was merely a consequence of the original pact. (see *752*)

316 – Threats can be the result of a coalition, or, less overtly, of the neutralisation of certain forces where this is necessary for the balance of power – this was the outcome of the Germano-Soviet pact of 1939. (see *755*)

Threats can also arise out of badly-managed internal breakdown, as was demonstrated by events in the former Yugoslavia and the former USSR.

317 – Decisions taken by international conferences can operate to the benefit or the detriment of third countries; agreements on non-intervention in a dispute are an example. Following meetings between Talleyrand, the French ambassador to London, and Wellington, an international conference was held in 1830 to discuss the consequences of the Belgian uprising against The Netherlands: the result was a new State with independence, boundaries and neutrality. Holland came to accept this only later, but in the meantime there was no military intervention by the great powers, despite their initial intentions.

318 – There are many examples in history of large States unhesitatingly entering into treaties by which smaller ones were sacrificed. In exchange for concessions made to France by the Treaty of Campoformio in 1797, confirmed in 1801 at Luneville, Austria succeeded in annexing the Venetian Republic and the Archbishopric of Salzburg, neither of which were previously subject to it.

319 – Ill fortune awaits weak States that do not pay sufficient heed to the cynical inequalities of international society and neglect to protect their interests by careful negotiation. The Munich agreements of 29 September 1939 changed the map of Europe without any consultation of the populations concerned, and were forced on Czechoslovakia which had not been party to the discussions. (see *755*)

§2. Implementing the strategy

320 – Even though the ways and means may differ, all activities involving competition, victory or domination are made up of a fine blend of the art of design and the art of implementation.

The weaker or more exposed a State, the more attention it must pay to its defensive strategy.

321 – It would be dangerous to view negotiation only in terms of tactics. As the expression of a policy, negotiation applies, and implies, a strategy whenever it follows a design, in other words, a process of deliberate and ordered thinking motivated by the long-term vision of lasting and fundamental interests. The princes of the Italian Renaissance practised a diplomacy limited to responding to short-term quarrels that were bitter and cynical, but inconsequential: its historical importance lies in the methods they used, not in the results. (see *2326, 2352*)

322 – Clausewitz defined military strategy as the use of engagement for warlike ends.[79] In the field of diplomacy, too, it determines how methods such as negotiation shall be used to serve the ultimate purpose of the action.

But the systematic nature of strategy should not lead to a belief that it can only be used offensively. A wait-and-see posture can have both strategic content and diplomatic significance.[80]

323 – A strategy should not be immutable. Its central themes will change with each succeeding era. Over the last two centuries, the major themes of diplomatic negotiation have changed to reflect, successively, the ideology of revolution, Romantic nationalism, the concern for collective security and nuclear strategy. (see *1697*)

However, the lack of realism or application evident in some international debates shows that strategy is only meaningful if it adapts to circumstances. Negotiation is both one of the conditions and one of the criteria for its effectiveness. (see *2230*)

Negotiation teaches how to generate ideas. (see *333*)

The unity of the manoeuvre

324 – In principle, as expressions of a strategy, war and negotiation should complement each other. The same applies when they are put into practice. (see *2325*)

Machiavelli taught that a nation should never gamble its entire fate using only part of its forces: it is an imprudent statesman who does not use all available means, diplomatic and military, to achieve success, or deploy them in powerful combination to face the decisive test.

325 – It is up to those in political power to decide on the stakes and the risks, and these will bind the soldiers and diplomats. If they do not, they leave their executors, however well chosen, to confront responsibilities which should not be theirs. (see *2327*)

In this age of communications, the strategist must explain and justify his thinking if he wishes to be followed. (see *2325, 2626*)

326 – *A negotiation is merely a point in the implementation of a broader strategy, whose author may not withdraw from play.* His role, to the extent that he is in a position to, is to adapt his guiding theme to the circumstances and to the progress of the manoeuvre, while all the time holding to his chosen political line with enough intransigence to gain support for it.

327 – A relationship of complementarity is thus established between the strategist and the diplomat: while the former may not divorce himself from the results achieved by his representative, the latter will happily appeal to higher imperatives as the case may be, to put the other party under pressure or delay the unsatisfactory outcome of a negotiation. (see *2363*)

One of the missions of the tactics might be to conceal the aim of the strategy.

---

79 K. von CLAUSEWITZ: *On War*, Berlin, Dümmlers Verlag, 1832, III, 1.
80 C. POIRIER and F. GERE: *La Réserve et l'Attente*, Paris, Economica, 2001, p. 34 *et seq.*

328 – At the political decision-making level, pragmatism, so widely applauded, is not only contrary to general thinking on the subject, but also leads each situation to be viewed in isolation as if each had its own particular solution. Waiting to see what happens is a sign of insularity. (see *1710*)

Without a strategy, the negotiator has no criteria by which to judge what is appropriate or timely, and the negotiation becomes a pointless and dangerous exercise. (see *2327*)

329 – It is extremely unwise to expect the negotiation itself to determine the choice between different possible outcomes. This rule applies even to the British: despite being represented by Nelson, among others, Britain embarked on discussions with France in 1802 on the basis of a conception of its interests that was purely commercial and opportunistic. It very soon regretted having ceded Malta and the Cape, and having, in so doing, implicitly acknowledged as a *fait accompli* the transformation of the continent of Europe, brought about by Bonaparte's military and diplomatic successes. There was nothing left for it to do but prepare for another war. (see *2152, 2335*)

330 – The statesman must distinguish what is merely tactical for his country from what is of strategic importance. But he can only do this by a careful evaluation of the results of the negotiation he himself has set in motion or is conducting. Thus, the Munich agreements, which contained a special item dealing with the question of the balance of power in Central Europe, should have been judged at the time not on the basis of tactics (as a manoeuvre designed to appease the ambitions of a dictator), but at the strategic level: the only possible result was the dislocation of the system set up under the Treaty of Versailles, and the collapse of the League of Nations. For those who had made the concessions, Munich was not so much a case of losing a battle as of losing the war.

331 – It is often in the interests of the author of a manoeuvre to conceal the underlying strategy from his partners if he wishes to keep his objectives hidden. (see *2600*)

The satisfaction of having reached a compromise should not, however, obscure the overall consequences, even long term, of the agreement: *the gains and losses in a negotiation are rarely immediate.*

332 – In an important negotiation, the party with the best chance of securing a lasting advantage is the one with a strategic view. Roosevelt arrived in Yalta without a clear conception of the future of the European continent: Stalin was able to impose his own, in other words, a partition into zones of influence which proved very durable.[81] It was to take a profound political and cultural upheaval before that strategy was finally defeated. (see *2342*)

333 – A new strategy can emerge as the logic of a negotiation unfolds. By reaching agreement with Hitler in August 1939, Stalin was in effect confirming Germany's desire to attack and destroy Poland. Forced to take part in dismembering that

---

81 C. MAREK: 'Retour sur Yalta', *RGDIP*, 1982, p. 480.

country in order not to let the Russian and Ukrainian populations escape, he steered the Soviet Union onto a new course, that of territorial expansion.[82] He lost no time in securing the first strategic result, by annexing the three Baltic States, followed by part of Finland and Romania. From that point on, the secret Germano-Soviet agreements resulted in the two powers coming head to head, then in competition in the Balkans, then finally into open conflict. Stalin drew a second strategic lesson from this: starting from before the end of the Second World War, he surrounded his country with a protective buffer of subject nations.

The reemergence of Germany as a major player on the strategic stage came about because of the success of the negotiations that allowed it to reunify.

334 – The art of negotiation, like that of war, rests on seeking out and exploiting the weak points of the other party. The shift in diplomatic manoeuvres to different geographical arenas can coincide with the appearance of points of low resistance on each side, also with the tendency of open conflict to become more localised. Russia, for example, has always been exposed on its eastern flank, and a diplomatic strategy for Asia is vital to its territorial unity.

Vulnerability invites challenge. This is true of technically sophisticated western civilisations, in particular that of Europe. Part of the function of negotiation is to help establish where a State's weak points are. (see *388, 1677*)

The changing nature of American vulnerability explains the succession of strategic concepts adopted in Washington, the diplomatic consequences of which affect the whole planet.[83] The brutal experience of terrorism serves to reveal and confirm the vulnerability of modern society. (see *854, 1698, 1773, 1873*)

335 – Thus, the diplomat is held to the same rigorous discipline in his thinking as the soldier; he has to guess the strategy of his partners and his opponents, while at the same time refining and adapting his own. (see *2330*)

The increase in dialogue and exchanges between the United States and the former Soviet Union resulted in their governments agreeing, in 1972, to avoid any strategic conflict. In arming itself, thirty years later, with a system of defence against ballistic missiles and raising the issue of preventive nuclear operations, the United States has compromised the future of those agreements and this might lead other States into strategic reactions. (see *345, 1712, 1714, 1732, 1738*)

336 – Negotiation does not work well if the chosen objectives are inconsistent. A diplomat must be ordered in his thinking and his actions if he wishes to gain credibility and respect. The same principle operates in alliances and also in business.

A unified strategy can be put into practise using a variety of different tactics, but not by the use of disordered manoeuvres. (see *2326*)

Realism

337 – Diplomacy takes account of powers and interests that actually exist, but not of dreams or sentiment. It is not motivated by passions or illusions, as were all the

82 M. BEAUMONT: *La Faillite de la paix*, II, Paris, PUF, 1961, p. 861.
83 L. POIRIER and F. GERE: *La Réserve et l'Attente*, Paris, Economica, 2001, p. 71.

sovereigns that came after Charlemagne who tried in vain to reconstitute his Empire. It must be the product of the most clear-headed and detached analysis possible of the consequences of a situation or an act. (see *2343, 2353*)

Risk assessment depends on the prevailing circumstances and on the ability to forecast the behaviour of other players on the international stage. (see *1706*)

338 – The negotiator as strategist must pay attention to the lessons of history and geography which have much to tell about the main causes of major confrontations, and the places where these have most often occurred. It is possible to identify those areas where long-standing antagonisms have arisen, some of them going back over thousands of years.[84] At times, war has exercised a real fascination over the human mind, for reasons which have as much to do with the unequal distribution of wealth as with the emergence of all-conquering ideologies. Finally, there are certain cities and capitals which have become favoured centres for negotiation, threats and manoeuvres because of the concentration there of the elements of diplomacy – human, financial and physical.

339 – Geopolitical research has explored the main strands of human experience out of which strategies are born.[85] They contain lessons for the diplomat about the features that unvaryingly characterise positions and manoeuvres, and in particular the need to reconcile the principles of defence with diplomacy. Russia, in spite of decades of Soviet rule, was able to reemerge with its traditional identity intact. (see *320, 2367*)

In truth, however, even in Europe, where war and negotiation have been carried on for centuries, strategy has been insufficiently studied.[86]

340 – There is a logic in the process of diplomacy. It is easy to understand why Britain's strategy was aimed at avoiding the dangerous build-up of power on the continent, and how Italy's main priority has been to focus on the intentions of the dominant naval power in the Mediterranean. Germano-Slavic antagonism has left the marks of two thousand years of fighting between a succession of different enemies on Central European civilisation, and made it ethnically and politically fragile. The whole history of France has been dominated by the need to cover three geographic fronts, the Rhine, the Alps and the Pyrenees, as well as maintaining the security of the Western Mediterranean and the Atlantic shore.

341 – An observer could pursue the process of deduction further, identifying features in a given diplomatic manoeuvre that derive from the character and circumstances of its author.[87] Italian imagination can be contrasted with German realism. French diplomacy is fashioned out of logic, clarity and independence; it is characterised by pride and a tendency to improvise, and it seeks in vain to hold up carefully-worded treaties against the open floodgates of history.[88] British foreign

---

84 G. BOUTHOUL and R. CARRERE: *Le Défi de la guerre*, Paris, PUF, 1976.
85 H. J. MACKINDER: *Democratic Ideals and Reality*, London, 1919.
86 J.-B. DUROSELLE: *L'Europe de 1815 à nos jours*, Paris, PUF, 1964, p. 326.
87 G. ALMOND: *The American People and Foreign Policy*, New York, Praeger, 1950.
88 A. SIEGFRIED: *L'Ame des peuples*, Paris, Hachette, 1950, p. 89.

policy, neither systematic nor rigid, is adept at using tactics to the best advantage. It combines moral authority, correct behaviour and perseverance with empiricism, flexibility in its choice of means and a rejection of legal constraints.[89] (see *2247*)

342 – Nothing is so damaging to negotiation as an error of political strategy. After 1919, the British were convinced that Germany would succeed in changing the situation that resulted from the Treaty of Versailles; they let it be known, therefore, that they would not object provided the manoeuvre consisted only of establishing a better balance in Europe by peaceful means, and, of course, that it had no impact on British interests. But they made the mistake of not revising this approach radically after the advent of Hitler, who made no secret of his offensive ambitions. Because they did not restore the balance in time, firmly and completely, by coming to the aid of France, the British condemned themselves to war. (see *2336*)

343 – The success of a negotiation depends on the accuracy of the analyses that underpin it. The interests at stake, the forces in the balance, the issues to be resolved and the personalities involved must all be accurately assessed. Judgements have to be made about all the usual factors and also any contingencies – people, passions and interests. Any eventuality of history or forecasting suggestion that might be relevant should also be considered, depending on its probability. (see *2109*)

344 – Everything changes, including those geographical factors that seem to be among the most stable: the cities of the Mediterranean were supplanted by the Atlantic ports after the discovery of America, and the route around the Cape, abandoned by Europe once the Suez Canal was built, has again taken on huge strategic importance.

The aims of strategy are renewed and developed when negotiation achieves its objectives: imperialism evolved through its progressive expansion.

345 – Forecasting on a worldwide basis is made difficult today by the progress in military technology, its dispersal throughout the world and the uncertainty surrounding the conditions for its use and what its effects will be. New strategic concepts have injected an element of unpredictability into negotiation. This is further evidence of the influence of military science on the methods of diplomacy. (see *2077*)

The strategic doctrine of the United States underwent profound change to take account of the diverse threats that replaced the monolithic rivalry with the former Soviet Union: a new diplomacy was born, founded on the prevention and punishment of irresponsibility and 'adventurism', as well as on the protection of airspace, outer space and cyberspace. (see *334, 735, 972, 1698, 1802*)

346 – Before beginning a negotiation, it is advisable to know the positions taken by the opposing party, its real interests, ambitions and weaknesses. If this analysis is based on recent intelligence, verified and corroborated, it can lead to conclusions very different from those that might otherwise have been reached in a given situation, based for example on previous dealings. *The intuition with which this*

---

89 H. NICOLSON: *Diplomacy*, Oxford, Oxford University Press, 1945, Chapter 6.

intelligence is used must be broad enough to encompass the entire scope of the negotiation. (see *2010*)

347 – Only afterwards can sentiment come into play, to lend support to a viewpoint but not to override it. Ignoring it is dangerous, however; sentiment forms the basis for the most lasting personal and collective bonds, as well as being the cause of the worst failures. Metternich was the last of the statesmen raised in the climate of sceptical and cosmopolitan rationalism of the eighteenth century, and it was his refusal to adapt to the spirit of Romantic nationalism that brought about his downfall in 1848. (see *1863, 2324*)

348 – Since negotiation forms part of the implementation of a strategy, its success cannot necessarily be judged by reference to what was intended at the outset. Its ultimate objectives are not always defined in advance, nor the path to them laid down. Some propositions can be subject to compromise, while others cannot. (see *803, 2370*)

349 – The negotiation may not produce complete agreement, either because the dispute remains partly open or because each of the parties interprets and implements the result in a different way. In both these cases, though, the door remains open for a further diplomatic initiative.[90] What matters is that communication has taken place and that each party has derived some benefit from it. (see *796*)

350 – The results of a negotiation are not always the ones expected. When they turn out badly, or contradict the whole purpose of the exercise, the reason is often strategic error. (see *2219, 2221*)

351 – The source of the error may lie in the objective. In causing the disappearance of the double Austro-Hungarian monarchy in the interests of the principle of nationality, the 1919 Treaties set up a patchwork of small countries with arbitrary borders at the heart of Europe, impossible to defend and unlikely to regroup. The Danube region was thus opened up to control by a great foreign power – Germany initially, and later the Soviet Union until its collapse.

352 – Once the objective is chosen, the next step is to reach a position from which it can be achieved. It was not enough, in 1919, to decide that neither Berlin nor Vienna should ever again be capable of endangering peace in Europe; it still remained to lay the groundwork for that peace, instead of storing up potential sources of conflict. The system of alliances that was supposed to act as a counterweight to Germany was useless if France took no steps to maintain it, even retiring behind a fortified line from which it was unable to come to the aid of its allies.

353 – A mismatch between ends and means will assume serious proportions if the means prove severely inadequate to the task. By refusing to engage after the First World War, the Anglo-Saxon powers condemned to failure the attempt to create a

90 F. C. IKLE: *How Nations Negotiate*, New York, Harper Row, 1964, p. 20.

new European order since France, the only country able to guarantee it at the time, had neither the power nor even the intention to do so alone. What was the point of the precautions Great Britain had allowed to be written into the treaty, if it already foresaw, in 1919, that it was not going to use them?[91] (see *2369*)

354 – A good negotiation does not limit itself to achieving agreement: good sense requires the consequences to be thought through as well. If the parties fail to agree on their reactions the first time they are put to the test, a split will be inevitable, even before the treaty has been in place for long enough to survive through force of habit and proven elasticity. (see *812, 2338*)

355 – It is often the party wishing to preserve some reason for intervening who will anticipate, if not predict, difficulties. (see *2241*)

The 1919 negotiation offers a convincing, if unfortunate, example. However, those involved should have been forearmed, as the implementation of peace treaties had for centuries been at the root of the major crises in Europe.

356 – An elegant façade can often disguise an uninhabitable building. *Whether military or diplomatic, a good strategy is not made up of proclamations, intentions, stray impulses or illusions: it is the product of a clear will backed by sound thinking.*

International reactions to the Yugoslav and Soviet crisis were timid and inadequately thought out: they did not express any underlying strategy. (see *1975*)

357 – Whatever the outcome of a negotiation might be, it does not, in practice, bring matters to an end. They will simply continue on a different course, and the politician must pay it continued attention. (see *798*)

As in the art of war, exploiting a victory requires measure, energy and forbearance. And every good diplomat aims to mitigate the effects of defeat, from the moment the unfavourable agreement is concluded. After 1919, Germany's leaders made no secret of their intention to bring about changes to the situation put in place at Versailles, but Stresemann wanted to do it peacefully, and Hitler by force.

358 – Each party will naturally seek to use the negotiation and its outcome to serve its own best interests for the future. *If no agreement has been reached on an issue, it will be very difficult to do so at a later stage.* (see *796*)

359 – Prudence suggests that any gains should be firmly secured, before proclaiming victory. Failure to do so encourages fresh instability by creating the risk that the gains will not last. Louis XIV made a succession of unwise moves throughout his long reign that had the effect on several occasions of uniting the crowned heads of Europe against him, made anxious by his recurring hegemonic tendencies.

As La Fontaine reminded us, an insolent victor merely prepares the ground for his own future defeat.[92]

---

91 M. BAUMONT: *La Faillite de la paix*, I, Paris, PUF, 1960.
92 'Tout vainqueur insolent à sa perte travaille', Fables, 1668–1693.

Chapter II:
Diplomatic Negotiation and Trade

360 – All human activity involves speculation: speculation is about winning combinations that maximise the value of assets and put them to the most advantageous use, depending on events and the needs of the moment. The search for new ways and means is what drives social relations.

361 – The circulation of people, goods and ideas is the key to modern civilisation: mankind's golden ages have been those when interchange was at its height. Many radical discoveries have come about as a result of the search for benefit. Routes and empires, as well as centres of culture, have most often been those of wealth and trade.

362 – The progress of nations has thus been bound up with their progress in trade, with its constant interactions and keen competition, whatever its object and purpose.

The first political manoeuvres took place at the heart of this web of human and business relations; the cities of Ancient Greece and the principalities of the Italian Renaissance are evidence.

363 – *The methods used in diplomacy were fashioned out of those of commerce.* In the beginning, there was no distinction between the two: with time, bargaining refined itself into negotiation, dealings into treaties and pacts into peace. But the connection persisted, basically because both have their origins in the same principle – the meeting of minds and interests. This, facilitated by direct contacts and enshrined in written form, was to impart a more lasting, balanced and stable quality to relations between princes and peoples. In this difficult environment, force and trickery were no longer the only rules that applied.

364 – Because of its origins and its mercantile approach, the art of negotiating applies good sense and favours compromise. The customs that govern how it is conducted are mostly not written down. They address the needs that experience has shown will arise, and they are applied in professional circles as a useful legacy from the past. Some negotiators may show a tendency to moralise, but they are usually overtaken by considerations of interest or necessity.

365 – A legacy of trade, negotiation rejects all excesses and all absolutes, in its methods as in its objects. Therefore, its practice does not favour the tactics of confrontation and domination, fanaticism and proselytising but is based instead on moderation, prudence and forbearance. One of its fundamental tenets is that *it is better to persuade than to compel, to contract than to exact, to buy than to seize.*

366 – Harold Nicolson described this admirably when he said that British diplomacy had been successful precisely because it was founded on the solid

commercial principles of moderation, plain dealing, good sense, credit, knowing when to compromise and a distrust of the element of surprise and of anything exaggerated or ostentatious.[1] (see *179*)

367 – A commercial transaction produces a specific benefit, often limited and temporary. However high the stakes, their value can be measured. This applies with equal force to trading agreements or other international instruments that deal with a particular subject. It is not, however, true of full-scale diplomatic manoeuvres or historic treaties, where the desire for power of whole nations comes into play. Values are involved here that can neither be measured nor compared one with another – these are fundamental and complex considerations that defy both systematic quantification and marketplace empiricism. (see *2115*)

As Montesquieu wrote, one should not apply the principles of private law to matters governed by the law of nations.[2]

368 – The main advantage of a realistic and moderate approach to international issues is that it sets limits on the oversimplified Manichean rhetoric in which governments indulge when they want to mobilise domestic opinion or rally wavering countries to their cause. *A pragmatic approach is better suited to the complexities of real life than are the systematic simplifications used in military combat.* (see *1678*)

Section 1: The balance of interests

369 – The great secret of negotiation is that it brings out the mutual benefits to the parties.[3] Men and nations trade because it is in their interests to do so; they reach agreements and collaborate because that is their instinctive response to the tendency that makes them compare what they have with what they want.

In present-day international society, each State has the sovereign power to decide on its own interests. This is how it expresses the right of its people to self-determination. (see *606, 1772, 1781, 2320, 2670*)

370 – The desire and need for a given commodity will determine its price and provide the impetus and direction for exchanges between nations. According to the traditional model, trade allows a product that is in surplus in one country, and therefore of no interest to it, to be sought and obtained by the other. Today, in addition, agreements between States may result in the creation of a worldwide surplus of wealth, the benefits of which are shared not only among them but possibly with others too. When a country is developed, the benefits extend beyond the formal bounds of its own territory.

371 – Once these principles are clearly established, the numerous detailed rules applicable to private transactions are of no relevance to diplomacy.

---

1 H. NICOLSON: *Diplomacy*, Oxford, Oxford University Press, 1945.
2 C. de MONTESQUIEU: *De l'esprit des lois*, XVII, Geneva,1740, p. 20
3 F. de CALLIERES: *De la manière de négocier avec les souverains*, Paris, 1716, with a later edition in 1750.

In practice, tactics in diplomatic negotiation are rarely a matter simply of getting the parties' interests to converge. In trade, a deal takes shape and is concluded because each partner expects to obtain some specific advantage from moving closer to the other's position. In diplomacy, by contrast, the forces ranged against each other, which may sometimes even be in conflict, are powerful and fundamental.[4]

372 – The considerations at play in diplomacy are many and varied, and are not simply a matter of weighing up the advantages. They involve the political objectives of each nation, which may or may not be rational, on such issues as its independence, social harmony, defence and prestige. The very purpose of power is furthermore tied in with the notion of the State and the development of relations between States. This objective is still alive within the European Union. (see *1249, 2134*)

§1. Trade between nations

373 – Where goods go, people will follow,[5] this is the consequence of the enhanced possibilities for communication that exist in a world brought ever closer by technical progress and economic liberalisation. (see *1819, 1933*)

The intense activity of the commercial banking networks, as well as modern techniques of advertising, contribute to the economic and cultural expansion of States, as does the presence of their nationals abroad, as long as emigration does not reach levels where it gives rise to fear and distrust.

374 – Relations between States are guided by the need to take account of others. Negotiations are made a great deal easier if the States concerned are open to external contacts and comparisons. However, differences in levels of development do not favour interaction; technological and commercial relations often work better between States in competition with each other than between States that are too dissimilar. (see *1353, 1916*)

The development of organisational diplomacy owes much to economic multilateralism. It was commercial negotiation that brought the European Common Market into being and gave it stability, and it was the effectiveness of its regulations which then won it the respect of other States. It is in the field of finance and economics that 'summit' negotiations are most efficient, even if they do not always produce tangible results. (see *1360, 2485*)

375 – The world's wealth is said to depend on trade; refusal to deal can amount to a political sanction. Certain powerful States will only provide services on condition that their negotiating partner makes concessions on other points: the diplomacy of the 'package deal' has added a new dimension to the notion of reciprocity between States. (see *667*)

4 J. FRANKEL: *National Interest*, London, Pall Mall, 1970.
5 C. de GAULLE: Press conference, 9 September 1965, in *Discours et messages*, IV, Paris, p. 375.

Wealth

376 – Money has always served as a tool of diplomacy. There is more to this than the covert – though sometimes admitted – role played by foreign aid, such as the practice of English subsidies historically known in France as 'Saint George's cavalry'. At the beginning of the twentieth century, the level of national savings in France had put the exchequer in such a comfortable position that the government was able to implement a selective policy of foreign loans, thereby reinforcing its international standing. At the same time, the increase in US investments in South America explains, at least partially, why it ousted Britain from the position of dominance it had held for a century on that continent because of its trading relations.[6]

377 – Today, it is the oil and gas producing countries that have become the focus of attention, not only on the part of those whose interests lie in the management of money but also of those running the risk of financial stringency: the fact that, coincidentally, the peoples involved are often Muslim has had the obvious effect of strengthening the cultural and strategic position of Islam.

Reaction to the invasion of Kuwait by Iraq would not have been the same if Kuwait had not possessed considerable oil reserves.

378 – Many positions of dominance have foundered through lack of money. The effects of the economic impoverishment of the Iberian Peninsula were felt especially acutely as soon as other powers were able to interfere with its maritime communications and sometimes cut them off altogether. Thus began the decline of Spanish diplomacy in Europe. And it was because both Tunisia and Egypt had to resort to European financial assistance in the nineteenth century that control of first their debts and then their policies fell into foreign hands.

379 – Statesmen, ambassadors and negotiators have all benefited from having links with the banking world: as well as providing them with a network of informants, loans were available when needed. In times of prosperity, this served the merchants of Lombardy, Florence and Venice well. When Charles V was elected Emperor in 1519, against the rival candidate, the French king François 1, this was in reality the triumph of one banking dynasty over another: the Fugger family over the Medicis. However, the costs of the exercise were such that the Habsburg victor was forced to hand over Venezuela as a pledge to some of his creditors.

380 – Rivalries between financial groupings have dominated the political history and geography of the western world, and can explain the rise and fall of powers, the alliances and the quarrels that have come and gone over land and sea. There was a time when Venice and Genoa, Pisa and Florence, Augsburg, Antwerp and Amsterdam were all fighting over credit and power; the Hanseatic League was held together by trade in the seas of Northern Europe.

381 – In more recent times, competition between major corporations has influenced and sometimes driven colonial expansion. Either at the request or the

---

6 P. RENOUVIN: *Histoire des relations internationales. Le XIXe siècle, l'apogée de l'Europe*, Paris, Hachette, 1955, p. 321 and 344.

insistence of governments, or because they themselves had obtained government backing, private enterprises succeeded in turning the railways, for example, into a vehicle for European political and cultural penetration into the heart of the new continents.

382 – Today's preoccupation with money is no longer about the jingling of coins; business relations have become far more complex. *One of the most striking and dominant features of contemporary negotiation is the importance attached to delicate financial and commercial considerations.* All countries with an open – and thus increasingly specialised – economy will be keen to follow the rises and falls in their trade, balance in goods, services and knowledge, as well as the crises in certain currencies. (see *1920, 1968*)

Trade

383 – Commerce increases the sum total of wealth,[7] and negotiation effectively oils the wheels. Furthermore, by helping to ensure that overproduced goods are redistributed and consumed, it mitigates the effects of the accumulation of surpluses, which might otherwise be mobilised in readiness for war.

But commerce cannot prosper without credit, and the absence of security reduces it to the level of barter: direct and immediate exchange can be a sign of decline in international confidence. (see *483, 1805, 1935*)

384 – Commercial and technological competition must be voluntarily accepted by the State if it is not to be driven to take early preventive or protective measures that interfere with the free interplay of trading initiatives. Diplomacy has a major role to play in carrying out policies of national development that are open to the outside world; that role is to provide information, warnings and forecasts, to reach accommodations and set matters straight when needed. It thus supports the private sector. (see *1935*)

385 – In societies founded on commercial prosperity, accounting for between 15 and 20 per cent of worldwide trade, the negotiator must learn the lessons of economics and finance as he does those of war. The erosion of certain currencies and the rise in oil prices did much to weaken Europe's diplomatic potential during the 1970s.

At the international level, each economic event takes on a political dimension; likewise, all political uncertainty has a price. (see *1829*)

386 – Some diplomatic positions have an impact on currencies and trade. However, the dominant powers are still not always aware of the onerous impact they have on others. The political and military neutralisation of Europe, so feared by western strategists, might one day come to pass, simply because of its extreme economic vulnerability, especially with regard to sources of energy, raw materials and external transport links.

---

7 E. de CONDILLAC: *Le Commerce et le gouvernment considérés l'un relativement à l'autre*, Paris, 1776, I, p. 6.

387 – *The link between the spirit of trade and the desire for power is closer than is generally realised.* One only has to observe the major role played by the armaments trade in the economies of several countries, whether in budgetary expenditures, industrial production, exports or imports. Almost all advanced technology is defence-related. (see *82*)

388 – However, this link goes deeper still. While, in business theory, the laws of the market safeguard peace by spreading prosperity, in fact the mechanisms of profit, yield and free competition are rooted in conflict, where the strongest win and the less productive are annihilated with complete disregard for ethics. (see *1922*)

Between competing claims and interests, trade knows conflict as well as conciliation, and it uses negotiation.

The civil and military authorities in the United States extol the virtues of the market economy, but at the same time they distort its normal workings, using a variety of measures that favour private enterprises with links to their strategic aims. They are not alone in exploiting globalised business and techniques: not all of China's exporting industries comply with intellectual property and trademark conventions.[8] (see *1807, 1813, 1963*)

389 – Capitalism is, in this sense, a doctrine of force and sometimes of violence: it exists in a perpetual state of economic tension, which rises dramatically at times of shock or crisis. Warfare of this kind is increasing in intensity all the time and extending into new areas previously untouched by foreign competition, such as culture and agriculture. (see *1627, 1974*)

390 – At the same time there are some entities that fall outside the scope of control either of the State or the market, like the transnational corporations that are the embodiment of the expansionist power of certain dominant economies. Here, the market no longer fulfils its theoretical regulatory role, but it will operate to the advantage of the strongest unless the balance is restored by negotiation. (see *1812, 1869*)

391 – Socialist or State-controlled economies, too, are beginning to show the same tendencies because it is the State that bears the economic risk. The connection between politics, war and economics is even more entrenched here than it is elsewhere, and it dominates the entire diplomatic scene. (see *1923*)

Having control of the economy politicises a State's foreign trade and produces effects on its partners.

392 – There are legitimate doubts about whether authoritarian systems are capable of facing up to worldwide competition without this degenerating into confrontation. It is not clear that a totalitarian ideology offers the best climate in which to prepare a nation for the challenges of international society. For one thing, technological, commercial and financial advance is not in itself a sufficient goal for a nation to aspire to: it is incapable of realisation in the short term, nor can it generate the necessary enthusiasm. Added to which the availability of accurate

---

8 G. LAFAY: *Comprendre la mondialisation*, Paris, Economica, 1998.

information, a key element in competitiveness, is not assured where there is only one official party line. (see *2359*)

393 – *Negotiation is an exchange of signals as well as services. States that reject the free movement of goods, people and ideas will become impoverished and ossified.* The scale of this problem came to light, during the debates at the Conference on Security and Cooperation in Europe held in Helsinki in 1975. While the Western countries viewed free access to information as a factor favouring competition and rapprochement between nations, the Soviets refused to give any facilities or freedoms that could have dangerous consequences for their political regimes. In the end, openness won through, but not without upheavals along the way.

394 – The pursuit of its trading interests is therefore seen as one of the preconditions for a nation's development. For a century, moreover, the philosophy of free trade has undoubtedly been responsible for an intensification in diplomatic negotiations, whether in the use of bilateral procedures or in major international conferences.[9] (see *1942*)

This liberalisation has also benefited the many types of illicit traffic, including those in arms, drugs and money, that contribute to the present global insecurity. (see *1678*)

395 – It must be recognised today that peace cannot be maintained without a better distribution of wealth, a market organised on fair and stable principles and real progress in the struggle against developmental inequalities and the mounting burden of debt; in other words, without continuous negotiation between States on economic and financial issues. Once it is harnessed in pursuit of these objectives, as it was under the Treaty of Rome, diplomacy takes on an increasingly forward-looking character. (see *1251, 1807*)

396 – There is no clear or generalised link between the accumulation of assets and the increase in the power of States.

The reason is that commercial dependence and economic specialisation limit the diplomat's freedom to manoeuvre, as can be seen from the growing solidarity between the members of the European Union. This was the assumption which underlay, at least in part, United States policy towards the former Soviet Union: it relied upon the fact that it was in the Soviets' interest to prevent the eruption of violence.[10] (see *1935*)

397 – The very nature of the world economy has been transformed by the growth of centres of private financial power on a scale altogether different from anything that existed before the Second World War. Corporations with turnovers exceeding the national product of large numbers of – not insignificant – States carry on their activities with no consideration for national boundaries, now that it is possible to transfer capital as well as personnel, methods and data, orders, services and

---

9 J. M. JEANNENEY: *Pour un nouveau protectionnisme*, Paris, Seuil, 1978, p. 18.
10 A. ADAHL: 'Economic Inter-Action and East-West Détente', in *Beyond Détente*, London, Sijthoff, 1966, p. 67.

products between one free-market country and another. They, too, are subject to the temptation to use force. (see *1815, 1914*)

The monetary and financial crisis in Asia in 1997 and 1998 served to confirm the danger, for governments, of the fluidity, speed and secrecy with which banking transactions could be carried out. It also showed how contagious such disturbances can be. (see *16, 1675, 1995*)

Competition

398 – There can be no negotiation without acceptance of competition, implying that there must be sufficient domestic power to back it up. This will by no means always be military or political power, however. (see *1925*)

One of the features of politics is that power and skill go hand in hand at every level.

399 – In diplomacy as elsewhere, when faced with two evils one must choose the lesser, accepting it where nothing better is available. In business, too, a compromise is preferable to a breakdown in relations. (see *387*)

To ensure that competition does not degenerate into confrontation, it is necessary to negotiate. (see *2242*)

400 – Diplomacy and economics often get in each other's way. Sometimes one partner will take the calculated risk of resorting to force: Britain was alone in intervening in Egypt in 1882, and in doing so it stole a march on France which had shared with it control of Egypt's finances. At other times the interplay of interests distorts the facts on which a political manoeuvre is calculated: one example was the 1973 oil crisis, when it became clear that the policies of the world's industrialised nations had been based on an underestimate of the price of fuel.

401 – Relations between neighbouring nations are still more problematic, in that the vicissitudes of history, mutual fear, suspicion and rivalry build on each other to produce animosities that are difficult to erase. Distance is reassuring, but distance is reduced by progress.

Faced with the grave and complex challenges of international life, many States are now seeking to negotiate, especially in intergovernmental fora. (see *1804, 1917, 1977*)

402 – Every nation must arm itself for economic negotiations, as these involve concerns that sometimes override the demands of politics. Some States export to, or obtain supplies from, States with which they have no formal relations; others have no hesitation in relying on the same private capital whose very existence in their own territory they continue to block. (see *1926*)

403 – Commercial and financial relations will from now on be central to worldwide diplomacy, especially since their current state of crisis has become the principal arena of conflict and confrontation between political systems. *Until culture overtakes them, politics and economics will become increasingly indistinguishable one from the other.* (see *391, 1675, 1812*)

For military reasons, East–West trade was for decades under constant regulation by an intergovernmental committee, Coordinating Committee for Multilateral Export Control (COCOM) whose decisions were binding on western industry. A similar system of monitoring might one day be used in the fight against the proliferation of certain kinds of weapons or dangerous substances. (see *1762*)

404 – Whatever the expansion in worldwide or continental interest groups, it is the State that sets the framework for commercial competition, surrounds it with rules concerning defence, employment, balance of payments and protective measures, and decides whether or not it will practise reciprocity. The counterpart is not always the obvious one: some dominant military powers, for example, insist that countries where their troops are stationed should bear part of the cost of the deployment.

405 – Countries lacking the industrial, commercial or technical resources to fund their own defence and their own trade have only a limited scope for manoeuvre. But States have sometimes been known to pay for the departure from their territory of a foreign army, even that of an ally.

Even the wealthiest nations must put in place a diplomatic strategy that takes account of their needs in terms of energy, agricultural produce, raw materials and foreign trade.

Likewise, no major corporation can escape the constraints of a national industrial or business strategy that has been either influenced or sometimes even endorsed by the military establishment. (see *55*)

406 – It has become more and more difficult for any nation to be self-sufficient, even if some governments do manage to pursue their own strategies under the protection of isolationist regimes or protectionist regulation. (see *1939*)

In a world where the interests of one State must always be reconciled with the pride of another, isolation can quickly spill over into confrontation. (see *633*)

407 – The mere fact that two or more governments side with each other in opening a negotiation should not disguise the differences, or even the divergence, in their respective interests. None of them will be motivated by the same desire to arrive at the same conditions or the same timetable. Even within the sincerest of alliances, there will still be competition. (see *415, 964*)

There is no front that a good diplomat cannot hope to stretch further.

408 – Each protagonist therefore finds some scope to manoeuvre to its own advantage, and each one will seize every chance to introduce more flexibility into the diplomatic game. This can be seen when crises erupt from time to time between the United States and Europe, causing occasional damage to their relations.

409 – Agreement is easy between governments that are certain not to come into conflict. Unfortunately, given the changeable nature of politics, such a situation rarely arises. While Bismarck was in power, Britain and Germany enjoyed good relations, but the maritime and colonial policies of his successor Kaiser Wilhelm II brought that to an end.

§2. *Attempting compromise*

410 – It is their diversity that impels nations to trade. It is rare for States to find themselves in a comparable situation, even when they have a great deal in common. *Any agreement between governments is the product of circumstance. Both parties will react with a mixture of satisfaction and dissatisfaction. Neither will ever claim to be completely happy, but each of them will have derived some benefit.*

There is no peace without compromise, and no compromise without negotiation.[11]

The balance of interests

411 – Affluence and poverty are relative. However, when they come face to face, those who have plenty and those who have little have different ways of negotiating. And the party with neither the material wealth nor the advantages that flow from it will not always be the less aggressive of the two. Many wars of conquest have been started, and won, by peoples who had nothing to lose. (see **660**)

The relative weight to be given to what each party brings to the other is not the same, and this has a bearing on how the negotiation is conducted.

412 – For the negotiator with only limited means, everything matters, and the smallest setback in the negotiation will have grave consequences, and can even seem like defeat. His goals are clear and often definite, because he knows exactly what are his immediate needs, and will go about obtaining them with all the more tenacity. It is much more difficult for him to make concessions than for anyone else: General de Gaulle was never more of a thorn in the side of the Allies than when he was most alone. (see **453**)

413 – On the other hand, too great a margin of superiority will often create a level of self-confidence that does not make for good negotiation. It leads to error, not only in weighing up one's partner's capabilities, but also in the general understanding of what the discussion is about. Being in a comfortable position reduces the ability to adapt. It breeds complacency, meaning that a party might neglect to update its information, rethink its strategy and revise its tactics.

Wealth and power produce a tendency to underestimate the adversary's means and resolve: its readiness as well as its willingness to fight, resist or attack. (see **83**)

414 – Since the whole object of the exercise is precisely to allow for the making of mutual concessions, in other words to reach a compromise, it becomes pointless if one party has the absolute upper hand.

The possession of technology can distort a negotiation just as much as military supremacy, by allowing one party to dictate its terms. One of the ways the Soviet policy of exclusiveness manifested itself was by rejecting the American system of satellite telecommunications.

---

11 L. NOEL: *Conseils à un jeune Français entrant dans la diplomatie*, Paris, La Jeune Parque, 1948, p. 32.

Russia has not persisted in this attitude; it cooperates with other countries in this field as well as in matters relating to space, though not without some difficult negotiations (as, for example, over its use of the French base at Kuru, in French Guiana). (see *2067*)

415 – No State will allow another to do deals on its behalf on matters of vital concern. Great powers have often traded the fate of nations among themselves: the history of Poland is an example. But unequal treaties are not easy to characterise as such, especially when they are multilateral. (see *611*)

The tensions that result from too great a degree of inequality between the parties have the effect of paralysing the negotiation, despite the best intentions of some of their representatives: *the weak are suspicious and concerned for their dignity.* (see *668*)

416 – In its relations with others, no State will give away something for nothing.[12] But sometimes, the balance involves factors beyond the scope of the negotiations themselves, irrespective of whether there are two or more parties involved.

Tying a negotiation to extraneous considerations carries the risk that the solution found to the matter actually in hand will be unsound or precarious.

417 – Within each camp, there will also be a negotiation going on. A balance will tend to be reached between gains and concessions, depending on the circumstances and the tactics used. Such a balance is indispensable if the agreement is to hold firm, in spite of the inequality between the parties.

418 – In the practice of negotiation, the weight each of the protagonists actually carries will be measured differently, depending on the tactical skills of its representatives, and sometimes on how many allies or client States it has. In multipartite meetings, medium-sized powers are able to use the ability of their ambassadors or the support of their partners to raise their game to a higher level than their interests or their international ranking justify, where this serves their political ends. (see *662*)

419 – In the business world, compromise is facilitated by having common measurements, most usually in the form of price, in other words, as objective as possible a way of valuing the subject matter of the discussion. In part, at least, trade is governed by the laws of supply and demand. Even where some of the factors are subject to variation, and change as a result of speculation or market forces, that relationship is always present in normal commercial dealings, depending on the talents or needs of the trader. No such consistent measurement is available in political negotiation. (see *1877*)

420 – What the stakes are and whether the outcome is the right one are questions that depend essentially on the time, the place and also the parties to the negotiation. Subjective considerations nearly always come into the equation, and this, for States, means political ones.

12 C. de GAULLE: *Mémoires de guerre*, Paris, Plon, 1954–1959, III.

Between States, what is agreed depends on the circumstances. Asking for something in return is not a strategic objective.

421 – While the diplomatic negotiator must of course look for what the other side can offer, the possibilities for give and take must be subject to careful assessment. Even between unequal States, the only way to obtain agreement is by striking a balance between mutual commitments, and it is up to each party to make its own assessment of how these compare. *The same stakes can be of differing value to each protagonist, depending on how pressing are its respective needs.* (see *80*)

People motivated not by interest but by vanity, militancy or ideology serve only to complicate or obstruct a negotiation.

422 – So delicate and subtle is the process of reaching agreement between States that, most of the time, the very fact of having reached a compromise – the fact that the dispute has been settled – determines how the parties value what they are giving each other.

After the event, and even taking account of the effect of power relationships that have nothing to do with the case in point, balance is achieved by the exchange of offers or concessions.[13] (see *303*)

423 – This is why diplomatic negotiation hesitates between the paths of law and empiricism, often relying at the same time both on principle and on the need to achieve a compromise, because it is necessary or advisable to reach a result. Reciprocity is the legal argument for giving a counterpart. (see *668*)

It follows that discussions that have no specific purpose are not negotiation. The fact that there are large numbers of national delegations gives impetus to a discussion and brings it publicity, rather than leading to a conclusion and a result. (see *2242*)

424 – It can even happen that the essence of the matter is a question of psychology, which makes it especially difficult to assess. The reciprocal threats and assurances exchanged between the superpowers would fall into this category: it is impossible to verify their true intentions, sometimes even the true facts.[14] (see *1702*)

425 – It can happen that the value of what is being offered is deceptive, because one of the parties has made an error of judgement. In 1801, by giving up his claims to the Nile, Bonaparte was able at the same time to make peace with Turkey, prove his sincerity to the Tsar, and exact a promise from London to withdraw from Malta, though this promise was never kept. He did all this before it became known that his lieutenant in Egypt had already capitulated. (see *1545*)

426 – Concessions should be handled with prudence and discretion: as soon as one is known about, it is taken for granted, and a fresh one will have to be made if the counterpart is not obtained quickly. It is possible to conduct a negotiation in such a way that the other party's efforts are concentrated around a certain demand or

13 I. W. ZARTMAN: 'Negotiating as a Joint Decision-Making Process', in *The Negotiation Process*, p. 67.
14 A. GROSSER: *Les Occidentaux*, Paris, Fayard, London and Beverly Hills, Sage, 1978, p. 341.

condition, and to put forward a response to this at the last minute: the long-awaited compromise destroys of the opponent's main argument and no new argument can be made in its place. (see *2246*)

427 – The counterpart offered might also consist of demonstrating one's political influence, according a privilege of protocol or recognising the other's moral authority, if this is all that is required to satisfy his honour. Pride and susceptibility, as well as concerns about one's place in the protocol, are also political motives.

428 – What the parties' mutual commitments are worth depends on a projection into the future: the results expected to flow from an agreement are among the reasons why it is reached. A government faced with a predictable manoeuvre might be tempted to negotiate something in return: in 1877, Austria obtained Russia's consent to the occupation of Bosnia-Herzegovina by giving its agreement to an attack by Russia on Turkey.

429 – Often, though, one danger is feared, but there is another lurking behind it that wipes out the benefits of the agreement. A criticism frequently levelled at F. D. Roosevelt is that he made concessions to Stalin at Yalta, only to have him declare war on Japan.

430 – Ignorance of the facts can lead a negotiator to argue about something that has already happened or something that is no longer significant because it has been overtaken by international events. At Yalta, again, Roosevelt thought that the Soviets would be inhibited from intervening in Central Europe by ethical or political considerations, though he knew that the field would be clear for the Red Army. Events were to confirm that his assessment of where the balance lay in the negotiation was flawed.

431 – The assessment of the likely gains, as well as of their counterpart, the balancing of which leads to the agreement being concluded, depends on the goal each party sets itself. When he was negotiating with Austria after the devastating military campaign of 1796, Bonaparte traded Vienna's abandonment of Belgium and Lombardy for the offer of part of what was held by Venice. With the peace of Campoformio, the uncertainties about the left bank of the Rhine were resolved to France's advantage. This allowed Austria to take possession of Salzburg and later of Venice itself, which France gave up in exchange for a share in its territorial possessions. Bonaparte thus achieved three objectives at the same time: peace, the establishment of the Rhine as the French frontier and the creation of the Cisalpine Republic in northern Italy.

432 – Leaving aside those cases where the counterpart is purely nominal, a distinction must be drawn between those cases where it forms an integral part of the negotiation and those where it is something extraneous, such as diplomatic backing, general financial aid or the possibility of commercial or cultural expansion. (see *1272*)

With the Treaty of Paris, in 1259, Louis IX of France (Saint Louis) gave back a large amount of territory to Henry III of England and received nothing in return except for Henry's agreement to serve as his vassal, with the title of Duke of Aquitaine. At that time, great importance was attached to feudal relationships.

433 – Each party must keep in mind the goal set when the decision was taken to enter into discussions. The concessions it makes, and the positions it gives up, will be measured against those obtained, there and elsewhere, which might be reflected in several treaties and a variety of obligations. The talks held at Locarno in 1925 settled the Rhineland boundaries, but when Germany refused to give the same recognition to Poland and Czechoslovakia, France decided to give its own guarantee to each of them, separately. The consequences were not long in coming. (see *832*)

434 – A given outcome might appear to be even-handed, but in reality puts one partner in a position of superiority. When Mussolini negotiated parity between the naval fleets of France and Italy, he expected it to bring him supremacy in the Mediterranean. And the 3:5 ratio between the Japanese and American navies agreed in Washington in 1922 gave Japan the upper hand in its zone of influence.

435 – For some, an examination of the counterpart is a matter of priority: Bismarck allegedly said, 'when someone asks me for something, I look first of all at what he is offering me'. But no treaty can give all the parties everything they want. The mechanism of mutuality is especially delicate in multilateral negotiation, where the primary object is to arrive at a situation in which all parties obtain enough to sign the agreement, even if it is only a matter of enhancing their vanity. (see *2445*).

Bargaining

436 – Everyone hopes to obtain as much as possible, but no one gets something for nothing. *Diplomatic negotiation is no stranger to bargaining: it starts with exaggerated claims being made and then refused, and continues with a balance of concessions until finally a settlement is reached, sometimes by wearing down the adversary who gives in simply in order to put an end to the matter.*[15]
Bargaining can sometimes obscure the real state of the negotiation.

437 – Bargaining is also a test of strength,[16] with some respecting only those interlocutors who engage fully in the fierce discussions that characterise this kind of dealing.
Some of the features present in negotiation are not found in commerce, and these are often psychological, like the sense of military security, a fondness for prestige and a tendency to rely on public opinion. All of them come at a price, as politicians are aware.[17]

438 – It is not enough to start by making extensive claims with a view to making concessions further down the road.[18] One must also have the power to negotiate,

---

15 V. WALTER: *Silent Missions*, Washington 1960.
16 T. C. SCHELLING: *The Strategy of Conflict*, Cambridge, Harvard University Press, 1960, p. 21.
17 C. LOCKHARDT: *Bargaining in International Conflicts*, New York, Columbia University Press, 1979.
18 F. WALDER: *Saint-Germain ou la négociation*, Paris, Gallimard, 1958, p. 41.

avoid being led into weakness and face the adversary from a strong tactical position. When Britain created the European Free Trade Association (EFTA), this was more than just a response to the setting up of the six-member European Economic Community – it was intended to strengthen Britain's hand in any subsequent negotiation for entry into the Common Market.

439 – The freedom to make extravagant claims is limited in time: if this is done during the course of an ongoing negotiation, it holds up progress. However, *it can be a good ruse to give the appearance of having only a small negotiating margin.* This can also work to the advantage of the adversary, to the extent that he expects an adverse reaction from his principals, and the final compromise will be greeted all the more favourably.

440 – Preparation before the negotiation plays a decisive role. This is not just a matter of knowing as much detail as possible about the facts and the limitations to which the operation is subject; it is also necessary to understand the political context and the psychological climate. Approaches can be made by third parties acting entirely on their own account. Sounding out a partner does not mean opening discussions, but can help to define what they will cover, the order in which they should be conducted, the timetable and conditions. *Negotiation implies communication: channels must be found for it that are more or less secret.* (see *2007, 2415*)

441 – Preparations for the negotiation are among the personal responsibilities of the lead negotiator. Studying the file, making an assessment of what the parties have to gain or lose, identifying with the cause, deploying resources, deciding on overall tactics and predicting those of the opponent – all of these are stages requiring painstaking and in-depth application, and the result should be that it is possible to predict the other party's intentions as well as what it will do.[19]

442 – The initial meetings or opening conversations call for the same degree of finesse, especially on the part of the organiser or the person presiding. It is his responsibility to put the participants at their ease and see to it that the prevailing atmosphere between them is one of mutual understanding, even harmony. The party in the best position to do so should be the one to make the first overtures, and should establish contact without excessive formality. Diplomacy is the art of dialogue, but dialogue still has to be opened up. (see *536, 2438, 2442*)

443 – The desire to reach agreement is at times so strong that parties will go to great lengths to understand the wishes and thoughts of the other side and how these are expressed: this was Henry Kissinger's observation during his meetings in China.

444 – Some statesmen, not wishing to appear conciliatory and therefore easily influenced, pride themselves on being highly regarded and much in demand because of their reputation for being meticulous and sensitive. This attitude can only be justified when it is used on behalf of governments and countries that are

---

19 T. C. SCHELLING: *The Strategy of Conflict*, Oxford University Press, 1963, p. 57.

themselves in a position of strength. While it might not be to their immediate advantage, the most powerful should never refuse to communicate or make this dependent on reciprocity. (see *304*)

445 – There are those who, for reasons of temperament, favour the advantages of the unilateral initiative in order to avoid having to enter into a game of mutual concessions. It suits them to be on the offensive because it enables them to choose their ground. But they will finally agree to use the methods of negotiation if it can be carried on within the framework of their manoeuvre. Those who use violence have always been subdued by negotiation. (see *93*)

446 – As for those who are motivated by religion or ideology, nothing should arouse more suspicion than their offer or acceptance of concessions. Their faith does not allow them to negotiate their principles, so when they propose compromise, it is only as a means of weakening their opponent, waiting for an opportunity to attack and to rally them to their own side. (see *1867*)

Sometimes the negotiator is so certain of being right that it blinds him to reality: when President Wilson set out his principles for the Armistice in 1918–1919, their terms were so rigorous that they could not be applied.

447 – The search for agreement will often lead to the difficulties breaking down, allowing issues that are capable of resolution to be resolved, and isolating those that will be the subject of subsequent bargaining. Diplomacy follows a natural pattern of successive compromises, leading sometimes to a whole package of compromises as the end result.[20] (see *1540*)

448 – There are those who rejoice in being able to find, at the right moment, a solution that enables each party to save face. *In practice there is an art to dialogue and debate, consisting of making one's arguments to the best effect at the right time.* (see *2449*)

As one ambiguous outcome succeeds another, intransigence becomes blunted.

449 – In some respects, the diplomat could be compared to the speculator: he loves the game and plays it for its own sake. His tastes do not change, and nothing appeals more to him than indirect approaches, clandestine meetings and oblique transactions. His failing is a tendency to negotiate no matter what the circumstances, even at the expense of political goals.

But the progress of the discussions will not be artificially aided where one party does not know or understand what the real issues are: no game should be lost because of misunderstanding or an excessive desire to be courteous.[21] (see *2428*)

450 – The outcome of the discussions must also be the subject of careful reflection. Surprise results and victories snatched under psychological pressure should be avoided, especially in the case where, in a final effort to force its opponent's hand, one party sends in a new negotiator, often of high rank, whose brief is to dispose of any remaining hesitation, overcome any last resistance and settle the matter.

---

20 O. YOUNG, etc.: *Bargaining, Formal Theories of Negotiation*, Chicago, University of Illinois Press, 1975.
21 C. DUPONT: *La Négociation*, Paris, Dalloz, 1999.

§3. Mediation

451 – Good tactics require the use of every possible means to induce one's opponent to change his behaviour. While still respecting the freedom of choice of the parties to the negotiation, this can be done obliquely. (see *639, 2628*)

Following a well-tried business formula, a third party, be it friend, enemy or neutral, can play a role in the negotiation, despite having no interest in the matter.

452 – It is in the interest of powerful States to flatter others by asking them for support or some form of service, or promising them some benefit – even going as far as revising a treaty that is unfavourable to them or handing over another State's possessions. When, in 1898, Britain wished to free itself from Kaiser Wilhelm II's opposition to its policies in the Transvaal, it went about this by promising Germany the greater part of Portugal's colonial possessions in Africa.

453 – It is not unusual for a manoeuvre to be carried out through the intermediary of a third State where its own interests are sufficiently similar. Each State finds itself cast in its own role, like characters in a play. The major modern powers are past masters at this game, which allows them a large measure of flexibility in their negotiations and also gives reassurance to the parties they are dealing with. (see *1147*)

As for weaker States, the indirect approach respects their sensibilities and obviates the need for them to make open concessions. (see *412*)

454 – These methods introduce an element of uncertainty, casting doubt on the durability or stability of the outcome. Governments take whichever path offers them the most advantages in the short term. Those with extensive ambitions are tempted to overstep the limits of their normal role. All of them will be tempted to use blackmail on those States that have signed a treaty relying on their help. And no State wants to see its intervention succeed if this means that more powerful States will have no further need of it. (see *1119*)

455 – Where there is equality in terms of power, the only factor that will prompt a free ruler or an independent State to choose one side over the other is the benefits and favourable treatment on offer.[22]

There is no place for gratitude between nations: the payback for giving support lasts only as long as that support is needed.

456 – Using a third party in a negotiation can help to weaken one side and, in an indirect way, to modify its behaviour. Two partners concerned about the balance of power between them can be brought closer or driven apart by using this tactic: for 200 years, all that it took to make Turkey declare its opposition to a given country was to suggest that the country in question was siding with Russia.

457 – Not infrequently, the outcome of a negotiation will have consequences for a country that was not party to it, if, for example, it limits that country's freedom of manoeuvre. It should come as no surprise that such collateral effects can also be beneficial. As an example, the Nuclear Non-proliferation Treaties signed during

---

22 F. de CALLIERES: *De la manière de négocier avec les souverains*, Paris, 1750, p. 111.

the Cold War by the United States and the USSR became binding on Russia as its successor, to Russia's benefit. (see *335, 753, 1702, 1731*)

458 – The best kind of diplomatic manoeuvre is one that allows a State to profit painlessly from the efforts of others. The statesman wishing to use his resources sparingly will make sure he acts in line with the actions of those powers that could obstruct or prevent his manoeuvre.

When in 1854–1855 the Crimean War and the negotiations that followed brought Russia to its knees, Austria could note with satisfaction that it had needed to do nothing to contribute to its downfall, other than having issued a demand for negotiations at the instigation of France and Britain.

459 – It is often possible to negotiate by sheltering behind the acts of a third party. For long years, the Ottoman Empire showed no hesitation in invoking the terms of the London Agreement of 1841, a treaty which was contrary to its sovereignty, in order to close the Dardanelles Straits to warships; acting as the guardian of the treaty enabled it to shore up its independence and its territorial integrity, for a while at least.

In the natural order of things, great destinies permit small ones to flourish. Nations can gain in wealth and influence under the protection of those with more power.

460 – The methods of conciliation that have grown out of the experience of traditional diplomacy, allowing for third parties to facilitate negotiations between the parties around the table, often bear a strong resemblance to those used in commercial circles.[23] But a negotiation conducted by a third State will be open to suspicion and easily undermined if there is insufficient common interest to sustain it: the mere fact of transmitting messages or making friendly intercessions can put the third State in a position to gain an advantage or to draw a dispute out into the international arena. (see *643*)

461 – Assistance from a third party can not only stop the conflict degenerating into the use of force, but it can also lead to both sides seeking an acceptable settlement. The General Act drafted by the League of Nations Assembly in 1928 put forward a range of procedures of this type for the peaceful settlement of disputes: in spite of being framed in somewhat hesitant language, it gives different methods that vary according to the scope of the role of the third party negotiator. This ranges from verifying the facts and establishing contact between the adversaries, to suggesting how a settlement might be reached or what it should contain. (see *1136*)

462 – Whether it is *ad hoc* or formally mandated,[24] voluntary or induced, and irrespective of whether the task is conferred on one prominent person or a panel, institution or State, *intervention can only be effective if each of the protagonists*

---

23 R. GENET: *Traité de diplomatie et de droit diplomatique*, Paris, 1932, III, p. 540.
  J. STONE: *Legal Controls of International Conflict*, London, Stevens, 1954.
24 UN: *Systematic Survey of Treaties for the Pacific Settlement of International Disputes*, New York, UN 1948.

accepts it. A party will manifest its willingness to negotiate by choosing the safest, quickest or easiest method, depending on the case, but it is rare for any one method to meet all three of these criteria.

Initiatives designed to rationalise the recourse to third parties in order to encourage or impose procedures of investigation, mediation, conciliation or arbitration, such as those to be found in the Final Act of the Helsinki Conference, the proceedings of the Council of Europe or after one of the OSCE conferences – for example, the one held in Stockholm – usually run into opposition from States because they deprive them of the freedom to choose the intermediary and define his mission. (see *2243, 2417*)

Since sovereign States are under no legal obligation to accept it, the effectiveness of this kind of intervention therefore depends on the third party in question demonstrating impartiality, independence and authority.[25] (see *1147*)

463 – Generally speaking, there are no precise rules governing the form such interventions can take: at the Congress of Munster, the mediation was done in writing. The purpose of such interventions and the effect they have depend entirely on the acceptance and goodwill of the parties; the methods they use are those of diplomatic negotiation.[26] This means that they can only work where the balance of power between the protagonists is not so uneven that one of them will look for a good pretext to reject any compromise and where they are conducted in such a way as to bring out clearly what the dispute is exactly about, and what each of the protagonists is seeking to achieve.[27]

464 – Conflict prevention or resolution can be made easier if reliable data can be gathered, uninfluenced by any considerations of vanity or prestige and also by the use of adversarial techniques to verify the facts alleged and the way they have been interpreted. This function is sometimes fulfilled by inquiries entrusted to prominent persons, commissions or international organisations, and these usually presuppose the cooperation of the parties to the dispute as a sort of preliminary negotiation. (see *2034*)

465 – Sometimes, though, even more direct ways can be found to influence the parties' behaviour. *Good offices, whether spontaneous or specifically requested, are intended to open up the way for direct contact and discussions between the protagonists, without going into the merits of the case* (Hague Convention of 1903, II, Article 2). This use of authority and influence often works because it is discreet, and it can sometimes lead to the dispute being settled voluntarily.[28] The 1494 Treaty of Tordesillas, which divided the New World between Spain and Portugal, was based on a proposal made by Pope Alexander VI. By contrast, when Britain offered to use its good offices during the 1870 war between France and Germany, this was not accepted.

---

25 V. PECHOTA: 'The Quiet Approach: a Study of the Good Offices Exercized by the UN Secretary General in the Cause of Peace', in *Dispute Settlement Through the UN*, New York, Oceana, 1977, p. 517.

26 J.-P. COT: *La Conciliation internationale*, Paris, Pedone, 1968, p. 17.

27 E. EDMEAD: *Analysis and Prediction in International Mediation*, New York, UNITAR, 1971.

28 E. SATOW: *A Guide to Diplomatic Practice*, London, Longmans Green, 1957, II.

466 – *Mediation goes one step further, because it entrusts the third party with negotiation*: he can take part in the meetings, explore ways and means and even suggest a possible basis for a settlement which both sides might find acceptable. This, at least, is what happens where the intermediary is disinterested and motivated by goodwill. By contrast, the offer of mediation Austria made to Napoleon in 1813 came closer to betrayal, since at the same time Metternich was establishing communication between the plenipotentiaries, he was also attempting to win financial backing from Britain and planning the ultimatum that would enable him to break his alliance with France. As to Napoleon III's mediation between Prussia and Austria, in the end it turned against his own interests.

467 – With a mandate from the member governments giving it the power to bind them, the Commission of the European Community conducts negotiations on their behalf within its sphere of competence. It also plays a part in formulating the positions the governments will adopt by agreement, when they then instruct the Commission.[29] (see *187, 1287, 1290*)

468 – Conciliation, when the parties agree to it, follows whatever negotiating procedure they decide upon. Most of the time this will involve an examination of the case by prominent experts or commissions with special skills, who will put forward a solution while leaving each of the parties free to make its final decision.

469 – In practice, as well as in most writing on the subject, *conciliation is not really a legal means of dispute resolution; rather, it is the pursuit of negotiation in new forms and with the help of new players*. If particular procedures are applied, especially those used by commissions to find an impartial way of bringing the parties closer, these are neither rigid nor binding, and they often derive from bilateral or multilateral treaties negotiated in the past. Any solution proposed only has authority for the protagonists if it is intrinsically legally or ethically sound, or because it comes at the right time: even so, they will have to think hard before rejecting it.

470 – Conciliation is progressively moving away from the traditional form of discreet diplomacy towards a public, institutional model, with various international organisations now considering it their mission to encourage and monitor it. In any event, however widespread the practice becomes, and however much publicity it attracts, conciliation demands the greatest possible flexibility and can only go forward with the consent of the States concerned. (see *1548*)

471 – *Arbitration, likewise, rests on the consent of the States, which may be given in advance or take the form of a treaty obligation*. It is used only where both parties agree that their dispute is a suitable one for this form of resolution, and this in itself presupposes that they negotiate. In the end, it can only produce a meaningful decision if the parties agree on the procedure to be adopted, and this in turn usually depends on the quality both of the discussions between the parties and the decisions of the arbitrator.

---

29 E. JACKSON: *Meeting of Minds, a Way to Peace through Mediation*, New York, McGraw Hill, 1952.

Since it was set up in the Hague in 1899, the Permanent Court of Arbitration, which in fact is neither a court nor even a permanent institution, has been seized of relatively few cases. The General Arbitration Act of 1928, amended in 1949, the object of which was to promote arbitration as a means of avoiding hostilities, remains somewhat theoretical. In practice, States show great hesitation in committing to procedures over which they have no control. (see *1122*)

472 – Arbitration is no substitute for negotiation, because it is not always – and not only – conducted on the basis of law: arbitration cases can also be decided on arguments of analogy or on principles of good faith, equity or even amicable settlement. This last is really only a matter of finding a convenient and timely solution, at which point the process starts to resemble mediation. In practice, as between States, arbitration is not a true form of dispute resolution by a legal tribunal, but more of a diplomatic process. During the negotiations on the draft treaty setting up the European Coal and Steel Community, the States involved took the unusual step of designating an arbitrator, by agreement, to assist the process by deciding any question on which they were deadlocked.[30]

473 – There are some instances in the business world where the intermediary has a wide-ranging and long-term role; usually, this person facilitates the settlement and receives a reward. The same pattern can be seen in international relations: the role played by the third State is ambivalent, giving rise to questions about what it expects to gain from its involvement. A State in this position must take care that its efforts in bringing the opposing sides closer together do not prompt them to call its good faith into question or accuse it of playing a double game.[31] The mediator or *amiable compositeur* is therefore well advised to cultivate a working atmosphere of understanding, sympathy and shared involvement.

474 – These procedures require careful consideration, if only because they introduce additional variables into the negotiation, factors which have to do with the individual intermediary.[32]

475 – There are often quite subtle reasons why States offer others their services as mediators or conciliators. The quest for prestige, the concern to keep the peace and the desire to maintain calm within one's sphere of influence are goals that can easily be stretched to accommodate the pursuit of political or economic interests. Napoleon understood this well when, in order to win Tsar Alexander over to his side upon his accession, he accepted the new Tsar's offer to mediate in his dispute with the Ottomans in 1801.

But the mediator should also pay heed to the fact that he may be expected to guarantee the resolution of the dispute. (see *835*)

---

30 P. REUTER: *Organisations européennes*, Paris, PUF, 1970, p. 49.

31 F. TERRE: 'L'internationalité du juge dans l'arbitrage', in *L'Internationalité dans les institutions et le droit*, Paris, Pedone, 1995, p. 219.

32 H. TOUZARD: *La Médiation et la resolution des conflits*, Paris, PUF, 1977.

    A. BROUILLET: 'La médiation du Saint-Siège dans le différend entre l'Argentine et le Chili sur la zone australe', *AFDI*, 1979, p. 47.

476 – It is not uncommon for a mediator to modify the questions and requirements of the parties that he is transmitting, to reflect his own concerns. Austria did this during the dispute between Russia and Turkey in 1737, and the following year France did the same: each of the intervening powers sought to favour its ally. Austria added its own requirements to those of the Tsar, but France used its diplomatic skills to dissuade Turkey from accepting them and salvaged Turkey's position by getting Russia to accept mediation by France instead.

One side can sometimes be weakened by the intervention of a third party. When the War of the Austrian Succession broke out in 1741, the British mediated between the Habsburgs in Vienna and the Prussians in Berlin. The result of this was that France lost the support of Prussia, whom they had sometimes relied on in the past as an ally against the Habsburgs.

477 – All mediations, conciliations and arbitrations should, in the interests of prudence, be made the subject of a prior formal agreement between the parties covering the subject matter of the intervention, its purpose and even the manner in which it will be conducted. Whether or not it goes forward will in any event depend on the goodwill of the parties, but they would nonetheless be well advised to protect themselves against any effects it might have later on their own ability to negotiate or manoeuvre. (see *1144*)

Section 2: Trust and skill

478 – Even at the highest levels, diplomacy can sometimes take crude and ruthless forms. Negotiation, however, has to be planned with careful thought and carried out with subtlety and skill.

It is easier to arouse distrust than it is to build trust; trust is fragile, but suspicion is lasting.

479 – In spite of the profound upheavals in diplomatic relations brought about by the advent of nuclear weapons, there is nothing new here; human nature remains the same, even if the conditions of life in modern society are very different. (see *2425*)

The methods used in diplomacy have been fashioned and honed over centuries of practice. But what determines success in the end, as in war and politics, is the personal capabilities of those in whose hands it lies to take decisions and act on them.

480 – As Machiavelli wrote on the subject of war, recognising an opportunity and seizing it is worth more than anything else. The proposition still holds true. One cannot always count on events taking a particular course, since they will be dictated by their own peculiar logic, no matter how strongly held or valid are the political principles involved.

481 – If a negotiator has mastered his art well, he will be able to justify and promote his government's position by words, gestures and manoeuvres, win over the maximum number of partners to his side and find ways of reconciling with his opponents without conceding on critical issues or accepting rash commitments.

Once he has won the confidence of his negotiating partners, a diplomat can prepare the ground for a conclusion based on mutual trust. Sometimes it is useful to show how far removed from rigidity and intransigence is the tactical versatility of nations generally recognised as having a particular talent for diplomacy. (*2437*)

§1. Good faith

482 – There are many ways of transacting business, whether one is a government or a private company. Where the agent is acting clearly and openly on behalf of his principals, it becomes a formal negotiation. Where his purpose is to gather information and build personal contacts without the government being responsible for what he is doing, it is merely informal. But when discussions are carried on entirely on a private basis, the public authorities have even less involvement, and there is no way of making known the outcome. (see *2414*)

Where an individual feels bound to give his personal word of honour, this requires extreme caution. (see *686*)

483 – The choice of approach will depend on what is right at the time, and this will mostly be influenced by the nature of the issues on the table. This choice must also be understood by the other party to the discussions proposed.

There can be no negotiation without prudence: unless there is trust, there can be no meeting of minds. (see *1805, 2077*)

484 – The sincerity, legitimacy or effectiveness of a given initiative can never be presumed, any more than the authority of the person behind it. The need to have these things established is even more obvious when one is working outside the normal institutional framework.

A person who negotiates does not necessarily do so with the intention of reaching an agreement: if he is motivated by the desire to conquer, proselytise or destroy, he is more likely to be using negotiation as a means to weaken, convert or dominate his opponent. (see *2227*)

485 – Good faith responds to an attitude of loyalty, probity and trust in relations with the other party. It consists of respect for the law and for one's commitments, exactly as they are. Disloyalty and deception are alien to good faith, as is anything stupid or frivolous. (see *571, 739*)

Good faith does not prevent anyone from selecting a partner based on what he expects to achieve from the negotiation. (see *329*)

486 – Just as credit is indispensable to a developed economy, good faith should be the ethical and practical cornerstone of relations between States.[33] This was affirmed in 1974 by the International Court of Justice in the *Fisheries* Case (ICJ *Rep.* 1974, p. 39). But this statement still has only relative value: as can be seen from Article 26 of the Vienna Convention on the Law of Treaties, the very meaning of the notion is not clear.

---

33 F. C. IKLE: *How Nations Negotiate*, New York, Harper Row, 1964, p. 87.

487 – It is sometimes necessary to dissimulate when conducting affairs of State. It has been said elsewhere that only prudence can ensure the success of a negotiation. *But, in political dialogue, prudence and dissimulation are not synonymous with bad faith.* It is in the very nature of the exercise for each party to give itself the best chance of success and try to obtain the best possible result. In doing so it will keep information to itself, disguise what it really wants and only reveal its hand at the last moment if its adversary's intentions are unclear. Where the rules of the game are known, they do not destroy one's reputation or credibility. (see *2603*)

488 – No general could be criticised for having deceived the enemy in order to save his army. Should a diplomat be brought to book for having used skill or cunning to protect or promote his country's vital interests by leading his opponent into error?

Good faith does not exclude distrust, just as giving credit does not rule out seeking guarantees.

489 – Bad faith should not be presumed, but nor is good faith ever a foregone conclusion. It is, furthermore, difficult to prove, only revealing itself as the negotiation unfolds. Hence the importance of respecting the usual procedures if the enterprise is to succeed. Faced with an interlocutor of doubtful probity, the negotiator is constantly on his guard: he must know how to convince the deceiver that he believes him, in order to beat him at his own game. (see *1556*)

Good faith is an expression of esteem, and it must be mutual.[34] *When it is, it gives rise to binding obligations, for example, in the implementation of treaties.* (see *668, 1259*)

490 – Good faith must be present throughout the entire negotiating process. The discussions must be carried on in a spirit of honesty and effectiveness, which means that the parties at the table must not indulge in any conduct that is contrary to their purpose. The systematic withholding of information, or a posture of outright rejection, self-promotion or exaggeration will be doomed to failure. Ambiguity and contradiction in words or deeds should be interpreted in the manner least favourable to their author (*Temple of Preah Vihear* case, ICJ *Rep.* 1962, p. 42). Failure to abide by agreed procedures and timetables, or to give serious consideration to the other side's proposals, often appears inconsistent with the conduct required of the negotiator.

491 – Some individuals have a natural inclination for bargaining. They make prolific statements, contradict themselves without scruple, always have an escape route planned and use such confused reasoning that all manner of hypotheses begin to seem plausible – all this is designed to defeat firmness and clarity, the two things they wish to avoid.[35] (see *2241*)

Promises are easily given, but they are respected in bargaining because they are a necessary part of it. (see *436*)

---

34 P. M. EISEMANN: 'Le *gentlemen's agreement* comme source du droit international', *Journal du droit international*, 1979, p. 326.

35 C. LOCKHARDT: *Bargaining in International Conflicts*, New York, Columbia University Press, 1979.

492 – This type of behaviour is nonetheless different from resort to intrigue, which casts suspicion on the negotiator by undermining his authority and diminishing his reputation. Sometimes the very credibility of his government is called into question. Bragging and betraying confidences do not redound to the credit of their author; rather, they often give ammunition to the opposing side or provoke it to make even greater demands.

493 – Statesmen unfailingly use all the means at their disposal in pursuit of their policies when there are major threats to be averted, such as an alliance of rivals that has to be brought down or an unfavourable treaty whose impact must be mitigated. Before the advent of Machiavelli, Louis XI of France based his entire diplomacy on duplicity and underhandedness, thus creating a climate in which everyone else's acts were greeted with the same distrust, anxiety and disbelief as his own.

In fulfilling his mission, the negotiator should not fail to remind those instructing him of the principles of good faith, should the need arise.

494 – Clever tricks should not be overused.[36] That said, the traditionally held view of diplomacy is that it is based on duplicity and deceit. The Romans were possessed of such a will to dominate that they never made peace in good faith; if Montesquieu is to be believed, their treaties were only ever really a lull in the fighting, and the conditions they imposed invariably triggered the ruin of whatever nation accepted them.[37]

495 – Resort to trickery adds to the uncertainty on the part of the adversary while reducing it on the side of the perpetrator. But even the cleverest will end by being caught in his own trap, and intrigue is detrimental to negotiation even when it seems to be helping it along.

Practices that are frowned upon in trade are equally undesirable in diplomacy, because they falsify the agreement between the parties or prevent agreement being reached at all.

496 – Even though, according to Machiavelli, it is absolutely necessary for a prince to have a perfect command of the art of simulation and dissimulation, no negotiation can succeed if it produces a feeling of distrust either on the part of one's allies or one's opponents. It makes no difference whether it is the underlying intent, the methods used or the people carrying them out that have produced this reaction. Nor does it matter whether the distrust attaches to the substance of the dispute or simply to appearances. Richelieu astutely observed that people distrust anyone whose actions suggest an excess of sharpness or subtlety.[38]

497 – Even if the negotiator does not actually deal in falsehoods, he must know how to conceal the truth where this is necessary in order to succeed. He will know

---

36 FREDERICK II of PRUSSIA: *L'Anti-Machiavel*, Chapter 26.
37 C. de MONTESQUIEU: *Considérations sur les causes de la grandeur et de la décadence des Romains*, Amsterdam, 1734, VI.
38 Cardinal de RICHELIEU: *Testament politique*, Paris, Laffont, 1947, p. 350.

how to keep a confidence, especially where his own instructions are concerned, and he will give nothing away about his objective, his reasons or his mandate, but will stop short of abusing the technique of manoeuvre. Good faith has no place for deceitfulness but, as Talleyrand said, it does permit the use of restraint, and he was in a position to know.

498 – Dishonesty works against the very purpose of negotiation, which is to bring about an agreement between sovereign powers. While skill, dissimulation and cunning are perfectly legitimate, lies on the other hand are not, as they can be verified or detected. (see *739*)

499 – In a society as unorganised as the international world, everything a State does, each action and reaction, will provoke an opinion on the part of someone else: whether or not this is the desired effect, it engages the author of the act, simply because each State is deemed to be willing and able to look after its own interests. (see *512, 768*)

500 – In every conversation, there is a risk of misunderstanding: the negotiator should be ready for this, just as he needs to be on his guard against any traps. *It is not enough to be the most determined; it is necessary to be the most clear-sighted.* In 1813, Napoleon fell victim to the illusion that his alliance with Austria, shored up by his marriage to Marie-Louise, daughter of the Habsburg Emperor, would survive his defeats in Russia and his problems in Germany. (see *774*)

501 – Good faith must continue even after the obligations are entered into (Vienna Convention on the Law of Treaties, Article 26). True, a treaty becomes binding only after it is ratified, and ratification is still discretionary. But signature places each of the contracting parties under a duty to act consistently with its objectives, meaning that they must do their best to have the treaty ratified, and refrain from doing anything in the intervening period that goes against the agreement or makes it impossible to implement[39] (Vienna Convention, Article 18). While non-compliance may not be subject to any legal sanction, there will be sanctions in practice in the future relations between the States concerned. (see *667, 786*)

502 – The diplomat must use his talents for perception and guesswork to assess what lies behind the thoughts and actions of those he is dealing with. This is not simply a question of ulterior motives, however tempting it is to ascribe these to the other side. He must listen to and digest all the arguments, at the same time while making his own, in order to understand thought processes that are not necessarily the same as his. (see *509, 2405*)

503 – Of course it takes time to persuade, reassure and convince the other party: it is better to accept at the outset that this will take time than to have to go back to the starting point halfway through the process. Talks can never make headway if decisions that have already been taken are reopened at every stage and if the

---

39 J.-P. COT: '*La bonne foi et la conclusion des traités*', Revue belge de droit international, 1968, p. 140.

parties shamelessly avoid the issues. If a negotiation is to succeed, the successive partial commitments that are made along the way must be respected.[40] (see *524*)

504 – Reputation and credibility are confirmed or destroyed as the negotiation unfolds. At the beginning, the diplomat should devote as much effort to disguising his own true nature as he does to getting to know the nature of his adversaries. Little by little, though, defences come down, cracks appear in the mask and a kind of complicity or even liking builds up between those on either side of the table. (see *2425*)

505 – Trust, if it is to last, must be built on solid foundations – on the sound lessons of history and knowledge of human nature, starting with an understanding of the different characteristics of every field of activity. A negotiator will lose respect, even when he has no intention of giving offence, if, for example, he makes a mistake in a foreign language and says something that is against the established religious, moral or cultural principles of the country of those he is dealing with.

506 – The quality of the relations between negotiators is determined by how much they know about each other's countries, civilisations and often languages, and at the same time how ready and willing they are to understand how the other person thinks and in what ways he is different. (see *2010, 2408*)

The trade is learned by putting oneself in the other's place, but this should never mean forgetting one's own.

507 – Trust is not granted automatically; the less one knows about the other party, therefore, the greater the degree of preparation advisable before the first meeting. From the beginning, meetings should be conducted in such a way as to create an impression of security and confidentiality, so that everyone present will be encouraged to participate without fear or reserve, but rather in a spirit of active curiosity and willingness to understand the other party. (see *2405*)

§2. Tacit negotiation

508 – Not all nations have the same scale of values or the same concept of public affairs. For countless millions, the notions and customs of Western diplomacy have no meaning or relevance; to them, these belong to another civilisation. (see *2054*)

509 – Often, each camp will have its own logical approach and, as a result, its own ideas about negotiation:[41] one need only look at the different ways in which the French and the British approach a discussion. The long debates so typical of Africa, the bargaining dialogues of the Far East and the Mediterranean propensity for speech-making all follow their different rhythm, all serve a purpose and all, in their own way, produce an outcome.

40 F. C. IKLE: *How Nations Negotiate*, New York, Harper Row, 1964.
    A. PLANTEY: 'Paradigms in International Negotiation: the Example of Good Faith', in *Processes of International Negotiations*, San Francisco, Westview Press, IIASA 1989, p. 287.
41 E. T. HALL: *The Silent Language*, New York, New York University Press, 1959.

510 – Revolutionaries have different notions of faith, and also of good faith, from those of their adversaries. *The weak often prove to be more sensitive and unyielding than the strong.*

Another temptation to be resisted is the tendency to interpret behaviour as deceitful when in reality it is nothing more than the outward manifestation of an empirical approach: a pragmatist does not have the same vision of the world, mankind or history, as someone steeped in the ideas and culture of a legal or philosophical system.

511 – The quality of the communications between the opposing camps depends on cultural factors that are not easy to evaluate and so does the durability of their final agreement. (see *1842*)

The risk of misunderstandings increases as the negotiations broaden to include nations and leaders ruled by different ideologies. (see *1840*)

512 – Westerners underestimate the importance of tacit negotiation, despite the fact that this goes on more or less all the time, flowing as it does from the mere acceptance of the behaviour of a partner or an adversary.[42] Even if this assent is not put into words or reduced to writing, it is binding: *silence is one of the ways to express, if not always actual agreement, at least one's acknowledgement of a situation, or understanding of a draft or lack of objection to a given initiative.* This practice is not confined, for example, to international organisations, or to its extreme form, abstention. Many unilateral manoeuvres are carried out in the expectation that the other party will signal its acceptance by saying and doing nothing or by bringing its own behaviour into line.[43] (see *679, 860*)

513 – For some, tacit agreements should be understood and respected, and the very idea of putting them in writing gives offence. Others, by contrast, prefer to have things formulated and set down in words, and this is viewed as a necessity in the case of a major negotiation. But many compromises remain *de facto* because each of the parties regards them as temporary. (see *649, 709, 768, 1846*)

514 – Taking refuge in indecision is not the answer. Silence does not always amount to consent: where there is an obligation to reach an agreement in very precise terms, this requires positive commitment. On the other hand, informal exchanges of agreement or interpretation, even in the form of a press release, if it is issued jointly, are viewed as the product of a successful negotiation that gives rise to binding legal obligations between the parties (Vienna Convention, Articles 9 and 34 *et seq*).[44] (see *2199*)

515 – Silence might seem a very attractive option in moments of difficulty, but it is not always a very astute choice: it amounts to recognition that an issue has been decided between third parties, because it is taken as meaning that one has no say in the matter.

---

42 T. C. SCHELLING: *The Strategy of Conflict*, Cambridge, Harvard University Press, 1963, p. 74.

43 J. CASTANEDA: 'Valeur juridique des résolutions des Nations unies', *RCADI*, 1970, I, p. 302.

44 J. SALMON: 'Les accords non formulés ou *solo consensu*', *AFDI*, 1999, p. 1.

By avoiding an issue, there is a risk of intervening only after it is too late to resolve it.

516 – If an international agreement is silent, the inference will be drawn that anything that is not forbidden is not only permitted, but was in the contemplation of the other party and accepted by it. It is well known that the first strategic arms limitation treaty was interpreted by Moscow as giving it the freedom to produce certain weapons: it amounted to an invitation to them to do so.

517 – In diplomatic negotiation, silence will work in favour, if not always of the strongest, then of the most determined and the most cynical. In institutional negotiation, it takes the form of consensus and passivity. (see *766, 1566*)

§3. Time

518 – There are no rules to be laid down about how to conduct negotiations, other than to follow local customs and observe the rules of civility.[45] It is still true, though, that a diplomat has to work within a number of constraints, chief among which is the need to adapt to the various competing factors that determine whether his interlocutors can agree. (see *616*)

519 – Montesquieu said that success mostly depends on knowing how much time will be needed to achieve a favourable outcome: this is certainly true in diplomacy, and should serve to discourage both lack of foresight and precipitate action.

A nation's wounds need time to heal.

520 – The part played by the time factor in pursuing a policy is all the greater where the emphasis is on anticipating future events. However, *not all peoples or negotiators will have the same interpretation of the notions of time, speed and the future.*[46] (see *294, 1996*)

Manoeuvres are mostly carried out by making a series of rough estimates, depending on when the opportunity arises and, obviously, on the strategic direction. (see *2148*)

Opportunity

521 – If a settlement is to be well received, it is vital to know how to wait for the right opportunity, and to seize it when it arises. *Negotiating in good time is an essential attribute of the statesman as well as of the businessman and even the soldier.* (see *265*)

For the negotiator, the optimal moment is determined not only by looking at one's adversary, but by weighing up his strength, which requires, among other things, the ability to predict economic circumstances, how military operations will go or what attitude one's allies will take.

---

45 A. de WICQUEFORT: *L'Ambassadeur et ses fonctions*, Cologne, Pierre Marteau, 1690, II.
46 E. T. HALL: *The Silent Language*, New York, New York University Press, 1959.

522 – This ability to get the timing right is even more decisive because favourable opportunities go by very fast, which can have serious consequences when there is a lot at stake. The French *Directoire* could probably have achieved peace with Britain in 1797, but it was split into rival factions and did not take the decision in time: the demands made by Paris, along with British naval successes, meant that the discussions being held in Lille failed and the war went on, the same war that was to bring Bonaparte to power. By contrast, two years earlier, the third partitioning of Poland had wiped that country off the map of Europe in the space of a few months: its three neighbours, Austria, Russia and Prussia, had been quick to reach agreement, and the failure of the Polish uprising coincided with inaction on the part of France, its weakened ally. (see *267*)

523 – In this field as in any other, wasted opportunities are not repeated. There are certain diplomats who have made an art form out of delaying tactics, the main purpose of which is to disarm the other party and cause him to miss opportunities that would have favoured him.

524 – A diplomat with the will to negotiate will find the right gestures, messages and channels to get this across. Without moving his starting point too far in the direction of his adversary, during the preliminaries he will avoid any topic on which there is disagreement, any overblown posturings and threatening behaviour, and wait until the talks are under way to raise the stakes and bring more serious disputes to the table. *Sending signals is an art.* (see *275, 2051*)

With the growth in the press and other media, diplomacy has new communication channels at its disposal. (see *264, 2010*)

525 – By mutual consultation, examining the facts together and making a preliminary joint comparison of the information available, a start can be made on discerning the other party's intentions and capabilities with a view to making future plans. Relations between the Federal Republic of Germany and the States of Western Europe were normalised in stages, from 1970 until the historic moment when reunification brought about the disappearance of the German Democratic Republic and set the seal on the decline of Soviet power, even before the USSR had ceased to exist. (see *2044*)

526 – Sometimes it is most important to find the opening that will allow a dialogue to begin. After that, the negotiation will follow its own logical course, as can be seen from the regularisation and growth in Sino-American relations from the days when all the two sides did together was play table tennis.

Even drawing up a list of differences can make it easier to negotiate and pave the way for a compromise.

527 – Taken together, these factors explain why an important negotiation requires careful preparation. The spark of interest must be ignited in the parties, and enough confidence and willingness generated to bring them to the table, or at least to inhibit them from rejecting the idea out of hand. Pressure can be brought to bear on a recalcitrant State by intimating to one of its allies, if possible the most powerful, that stands to gain something from the dialogue, the more so since it can avoid having to bear the consequences itself. (see *507*)

528 – As Clausewitz might have put it, if one side has an interest in acting, it may be in the other's interest to await events. A State whose armies are winning on the battlefield will delay negotiating an armistice; a State in a phase of expansion does not advertise its claims if they might seem excessive; and a State wishing to manoeuvre or attack does not allow its hands to be tied or its intentions to be revealed. (see *242, 282*)

529 – It goes without saying that either party can always try to escape from a negotiation if the timing or the circumstances are not right for it, or if it fears that by opening discussions it will be taken to have acknowledged a given interest or accepted a given commitment. (see *283*)

530 – Aside from the case of military defeat, the question is whether it is possible to compel an adversary to negotiate or at least to hold talks. Meetings come to mind – long conferences, some of them – like the notorious one held in Paris in 1951, which consisted of negotiations to avoid negotiating, and where the parties could not even agree about the agenda or whether it was even appropriate to discuss a certain issue. Some conferences have scarcely been opened when they are aborted by the non-appearance or manoeuvrings of one of the delegations, as happened in 1960 when Khrushchev used the American spy plane incident as a pretext to put an end to the meeting of the Four Great Powers at the Elysée Palace. And there have been others, such as the long Paris Conference on Vietnam in 1972, when the parties went on repeating the same allegations in a sort of dialogue of the deaf, while the real business was being transacted elsewhere.

531 – The so-called diplomacy of the empty chair is based on the same refusal to be drawn into a system of negotiation of which one does not approve, or when one is fearful of being bound by the consequences. The French have frequently adopted this posture, for example, at the UN General Assembly, whenever items were on the agenda that they considered to be within their domestic sphere of jurisdiction, such as Algeria, or again at the Disarmament Committee which met from 1962 to 1978 in Geneva, when all the while the major powers were continuing to develop their bombs and missiles.

532 – Most of the time, it is difficult to force one's approaches on a reluctant partner; perhaps more difficult, even, than inducing an enemy to fight. Of the various devices that have been used – ranging from pressure, surprise and isolation, to winning over allies – few of them produce results in time to preserve the benefits of a well-calculated initiative. (see *273*)

The more the claimant softens his position, the more inflexible the adversary will become.

533 – Institutions and mechanisms have been set up to provide a framework for negotiation that is both favourable to it and based on principles of equality. Some of these make negotiation compulsory, as is the case with Article 2 (3) of the UN Charter. But they cannot guarantee a positive outcome: agreeing to negotiate is not a promise to agree. All they can do is to delay, if not always prevent, unilateral manoeuvres. (see *749, 1652, 1783*)

534 – This is enough as a starting point, as can be seen from the reactions of those States that take no part in these procedures or reject them altogether, and dream

up alternatives in order to paralyse or sidetrack their workings. The founding of the International Energy Agency by the European Organisation for Economic Cooperation (precursor to the OECD) was designed to open up the closed circle of European Atomic Agency Community (EURATOM). Likewise, the Western European Union was used as a way of deflecting French opposition to Britain's entry into the European Common Market.

535 – There are still those who resort to the use of intimidation or coercion, a real temptation for the strongest, but no fruitful negotiation can be induced or conducted on this basis, nor, *a fortiori*, will it produce lasting results. (see *88*)

But a simple proposition, if repeated obstinately and often, will have its effect on opinion and make it more difficult for weak regimes to resist.[47]

536 – The diplomat would be well advised to look at how things are done in the world of business: it is better for him to create a situation in which it is in the interest of all parties to negotiate and, if possible, to reach agreement. He should not, therefore, dismiss any line of inquiry that might give him a better understanding of the precise position of his partners, or rule out any gesture that might increase their level of trust. He needs to put them at their ease in order to win them over – though, if agreement is what he wants, he should not give the impression of being too keen.

537 – On the other hand, faced with an adversary who has no choice but to negotiate, there is no need to let him dictate the timing: it makes more sense to seize the moment when he will be at the greatest disadvantage. (see *282*)

§4. *Duration*

538 – In order to succeed in the initial approach and the discussions themselves, it is not good to act in haste or under pressure. Nor is it advisable to be in too much of a hurry to bring matters to a conclusion, unless circumstances are likely to change so radically that the entire strategy will be jeopardised. As La Fontaine put it, having patience and time on your side is worth more than either strength or anger.[48]

The negotiator must always take the time to set out his point of view and the factors affecting it, sometimes even his scruples, allowing them to operate on the minds of the opposing camp.

539 – By contrast with business, where the gains to be derived from a negotiation depend on speed, there is nothing to be gained from hastily conducted negotiations if this is incompatible with the seriousness of their content, even allowing for the fact that the politician will be tempted by the idea of spectacular success. If he sees his adversary either delaying or rushing ahead, the diplomat will never fail to ask why.

However, deadlines can force concessions to be made: in order to succeed, one must have time on one's side.

540 – It is better to play for time or avoid the issue than face rejection or to give in to unfavourable conditions. The negotiator will pursue his course with calm and

---

47 H. A. KISSINGER: *The White House Years*, Boston, Little, Brown & Co., 1979.
48 J. de la FONTAINE: '*Patience et longueur de temps font plus que force ni que rage*'.

prudence. He must not hesitate to repeat his arguments or to put questions to the other side.

There are various devices he can resort to in order to avoid a problem or prepare for an attack, among them being calculated hesitation, diversions, last minute hitches, histrionics or tactical withdrawal. (see *283, 294*)

541 – While they wait for the full and definitive resolution of a dispute, parties will sometimes agree on a *modus vivendi*, in other words, a limited and temporary compromise formula to allow the main negotiation to go forward.

The wish to reach a conclusion without becoming mired in sluggish procedures has led an increasing number of parties to adopt a simplified form of 'executive agreement'. (see *781*)

542 – The mood of the participants has an effect on how the negotiation proceeds. A party wishing to gain time will find a pretext for delay, and one wishing to skew the other party's predictions will engineer some allegedly fortuitous event. A party that wants to prevent a delegate from pulling together his argument will bring the meeting to an abrupt end.

That said, there is nothing to stop an opponent from attempting the reverse manoeuvre. It is as well to give the appearance of being at ease if one does not want to look rushed or startled. (see *503*)

543 – Timing determines whether a proposition can be allowed to mature or if it must be rejected. The negotiator must know how to judge how much he can achieve and how long it will take him. *The most successful negotiation is the one involving the smallest concessions*, even, if possible, something the adversary was already entitled to receive. (see *426, 2441*)

544 – The negotiator waiting for the right moment often shies away from direct attack, and puts off the discussion of thorny issues until the day when he can approach them in his own way.

The best way to fend off the effects of a manoeuvre is to prevent it from being completed and then to divert or paralyse the unwelcome initiative.

545 – Depending on the nature of the subject matter and the degree of interest of the parties, some discussions produce rapid agreement, while others drag on for months or even years. It is not unheard of for the intervals between talks to be longer than the time actually spent in discussion.

546 – These breaks in negotiation can often be put down to human nature with its indecisiveness, its fear of taking risks and its inability to grasp issues that are too complex or that require long-term prediction of what the future holds. (see *2148*)

When the environment is too unstable, negotiation can only succeed if it advances by very small steps.

547 – A slowing down or suspension of discussions can give the parties the chance to form a clearer idea of what has been decided in order to avoid going back later over the same ground. It also allows them to think through all the possible consequences, or, if there is time, use the new situation as the basis on which to

plan their next objective and how to go about it. Metternich prolonged the discussions being held in Vienna in 1814–1815 for all these reasons, until the unexpected return of Napoleon from Elba put them into abeyance.

548 – It would be wrong to conclude from this that nothing ever happens during periods of suspension: it is at such times that wars are declared. During hostilities, too, there are quiet periods, used for rest and observation, and these can be propitious for the opening or reopening of talks.

549 – Having a sense of timing also allows one to offer concessions when they are welcome and helpful, in other words, at the point at which they can contribute to moving the discussions forward and reaching agreement. It is no good waiting until advances made by the other side have robbed them of their utility.

550 – No proposition should be made too early on, for example, if it benefits an interlocutor of whose political leanings one is not sure.
  Precipitous action is open to the criticism that it makes one side imprudent and the other distrustful.

551 – Like the businessman, the negotiator must know how to take the rough with the smooth, never to be tiresome and never to rush. The point each party is aiming to reach is never the same: he must therefore wait to seize the moment when his interlocutor is ready to bring matters to a conclusion, either because of new developments or the logic of his own policy. According to Talleyrand, the essential virtues of the diplomat are patience and prudence.[49]

552 – The use of time in negotiation can have a bearing on the outcome. The choice of an agenda or a timetable often produces the first confrontations, where principles are concealed in debates over procedure, and which can sometimes be very revealing as to the hidden intentions of the representatives, the issues that particularly interest them and those they are anxious to dispose of quickly. It can sometimes betray their desire to delay agreement.

553 – Even the fixing of the times of meetings deserves attention: one delegation might wish to gain more time or deprive another party of it. The delays and tedium of ceremonies and organised festivities can be liberating for one and exhausting for the other or they can induce a shared desire to reach a compromise at the first opportunity.

554 – The overall organisation of work can make life difficult for some negotiators, interfering with their work, their reflection and their consultations with colleagues, especially when they are abroad. Thought should be given to these aspects ahead of time. (see *565*)
  A speaker who is kept on his feet will become tired and irritable.

555 – Research has been done into the effects of time pressure on negotiations,[50] and shows that by no means all of them are beneficial. Setting a deadline is

---

49 J. ORIEUX: *Talleyrand ou le Sphinx incompris*, Paris, Flammarion, 1970, p. 304.
50 D. PRUITT and J. DREWS: 'The Effect of Time Pressure on Behavior in Negotiation', *Journal of Experimental Social Psychology*, 1969, 5, p. 43.

perceived as a form of coercion, if not an actual threat. It is one technique for resolving crises, however, and it features, for example, among the practices of the European Community, where it encourages compromises to be reached as a package. (see *1262, 1845*)

556 – In any case, unilaterally setting a time limit for a negotiation amounts to an expression of domination, or even a formal notice or ultimatum, whether it is done in advance or during the course of the discussions, as the Soviets did in 1951 to put an end to the interminable proceedings at the Conference of the Four Great Powers. (see *92*)

557 – The fate of a negotiation depends on the consequences of failure. If this constitutes an unacceptable risk, it means that there are dangers involved in maintaining an inflexible posture, because the one who can keep this up the longest will win the day.[51] (see *2152*)

Following the same logic, moving forward with a dispute often acts as a stimulus to negotiations.

558 – Time brings its own solution to many problems. *The exact value of any counterpart can be measured in terms of one's own political position, but might also depend on speculation about the future or a prediction that a given development will take place.* In diplomacy, it is important to understand how long things take. As far back as 1790, London had begun to consider setting up a United Kingdom of The Netherlands along the entire continental shores of the North Sea, entrusted to the Orange-Nassau dynasty, in response to the Belgian revolt against the Emperor of Austria. It was only after the negotiations of 1814, however, that this plan came to fruition, and even then it did not last. (see *820, 2076, 2333*)

559 – With time, as with the substance of the matter, no commitment and no claim are worthy of consideration if they go beyond the bounds of what is reasonable. When Stalin was putting together the forecasts on the basis of which he would negotiate at Yalta, he felt satisfied that Roosevelt did not think it was possible to keep American troops on European soil for more than two or three years after the end of hostilities. Both of them were wrong. (see *2105*)

Venue

560 – The venue chosen for an encounter can have a bearing on how it will unfold. This has become an increasingly important consideration now that diplomatic manoeuvres are carried on around the world, including in countries whose climate is less than conducive to work. (see *284*)

561 – The negotiator operating on his home ground has the advantage in every respect. He can go about his business without having to deal with potentially troublesome ancillary matters such as his delegation's living accommodation and working conditions and the confidentiality of their information. It also leaves the

51 C. OSGOOD: *An Alternative to War and Surrender*, New York, Urbana, 1962.

host country free to choose what facilities it can or will make available to the other side's delegation. (see *1024, 1025*)

562 – Unless he is in a position to be able to insist on a neutral venue, the diplomat will be dependent on the host country to provide a number of necessary services. He must take stringent precautions to protect his working quarters and his communications, at a time when modern technology makes it possible to intercept even the best-protected information. (see *2011, 2606*)

563 – In either case, however, the negotiator must act promptly and decisively to ensure the best possible conditions for his work. Diplomatic representations play an appreciable role here, and it is the responsibility of the local ambassador to look after the needs of negotiators sent from his capital.

564 – The choice of the exact venue for an international meeting will of course depend on what is available. Not all Heads of State can set up camp in a Field of the Cloth of Gold or, like Napoleon at Tilsit, make use of an island in the river. The Berlin negotiations of 1971 were held in the council headquarters of the Allied Command, in the American sector: the Westerners took this as confirming that the negotiations were a continuation of the earlier four-party talks, while the Soviets took it as an acknowledgment that East Berlin would not be part of the discussions.

565 – Geographical accessibility is also a consideration, as can be seen from the progress of the talks at Yalta. Nowadays, no negotiator would agree to hold meetings in a place that did not have fast and reliable communication links with his capital. (see *2056*)

566 – The prospect of conflict has a moderating influence on the laws of hospitality. A delegate receiving a frosty welcome will wait and see if the working conditions turn out to be any better. If they prove to be inadequate from the point of his security, communications and his need to spend time in reflection, he will withdraw from the discussions until these problems are dealt with.

§5. Dexterity

567 – While force often takes the form of a series of rapid strikes, negotiation opens up the way for gamesmanship and calculation, and is played out amid nuances, digressions, subterfuge and hidden meanings. A good negotiator will take pains to ensure that the limits of the debate are clearly laid down and the outcome is free from ambiguity. *Whether or not an agreement is respected often depends on the precautions taken at the outset. They can also be decisive if it comes to proving that the agreement actually existed.* (see *2447*)

568 – As practised nowadays, negotiation resembles a conversation: it must be conducted in a pleasant and courteous manner. The parties may appear unconcerned, but they must never show contempt or tactlessness. Certain habits, certain allusions or expressions might cause offence to the other party and make agreement impossible. The negotiator will avoid attitudes that force the other party into submission as well as personal attacks or anything that causes humiliation or insult.

569 – In any alliance or coalition, it is the most powerful and the one with the fewest constraints on his freedom of action who will be tempted to take the lead in the collective negotiation. This is to be avoided, if he does not wish to annoy, worry and alienate his allies. When France was holding talks with Germany in 1938 about the fate of Czechoslovakia, it gave the appearance of having forgotten that the USSR, too, had given that country a guarantee. Stalin did not fail to understand the reality: in spite of the Franco-Soviet pact, Paris did not in fact view him as an ally. (see *869*)

570 – The attitude of the negotiating partners is of key importance in this respect because it reveals a great deal about their true nature and the moves they are likely to make. The negotiator knows how to put his personality, voice and gestures to work in his cause, and thus he avoids the use of telephones and other communications media that obstruct personal contact with his interlocutors.

571 – Simply because a negotiation goes easily, it should not be assumed that agreement on the substance will automatically follow. *Negotiation is not a matter of sentiment, and good faith is founded on lucidity, in other words, on a thorough and honest appraisal of the items in issue rather than on exchanges of pleasantries or outward displays of cordiality.* (see *486, 2244*)

572 – The statesman sees political manoeuvres as the way to achieve a variety of ends, and these may even be contradictory. He might seek support from powers that do not get on well together, or he can be ready to take advantage of future turns of events that are still unclear. Gamesmanship is the very essence of diplomacy, and it is vital to keep all one's irons in the fire.[52] The same is true of private business.

573 – Negotiation is a dialogue. As La Rochefoucauld wisely said, you must listen to those who are speaking if you wish them to listen to you. Freedom to respond is a precondition for sincere dialogue. Such an attitude implies open-mindedness, attentiveness and the ability to retain what has been said.

There is always something to be learned from the other side's explanations, even if only about its motives. In some debates, the one with skill is the one that has the last word. (see *2438*)

574 – The diplomat can learn a great deal from the patient, friendly and attentive manner in which a salesman approaches his customer, putting himself in the customer's shoes in order to persuade him and refraining from expressing his own reactions of resentment or disillusion. Adopting a courteous manner enables him to take the risk of taking a firmer position on the substance of the issue, if he does not think it will be possible either to reach agreement on a particular point or accept a compromise.

575 – *The negotiator, unlike the politician, does not easily close the door on discussion, whether out of conviction or sentiment.* Temper, vanity and histrionics are alien to him. There is no room for arrogance, timidity, distrust,

---

52 S. and I. HOFFMANN: *De Gaulle, artiste de la politique*, Paris, Seuil, p. 340.

presumptuousness, hesitancy, impulsiveness, likes or dislikes. The unwise, the vulnerable, the vain and the impatient will all be given short shrift. (see *309*)

576 – At every stage of a negotiation, it is necessary to reflect and to calculate. The essence of the process is to be able to reconcile facts and variables coming from two or more camps, each one of which is different from the others. But these are positive attributes, implying not only qualities of wise restraint and the ability to reflect before making a decision, but also imagination and the capacity to adapt and formulate a reply, as well as a sound knowledge of how the world works.

577 – In negotiation, prudence means meeting each situation or argument with a precise, measured and timely response. Certainly, there is no harm in spontaneity, if conditions are favourable and its effect can be gauged. And, in extreme circumstances, a diplomat must know how to be audacious. Clausewitz admired Frederick II of Prussia for his ability to combine brilliant coups and wise restraint, both of them qualities of someone who had learned from experience and mastered his role.

578 – It can sometimes help to allow a minor player to take the lion's share of the negotiating, in order to keep the powder dry and preserve freedom of action for as long as possible.
Commitments should be made as late and as sparingly as possible.

579 – Every concession, even if it is negligible or the result of an error, should be accepted and noted, whatever the rank of the person making it, because it aids the process of making inroads into the opponent's position; however, it also deserves some gesture in return. The parties progress from one partial agreement to the next, moving closer, flexibly and by stages, to an agreement that will give each of them what they need as well as respecting each other's interests.[53] (see *280, 2148*)

580 –Diplomats agree that the interests of negotiation are best served when the parties have a realistic view of the situation and give a clear account of what they want. Some, though, advise that motives and intentions should be carefully disguised.
Experience suggests that there is something to be said for revealing the objective of a given initiative in order to help the parties reach a broad understanding of what their talks are intended to achieve. Nor is the negotiator in a position to prevent the other party from asking these questions, and wanting to know what are the concerns and wishes of the others.

581 – Often, what a negotiator does will produce results within the opposing camp. If he is skilled, he will lead his interlocutor to make the desired deductions and take the desired actions, either out of solidarity or interest, or by persuasion or pressure, or even because of the simple logic of the way the facts are presented. The highest form of this art is to lead one's adversary into doing something that will weaken him or cost him resources, effort, prestige or popularity, draw him into a dangerous or one-sided contest or earn him the hostility, envy or plain indifference of others, thus contributing to his isolation – all this while leaving him an escape route.

---

53 F. C. IKLE: *How Nations Negotiate*, New York, Harper Row, 1964, p. 87.

582 – Sometimes it is necessary to clear other potentially interested parties out of the way in order to move ahead with a negotiation. Where threats are not available, offering to compensate a third State for its neutrality is convenient as this can be done to the detriment of one's adversary. Russia behaved in this way on various occasions during the gradual dismantling of the Turkish Empire; similarly, the price paid for the Germano-Soviet agreement of 1939 was the dividing up of Poland.

583 – It is certainly possible to carry on parallel talks with two or more interlocutors, in secret. This can be kept up for some time, but not indefinitely: once the preliminaries are over, a choice has to be made. Stalin had in fact been playing a double game until the Germano-Soviet pact of 1939 put an end to it.

584 – The diplomacy of great political encounters should not overshadow the diplomacy practised in the many international conferences and organisations. This is where procedures, working methods and rules have been formulated that now provide the framework for traditional negotiations. (see *1540*)

585 – Negotiations in business are characterised by the absence of formality. The diplomat, by contrast, must understand that, in his world, the procedural choices he makes will inevitably have an impact on the outcome of the exercise. They may have the effect of modifying the balance of power between the parties, and he must adapt his strategy accordingly. (see *1026*)

586 – Sometimes a diplomat will take on the role of the devil's advocate in his exchanges with his political masters.

Negotiation, though, is more than a mere debate – it is a confrontation. All discussions should be directed towards one goal, which is to succeed.

587 – Speeches and manoeuvres are made in the hope of weakening the opponent, not only by their content, but also by the impact they produce. When facing allies, the initial attack should be directed against the least strong. The front a delegation presents may include a weak point, and it is good tactics to widen the breach. And by seeming to attribute more importance to one secondary player than to another, it is always possible to upset the cohesion and good relations within the opposing camp. (see *2464*)

588 – The list of stratagems is inexhaustible. It includes drowning one's opponent in a welter of procedure, haggling, sheer eloquence or confrontation; there are also devices for evading the consequences of discussions that have got off to a bad start or taken an unfavourable turn.

All negotiations are thus punctuated by incidents which – though no one will admit it – have in fact been caused deliberately.

589 – Beyond all the tactics, procrastinations and manoeuvres, there is an overall purpose to negotiation that imposes a certain discipline on diplomacy; that purpose is to reach, and sometimes publish, a formal agreement. This notion of contracting, if not the associated formalities, is derived from business practice. (see *710*)

590 – Diplomatic negotiation throws up the same problems as trade, but these are exacerbated by the appearance of legitimacy States confer on the worst kinds of

specious methods. *Once the matter is concluded, no amount of frenzied activity, repentance and belated refusals will avail.* (see **2324, 2332**)

591 – The negotiating partners will be called upon to give a variety of guarantees. Setting down any long-term obligations in a treaty and backing them with guarantees is only the first stage in the diplomatic process. Only after signature does the next stage begin, in which any credibility stored up earlier in the process may be put to use. (see **824, 2335**)

592 – The negotiator does not like to see negotiations break down. It places numerous procedural hurdles in the way of parties wishing to reestablish a dialogue. It can also leave a general impression of guilt, which gives rise to great sensitivity on the part of public opinion and wipes out the beneficial effects of any sense of mutual understanding that the parties might have established at the beginning of the relationship. (see **484**)

593 – Rather than let matters reach this point, one solution the diplomat can offer his principals is to suspend the discussions, so that they can be resumed without undue formality when the climate improves. The negotiator who decides to do this will find no shortage of plausible excuses.

594 – Moreover, diplomatic exchanges are rarely without some utility. Their collateral effects are often worth more than the main objective and can still be garnered even if no agreement is reached. These might include the opening of direct relations, prevention of unilateral action or the prevention or thwarting of attempts at coercion. Such exchanges can bring about changes in the surrounding environment or allow propaganda or psychological messages to be spread either domestically or internationally; third countries can be influenced, and the weakness or uncertainty of an adversary can be demonstrated. (see **508**)

595 – It is difficult to be objective at all times about the negotiation one is engaged upon, without succumbing either to optimism or pessimism. A golden rule in all cases is never to conceal the difficulties in a negotiation. Precisely because these things are normally predictable by anyone with insight, they must be brought out onto the table and discussed.

596 – The negotiator must never, in this context, allow himself to step outside his role and expose himself to criticism, for example, by being too bold or too careless. It is dangerous to allow hopes to be built on the basis of a solution that is unlikely, or on one that is merely probable: failure will then be seen as a sign of incompetence or duplicity. (see **2629**)

597 – The failure of a negotiation must never be taken as a personal humiliation or as an act of hostility: instead, the lessons of experience must be learned.

National interest justifies political realism and provides the driving force behind displays of power and tactics. It is changeable, and it is also relative. All forms of international contact, whether bilateral or multilateral, serve a purpose by providing a clearer picture of where the interest of any nation lies. (see **369, 2134, 2333**)

Chapter III:
Diplomatic Negotiation and
the Rule of Law

598 – In the absence of common ideology, superior authority or impartial constraints, the whole edifice of peaceful relations among States depends entirely on their will, whether express or tacit. In spite of the acceptance by governments of general principles, international agreements remain the principal source of international law, in which the State both creates and formulates the rules, and at the same time upholds and applies them.

States have full powers to decide on the timing, the subject matter, the form and the terms of the commitments they make. Most of the time they act by mutual consent, but sometimes they choose to act unilaterally. When the suspension of nuclear testing was announced by the powers concerned and put into effect by them, this was the result of tacit negotiation.

599 – Even custom, which plays a major role in international affairs, can only be effective if it is sufficiently widespread and lasting to be recognised as an expression of the agreement or the established practices of States. (see *2203*)

600 – This means, in fact, that the continuous process of reconciling the different interests of sovereign powers can only be carried on through diplomatic negotiation, which is indispensable if the rule of law is to be upheld, developed and respected in relations between States. This is true even of those legal instruments that are not agreements as such, but whose drafting in international fora is in reality an expression of the will or at least the consent of the parties present: what results is an agreement between States that is more or less explicit. (see *1540*)

The normal workings of diplomacy have evolved into a permanent multipartite negotiation. The public does not see it in such clear terms, as these discussions range over a whole spectrum of subjects and do not always end in dispute. It is easier to apply international norms in countries that adopt a monist theory, in other words those in which international norms duly laid down and promulgated automatically become part of domestic law.

601 – The fact that international law evolves mostly out of bilateral or multilateral negotiations between States gives it a strongly political character. On the one hand, because of the conditions under which it is formulated, it can easily be turned into the instrument of political strategy of one country or a group of countries; on the other, both its content and the degree to which it is respected depend on the extent to which governments are prepared to accept justice and lawfulness.[1] (see *2359*)

---

1 S. HOFFMANN: 'Quelques aspects du rôle du droit international dans la politique étrangère des Etats', in *La Politique étrangère et ses fondements*, Paris, Colin, 1954, p. 239. C. CHAUMONT: 'Cours general de droit international public', *RCADI*, 1970, I, p. 333.

Negotiation not only moulds and establishes the rules and the institution, but also allows exceptions and modifications whenever the powers involved so agree. It is thus their only real means of adaptation and development.[2] (see *851*)

602 – In relations between States, the political dimension overrides the legal; the gulf between law and compromise is as wide as that between words and action. As the French political leader Georges Clemenceau said, history consisted of men proclaiming what was right while doing what was wrong.[3]

Precisely because its legal effects are binding on sovereign States, however, negotiation must be subject to legal discipline: this determines if and when negotiation can take place, how it should be conducted and, ultimately, whether or not its exercise is valid. (see *1613*)

Section 1: Reconciling sovereignties

603 – The main principle in international affairs is that States are sovereign and autonomous: their domestic systems answer to their own laws, and their authorities form their own views as to what is legitimate or timely, especially where foreign policy is concerned. (see *2304*)

No nation or institution has the right or the capacity to impose its point of view on any subject. *No State is the master of the political game, though each of them may try to be.* (see *74*)

In Europe, new sovereignties have appeared with the revival of nationalism, and this poses difficult legal problems of State succession. The issue was examined, in part, under the aegis of the United Nations: as for treaties, in the Vienna Convention of 1978 on State Succession in respect of Treaties, and as for debts and assets, in the Vienna Convention of 1983 on Succession of States in respect of State Property, Archives and Debts. (see *652*)

604 – If there has been a redoubling of efforts to introduce legal order into the international arena, these are only slowly and partially beginning to show results. The short history of the League of Nations showed the triumph of historic nationalisms over an ideal of international cooperation that was generous in spirit but abstract and distant.[4] (see *2265*)

605 – The very fact that States coexist obliges them, nonetheless, to consider each other in their behaviour. Progress has reduced their autonomy and forced them to bend to rules that were foreign to them, ever since it became clear that the needs of nations were common or even identical. Reality forces sovereigns to compromise, making diplomatic negotiation the cement that binds them together in what is now known as the community of nations – a phenomenon that could better be described as a society of States in which new relationships of solidarity are gradually forming. (see *78, 2253*).

2 R. ARON: *Paix et guerre entre les nations*, Paris, Calmann-Lévy, 1962, p. 117.
3 G. WORMSER: *La République de Clemenceau*, Paris, PUF, 1961, p. 357.
4 C. de VISSCHER: *Théories et réalités en droit international public*, Paris, Pedone, 1960, p. 83.

§1. Sovereignty in negotiation

606 – In diplomatic relations and at diplomatic conferences, the principle is that all sovereign powers are equal – or, as Grotius put it, States or Heads of State whose acts do not depend on anyone else, except where they are bound in advance under a treaty. (see *369, 2335*)

Sovereignty is an absolute notion.[5] Forged by centuries of history, it is sustained by politics as well as law.

607 – The notion of sovereignty has generated a wealth of literature and a variety of theories. Ever since the Treaties of Westphalia of 1648, founded on the sovereign equality of the kingdoms and principalities of Europe, it has been put into practice on an everyday basis, backed by treaties in force and in particular by the UN Charter, Article 2 of which refers to the 'sovereign equality of States'. The International Court of Justice applied it in the *Corfu Channel* case (ICJ *Rep.* 1949, p. 18), and it is enshrined in the 1969 Vienna Convention on the Law of Treaties (see the annexed Declaration on the prohibition of military, political or economic coercion in treaty-making).

608 – *Sovereignty is the assumption on which negotiation is based, but it is also its subject, either where States, especially new States, assert the attributes of sovereignty or where its limitations are under discussion, as when States adhere to treaties or to international organisations or integrated systems whose very object is to dismantle it.*[6] (see *1503, 2298*)

The advent of the technological civilisation has consequences for the traditional notion of sovereignty. The international environment has become more fluid with delocalisation of the notions of law and rights and national ambitions expanding into new areas, some of them uncharted. All these factors, together with the many other ways in which people and goods have become mobile, have robbed diplomacy of the simple certainties and stability on which it could once rely.

Capacity and will to negotiate

609 – Public international law determines the consequences that flow from the principle whereby a sovereign nation is free to deal and contract to suit its own purposes, inclinations and formal requirements. It has been said that a State need not consider itself bound by any measure on which it had not been able to decide on terms of equality.[7]

Sovereignty gives each State the immediate and exclusive right to negotiate on any matter that affects its future or its interests.

---

5 C. CHAUMONT: 'Cours general de droit international public', *RCADI*, 1970, I, p. 333.
6 R. BADIE: *Un monde sans souveraineté. Les Etats entre ruse et responsabilité*, Paris, Fatard, 1999.
7 C. de GAULLE: *Mémoires de guerre*, Paris, Plon, III.

610 – Part of the Sovereign State's role and responsibilities is to ensure that its rights are protected. No one may obstruct its will to do so. It can neither be obliged to negotiate and make treaties nor prevented from doing so, in whatever form and on whatever subject it chooses, provided it observes the fundamental principles of international law. It cannot be forced into an agreement (*Advisory Opinion on South -West Africa*, ICJ *Rep.* 1950, p. 133), it is free to negotiate, subject to respecting Article 2(3) of the UN Charter and it retains its freedom of action to the extent that it has not bound itself (*Haya de la Torre* case, ICJ *Rep.* 1951, p. 71) or transferred or shared its capacity to do so. (see *217, 1360, 1476, 1532*)

611 – States will normally ensure that decisions are not taken without their participation in issues which could affect their interests: this is one of their essential diplomatic functions. (see *415*)

However, in the present international environment,[8] *no State may claim as of right to take part in a negotiation or conference even if it considers that its interests are threatened.* (see *1605*)

612 – On the contrary, competition for a predominant position tends to have the effect of limiting the number of parties involved in a treaty. However surprising it may have seemed at the time, it was only because the Piedmontese made such a contribution to the Crimean War that Cavour was allowed to be present at the Paris Congress in 1856 and to put the Italian question on the table.

613 – There are advantages and disadvantages to being represented at a negotiation. Even where no obligation is incurred, taking part gives an opportunity to observe the discussions and exert influence, as can be seen from the consistent practice of British diplomacy. It can also serve to establish one's rank or legal capacity: General de Gaulle needed to use every ounce of his skill and energy to have France readmitted to the circle of the Great Powers in 1945, having not been invited to the Yalta Conference. (see *1018*)

614 – At least in theory, there can be no true negotiation between entities that are not sovereign States, but exceptions can occur, where, for example, an authority seeks to assert its international ambitions. However, this remains an unpredictable process, fraught with difficulties, as can be seen from the attitude of France towards Quebec and the external negotiations of the European Community. (see *655, 1301, 1485*)

The nature and role of regional or territorial communities, and the place accorded to them, is a matter for the domestic constitution of each of the countries concerned; depending on the case, there may be a greater or lesser degree of decentralisation. Some States have a federal structure, and the legislative autonomy of the constituent parts can complicate the central government's efforts to implement foreign policy.

In France, as well as the rest of Europe, the growth in communications has enabled flexible forms of regional entity to come into existence that cross national frontiers (see the 1980 Madrid Convention). These negotiations are not diplomatic

8 P. REUTER: *Introduction au droit des traités*, Paris, PUF, 1985.

in character. The Alpine community which has existed since 1978 and covers part of Austria and Slovenia gained recognition by the governments concerned, in 1988, of its special competence in the fields of transport, culture and the environment. In France, the regions are allowed by law to maintain relations with foreign local authorities on their borders. This possibility was extended to all local authorities provided they comply with international obligations. The European Union has a regional policy with its own budget. However, there are differences in status and competences between the regions of the different European States.[9] (see *1251*)

In federal States, where other entities, such as states forming part of the federation, have a diplomatic role, this is by derogation.[10] (see *8*)

615 – The fact that notions of 'State' and 'people' are not identical is a highly sensitive issue. A people can be a subject of law, but it cannot take an active part in the formal procedures required for international negotiation. Also, the conflicts that underlie negotiations do not break out only between States. Law gives place to realities when the success of peacemaking depends on the cooperation of particular groups or personalities, and procedures have been devised to enable them to take part in talks. This was the case with national liberation movements, which were allowed to appoint observers in some international organisations.

The application of international law to national insurrections implies the recognition of what has been described as an emerging form of international belligerency. (see *681, 687*)

Nonetheless, the disintegration of certain States, in Europe and elsewhere, with its attendant bloodshed has cast doubt upon the traditional notion of international negotiation. (see *1878*)

Independence

616 – The essence of independence, for a nation, consists in having the freedom to determine its own policies without being obliged to submit to another's authority and to exercise its options free from any extraneous pressure and in having the right, where a matter is decided by agreement or compromise, to take part and express its views at its discretion. (see *16, 77*)

The only cases where negotiation is obligatory are determined by political considerations: military defeat is one of them. This does not mean there is an obligation to reach agreement. However, the UN Security Council sometimes shows a tendency to sanction a government for refusing to negotiate, as was seen in the Iraq crisis. (see *1697*)

617 – No independent State can be answerable to another or abandon the exercise of its own basic prerogatives. The European Community shows that even the most powerful mechanisms of integration have their limits: they may forge ever closer links between the countries of Europe, but they do not deprive them of the essential

---

9 'Les relations internationales des régions en Europe', in *Etudes internationales*, Quebec, Laval University, 1999, IV.

10 E. ZOLLER: *Droit des relations internationales*, PUF, 1992, p. 16.

attributes of sovereignty; these nations continue to be States, endowed with their own public powers, conducting their own diplomacy and taking part in the most important international negotiations. (see *1358, 1489*)

618 – *In legal terms, independence confers the capacity to deal with others from a position of free and equal self-determination.* Obviously, every treaty or agreement entered into with a foreign power limits the State's freedom of action, as do decisions taken collectively within an international organisation. The sovereign parties retain the freedom to make their own judgements on the advantages and disadvantages before committing themselves. The US Senate, for example, rejected as unconstitutional any automatic obligation to engage in any Atlantic military action; furthermore, it has refused to ratify a number of major treaties, including the 1999 treaty prohibiting nuclear testing. (see *688, 1795, 2579*)

619 – Because, according to Article 6 of the 1969 Vienna Convention, every independent State has the capacity to enter into treaties, diplomatic negotiation is one of the commonest ways in which sovereignty manifests itself. It is also the most important and the most exclusive. In the absence of clear and express agreement, no provision or stipulation may be interpreted so as to limit or delegate that power.

620 – The feature that most clearly distinguishes a confederation of States from a federal State is the latter's capacity to conduct foreign negotiations. The fact that members of the Soviet Union such as Ukraine and Belarus for many decades held seats in international organisations did not mean that they had freedom to negotiate.

621 – The fact that a State has a coherent federal structure cannot always prevent some of its members conducting external negotiations within their spheres of autonomy.

The evolution of the British Empire shows how the dominions and colonies progressively formulated and imposed their desire to conduct their own diplomatic negotiations and how this paved the way for their accession to sovereignty.

622 – Independence is a paradox when it opens the door to all kinds of pressures on national ways of life and cultural originality. Globalisation and interdependence in finance, trade, the media and ideology have different consequences for the rich than for the poor.

Independence gives increased potential to the strong for negotiation and domination, but for others it often accentuates their weaknesses, deficiencies and inferiority; when such countries do not know how to implement a comprehensive, independent and flexible policy, regulations can work against their interests.

623 – Historically, for a State, subjugation begins when it gives away its power to deal with others. From then on, depending on how much of its power has been transferred or usurped, it is the dominant power that not only defends it against dangers within and without, but also negotiates on its behalf, if it has retained enough of its personality to enter into separate commitments. This was the kind of protectorate regime European States imposed on their impecunious debtors, and it came to be recognised at the international level.

624 – Sovereignty without independence is an illusion. The official sovereign is not always the one who holds the real power: there are some hegemonies that observe the formalities of diplomacy and the appearances of freedom.

In its most extreme form, this alienation knows no limits: in 1896 France unilaterally proclaimed the annexation of its protectorate of Madagascar, and in 1958 it used the same method to declare that act abrogated.

625 – Freedom must also involve the exercise of will, if it is not to remain empty and devoid of meaning, at a time when domination is not so much overt as indirect and disguised, and consists more of economic exploitation than of political sway. Sovereignty cannot be merely a matter of refusing subjugation – it must necessarily involve seeking to influence, if not to dominate, other competing sovereigns. (see 30)

A negotiation is a meeting of wills.

626 – The will to exercise the attributes of sovereignty underpins foreign negotiation. However, *in some of the present-day systems of international organisation, States give up part of their negotiating power in favour of an institution that brings them together and represents them.* This does not mean that they lose their independence, but it changes the way in which they conduct their foreign policy.

Where a country is represented by another for the purposes of certain international acts, this does not impair its independence as long as the representation is neither total nor definitive (Article 6 of the Vienna Convention of 1961).[11] (see *1432*)

627 – Negotiation often serves as an affirmation of independence: after 1922, the Treaty of Rapallo put both Germany and Soviet Russia in a position to show the Allies that they wanted diplomatic autonomy.[12]

Furthermore, taking part in foreign relations and foreign activities is a powerful factor for progress, contributing to changing the patterns of domination and to the splitting up of monolithic political blocs.

628 – The will to assert oneself is what motivates negotiation; without it, subordination is the only course left.

But the spirit of national independence should not be taken to extremes: the world being what it is, so small and confined, there is in reality no complete independence.[13]

There is nothing immutable, unvarying or sacramental about independence. And this is what gives hope to the diplomat: the hope of overcoming quarrels, reconciling interests and transcending passions.

629 – History also shows that peace has always suffered from the rejection of certain ideals, nations and individuals by others. People must meet, in order to

---

11 A. SERENI: 'La representation en droit international', RCADI, 1978, II, p. 73.

12 J.-B. DUROSELLE: *Histoire diplomatique de 1919 à nos jours*, Paris, Dalloz, 1978, p. 62.

13 C. de GAULLE: 'Discours prononcé à Dakar, 13 décembre 1959', in *Discours et messages*, III, Paris, Plon, 1970, p. 152.

know each other. For many years Muslim and Eastern countries lived at the margins of the society of nations. The fact that they have opened up to international exchanges has not diminished their individual character. (see *2048*)

630 – The desire for independence should not, obviously, lead to a breakdown of relations and isolation. It is not in any country's interests to suspend all diplomatic relations and refuse all external commitments. On the contrary, it could protect its freedom by contracting with other powers, particularly with those States whose long-term interests show enough similarity with its own. Smaller States find the best form of protection for their independence in alliances.

The right to a currency is one of the sovereign rights of a State. But this can be the subject of negotiation about exchange rate parity and guarantees, equalisation mechanisms and even a common currency (the euro, for example). The world economy is tending towards the creation of zones of monetary solidarity based around the main poles of activity. (see *1347, 1920*)

631 – In addition, for nations as well as individuals, solitude is difficult to bear. It is the many and varied relationships formed between the peoples on this increasingly crowded planet that define international society; the moral or sometimes sentimental aspirations they express are growing stronger. (see *1679, 2255*)

632 – The existence of States that take no part in normal diplomatic relations does not present any real obstacle to international activity. For centuries, the presence of peoples on the southern shores of the Mediterranean whose religion kept them out of normal inter-state relations and who engaged in maritime piracy never prevented each of the European States from pursuing its own policy in relation to them. Their isolation limits the fragile impression of security that comes from international cooperation, even when this is marred by discord, but it certainly does not justify the use of measures of coercion against the isolated State, as happened in the case of China at a time when it had no intention of opening up to exchanges with the West. (see *539*)

633 – Precisely because they refuse to be bound by common rules, some countries can appear recalcitrant, and even to threaten revolution: this was the case with the USSR after 1917 and China after 1949. Soviet Russia, however, which started out by condemning the methods of traditional diplomacy, came round to the idea as soon as it saw that these methods could help it achieve its objectives. And one of the reasons France gave for restoring links with China in 1964 was that increasing the number of contacts between peoples furthers the interests of wisdom, progress and peace.

634 – Some revolutionary doctrines have challenged diplomatic methods and advocated direct relations between peoples: it has proved impossible to apply them for any length of time. The way ideologies have developed in France, Russia and China at different times in history has proved very revealing in this regard.

Non-interference

635 – A nation's right to self-determination is a prior condition for its freedom and the validity of the external commitments it undertakes. The principle goes back

further than is generally believed. Taking an example from French history, the Comtat Venaissin was a territory that belonged to the Vatican until its population voted in 1791 to make it part of France. (see *369, 2642*)

636 – However, the tendency to interfere in the business of others has proved persistent. In relations between States, it has often been motivated by the imperatives of religion (in the Middle Ages as well as more recently), the legitimacy of monarchy (under the French Revolution and throughout the nineteenth century)[14] and humanity and civilisation (against piracy wherever it has occurred).[15] (see *1891, 2290, 2312*).

This tendency manifests itself in those that set up regimes or sovereigns in other countries in thrall to them, in order to benefit from their cooperation in war or negotiation. Quarrels of this kind were frequent in the days before the right to vote became widespread: throughout the nineteenth century, new thrones were offered to the great families of Europe, after careful political calculation. (see *124*)

637 – The gulf between principle and reality gives cause for concern, especially now, in the face of a proliferation of cases of more or less discreet interference, in which the Great Powers are tending to interpose another State to act where they cannot themselves do so overtly. (see *78*)

Interfering in the domestic politics of a State can dispense with the disciplines and uncertainties of negotiation and impose on a government a strategy that is alien to its thinking. (see *2333*)

638 – Interference can be more or less clear or intentional. When, in October 1918, US President Wilson declared that peace could not be negotiated with Germany's former leaders who had been responsible for the war, this brought about first the abdication of Kaiser Wilhelm II, and then, in November, revolution in Prussia. And it was an Anglo-American good offices mission following incidents that took place in Sakhiet, in Tunisia, that triggered the fall of the French government and the revolt of Algiers in 1958. (see *240*)

The history of negotiations between the United States and Panama shows how the desire to interfere for strategic reasons prevails over respect for national sovereignty: the Canal Zone was the object of successive treaties in 1977 and 1978, and finally of military intervention in 1989.

639 – It can happen that emissaries of a third party, official or not, intervene in talks in order either to paralyse them or to help them along, sometimes with a view to ensuring certain interests are respected. At the Geneva Conference in 1954 on the future of Vietnam, France came under heavy pressure from the British and American representatives. And when the time came to negotiate the setting up of the European Coal and Steel Community, the United States helped by cooperating in very specific areas. (see *452*)

---

14 P. RENOUVIN: *Histoire des relations internationales. Le XIXe siècle*, I, Paris, Hachette, 1954, p. 42.
15 R. ARON: *République impériale. Les Etats-Unis dans le monde (1945–1972)*, Paris, Calmann-Lévy, 1973, p. 239.

640 – Subject to certain conditions, international organisations may also interfere in the sphere of domestic competence (see Articles 2 and 7 of the UN Charter). The notion of the 'reserved domain' of States remains unclear; this has to be the subject of specific negotiations because its delimitation is the product of shifts in the balance of power.[16] (see *1661, 2250*)

In certain dramatic instances, humanitarian aid provides the spur for interference through a broad interpretation of Chapter VII of the UN Charter. Threats to peace, breaches of the peace and acts of aggression are taken by the Security Council as permitting intervention where the political context permits, as with the investigations into war crimes committed in the former Yugoslavia. (see *729, 834*)

641 – Interference is sometimes based on the outcome of a diplomatic negotiation. The implementation of the Treaty of Vienna, and the defence of the political equilibrium it had created, led Metternich to influence the internal affairs of several European countries. And the agreement signed in Moscow in 1944 between Stalin and Churchill on the sharing of influence in Western Europe and the Balkans contributed to a civil war in Greece in which the British army intervened in 1945.

642 – Gone are the days when powers could decide the fate of whole territories without consulting their populations, as happened at the Berlin Conference that divided up Africa. But the international environment is ever changing and renewing itself, and this means each government must be vigilant and decisive. The struggle to do so is useful, as it stimulates competition, innovation and progress.

Great Powers find it more convenient to exercise pressure by indirect means. Any confrontation can serve as the pretext for intervention: some will seize the opportunity to exacerbate the dispute, while others will play a mediating role, according to their interests. (see *452, 2312*)

Mediation is usually dictated by an empirical approach to international relations: it is not systematic, but often temporary. (see *451*)

643 – Often, where one State proclaims a doctrine of non-intervention, the intention is to prevent another, better-placed, State from involving itself in a matter that does not concern it: Britain used this tactic to protect Cavour's Italian policy against Austria. But this type of manoeuvre does not always succeed: the Spanish Civil War attracted widespread international intervention after 1936.[17] A decision not to intervene militarily or economically does not mean that there is no scope for diplomatic action – in fact it promotes negotiation rather than paralysing it. (see *317*)

644 – Collective intervention often provides a way of neutralising the opposition of another party or any attempt on its part to raise the stakes: Poland's fate depended many times on the collusion of its neighbours, who were negotiating together directly against its independence. There is a tendency to favour neutral mediation to bring about the peaceful resolution of disputes between States. (see *1548, 1552, 2167*)

---

16 C. de VISSCHER: *Théories et réalités en droit international public*, Paris, Pedone, 1960, p. 283.
17 C. de VISSCHER: Ibid., p. 301.

A dispute between Eritrea and Yemen concerning the Hanisch Islands was decided in 1999 by independent arbitration under the auspices of France.[18]

645 – The right to interfere in an emergency has been recognised by the United Nations.[19] Several debates have taken place in the General Assembly about real threats to mankind (see GA Resolution 43–131 of 8 December 1988) or the environment, an area in which political frontiers are of no effect. Other UN organs, too, have faced the issue. The Security Council, for its part, has relied on Chapter VII of the Charter in deciding that certain States' activities were such as to threaten international peace and security, and thus to justify intervention in their internal affairs.

Events in Yugoslavia even gave rise to talk of a duty to intervene, and in 1992 the Security Council voted to set up an impartial Commission appointed by the Secretary General of the United Nations to investigate war crimes alleged to have been committed in that country. In 1993 and 1994, it set up a Tribunal for the punishment of the 'crimes against humanity' committed in the former Yugoslavia and another Tribunal for crimes committed in Rwanda.[20] More recently, a Tribunal has been established jointly with the government of Sierra Leone with jurisdiction over crimes against humanity committed in that country. (see *628, 723, 1135, 1609, 2235*)

The first of the recent crises in Iraq triggered debates in which various forms of intervention were discussed with a variety of complex objectives– including the punishment of aggression, humanitarian aid and concerns about human rights – issues fraught with difficulty. The Security Council gave effect to General Assembly Resolution 45–100 of 14 December 1990. (see *729*)

646 – History teaches that it is both unjust and wrongful to fail to respect the personality, rights and honour of even the smallest States. All nations have an equal need for dignity, and States will sometimes suffer deprivation and refuse foreign aid where the process of negotiating for it offends their sensibilities. (see *85*)

Even when it is motivated by humanitarian considerations, any interference in a State's domestic affairs can only be temporary and clearly defined; its objective must be limited, and it must be carried out with prudence in a way that complements the actions of the competent national authorities. Excesses must be avoided.

Precisely because it appeals to their sense of mutual respect and responsibility, negotiation can successfully police relations between States and ensure that they keep their word. (see *673, 2639*)

Responsibility

647 – The Sovereign State answers for its own conduct, for the activities of its officials and citizens and for the use made of its territory and dependencies. To its

---

18 J. F. DELOBELLE: 'Le différend entre l'Erythrée et le Yemen', *AFDI*, 1999, p. 554.
19 M. BETTATI and B. KOUCHNER: *Le Devoir d'ingérence*, Paris, Denoël, 1987. M. BETTATI: *Le Droit d'ingérence*, Paris, Odile Jacob, 1996.
20 E. DAVID: *Principe de droit des conflits armés*, Brussels, Bruylant, 1999.

partners, a State must in principle be viewed as a cohesive entity: unless otherwise determined, the commitments it makes are binding on all its authorities, nationals and territory. (see *2319*)

648 – The notion of responsibility is one that comes into play both in the procedures and the outcome of negotiation, because it is present in all aspects of a State's relations – in its duty to carry out its commitments, iron out problems, re-establish legal order and make reparation for any damage or offence. *The international system presupposes that the State is capable of respecting its obligations* and in particular that it will not allow its nationals or its territory to be used for purposes that are not in conformity with international order and its own foreign obligations (see *Corfu Channel* case, ICJ *Rep.* 1949, p. 29). (see *1650, 2321*)

649 – The use of the power to negotiate imposes responsibilities on each of the partners. This obligation does not attach only to specific acts. Attitudes such as acquiescence and implicit renunciation or delay in resolving issues have legal effects in relations between States. Leaving aside responsibilities vis à vis the international community as a whole, such as those imposed by international institutions, mostly on the more powerful States,[21] most obligations are owed to specific and identified States. (see *Barcelona Traction* case, ICJ *Rep.* 1970, p. 32) (see *512*)

650 – Force majeure may be invoked to explain a State's failure to comply with an obligation where it encounters an insuperable obstacle outside its control. Such a state of necessity must be examined in negotiation between the partners, so that they can agree about the consequences that are to follow: this might happen, for instance, where a State has stopped making payments.

As between States, no excuse exists as of right.

651 – Clearly, since there is no means of legal recourse against a State at the international level, it is difficult – in fact, most of the time impossible – to invoke its responsibility in a peaceful manner, except where the international community or part of it refuses to recognise the effects of an agreement that is obviously vitiated. However, courts consistently uphold the principle that the violation of an international obligation carries with it the duty to make reparation. (see *1661*)

652 – The notion of responsibility provides the basis for prolonging the effects of certain negotiations by virtue of State succession or succession among international institutions and at the same time sets limits to it, as can be seen from the Final Act of the Paris Conference of 30 May 1972 on the taking over of the rights and obligations of the CERS and CECLES by the European Space Agency. (see *1478*)

But, with the exception of boundary treaties, the slew of problems resulting from decolonisation has made legal continuity very uncertain. It has become even more difficult in the context of the break-up of some of the States of Central and Eastern Europe. A number of diplomatic agreements were necessary to regulate the

---

21 R. J. DUPUY: 'Le fond des mers, heritage commun de l'humanité et le développement', in *Pays en voie de développement et transformation du droit international*, Paris, Pedone, 1974, p. 235.

succession to the former Czechoslovakia. There is still some uncertainty about the obligations assumed by States that came into existence as a result of the dismemberment of the USSR. (see *76, 1744*)

The case of Yugoslavia was even more complicated. Under the General Assembly Resolution of 22 September 1992, the Federal Republic of Serbia and Montenegro did not succeed as a matter of right to the seat occupied by the Federated Socialist Republic of Yugoslavia. (see *808, 1650, 1989*)

653 – Because they exist as autonomous structures, international organisations can express interests that are distinct from those of their members. To this extent, whether they are worldwide or only regional in scope, they become new partners on the international negotiating scene. (see *1175*)

The question arises whether they have their own real and permanent responsibility when operating at the level of international negotiation or whether they do not sometimes have the perverse effect of diluting the effectiveness of international commitments. (see *1179, 1599, 2622*)

654 – International institutions, as entities, have neither territory nor population nor any sovereign authority. In practice they depend on the will of States from the moment they are set up and in everything they do. They can never arrogate to themselves diplomatic prerogatives beyond the scope of their particular mission, and they are not in practice permitted independent representation in international negotiations. If the regime of the European Union is an exception to some of these principles, this does not override the privileges of the States: on the contrary, it serves to confirm the difficulties encountered when international functions are exercised by authorities whose responsibility is not suitably delimited. (see *1196, 1197, 1380*)

655 – Responsibility underpins all international negotiation, and is essential to give it meaning and scope. It also sets the limits, in the sense that it embodies the very real constraints imposed by domestic politics on the actions of statesmen and diplomats.

To negotiate or contract with an entity that lacks responsibility has no effect in diplomatic terms. This is especially true in times of crisis. (see *658, 684, 2230*)

§2. Equality and reciprocity

656 – As between States, legal equality is not only a principle affirmed by the UN Charter (see Article 2), but also one of the preconditions for negotiation. It enables each State to insist that no other may claim, in their mutual relations, more extensive rights than it enjoys itself, nor free itself of any of the obligations all States have to the international community as a whole.[22]

657 – *In negotiation and especially through negotiation, all States have an equal capacity to make their voices heard, claim and exercise their rights and assume and carry out their obligations.* None of them may be discriminated against or receive

---

22 M. SIBERT: *Traité de droit international public*, I, Paris, Dalloz, 1951, p. 182.

preferential treatment, and all of them must make use of the whole range of prerogatives deriving from their sovereignty and independence (see *Advisory Opinion on South-West Africa*, ICJ Rep. 1950, p. 133). (see *50*)

658 – Diplomatic negotiation only has any real value if it is based on freedom, in other words if it proceeds from equality of will and results in commitments freely entered into by each of the responsible authorities. Great nations are wrong when they sometimes imagine that they have solved problems by reaching agreement among themselves without negotiating with others.[23] (see *89, 655*)

659 – Though it may be weakened by lack of resources, a sovereign nation will never cease to value its intrinsic identity or to require it to be respected. Public opinion had little time for the doctrine of 'limited sovereignty' constructed by the USSR in 1968 to justify the intervention of Warsaw Pact forces in the internal affairs of its 'satellite' countries. (see *142, 646*)

660 – However, it is impossible to conduct a negotiation, which is an essentially political activity, without being aware that there is tremendous inequality, in practice, between those taking part, depending on their power, resources and situation, and also on the character of their population and the quality of their leaders.[24] Some Member States of the UN are simply archipelagos or islands with only a few thousand inhabitants. (see *251*)

Not all States, then, bring the same intensity or commitment to international negotiation. This is obvious in the military, finance and business fields. (see *2293*)

661 – Inequality of power also means inequality of responsibility, and technological advances are causing this to increase. It has long been admitted that certain major States have set themselves the collective mission of organising world affairs and keeping the peace.[25] While President Wilson put forward a far-reaching interpretation of the equality of nations, in 1918, this principle never prevented disequilibrium from arising between the Anglo-American negotiating partners as soon as there was a change in the balance of power. (see *1032, 1574*)

662 – *When the principle of sovereignty is put into practice, it fulfils its intended purpose of placing the partners on an equal legal footing.* This is the main concern underlying the formal aspects of negotiation – as well as of protocol – and the procedures adopted within international institutions.[26] (see *1136, 1536*)

However, the great nations are accorded a special place in such organisations out of a simple desire to secure their voluntary cooperation.[27] The privileges

23 P. H. SPAAK: *Déclaration du 19 avril 1962*, cited by P. REUTER, *Organisations européennes*, Paris, PUF, 1970, p. 69.
24 R. P. ANAND: 'On the Equality of States', in *The Theory and Practice of International Relations*, Englewood Cliffs, Prentice Hall, 1966, p. 23. R. W. TUCKER: *The Inequality of Nations*, New York, Basic Books, 1976.
25 H. NICOLSON: *The Evolution of Diplomatic Methods*, London, Macmillan, 1954.
26 B. BOUTROS GHALI: 'Le principe d'égalité des Etats et les organisations internationales', *RCADI*, 1960, II, p. 9.
27 L. M. GOODRICH: 'The Maintenance of International Peace and Security', in *The Theory and Practice of International Relations*, Englewood Cliffs, Prentice Hall, 1966, p. 393.

offered to the then Soviet Union and the United States in the United Nations Security Council were the condition their respective governments imposed for accepting the UN Charter. Though the USSR as such no longer exists and the composition of the Security Council is criticised, the legal position thus established has stood the test of time, and might continue, as long as the veto is not misused for political reasons. (see *1113*)

663 – Weaker States are often able to use their free and equal self-determination more skilfully in diplomatic manoeuvres than the most powerful: out of fear of domination by the great powers, the former try to maintain a state of rivalry between the latter. Such States are always prudent when taking on the role of mediator, knowing that if their mission is a success they may be left on the sidelines. (see *412*)

664 – It is a nation's prerogative to reserve matters relating to its constitutional competences to be decided under its domestic law. No nation can concede an essential component of its independence. This reservation is often very convenient; American or British negotiators frequently plead that what they do is subject to scrutiny by the Senate – even its individual members – or by Parliament.

665 – Legal dependency on another power places nations and their leaders in a subordinate position from which they cannot negotiate where the domination begins and ends, or who is exercising it. This was the case for both Egypt and Morocco during the time they were under protectorate regimes. More recently, the political and diplomatic dependency of the States of Eastern Europe was swept away as soon as the USSR began to weaken.

The fate that befell the nations that made up the former Yugoslavia has seen the reappearance of forms of government that resemble protectorates.[28] (see *1132*)

666 – Just as the arguments made in favour of reciprocity have changed, equality tends no longer to be a precondition for negotiation, but its actual objective.[29] Prospective negotiation is much concerned with putting parties in a position of greater equality of opportunity, especially with a view to development: this is what justifies the preferential treatment, protection and advantages that are expected to reduce inequalities between nations. (see *416, 2191*)

667 – Where there is both sovereign equality and a practice of exchanges between States, this makes reciprocity in diplomatic negotiation particularly important, whatever the topic, subject to any practices or agreements making an exception to this principle.

Reciprocity is a basic condition for international relations. (see *375, 423, 455*)

668 – Reciprocity is at work all the time in both diplomatic and business negotiations, introducing symmetry into the parties' behaviour, achieving a balance between advantages gained and obligations undertaken, and formulating reservations, all of them preconditions for the meeting of minds necessary to make

---

28 F. PAGANI: 'L'Administration européenne de Mostar', *AFDI*, 1996, p. 234.
29 C. CHAUMONT: 'Cours général de droit international public', in *RCADI*, 1970, I, p. 402.

the contract valid and stable. This is not simply a question of treating both parties in the same way and respecting their equality in legal and protocol terms, since both of these are underpinned by a whole raft of ceremony, often going back for centuries. It means, most of all, ensuring that there is a fair and harmonious balance between what is given and what is received, though these may take very different forms; it can also involve the giving of mutual guarantees whereby both parties are made responsible. (see *649, 1715*)

669 – Reciprocity is the basis of respect for commitments: it can even be described as the main guarantee that they will be real and lasting (see Vienna Convention, Article 35). It is accepted that a Minister of Foreign Affairs may be questioned, in Parliament or the courts, about whether third States have properly carried out their commitments, in order to determine the precise effect of an international provision in domestic law. While in certain legal systems (see the French Constitution of 1958, Article 55) treaties or agreements duly ratified or approved have primacy over domestic law, this is not true of major international rules, unless the other party has applied them. (see *489, 837, 1598*)

670 – Reciprocity also comes into play in implementing a variety of conventions and agreements, in the treatment of foreigners, and in building the trust necessary for international law to progress. Where it is refused, there is a right of unilateral response requiring no negotiation: this takes the form of denunciation of agreements, retaliation or reprisals (which differ from one another because retaliation does not involve the use of armed force).[30]

671 – Reciprocity not only rules out grossly unequal terms, but it also prohibits revenge: the strength of the response must be in parallel with the original conduct. The threat of trouble, or even of proportionate sanctions, has the effect of deterring the other party from breaching its commitments, unilaterally resorting to force, or making unjustified manoeuvres. *The power to retaliate is one of the privileges of sovereignty; limiting it is one of the objectives of organised international society.* (see *1277*)

672 – Reciprocity acts as a brake on the excesses that could arise where there is no international law-making power. It has a law-making effect because it promotes balance between attitudes and commitments, and due consideration for good faith and credit. Because of reciprocity, negotiation is disciplined and productive, custom becomes established and – sometimes – treaties are applied.

673 – Since it is difficult to make the punishment fit the crime, *what reciprocity brings to relations between States is order rather than justice.* Its merit is that it does so by a natural process that leads to the self-limitation of power and encourages diplomatic negotiation even between the weakest States, which still want to be able to offer their partner some counterpart. This might take the form of opening up to their interests, nationals or influence, bringing stability to a region under threat, or offering to make available raw materials or communication routes. (see *837*)

---

30 E. DECAUX: *La réciprocité en droit international*, Paris, LGDJ, 1980.

674 – Concern to ensure a level playing field has led the emerging and developing States to invoke the non-reciprocity of concessions to obtain the advantages necessary for the progress, or even the survival, of certain nations (General Agreement on Tariffs and Trade, IV, Articles 36, 8).[31] Non-discrimination is therefore moving in the direction of 'compensatory inequality',[32] or 'advantageous inequality',[33] in other words towards rejection of automatic reciprocity.[34] (see *2190*)

The desire to eliminate imbalances has also reached the fields of information and communication.[35] (see *1851*)

§3. Eligibility to negotiate

675 – True diplomatic negotiation can only take place between Sovereign States capable of expressing their wishes, being represented, and entering into commitments. (see *1516*)

But new entities, sometimes with limited negotiating capacity, can appear as a result of agreement between States. For instance, the Palestinian Authority was born out of the Oslo agreements (signed with Israel in 1993) and the Palestinian State was recognised by the UN Security Council by its Resolution 1397 in 2002. (see *1175, 1368, 1401*)

Recognition

676 – A State must be recognised by others if it wishes to be able to contract with them, and they in turn must accept all the consequences of the appearance of this new partner. Non-recognition is a political act.[36] (see *13*)

But recognition does not imply any obligation to negotiate, nor even to enter into diplomatic relations.

677 – The accession to independence of a substantial number of States has confirmed that official negotiation implies recognition of the other party, while leaving a great deal of flexibility as to how this should be done: by formal declaration, official correspondence, diplomatic agreement, the opening of diplomatic relations, or official visits, for example. While the legal nature of recognition is the subject of theoretical debate, in practice it is only relevant in the relations between the States concerned.

---

31 S. EL NAGGAR: 'the UN Conference on Trade and Development: Background, aims and politics', *RCADI*, 1969, III, p. 245. T. FLORY: *Le GATT, droit international et commerce mondial*, Paris, LGDJ, p. 196.

32 G. FEUER: '*Réflexions sur la Charte des droits et devoirs économiques des Etats*', RGDIP, 1975, p. 294.

33 G. de LACHARRIERE: 'L'influence de l'inégalité de développement des Etats sur le droit international', *RCADI*, 1973, II, p. 251.

34 G. FEUER: 'Les principes fondamentaux dans le droit international du développement', in *Pays en voie de développement et transformation du droit international*, p. 227.

35 S. MACBRIDE, etc: *Many Voices, One World*, UNESCO, 1980.

36 M. LACHS: 'La reconnaissance et les problèmes de la coopération internationale dans les traités', in *Mélanges en l'honneur de G. Gidel*, Paris, Sirey, 1961, p. 412. S. TALMON: *Recognition of Governments in International Law*, Oxford, Clarendon Press, 1998.

678 – Where States have already accepted unofficial procedures, personal contacts and manoeuvres in the course of resolving a dispute, even where their authorities interpret them differently, these preliminaries are often dispensed with. *A State that grants recognition to another, or negotiates it, will take its own rights and interests as its starting point.* It must act in good time, because events have a way of swiftly taking over.[37]

It is doubtful whether the recognition of several of its component parts, which came about in a piecemeal fashion and without conditions being imposed as to human rights or the status of minorities, did anything to improve the crisis in Yugoslavia. In that case, serious differences of opinion between the Member States of the European Union proved, if proof were needed, how much the recognition of a State depends on politics and sovereign prerogative.

679 – Recognition of a State is often tacit. Furthermore, it is not necessary in order to condemn the aggression of a third party (according to the United Nations definition of aggression) or to open diplomatic talks. On the other hand, it is normally required before signing a treaty, which is a formality that depends on the legal capacity of the parties. When France's territories in Africa gained their independence, two types of agreement were drafted in parallel, one transferring powers to the new States and the other setting out their cooperation with France, but the latter were signed only after each State had proclaimed its sovereignty on the basis of the former.[38] (see *512*)

When the crisis erupted in Yugoslavia, 12 Member States of the European Union attempted to set down a code of conduct for recognition of the new States, that recalled the principles of the United Nations Charter, the respect for minority rights, respect for borders and disarmament commitments, and contained an undertaking to arbitrate. This initiative had no effect on the way the local powers behaved. The entities in question were too uncertain in their composition, and fraught with too many problems and conflicts. (see *678*)

680 – International practice tends to limit the effects of constitutional changes on relations between States. Recognising a regime or government in order to bring it into diplomatic negotiations in practice opens the way to involvement in its internal affairs, with all the blackmail, pressures, and rivalry that entails. It also requires procedures to be adopted, choices to be made and positions taken for which third States would rather not be responsible.

In many cases, governments look to the negotiation itself, which will implicitly resolve the issue of recognition, to open up normal diplomatic relations.

681 – To negotiate with an entity is to recognise it: while that entity might not be clear about its nature, in international life it will invariably become what it represents.

Recognising one's partner can have important consequences internally by conferring or consolidating legitimacy: the first phase in the diplomacy of

---

37 R. ARON: *Paix et guerre entre les nations*, Paris, Calmann-Lévy, 1962, p. 127.
38 G. NERA: *La Communauté*, Paris, PUF, 1961.

liberation movements is to establish that they represent a nation (for example the Oslo Agreements of 1993, whereby Israel and the Palestinian Liberation Organisation recognised each other).

682 – Where one of the parties to a negotiation or discussion within an international organisation is not formally recognised, there are some groups aspiring to independence that have been represented by personalities discreetly included in the delegations of the States officially participating: accommodations like this are commonplace at the UN General Assembly.[39] (see *615*)

Representation

683 – For negotiation to take place, the conditions under which States take part must be laid down: in other words, it must be known which authorities can validly act in their name, or more precisely, following the traditional distinction, who has the legitimate authority to deal and to enter into treaties. The practical problem arises at this level: *any way of negotiating is valid, but the engagement must meet the necessary legal and political criteria, knowledge of and respect for which are the cornerstone of all worthwhile diplomacy and of international law as a whole.* While relations between governments can sometimes be carried on by unofficial or private means, as where they do not formally recognise each other, no private company or individual can bind them internationally.[40] (see *1462, 1501*)

While the methods used in negotiation involve discussions between increasing numbers of entities as intermediaries, the first sign of serious trouble will reveal that it is the governments that are the true protagonists.

684 – It is only to be expected that politicians and lawyers are concerned about the value of the commitments they have obtained, in other words the capacity of the person making them. There is no imperative norm in this area, however, because every State has the competence to decide the terms on which its own constitutional powers will be exercised. (see *655, 2633*)

685 – *In principle, every State is free to establish and choose the authorities that represent it, as well as the procedures it uses to prepare and conclude negotiations and implement their outcome.* But in practice, there is an increasing degree of harmonisation (as to the executive prerogative, the powers of negotiators, the drafting of documents, the format and language of agreements, and also signature, ratification and so on). An exception to this is negotiation by the European Union, which has features of its own. (see *609, 1184, 1391, 1448*)

686 – National authorities bind their countries by the procedures they accept, the signatures they give and also the declarations they make. Except where there is clear and serious breach of their fundamental public policy, they cannot invoke irregularities or mistakes arising out of internal policies in order to escape from the obligations so assumed. (see Vienna Convention of 1969, Article 46).

---

39 C. LAZARUS: 'Le statut des mouvements de libération nationale à l'ONU', *AFDI*, 1974, p. 173.
40 P. M. DUPUY: *Droit international public*, Paris, Dalloz, 1992, p. 176.

Although the notion of being 'honour bound' is shrouded in vagueness, *the essence of a gentlemen's agreement is that it is concluded by official representatives in their own name and without engaging their governments:* it is limited in effect and in time, and based entirely on the good faith of the individuals concerned.[41]

687 – The answer to the question whether or not a partner is properly represented is not to be found only by looking at the constitutional regime of the country in question, but also requires an evaluation of the political weight of those representing it. The problem becomes even more difficult in the case of populations that are seeking to achieve independence but are not yet in a position to express themselves freely or designate those who will represent them. (see *615*)

The degree to which any envoy or authority is representative depends on the power relationship. Diplomats are aware of this.

688 – The prudent negotiator will not be taken in by appearances, nor will he make concessions to emissaries who do not deserve them. All his efforts would thereby be wasted and would have served only to weaken his own ability to reach a settlement. It is his business to seek out where the true power lies, in the hands of which institution, which person and sometimes even which country, and direct his efforts towards those who have the capacity to give binding commitments. He is also expected to adapt his tactics to reflect the inevitable changes in the balance of power and influence operating on both domestic and foreign politics, at home and abroad. (see *2405, 2633*)

689 – There are various procedures available in diplomatic practice for verifying the credentials of negotiators. International meetings begin with this, although it is relatively less important within international organisations, except where there is a dispute over whether a government, authority or emissary is legitimate or properly represented. It was during an exercise of verification of powers that the China of Beijing was called to take the place of Taiwan at the United Nations in 1971.

690 – Each State appoints its delegate, sets his mandate and establishes his powers according to its own rules. *There is generally one single document, drawn up normally in the name of the Head of State, that appoints the negotiators and sets out the acts they are empowered to perform on behalf of their principals* (Vienna Convention of 1969, Article 2). (see *1047*)

It is part of the function of every diplomatic mission to negotiate with the government of the receiving State (Vienna Convention of 1961, Article 3)

691 – It is not the negotiator's prerogative to choose with whom he negotiates.[42] (see *295*)

In diplomatic negotiation, the following are deemed to represent their State, without the need for justification: Heads of State or government, Ministers of

---

41 C. ROUSSEAU: *Droit international public*, Paris, Sirey, 1970, p. 72. P. M. EISEMANN: 'Le *gentlemen's agreement* comme source de droit international', *Journal de droit international*, 1979, p. 326.

42 J. W. SCHNEIDER: *Treaty-Making Power of International Organizations*, Geneva, Droz, 1963, p. 64. A. de WICQUEFORT: *L'Ambassadeur et ses fonctions*, 2, Cologne, 1715, II.

Foreign Affairs, heads of diplomatic missions, and representatives officially accredited to a conference or an international organisation. (see *2461*)

692 – Unless they are subsequently validated by a constituted authority, the acts of persons who do not have representative capacity have no official force, though this does not prevent them from contributing to initiating and developing diplomatic manoeuvres. (see *1053, 2414*)

693 – Powers are often signed by the Head of State, intended for a particular negotiation and sent or handed to the negotiating partner. The credentials of some plenipotentiaries are also limited, either to relations between the sending State and the accrediting State, or to international meetings in general. (see *1008*)

694 – Heads of State or government represent their States for all purposes in all negotiations where they have the constitutional power to negotiate (General de Gaulle and Chancellor Adenauer signed the Franco-German Treaty of 22 January 1963), as do Ministers of Foreign Affairs. The fact remains that these principles can be difficult to apply when a State is dismantled, as can be seen from the transfer of powers from the USSR executive to that of Russia. (see *2488*)

Other negotiators must produce full powers appropriate to the meeting and allow them to be verified, unless it is clearly understood that their partners neither intend to require such demonstration nor usually do so (Vienna Convention, Article 6). If powers are notified, this can give rise to discussions about their drafting.[43]

695 – The existence of powers in due form is a precondition for the validity of a signature, but not, strictly speaking, of a negotiation. Major negotiations can be cited which were conducted by unofficial or private representatives, who had no legal authority but instead enjoyed the confidence of their sovereigns or governments: thus parliamentarians, merchants and journalists can and have been called upon to carry out highly sensitive diplomatic missions. (see *2415*)

In practice, governments are becoming less concerned with irregularities in powers, as high-speed communications mean they can easily verify whether a party intends to negotiate.

696 – Powers become less important as ratification becomes more so, since it is the basic precondition for the binding nature of the outcome of the negotiation. Refusals to ratify treaties confirm this rule. (see *780, 785*)

The development of negotiations within organisations or integrated systems has reduced the number of occasions on which special credentials are required; there are more and more collegial negotiations, in which the traditional precautions of diplomacy and protocol no longer feature. (see *1256, 2467*)

697 – From the start of a negotiation, a State should make known any limits or restrictions on the power of its official to negotiate (Vienna Convention, Article 47).

---

43 Ibid; p. 16. M. de MAULDE LA CLAVIERE: *La Diplomatie au temps de Machiavel*, II, Paris, 1892, 2, p. 86.

While the notification of powers allows the capacity of those taking part in a negotiation, or representatives at a conference, to be verified, there is no requirement to verify what directives they have received from their authorities.[44] Though these instructions are not binding on third countries, they often have an immediate effect on the decisions and workings of international organisations where these require unanimity of the Member States. (see *2419*)

698 – One of the aspects of the responsibility arising out of sovereignty in the field of negotiation is that every State must ensure that its representatives have its legal and political backing. This obligation can have serious consequences.

699 – It is up to every sovereign or government to satisfy itself as to the loyalty and discipline of its envoys, because it is responsible for their acts, irrespective of their grade or mission.

700 – No negotiator may accept orders from any authority other than his own, in other words that which is granted under his own country's system of government. The Romans used to threaten negotiators in person as a way of discouraging delaying tactics.[45] *Diplomatic immunity is one of the conditions for the validity of commitments entered into: an envoy who is subjected to violence loses his power to negotiate.*[46]

701 – Harold Nicolson remarked that there could never be a satisfactory outcome to negotiation if the different emissaries were put to death on arrival. Rome recognised the principle of inviolability of the official messenger, but those on a diplomatic mission remained exposed to all sorts of dangers: even if they came by sea bearing gifts, or showed the white parliamentary flag, they were still not safe from all risks.

702 – Now, every day, emissaries set off by air, road or rail without any formality or privilege attaching to their business. However, immunities are still necessary for freedom of negotiation, insofar as this implies derogation from national policing rules. (see *1056*)

Section 2: Norm and contract

703 – Never has international society seen so many dealings and institutions, and never have established theories and long-standing habits been so much at the mercy of events. And yet, States still only have a finite number of procedures for reconciling their ambitions and settling their disputes: these involve too many factual elements for their study to be confused with the body of rules and principles that today constitutes international law.

704 – Even when dealing with the boldest advances of modern technology, negotiation still follows its traditional pattern. Revolutionary powers might have

---

44 Ibid., p. 124.
45 H. NICOLSON: *The Evolution of Diplomatic Methods*, London, MacMillan, 1954.
46 A. de WICQUEFORT: *L'Ambassadeur et ses fonctions*, Cologne, 1715, I, 15.

ignored or overturned the habits and conventions of diplomacy, but they often revert to them, satisfied with the convenience and security they offer.

705 – For centuries, political situations have been too complex to be accommodated by a purely bilateral approach to negotiation. But only on 9 June 1815, the date of the Final Act of the Congress of Vienna, was a series of bilateral treaties first linked together and recapitulated in a way that amounted to a multilateral settlement. (see *998*)

706 – Bilateral and multilateral agreements, treaties and conventions, are the most highly-developed products of international negotiation. They sometimes do more than settle a political dispute or establish a balance between what each party to a transaction has given and received. In a growing number of cases, their effect, or even their object, is to put in place new rules governing relations between States. This normative aspect extends to setting up institutions: the majority of international organisations owe their existence to a diplomatic treaty. (see *1598*)

The diplomatic treaty is the necessary, but voluntary, instrument whereby the interests of States are reconciled and made to work together: it overrides the bounds of sovereignty, and as such is deserving of the greatest legal caution. The codification of the law of treaties, drafted by the UN International Law Commission, took the form of a convention which itself bears the hallmarks of a diplomatic treaty (the Vienna Convention of 23 May 1969), though a number of States have not ratified it. Its general nature is mainly explained by the fact that it is based for the most part on well-established custom. The Convention has been in force since 1980.

707 – *Alongside those voluntary agreements that are negotiated like contracts and take a contractual form, there are growing numbers of tacit engagements that result simply from a meeting of minds or from unilateral acts.* Many commitments are given or accepted in this way, often major ones, such as those undertaken within international organisations. (see *85, 1567, 2186*)

708 – Other international commitments emerge from a system that is very flexible, whereby one government lets the other know what it can and intends to do, and at the same time takes note of the other's position. This leads to a form of empirical understanding, better suited to dealing with complex subjects and difficult technical terminology than the strict legal formalism of the diplomatic treaty. When, in 1958, Great Britain, the United States and the Soviet Union decided to suspend nuclear testing, they did so by a series of unilateral measures, then subsequently changed their minds. Even so, these same three States made identical statements to the Security Council in 1969, binding themselves not to use nuclear weapons in any attack. (see *1785*)

709 – These methods were worked out in talks between the Great Powers aimed at limiting the use of strategic weapons. At the time, because of the secrecy surrounding discoveries and the changes in technology that were going on, none of the partners was in a position to assess exactly what the other was offering; each one willingly put forward its proposals to be weighed against those of the other

party, and the result was a kind of contract, parts of which were formally recorded. (see *1737*)

710 – There may be variations in the modes of engagement, but these can only have legal effect if they comply with some of the principles that have emerged from centuries of practice: negotiation is a legally regulated exercise. However, not all diplomatic discussions lead to the signing of a treaty, as can be seen from the ending of the Helsinki Conference. (see *2200*)

§I. Respect for principles of law

711 – In a general sense, modern society underestimates legal and moral norms, both those that justify conduct and those that punish it: greater importance is attached to economic profit and technical efficiency. Neither of these is compatible with established precepts, tending instead to undermine the status quo.

In the international arena it is all the more tempting not to apply the rules, since innovation and surprise can sometimes yield decisive tactical rewards. (see *1595*)

712 – The edifice of international law is always under threat, because relations between States are mostly ruled by the promise of reciprocity, threats or interest. Even in Western Europe, there has never been much collective sense of solidarity, either among leaders or the peoples themselves.

As long as negotiation does not seek to apply higher ideals, it is unlikely ever to have the effect of improving international ethics.

713 – This moral irresponsibility is not alleviated by international organisations themselves, since they show hardly any interest in identifying with and championing political responsibility: despite the need for worldwide economic and technical rules, this is the way the system works. In fact, the reverse is true: the work done at many multilateral meetings is imprecise, equivocal and unfinished, and this tends to mean that the rules that emerge from them – rules that are moreover often drafted in several languages – are lacking in essential legal clarity. *Each of the parties takes away what suits it from the negotiation and the debates going on around it.* (see *2220*)

714 – In a society where the natural order is allowed to prevail, the law of the strongest will tend to dominate. At the very time when there is a need for growing solidarity among nations, the random and unpredictable nature of factors both economic and ideological, the power of ambition and the impulse to possess or attack have severely undermined the effect of more generous or humanitarian statements. (see *389*)

715 – Diplomatic manoeuvre is undoubtedly freer in times of tension or even war, when nations allow their leaders more initiative, accept the arbitrary, and take what they can by using force or trickery, in a spirit of unscrupulousness or even cynicism. The fact remains, however, that *any effort to introduce order into relations between States tends to bring with it disciplines that limit the use of force, and favour diplomatic negotiation instead.* (see *2158*)

716 – The coexistence of States, like the lasting reconciliation of their interests and ambitions, presupposes the peaceful settlement of their disputes. The quest for this prompted the two Hague Peace Conferences and the instruments that emerged from them. (see *1738*)

Aside from the permanent institutions and frameworks for the resolution of disputes between States, specific bodies have been set up, by negotiation, to fulfil this function, such as the Iran–United States Claims Tribunal in The Hague.

717 – The Helsinki Conference (and those that came after it under the CSCE and later the OSCE) added to the rules already in force, for Europe at least, the principles of respect for sovereignty, international integrity, the inviolability of borders, non-interference in internal affairs, good faith in carrying out contractual obligations, and cooperation between States. However, the experts who met to implement the Final Act of the Conference, seeking principles for a system of peaceful resolution of international disputes, ran into serious difficulties, as there were still so many totalitarian political regimes.

Since the collapse of Communism these principles have been called into question: States have become dislocated, issues have arisen over frontiers, and humanitarian interference has increased. The peaceful settlement of disputes remains a pious hope (see the Stockholm Conference of 15 December 1992).

718 – The negotiator must take care not to confuse security with immobility, or change with revolt. For many powers, the real object of diplomacy is to maintain the established order, while others, not disguising their discontent, look for ways to undermine the entire international system. (see *2188*)

719 – Peace is more than just a legal institution, it is the fruit of the stabilisation of the international environment. It is rather a process of progressive adaptation of forces, law and interests to a certain set of ideological principles that depend on the environment around them.[47] (see *150, 154*)

The negotiator must be wary of any manoeuvre that could have the effect of breaching an accepted norm.

720 – The need for stability explains why custom and precedent have played such a predominant role in diplomatic discussions and initiatives: consistent practice shows how partners have adhered to solutions that are in some sense law-making. The negotiator must therefore take care not to allow procedures or conduct to be adopted that are unfavourable to those whom he represents, but should on the contrary put in place procedures that promote their views and are compatible with their means. (see *2203*)

721 – Law often ratifies the facts, even more in international life than in domestic legal systems. The starting point for negotiation is reality. The division of Germany and the international recognition of the two Republics, which lasted for several decades, resulted from the military occupation and the Cold War.

47 H. A. KISSINGER: *A World Restored*, Boston, Houghton Mifflin, 1957.

722 – The behaviour of peoples is different from that of individuals: as Montesquieu said, it is absurd to decide the rights of nations on the basis of the same maxims that apply between individuals.[48] Formulae practised in diplomacy could be criticised as unethical in interpersonal relations.

But sovereign power, however absolute, consecrated and inviolable, does not and may not, as Rousseau wrote, exceed the bounds of generally accepted convention.[49] This is true, too, of the freedom of States to manoeuvre and negotiate.

723 – According to doctrine, there are certain fundamental norms whose breach renders the acts in question void, even where they result from an agreement between sovereign powers. The Vienna Convention of 23 May 1969 (Articles 53, 64 and 66) sets out this principle and how it is to be respected. The International Court of Justice is bound to apply 'the general principles of law recognised by civilised nations' (Article 38 of the ICJ Statute). The same is true for the International Criminal Court (Treaty of Rome, 1998). (see *645, 729*)

724 – Thus, without endorsing a principle that is much disputed when it appears in treaties, *there are certain rules (jus cogens) ratified by the international 'community' as a whole, that must be taken as not negotiable, meaning that they cannot be overridden by the words or deeds of diplomats.* The autonomy of will of States nonetheless leaves only limited scope for a worldwide public policy. (see *1862*)

725 – The basis and content of these principles are open to discussion, because they have varied. Not much is left from the ancient world or the Christian Middle Ages, because diplomacy has lost its sacramental quality through constantly adapting itself to the needs of the moment over the years. It would seem inconceivable today to lay down a mandatory link between government and religion, in the way the Peace of Augsburg did in 1555 for feudal Germany, and equally misguided to advocate the 'Alliance of Perpetual Peace' of the Abbé de Saint Pierre in France, who was arguing the case for a confederation of European States as long ago as 1713.

726 – It goes without saying that these rules are not mere formulae resulting from the knowledge and application of legal precedent; they are closer to natural law, based on man's conscience and reason following the ideals already put into words by Grotius.[50] Some of these principles can produce contradictory results when applied: the authors of peace treaties often hesitate between the incompatible consequences of norms of equal value. This was the case with the conflict between the principle of territorial integrity and that of nationalities, particularly in deciding the fate of the intermingled populations of Central Europe or the Balkans.

727 – While it may be difficult to agree on the rules of diplomacy and on what is meant by a norm 'accepted and recognized by the international community of

---

48 C. de MONTESQUIEU: *De l'esprit des lois*, Geneva, 1748, XXIV, 18.

49 J.-J. ROUSSEAU: *Du contrat social*, Amsterdam, 1762, II, 4.

50 H. de GROOT: *De iure belli ac pacis*, Leiden, 1625. C. ROZAKIS: *The Concept of Jus Cogens in the Law of Treaties*, Amsterdam, North Holland, 1976.

States as a whole as a norm from which no derogation is permitted' (Vienna Convention on the Law of Treaties, Article 53),[51] denying a people the right to decide their own fate, cooperating in aggression, and dividing up or annexing a Sovereign State must today number among the international acts considered unethical or unlawful, which the Vienna Convention would allow to be treated as void because they derogate from rules that are imperative, absolute and general (see the UNGA Resolution of 14 December 1974 defining aggression).[52]

728 – The Convention on the Prevention and Punishment of the Crime of Genocide is an example of how these concerns translate into a legal document: the intention to destroy a human grouping defined by race, religion or nationality taints every diplomatic manoeuvre with nullity even where there has been no clear resort to actual violence (Convention of 7 December 1948; Advisory Opinion on *Reservations to the Convention on the Prevention and Punishment of the Crime of Genocide*, ICJ *Rep.* 1951, p. 15).

The notion of international criminal responsibility has emerged progressively from the debates and work of the United Nations. (see *723, 2253, 2275*)

729 – Opinion also condemns those practices that could be viewed as unfair or brutal, contrary to humanitarian rules or customs, or abuse of a dominant position, to borrow the language of the Treaty of Rome which set up the European Economic Community: interference in the affairs of an independent country, the open use of armed coercion, resort to slavery, or the acquisition of territory by force. Any negotiation in the furtherance of such ends must be prohibited.

At times of severe national crisis, the United Nations (see General Assembly Resolution of 8 December 1988) has often found that States have a right or even a duty to interfere for humanitarian reasons, authorising them to undertake massive aid operations against the will of their normal diplomatic interlocutors or even where these latter have disappeared. Questions remain about the basis, motives and limits of these interventions in some States' internal affairs. Once it has begun, this process can prove to be dangerous and unending. The extreme difficulty of understanding and dealing with certain of these ethnic and cultural flashpoints can condemn the best-intentioned international initiatives to failure, and discredit the organisations that have undertaken them.[53] (see *645*)

730 – Still, the repeated violation of the neutrality of certain countries during the wars of the past century, as well as the many open interventions in the internal affairs of small nations, argue for the exercise of great prudence when considering what sanctions to apply to such abuses of power and violations of the most solemn treaties. The United States was condemned by the International Court of Justice for its intervention in the affairs of Nicaragua, but its reaction to the ruling was one of indifference (see ICJ *Rep.* 1986, p. 14).

51 C. CHAUMONT: 'Cours général de droit international public', *RCADI*, 1970, I, p. 462.
    M. VIRALLY: 'Réflexions sur le jus cogens', *AFDI*, 1966, p. 5.
52 J. SZTUCKI: *Jus Cogens and the Vienna Convention on the Law of Treaties*, Vienna, Springer, 1974.
53 M. BETTATI: *Le Droit d'ingérence*, Paris, Odile Jacob, 1998.

731 – It is not unusual for governments represented at international meetings to declare that their mutual relations are founded on good faith, non-interference, the rejection of coercion, equality between nations and the respect for peoples' right to self-determination. Statements like this should not cause the diplomat to lower his guard: each State, with cold-blooded realism, seeks to foster its own interests under the cloak of great principles, sometimes claiming to teach others a lesson in the process.

Such is the harsh reality of international life that it is often enough for one partner to adopt an attitude at total and cynical variance with the rules for others to feel compelled to follow. (see **637**)

This explains the wariness of diplomats when faced with arguments about the duty to interfere for humanitarian, or allegedly humanitarian, reasons.[54] (see **645, 2159**)

732 – Freedom to negotiate is also limited by commitments previously entered into, whether unilaterally or by agreement. This explains why some powers make it a rule to preserve their autonomy of manoeuvre in all circumstances, so as to be able to confront the greatest variety of situations without having to consider anything but their own immediate interests. It also explains why others seek to conclude multiple non-aggression pacts or treaties of amity in the hope, not always borne out, of keeping hostile diplomacy at bay.

733 – Because legal norms are considered as reference points of moral value, recourse to them is a potent diplomatic weapon. (see **232**)

The negotiator may not ignore or underestimate the support the law can provide, both by its main universally recognised principles and the particular rules and treaty provisions in force: an argument based on a pre-existing international convention, the regular practice of other States or the general legal fabric of which the agreement being drafted will become part, if applied, will carry great weight in terms both of policy and logic. (see **2205**)

734 – One or more of the powers in a manoeuvre might even plead fundamental principles in order to assume the role of accuser or judge of the attitude of other States. *A convenient tactic is to weaken the position of the adversary by levelling accusations against it, rightly or wrongly.*

735 – *Little by little, an impartial legal consultative function is emerging that will facilitate the task of the negotiator:* the secretariats and legal departments of the major intergovernmental organisations, especially those of the United Nations, the International Labour Organisation and the European Union, are making a contribution to the stabilisation and development of international law.

§2. The validity of commitments

736 – In clearly providing for the nullity of treaties, the 1969 Vienna Convention on the Law of Treaties, despite not having been ratified by all States, indirectly laid

---

54 M. BETTATI and B. KOUCHNER: *Le Devoir d'ingérence*, Paris, Denoël, 1987.

down and defined the conditions with which international negotiation must comply. This means that, in practice, where the terms of the negotiation are in balance, they can generally not be severed one from another.

737 – Some of these principles are a matter of international public policy: these place real limits on the freedom to negotiate, depending on the object or purpose of the manoeuvre. Where its result is unlawful or unethical, the whole negotiation may be tainted with nullity and be held void *ab initio*. A diplomatic treaty may be affected in whole or in part (Vienna Convention, Article 53).

There are conditions applicable to all official negotiations, that serve to ensure that the treaty is validly entered into and consent is freely given on both sides.

Relations between the parties

738 – If its outcome is to be legally valid, a negotiation must fulfil certain conditions, many of which have to do with the meeting of minds of the contracting parties. In practice this means ensuring that the consent of the parties is not so distorted as to be rendered null and void. (see *490*)

739 – Prudence is required when transposing the traditional theories about factors vitiating consent to the international level: misleading manoeuvres, trickery and fraud have bedevilled negotiation for centuries. It is up to each party to arm itself against the diplomatic consequences of such methods (see Vienna Convention, Article 49). A vigilant negotiator will be sure to verify the accuracy of the facts on which his consent, or assent, is based.

740 – Once the contract is signed, it will be difficult to argue that it is void by reason of fraud: the perpetrator is neither required nor even allowed to plead his misdeed, and on the victim's side, even if concern for his reputation allows him to admit his thoughtlessness, it will usually be too late, given the speed with which major treaties take effect. It serves little practical purpose to argue that the Munich agreements were damaging to the Western countries, even if in 1938 they could have claimed ignorance of Germany's aggressive intentions.[55]

741 – While neither perpetrators nor victims are anxious to boast about it, it is possible for a negotiation to be tainted by corruption (see Vienna Convention, Article 60). Diplomats and even statesman do exist who are susceptible to favours and money, and history is not short of examples. It is rare, however, for these vices to be used as an argument against the validity of the treaties they made.

742 – In some countries, there are procedures for ratification after parliamentary scrutiny that can provide an opportunity to sanction the dishonest negotiator. Since they carry the threat that the treaty will be rejected, they should deter and paralyse any attempts at corruption. However, there are notorious trials and scandals to show that trafficking in influence is still common in the modern world.

---

55 J.-B. DUROSELLE: *La Décadence*, Paris, Imp. nationale, 1939, p. 351.

743 – Except where they concern a secondary issue having no influence on consent, or can be dealt with by a drafting correction, mistakes can be such as to vitiate the will of one party to the agreement; this argument can be invoked where the mistake concerns a fact or circumstance that was believed to be true at the time of signing the treaty and was one of the essential bases on which consent was given (Vienna Convention, Article 48). Obviously, mistake may not be pleaded by the party responsible for it, or by an accomplice or a consenting victim. (Case of *Temple of Preah Vihear*, ICJ Rep. 1962, p. 42.)

744 – There have been negotiations that were tainted by a seriously flawed view of the material facts. Thus, the north-eastern borders of the United States laid down by the Treaty of Paris in 1783 gave rise to multiple disputes because the maps at the time were inaccurate, and new negotiations had to be opened. It is no surprise that French Guyana, a territory not yet explored at that time, was incorrectly delimited in the Treaty of Utrecht in 1713. Worse still were the diplomats who put together the agreement between Austria and Poland in 1773, which stated that the boundary would follow a river that did not actually exist.[56]

745 – The desire to protect international conventions and the rights deriving from them means that most States and international tribunals will refuse to countenance different interpretations, even when these are shared by both parties; there have, however, been some cases where the parties went to arbitration in order to resolve the dispute, such as the 1999 arbitration between Eritrea and the Yemen over rights to the Hanisch Islands.

746 – Negotiators must therefore be careful not to make mistakes, or be deceived, during the preliminary phase of a diplomatic agreement, and most of all during the preparatory phase of the many commitments they undertake within international organisations: only rarely do all interested parties agree to rectify a diplomatic instrument. Material errors in a commercial treaty signed in 1853 between the United States and Paraguay gave rise to armed conflict. (see *774*)

747 – *Managing coercion in diplomacy is a central issue in relations between Sovereign States.* (see *86, 530*)

Clearly, the use of violence or physical or psychological pressure against an envoy vitiates his formal acts (Vienna Convention, Article 51), and jeopardises his role as a representative.[57]

748 – The real problem lies rather with coercion directed against a State itself, which is very difficult to isolate from the normal consequences of inequalities of power, except in those cases where methods are used that are contrary to international order, such as the threat of military force, subversion or plotting. A negotiation carried on under overt military force is without effect (Vienna Convention, Article 52). Czechoslovakia never consented to be bound by

56 A. ORAISON: *L'Erreur dans les traités*, Paris, LGDJ, 1972
57 G. A. CRAIG: 'Totalitarian Approaches to Diplomatic Negotiation', in *The Theory and Practice of International Relations*, 1970, p. 244.

the Munich agreement, signed in 1938 against its interests and in its absence. (see *104*)

History and practice, however, do not allow unequal treaties to be assimilated to unlawful treaties.

749 – The United Nations Charter condemns resort to the threat or use of force which is incompatible with its objectives, and lays down procedures to ensure that this duty is respected, as well as the legitimate right to individual or collective self-defence (Article 57). This rule is confirmed by the Vienna Convention, in Article 52 and also in the Annex on the prohibition of military, political or economic coercion in treaty-making. (see *1652*)

750 – However, while these prohibitions may be respected in the modern world, they have little effect on actual negotiations, in which the party exerting pressure dresses it up, seeking to justify it by the legitimacy of its claims or by the fact that its partner has done wrong. An international court cannot take accusations of coercion into account without concrete evidence (*Fisheries* Case, ICJ *Rep.* 1973, p. 14).

Moreover, it is inherent in a peace treaty that it is negotiated under the threat of force: it is difficult for the loser to plead that his consent is invalid when he would not hesitate to use the same methods on his adversary.[58] (see *91, 137*).

751 – At the procedural level, one defence against all forms of pressure can be found in the multilateral nature of negotiation. *Where commitments are public and in balance, this makes it difficult for the stronger party to manoeuvre against the weaker.* Where consent is not accompanied by formalities and publicity, the obligation appears less onerous.

On the other hand, bilateral negotiation will never be entirely free from these risks: herein lies the peculiar difficulty of the art, in which the intentions of the parties can rarely be reconciled or even revealed. (see *104, 144*)

Third parties

752 – The question of the effect of negotiations on third States who are not represented at them has long been the subject of doctrinal and political debate. The growth in international regulation has somewhat diluted the body of prescriptions designed to ensure that the need for States' consent is scrupulously respected. Sometimes the needs of global society must override the abstention, default or selfishness of any one of the 190 or so independent States. (see *1021, 1516, 2204*)

753 – While undoubtedly conventions exist whose effects extend beyond the contracting parties (see the Treaty of 1 December 1959 on Antarctica), and whose object is universal in scope, in general terms the rule under the Vienna Convention (Article 34) is to the contrary: a third State must expressly accept an obligation before it can be held bound by it (Article 35), though its consent to a

---

58 J. BASDEVANT: 'Règles générales du droit de la paix', *RCADI*, 1936, IV, p. 471.

right may be presumed where there is no indication to the contrary (Article 36).[59] (see *1021*).

754 – Some schools of thought rely on the universal character of an international institution in order to invest it with unlimited powers (*Advisory Opinion on Namibia*, ICJ *Rep.* 1971, p. 20): *the fact is that the deliberations and activities of multilateral conferences and the increasing number of reservations to conventions make the notion of a 'party' unclear.* (see *1516*).

755 – The balance of power in the world is fragile; a coalition or an alliance could jeopardise it. The Great Powers, acting together, have always tended to confuse their own interests with those of the community of nations as whole, and to confront smaller countries with, or impose upon them, decisions in which they have played no part.[60] (see *316, 319*)

The coalition of certain majorities produces the same effect today in multipartite conferences, giving rise to norms that are declared to be universal.

756 – It is rare in international negotiation for one State to contract on behalf of another. By contrast, once a treaty is signed, the frequency of resort to the most-favoured nation clause tends to spread the benefits more widely. This was the method adopted within the GATT to encourage the reduction in discrimination and trade barriers, and promote economic globalisation. The World Trade Organisation (WTO), which succeeded it in 1994 in Marrakech at the end of the Uruguay Round, has continued this work, aided by patient negotiations and successive conferences of plenipotentiaries. (see *1046, 1102, 1632, 1942*)

757 – It is also true that the reach of the norms contained in certain treaties can be enlarged, by express adhesion, implied acceptance, or custom, to cover States that did not take part in the original negotiation (*Continental Shelf* cases, ICJ *Rep.* 1969, p. 3). (see *1416, 1516, 1604*)

Many normative treaties make it easy for third States to accede on terms that are becoming simpler and more flexible.

758 – In a world that is heading in the direction of global or collective regulation, the principle that a negotiation has no effect on third States is often more real in theory than in practice. (see *2199*)

No government can be indifferent to negotiations between others: this is why the setting of criteria for participation in negotiations or at a conference often gives rise to disagreement. (see *1022, 1023*)

§3. Concluding the agreement

759 – From the earliest times, human populations have devised special ceremonies to mark the conclusion and promulgation of important negotiations, particularly

---

59 M. VIRALLY: *L'Organisation mondiale*, Paris, Colin, 1972, p. 14.
60 P. CAHIER: 'Le problème des effets des traités à l'égard des Etats tiers', *RCADI*, 1974, III, p. 589. P. M. DUPUY: *Droit international public*, Paris, Dalloz, 1992, p. 205.

those involving alliances and peace treaties. Many primitive tribes sought to bind their partners by religious or magical practices, gifts and sacrifices intended to lend a sacramental character to the commitments they made. In Rome, declarations of war and peace were accompanied by a solemn public ritual.[61] And the great meetings of sovereigns during the Middle Ages and the Renaissance took on a diplomatic significance by virtue of the protocol alone, even though they often produced no written instrument.

760 – Negotiation often goes hand in hand with the drafting of an instrument. But both theory and practice are today tending away from imposing specific formal conditions for the validity of international undertakings. The agreement and the document that records it are not the same, even if the parties also negotiate about the form this document should take.[62]

The contract

761 – International negotiations between States produce an extraordinarily diverse catalogue of bilateral, multilateral and even unilateral instruments: solemn pacts and treaties requiring the involvement of Heads of State and subject to ratification; conventions whose subject-matter is legal, administrative or technical; agreements in a more or less simplified form; exchanges of letters or notes deriving validity from their use of identical language; memoranda approving, recapitulating and summarising facts and arguments, as agreed by the parties; administrative arrangements between public services for the implementation of conventions; protocols setting out detailed facts and summarising the parties' positions in the light of subsequent changes to the law, or setting out the results of negotiations; collective or even unilateral solemn declarations closing the talks and sometimes announcing a programme of action; verbatim records or minutes setting out acts or discussions when the parties have approved them;[63] press releases whose text is agreed by the delegations; agreed annexes to an official instrument, or riders that modify one. This lack of precision in terminology is exacerbated by the number of languages in use.[64] (see *686, 2623*)

As between private companies, the main instrument in use is the contract. Their transactions are conducted on markets and under conditions that are more or less free depending on their field of activity and on the States involved, many of whom seek to interfere in their dealings. (see *1818, 1930*)

762 – There is no doubt that when a State gives its consent, it is bound, irrespective of how that consent was expressed. The wise negotiator will proceed with caution, however: when François I of France and the Emperor Charles V agreed in 1559,

---

61 H. NICOLSON: *The Evolution of Diplomatic Methods*, London, New York, MacMillan, 1954.

62 J. BASDEVANT: 'La conclusion et la rédaction des traités et des instruments diplomatiques autres que les traités', *RCADI*, 1926, p. 539.

63 P. RENOUVIN: *Histoire des relations internationales. Le XIXe siècle*, I, p. 94, Hachette, Paris, 1995.

64 G. PAMBOU TCHVOUNDA: *La Conférence au sommet*, Paris, LGDJ, p. 318. J. F. PREVOST: 'Observations sur la nature juridique de l'Acte final d'Helsinki', *AFDI*, 1975, p. 129.

and again in 1598, to permit French ships to sail as far as the Tropic of Cancer without being treated as enemy vessels by the Spanish, nothing happened as a result of their oral understanding. (see *490*)

763 – It is important to ensure that the results achieved in the discussions are not undermined by unfair or hasty manoeuvres. There is a very ancient tradition of carefully recording them in some form for posterity, even to the point of carving them in stone. *Negotiation suffers, however, from the haste of certain politicians who often give their agreement on the basis of ill-conceived and badly drafted texts that are unfinished or inconsistent, and attract an accumulation of declarations and interpretations in their wake.*

764 – Today, when an agreement is reached, a joint official document is usually drafted, in other words a text that can serve as evidence and as a reference. As the word 'diplomacy' itself implies, and as Article 2 of the Vienna Convention recalls, *the written word plays a primordial role in this field.*

Keeping a record of conversations does not suffice to capture the unfolding of a negotiation that might be invoked against a partner, nor is it recommended in practice:[65] a meeting is not a treaty.

765 – If, at least some of the time, they are to constitute the law between parties as reluctant to be bound and as elusive as States, these official acts must be drafted, verified and preserved with the greatest care.[66] *The prudent negotiator always tries to prepare his own draft of the text he wishes to see adopted: even if the language is not exact, the logic of the way the ideas are presented will influence the other party.*

Astute negotiation can alleviate the burden of some clauses and deflect the force of unfavourable language.

766 – In diplomacy nothing is worse than texts that are silent, because this amounts to accepting the will of the strongest or most enterprising (see the Yalta Declaration, 11 February 1945). (see *516*)

All the verbal assurances in the world will not save a party from its own imprudence, or hold back an aggressor. This was the case with many of the negotiations between the Allies in 1944–1945, when Stalin came off best: the future of Central Europe was decisively and unfairly determined because the West was silent on what were to be the definitive borders of Poland.

767 – A good negotiation should not decide anything more or less than is necessary.

In the absence of agreement, it is better to maintain the status quo resulting from common tacit consent. Treaties concluded at the last minute to influence voters or for reasons of vanity often remain a dead letter. (see *513*)

768 – An exchange of unilateral declarations can be one of the outcomes of negotiation. Similarity of attitudes might create a rule, but the question remains as to whether it will prove lasting, or give rise to legal obligations capable of limiting

65 V. WALTERS: *Silent Missions*, New York, 1978.
66 C. THAYER: *Diplomat*, New York, Harper Row, 1959, p. 98.

State sovereignty. Such practices introduce a further element of vagueness and uncertainty into international negotiation. (see *512, 709*)

Between States, nothing goes without saying, or without being written down – thus, agreements should be put in writing, as clearly as possible. (see *2200*)

769 – All progress in international law depends on treaties being respected, whatever the motive: good faith, fear, or interest. Even before the signatures that set the seal on the text, it is important to avoid allowing divergences of view or disputes to arise over what has been agreed. The experienced negotiator will ensure that the treaty is drafted in the most appropriate language, and will steer clear of imprecision as well as of inflexibility. (see *2241*)

770 – One cannot pay too much attention to the text. This is not merely a matter of material errors in a legal instrument, as happened in an agreement between France and Yugoslavia in 1958, when francs and dollars were confused, or of divergent translations of a treaty, as with the Russian version of Article 37 of the United Nations Charter. Lengthy procedures were needed in China in order to have corrections made to the Chinese text of the Convention on the Prevention and Punishment of the Crime of Genocide, approved by the United Nations in 1948. (see *743*)

771 – Frederick II of Prussia advised that the punctilious grammarian should always precede the skilful politician.[67] The agreement the two sides have reached must be set down in the greatest possible detail if later challenges are to be avoided. The signature in 1801 of the concordat between the Papacy and France came only after nine successive drafts had been produced, some of them reviewed by Bonaparte himself. There was a time when notaries, especially pontifical notaries, verified the validity and accuracy of draft diplomatic agreements.

772 – The fact is that the drafting of the final documents often requires the terms of a negotiation to be more clearly defined, and this can delay the time limits. The most difficult debates often centre on the texts, especially where these will have to be published. The overuse of statements with no real meaning may also be a way of avoiding an impasse.

A dispute over words is litigation in the making.

773 – Originally Latin and later French, primarily because the diplomacy of Louis XIV was the most effective and best organised of his time, the language of diplomatic negotiation has varied, with English now extending its hold, though generally speaking with no corresponding improvement in its technical quality.

Today, in this field, there are no longer any rules or customs, which leaves abundant scope for problems of interpretation, translation and reference: many disputes are fuelled by the absence of reliable and recognised points of reference for the parties. (see *2055*)

774 – No amount of precautions will be proof against error; nor does good faith offer protection against its effects. The negotiation must be resumed, a matter of

67 FREDERICK II of PRUSSIA: *L'Anti-Machiavel*, Chapter 26.

extreme sensitivity where the correction of a treaty is involved (Vienna Convention, Article 79). (see *743*)

Signature and its value

775 – The diplomatic negotiating procedure closes, once a concrete result has been achieved, with the signature of an agreement, in other words by each leader in the negotiation or the head of each national delegation placing his or her signature on the document, at the end of the text. This act is performed by plenipotentiaries with the necessary powers. Signature is often preceded by verifications that use a variety of methods, confirmed by initialling the documents; the same techniques are used to authenticate any attachments. (see *1440*)

776 – In principle, signature determines the text and the date of the agreement. It also determines its binding force, except where the treaty has to be ratified, in which case this process is a precondition for its taking effect, provided there is no stipulation to the contrary, for example in the wording of the powers. Refusal to ratify will deprive the signature of its legal effect.

777 – Today, large numbers of negotiations end without any formal document being signed: the text is finalised and authenticated within the framework of an institutional process, for example in a multilateral conference or after a vote. (see *2235*)

There is a legitimate comparison to be made between the rigorous observance of law and protocol in traditional diplomatic engagements and the lack of precision that marks the end of many negotiations within international organisations (see UNGA Declaration No. 29-3348 of 17 December 1974 on the Eradication of Hunger and Malnutrition). (see *2174, 2181*)

778 – Votes are sometimes cast, agreements reached and signatures given *ad referendum*: the act authenticates the text but does not express definitive consent on the part of the State concerned. The outcome of the negotiation remains suspended until confirmed by the competent authorities, whose attitude is either not yet determined or not known to anyone other than their own representative. When confirmation is given, the decision or signature becomes final, with retroactive effect (Vienna Convention, Article 12).

779 – It is rare for a political authority to leave the result of an important negotiation for its representative to judge: having issued him with directives and instructions at the outset, it reserves the right to make sure these have been complied with. Approving an agreement means consenting to be bound by the obligations that have clearly emerged from the negotiation; failing to approve it means refusing some or all of them. (see *1443, 2420*)

780 – The negotiator's signature only binds his authorities if they express their consent to be bound. This act, which is variously described (Article 2 of the Vienna Convention refers to ratification, acceptance, approval and adhesion), allows the conformity of the negotiation with the policy line to be verified, and all its consequences in the domestic sphere to be examined. It sets the final seal on the

treaty.[68] It is a guarantee against error, or infidelity or inaccuracy in language,[69] and provides one last opportunity for reflection.[70] (see *2572*)

781 – The need for ratification serves to distinguish the negotiation of treaties that bring into play the solemn authority of Heads of State from that of more simplified agreements, often of an administrative nature, where signature, approval or an exchange of documents will suffice[71] and also from the deliberations of international organisations that culminate in a vote or the adoption of a text. This distinction does not alter the political responsibility of the envoy vis à vis those who entrusted him with the mission. (see *2573*)

782 – The conditions for validity and ratification are a matter for the domestic laws of each State. The decision lies with the authority or authorities that are able to bind the State under its constitution: the competences and procedures involved are varied and complex, depending on the country and the nature of the commitment. (see *2579*)

783 – The State is morally and politically bound from the moment the agreement is signed, and must refrain from doing anything in conflict with its undertakings. In one sense, the outcome of the negotiation is crystallised. Refusal to ratify a treaty negotiated by an ambassador with full powers should be forbidden.[72] (see *698*)

784 – In the vast majority of cases, the executive powers will have been kept informed of the negotiations and will approve the outcome. But they may do so only subject to their right to interpret or refuse certain clauses. They will hesitate to ratify, or to begin the ratification process, if their view of the outcome of the negotiation is altered by the last-minute pressure of public opinion, or if the legislature appears reluctant to endorse it. (see *2625*)

In States with a complex constitutional structure, such as Canada or Russia, the implementation of certain treaties requires the endorsement of the local authorities.

785 – There are many examples in history, some of them well known, of the legislature refusing to ratify or rejecting treaties. The United States Senate did this with the League of Nations Pact, and the French National Assembly rejected the draft European Defence Community agreement, ending two years of uncertainty. In other cases, ratification is made subject to interpretation clauses or reservations, which can have the effect of modifying the outcome of the negotiation.

The experiences of the Maastricht and Nice Treaties showed how sensitive these issues can be, especially if public opinion is consulted. (see *1359*)

---

68 A. de WICQUEFORT: *L'Ambassadeur et ses fonctions*, Cologne, 1715, II, 15.
69 C. DUPUIS: 'Les relations internationales', *RCADI*, 1924, I, p. 287.
70 P. REUTER: *Droit international public*, Paris, PUF, 1973, p. 85.
71 C. CHAYET: 'Les accords en forme simplifiée', *AFDI*, 1975, p. 1. A. CRAS: 'Les *executive agreements* aux Etats-Unis', *RGDIP*, 1972, p. 973.
72 H. NICOLSON: *The Evolution of Diplomatic Methods*, London, New York, MacMillan, 1954.

786 – It has been said that the principle of good faith is accorded less weight during the ratification process than in the negotiations themselves.[73] (see **501**)

The negotiator is well advised, therefore, to pay timely attention to the legal and political conditions attached to the future ratification of the commitments his interlocutors are making. (see **696**)

787 – The more political – and thus important – the negotiation, the more risks the obligation to ratify presents for the envoy's credibility and the more dangers for his interlocutors, who may find at this late stage that their concessions have brought them nothing. It is also an argument for keeping a close eye on how public opinion is likely to react to a negotiation. This advice applies not only to those whose own national positions are not secure, but also to their interlocutors, who must constantly weigh up the risks to which they are exposing themselves in making an agreement without being sure of what their adversary will ultimately want. They only have themselves to blame if the concessions they have made turn out to have been in vain.

788 – Once it is formally minuted, the exchange, notification or deposit of instruments of ratification (with a State or an organisation designated in advance) means that the parties can consider the outcome of the negotiation to be definitive: the agreement becomes binding on each of the States concerned. (see **1599, 1664**)

Publication

789 – Publication of commitments made reveals the negotiation behind them. Publication is a guarantee of performance because it is a condition precedent for relying on the commitments, though not a necessary condition for their entry into force. That, like any other stipulation, is a matter for negotiation, and, in the absence of any provision to the contrary, it is triggered by signature or ratification.

790 – In response to the condemnation by President Woodrow Wilson of secret diplomacy, first the League of Nations Pact (Article 18), then the United Nations Charter (Article 102), and subsequently various other institutions such as ICAO and IAEA, began to provide for registration (meaning deposit with the Secretary General, who acknowledges receipt) of agreements concluded between their Member States.

Even from the time of the League of Nations, legal opinion has been divided as to whether failure to observe this obligation makes the instrument void, not valid as against third parties, or of only relative effect.

791 – The sanction for breach of Article 102 of the Charter is limited to bringing proceedings before international tribunals: the substantive outcome of the negotiation remains in effect. In fact, though the Vienna Convention sought to extend the obligation to publish (Article 80), it is not always complied with, and the International Court of Justice is powerless to do anything. (see **1653**)

---

73 J. P. COT: 'La bonne foi et la conclusion des traités', *Revue belge de droit international*, 1968, p. 150.

792 – The conditions for publication, like those for entry into force, are often the subject of negotiation, but these are only of very limited effect because the conditions only come into play after the negotiation has ended. However, it is worth mentioning those clauses whereby the adherents to a multipartite agreement agree that it will take effect as soon as a certain number of them have completed the procedures necessary to confer validity on it and to notify it (the majority of States represented at a given conference, for example).

793 – The more difficult it is to bring a negotiation to fruition, the more care should be taken to protect the results achieved.

Chanceries are right to attach great importance to the archiving of documents, in other words storing them in a secure place, labelled and filed in such a way that they can easily be retrieved.

794 – International organisations, in particular the Secretariat of the United Nations, have played an increasing part in the codification and publication of international legal instruments of which they are often the designated depositaries. The considerable work still to be done will be made easier by developments in information technology.

The General Secretariat of the Council of the European Community may act as depositary for treaties binding on Member States.

795 – In spite of these principles, it is possible to agree that an accord should remain secret, at least for a certain period of time. But, as the French writer La Rochefoucauld said, few secrets last for ever, nor do people's scruples about revealing them.[74] *Each party is bound, in principle, to consult the other or the others before divulging anything, unless they have agreed: there have been notorious diplomatic incidents caused by one party passing on information about a confidential negotiation.* (see **2611**)

§4. After the negotiation

796 – Committing to negotiate means undertaking to behave in such a way that negotiation is possible and may be productive, but not to actually resolving the dispute (*North Sea Continental Shelf Cases*, ICJ *Rep.* 1969, p. 47). Doctrine makes a distinction between an obligation of means and one of result. So does the practice: the negotiators of the Treaty of Versailles heeded the requirements of President Woodrow Wilson, but to no avail, as the United States ultimately refused to join the League of Nations.

797 – The temptation should be avoided of considering that the proliferation of treaties has had a beneficial effect on the international community: *useless conventions weaken those that are necessary.* Few treaties, no commitments, was Montesquieu's watchword. (see **2219**)

---

74 '*Il y a peu de secrets de tous les temps, et le scrupule de les révéler ne dure pas toujours*'.

798 – There is a common propensity among negotiators, as with all human beings, to think that their activity must produce a lasting result. Often, they try to construct agreements they hope will stabilise their international relations.

But no state of affairs is definitive, no development can be halted, and no balance is permanent. *A treaty or contract alone is no guarantee that aspirations will be satisfied: this requires constant adjustments to policy and conduct starting from the moment there is a meeting of minds.* (see *357, 977, 1849*)

799 – Even within an alliance, no responsible country will give up the exercise of its will or its judgement for the benefit of another: decisions must be made by agreement, in other words by constant consultation and fresh negotiations. Otherwise, some nations will cease to consider themselves bound by their obligations, or to devote the means to fulfil them, or even cause the coalition itself to disintegrate. (see *961, 966*)

800 – The signing of a treaty should therefore not be regarded as the end of the negotiation. The world and society continue to evolve, and this deters the diplomat from simply defending the established order at any price (as the Holy Alliance did for the first half of the nineteenth century). On the contrary, he must, without fail, maintain relationships with his interlocutors that are effective, solid and flexible. This is the only approach that will avoid disagreement between allies.

One of the criteria for a successful negotiation is that it opens the way for new discussions. (see *349*)

801 – Cardinal de Richelieu advocated caution in making treaties, but total scrupulousness in complying with them. This is not only a principle of ethics, but a rule of legal and political wisdom (*pacta sunt servanda*: Vienna Convention, Article 26).[75] But negotiation allows treaties to evolve, by agreement between the parties: this is the true path to peaceful change.[76] (see *2239*)

802 – The process of negotiation means that the outcome will be presumed to be valid. It is often repeated that conventions arising out of a proper negotiation have binding force:[77] any argument that a treaty is void for lack of consent must be raised in good time (*Temple of Preah Vihear* Case, ICJ *Rep.* 1962, p. 42). Even partial agreements concluded during the course of the discussions must be honoured.

Failure to live up to one's word can have irreparable and disastrous consequences in ethical terms.[78]

803 – It is not always obvious what the outcome of a negotiation actually is. Stipulations are subject to interpretation, and doubts about their meaning and scope are the more legitimate where they involve obligations that are often lasting and onerous, or where their language is obscure, contradictory or ambiguous,

---

75 H. de GROOT: *De jure belli ac pacis*, Leiden, 1625, I, 3 and 21.
76 P. de VISCHER: *Théories et réalité en droit international public*, Paris, Pedone, 1960, p. 408.
77 E. de VATTEL: *Le Droit des gens ou principes du droit naturel*, Neuchâtel, 1758, IV, 4.
78 L. NOEL: *L'Agression allemande contre la Pologne*, Paris, Flammarion, 1946, p. 227.

especially as a result of many languages being used, or because the parties were prepared to accept a text that is ambiguous, imprecise and incomplete in the absence of total agreement about the result of the negotiations. (see *354, 357, 2193*)

804 – The more negotiation is dominated by political considerations, the more carefully the outcome should be scrutinised. The slightest divergence in application might claim to be justified by an interpretation of the agreement, or it might result in its being denounced.

It is sometimes difficult to produce a text that fits the factual situation. This has notably happened with attempts to define polluting substances and their effects in implementation of the Kyoto Protocol. (see *2055, 2193*)

805 – To seek the precise meaning of a document is to try to find what its authors wanted. This will have been expressed during the negotiation, but may have been coloured by other conventions, or international custom or practice (Vienna Convention, Article 31): the very density of diplomatic relations means that these legal and terminological points of reference are becoming increasingly relevant, and it will be essential for negotiators to know them.[79] (see *1618*)

In the European Union, the European Court of Justice in Luxemburg is responsible for interpreting the instruments setting up the Communities, and also for decisions taken by the Community institutions in implementing them.

806 – Problems of interpretation can often only be solved by going back to the beginnings of the agreement: it might be that only the negotiators or their principals are able to say what was the agreed meaning of the terms, provide and clarify the *travaux préparatoires* (*Fisheries Cases*, ICJ *Rep.* 1973, p. 14 and 1974, p. 39), state whether the agreement was to be reciprocally applied, indicate what was meant, or reach agreement on a problem common to both parties. This explains why the executive plays the leading role in diplomatic negotiation. (see *2508*)

§5. The duration of the commitment

807 – The duration of commitments mutually undertaken by parties to a negotiation is the subject both of doctrinal uncertainty and of disputes at a practical level.

The simplest formula is express agreement between the parties on the length of time the agreement is to remain in effect. At the time they decide when it shall enter into force, they can provide for the possibility of extension, which might even be tacit. (see *881*)

808 – The binding force of treaties means that it is not open to either of the parties, or their successors, to decide to put an end to their obligations. However, the signatories cannot be expected to have intended what they negotiated to be valid

---

79 G. BERLIA: 'Contribution à l'interprétation des traités', *RCADI*, 1965, I, p. 287.

for all time, nor would it be in their interests to waste time shoring up the legal appearances of a treaty that has already been breached.

The dislocation of the former Yugoslavia confirmed how extremely difficult it is to define a 'successor State', whether in terms of its population and territory, the factors by which it is essentially delimited, or its constituted powers, rights and obligations (Security Council Resolution of 19 September 1992). (see *603, 652*)

809 – Human actions are aggravated by those of time: circumstances do not stay the same, even if the changes are superficial. There are thousands of reasons that can be used to explain or even justify delay, reluctance or refusal to carry out diplomatic agreements. (see *924*)

810 – Part of the diplomat's task is to address these questions in time, in other words before the end of the negotiations. In the case of a bilateral negotiation, he must foresee which are the clauses in the agreement as a whole that his adversary will seek to distort, breach or allow to fall into disuse, and draw the necessary conclusions as to precautions to take or responses to have ready: the moment one or more States make up their minds to reject it, the principle of integrity of a treaty (Article 44 of the 1969 Vienna Convention) becomes merely academic. (see *960, 2080*)

Precautions are all the more advisable as it is usually the most important stipulations that are the most exacting, and thus the most vulnerable.

811 – In multilateral negotiations, the risk is not only that treaties will not be implemented, but that one of the parties will withdraw, leaving the others to assume its obligations.

812 – After a negotiation, the parties' interests will still be divergent and even opposing, in spite of the sometimes *ad hoc* and temporary agreement they have reached. Often, the wishes of one will remain, or become, the exact opposite of what the other wants: this is why treaties are so rarely amended. (see *354*)

813 – Obligations can be extinguished if both parties so wish: this involves a negotiation. However, it is not easy to obtain the consent of the party favoured by the status quo.

814 – In order to avoid widespread resort to denunciation, whether or not this was provided for at the time of negotiation, a radical change in the legal or factual circumstances that pertained at the time the treaty was signed, and on which the agreement was predicated, must be accepted as justifying a request to modify some of its stipulations or rescind those clauses that are found to be moot or obsolete. For practical and legal reasons, this is best done by a new negotiation.

815 – If it is difficult to conclude a treaty, it is even more difficult to revise it, which explains why there are more new agreements than modified ones. In order to preserve the balance of the relationship, diplomats sometimes prefer to start the entire negotiation again from the beginning.

816 – Within international organisations, negotiation of amendments is easier than revision, which is more thorough.

Revision clauses, often detailed, are on the increase, particularly in treaties creating institutions, and more generally in multilateral agreements (see Article 109 of the Charter of the United Nations). Under these, it is rarely possible to avoid a negotiation on the modifications to be decided upon, the principle underlying them, or the effect they will have on all the parties to the original agreement, in order to ensure that the same text applies to each of them.

817 – The growth of prospective negotiation has had the effect of giving a new importance to the renegotiation of commitments: where this is provided for in advance, and facilitated by clearly defining the length of time conventions remain in force, it takes on a dynamic normative role in improving international relations. (see *1825, 2204*)

818 – In practice, the best precautions are the ones that are announced and provided for at the time of the negotiation. Clauses providing for exclusions or allowing for temporary derogation fall into this category: these can be invoked if problems arise of a serious but temporary nature in the performance of certain obligations, without undermining the treaty as a whole (Vienna Convention, Article 72), and their application can be discussed by the governments concerned within an international institution. (see *1545*)

819 – There are several ways in international negotiation of avoiding the danger that agreements will be denounced. For example, the contracting parties can provide that reasons for challenging the treaty shall be notified, together with advance notice of denunciation to allow for a possible new negotiation to take place (Vienna Convention, Article 65; see also the Treaty of 5 August 1963 on the partial halt to nuclear testing, and the Non-Proliferation Treaty of 1 July 1968).

820 – It is for the governments that must take these decisions to weigh up the circumstances justifying the denunciation or suspension of commitments: the wise negotiator should be prompted by this to seek commitments from his partners that are limited in time, as these will be more likely to be respected. (see *558*)

The best agreement is one that takes effect straight away and can be speedily implemented.

821 – In short, the wise will learn the lessons of experience: *credit is as necessary to international relations as it is in commercial transactions*. What prompts governments to respect their commitments, in a world where negotiation takes place on a daily basis about a wide range of issues, is self-interest, concern or fear of being treated the same way, careful calculation of what will serve them in the long term, and knowing that their peers are watching what they do. Frederick II of Prussia wrote that honesty and wisdom required even princes to abide scrupulously by their treaties.[80] (see *481, 2239*)

822 – Every State that has achieved its main objectives thereby becomes a staunch defender of the status quo, and uses its diplomatic skills in the interests of peace,

---

80 FREDERICK II OF PRUSSIA: *L'Anti-Machiavel*, Chapter 26.

stability and reconciliation: the Berlin government adopted this attitude after 1871, as did the Moscow government after 1945.

Breach of a norm, an institution or even a custom will be met with a reaction of solidarity on the part of all States whose interests they serve: this provides a means of policing international relations.

Guarantees and sanctions

823 – In the current dysfunctional and amoral state of international society, no precaution will be of lasting effect between sovereigns – in other words, between States.[81] (see *923, 957*)

It is extremely rare for the diplomatic conduct of a State to be sanctioned by a court, even where breach of a specific obligation is involved. The only example to the contrary is the European Community. (see *1673*)

Furthermore, an international court or tribunal requires a diplomatic treaty to set it up, which in effect means it requires the agreement of the very States who will be subject to its jurisdiction. (see *2139, 2236, 2240*)

824 – Alliances remain unpredictable, even the most solemn, when the players are only interested in maintaining the balance of power: just as Metternich had played off Napoleon against Tsar Alexander, Stalin tried, up to the end, in 1939, to keep one foot in both camps. (see *2239*)

825 – From a partner's point of view, any doubts will prompt it to seek sureties, the first of which will be to induce the other to take a step from which there is no going back. This step might involve abandoning its defences, dismantling its strongholds or scuttling its fleet. Most of the time, it involves war:[82] this was what France demanded of Britain 1914. (see *947*)

826 – The fact that, as between States, the value of a commitment often depends on whether it is more in that party's interest to honour it than to breach it, injects an inevitable element of uncertainty into political promises and makes it particularly important that treaties are respected, whereas it ought to be possible to justify this on ethical grounds alone.

827 – The diplomatic arsenal, like that of trade, also contains ways and means of guaranteeing that agreements are carried out, and resort to them is not uncommon: occupation of territory, the surrender of strongholds, the grant of financial privileges, the allocation of resources, and the abandonment of human populations.

The nature of these pledges and how they are used vary according to the accepted values of the different civilisations.

828 – Rome demanded hostages to ensure the respect of its subject peoples, and treated them well as long as the pact was honoured. The future king of the Franks,

---

81 A. de WICQUEFORT: *L'Ambassadeur et ses functions*, II, Cologne, 1690, 12.
82 J. CAMBON: *Le Diplomate*, Paris, Hachette, 1926, p. 17.

Pepin, was sent to the king of the Lombards who adopted him, as a guarantee of the alliance he had been offered by the boy's father, Charles Martel. And many were the daughters of princes who were offered in marriage in order to seal an agreement. Proudhon was in favour of the taking of hostages: if they were well chosen, they would use their influence to induce their fellow citizens to abide by the agreement and make sure nothing happened that would result in their own personal suffering. In modern times, hostage-taking has become a means of exerting pressure independent of any diplomatic process.

829 – Today, the giving of an oath is no longer relied upon, whereas, centuries ago, princes who were freed on the strength of their word would go back to prison to honour it: in 1842, the conclusion of an alliance at Strasbourg between Charles the Bald of France and Louis of Germany was consecrated not only by the two kings swearing an oath, but by their armies, too, swearing to abandon them if they did not keep their word.

830 – Among the last well-known examples of the pledging of a security was the occupation of the Ruhr towns in 1921 by French and Belgian troops in order to make Germany pay reparations: the episode ended ingloriously, with an evacuation. It would be difficult today for world opinion to accept a national military presence on foreign territory. Where this continues for an extended period it creates problems internally and externally. Intervention by troops stationed abroad against the local authorities could moreover be subject to the general condemnation of aggression.

831 – Participation in major financing or technical projects creates commitments that are more solid and vital than any alliance, as was shown by the study of the consequences of the building of the Aswan Dam for Egypt's diplomacy, and by the growth in economic and trading cooperation between the former Soviet Union and the United States. (see *1968*)

832 – Resorting to the guarantee of a third country is a frequently used diplomatic practice, particularly among the lesser powers. This precaution exposes some States to responsibilities that are too onerous, without always being effective, as can be seen from the abandonment of Czechoslovakia in 1938, not only by France and Britain, but also the USSR. Since 1967, one of the themes of negotiation in the Near East has been the replacement of the practice of taking territory as security by resort to the protection or guarantee of third powers; this happened in 1918 with the French border on the Rhine, though the Franco-British and Franco-American treaties of guarantee were never put into effect.[83] (see *931*)

833 – These processes have often been supplemented by the intervention of international organisations, often in a good position to monitor the implementation of treaties, whether or not entered into under their auspices, because the resources put at their disposal by certain States enable them to do so. (see *1450, 1638*)

---

83 G. WORMSER: *La République de Clemenceau*, Paris, PUF, 1961, p. 355.

The Constitution of the Free City of Danzig was set up under the guarantee of the League of Nations in 1920.

Negotiation of the goals and methods of international investigations will take on increasing importance. (see *2037*)

834 – Some powers rely on international forces to ensure compliance with ceasefires in conflict zones, or clauses in peace treaties. These military contingents are there with the consent of the States concerned, and may not intervene in their internal affairs. The withdrawal of the machinery put in place by the United Nations after the Suez crisis triggered one of the wars between Israel and Egypt, in 1967. (see *1661*)

Originally destined to supervise military truces, the peace-keeping forces of the Security Council have seen their mission expanded to cover activities of a political nature, for example in Namibia, Cambodia and Yugoslavia. (see *729, 1698, 1784, 2159*)

835 – The giving of guarantees can only result in negotiation expanding to include those whose cooperation is necessary for this: in practice, if a guarantee involves an obligation on the part of a sovereign power, it must be given by treaty or formal diplomatic instrument. Even where the commitment is a collective one, it is rare for nothing to be required in return.[84]

836 – Some politicians have taken the view that States might be forced to respect their undertakings by verification of their conduct or the threat of various types of sanctions: economic, financial or moral, rather than military. Formal agreements are giving way to notions such as these, thanks to the cooperation of certain powers and the growth of international organisations. The exercise of this power is not automatic: it, too, presupposes a negotiation even when its subject is the application of humanitarian law.[85] (see *1653*)

The Yugoslav crisis led the United Nations Security Council to decide to impose a series of increasingly severe embargoes on Serbia in 1991–1992, as well as to deploy a multinational intervention force.

837 – In seeking legal effectiveness for compliance with international obligations, ways must be found to circumvent the lack of binding sanctions on States. Negotiation serves two purposes: verifying the implementation of norms, as for example in disarmament or human rights, on the one hand, and the use of public, even adversarial, procedures to inquire into alleged violations on the other.

The verification of treaty implementation can be made easier where the engagements are said to be 'transparent' (arms limitation treaties, such as the 1972 ABM treaty) and where consulting committees of experts or negotiators are brought in. This latter solution is usually adopted when State obligations involve legal questions (eg. labour conventions) and commercial issues (eg agreements made under the GATT and now the WTO), where third-party mediation is possible, though, even there, it is not always effective. (see *1740, 2029*)

---

84 R. GENET: *Traité de diplomatie et de droit diplomatique*, III, Paris, Pedone, 1932, p. 371.
85 M.-F. FURET, J.-C. MARTINEZ and H. DORANDEU: *La Guerre et le Droit*, Paris, Pedone, 1979, p. 232.

838 – In reality, in almost all cases, it is left to the discretion of States to respect their commitments.[86] But refusal to honour an obligation freely entered into will never fail to provoke a reaction on the part of the partner. A balance needs to be maintained between the sanction and the breach complained of. A unilateral act always carries the risk of uncertain repercussions: the denunciation of a treaty, or the rejection of a precautionary measure can trigger the breaking off of diplomatic relations, or even war, in other words it can jeopardise the whole fabric of legal bonds that have been created by negotiation between the parties concerned. (see *93, 671*)

From the time of signature of the Treaty of Versailles, those responsible on the German side wanted to have it revised. Major gains were obtained by negotiation under the Weimar Republic: the evacuation of the occupying armies, the rectification of certain frontiers, and the grant of facilities to German minorities.[87] But the rupture appeared as soon as diplomacy gave way to a Pan-German policy.

839 – Negotiators are sometimes prudent enough to state the duration of the commitments or to provide for their revision or termination. Where they have not done so, no political situation may be considered as incapable of change or breach, and so the possibility has to be admitted of adapting the law to circumstances as they unfold: this is one of the missions of diplomatic negotiation. (see *2240*)

840 – *Negotiation does not only precede a commitment; it is also used when undoing it*. As A. Siegfried said, there exists, or rather there used to be practised, an art of breaking commitments, made up of practices sometimes as complex as the ones used in making treaties.

841 – Wisdom would suggest that failure to apply contractual clauses, their modification or denunciation, should form part of a broader diplomatic manoeuvre that gives warning of these actions and explains the effect they will have. However, it has to be admitted that governments often prefer to take unilateral, sometimes sudden, action: history shows that it is the most important treaties from the political or military perspective that are subject to the most obvious, if not the most flagrant, violations.

In the future, true preventive negotiation will develop, one that is capable of paving the way for and maintaining harmony between the views and ambitions of States, as well as respect for good faith in their mutual relations. (see *1738*)

The more decisive the negotiation, the more fragile is its outcome.

86 J. BARBERIS: 'Les liens juridiques entre l'Etat et son territoire', *AFDI*, 1999, p. 132.
87 P. RENOUVIN: *Histoire des relations internationales. Les crises du XXe siècle*, Paris, Hachette, 1957, I, p. 227.

Part II:
Institutional Negotiation

842 – The modern concept of the State provides the structure, definition and stability that enables peoples to organise themselves and express their individual character. It has resulted in a veritable proliferation of territorial, ethnic and political entities claiming to be recognised as nations and seeking to exercise the privileges of sovereignty. The newer these are, the more susceptible they will be. (see *2305*)

843 – The population of the planet is ever increasing. With interdependence of peoples comes growing threats. All large-scale plans for the future must take account, at the same time, of the complementarity of national economies and the power wielded by the transnational businesses and forces that continue to expand and compete without regard for legal or geographical frontiers. Pressures are steadily growing, too, on the ecological environment. (see *1808*)

844 – The intensification of negotiations between States provides the beginnings of an answer to this contradiction between the deep divisions in mankind and the increasing interdependence of its different peoples because it offers organic, evolutionary but sustainable ways to develop the 'community of nations'. (see *2256, 2274*)

845 – States are free to negotiate any form of cooperation, alliance or project on which they can agree. One of the trends in modern negotiation is the appearance of so many different forms of association among States, in the Pacific, the Caribbean, Southern Asia, Central America, South America and West, Central and East Africa. (see *842, 1099, 1104, 1205, 1812, 1915, 2137*)

These groupings of States take disparate forms depending on the type of solidarity they express. Some of them exist to respond only to dangers that arise while others reflect fundamental choices such as a refusal to align with the Great Powers or to engage in capitalist competition.

Alliances, however, often involve major and lasting commitments. Modern day negotiation within alliances, with its complex organisation, is taking on an institutional character. (see *990, 1938*)

846 – As a result of negotiation, these groupings are organised in a variety of ways. While diplomatic treaties are common, organisations also exist that are based on alignment of conduct, such as the Nordic Council that grew out of the Baltic Council in 1993, and there are powerful bodies like the Commonwealth that have no written foundation. Within federal systems, too, sub-groups negotiate among themselves under cover of a declared unity vis à vis the outside world.

847 – These groupings vary in their geographical extent. The Organisation of American States (Bogota Charter, 30 April 1948) does not prevent specific Latin American organisations coming into existence, such as those set up by the Montevideo Treaties of 18 February 1960 and 12 August 1980 or the Treaty of Asunciòn of 26 March 1991, in force since 1995, alongside the Central American collective under the San Salvador Charter of 14 October 1951. (see *1643*)

The history of that organisation shows how the crushing weight of one member State – in modern times, the United States – can ultimately distort all negotiations within an institution and, consequently, its role in diplomacy. (see *1527*)

848 – The Arab League gives expression to cultural, even religious, solidarity (Treaty of 22 March 1945), while considerations of this type are excluded a priori from the United Nations and its entire machinery (see UNGA Resolution 2625, the Declaration of Principles of International Law Concerning Friendly Relations and Cooperation Between States). Notwithstanding this, the Islamic Conference of 55 countries, set up in Jeddah in 1962, is a 'regional organisation' for solidarity and cooperation between Muslim peoples on three continents.

The *Organisation internationale de la Francophonie* (International Organisation of French-speaking Peoples) has both periodic conferences of Heads of States and governments, with summits in Hanoi in 1997, Moncton in 1999, Yaoundé in 2001, Beirut in 2003 and Bucharest in 2006, and a cultural and technical cooperative body, the *Agence intergouvernmentale de la Francophonie* (formerly the ACCT), set up by the Niamey Conference in 1970. (see *1949, 2214*)

849 – The concerns about defence and mutual military assistance that prompted the founding of the Western European Union (the Paris Treaty of 1945 and the Brussels Treaty of 1948) occupy the other end of the spectrum from those – nonetheless very strong – that underpin the various African monetary unions and the common customs areas which have had the effect of reinforcing economic interdependence more or less worldwide.

The private sector economy, and also professional and cultural activities, are caught up in a worldwide network of communication and have adopted some of the practices of multipartite negotiation and international organisation.[1] (see *1680, 1915*)

850 – As for the Commonwealth, this is an immense worldwide association of States with disparate domestic regimes and different foreign policies, whose members enjoy special relations both at the bilateral and the multilateral level. Even where divergences cannot be completely overcome, negotiation between the partners is made easier by their traditional solidarity and by having specific institutions (the Secretariat and the conferences of Heads of Government and ministers). In its relations with the rest of the world, on the other hand, the Commonwealth has no power to negotiate on its own behalf or that of its members.

---

1 J. TOUSCOZ: *Droit international*, Paris, PUF, 1993, p. 185.

851 – Whether these are intergovernmental organisations, systems of law, assemblies based on the parliamentary model or even institutional expressions of integration, the whole flourishing apparatus derives from agreements between governments, and inexorably strengthens the fabric of their mutual relations. (see *1956, 2284*)

Coming on top of the changes already wrought by multilateralism in the way diplomacy functions, this continuing trend towards organisation is altering the nature and the aims of international negotiation. This is how the principle of the most-favoured nation clause, enshrined in the GATT, has come to play a part in the globalisation of the world economy. (see *706, 756, 2476*)

Relationships tend to become institutionalised but they will not lose their own character as long as States retain their sovereignty. (see *2265, 2485*)

Chapter I:
Alliances

852 – From the earliest times, even the most primitive and xenophobic of nations have made pacts when going to war: joining forces brings superiority on the battlefield.

The main object of an alliance is to increase the partners' ability to resist aggression. It functions as a coalition when attacking, but also serves a deterrent purpose once the promise of mutual assistance becomes known. (see *111, 168, 238, 239*)

853 – No alliance is indefinite: sometimes States reach agreement in order to attack, conquer and share, because of the advantage they derive from joining forces. That was the plan for the Berlin-Rome Axis before the Second World War. Today, such an objective would be contrary to the UN Charter and would thus remain secret. (see *114, 117*)

854 – Modern civilisation with its technological complexity has multiplied and diversified the risks, especially internationally. These risks encourage States to act with prudence and make alliances unpredictable. This leads the Great Powers to maintain their independent tactics, which are therefore no longer 'institutional' in character. (see *334, 335, 1678*)

855 – Aside from their immediate tactical concerns, rapprochement between some States can represent a more long-term community of interests: treaties entered into on this basis are among the wise manoeuvres that contribute to the balance of power and influence.[2] One example is the tradition of seeking an ally at the enemy's rear, which has been a theme of French policy on the continent of Europe for a thousand years. Other examples are pacts between powers united not only because their fears are the same, but because their interests also converge. (see *380, 844*)

A rapprochement between nations naturally causes those it threatens to do the same: negotiation generates other negotiations. (see *945, 1700*)

856 – An alliance is also the expression, in the diplomatic arena, of community of destiny, sentiment and culture between nations: though not governed by any particular pact, the long relationship between the United States and the United Kingdom could be so described.

---

2 H. J. MORGENTHAU: 'Alliances in Theory and Practice', in *Alliance Policy in the Cold War*, Baltimore, Johns Hopkins Press, 1959. G. LISKA: *Nations in Alliance*, Baltimore, Johns Hopkins Press, 1962.

These 'institutionalised' communities can also be of a scientific or technical nature: common or coordinated programmes for research, development and manufacture of armaments are the subject of alliances (for example, the 1996 military cooperation agreement between Israel and Turkey) and enable them to last (see the European Framework Agreement of 27 July 2000). The same cannot be said of 'partnerships' (as between the European Union and Russia in 1995), or *ad hoc* operations, like the docking in space of the Atlantis shuttle and the Mir space station in June 1995. By contrast, the 'partnership' between Russia and China in 1996 was accompanied by a military treaty in 1997, revised in 2001 and signed by four Central Asian States (the Shanghai Group against so-called separatist movements). (see *947, 1692, 1769*)

857 – Never has the world seen such intense activity in the negotiation of alliances as during the second half of the twentieth century: so widespread was the phenomenon that questions were raised about the compatibility and applicability of the commitments that resulted.

Some States, such as the United States, are at the centre of a veritable system of bilateral and collective alliances covering the whole planet, requiring constant negotiation to keep them in place, maintain their coherence and regulate their consequences.[3] (see *2338*)

858 – The spread of systems of alliances in opposition to each other causes collective security to break down. Their collapse makes it easier to revive solidarity between States, but provides no guarantees, given that dangerous forces are now free to manoeuvre.

Reconciling these two strands of diplomacy is difficult: it might prove impossible.[4] Where strategies are fundamentally opposed, negotiation cannot bridge the gap. (see *1781*)

Section 1: The nature of alliances

859 – States work together in many different configurations – transient or lasting, broad or restricted, depending on circumstances and on the crises that may arise in relations between peoples. (see *169, 1692*)

860 – Solidarity in times of trial and difficulty is often the product of a tacit agreement, itself born out of a tradition of friendship, fear of the same enemy, the certainty of not coming into conflict or a combination of interests. Such was the case with the *Entente Cordiale*, which, though originally signed for colonial reasons, led Britain and France to face two great wars side by side and also led the United States to provide support to the European democracies. (see *109*)

861 – Countries that are united only by a common danger do not want to enter into mutual obligations that outlast their immediate need for security. (see *797*)

---

3 J. E. KING: 'Collective Defense: the Military commitment', in *Alliance Policy in the Cold War*, Baltimore, Johns Hopkins Press, 1959.
4 A. WOLFERS: 'Collective Defense versus Collective Security', ibid., p. 49.

862 – The pooling of forces in order to overcome an adversary is enough to form a coalition: coalitions are creatures of circumstance and their objectives are generally short-term. The commitments they involve have no solid foundation. Each partner continues to be in competition with the others. The Triple Alliance, the brainchild of Bismarck in the 1880s, brought together three Empires with a history of fierce antagonism: only a major strategy could keep it alive, and the lack of one soon made itself felt (see *165*)

863 – Spheres of influence are not defined by legal stipulations; their limits are flexible and they adapt to whichever power is predominant and rarely give rise to obligations. On the other hand, *an alliance rests on commitments that can only be embodied in a formal treaty.* (see *130, 1692, 1754*)

864 – Although there are doctrinal differences on this point,[5] by contrast with the numerous agreements that govern commercial, technical or financial cooperation between States, a true diplomatic alliance means, most of the time, a commitment to give mutual aid or assistance in the event of war: the object of the alliance is military even if it only refers to the maintenance of peace and security. *Combat is the test of the true strength and sincerity of intentions.* (see *234*)

865 – Alliances can be singled out from the great mass of diplomatic treaties because they are directed against an actual or potential enemy. It is this consideration that brings the alliance into being and gives it meaning and scope, strength and durability.[6] It demands a strategy that goes beyond mere concerted action. (see *1359, 1714, 2325*)

§1. The pact

866 – Whatever name is given to the treaty itself, an alliance is the product of a pact between States that are, and remain, sovereign. It can be binding on two nations or on several. While, in the latter case, it can, in theory, be broken down into a series of bilateral relations that may be treated separately, and while in practice direct negotiation between the members is accepted and even encouraged, it is doubtful in reality whether its organisational structure and workings could be replicated simply by aggregating these component relations. (see *2313*)

867 – An alliance is not simply an amalgam of States. However strong their shared cultural values, however frequent the exchanges between them and however similar their political regimes, their union will remain vulnerable as long as it is not capable of rapid response. A nation wanting to give a joint response to external challenges bears risks of being overwhelmed by the need to keep short-term interests and bilateral exchanges in alignment.[7] (see *1512, 1520, 2313*)

---

5 L. CAVARE: 'Considérations sur les traités d'alliance', in *Mélanges Gidel*, Paris, Sirey, 1961, p. 127.

6 B. BOUTROS-GHALI: *Contribution à une théorie générale des alliances*, Paris, Pedone, 1963.

7 K. DEUTSCH: *Political Community at the International Level*, New York, Doubleday, 1954.

What cements an alliance is the privileged status it gives to bilateral or multilateral communication. (see *2050*)

868 – Following time-honoured tradition, modern customs exist to formalise the conclusion of a pact to make it clear what protection each member can expect from it in times of need. But bonds of this kind do not always need to be enshrined in documents or attended by ceremony. (see *763, 768*)

869 – It will not always be clear from the beginnings of a given diplomatic manoeuvre that an alliance exists, what its objectives are or whether it is solid: the famous Franco-Russian alliance at the end of the nineteenth century was slow to take shape. It is not unusual for common cultural concerns or close economic interdependence to be the first signs of awareness that there is potential for political and military solidarity.

An alliance sets the seal on an existing rapprochement between States rather than causing one to happen. (see *1847*)

870 – However, the mutual obligations within the alliance should be completely and precisely set down, especially if they include a promise of military intervention. Such clauses merit careful negotiation, and if their implementation is to be assured they must be in writing; their consequences are such as to require formal ratification. (see *781*)

A government that fails to engage in serious debate about such strategic commitments will prove to be an indecisive and unreliable partner.

871 – Where it results from a treaty, the commitment will come to be known about not only by virtue of its approval under the constitutional rules of each State, but also, particularly in a democracy, because it is published. This means that an alliance serves as a warning to third parties, discouraging them from any ill-considered action. (see *2572*)

872 – By contrast with what happens with defensive pacts, States that ally their forces for the purposes of attack often keep their planned manoeuvres secret in order to surprise their adversaries before they have had the chance to unite or respond. (see *2600*)

873 – Generally speaking, publication does not extend to operational provisions whose existence the adversary suspects, though he does not know their contents. Even in 1914, the French Parliament still did not know about the secret clauses in the Franco-Russian alliance.[8]

874 – The negotiation of alliances is thus a major part of diplomatic manoeuvre. When skilfully unveiled, such plans can deter a power from adopting a posture of provocation, or prevent a hostile front from being formed: at the end of the nineteenth century, Germany succeeded in delaying the rapprochement between France and Britain by offering its friendship first to one and then the other.

---

8 H. NICOLSON: *The Evolution of Diplomatic Methods*, London, New York, MacMillan, 1954.

875 – Sometimes, the mere appearance of a military solution is enough to deter aggression. This is especially true in a world dominated by fear of nuclear weapons no one wants to be used. Otherwise, converting the possibility of mutual assistance into a public obligation will have the desired deterrent effect, especially on public opinion.

876 – Many States have been, and still are, attracted by neutrality where alliances are concerned: their refusal to commit themselves can be explained not only by their lack of interest in the quarrels of others, but also by a desire to open up and maintain negotiations on a freer, broader and more fruitful basis than a predetermined or rigid diplomatic framework would allow. (see *191*)

877 – The untold destruction threatened by nuclear weapons makes them less credible: in addition to the horror they arouse, the neutralisation of strategic forces has generated, at the same time, a desire on the part of many nations for freedom to manoeuvre, unfettered by commitments, and also an attitude of irresponsibility on the part of some of their leaders. (see *1762*)

The same could be said of other weapons of mass destruction as well as their delivery systems. (see *1714, 1715*)

878 – It is easy to understand why some governments practise a diplomacy principally based on the rejection of treaties of alliance in favour of a network of favoured but pragmatic relations. (see *854*)

States anxious to maintain a free hand, and in a position to do so, are uncomfortable in alliances, even when they play the leading role: throughout the nineteenth century, Britain supported Turkey against Russia as a matter of principle, but it did so without ever offering a binding commitment.

879 – It is far from settled that a State's power can be measured by the extent of its clientele. In the modern world, dominated by powerful interest groupings, no State, weak or strong, can embark on or wage a military, financial or economic conflict without having first made sure it could count on adequate support. The reciprocal nature of this cooperation leads to the formation of alliances. (see *857*)

§2. The bond

880 – According to the French writer Proudhon, alliances between States are by their nature difficult and short lived, limited to a specific purpose and have little to recommend them. They are, he said, a breeding ground for defection and ingratitude.[9] (see *371*)

Before they were seized by Macedonia, associations between the cities of Greece were formed and broken with ease, except for those that were founded on religious fear or out of respect for a sanctuary. The political architecture that resulted from the Treaty of Vienna in 1815 had already begun to disintegrate before 1830.

---

9 P. J. PROUDHON: *La Guerre et la Paix*, Paris, Rivière, 1927, p. 298.

881 – Pacts sometimes state how long they are to last, but this serves no purpose. The alliance stands or falls by the strength of the bond that holds it together, in other words the mutual benefits the relationship brings. Legal bonds count for less than common interests.[10]

It is an enemy that causes alliances, but an ally that is betrayed.

882 – The appearance of the same risk or danger naturally dictates how the countries under threat will respond. Where they share similar fears and concerns, the greater the disproportion between their forces and those of the common enemy, the closer they become: in the sixteenth century, the power of the Romano-Germanic Emperor Charles V led the King of France and the Ottoman Sultan to reach an understanding.

883 – Each partner perceives the danger in its own way, depending on its past, its interests and where it is vulnerable. The more States are involved in an alliance, the more it will be weakened by their differences in judgement. There are some who have questioned how much pluralism an alliance can withstand, but without arriving at an answer. In the 2003–2004 conflict in Iraq, only some of the members of NATO agreed to intervene alongside the United States.

884 – Within an alliance, cohesion will increase when the balance of which it forms part is tilted against its interests. Once the binding influence of the fear of French power was no longer there, the Holy Alliance, concluded in 1815, degenerated into a federation with limited objectives which rapidly fell prey to internal strife. (see 149)

He who cannot dismantle a hostile alliance must find a way to tranquilise it.

885 – A failure that can be repaired will reinforce the coalition: respect for the pact will increase with the threat of defeat, as long as the fear is not so great that it causes the alliance to fall apart. But, a reversal often follows shortly afterwards.

886 – Military considerations are not the only ones that come into play. Depending on the degree to which the partners' values are shared, an alliance can be the expression of a simple tactical coalition or strategic interdependence: there was never any lasting understanding between Britain and Russia, for example.

887 – An alliance has been described as being a matter either of choice, sentiment or convenience. Undoubtedly, each individual country will proceed by selecting favoured partners on the basis of certain criteria, and on condition of reciprocity. Thus, States' political regimes influence the alliances they belong to as well as how they behave within their own borders.[11] (see *2613*)

888 – Interest does not last and friendship is dependent on circumstances, but natural affinities are often powerful and go back a long way: they can arise out of the type of civilisation (as with the bond in the Middle Ages between the Hanseatic cities and those of the Rhine) or culture (between Latin countries, for example, or

---

10 H. J. MORGENTHAU: quoted by T. W. ROBINSON in *The Theory and Practice of International Relations*, Englewood Cliffs, Prentice Hall, 1970, p. 205.

11 R. NEUSTADT: *Alliance Politics*, New York, Columbia University Press, 1970.

Scandinavian or Anglo-Saxon ones), or proximity (as between Canada and the United States) or, most of all, history: some of these choices are based on ancestral or instinctive enmity. (see *1863*)

Such affinities can facilitate the mutual consultations that are a tacit expression of alliance.

889 – As might be expected, the assurance each partner receives from the others is reinforced by closeness of ideals, beliefs and social systems, but it is not easy to agree on what makes for lasting political closeness: there are often too many differences or variations in their objectives, their analysis of a situation or the hypotheses on which they operate. As to geographical proximity, the only advantage it offers the alliance is that of convenience. (see *1890*)

890 – The interest each party has in maintaining the agreement may be strong enough to overcome wide disparities in the types of civilisation the parties represent: religion proved no obstacle to the sixteenth-century alliance between the King of France and the Ottoman rulers. However, cultural obstacles are nowadays difficult to surmount in countries where public opinion can express itself freely. (see *1865, 2613*)

891 – No alliance can survive in the long term if it goes against the nations' most deeply felt aspirations. It served no purpose for King Carol of Romania to enter into a secret treaty with the Austro-Hungarian Empire in 1883; when the First World War came, the two countries found themselves in opposing camps. (see *2634*)

892 – Blood ties are another way of cementing an alliance: for centuries, princely marriages brought peoples together, at least for a while. This is why the Habsburg Emperor Maximilian took care to install his children and grandchildren in Spain, Hungary and Bohemia. Philip III of Spain married his daughters to Louis XIII and the Emperor Ferdinand III and his granddaughters to Louis XIV and the Emperor Leopold I.

But history bears out common sense in one respect: such marriages are no proof against fickleness, even when backed by diplomatic treaties.

893 – The value of an alliance resides most of all in the resolve of its members. *No form of support will suffice unless a State makes most of the effort by itself and for itself*. It must feel strong enough to make its plan succeed even if its 'brothers in arms' should fail, as the French Cardinal de Richelieu advised in his *Testament politique*.

The most effective support for the alliance will come from those States with an interest in maintaining its integrity and autonomy; the need to maintain the balance of power will contribute to its stability.

§3. Equality or predominance

894 – The fact that two or more States have entered into an alliance does not mean that relations between them will be free of problems, especially where there is too great a gap between the partners' ideals and the means they have for achieving them. (see *155*)

895 – An alliance between countries that are too dissimilar in strength or ambition will thus be difficult to create and even more difficult to maintain as soon as a grave external threat arises that forces each of them to make concessions. It was already clear even to Grotius that too great a degree of inequality between allies will spoil the alliance.[12] *Some pacts are really treaties of guarantee*, where, for example, they apply to the territory of only one of the allies. (see *154*)

896 – Unless the union is to be allowed to disintegrate, none of the allies will have freedom to manoeuvre externally unless the others agree to reduce their own commitment; they must therefore be consulted, even to the point of acceding to their concerns. To see this at work one need look no further than the history of the relations between Vienna and Berlin prior to 1 August 1914. (see *569*)

897 – It has been said that no one can escape the obligations of power.[13] It is always useful to have powerful backing. In an alliance, the most powerful member is usually alone in being in a position to give effect to its own decisions, against its adversary first of all, but also vis à vis those who depend on it for their liberty or prosperity: *an alliance can become the breeding ground for predominance*. (see *133, 2283*)

898 – A dominant State is led to intermingle its own interests with those of its allies, but expects them to give it the support it needs in its own moves: what matters to it is effectiveness. But it must remember that, on the other hand, its partners will be wary of condemning themselves to be subordinated, sacrificed or even abandoned. (see *135*)

899 – Inequality in an alliance will have a natural tendency to extend to all the elements necessary for the strategy and tactics adopted by the dominant power. (see *1653*)

With the Romans, alliances followed a policy of conquest, protectorate and annexation, especially with regard to those peoples that had not been comprehensively defeated, with whom Rome made a peace that preserved their nominal independence, the *foedus*.

900 – The partners are rarely in balance, either in what they intend or in the means they have. The alliance must be sincere and solid before one of the allies will agree to give serious reinforcement to another.[14]

A chance friend may become a future enemy: the risk is all the greater if that ally increases in autonomy.

901 – It could even be thought that equality of strength among the participants might, except in cases of extreme danger, become a factor for disunity where diplomatic negotiation between them does not ensure that their strategies remain attuned.

902 – Besides, generally speaking, the great powers must take account of the risks to their overall strategy that might arise from the imprudence of their allies or the

---

12 H. de GROOT: *De jure belli ac pacis, libri tres*, I, 1625, p. 278.
13 R. ARON: *Paix et guerre entre les nations*, Paris, Calmann-Lévy, 1962, p. 145.
14 Ibid., p. 40.

commitments made by them to third countries: they would not wish to lose their freedom of decision and be forced to go further than they had intended. (see *1757*)

The strongest do not agree to be treated in the way they treat others.

903 – By threatening to withdraw its support, the dominant country can effectively restrain its allies. It does, however, need to be aware of the concern or irritation that this kind of pressure can engender. The best alignment is one that is not imposed but negotiated.

904 – To the powerful, consulting partners or seeking unanimity paralyses its intervention, especially where this has to be rapid or even massive in order to have an effect. Even today, it is not uncommon to see alliances justifying bringing a recalcitrant member into line or developing into a form of protectorate. *The ability to impose one's will acts as a disincentive to discussion.* (see *623, 971*)

905 – As for the States under domination, they will progressively but ineluctably turn away from shouldering their responsibilities effectively. The protection they enjoy little by little makes them a burden and a weak link for the alliance as a whole. (see *142*)

906 – In some alliances with many members, a shared anxiety develops as to the ambitions and pretensions of the more powerful. This leads the other partners to favour formal and continuing consultations, in other words, the mechanisms that can support their position. This concern sometimes obliges them to regroup to increase their strength, just as they would do in an international organisation.

907 – By offering scope for reconciling the multilateral with the bilateral, such a grouping can encourage the development of favoured interchange between certain of its members.

A collective alliance can provide an umbrella for a succession of preferences as long as these are not exclusive.

908 – Whatever state of harmony may reign among the allies, small nations often find it difficult to be dependent on security that is not of their own determining, without taking certain precautions: it is in their interests, therefore, to pursue discussions with third parties, and there is nothing wrong in this, since they are not in a position to pronounce on the strategy of the alliance as a whole. (see *140, 527, 1756*)

909 – It follows that it is unwise, in an alliance, to look only at whether it works as a whole; the uncertainty that overshadows respect for international obligations means that each partner will keep open the possibility of calling upon those whom it can and must count on for support.

910 – If a leadership role is impossible, the next best course for a State is to retain control over its resources and its independence, as fully as possible and for as long as possible. Subject to this, taking part in a concerted action is legitimate, especially when this no longer raises secondary issues.

911 – But why approach a minor player when the master himself is available? *The only countries that third parties will take seriously – the only ones, to them, that*

count – are those that are able to exert a material or moral influence over the behaviour of their own allies. In 1802, knowing that the Emperor Francis II was not going to reconfigure Germany in the way that he wanted (in other words, not to the benefit of France) Bonaparte resolved the matter directly with the Tsar, who was flattered to be called upon to intervene and who shared the same concern: the Emperor had no choice but to cooperate, receiving Trentino in return.

912 – It can happen that, within an alliance, it is not always the same country that dominates. The coalition against Napoleon in 1814 and 1815 was led first by Metternich, who had brought together the States of Central Europe, and then Castlereagh, who mustered further support as well as funds, but it was finally Tsar Alexander of Russia, who was in Paris with his army, who took the lead.

913 – The Atlantic Alliance, signed in Washington on 4 April 1949, at that time represented a departure from earlier pacts in that it dealt with nuclear weapons. The Warsaw Pact, concluded in response to it, did likewise.

Relations between the two greatest powers were made up of both rivalry and complicity. Far from diminishing, the negotiations between them involved calculations and strategic ambitions their allies could not share and the risks they addressed were so grave as to threaten their very existence. At that level, the course the discussions took, and whether they ended in agreement or were broken off, could only be determined by decisions taken at national level, irrespective of the degree of alliance. (see **946**)

914 – Deterrence is all about handling certainty and uncertainty at the same time: the political resolve of the protagonists will be matched by the care they take to conceal their methods and tactics. Likewise, the use of nuclear weapons is a matter entirely for national decision: their allies will have no choice about any aspect of the strategy, assuming they are even aware of it. (see **1711**)

This is what happens with summit negotiations.

915 – After the Second World War, and in the decades that followed, each of the great Powers viewed itself as being alone, on its side, in having worldwide aspirations.[15] The extension across the globe of the range of weapons, as well as of political manoeuvres, exposed States of secondary rank to involvement in conflicts that did not concern them and that they could have done nothing to prevent.

The break-up of the USSR, with its governmental, diplomatic and military machinery, created an area of instability that stretched over two continents and opened up new arenas for competing influences, boundary disputes and ethnic conflict. As a result, new polarisations have appeared in European and Asian diplomacy.

916 – With relations between the dominant States and their partners more unequal than ever, tensions built up within alliances could only be kept in check by the threat from the other side. They were held together, more than ever, by the arms race

---

15 R. ARON: *République impériale. Les Etats-Unis dans le monde (1945–1972)*, Paris, Calmann-Lévy, 1973.

and the potential for conflict between the two camps: it was the Red Army that cemented the Atlantic Alliance, just as it was the fear of encroaching capitalism that bound together the Communist world in a pact that has since vanished.

The dissolution of the Warsaw Pact left some of its members uncertain as to their defence strategy. Three of them, Hungary, Poland and Czechoslovakia, as it then was, signed an agreement at Visegrad in 1991 with the aim of coordinating their security without actually forming an alliance and turned towards the West. For the majority of these former 'satellite-States', assession to the Atlantic Alliance meant securing the protection of the United States. (see *854, 946*)

917 – The State that finds itself in the position of dependence under a pact will be tempted to disengage itself from the common strategy and decrease its contribution to the common effort. Commentators have found that there is a tendency for the distinction between allies and neutrals to become blurred; the mutual guarantees of the Great Powers breed respect for their spheres of influence and discipline in their respective camps.[16]

918 – There is a balance between formal legal unity and the pluralism of national identities. *The cohesion of an alliance depends on the balance between the sacrifices it may require and the advantages it brings.* Each government judges this on the basis of its own priorities and policy imperatives. (see *2352*)

919 – States wish to preserve for as long as possible the freedom to choose between the unity of the manoeuvre and the diversity of its component parts. They want the agreement to be the product of their will rather than that of the group to which they belong.

Weak or strong, each of them should bear in mind the expert advice of Talleyrand: keeping allies requires care, consideration and mutual advantages.[17]

Section 2: The diplomatic effect of alliances

920 – In human society as in nature, the reality lies somewhere between the absolute autonomy of the individual and the complete cohesion of the systems.[18] An alliance is a form of the collaboration between sovereign States: it limits, but does not obliterate that sovereignty, in other words their fundamental freedom of choice. On the other hand, it helps them in their negotiations. (see *154, 281*)

Calling upon an ally must be an independent act.

921 – Taken as a whole, the alliance is destined to manoeuvre within the international environment as a function of the balance of the powers contained

---

16 H. A. KISSINGER: *The Troubled Partnership*, New York, McGraw Hill, 1965, I, p. 34.

17 '*Les allies ne se conservent qu'avec du soin, des égards et des avantages réciproques*', J. ORIEUX: *Talleyrand ou le Sphinx incompris*, Paris, Flammarion, p. 295.

18 L. de BROGLIE: *Continu et discontinu en physique moderne*, Paris, Albin Michel, 1941, p. 116.

within it: it is a result of negotiation at the same time as giving rise to it.[19] (see *1066*)

Community of interests and sometimes of destiny makes itself felt before and during a war as well as after the hostilities. A State harmed by such solidarity will necessarily seek to erode it. (see *2281*)

922 – Efforts were made in the United States to put forward a simplified doctrine of alliance, notably by the use of modelling techniques.[20] But, serious doubt can be expressed as to whether it is even possible to propound a general theory of alliances, especially in the light of the Atlantic experience.[21]

923 – No balance of power is ever established for all time: *no treaty is eternal, either in its initial concept or in its legal architecture*: did not France and England sign a 'perpetual peace' in 1518? (see *169*)

924 – Circumstances change and common dangers recede, and this removes the main justification for the mutual concessions that bring about an alliance. Established after the defeat of Napoleon in 1815, the 'Holy Alliance' fell into decline from the reign of Louis XVIII of France; the Allies of the First World War fell out during the negotiation of the Treaty of Versailles in 1919; and those of the Second World War grew apart once hostilities were over. (see *810*)

925 – Once an alliance is concluded, close relations should make it possible for surprises to be avoided. Each member must hold itself ready to fulfil its commitments, but should not let its partner have *carte blanche*: every form of support has to be negotiated.

Moreover, a degree of uncertainty about how the obligations under a pact are to be interpreted can serve to deter an enemy.

926 – Even the most perfect of organisations will be eroded by the passage of time; the tighter and more onerous the coalition, the more wearying the burden will become.

An alliance treaty will begin to produce effects that are counterproductive from the moment it proves its worth in warding off the danger that led to its creation. (see *799*)

927 – During hostilities, the entire foreign policy of the warring parties will be coloured by the commitments of solidarity they have made. At times of great danger, they prefer to use their diplomatic skills to recruit new members to their cause. (see *222*)

Sometimes, driven by weariness or fear of the enemy, one ally will negotiate in secret to stop the fighting or even denounce the pact: this is when the inevitable

---

19 H. GRANFELDT: *Alliances and Ententes as Political Weapons*, Bromma, Fahlbeck Foundation, 1970.
20 H. STARR: *War Coalitions*, New York, Lexington Books, 1972.
21 O. HOLSTI, P. HOPMANN, J. SULLIVAN: *Unity and Disintegration in International Alliances, a Comparative Study*, New York, Wiley, 1973.
   M. NAIDU: *Alliances and Balance of Powers*, New York, St. Martin's Press, 1974.

divergence in political objectives comes into the open. The abandonment of Czechoslovakia by its western allies at Munich in 1938 was done with no fighting, no glory and, ultimately, to no purpose in bringing about peace. (see *813, 840*)

928 – Conducted in secret, these direct conversations must of necessity be hurried: a party so exhausted that it is forced to negotiate with its adversary will no longer have the strength to confront its ally.

After his accession, Charles I of Austria made several unsuccessful attempts to put an end to the First World War or extricate his country from it: neither his sincerity nor the quality of his tactics were enough to overcome the coercion of the German alliance.[22]

§1. Alliances in negotiation

929 – The mutual engagements that flow from a treaty explain why no alliance can be open to the outside world. Its members are finite in number; the adhesion of a new partner can alter the internal balance of the mechanism or make it unexpectedly vulnerable, and this means that it requires the approval of all members. The enlargement of the Atlantic Alliance to include States from Central and Western Europe and the Baltic region was mainly diplomatic in nature (the mutual guarantee is that the zone is 'nuclear-free'). (see *916, 946, 1700, 2282, 2287*)

930 – The predominant role played by political and military considerations in commitments made between allies can mean that some pacts are mutually incompatible. The USSR denounced the Franco-Soviet treaty of 10 December 1944 when the former Federal Republic of Germany became part of the Atlantic Alliance in 1954.

Events themselves will put an end to contradictory commitments and bring priorities or preferences to light. Even during Bismarck's lifetime, and in spite of his ingenuity as a tactician, rivalry between the Austro-Hungarian Empire and Russia in the Balkans showed how artificial had been the system set up by the 'Agreement of the Three Emperors' by forcing Germany to choose between its two allies.

931 – The question especially arises when one power is faced with the need to transform, and constantly adapt, its various local commitments into a group strategy.[23] Not only might there be contradictions between different pacts, but it might also be impossible to give effect to guarantees, either because the means are lacking or because of divergence between the clauses that trigger the obligation to provide assistance. Too many alliances will make all the partners vulnerable. (see *967, 2338*)

932 – Exclusive groupings, which alliances put on a formal footing, have the effect of compartmentalising the diplomatic terrain. The coming together of the

22 G. PEDRONCINI: *Les Négociations secrètes pendant la Grande Guerre*, Paris, Flammarion, 1969.
23 H. J. MORGENTHAU: 'Alliances in Theory and Practice', in *Alliance Policy in the Cold War*, Baltimore, Johns Hopkins Press, 1959.

European powers had a compensatory effect, but this was neutralised by the end of the nineteenth century by nations forming themselves into rigid blocs. Paralysis in the evolution necessary to maintain the balance of power is often attributable to an excess of formal legal structure. (see *2287*)

933 – The temptation to oversimplify the political scene should be avoided. Newcomers have no desire to take up the quarrels of others and, in principle, will not agree to be bound by commitments undertaken before they were in a position to express their own wishes.

934 – When governments want to recover their freedom to act and react, everything they do will tend to weaken the cohesion and alignment of monolithic groupings in an effort to free themselves from external constraints which serve no further purpose or have come to present a danger.

935 – However, when an alliance is broad or powerful, States that have not become part of it can find themselves bound by the limitations it imposes. (see *314*)

936 – When a nation feels isolated, or senses that it stands alone, this can threaten international relations: alliances generally serve to give them structure. Far from compromising the security of third States, under constant threat of falling prey to the ambitions of others, they in fact bolster it. The sum total of the various relations between States has the effect of preserving the overall status quo.[24]

937 – Even the greatest of enemies can have an interest in stabilising the international environment, either because they fear falling victim to potentially unfavourable developments or because they wish to take time to plan a manoeuvre to be put into effect when the time is right. Their converging efforts can stifle the stray impulses of their allies towards independent action and avert the dangers of confusion. This could be seen at work at the time of the opposition between the Atlantic Alliance and the Warsaw Pact. (see *822*)

938 – An alliance can only fulfil this role, however, in pursuance of a strategy – a single strategy, common to all the members. Alliances beset by internal contradictions merely cancel each other out. Even in ancient times, Philip of Macedonia regulated the relations between the cities of Greece in order to bind them into his Pan-Hellenic policy. (see *1527, 2325*)

An increase in military force is only meaningful if it serves a policy accepted by all the allies.

939 – Alliances have no absolute virtues.[25] Where they are ill-conceived, they can be a fresh source of vulnerability. It is dangerous to become the ally of nations engaged in too many quarrels.

Some alliances set limits in advance to the scope of their actions: this precaution has led to the Atlantic Alliance being vulnerable in those parts of the

---

24 C. von CLAUSEWITZ: *On War*, VI, chapter 6.
25 '*Les alliances n'ont pas de vertus absolues*', C. de GAULLE: 'Conférence de presse du 14 janvier 1963', in *Discours et messages*, IV.

world where the treaty does not allow it to take the initiative but where some of its members wish to use it as an instrument of political stability and military security (several member States of the OSCE are in Asia). (see *1241*)

940 – It is extremely difficult to identify in advance the weaknesses of a future ally; these will be all the more serious for being unpredictable and thus unexpected. The internal equilibrium of the pact will compensate for some of them where external threats are concerned. Sometimes, though, far from cancelling each other out, weaknesses merely multiply.

941 – An attack can overthrow an ally and throw into disarray the balance of power that had been built on its cooperation. *Thus no great power should be without the means to execute its policies in the event of one or other of its allies no longer being there.*

942 – One of the objects of a manoeuvre could be to strike at the dominant power through its ally: many countries have been led in this way into wars that were unplanned, badly timed, unpopular and disastrous.

943 – However formal or finely tuned the alliance, its effects will always be less than perfect: there is no such thing between nations as a perpetual, total and absolute guarantee. As La Fontaine's fable says, 'No treaty on this earth could make a cat be grateful.'[26] (see *799*)

944 – Even where the pact lays down the conditions in which it will come into play, and the territories it covers (which can sometimes be those of third States), allies are forced by the growing difficulty of limiting open, albeit localised, consequences to keep up a constant negotiation as to the scope and effects of their commitments. The parties may have made provisions in the event of attack, but they will not always have clearly defined what constitutes a threat, or stipulated the conditions it must fulfil to trigger their obligation of mutual assistance.

945 – The obligations in an alliance are, moreover, frequently cast or expressed in conditional terms, either because of the geographical distance between them, or through military precaution, or because of a combination of other, inconsistent, commitments entered into in other quarters. By contrast with the North Atlantic Pact, the Brussels Treaty of 1948, amended by the Paris Treaty of 1954, contains a clause (Article 5) providing for automatic mutual assistance between the countries of Western Europe. Such a stipulation – especially one signed by the United Kingdom – is rare.
Even an automatic guarantee presupposes negotiation to secure the consent of the party being assisted before it can be implemented.[27]

946 – An alliance is normally a manifestation of policy, so it is only to be expected that those members that derive the greatest benefit from it do what they can to ensure their continued protection, beyond what the treaties require. (see *824*)

---

26 'Aucun traité peut-il forcer un chat à la reconnaissance?' J. de la FONTAINE, *Le Chat et le Rat*, translation by Craig Hill, *Beasts and Citizens*.
27 J. VIGNES: 'La place des pactes de défense dans la société internationale actuelle', *AFDI*, 1959, p. 37.

The disappearance of the threat of confrontation in Europe has deprived the Atlantic system of its strategic purpose. In order to keep the organisation in being, and because it suited the dominant power to do so for its own purposes, the Alliance went so far as to invite its former antagonists, including Russia, to participate.

The Founding Act on Mutual Relations, Cooperation and Security between NATO and the Russian Federation, signed in Paris on 27 May 1997, marked at the same time their mutual recognition and strategic complicity.[28] Russia is back on the joint permanent council, and 26 European States are now involved in this rapprochement, the most recent, as of 2004, being the three Baltic States, Romania and Bulgaria. (see *916, 977, 1735*)

After fifty years, the Atlantic Alliance has, since the Washington Council of NATO in 1999, become a sort of collective security pact the effects of which could extend over all possible flashpoint areas, including Asia, if so required by the UN Security Council, following the Balkan model. (see *1700*)

947 – It takes an irrevocable act or position to make a State subject to an alliance. On 5 September 1914, the three States in the Entente between Britain, France and Russia undertook not to conclude a separate peace with the central Empires: this precaution was rendered useless in the face of the Russian Revolution or the breach of political solidarity that went with it. (see *837*)

948 – The restraints imposed by pacts can sometimes mean that they are ill-adapted to a new situation. If they are not reviewed, the partners will start making their own alternative plans.

In times of trouble, the statesman monitors what his allies are doing. It is often when he needs them most that they will be most tempted to invoke a reservation or avoid their obligations. If the pact breaks down, the last in the fight will be the one that suffers.

949 – Thucydides wrote that fear of the consequences of breakdown is one of the things that binds alliances together: the allies of Alexander, Caesar and Napoleon were held to their agreements by fear.

950 – *A State against which a coalition is formed must adopt the tactic of doing, and saying, nothing that might consolidate it*; it must not only refrain from any action that might have the effect of bringing the members closer, but – especially if it intends to attack – also do whatever it can to undermine and obstruct the solidarity between them. (see *884*)

951 – One good tactic is to approach the minor players to obtain information from them about the intentions of the main adversary and also to instil doubt, concern or envy in them. It is sometimes easy to prove to one of the partners that it cannot count on the others, especially if it is a small country and easily discouraged.

953 – In the end, one can never 'rely in any degree on alliances formed through necessity'.[29] Nothing could stop Austria from abandoning the French camp in

28 F. GAUTIER: 'Accords et engagements politiques en droit des gens', *AFDI*, 1997, p. 82.
29 '*S'assurer sur l'alliance qu'a faite la nécessité*', J. de la FONTAINE: *Le Chat et le Rat*, Fables, 1688–1993 and translation by Craig Hill, *Beasts and Citizens*, Concord, Mass., Palm Press, 2003.

stages that coincided with growing doubts on the part of Metternich about Napoleon's chances: under cover of third party intervention and with financial backing from England, it managed to pass from one camp to the other in the space of a few months. (see *466*)

954 – Where possible, an alliance is more swiftly overturned if this causes damage to a powerful member: it is less dangerous, and more profitable, to protect a weak State whose very existence is threatened than to join forces with a large State whose adversary is winning.

955 – *No legal provision will ever prevent a State from defending its vital interests from anyone that threatens them, if it senses that it is in a position to obtain a favourable outcome.* This is why alliances fluctuate and why their composition inevitably varies with the balance of power. (see *415*)

956 – In the final analysis, for strategy, the configuration produced by an alliance, unless it is the object of constant monitoring, is scarcely less changeable than would emerge from a straightforward coalition, except where the effect is one of hegemony.

§2. Negotiation within the alliance

957 – Frederick II of Prussia observed that events would decide which of the allies would reap the rewards of the alliance.[30] Each of them hopes for some advantage, as it is difficult for a State to subordinate its vital interests to those of another or of a collective grouping.

No alliance can respond to all of the objectives and concerns of all its members: sooner or later, their interests and wishes will start to diverge.[31] (see *823*)

958 – Some disagreements can and should be overcome. As Anthony Eden, who was for years in charge of Britain's foreign affairs, remarked, if allies took concerted action only when they all held identical points of view, the very notion of alliances would be meaningless.

959 – An alliance is not a stable, homogeneous or hierarchical grouping because each of its members retains its own personality, and so it is up to those who decide on its strategy to bear in mind what Henry Kissinger described as the acceptable margin of disagreement. *The understanding must be sufficiently close to maintaining a constant flow of consultation: alliances should be put to good use.* (see *800*)

960 – Steps need to be taken in good time to avoid the partners becoming estranged, their deepest aspirations coming into conflict or their needs or interests diverging. The more broadly based the alliance the greater these risks will be: there

---

30 'L'événement décide lequel des alliés retire les fruits de l'alliance', in L'Anti-Machiavel, Chapter 26.
31 H. A. KISSINGER: *The Troubled Partnership*, New York, McGraw Hill, 1965.

will be a wide variety of threats to confront and concerns to reconcile, not always easily. But, where an ally takes independent action this can serve to validate its commitment under pressure.

961 – The broader the alliance, the more diverse the motives for joining it, the more unpredictable its members' reactions and the easier it is to uncover their secrets. It is therefore strongly advisable for members to consult each other continuously. This is a way of heading off differences of view, remaining vigilant about the dangers of infiltration and making plans of attack or counterattack. (see *799*)

962 – The closer the risk of conflict, the more allies must favour political consensus over military manoeuvre. Fear of the ill-considered act or the *fait accompli* generates a climate of distrust that is not conducive to effective deterrence or counterattack. The divergences that appeared within Europe during the war in Iraq in 2003–2004 revealed the lack of political cohesion within the European Union as well as the Atlantic Alliance centred around the United States, despite the existence of active institutional structures. (see *93*)

963 – As long as the events that triggered the alliance do not amount to an emergency, its members will discuss its disadvantages. Their obvious preference is for burdens and responsibilities to be shared equally. Still, it is necessary for the partners to agree on a common, albeit often sensitive, reading of the state of the international environment: every alliance must make use of the communication between its members.

964 – Though it cannot allay the concerns of nations and prevent them competing with each other, an alliance can sometimes provide a closed environment in which they can compete, disagree or even come into conflict. Hostilities can go as far as open combat or the threat of war: a situation of this kind was provoked between Greece and Turkey by the events in Cyprus, despite both of them being members of the Atlantic Alliance. (see *408*)

965 – Where there are opposing interests within the same camp, this can spoil an entire negotiation: the disputes that led up to the conclusion of the Treaty of Versailles in 1919, which proved difficult to resolve, were disputes between allies.

Many alliances oblige their members to agree to the peaceful settlement of internal disputes. Article 8 of the Brussels Treaty of 17 March 1948, amended on 23 October 1954, makes a distinction for this purpose between legal disputes and political disagreements.

966 – The role of negotiation is to maintain overall harmony while, at the same time, ensuring that the diversity of the parties is respected, that the members' efforts are channelled in the same direction to face a perceived common threat and also that the alliance itself is able to respond to a sudden common danger while leaving each member free to address its own individual needs.[32]

---

32 H. A. KISSINGER: *The Troubled Partnership*, New York, McGraw Hill, 1965.

967 – The institutional framework of an alliance must provide facilities for the resolution of internal disputes: however, the more widely spread the alliance, the heavier, slower and more inefficient these procedures risk becoming. Thus, some partners, perhaps at the request of one of them, will prefer to consult together and reach a decision on their own, rather than risk a conflict that could lead to the break-up of the alliance as a whole.

968 – When mutual trust evaporates and policies no longer converge, even an internationally dominant alliance will be undermined. The negotiators must overcome disaffection and disagreements and the 'wise men' now frequently called upon in major international fora, may be on hand to propose goals and ways of adapting.

969 – A State that attempts to dissolve the pact or weaken the commitments undertaken will choose the course of obstruction as long as it does not have to confront its partners but can still count on their support. It plays upon any divergences and may even provoke them in order to increase its own freedom of manoeuvre without breaking up the pact.

In an alliance, reservation is a sign of impending flight or default.

970 – Although this need will be eroded by familiarity, one of the objects and purposes of an alliance must still be to improve the conditions under which the partners can negotiate, and to make it permanent if not actually institutional. There will always be the risk that potentially opposed interests may jeopardise the understanding, and the longer this opposition continues, the worse that risk becomes.

971 – The recalcitrant ally has always been difficult to deal with. This is more than ever true under the nuclear umbrella. It requires powers of coercion amounting to supremacy to go as far as the military invasion of Czechoslovakia in 1968. Once sanctions are imposed, opposition to them will stiffen. It is important not to offend national pride when appealing to public or media opinion.

Within an unequal alliance, war becomes a means of keeping order.

972 – Power can only be seen to be real if it is put to the test. Only then will it become clear which parties determine how the pact is to be applied or what the fate of the alliance is to be, and they are the ones that will decide when to attack and at what point deterrence must give way to counterattack. *No dominant State will allow a commitment to be fulfilled automatically or accept its allies' attempts at autonomous action.* But the very fact of its protection might lead one of them into acts of rashness or provocation, or 'moral hazard'. (see *345, 1760*)

973 – Alliances sometimes have to take straightforward and rapid action. The consultation and involvement of too many players can delay or paralyse action at the very moment when it is most needed. The longer it takes and the more ponderous the processes to produce collective action, the more compromised its ability to respond to the urgent needs of its members: efforts to avoid inequality can, if badly handled, lead to ineffectiveness.

974 – Concentrating the decisions and powers in the hands of the most powerful ally produces disquiet and misunderstandings, and deprives its dealings with others

of much of their effect. In ancient times, the dismissive attitude of Athens towards the Ionian cities under its sway caused it to be isolated and ultimately to lose.

975 – The dominant power finds it easy to put aside the procedures and constraints of diplomacy as soon as equality and reciprocity in relations between independent sovereign States cease to be of real concern. It imposes its own interpretation of the pact, and fails to adapt to pursue the ends and means of the alliance.[33]

The United States succeeded in having most of the financial burden of their intervention in Iraq in 1991, as well as part of the burden of the military presence there in 2003–2004, borne by their allies.

976 – There exists an internal diplomacy within alliances tending to turn each one into a disciplined and balanced system. This ensures in particular that timely account is taken of the concerns of those members not in a position to insist, and that restraints are placed on those inclined to take excessive liberties where their commitments are concerned.

Preparing for the unforeseeable often means increasing one's influence before the event occurs.[34] (see **2295**)

977 – Within an alliance, each sovereign State is responsible for weighing up its own interests and also pursuing them. The legal framework thus needs to be sufficiently flexible to allow for changes, even at the risk of ambiguity. The greater the number of partners, the less lasting will be a rigid and restrictive alliance, by contrast with one that is pragmatic and flexible. The enlargement of the Atlantic Alliance in 2004 to include seven countries from Eastern Europe and, especially, the three Baltic States, where there are large Russian minorities, might serve to weaken the alliance as a whole. (see **946, 2797**)

On the other hand, alliance permits responsibilities to be shared if not actually diluted: many interventions in times of crisis are undertaken by multinational forces, such as those of the United Nations or NATO (the Berlin negotiation of 1996 was one example). (see **1599, 1723, 1725**)

978 – The desired objective will determine the manoeuvre. This might take the form of stabilising interests and forces rather than achieving the sudden and short-lived supremacy of the coalition in a confrontation.

Within the legal framework of the European Union, in order to confront certain crisis situations, some of the members behave as if they were part of an alliance. The first intervention, in Bosnia in January 2003, was a civil policing operation, and this was followed by a political intervention by a contingent drawn from thirty countries, acting on a mandate from the United Nations, in the Republic of Macedonia in March of the same year. Then, in June 2003, at the request of the Security Council, a military operation, Artemis, in the Democratic Republic of Congo, paved the way for a later UN deployment. These operations were negotiated in close liaison with NATO. (see **1493, 1359**)

33 H. NICOLSON: *The Evolution of Diplomatic Methods*, London, New York, MacMillan, 1954.
34 H. A. KISSINGER: *The Troubled Partnership*, New York, McGraw Hill, 1965.

979 – Only negotiation allows internal crises to be avoided or resolved. This sometimes calls for great firmness, where one power wishes to avoid being drawn by one of its allies into commitments beyond those it has agreed to make. Each one must discipline its own allies, and not allow third parties to become involved.

980 – Just as the alliance carries out its manoeuvres on the international plane, the sub-groups that can form within a multipartite alliance will have their own dynamic. Even when they respect the overall strategy, their objectives can compromise it, and competition between them can undermine commonly agreed tactics, especially when these are not respected.

981 – It can be a matter of concern for the powers to see smaller groupings springing up within their alliance, especially where they have no control over them. The United States wanted to have decisions taken by the Western European countries within the European Communities subjected first of all to Atlantic-wide coordination, but this proved unacceptable, and all the Europeans would agree to was a regular exchange of information (see the Ottawa Declaration of 18 June 1974). The 2003 Iraq war revealed that real conflicts existed between the strategies of the European members of the Atlantic Alliance. (see *1244*)

982 – Fear of internal disputes or break-up leads the dominant State to take an interest in its partners' regimes and political leaders, and sometimes intervene in their domestic affairs: the reason given by the Warsaw Pact for expelling the Czechoslovak leaders in 1968 was that they posed a threat to the general interests of the socialist community. The Pact itself was dissolved in 1990. (see *641*)

983 – Not only can an alliance not hope to eliminate negotiations between its members, but it provides them with a favourable setting and invests them with increased importance. *Having started out as a way of provoking cooperation among the partners, an alliance can sometimes undergo what looks to its leaders like a process of integration*: in order to be successful in military and diplomatic terms, it must extend over other sectors as well.

984 – It is therefore no bad thing for treaties to contain clauses regulating negotiations between the signatory States, either through consultation procedures or implementing mechanisms, or even by setting up multilateral machinery for administration and cooperation. In the case of a collective alliance, it may have a permanent management body.

985 – Negotiation is thus, at any rate partially and progressively, giving ground to a command structure. This, at the time, was how the Atlantic Alliance grew up in the face of increasing danger, because it was not thought possible for fifteen or so States to defend themselves on such an extensive front without coordinating their resources and policies. (see *1631*)

986 – It should be remembered that, from 1912, the growth of German power forced France and Britain to strengthen their practical ties and seek to protect their *entente* against the caprices of the cabinet or the majority. Headquarters agreements were signed to reinforce the existing diplomatic cooperation, aimed at sharing the responsibilities and costs of the common defence effort.

987 – Modern military alliances go as far as the integration of their members' armed forces into compact units, and the alignment of their diplomatic and economic strategies: they seek to address all the problems associated with the pooling of resources necessary to achieve their common strategic potential. (see *1630*)

However, the breaking up in 1990 of the Warsaw Pact signed in 1955 meant that Central and Western Europe were no longer alienated from each other, which brought with it a new sense of negotiating freedom for the countries in those regions. (see *916*)

The question remains whether the Community of Independent States that took the place of the USSR is really an alliance: it does have a collective security agreement (signed at the Tashkent conference on 15 May 1992), though its member States – Russia, Byelorussia, Armenia, Azerbaijan, Georgia, Kazakhstan, Kirghizstan, Uzbekistan and Tadjikistan – are not clearly listed, and a united army. (see *1785*)

988 – Strategic planning is designed to deal with emergencies, and is dependent on the will of whoever has the power to attack or counterattack if it is to work, though all parties to the coalition must contribute resources. It therefore increases the gulf between the risks minor powers take, for example, in harbouring another State's armies and weapons, and the advantages they stand to gain from being part of a common defence system.

989 – The Atlantic Alliance has set up systems for coordination. Its policy direction is fixed by unanimous agreement by a council of delegates from all the member States. This council, normally made up of permanent representatives (since the Council of Ministers held in Lisbon in 1962), has adopted the methods of work and decision-making of an international organisation, but remains a diplomatic institution. This is in contrast with the strategic command and also the armed forces and civil administration, which make up a vast hierarchical international structure, with its own legal personality since 1950, and which depends on having a permanent, integrated headquarters. (see *1514*)

990 – The inequality of forces, the weight of the machinery and the differences in strategic concerns have led some powers to reserve the most important negotiations, if not the actual decision-making power, to themselves, in spite of the misgivings of the others. *An alliance becomes an instrument of strategy: the balance of power and will within it determines which State will benefit most.* (see *126*)

Chapter II:
Conferences and Organisations

991 – Since the end of the Second World War, interactions between States, groups of States and also private sector companies have multiplied, becoming more complex and long lasting. Multilateralism in international relations, in a variety of forms, continues to grow. It calls for tactics suited to balances of power and combinations of interests that are both less stable, and more nuanced and unpredictable, than those found in bilateral negotiation. (see *1062*)

992 – The international environment is becoming richer and denser. This requires an effort on the part of States to create structures and norms to keep it from breaking down, and fulfil its needs for dialogue and solidarity. Without abandoning the ways and means of traditional diplomacy, modern society is fashioning the instruments it needs for its own administration and development.

993 – These new methods of negotiation have gradually come to be used in multiple international meetings, some of which address immediate needs while others take a more lasting form. The forces, influences and interests at work are many and varied, and the political will that develops not only encompasses but also transcends the will of any one of them.[1] (see *2489*)

994 – Within these constantly evolving patterns, it is not easy to draw a distinction, where negotiation is concerned, between multilateral conferences and international organisations. *Conferences often give birth to institutions and rules; on the other hand, negotiation within organisations generally takes place through conferences.* All of these serve to provoke, stimulate and regulate the dialogue between States, opening up new possibilities and new opportunities. All forms of dialogue are increasing in importance as instruments of policy, diplomacy, finance and administration.

995 – Conferences and organisations also become the focus of negotiations in order to solve their own internal problems and adapt their role to the international environment. Two constraints reduce their effectiveness: they must overcome not only the reserve and slowness that typify international negotiations, but also the weight and inertia of machinery that is becoming ever more structured and complex.

---

1 E. SATOW: *A Guide to Diplomatic Practice*, London, Longmans Green, 1917; *International Congresses*, London, HMSO, 1920. J. KAUFMANN: *Conference Diplomacy*, Leiden, Sijthoff, 1988.

996 – The international organisation has itself become a negotiating objective for those who see the future of the global community as one of increasing interdependence, if not the beginnings of a kind of integration, as in Europe.[2] As international dialogue brings out the common interests between nations, whether these are similar or complementary, this dialogue itself will be reinforced.[3]

997 – The main consequence of this evolution is that the number of international institutions, intergovernmental or otherwise, has multiplied. The proliferation of negotiations taking place within these organisations has had the dual effect of multiplying and diversifying their structures and creating innumerable working units. (see *1103, 1993*)

Section 1: Multipartite conferences

998 – Since time immemorial, the representatives of sovereigns or powers have met to discuss matters of common interest in order to agree, if possible, on common positions. The widening of the circle of nations, the growth in transnational activities and ease of travel provide more opportunities than ever for such meetings, official or not.

999 – From the Peace of Westphalia in 1648 onwards, many congresses or conferences have been organised in order to resolve disputes between princes or nations.[4] These disputes have sometimes degenerated into overt hostilities: what matters then is to succeed where force of arms has failed, to gain time or even embark upon peace initiatives. Often, the objective is to prevent opposing interests from escalating, especially where the countries threatened do not want war. The initiative for a meeting can also come from a State wishing to establish its influence by interfering in a discussion between other parties. (see *63, 452*)

1000 – It should be possible to differentiate between diplomatic conferences according to their subject matter, their participants, the occasion on which they are held, their procedure and the consequences they produce: seventy-five different types of meetings have been identified, some not official and some involving representatives of administrative and semi-public, or private, entities.[5]

1001 – Great political conferences are characteristic of what has been called the new diplomacy,[6] summit diplomacy in particular,[7] in other words, negotiation that

---

2 D. MITRANY: *A Working Peace System*, London, Oxford University Press, 1943 and 1966. K. W. DEUTSCH: *The Analysis of International Relations*, Englewood Cliffs, Prentice Hall, 1978.
3 F. C. IKLE: *How Nations Negotiate*, New York, Harper Row, 1964.
4 E. de VATTEL: *Le Droit des Gens*, London, 1758, II, XVII, §330.
5 E. PLISCHKE: *International Conferencing and the Summit: Macro-Analysis of Presidential Participation*, Philadelphia, Orbis, 1970, p. 674.
6 S. D. KERTESZ, M. A. FITZSIMONS, etc.: Diplomacy in a Changing World, Notre Dame University Press, 1959.
7 S. D. KERTESZ: 'Summit and Personal Diplomacy', in *The Quest for Peace Through Diplomacy*, Englewood Cliffs, Prentice Hall, 1967.

takes place between those with supreme political authority. Their multiplication is especially notable in the United States, whose Presidents, starting with F. D. Roosevelt,[8] have personally taken part in an increasing number of bilateral and multilateral encounters of this kind. But any study of this form of negotiation must distinguish between multilateral dialogue and the mere continuation of traditional bilateral relations between sovereign States. (see *705, 2189, 2485*)

1002 – Before the League of Nations existed, the beginnings of a system of international organisation[9] dominated by the major European powers could already be seen in the 'European concert'. This informal, flexible organisation proceeded mainly on the basis of conferences of plenipotentiaries at which the unilateral actions of each power were either contained or endorsed by the others. It did, however, lead to self-discipline, constant monitoring of the field of manoeuvre and pressure on third parties, those smaller countries whose freedom of action was thereby limited but which were assured of protection. (see *149*)

1003 – Since the beginning of the nineteenth century, major negotiations between sovereign powers have been carried on in multilateral diplomatic meetings.[10] The procedures of conferences of plenipotentiaries have been used to harmonise political strategies (the Berlin conference in 1885 and the Yalta and Potsdam conferences of 1944 and 1945 respectively are examples), to draw up peace treaties (as in the Peace Conferences in France after the First World War), to set up international organisations (the San Francisco Conference of 1945 where the UN Charter was adopted), and lay down a variety of new rules of international law (the Paris Congress of 1856 and the Peace Conferences at The Hague in 1899 and 1907).

1004 – This method is also used to verify the implementation of major multipartite conventions; one such case was the Helsinki Agreements on Security and Cooperation in Europe.

The Conference for Security and Cooperation in Europe offers a good example of the tendency international initiatives have of prolonging their own existence and forming themselves into structures: the Paris Charter of 21 November 1990 set up bodies and mechanisms that became obsolete, in part, with the dislocation of some of the States of Europe and the USSR. The partners never reached agreement, however, on the practical role the institution might play in major crises in Europe. (see *1122, 1241, 1700, 1793*)

1005 – These political encounters have been supplemented by the current practice of convening meetings in order to standardise regulations and custom (examples are the Conference on the Codification of International Law in the Hague in 1950 and the Conference on the Law of the Sea that began in 1972 and ended in 1982 at Montego Bay), regulate sectors of activity or set up institutions for the

---

8 M. P. HANKEY: *Diplomacy by Conference*, London, Benn, 1946.
9 S. HOFFMANN: *Organisations internationales et pouvoirs politiques des Etats*, Paris, Colin, 1954.
10 R. GENET: *Traité de diplomatie et de droit diplomatique*, Paris, Pedone, 1932, III.

development of cooperation between States at global level or within certain continents such as Europe or the Americas. (see *1596*)

1006 – Whereas, originally, technical conferences were used as a way of satisfying the desire to facilitate all kinds of communication between countries and continents as they freed themselves from the excessive constraints of traditional frontiers, they later became increasingly frequent in various sectors where the need arose for longer-term cooperation between national administrations. *Major conferences today require months or even years of preparation and their participants can number hundreds or thousands.* (see *2056*)

1007 – The techniques used in institutional conferences have progressively moved away from those of formal diplomatic congresses, and they now include a new normative power that plays an important constituent role.

Certain negotiations, especially those concerning networks (telephone or data transfer, for example) can only be concluded on a multilateral basis. (see *1834, 1968*)

International law in these areas is under radical development through a variety of technical conferences.

1008 – Among the various possible classifications, the most useful for the purposes of negotiation draws a distinction between conferences of plenipotentiaries deliberating on behalf of their governments, drawing up diplomatic instruments or managing an international institution, and administrative or technical sessions limited to working towards the harmonisation of the positions of the States represented, based perhaps on expertise, proposals from delegates, or the legal, economic or scientific studies that are often carried out by international secretariats. (see *690*)

1009 – The rules of UNESCO, for instance, make this distinction between meetings of a representative nature attended by delegates of governments or international organisations (which may even be non-governmental), and non-representative meetings such as congresses, consultative committees, meetings of experts and colloquia. (see *692*)

1010 – Even when they are official, conferences attended by representatives who do not have powers can serve only to produce reports or drafts for submission to the governments concerned, since their members do not have the capacity to enter into agreements; even so, they still often fulfil a real political function by providing a forum for preparatory negotiations to take place.

1011 – International negotiation adapts quite naturally to the changing form and nature of relations between governments: negotiation is the key to the preparation of meetings of a highly technical nature, as well as being essential to the success of the most important assemblies of plenipotentiaries, political leaders or diplomats.

§1. Preliminary negotiations

1012 – Leaving aside the rare cases where one power is compelled by some clear overriding necessity to issue an urgent collective invitation, convening an international conference requires a number of preliminary issues to be addressed, mainly having to do with the participants, the subject matter, the venue, the timing and the procedure of the meeting.

These preliminaries are usually the subject of bilateral negotiations, since the prior agreement of the governments concerned is the condition of their attending the conference. (see *1557*)

1013 – Whether a meeting is convened by one State or more, the participants must agree on its subject: thus, even setting the working agenda will require sometimes sensitive discussions enabling the relative strength of the parties, the items in dispute and potentially useful approaches to be considered.[11] No conference, according to Harold Nicolson, should be organised without the participants first agreeing on its scope and on the programme, and seeking assurances, initially by ordinary diplomatic channels, that their respective points of view are not totally irreconcilable.[12] Preparation contributes to the success of a meeting, and it must therefore take account of problems of substance.[13]

In too many meetings, the agendas are vague, composite and interminable, and this undermines their effectiveness. (see *2220*)

1014 – Principles agreed upon at the start of a conference may be adjusted along the way, but the procedures for doing this go further than those of traditional bilateral negotiation, as they involve securing the agreement of all the participants. The desired result can be achieved by oblique approaches and parallel conversations.

Diplomatic discussions may take place between some of the participants outside the official sessions to adjust the direction or the pace of the collective effort.

1015 – The preparations for a meeting determine not only the agreement of the States it brings together, but also the quality and the speed of the work achieved. In principle, the conference can determine its own ways of working, but it is helpful if the main procedural issues can be dealt with before the official sessions begin, either by preliminary conversations, exchanges of notes or restricted meetings, since these are crucial to the successful conduct of the meeting, even in the eyes of the public at large. *Many preparatory measures go beyond their apparent purpose: reaching majority agreement on the rules anticipates decisions on the substantive issues.*

1016 – Since the days of the League of Nations, part of the mission of certain international organisations has been to prepare for, convene or arrange for the convening of intergovernmental conferences on matters within the scope of their competence (see Article 62 of the UN Charter: Economic and Social Council), and even to establish the list of States that will be invited to take part.[14] The advantage

11 J. de BOURBON-BUSSET: *La Grande Conférence*, Paris, Gallimard, 1963, p. 49.
12 H. NICOLSON: *Diplomacy*, Oxford University Press, 1945, Chapter 7.
13 H. A. KISSINGER: *The White House Years*, Boston, Little, Brown, 1979.
14 UN: *Répertoire de la pratique suivie par les organes des Nations Unies*, New York, UN, III, p. 209.

of this procedure is that it paves the way for major developments in multilateral law-making negotiation, without this having to be preceded by the formalism of traditional diplomacy with its bias towards unanimity: the organs of the institution will, by consensus if need be, resolve issues about the procedure, agenda and participation, and formulate the internal regulations permitting the work of the meeting and its voting to go forward. (see *1127*)

1017 – In general, therefore, it is the head of the institution who is responsible not only for preliminary studies and tasks, but also for making certain political approaches. This practice contributes to the growing influence of international secretariats in the field of law-making negotiations. (see *1558*)

1018 – Decisions as to which powers should be represented at an international conference are taken on the basis of criteria and methods that vary considerably: there is no obligation to include all States having an interest in the outcome of the issues under discussion.[15] Sometimes the list is drawn up on the initiative of one or more of the powers issuing the invitation, which can resolve any disagreements among themselves. At the other end of the scale it can be highly flexible, even to the point of extreme vagueness, in cases where the meeting is organised by an international secretariat. (see *603, 753, 1515*)

1019 – Major international conferences reflect the inequality between powers: the States most frequently represented are those whose participation is necessary to resolve the issues in hand. Diplomacy must remain flexible here, while complying with precedents and procedures. *The very presence of a State at important political meetings can itself be the object of intense negotiation involving considerations of interest, prestige and effectiveness* (the expansion of the G4 countries to the G8 or G9 is a case in point). When France invited the German Princes to the Congress of Munster that brought about the Peace of Westphalia, in 1648, it did so in order to maintain the divisions within the Romano-German Empire.

1020 – A multilateral conference can be opened to third States or international organisations that will have no part in the final decision. Associate or observer status allows them to stay informed and perhaps to state their views, but not to take part in the decision.[16] (see *755*)

1021 – A conference can allow for non-participating States to adhere at a later date, as the negotiation may have suffered from their absence. The trend is towards increasing numbers of States being represented at international conferences. (see *1605*)

1022 – When a negotiation becomes multilateral or global, this can lead some powers with widespread interests to expect to be able to intervene at a later date

15 P. CAHIER: *Le Droit diplomatique contemporain*, Geneva, Droz, 1962, p. 380.
16 UN: *Répertoire de la pratique suivie by les organs des Nations unies*, New York, UN, I, p. 699 and III, p. 591. R. GENET: *Traité de diplomatie et de droit diplomatique*, Paris, Pedone, 1932, I, p. 97 and III, p. 160.

in discussions held to review the commitments that have been made. After the Second World War, the opposition of the Western co-signatories paralysed Russia's attempts to force Norway to accept modifications to the legal regime of the Barendts Sea.

1023 – On the other hand, not being invited to a conference can mean losing control of a negotiation, at least in its preparatory phases. Not only is the State concerned deprived of knowledge of some of the relevant facts, but it is also faced with the threat of not featuring among the authors, signatories or beneficiaries of the final arrangement.

1024 – The choice of venue for an international conference is not immune from political considerations. This is sometimes an expression of respect for the dominant power (the United Nations and the Atlantic Alliance were created in the United States, in 1945 and 1948 respectively, and it was also the setting for the Camp David Conference on the Middle East and the Dayton Conference on Bosnia, among others), or it may simply set the seal on that State's diplomatic and moral receptiveness. There are times, by contrast, when it is based on considerations of neutrality, or the absence of any commitments or interests on the part of the host country: many meetings are held in Switzerland for this reason. Another factor is geography: poles of diplomatic activity exist such as Paris, London and New York. (see *560*)

1025 – Holding an international conference on one's territory means that a State has to issue invitations, and thus take a view as to who should and should not be there. It also provides an opportunity for each participant to have its favoured interlocutor present, as General de Gaulle did during the short-lived Conference of Four (France, the United States, Great Britain and the USSR), held at the Elysée Palace in May 1960. Moreover, secretariats are often recruited on the spot, which can itself affect the drafting and distribution of working documents and draft agreements. (see *1037*)

§2. Multilateral participation

1026 – It is characteristic of the international conference that it has completely transformed the traditional methods used in negotiation. Not only have information and communications networks grown up as part of it, but an independent system has established itself with its own rules on protocol, the use of languages and the procedure for deliberations, decisions and voting. (see *2284*)

1027 – In practice, as a result of the conditions in which they function, international conferences have evolved into organised bodies with their own complex balance of power and ways of resolving differences, producing opposition or coalition depending on the number of parties represented and their strategy.[17] (see *1519*)

---

17 M. SIBERT: 'Quelques aspects de l'organisation et de la technique des conférences internationales', *RCADI*, 1934, II, p. 389. E. SATOW: *A Guide to Diplomatic Practice*, London, Longman Green, 1958, p. 303.

Negotiating procedure

1028 – Within a conference, what determines the strategy of each negotiator is not simple antagonism, bilateral exchanges or systematic polarisation, but a pattern of manoeuvres made for complex reasons, played out within the framework of the meeting and following its particular procedures. (see *154*)

1029 – This explains why delegates pay so much attention to every aspect of the conditions under which they find themselves working. Choices which appear to be of secondary importance, such as which plenipotentiaries to admit, the order in which the business will be dealt with, how certain procedures are applied, the setting up of working, studying or drafting groups and the way voting is handled, can affect the outcome of the negotiation. Internal rules, and the customs engendered by their practice, make negotiations between governments subject to collective disciplines designed to ensure that they produce coherent results.[18]

1030 – This also accounts for the attention devoted to the agenda of the meeting: a discussion about this will often provide a first indication of national positions. The same goes for the seating arrangements at the negotiating table, which has been the subject of long and difficult discussions.

To give the representative a seat is to recognise the authority that mandates him.

1031 – The rules that govern the conduct of international conferences tend either to preserve or reestablish legal equality between those present. The way participants are ranked, the order in which they take the floor, the voting procedure and the order of signature can be determined objectively by neutral techniques such as alphabetical order, drawing lots or taking turns. Documents and written minutes must be drawn up and circulated on a non-discriminatory basis.

1032 – This equality of treatment is given legal expression whenever a vote is taken, but otherwise is not always apparent in practice: the more vital a participant's agreement is to the success of the discussions, the stronger its position and the freer it is to set the terms for its participation. (see *156, 662*)

1033 – There is one generally accepted form of directing meetings: the chairmanship, on which the progress of the negotiation, the steering of relations between participants and the formulation of concluding statements often depends. This is a point on which the States present like to agree, despite the existence of a custom, whereby, unless it is otherwise provided, the power issuing the invitation fulfils this role, at least for some of the plenary or official sessions. (see *1024, 1143, 1274*)

---

18 F. S. DUNN: *The Practice and Procedure of International Conferences*, Baltimore, Johns Hopkins Press, 1929. W. D. PASTUHOV: *A Guide to the Practices of International Conferences*, Washington, Carnegie Endowment, 1945.

1034 – Different systems have been used to deal with this issue: for example, the chair can be held by rotation or by turns. At the so-called North–South Conference on international economic cooperation, held in Paris in 1975, the decision was taken to have two co-chairmen, one from a developed country and the other from a developing country.

1035 – Little by little, the office of chairman is becoming more clearly distinguishable from the representation of his country: there are even cases of eminent people continuing to preside over the work of a conference after the government that appointed them is no longer in power. In practice, the role played by the chairman of a conference as mediator, conciliator and arbitrator creates a duplication of functions that often calls for the position to be filled by elections or by drawing lots. (see 2467)

1036 – The person occupying this position must exploit its full potential: as the chairman sets the scene for the discussions, it is in his power to steer, complicate or suspend them. Sometimes his contribution can be the decisive factor in whether they succeed or fail, as was the case of Bismarck, whose adroitness in presiding over the Congress of Berlin attracted universal appreciation. By contrast, depending on his character, the role of chairman might inhibit a negotiator from giving the fullest expression to his own arguments: this, as Stalin probably foresaw, happened with Roosevelt during the Yalta Conference.

1037 – A good negotiator must know how to deploy, within the limited time available, all the possible manoeuvres afforded by multilateral conferences, which are very different from the procedures used in bilateral negotiation. *A good negotiator must not only know and make use of the rules of procedure, but closely follow the overall political configurations and how they evolve.* Interests combine and change in subtle ways, following the particular logic of each delegation and the developments in a political environment that each of them perceives differently.

1038 – In resolving political issues in a multilateral forum the diplomat is encouraged to improve his position by playing on divisions or rivalries between his adversaries. Some he weakens by isolating them, thus undermining their argument. Others he rallies to his cause, by presenting his case to them with skill, force or solemnity, as the occasion demands.

1039 – Conference tactics imply a knowledge of how to make use of the internal rules, take advantage of the preparatory work being done by the executive secretariat, speed up or slow down the debates and either contribute to the excessive number of proposals on the table or criticise them.

Documents also deserve close attention, even those that are routine in character: certain minutes can be binding and may contain simplified forms of agreement. (see 761)

1040 – Within these conferences, no party can avoid the obligation to keep the overall negotiation in its sights. There are procedures to make sure it is conducted appropriately, and rules to ensure a consistent result, but it remains subject to external pressures.

1041 – This form of negotiation owes much to certain parliamentary methods, in that its subject matter gives rise to general policy debates, it involves common working procedures and the formation of majorities, and it culminates either in a vote or a consensus. But this comparison cannot be generalised: *the more important a conference is in political or technical terms, the more closely it will adhere to traditional diplomatic methods.* (see **2617**)

1042 – Multilateral public procedures open up manoeuvres for negotiators that give new life to their art. They must know how to turn to their advantage the whole raft of events taking place outside the debate itself, in particular the reaction of public opinion. They can even draw on them for arguments that have only the remotest connection with the matter in hand.[19] (see **2399**)

1043 – Harold Nicolson took the view that moveable or periodic conferences went against the principle that the only useful negotiation was done on a continuous and confidential basis.[20] Private conversations might still be courteous and reasonable, but if issues were thrown open to public debate before the desired objective was achieved, the negotiation would almost certainly fail. (see **2617**)

1044 – However, holding an official conference does not necessarily mean a public debate, or one in which everyone takes part: as long ago as the Congresses of Munster and Nijmegen, in 1646 and 1675 respectively, many of the discussions were carried on by written communication. An intense amount of diplomatic activity is conducted on the sidelines of numerous international bodies, beyond the mere exchange of information between national delegations.

During an international conference it is possible for all parties to conduct multiple negotiations in parallel to the main debate. (see **2295**)

1045 – Such is the usefulness of these encounters that some institutions, such as the European Union and the Council of Europe, encourage consultation and cooperation between the representatives of their members at major international meetings. (see **1315**)

National representation

1046 – Longer and more frequent conferences of all kinds are being held in response to the needs of world society. Diplomats can no longer meet these needs, being neither sufficiently numerous nor appropriately qualified: as an example, the American delegation to the tariff negotiations in Geneva in the 1960s numbered about forty people, all with different roles, and the GATT negotiations in 1992–1993 involved delegations from more than a hundred countries, as well as hundreds of experts.

19 D. RUSK: 'Parliamentary Diplomacy, Debate v Negotiation', in *World Affairs Interpreter*, Los Angeles, 1955, p. 121.
20 H. NICOLSON: *The Evolution of Diplomatic Methods*, London, New York, MacMillan, 1954.

1047 – *Subject to any mutual commitments, each State is free to decide for itself who shall represent it at international conferences, and the numbers, rank and capacity of those persons.* Aside from diplomatic meetings, the delegates sent, whether on an occasional or regular basis, are mostly specialists in the subject under discussion, drawn from very broad backgrounds, which does not prevent them from conducting skilful and effective negotiations. The growth in the practice of committee negotiations means that delegations are becoming ever larger. (see *690*)

1048 – Experts are sometimes invited to take part in the specific part of the discussion that concerns them, and in practice the negotiation of procedural questions is resolved by allowing politicians to call upon their technical advisers on a reciprocal basis: usually, it is the conference itself that decides when experts should come and go. This practice has had the effect of strengthening the advisory role of secretariats and international bodies. (see *2456, 2470*)

1049 – The characteristic feature of 'expert diplomacy' is that it is conducted on the basis of written orders. The directives issued to delegations are instructions that bind all the members, especially if they are not nationals of the country they are representing. These are not merely technical documents; they must enable the delegates to see how their role fits into an overall strategy, which means they may not ignore the political aspects of the issues to be discussed. For this reason it is advisable for them to be reviewed, if not actually drafted, by those responsible for the State's diplomatic activity. (see *2419*)

1050 – The occasional negotiator is bound to follow the instructions received, and this applies to his general conduct as well as the debates in which he takes part. If they are insufficient or incomplete, or inapplicable, it is up to him to see that they are properly supplemented, which may be done through national diplomatic channels. This must be done, for example, if the conference is setting up new institutional structures, or committing to additional expense.

1051 – In many conferences, in practice, it is not possible for the negotiator to obtain specific instructions from his national authorities. The temptation in that case will be for him to align himself with the positions of those delegations that are closest.

   Geographical or ideological solidarity operates as a substitute for diplomatic instructions: this can especially be seen with the representatives of many developing countries within the United Nations.

1052 – So important it is for each delegation to ensure that its instructions are up to date that the proceedings must sometimes be suspended. The Conference on International Economic Cooperation, held in Paris between 1975 and 1977, was interrupted several times to allow its participants to make return visits to their respective capitals. (see *2429*)

1053 – Measures must be taken at national level to confer regular and official negotiating powers on those selected for this purpose: many international meetings begin with the deposit of powers and the verification of the credentials of the participants, which frequently gives rise to sensitive issues requiring consultation with the capitals concerned. (see *693*)

1054 – The level of powers needed to authorise a person to speak and act on behalf of a government depends on the nature of the commitments he will be making. In the case of a diplomatic treaty, these must be specially drawn up and signed, and they often take the form of full powers.

1055 – But diplomacy by conference, as it has been called, also provides a way for leaders to steer the negotiation themselves, and even conduct the negotiations in person in restricted meetings.[21] Person to person negotiation is more rapid, flexible and productive, provided misunderstandings and leaks can be avoided. Some of these conversations must nonetheless remain confidential.[22] (see *2487*)

1056 – Treaties and headquarters agreements, as well as the laws and current practices of some States, tend to confirm the quasi-diplomatic status of delegates sent by States to multilateral conferences and meetings set up by international organisations. Immunities and facilities enable them to carry out their missions in complete independence. These are determined by the duration of the meeting and the official's rank: heads of delegation are often assimilated to heads of diplomatic missions (see the 1969 UN Convention on Special Missions). (see *701*)

1057 – It is established that national representatives are not subject to restrictions concerning their liberty, immigration and travel, transfers of currency or use of codes and mail. Their personal baggage, correspondence and working documents are inviolable. Acts done in the exercise of their functions are covered by immunity from jurisdiction, even after their mission is ended.[23]

1058 – The principle of reciprocity, frequently applied to diplomatic exchanges, ensures that these protections are respected, but problems still arise, as was seen from the case of the Palestinian delegation to the United Nations.[24] In 1988 the PLO office in New York was closed, and the UN General Assembly requested an Advisory Opinion from the International Court of Justice. The Court took the view that the case should have been submitted to arbitration as provided in the headquarters agreement.

§3. Balances and choices

1059 – International conferences are becoming more frequent, and their fields of competence are extending, especially into areas where the technical nature of the

---

21 D. G. ACHESON: *Meetings at the Summit*, Durham, New Hampshire University Press, 1958.
22 M. P. HANKEY: *Diplomacy by Conference*, London, Benn, 1946.
23 M. OESER and R. MEISSNER: 'Zu einigen Grundproblemen der Kodifikation und Weiterentwicklung des Völkerrechts Über die Vertretung der Staaten in ihren Beziehungen zur internationalen Organisationen', in *Deutsche Aussenpolitik*, Berlin, RDA, p. 915.
24 E. ZOLLER: 'Sécurité nationale et diplomatie multilatérale, l'expérience des Etats-Unis comme Etat hôte de l'ONU', *AFDI*, 1988, p. 109.

subject matter is a deterrent to politicians. *The programmes they examine, the agreements and rules they produce and the commitments they engender are many and varied.*

1060 – These working bodies are designed to fulfil the institutional needs of new international solidarities that have grown up, some of them worldwide, some not. The subjects addressed in their debates become more and more specialised and diverse, and at the same time, they open up ever more far-reaching and global perspectives.

1061 – Thanks to this method of negotiating, which is general, sometimes based on majority decisions and often conducted on the basis of anonymity, the product of these discussions and deliberations does not bear the stamp of any particular nation. It allows for continuous consultation, cooperation and even mediation between the interests of different States, aided by bureaux staffed by officials of widely differing nationalities.

1062 – It is rare for the delegations to a multipartite conference to divide into two opposing camps. Tactics take novel forms, as the interaction is more complex and fluctuating than in a traditional exchange. Negotiations are divided up according to the major working topics, with committees or subcommittees set up whose task is to put forward partial settlements or draft resolutions: this is an endless source of internal problems of organisation.[25]

1063 – Conferences can serve to reinforce the position of one of the participants on substantive issues. Either it can take the initiative to convene the event knowing that doing so might bring it some advantage, or it can secure some position of authority such as the chairmanship of the meeting: this was the role that fell to Metternich at the Congress of Vienna.

1064 – While some statesmen have made remarkable use of the tactical possibilities offered by the broad landscape of international conferences, many commentators take the view that these are not conducive to good diplomatic practice because they are slow, cumbersome, costly and misleading. *These meetings have become so numerous and frequent that they create an unhealthy dependency and multiply the risks of overlap and contradiction. (see 2620)*

1065 – Often, polarisation in the diplomatic arena resurfaces in multilateral negotiations. Participants in a conference can form themselves into coalitions and split into opposing camps according to their political, economic and linguistic affinities, or their hostility to one configuration or another: *whether the dominant powers are in opposition or alliance, they cannot fail to influence the will of others and their capacity to negotiate.* (see *276, 921, 1127*)

1066 – During the 'North–South' Conference in Paris, the participants separated into interest groups. Subsequent debates (such as the Cancùn Conference in 1981) revealed the lack of agreement between the nations in the industrialised camp,

25 N. L. HILL: *The Public International Conference*, Stanford University Press, 1929.

while the developing countries succeeded in overcoming their economic and social differences, opposing interests and political rivalries in order to make common use of some of their negotiating weapons, among them – petrol.

1067 – The techniques adopted by international conferences often limit their achievements: consensus is no guarantee of execution, reservations serve to complicate the international legal machinery and overlapping competences result in contradictory norms.[26] Giving publicity to the work can raise hopes, when in fact the real debates are happening somewhere else; if the will to reach a conclusion is anything short of unanimous, the proceedings risk becoming mired. Professional, ideological or other groups use a variety of means to exert influence or threats from the outside, or sow dissent. (see *2228*)

1068 – This explains the exceptional role played in negotiation by form and terminology: the choice of expressions provides an instrument for measuring the spirit of conciliation, the degree of respect for the partners and the degree of understanding of their concerns. (see *2171*)

1069 – It is difficult to hold important international conferences without attracting public curiosity. Quite the reverse: by contrast with the informed and confidential discussions that take place between professionals, participants are encouraged to pay much attention to reputation and prestige, to disregard the confidences and subtleties that are a necessary part of good policy and to be inappropriately argumentative and intransigent. By sometimes deflecting the participants away from an open exchange on the real issues, international conferences make their resolution more problematic and unpredictable. In practice, diplomacy is normally conducted through a process of mutual concessions, but these become more difficult to balance against a background of inflamed public debate.

1070 – Far from raising the level of the discussion to that of political compromise, the usual effect of these conferences is to reduce it to the lowest common denominator the parties can find. Negotiation will be subject to the constant threat of public accusations, partisan charges and the use of vague and arbitrary concepts. Too often, in conferences, the real problems are missed and effective negotiations evaded or postponed.

1071 – But this is not an absolute condemnation. Multilateral negotiation does offer the diplomat constantly renewed possibilities, if only he knows how to use them to further his own interests: it opens up a whole range of tactics, postures, ways and means, and facilitates contacts both inside and outside the meetings themselves that are productive because they are informal and can be pursued in parallel.

Shifts may occur in the opposing camps to which the participants belong, as the interests of the members of the same group will not always be identical. (see *2617*)

26 M. BEDJAOUI: *Pour un nouvel ordre économique international*, Paris, UNESCO, 1978, p. 177.

Of great interest are those cases where a meeting, with terms of reference fixed in advance, has enabled a transaction to be moved forward or a dispute to be resolved.

1072 – Conference procedure gives a varied and flexible dimension to diplomatic exchanges, as long as confidences are respected where necessary. Military, financial or other experts can be called upon, which facilitates agreement on the technical aspects of the issues. *Alongside the plenary discussions, preparatory or restricted meetings take place where the real work is done. Here, a delegate can communicate by making a declaration in public, or sending notes or emissaries, as the occasion demands.* The judgement of posterity on the Congress of Vienna, when no plenary meetings were actually ever held, serves to confirm how effective these procedures can be.

1073 – Governments will, however, be constrained to manage their participation in international conferences because they are so numerous, expensive and lengthy, and also because they overlap. They will do this by re-establishing the role played by diplomatic channels and missions, and at the same time, by placing more and more of their technical negotiations within the existing international organisational framework.

1074 – The coordination that can result from these contacts allows initiatives to be shared, manoeuvres to be toned down, and alliances extended. In any event, it provides a way of overcoming the problems of isolation in a negotiation, a position in which France found itself at the Washington Conference in 1974. France subsequently abandoned this position, when in 1992 it adhered to the International Energy Agency set up within the OECD.

1075 – However sophisticated the preparation and however assiduous the secretariat, no multilateral negotiation can succeed where there is no will to agree, or in the face of discord on major issues of policy.

An international conference is a temporary meeting: it has no way of pursuing any diplomatic line of its own.

1076 – The successful outcome of a congress depends on the atmosphere in which it unfolds. This type of diplomacy requires good relations to be maintained between those representatives whose interests are similar, and, likewise, cultural differences or varying sympathies must not paralyse the process of rapprochement of the delegations, or degenerate into confrontation. (see *1878*)

1077 – The results of international conferences do not always meet the expectations they have aroused, nor do they depend entirely on the quality of the work done. A negotiation must be held to decide on the conditions to be met before the outcome is treated as final, especially with regard to consensus, voting and reservations. (see *1565*)

1078 – According to traditional diplomatic principles, there must be unanimity of the countries concerned before a decision can be treated as final, but where there is a sufficient majority to reach an agreement, minority objections tend to be set aside in the interests of an effective solution. Thus, the draft of a multilateral treaty may be regarded as adopted once two-thirds of the States present at the negotiation agree on its text and its entry into force (Vienna Convention of 1969 on the Law of Treaties, Article 9). The practice of consensus is another way of facilitating the conclusion of international negotiations. (see *1562*)

1079 – The partners must also agree on the publicity to be given to their work, unless one of their number takes steps unilaterally, for example, by using the media to exert pressure on its interlocutors, or those they represent. *The least that can be said is that major multilateral conferences attract press coverage, which is not conducive to the prudent silence that should attend any sensitive negotiations.* This means that they must sometimes be carried on in private, or even secret, meetings. This was the direction the G7 and G8 took for many years.

1080 – While traditional negotiation is an instrument of justice by substitution, which aims to achieve equality in exchanges and reciprocity in conduct, sociologists would describe the multilateral conference as closer to the distributive justice model, the object of which is to redistribute resources according to service, merit and, in modern times, need. It is also an expression of the development of interpersonal relations in an international setting. It lends itself to impassioned reactions such as the mass movements seen in Genoa, Seattle and Porto Alegre.

1081 – International *détente* has not always brought about *entente*, but it has acted as a stimulus to cooperation between nations. Still, the course of numerous multilateral assemblies shows how great is the distance that separates confrontation from concerted action: the 'North–South' Conference (Cancùn, 1981) was one such case, while it lasted. One essential message recurs – the need to maintain contact. (see *1930*)

1082 – Despite the continuing competition between States arguing over territory, resources and money, the great conferences have contributed to the birth of a common awareness of the major issues that humanity faces. Negotiation often leads to the formulation of rules of law of widespread application, or to the adaptation of pre-existing provisions to new situations. But it can also encounter machinations – some of them ruthless – that tend in the opposite direction, such as those of the so-called '*intermondialiste*' movement. (see *2162*)

1083 – The advantages of institutionalised multilateralism explain why some tacticians have sought to interfere in a negotiation without agreeing to be bound by it. The observer, protected by a status which prevents it from undertaking any commitment, or even taking part in the debates, obtains useful information from the discussions at which it is present, and discreetly influences the course of events in the direction of its own interests, paving the way for future bilateral negotiations based on its direct knowledge of the outcome.

1084 – Where a conference does not offer flexible enough procedures or solid enough guarantees to satisfy the concerns of the great powers, they will find ways to circumvent it: *the major States still want to retain the initiative, the choice of the diplomatic framework and the possibility to manoeuvre.* (see *1537*)

Section 2: International organisations

1085 – Multilateral negotiation is diversifying with frequent practice and the passage of time, and is still acquiring new instruments designed to address core interests in a comprehensive and lasting way.

1086 – International secretariats were set up in the wake of certain especially productive conferences, with the specific purpose of providing facilities favourable to the conduct of negotiation, in particular, access to a permanent, convenient structure for consultation or collaboration, thus enabling national concerns to be expressed and reconciled without excessive diplomatic formality.

1087 – Other bodies have been set up under international agreements whose purpose is to monitor their implementation, provide the means to carry them out or move forward with their work. Usually composed of representatives of the contracting parties, sometimes on a basis of parity, they provide the framework for ongoing negotiation in pursuit of the aims of the underlying agreement.

1088 – The political divisions resulting from the narrow concept of the nation-state or the process of accession to independence have also prompted attempts to regroup along continental lines, in Europe, South America and Africa, resulting in structures that vary in scale.[27]

The Lusaka Summit, held in 2000 at the initiative of the Heads of States, transformed the Organisation of African Unity (OAU) into the African Union, with 53 members, its own Central Bank, a Court of Justice, a development fund and the multipartite NEPAD plan. (see *1786, 1949*)

1089 – These initiatives are not limited to policy, on which agreement between States remains unpredictable. *As a matter of practical reality, national interests work together much better where there are elements of complementarity and solidarity.* This explains the proliferation of technical and specialised international bodies such as those within the orbit of the United Nations or the various intergovernmental economic organisations and also the inter-state establishments that have become so numerous in Europe. (see *1594*)

1090 – Once these bodies are in place, governments try to put them to the best possible use, giving them new functions and making increased resources available. One such task is to contribute to multilateral negotiation by collecting and compiling documentation, undertaking preparatory studies for intergovernmental meetings and devising proposals acceptable to all the governments present, harnessing diplomatic compromise to produce constructive cooperation. They are also charged with drawing up common rules and standards, managing new services, making investments, providing certain States with technical and financial support and entering into the necessary relationships with the private sector. (see *1516*)

---

27 P. H. TEITGEN, etc. : *Les Organisations régionales internationales*, Paris, Montchrestien, 1971. A. KONTCHOU-KOUOMEGUI: *Le Système diplomatique africain*, Paris, Pedone, 1977.

1091 – In response to the need for lasting and concerted action on the part of sovereign States, this apparatus has of course expanded, with each new mission providing an opportunity for national interests to come together or collide. It has become more rich and diverse as a result. *There are already more functioning international organisations than there are sovereign States, not counting the non-governmental companies and institutions, profit-making or otherwise, whose numbers run into thousands.* (see *1894, 1907*)

1092 – International life continues to be organised on the basis of agreement, respecting the legal equality of States, and the reciprocal nature of the commitments made by the parties. *Institutions serve to make negotiation more attractive and effective by opening up new domains.* (see *1508*)

On the other hand, though, *once a permanent communications structure is set up, its normative and organisational roles come into their own*: these are debated in theory but acknowledged in practice. (see *1510, 1596, 2223*)

1093 – Three quarters of intergovernmental organisations are not global in scale, and most of them have only small executive secretariat structures. However, international negotiation must respect their fields of competence and their activities, even where these overlap. (see *102*)

§1. The institution as a product of negotiation

1094 – The constitutive instruments of intergovernmental organisations are regarded as rules of law, objective and lasting. In truth, whatever name they might be given, most of these are treaties resulting from negotiations between sovereign States (the Central Commission for the Rhine was the product of the Congress of Vienna in 1815 and the European Danube Commission of the Paris Congress of 1856). Even the Nordic Council, which resulted from parallel decisions taken at national level, is the product of an international agreement. (see *606*)

International organisations can be analysed as voluntary associations of States.

1095 – The role of international, especially European, organisations in international cooperation, the powers accorded them and those they acquire, are enough to justify taking the greatest care when conducting and implementing the negotiations that create them.

Constitutive negotiation

1096 – The existence of these organisations imposes constraints – higher priorities, procedures, legal and financial obligations, among others – on all their participants. These constraints have to be examined and debated by each State at national level.

This negotiation has the merit of helping to resolve the many organisational issues that arise out of international conferences. (see *1012, 1016*)

1097 – Any institutional system in which negotiation takes place between States presupposes that national interests exist, and are defended. *If these political preoccupations become less pressing, the organisation loses its meaning, whatever its administrative machinery.* (see *2291, 2311*)

Organisational objectives are only of secondary importance where diplomatic imperatives are concerned.

1098 – Negotiation generally starts with questions of information: how it is collected, controlled and exchanged. Thus, at the OECD, the collective use of national information allows group reports to be produced that are often prospective in character. From information, it is only a short step to comparison, or even rationalisation: once national programmes are better known, they have the effect of encouraging, orienting and correcting each other. (see *2037, 2040*)

1099 – The consultation that precedes the taking of decisions at national level emerges as one of the principal functions of the organisational system, whose dynamic it serves to reinforce. States seek each others' opinions, which naturally leads them to cooperate in the face of challenges, discuss their mutual obligations and agree on common or parallel systems of rules, all of which reinforce the role of the collective groupings to which they belong. (see *2053*)

1100 – In its turn, by agreement of its member States, the organisation is granted the competence to set up the organs it needs to carry out its functions (see, as regards the United Nations, Advisory Opinion on the *Effects of Awards of Compensation made by the United Nations Administrative Tribunal (1953–1954)*, ICJ *Rep.* 1954, p. 57; also Articles 7 and 68 of the Charter), subsidiary institutions, of which there are hundreds, with different structures and means and even new entities. UN resolutions were passed to set up the United Nations Children's Fund (UNICEF) and other institutions such as UNRRA, UNRKA and UNRWA. (see *1152*)

1101 – Some of these bodies become specific centres for negotiation. The United Nations Industrial Development Organisation (UNIDO) was set up in 1967, with the agreement of the General Assembly, with the status of a Specialised Agency and its own decision-making organs. (see *1519*)

The Security Council has itself created specialist bodies to monitor the implementation of its decisions.

1102 – There has been a wealth of initiatives, further institutionalising the international environment. Some of them fulfil a double or triple role, meaning that governments have a choice of structures in which to pursue their cooperation: in Western Europe, this is the case with the environment and nuclear energy.

The response is often motivated by political as much as technical considerations, which explains the failure of the Havana Charter (1947–1948). The very name of its successor institution (from 1947 until the Marrakech Conference of 1994 it was known as the General Agreement on Tariffs and Trade, or GATT), made its object very clear: to promote commercial negotiations and provide them with a framework.

This is the mission of the World Trade Organization, which operates on the principle that international economic relations are based on freedom of exchange, though this is not fully in line with the principles of the European Common Market or the basis on which developing countries enter into association with it. (see *756, 1400, 1411, 1632, 1829*)

1103 – International administration, including that of Europe, already provides work for tens of thousands of officials from one hundred or so nationalities, working in almost all the world's countries and territories. It manages billions of dollars of funds and controls an increasing number of locations and documentary resources, working through a host of different organs. These do not, however, make up a homogeneous whole: every institution has its own place, composition, role and resources.[28]

1104 – In practice, however closely-knit this organisational fabric, inter-state negotiations still dominate. Governments set up these institutions, directly or indirectly, and governments decide their status, obligations and resources according to the objectives they have agreed upon together. In some cases, there will have been partial agreements between the governments concerned prior to setting up the organisations: the Berne Conference produced the first two International Labour Conventions, in 1905, while the ILO was not created until the Paris Conference in 1919. (see *1426, 1532*)

The Conference of West African States has actively engaged in negotiations, and this is now beginning to happen in Central Africa, where the Central African Economic and Monetary Community now has six member States. As for the Association of South–East Asian Nations (ASEAN), it is threatened by the instability of several of its members. On the other hand, the Gulf States Cooperation Council, set up in Riyadh in 1980, meets almost every year; its members control almost half the world's petroleum resources, and it also cooperates on issues of security and trade. (see *845*)

1105 – In creating an international organisation, States subscribe to its mission and the disciplines this imposes. They also undertake specific mutual obligations: respect for the underlying principles, independence, missions and procedures of the institution. *Here, again, the reciprocity of attitude and commitment found in diplomatic relations can be seen, with each government wanting the others to follow its example, even where they are reluctant.* (see *1518*)

Likewise, in joining an organisation, a State accepts its missions and procedures. The admission of China to the WTO came only after some forty agreements were signed on different products or services, some of them, such as those with the European Community and the United States, highly complex.

1106 – Each international organisation is entrusted with specific missions, and will therefore use particular procedures for the negotiation and drawing up of rules of

28 C. W. JENKS: *The Proper Law of International Organizations*, London, Stevens, 1962.
A. PLANTEY: *International Civil Service: Law and Practice*, New York, CNRS, 1981.
La fonction publique internationale (F. Loriot), Paris, CNRS, 2005.

international law. Proposals have been put forward to harmonise and standardise this extremely complex and differentiated system, but they have fallen foul of the individual character of the bodies and methods of each different institution and the consistent way in which each one applies its own customs. International administration has already established its own profession and the routines that go with it. (see *1993*)

1107 – The more political the way of approaching the issues, the greater the degree of structural and functional flexibility governments will require from an international organisation.[29] (see *1539, 1807*)

1108 – International society has been moving rapidly in the direction of national independence, and this means that the number of members of international organisations has grown steadily since the Second World War. This movement will naturally slow down, but its effects can already be seen not only in the constitution and workings of the institutions concerned, whose organs and procedures have adapted to this radical shift, but also in the work they are doing.[30] (see *2293*)

1109 – The composition of the ruling bodies of the major world institutions, the United Nations first and foremost, has expanded and will continue to do so. Increasingly cumbersome working and negotiating procedures have led to greater use of consensus. Their output has become more complex and uncertain, both in legal and practical terms.

Equality of the members

1110 – Although international organisations are set up to work in favour of all their members, the advantages States actually derive from them vary depending on their position. These disparities continue to increase. (see *1535, 1653*)

1111 – International institutions normally devise their organs and procedures in such a way as to avoid any discrimination between the member States, all of which are represented within the organs or bodies on the same basis. One of the main reasons why small countries favour the United Nations is that this organisation acknowledges their sovereignty by giving each of them the opportunity to have its views heard on major issues of worldwide importance, and a public platform to defend its interests. (see *1536*)

1112 – But the disparity between States created by the fragmentation of international society is too great in practice for international organisations to ignore. *Governments have been forced to manage the rule of equality so as to avoid the paralysis that can result from unwieldy plenary meetings and interminable debates, and decisions that fail to reflect what is possible or where the real responsibility lies.* Executive councils or committees are set up to limit the ongoing negotiation to a reasonable number of delegations, rotating on the basis of

---

29 M. P. HANKEY: *Diplomacy by Conference*, London, Benn, 1946.
30 W. FRIEDMANN: *The Changing Structure of International Law*, London, Stevens, 1964.

geographic zones, and voting methods have moved towards weighted voting, consensus, and implied consent.

1113 – Despite legal appearances, and against the wishes of a number of powers, inequality between States has even been formalised in several international institutions, and in particular in the United Nations Security Council. (see *131, 1536*)

It is current practice for the councils of many institutions to include the representatives of the great powers. In the International Labour Organisation, ten of the members of the governing council must be representatives of countries whose inclusion is based on their industrial importance. (see *662*)

1114 – A further source of inequality between partners arises because some States do not have adequate personnel available, either in terms of numbers or quality, to ensure that their interests are represented in the working and deliberative bodies. (see *735, 1214*)

1115 – An analysis of votes[31] shows how power politics have developed in the international system with the object of controlling the majorities and the administration. Coalitions, automatic alignment, diplomatic pressures and demagogic threats all undermine the supposed universality of the major institutions, and this sometimes benefits the favoured powers or groups of States. *Faced with demands for increased powers within the organisation by those that control it, the best other States can do is preserve their freedom of manoeuvre for as long as possible.*

1116 – The international organisation tends to give new meaning and content to the notion of equality between States: they find themselves bound by obligations that are not the result of *ad hoc* agreements, but are intended to be objective and general in nature, like legislation in a domestic legal system.

There is still scope for debate as to whether or not international organisations work in favour of the dominant powers. (see *1650*)

1117 – One thing is certain: their rules of operation serve to prevent the most powerful countries from taking over the reins, as multilateral procedure frustrates overt coercion. On the other hand, the distrust in which the major States hold each other and are held, serves to keep them out of many positions of direct responsibility, whether in decision-making posts or with regard to specific operations: symptomatic of this is the fact that, in the early days, the international forces of law and order consisted mainly, if not exclusively, of contingents from middle-ranking countries. (see *1535*)

1118 – Certain institutions can, at a given time, contribute to the success of diplomatic manoeuvres by the strongest States or groups of States. At the beginning, the United States controlled the United Nations; later, the United Nations was to serve as the vehicle for programmes that went against US policy.

---

31 M. BEDJAOUI: *Pour un nouvel ordre économique international*, Paris, UNESCO, 1978, p. 151.

Paralysed for over forty years by the opposition of the Great Powers, the machinery of the United Nations is today faced with excessive demands. (see *834*)

The United States used Security Council resolutions to justify its war against Iraq in 1990–1991. This was not the case in 2003–2004, when the limits of decision-making capability within the United Nations became apparent. (see *136, 1233, 1675*)

1119 – Faced with the threat of domination of the diplomatic system in its present form, the role of non-dominant States – the only way, in fact, for them to make their presence felt – is to mediate, redress the balance, promote initiatives and open up debates. They must aim to paralyse or break up alliances between the most powerful, or align themselves in order to play their own part in the overall diplomatic manoeuvring. (see *454, 2298*)

1120 – States will gradually learn how to make the best use of the possibilities intergovernmental institutions offer them by using these bodies as a framework in which to negotiate and put together broadly based, long-term programmes which their administrations can then abandon if they see fit.[32] This means that negotiations work to benefit broader interests, rather than being limited to single, short-term pragmatic concerns. (see *1214*)

1121 – The United Nations Economic Commission for Europe has proved to be a favoured meeting place for representatives from countries with different social systems. The volume of work, the technical nature of the issues addressed and the role played by the secretariat have had the result of reducing formalism in negotiation in favour of a pragmatic approach that is flexible and effective.[33]

1122 – The international system will, probably, devise ways of regulating conflicts between States in order to promote peaceful settlement. A variety of proposals have been made, with a view to setting limits on the unilateral actions of governments and improving the implementation of the UN Charter.[34] (see *1651*)

In 1957, for example, the Council of Europe proposed conditions for the peaceful settlement of international disputes (Convention of 29 April 1957). In Stockholm in 1992, the CSCE put forward a proposal for conciliation and arbitration procedures to the European States. (see *257, 471, 1004*)

§2. Institutionalised multilateralism

1123 – As well as the multilateralism of international conferences, the organisation can offer the advantages of a permanent staff, a neutral location and the active participation of the secretariat, as well as, sometimes, a new dynamism and purpose.

---

32 M. HILL: *The United Nations System: Co-Ordinating its Economic and Social Work*, Cambridge University Press, UNITAR, 1978.

33 UN: *Three Decades of the UNECE*, doc. E/ECE/962, New York, 1978.

34 S. D. BAILEY: *Peaceful Settlement of Disputes; Ideas and Proposals for Researches*, New York, UNITAR, 1971.

The effectiveness of an institution depends in particular on the ease with which it can function, and the flexibility of its procedure. States can rarely resist comparing the respective advantages and disadvantages of these mechanisms.

1124 – At the same time, every institution, from the moment it comes into being, creates its own logic based on its common principles of action and its specific missions. Balances of power, circuits and internal routines develop; it must adapt in order to survive. Diplomatic negotiation must take account of these organisational constraints.[35] (see *1511*)

Intergovernmental negotiation

1125 – The primary reason for setting up international organisations is to use their organs, procedures and workings to facilitate and exploit encounters and agreements between governments. Such an organisation can function on different levels, and in different policy and technical sectors. But, taken as a whole, the changes it brings about in negotiating methods amplify the effects of multipartite conferences. (see *1016*)

1126 – Discussions are guided by procedures, precedents and rules such as those documented in the collected works on the practices of the General Assembly, Security Council and other UN organs.[36] More than this, they form part of a predetermined system producing balances and trends, one of the effects of which is to increase the volume and scope of international negotiation.

1127 – Each organisation has its own structure, imposing procedures, mechanisms and regulations on multilateral negotiation that amount to so many limitations on the partners' freedom to manoeuvre. The resulting rigidity might explain why some governments prefer the traditional path of direct negotiation. Many of the proposals for improving the UN system aim at rationalising the work and procedures of the Economic and Social Council as the centre coordinating the institutional machinery.[37] (see *1065*)

1128 – The organisational framework of a negotiation determines its subject, who the protagonists are, the methods used and sometimes the rules by which it will be conducted. It also places obstacles in its way that themselves become institutionalised: the number of interests to be reconciled, and the number of possible power combinations, multiply very rapidly every time more actors become involved.[38] (see *2281, 2284*)

---

35 F. K. von PLEHVE: *Internationale Organisation und die moderne Diplomatie*, Munich, Olzog, 1972, p. 54. J. W. FELD: *International Relations: a Transnational Policy Approach*, Sherman Oaks, Alfred, 1979, p. 215.

36 UN: *Repertory of practice of United Nations organs*, I–V, with supplement and table of contents, New York.

37 M. HILL: *Comment introduire davantage d'ordre, de cohérence et de coordination dans le système des Nations unies*, New York, UNITAR, 1974.

38 M. VIRALLY: *L'Organisation mondiale*, Paris, Colin, 1972, p. 163.

1129 – A party agreeing to a diplomatic negotiation within an existing organisation must know that this will make a difference to its content, and either reduce or expand the scope of the discussion. Sometimes the institution can offer a State or group of States the opportunity, or even the right, to take sides or perhaps intervene in a dispute or discussion on the pretext of a collective and apparently disinterested procedure. At other times, on the contrary, it will tend to limit access to the members alone. This is the case with some negotiations between industrialised nations, under the specific structured umbrella of the OECD.

1130 – Another of the benefits of international organisations is that diplomatic contacts can be established between States that normally have no official direct relations. In times of tension, their sittings can offer irreplaceable opportunities to meet. (see *1520*)

1131 – Negotiating within an international organisation also implies that States accept, or even welcome, the interposition of a form of screen between their manoeuvres and the results they produce. *In practice, a diplomatic initiative involves consultation with partners, or their consent; it is sometimes hidden beneath multilateral or anonymous guises that make it look less unilateral.* However, it is rare for an organisation to be as opaque as the United Nations was during the Korean War, or the Organisation of American States when the United States intervened in the Dominican Republic in 1965. (see *1525*)

The Gulf War of 1991 was an example of the use of organised negotiation and intervention.

1132 – It is not uncommon for the intervention of an international institution to endorse the efforts of governments wishing either to bring about the resolution of a conflict, use the situation to strengthen their own positions or put pressure on one of the protagonists to redress the balance of power. (see *977, 1547, 1785*)

This was the interpretation given to the international interventions in Serbia during the Kosovo crisis. The machinery put in place to meet the demands of that situation was an unlikely assortment of overlapping treaties, institutions, competences and responsibilities. Based on Chapter VII of the Charter, the Security Council twice declared, on 23 September 1998 and 21 November 1998, that there existed a threat to peace and security in the region, and, in Resolution 1244 of 10 June 1999, following on from that of 14 May 1999, it contemplated intervention by States and the competent international organisations. In the same time-frame, the European Union also discussed the issue, in Berlin in March 1999 and Cologne in July 1999, as did the G8 summit held in Petersberg in May 1999, this latter also involving the United States and Russia. The execution of the Security Council resolutions showed the predominance of the NATO machine. (see *1493, 1785*)

1133 – Within international organisations, whatever their field of activity, issues are placed in a broader and more complex context; this might interest public opinion, but it requires each member to invest in the new strategic effort. (see *1910, 2616*)

1134 – Exchanges of ideas, information and arguments are sometimes easier in this setting than in one of traditional diplomacy. Held in check by third States or public opinion generally, aggressiveness is partially neutralised, and conflict is reduced by governments giving more frequent, detailed and complete explanations of their intentions, knowing that they must justify their position and rally the doubters.

1135 – Partners are inclined to work more effectively together, and to form groups depending on their interests, affinities and tactics, without their positions appearing too exclusively national.[39] The responsibility of each one for the outcome of the whole deliberation is correspondingly diminished.

In some restricted bodies, collective representation of groups of countries with closely allied interests allows negotiating techniques to be used that are compatible with the increasing workload of major international conferences.

1136 – The involvement of States that are not directly interested in the negotiation serves to open up the dialogue, erode national prejudices, smooth over conflictual tendencies and reduce or avoid the use of force. Such interposition is of course welcomed by those setting out to negotiate from a position of weakness or uncertainty. (see *461, 1515*)

1137 – When an international institution proceeds by holding large-scale diplomatic meetings, the interplay of transnational forces is made easier by opening up the forum to the representatives of elected assemblies, the media, pressure groups and professional or cultural organisations. *Publicity can sometimes serve as a stimulus to the discussions, and at other times thwart them; it creates a healthy fear of being held responsible for their failure.* (see *1898*)

1138 – The United Nations is an example of what one can expect from a representative assembly of States, with all their ambitions, interests, prejudices, strengths and weaknesses. But, it provides a meeting place and a favoured and permanent platform for the expression of national policies, the adaptation of international relations and, at the same time, diplomatic debate that appeals to the public beyond the governmental level.

1139 – This strong tendency for negotiations to become more multilateral is progressively opening up new possibilities and compromise solutions, ways that were previously blocked as well as escape routes, and allows temporary majorities to form as the occasion demands. It opens the way to an assortment of moves and allows reservations to be made, thus avoiding the loss of face that follows when concessions are made too quickly. *The institution presents its procedures in a favourable light, promotes the use of good offices and mediation, and consolidates agreements. It takes the edge off reciprocal concessions and advantages by applying them to the mutual exchanges of many successive partners.* (see *1567*)

1140 – The very exercise of the power to negotiate within international organisations shows how far political power has evolved, and how diplomatic manoeuvres have unfolded. As an example, the entire history of the United Nations has been marked by episodes of rivalry or cooperation between the nuclear powers,

---

39 M. VIRALLY, P. GERBET and J. SALOMON, etc.: *Les Missions permanentes auprès des organisations internationales*, I, Brussels, Bruylant, 1971.

and by the growing influence of newly developing countries.[40] The same phenomena have occurred in the technical institutions, which have also witnessed the great political and ideological quarrels of our time. (see *1228*)

1141 – Within an international institution, power configurations appear in which States or groups of States see their influence wax and wane, and their freedom of action enhanced or distorted.

States or groups of States whose influence is predominant thus follow one after the other, for instance, in the United Nations where certain delegations constitute real, and strong, pressure groups.[41] The 'Group of 77' now has 133 members. (see *1315, 1537*)

1142 – Even more than in conferences, the missions and regulations of international organisations force their members to adopt new tactics. *In this framework, the play of different manoeuvres can follow different patterns: the predominance of any one partner, the formation of clienteles and coalitions and the various roles can change.*[42] But the weaker the solidarity, the more work has to be done to coordinate: it is never ending.

1143 – The presidency increases in importance as the procedures become more institutionalised. National representatives are often called upon to assume the presidency by turns, which offers a guarantee of reciprocity. In addition, it is more and more common for presidents to have a permanent administrative secretariat, which is of course a department of the organisation, especially where the chairman of one committee is the most senior civil servant in the organisation. (see *1033, 1202*)

1144 – By bringing in new actors who are not involved in disputes, the institutionalisation of rules gives legitimacy to new kinds of claim and also favours the use of inquiries, good offices and mediation, thus exerting pressure on the parties to a dispute and forcing them to negotiate. Within an international organisation it is easier for both parties to agree to intervention by a third State. (see *452, 462*)

Procedure in international organisations encourages mediation in many cases. It makes it easier for member States to hold diplomatic contacts with each other, whether secret or official. Certain functions are especially well suited to conciliation, certain prominent persons may be called upon, or meetings organised, sometimes with an eye to appealing to public opinion.[43] (see *461*)

1145 – *Attempts to bring about the peaceful settlement of international disputes lead to conciliation of the practices of international conferences with those of*

---

40 V. WALTER: *Silent Missions*, Washington, 1945.
41 E. R. APPATHURAI: *Les Missions permanentes auprès des organisations internationales*, Brussels, Bruyant, 1975, p. 99.
42 R. W. COX and H. K. JACOBSON: *The Anatomy of Decision: Decision-Making in International Organization*, Yale University Press, 1973, p. 25.
43 A. PLANTEY: *Principes de diplomatie*, Paris, Pedone, 1992, p. 295.

traditional diplomatic negotiation.[44] Thus, before it holds public sittings, the Security Council often meets for the purpose of free and secret consultations, which in reality are negotiations. These exchanges range over a variety of subjects: the sharing and discussing of information to throw light on a case and prevent opinion from hardening, agreement about the procedure to be followed in the public sessions, a joint search for ways of resolving a dispute, drawing up a settlement, improving draft decisions or ironing out intemperate language or procedural delays.[45] (see *1537, 1547, 1652*)

1146 – The fact remains that attempts to institutionalise the great diplomatic conference, that is, the Security Council have not made it a representative or responsible worldwide government, with real powers. It is even possible for its principal function to be disregarded, as was the case with the intervention by the United States in Iraq in 2003. (see *834, 1518, 1784, 1894*)

Acting under the Council's authority, subsidiary committees exist whose responsibility it is to ensure that its resolutions are complied with: they are often the setting for sensitive negotiations, since their role depends on the delegates who sit on them, as with the Sanctions Committee. (see *1784*)

1147 – The Organisation for Economic Cooperation and Development (OECD) succeeded the OECE in 1961, numbering thirty industrialised States, together accounting for around three-quarters of worldwide production of goods and services. It is characterised by its large number of working groups which mix expertise, consultation and negotiations and also by the flexible rules it has adopted for decision-making: here, unanimity does not mean that a partial agreement, recommendation or decision will be binding on a Member State that abstained.[46] (see *1214, 1562*)

1148 – Conceived as an institution of general scope, the Council of Europe is empowered by its statute to develop cooperation between its members through treaties. It has thus provided the framework for over 100 conventions and agreements on a wide variety of subjects. (see *1239*)

The European Convention on Human Rights of 4 November 1950, together with its 14 protocols, was the product of delicate negotiations and also the beginnings of an original legal construction creating a direct relationship between private individuals and an international institution. The European Court of Human Rights has often found that States, including Great Britain and France, have wrongfully exercised their powers. (see *1152, 1249, 2171*)

1149 – The Committee of Ministers of the Council of Europe has become a true diplomatic conference, periodic and organised, in regular form. Acting mostly

---

44 J. D. BAILEY: *Peaceful Settlement of Disputes: Ideas and Proposals for Researches*, New York, UNITAR, 1971.

45 F. Y. CHAI: 'Consultation and Consensus in the Security Council', in *Dispute Settlement through the UN*, New York, Oceania, 1977.

46 M. SALEM: 'Du rôle de l'OCDE dans la mondialisation de l'économie', in *La Mondialisation du droit*, Paris, Litec, 2000, p. 329.

through recommendations, it enables agreements to be negotiated. Often at the instigation of the Parliamentary Assembly, it adopts draft agreements by a qualified majority, and puts them forward, by consensus, for signature or possible ratification by the States concerned, which are not necessarily members of the organisation. It also holds ministerial conferences on particular topics.

1150 – Because of the confidentiality of these procedures and the way the deliberations are conducted, it is possible for governments to agree on instruments that have the seal of approval of the entire Council of Europe and thus the backing of its reputation, although, legally speaking, they are not acts of the organisation itself.

1151 – The negotiating procedure has been further refined by the setting up of committees of experts charged by the Committee of Ministers under Article 17 of the Statute with producing drafts for it within a given time-frame. From the legal standpoint, the members of these committees are not regarded as representing governments, but in practice, they serve as a channel for official dialogue from the exploratory stage, and this makes it easier for the ministers to approve the texts produced. The work of these innumerable committees is coordinated by steering committees.

They have greatly enriched the repertoire of methods of international negotiation, especially because of the secret voting system of the Committee of Ministers and the role played by the Assembly.

1152 – The Council of Europe has also given birth to specialist multilateral institutions such as the Resettlement Fund, set up under the Resolution of 16 April 1954, responsible for granting financial aid to deal with the refugee problem, the Cultural Fund and the European Cultural Foundation and also the European Court of Human Rights. (see *1198*)

1153 – The International Labour Organisation presents a more restrictive form of negotiation, laid down in Article 19 of its Statute. Its conventions are adopted by a two-thirds majority of all the delegates present at the Conference, which includes industry and union delegates, and they become acts of the institution itself. Conventions are not opened for signature by government representatives, who undertake, instead, to put them forward for ratification by their national authorities. (see *1609*)

Relations between Parliaments

1154 – Peace and harmony between nations can only favour the establishment of sustained contacts between their political élites, especially the members of their national elected assemblies. Several private initiatives have come about in order to pursue this goal, the best known being the Interparliamentary Union.

1155 – As the product of diplomatic negotiations, international parliamentary assemblies are a new type of institution, which has sprung up mainly in Europe, both because of its democratic and representative constitutional regimes and because of its desire to involve political movements more directly in the unification of the continent. (see *1240*)

1156 – The Council of Europe, set up under the Charter of May 1949, was foremost among these great interparliamentary assemblies. A treaty of March 1948, amended in October 1954, set up the Western European Union, the same type of Assembly, with competence in the field of defence. At about the same time, in 1955, the Atlantic Treaty Organisation also set up a parliamentary assembly, but this had no official power.

1157 – There exist several other interparliamentary institutions in Europe. The Nordic Council has a plenary assembly consisting of parliamentary and government delegates, and deals with problems of cooperation between the five countries of northern Europe. The Baltic Assembly brings together the members of parliament of these three countries under a treaty dating from 1994; there was already a parliamentary conference on the Baltic Sea in existence since 1991. The Benelux countries, too, have their own interparliamentary consultative council.

1158 – The Assemblies of the European Coal and Steel Community, the European Economic Community and the European Atomic Energy Community became one single institution pursuant to the 1965 Merger Treaty. The resulting Assembly took the title of Parliament, and increased in importance not only because of the expansion of the Common Market, but also because it was granted effective powers and new methods of election following the negotiations in December 1991 in Maastricht and October 1997 in Amsterdam. After the Council of Nice in December 2000, and the accession of the States of Central and Eastern Europe, the allocation of seats has changed. (see *1295*)

1159 – In principle, international parliamentary institutions are composed of delegations chosen by the national assemblies of their members. It was decided, however, that members of the European Parliament should be elected by universal direct suffrage in each of the member countries. (see *1296*)

1160 – The Assembly of the Council of Europe is founded on a common ideological principle and transposes the principles and methods of parliamentary democracy to the level of an international organisation. As well as its original consultative role, it now acts to promote initiatives and progress on the part of European public opinion and also of its member governments, which it encourages to negotiate within the Committee of Ministers.

1161 – These first steps towards institutional collaboration between legislators have inevitably led to the development of a new form of international negotiation, one which creates direct relations not only between governments but also parliamentary delegations, that come together in assemblies with the power to take official public positions, albeit not enforceable against States themselves – and which, moreover, requires complex choices to be made between political parties, national representatives and different institutions. This has been referred to as 'parliamentary diplomacy'.

1162 – International parliamentary assemblies occupy a position where negotiations between sovereign States intersect with interdependencies of the kind that normally go unnoticed by diplomats and international civil servants. They set limits on the tendency of their members to be guided purely by national ties and make political or ideological rapprochement easier. (see 2593)

1163 – Institutions such as these provide fresh themes for reflection and action in diplomatic relations; they sometimes take initiatives that have the effect of broadening the field of collaboration between the countries concerned and contributing to the unification of the law.

1164 – In the current state of international agreements, no assembly is sovereign at international level. *All the assemblies in which parliamentarians come together, even those elected by direct universal suffrage, are set up under diplomatic agreements that determine their powers and attributes in such a way as not to jeopardise the prerogatives of national governments and legislatures.* (see 1287)

1165 – Apart from the institutions of the European Union, the role of these assemblies is purely advisory, except when they are setting their own internal rules of procedure and administration. They cannot engage the political or financial responsibility of governments, either separately or collectively.

1166 – The European Parliament is the only assembly with its own decision-making powers, or even the power to take decisions in specific areas concerning relations between Community institutions. It is vested with the power to vote on a number of managerial acts of the Community, as well as on draft international agreements. Since 1991, the European Council has given it broader powers, and in many fields it now decides by 'co-decision' with the Council. (see *1298, 1300, 1319, 1444*)

1167 – The role played by interparliamentary meetings in diplomatic negotiation should not be overestimated, nor underestimated. They provide opportunities for those in positions of political responsibility to meet, gather information and explain their views, in the knowledge that their written and spoken words are protected by immunity and that their procedures will be fair. (see *1858*).

1168 – Exchanging views and working together in close touch with public opinion leads to collective policy initiatives that go beyond the normal concerns of diplomatic reciprocity and government cooperation. This sometimes takes the form of votes on recommendations or resolutions, or meetings between members of governments and parliamentary committees, or joint meetings of the corresponding committees of each of the assemblies (for example, between the Council of Europe and the European Parliament). Sometimes it involves colloquia, congresses and conferences open to multiple participants, devised for the study of subjects of international cooperation, one example being the study of human rights in the Council of Europe and the European Union. (see 2592)

1169 – On the other hand, the very logic of the way parliaments are set up, and their particular working methods, emphasises their administrative aspects.

They have their own premises, officials and prerogatives, and their reports and debates both in committee and in plenary session reflect technical or policy groupings that go beyond national attachments, but find support in public opinion.

1170 – The traditional exercise of the parliamentary function within these assemblies has the effect of reinforcing negotiation between national executives. Thus the Parliamentary Assembly of the Council of Europe might favour or encourage official negotiations, and it might also be called upon to give its opinion on draft conventions at the request of the Committee of Ministers. In some cases it facilitates the ratification of treaties, either at the time of consultation or at a later stage, by creating pressure on governments.

1171 – The obligation to take a common position, publicly and in writing, on the answers to be given to recommendations and questions directed to the Councils of these organisations produces an interesting method of cooperation. *While this often results in agreements based on the lowest common denominator, for fear of deciding issues that are not yet settled between governments, it brings the executive branches together, sensitises them to public opinion and encourages them to address new topics of discussion and lay the groundwork for future solidarity.* The fact that these negotiations are taking place explains why the responses are often a long time coming.

1172 – The countless oral questions put in public sessions induce governments to take a position, which may be that of their country or of the joint executive body of the organisation. These oral statements are more political in nature than the replies to written questions, which are often complex, delicate or technical. They can sometimes be the starting point for a new negotiation, especially in the European Parliament, where even the Council of Ministers, or its President, as well as the Commission, are in certain circumstances required to take part in debates on matters of importance. (see *1301*)

1173 – The European Parliament holds hearings very like those of national parliaments: these are designed to obtain more information or, where the hearings are public, to assist in the formation and expression of opinions. They enable a variety of groups to be given a hearing at Community institution level in specific areas: youth, multinational business, medicine, nuclear energy and migrant work are examples.

1174 – Some international parliamentary assemblies, such as the Council of Europe and the European Parliament, have served as a platform for European governments to announce important political negotiations.

§3. The organisation as an actor in negotiation

1175 – With the establishment of institutions to which States have granted the power to act in the international arena, diplomatic privilege as the exclusive preserve of sovereign nations has come to an end. World society is turning to broader and more lasting forms of organisation. Sometimes the principles they follow are new, with anonymous multilateral procedures offering peoples and territories that do not have sovereignty, as well as ethical or professional interests, the chance to be represented in international technical, and sometimes diplomatic, activities, and associated with them. (see *654*)

1176 – These trends have resulted in the creation of organised international public services, in the form of institutions with legal, financial or technical powers that enable them to deal with other entities. *The degree of internationalisation of these institutions varies according to the wishes of the States that set them up.*[47] *But their existence and their actions continue to be underpinned by the will of the Member States.* (see *1242*)

Some of these services fall outside the scope of international law: negotiators may even prefer to have them set up and governed under the laws of the State where they are based, sometimes in the form of a commercial entity.

1177 – The international organisation remains a secondary phenomenon, the result of productive negotiations between States, which alone are the primary actors and fundamental partners on the international scene. (see *606*)

No international institution is recognised by States as an equal partner either in diplomacy or politics.

1178 – International institutions do not possess any of the essential characteristics of statehood. Their aims are defined by governments, which impose on them a dependency that is often limiting in terms of their objectives, decisions and resources – the kind of subordination that no sovereign State would accept if it weakened the exercise of its political responsibilities vis à vis the people it represents.

1179 – The legal personality of an international institution is distinct from that of States, since it is based not on the traditional notion of national sovereignty but instead on the clearly expressed intentions of the States creating it. *The object, duration and scope of this attributed personality are limited to those defined in the constitutive instrument of the organisation or implied by its drafting* (see *Advisory Opinion of 11 April 1949 on Reparations for Injuries Suffered in the Service of the United Nations (1948–1949)*, ICJ *Rep.* 1949, p. 174). (see *655*)

1180 – The major function of the international institution is to facilitate relations and promote cooperation between its Member States, and thus its competence will be general or specific, global or regional, depending on the wishes of its creators. This fundamental decision conditions the scope of the negotiations that can take place within it. On the other hand, organisations tend to prolong the effects of the concerted actions of their founding States, and so their duration is rarely fixed in advance.

1181 – Each party to a negotiation is entitled to interpret its outcome; any act that goes beyond the organisation's founding instrument, unless the Member States have agreed on it, can be the source of discord and is subject to further negotiation,

---

47 H. T. ADAM: *Les Etablissements publics internationaux*, Paris, LGDJ, 1957.

as witness the dispute over the activities of the United Nations, in the Congo and elsewhere, which certain powers regard as irregular. The European Union is alone in having a jurisdictional mechanism for the compulsory settlement of such disputes. (see *1302*)

1182 – The introduction of national interests into collective organisations has given rise to a new form of negotiation, carried out on behalf of Member States with third parties. However, the participants may always use negotiations between themselves to arrive at a single common position, and then decide on what conditions and by which authorities the joint negotiations shall be conducted, to give themselves the opportunity to examine and, as the case may be, approve the results produced.

This is the procedure followed in international trade negotiations, where the European Commission receives authorisation and instructions from the governments of the Member States. (see *1103, 1485*)

1183 – Among the attributes necessary for an international organisation to be able to fulfil its mission is the legal capacity to have rights and duties and to act on the international plane (see *Advisory Opinion on Reparations*, ICJ *Rep.* 1949, p. 174). Such capacity naturally extends to negotiating contracts and treaties with external entities, at both the national and the international level.[48] This capacity is exercised on conditions that the International Law Commission is seeking to codify, and the agreements so concluded are often subject to certain rules of international law. (see *1370*)

1184 – It is a matter for each State to make its own sovereign determination of which institutions or individuals are to represent it in international life. Within international organisations, by contrast, it is a matter for the founding governments to agree which authorities will be given these functions. (see *685*)

1185 – Governments exercise control over the external negotiations of international organisations: in practice each of them is bound in its entirety by commitments undertaken, hence the councils or assemblies in which the member countries are represented often have elaborate rules for the approval of such negotiations.[49]

1186 – Relations between international organisations include a very large number of administrative agreements entered into by the competent Secretaries General or Directors General, and taking a variety of forms. It is not uncommon to find clauses expressly providing for this in the constitutive instruments (see, for example, Article 63 of the UN Charter).

---

48 P. REUTER: Organisations européennes, Paris, PUF, 1970, p. 85. G. FITZMAURICE: *The Law and Procedure of the International Court of Justice*, BYIL, 1953, p. 2.

49 UN: *Répertoire de la pratique suivie par les organes des Nations unies*, III, p. 351. C. W. JENKS: 'Coordination: a New Problem of International Organization', *RCADI*, 1950, II, p. 157. T. A. M. ALTING von GEUSAU: *European Organizations and Foreign Relations of States*, Leiden, Sijthoff, 1962, p. 143.

The World Food Programme was the result of a coordinated initiative between the United Nations and the FAO. The European Commission, too, confers some of its tasks on autonomous agencies the status of which is defined in each case.

The Mercosur group has entered into a collaboration agreement with the European Community, which is its main trading partner: this is expected to lead to lasting political dialogue. (see *1643*)

The World Bank and the European Community together participated in the creation of the European Bank for Reconstruction and Development (EBRD). (see *1637*)

1187 – Many arrangements nonetheless exist that enable coordination or collaboration to take place between specialised bodies, on a quite informal basis between their senior officials, either by unilateral or parallel decisions or resolutions, or by an exchange of working documents, or simply by measures taken internally. One principle, however, remains sacrosanct: *no agreement between international executives can impose burdens on the Member States that they have not expressly agreed to accept.*

1188 – Discussions between international organisations imply mutual recognition of their legal personality and their particular aims, since each organisation is an autonomous entity whose own organs have specific decision-making powers. Such discussions may only proceed, therefore, with the agreement of the governments involved.

1189 – Less common are statutory clauses that allow negotiations between international organisations and sovereign States. The fact remains, though, that diplomatic practice is replete with agreements of this type, and the right of representation is increasingly used among organisations. (see *2468*)

1190 – One of the first issues on which an organisation needs to reach agreement with its member States, or some of them, concerns the conditions under which it will carry out its mission: the privileges and immunities necessary for its international functioning, the particular status of its officials and the rules applicable to its headquarters, documents and finances.

Some States compete with each other to attract the major international institutions into their territory.

1191 – Agreements with third countries are more rare: examples include the association agreements entered into by the United States, Canada and various European countries with what was formerly the OEEC. Aside from the European Union, few organisations admit the representatives of non-member States.

1192 – Certain institutions have the task of negotiating with governments not only in the normal pursuit of their statutory mission but also to secure new forms of support for national sovereignty: food aid, investments, financial and budgetary aid or technical assistance.

They also enter into agreements with national bodies, public or private, for the purpose of studies, works, technical expertise missions or the implementation of development programmes.

1193 – These functions expand and overlap in line with the growth in diverse forms of aid. They result in the creation of new institutions, taking various forms, and in some of them being granted the power to intervene officially in crises, to take action at grass-roots level and undertake the resulting negotiations, as has been seen from the practice of emergency forces. *In such cases, the international organisation acts as a substitute for the State, the normal player on the diplomatic stage.* (see *1132, 1651, 1981*).

1194 – Whether the existence of an international organisation is binding on a third party is an issue that has been extensively debated. The International Court of Justice took the view that this was not open to doubt in the case of the United Nations, since almost all the members of the international community belonged to it (*Advisory Opinion on Reparations*, ICJ *Rep.* 1949, p. 174).

1195 – In truth, the attitude of governments with regard to international institutions to which they do not belong is still dictated by what they think is in their interests. Their attitude will be one of reserve where they fear being made to take account of, and give consideration to, forces they do not control, and which might pose problems; it will be negative where the institution includes a State with which they have no official relations, In any event, the way is left open for a compromise.

1196 – As the instrument of the will of States, no international organisation can embark, on its own initiative, on any major negotiation: *the institution is not itself a pole of diplomatic activity, nor is it invested with any primary political responsibility, in other words, before a people.*[50] (see *655*)

The more important a negotiation is, the more likely it is to take place outside the governing organs of the multilateral institution.

1197 – While there is no doubt that an international organisation has the capacity to negotiate for the purposes of fulfilling the missions conferred on it, using the institutions attributed to it, the question remains whether it can be considered as an autonomous actor on the world stage, capable in its own right of altering the environment in which it finds itself, the main characteristic of which is mutability and proneness to conflict.

1198 – The balancing, or even confrontation, of the forces in play happens inside the organisation. Choices are made in order to adapt to the environment, since the organisation itself does not have autonomous authorities that could give it independent direction and impetus based on direct political responsibility, and it is run by officials or technical staff who are not subject to any democratic control.[51]

As an actor in negotiations, the organisation must inspire confidence: it is the duty of its leaders to meet this challenge.

---

50 J. W. SCHNEIDER: *Treaty-Making Power of International Organizations*, Geneva, Droz, 1963, p. 62. E. HAAS: *Beyond the Nation State*, Denver, Stanford University Press, 1964.

51 E. JOUVE: *Relations internationales du Tiers-Monde*, Paris, Berger-Levrault, 1976, p. 273.

1199 – The danger exists that a lack of a sense of responsibility on the part of international bureaucracy might create a political vacuum. Public service at this level is not subject to democratic power; instead, it can become dependent on the strongest or richest of the Member States.
The future of the institution depends on the dynamism, skill and standing of its head. (see *655*)

1200 – The role played by the Secretary General of the United Nations in negotiations has been enhanced by the stability, independence and experience of the holders of the office. This role has developed out of the founding instruments themselves, thanks to the trust shown by governments and the work of various intermediaries, public reports and secret processes.

However, the responsibility thus exercised by this highest of international officials is still subject to the political will of the governments, especially those represented in the Security Council.

Throughout various international crises,[52] the Secretary General's readiness to serve, his independence and moral authority, have equipped him with remarkable powers to mediate in cases where his knowledge of the situation made him aware that a dispute was imminent and where he was encouraged to do so by the agreement of the parties. One example is the mission carried out by Javier Perez de Cuellar in Iraq before the 1991 Gulf War.

1201 – Aside from the skills required to lead what is often a huge and complex administration, the true qualities of the head of an international secretariat are exactly those of a good diplomat. *His role is to negotiate, to make others negotiate, to understand negotiation and give it the best chance of success.*

1202 – Over time, one office has come to predominate. During the month he is in office, and in spite of the fact that the President of the UN General Assembly has priority in terms of protocol, it is the President of the Security Council who plays a decisive role in bringing together States that are in conflict. Not only is he skilled in the practice of calling upon colleagues for advice, individually or collectively, but he can also use their replies to give him the outline of a possible solution. This is why any preconceived ideas, haste or excess would serve only to weaken his capacity to negotiate. (see *1143*)

1203 – Once the system of an international organisation is set up and functioning, it can reinforce the political manoeuvres of its Member States vis à vis the outside world. The Pan-American character of the Organization of American States had an effect of this kind by reinforcing the reach of the Monroe Doctrine.

1204 – Sometimes, the international role of an organisation consists simply of giving its backing to particular work or decisions. This is the case of the

---

52 M. C. SMOUTS: *Le Secrétaire général des Nations unies*, Paris, Colin, 1971. R. DAYAL: *Mission for Hammarskjöld: the Congo Crisis*, Princeton University Press, 1976. J. PEREZ de CUELLAR: 'Le rôle du Secrétaire général des Nations unies', *RGDIP*, 1985, p. 273.

United Nations, which acts through the resolutions of its General Assembly and the decisions of its Security Council. The Council of Europe acts through its treaties, the OECD through the conclusions in its reports and the European Union through the law made by its institutions.

1205 – Despite their weakness, there are some international organisations today with a political will and legal personality distinct from those of their member countries. Built on strong common ground, some of them are designed not only to last but also to develop, by adapting their structure to meet their increasing responsibilities, even by scaling down where necessary. Authors sometimes present them as part of a new world legal order.[53] (see *1094, 1104*)

1206 – Governments must be ready to act within the resulting legal, financial and practical framework, even if this adds an extra layer of procedures, norms and entities, which changes the way they exercise their prerogatives. The more governments are involved, the less integration is possible.

This teeming proliferation of international machinery becomes, in its turn, a force for integration in relations between States: they will have to accept that their real interest lies in respecting the independence of these organisations and actively negotiating to ensure they function effectively.[54]

§4. An instrument of diplomatic manoeuvre

1207 – As a result of technical initiatives, every aspect of the intergovernmental administrative edifice is subject to growth and change. This branch of diplomacy is one of great promise, requiring increasing levels of qualification from those who choose to specialise in this field.[55]

1208 – These institutions and their machinery are the result of negotiation, and it is also by negotiation that they develop their activities along lines distinct from those of their parties and define a truly common policy to be pursued in any given area. Disagreements can be resolved by consultation, without the need to resort to the authorities to impose a ruling. (see *1630*)

1209 – Not only do international organisations provide the framework for negotiation between States, but they are also among the entities and actors involved in it. As such, they become the instruments of State policy to the extent that they are solid and coherent enough to be capable of manoeuvre.

1210 – At every level, the multiplying number of institutions has led to the imposition of more and more detailed multilateral disciplines. This has distorted the traditional competitive playing field and produced its own entire networks and

53 P. REUTER: *Organisations européennes*, Paris, 1970, p. 10. 'Organisations internationals et évolution du droit', in *Etudes offertes à A. Mestre*, Paris, Sirey, 1956, p. 447.

54 G. BURDEAU: 'Le FMI et la surveillance de l'espace monétaire et financier mondiale', in *La mondialisation du droit*, p. 261.

55 A. PLANTEY: *Droit et pratique de la fonction publique international*, Paris, CNRS, 1977.

systems that work against the methods of traditional diplomacy. *International management is self-sufficient and depends less and less on negotiation, even multilateral negotiation, instead favouring administrative or technical procedures:* this explains why, in an increasing number of cases, intergovernmental bodies are headed by senior international officials rather than national representatives. (see *1632, 1635*)

1211 – The very fact that States have felt the need to set up delegations to the main international administrations naturally tends to increase the amount of discussion in or around them: such an entity will be inclined to seek an increased role for itself.[56] Often, it is the meeting of these permanent representatives that directs the organisation. (see *2467*)

1212 – In addition, delegations to intergovernmental organisations know that it is in their interests to maintain contact at every level with the secretariat of the conferences they attend. The role played by international civil servants is beyond question, especially with regard to the procedure, organisation, and production and publication of the working documents on which the success or failure of a negotiation can depend. (see *1608*)

1213 – The interest all States show in the geographical distribution of important posts in both the international and European public service would suggest that the occupants of these posts exercise some influence. Certain senior officials are able to shed light on a conflict, identify what it is really about, and suggest possible solutions, assuming they do so discreetly. (see *1103, 1621*).

1214 – Many States have central administrations that are understaffed and under-resourced; they use international institutions in order to obtain the information they need to decide how to act. *This is why, for many negotiators in very different fields, the United Nations, through its debates and documents, is the main source of documentation and practical experience.* It is thus very important that its work should be of a high standard and its publications impartial. (see *735, 1928*)

One of the main missions of the OECD is to gather and make use of economic facts and statistics, and to provide an impartial forum for meetings, discussions and expertise at intergovernmental level. (see *1074, 1147, 1241, 1243, 1927*)

1215 – Some meetings serve as a testing ground for governments, who use them to assess how an initiative or attitude is likely to be received or how effective a given response will be. They are also able to anticipate or thwart the manoeuvres of others. Negotiation today requires both modern and traditional diplomatic channels to work closely together. (see *1174*)

1216 – Some of the greatest powers can be seen taking advantage of the scope for experimentation and manoeuvre international fora offer them, whether they use it for opening negotiations, exploiting a situation that has arisen or for purposes of

---

56 P. GENET: *Le Droit diplomatique contemporain*, Geneva, Droz, 1962, p. 414. *Les Missions permanentes auprès des organisations internationales*, Brussels, Bruylant, Carnegie Foundation, 1971, etc.

propaganda. Provided they respect the procedures and customs of the institution, these tactics are highly profitable in political terms, as indeed are those that serve to stay the organisation's hand when its intervention would be dangerous. (see *1549*)

1217 – Relations between States are also conducted on the fringes of these institutions. States have policy and strategic goals that lead them to cooperate, regroup and form coalitions in order to make their opponent take their will into account. Inevitably, these coalitions express themselves in the form of interest or pressure groups within the organisations.[57] (see *1198*)

1218 – Their first objective is to bear upon the decision-making processes by aligning national positions, usually starting with the most audacious proposition. This means that there is real moral coercion on those delegations that, without being instructed to do so, automatically rally behind the dominant position and thus contribute to the much-criticised automatic majority. (see *1051, 2174*)

1219 – There is thus a movement towards harnessing international organisations in the service of new strategies. The axes of power in world diplomacy are still in place, and some of the effects of this can be felt running through the multilateral institutional machinery: they can give – and change – direction, but they can also dismantle and destroy it. (see *2181*)

1220 – International administrations often tend to react by forming themselves into structured and autonomous bodies, independent from States, geared entirely towards fulfilling their constitutional function. This form of consolidation is not peculiar to them, but is a characteristic of all complex types of apparatus, in the corporate as well as the biological world. (see *1103, 1199, 1519*)

1221 – Even when not deployed in the service of the States which, alone or together, dominate an international organisation, the cohesion of its bureaucracy cannot fail to provoke a reaction on the part of governments anxious to maintain their freedom of political choice. *States lose no opportunity to assert their authority over a system with a tendency to free itself from their control and set itself up as an independent technical or diplomatic power.* (see *1960*)

1222 – Hence the interest governments have in giving careful consideration to the tasks and resources of the machinery they have created, and of which they are part: only by negotiation can they avoid becoming its prisoners. *Governments also make sure, in many international institutions, that no decision is final or binding unless its adoption was preceded by negotiation.* (see *1563*)

Where the degree of constraint is too great, States find pragmatic ways of avoiding it. Twenty or so European governments created a lightweight structure, named Eureka, for scientific and industrial cooperation between laboratories and businesses: each project benefits from public funding at national and community levels, which requires complex negotiation, notably in a conference of ministers who choose from among the high technology projects proposed by the enterprises

---

57 T. HOVET: *Bloc Politics in the United Nations*, Cambridge, Harvard University Press, 1960.

concerned. There is also the 'Esprit' programme, aimed at stimulating and coordinating technological research.

1223 – Even when it does not require unanimity, an international organisation must take nationalimperatives into account. Apart from rules that impose weighted voting, or require a qualified majority for any decision to be enforceable, some organisations offer States a form of appeal against measures taken against them by the majority in the Council of the organisation, as in the ILO and the ICAO. (see *1565*)

1224 – With the exception of parts of their management structure, international organisations are not autonomous; they are subject to major constraints, the greatest of which is the weight of influence of their Member States which, in the main, are the ones with the decision-making power. *Many international institutions serve to consolidate the role of States by providing them with new opportunities for expression.*

1225 – In this way the United Nations has had the effect of entrenching the phenomenon of the State by recognising the sovereign equality of independent States, promoting the self-determination of peoples with its consequences, and arranging for most forms of financial aid and technical assistance to developing countries to be handled at a national level.[58] (see *2309*)

The temptation is strong for some great powers to use international organisations as instruments of their own global policies.

1226 – Dependent on the will of others, and lacking the necessary freedom to engage in its own diplomatic manoeuvres, an international organisation is unlikely to exceed the mission its members agreed to because its very existence as a cohesive entity is at their mercy. Its role is limited to the function conferred on it, with the – often limited – resources allowed it by the main actors on the international stage, namely the States that set it up. It is often said that many governments do not contribute enough to multinational programmes, preferring bilateral aid in the form of grants or loans, which allow them to expand their trade or influence. (see *713, 1976*)

1227 – Leaving aside the special case of the European Union, the heads of international organisations, even the most powerful, only have very limited powers of diplomatic initiative; they have no prerogative enabling them to resolve political conflicts or bring pressure to bear of their own volition on Member States in order to ensure that commitments are respected. (see *1656, 1661*)

1228 – To the extent that the larger organisations have become the favoured instruments of certain diplomatic networks, even within the most specialised institutions, their debates are becoming more and more politicised and their work influenced by motives and considerations unconnected with their mission. (see *2619*)

---

58 G. R. BERRIDGE and A. JENNINGS: *Diplomacy and the UN*, New York, St. Martin's Press, 1985. M. C. SMOUTS: 'Réflexions sur les méthodes de travail du Conseil de sécurité', *AFDI*, 1982, p. 601.

Groups of States either try to have certain issues transferred from one institution to another, or reopen the debate in another forum if they are not satisfied with the outcome. This kind of argument does nothing to facilitate coordination at headquarters level. (see *1991*)

1229 – This development cannot be entirely attributed to the inadequate level of technical qualification of many national delegations. It is a symptom of deep-seated differences in the hierarchies of values nations accept or uphold. The global organisation provides both the setting and the means for intergovernmental negotiation and makes it possible for States to fashion arguments and priorities, or practise political or ideological exclusion, without regard for the particular purposes and functions of international administration.

1230 – The debates that take place sometimes cause the reality and seriousness of the problems in hand to be underestimated. While States themselves are concerned about losing control of their own system to forces that are powerful, blinkered, reckless and uncontrolled, international organisations have proved singularly ill-adapted to these situations which can result in sudden and widespread breakdown. (see *713, 2224*)

Starting in 1991, the crisis in former Yugoslavia showed how extremely difficult it is for international institutions, even when acting within the scope of their functions, to grapple with serious cultural and ethnic problems and find an effective response when confronted with a real challenge. (see *1132, 1675*)

1231 – What can the UN Security Council and General Assembly do in the face of 'antipersonnel' mines and growing stocks of all kinds of weaponry? What action can the financial institutions take to limit the chaos in currencies? What attitude will other organisations take towards the proliferation of multinational businesses, the march of technology and the increasing tendency to transfer data to private centres of research and decision-making?

1232 – The increasing expense and constraints of this machinery will lead governments to rationalise it and make it less inefficient and more coherent. There is still room for negotiation to harmonise the missions, programmes and resources of international organisations. (see *2230*)

1233 – These objectives are difficult to achieve, however, where the partners involved are too numerous or too disparate. Any agreement among them on the nature and substance of international society must be based on a common political philosophy and a desire for cooperation.

Powerful innate tendencies have a way of asserting their domination, in the end. It is in the nature of relations between sovereign powers that they are free to decide where their interests lie and with whom they wish to deal. *It is always difficult and precarious to seek to confine the will of several nations within the bounds of a collective strategy, as the experience of the European Union has shown. On the other hand, as long as plurinational systems are incapable of acting or reacting fast and effectively, determined governments will always be quick to seize the initiative or respond in their own way.* (see *110, 834, 1329, 1358, 1698, 1994, 2284*)

1234 – As a meeting place of peoples, routes and civilisations, Europe gives the appearance of a confined territory, parcelled out between populations that have been allies at some times in history and opponents at others, but have never been brought together for long periods in a broad, solid and cohesive union.

1235 – At a time when the capacity of the traditional State to continue to assure the security and prosperity of its inhabitants is under discussion, the States of Europe appear vulnerable. The entire continent is dangerously exposed to crises and conflicts between nations and civilisations, each legitimate in its own way. (see *1678, 1690, 1692*)

1236 – Despite its historical antagonisms, economic inequalities and cultural differences, advances in communications and exchanges are revealing the depth of the solidarity within European society and its need for unity. *Europe offers a particularly favourable ground for developing and perfecting negotiation between governments, between elements of civil society and between private enterprises.* (see *1849, 2287*)

1237 – There have been numerous attempts to give institutional form to this unique and close, competing but complementary, relationship. The idea of federalism was raised in some quarters long ago, and the drafts by Aristide Briand, debated in the League of Nations Assembly in September 1929 and recorded in the Briand Memorandum of 1930 on a federal union regime for Europe, prefigured the common market and some of the institutions of what is now the European Union.

In 1946, in Zurich, Winston Churchill launched the concept of the 'United States of Europe': this led to the creation of the Council of Europe in 1949. In 1947, General Marshall offered American aid to Europe on the condition that its States set up an organisation to administer it: this prompted the creation in 1948 of the Organisation for European Economic Cooperation, the precursor of the OECD. Also in 1948, in Brussels, the five European Allies, faced with the hostility of the USSR, created the Western European Union.

1238 – Europe is recognised today as a diplomatic, administrative and financial reality in negotiation worldwide. Several global institutions with headquarters elsewhere have established a presence there. The United Nations, for example, has an Office as well as an Economic Commission, set up pursuant to a 1947 resolution of the Economic and Social Council, in which European States (even those that are not members of the UN) and also the United States are represented, and which provided a forum for contacts and exchanges between the countries of Western, Central and Eastern Europe at a time when the continent was divided.

1239 – Europe, however, is far from clear as a concept, and can be understood in a variety of different ways. Its geographical, historical, ethnic, cultural and economic dimensions will not be the same for the purposes of legal construction as they are for diplomatic negotiations or in the ideological sense. (see 6)

Thus the frontiers of the European diplomatic system have fluctuated throughout history and are changing still, as a function of the political environment and the upsurge in new initiatives: there are as many as 48 Member States in the Council of Europe (since Georgia joined in 2004) and as few as 5 in the Nordic Council.

European negotiations often result in the creation of particular areas, based on their subject matter and on the political will of governments and the people, when they are consulted: thus, the 'Euro zone' is different in dimension from the 'Schengen area', the 'Eurojust' or 'Europol' zones.

1240 – Cooperation in Europe has led to some interesting developments in the whole concept of international groupings of States: these are more numerous now, and their functions are more varied. The negotiation that goes on within these entities is becoming increasingly complex and technical and its results more lasting.

It was in Europe, moreover, that the first intergovernmental unions appeared in the nineteenth century, in specific fields such as postal and telephone communications.

1241 – Western Europe has thus been the test bed for extensive, diverse and far-reaching kinds of international cooperation, both internal and external. Institutions proliferate, each with its own headquarters (agreed upon by negotiation between the governments), members and organs, its own geographical, functional and ideological dimension, and its own particular form of solidarity. Some of them have provided the vehicle for new initiatives: the OECD, for example, was responsible for setting up a European conference of transport ministers, a European monetary agreement and the International Energy Agency. (see *1962*)

The Conference for Security and Cooperation in Europe brought together 34 countries in Paris in 1990, not all of them European. Its successor organisation, the OSCE, now numbers more than fifty States, including several in Central Asia, such as Kazakhstan, Kyrgyzstan, Uzbekistan, Tajikistan and Turkmenistan.[1] This is a very broad framework for negotiation (see the Charter of Paris for a New Europe, 21 November 1990); the European Stability Pact of 21 March 1995 proved how effective it is for purposes of disarmament. (see *1004, 1122, 1700, 1752, 1793*)

1242 – The will to give recognition to ideological ties sometimes leads to political organisations being set up: however, the expression of real complementarities is frustrated or delayed by the traditional diplomatic methods practised in them.

---

1 V.-Y. GHEBALI: 'Le rôle de l'OSCE en Asie centrale', *Revue de Défense nationale*, July 2001, p. 122.

This was the case throughout the whole course of European unification after the Second World War, with the United States not only consenting but playing an active part, and at one point seeking to control the process itself. (see *981*)

Western Europe can thus claim the first international parliamentary assembly (the Council of Europe), the first attempts at military, administrative and jurisdictional supra-nationality and the first international election based on universal suffrage in every member State. (see *1155*)

1243 – Created in France in 1950, the Europe of the Communities was the product of two movements, one administrative and the other ideological,[2] and their coming together explains the unique and difficult nature both of the negotiations that set it up and of those that now take place within it. (see *1255, 1336*)

In practice, the creation of the European Coal and Steel Community (which remained in existence for fifty years, under the ECSC Treaty of 18 April 1951), the European Economic Community and European Atomic Energy Community under the Rome Treaties of 25 March 1957, introduced a new political objective into the traditional diplomatic system because these entities were superimposed on their component States while at the same time their responsibilities and functioning remained subject to negotiation by their governments.

Later, the mission and institutions of these European Communities came to be viewed as too complex and unwieldy: a Merger Treaty was negotiated in 1965 to unify the Council, Assembly, Court and Commissions of the Communities. The Single European Act of 1986 replaced the Common Market with the Single Market. In Maastricht in 1991, the European Council decided, on the basis of a proposal by the Commission, that the Communities would henceforth be known as the European Union. It added two new fields of competence, or 'pillars': foreign policy and security, justice and policing. In 1997, in Amsterdam, the Council made certain additions to the Single European Act and accepted the possibility of direct cooperation between governments. In 2000, the Council of Nice confirmed all these changes and adopted the Charter of Fundamental Rights. (see *1247, 1248*)

1244 – Meanwhile, in order to form a counterweight to the process of unification that was under way in Western Europe, the Soviet Union and its allies founded their own cooperation, the Council for Mutual Economic Assistance (COMECON), on 25 January 1949. This intergovernmental cooperative body was not limited to the continent of Europe. Its effectiveness was undermined by Russia's political, military, economic and ideological preponderance over its partners. (see *133*)

This international grouping in Eastern Europe tended to have the same integrationist effect as in the West, but mainly operated for the benefit of only one of the partners. It disappeared amid great confusion with the fall of the Berlin Wall when the new States began negotiating with the European Union.

---

2 R. SCHUMAN: 'L'Europe dans la politique extérieure de la France', in *Les Affaires étrangères*, Paris, PUF, 1959, p. 355. C. ZORGBIBE: *Histoire de l'Union européenne*, Paris, Albin Michel, 2005.

The Commonwealth of Independent States (CIS), founded at the Minsk Conference of 8 December 1991, has as its members twelve of the original fifteen republics formerly part of the USSR federation; it is only partly European, and includes a group of States that depend on Russian aid, such as Belarus, Kazakhstan, Kyrgyzstan and Tajikistan. (see *987, 1004*)

1245 – The Western European experience has added a new category of international organisations, one whose intergovernmental character is only of secondary importance. These are entities with responsibility for managing services of common interest to a number of countries, designed not in the classic form of a conference of plenipotentiaries or government delegates but rather as that of a joint enterprise. These international entities, one of the first models for which was the Bank for International Settlements, set up in 1930, have had a wide range of responsibilities, including the financing of railroad rolling stock (Eurofima), experimental nuclear reprocessing (Eurochemic) and, more recently, air security (AESA). Their legal forms vary from public entities to mixed or private companies.

The European Bank for Reconstruction and Development (EBRD) was set up by diplomatic treaty in 1990 with 43 Member States, which had risen to 58 States by 1999. It operates on the London markets under local law, as provided in its headquarters agreement. (see *1186, 1637*).

1246 – Negotiation between the partners takes place within these structures, following the methods used in the private sector. The delegates who take part in them sometimes represent national public services, and sometimes private or privatised entities. National concerns are still expressed, but more flexibly.

The technical success of some of these international initiatives cannot hide the lack of a collective strategy on the part of the governments. The European Space Agency is an example of this, as its programmes are the end-product of hard bargaining between 17 member countries. (see *1493*)

1247 – The European Union has pursued the objectives laid down in the Treaties of Maastricht (1991), Amsterdam (1997) and Nice (2000). But it has not made a strategic choice between the two challenges presented: to develop its core competences (as decided at the Council of Laeken in 2001) or to enlarge its membership (as decided at the Council of Copenhagen in 2003).

The long-planned process of enlargement, first of the Communities, then of the European Union, which began with six members, has resulted in a massive entity with 25 Member States since 1 May 2004, which will become 27 in 2007. Their numbers will probably grow still further. Within its bounds, several traditional poles of negotiation have reappeared, including those of the Baltic States, the States bordering the Danube and, later, the Balkan and Mediterranean poles. The centre of gravity of Europe is sliding towards the East of the continent in the direction of the Russian border. This entity of more than five hundred million people can no longer be managed on the same terms as were envisaged in the days of the Schuman plan. (see *1243, 1272, 1416, 2004*)

This realisation prompted a review of the founding treaties. The resulting episode of the draft 'Constitution' had no effect on the dimensions of the Union, which derive from the treaties of adhesion entered into by each of the new Member States.

1248 – By progressing beyond anything previously attempted before, and by devising novel institutions and mechanisms to serve the interests of cooperation between States, the European Union has provided the testing ground for a kind of diplomacy that has overtaken traditional negotiation. Within this community, the free exercise of traditional diplomacy and private negotiation cohabits with the legal methods and structures of a powerful organisation. A continuous process of arbitrage goes on that serves to reinforce the collective power enjoyed by the States that submit to its disciplines. (see *1339, 1491*)

At the time of the Maastricht negotiations, it was envisaged that the European Union would encompass all the competences and activities of the Communities, with the political cooperation of the Member States. The legal and diplomatic nature of this Union was to depend on the attitude of the different partners to certain highly controversial issues. However, the creation of a Union citizenship comprises very specific rights, such as eligibility to vote or the right to diplomatic protection, without replacing national citizenship.

1249 – According to its founding treaties, the European Union creates an area of liberty, security and justice, where human rights and the freedoms of movement and establishment are respected as well as the principles of the rule of law and democracy that are common to Member States.

Based on discussions in which both governments and Community institutions were represented, a Charter of Fundamental Rights was adopted by the European Council at the Biarritz Conference and the Nice summit of 2000, having the status of a declaration of principle. It is a more complete, and complex, document than the 1950 Council of Europe Convention on Human Rights. (see *1293, 2171*)

1250 – The numerous innovations thereby imported into the typology of international relations produce effects in two directions: on the one hand, between their members, however numerous, and on the other, vis à vis the outside world, which is obliged to take account of this new and coherent force in global affairs. This is what gives Europe its unique character and role in international negotiation.

Section 1: The framework for dialogue

1251 – European States have been negotiating for centuries: it was in Western Europe that the principles and methods of modern diplomacy were first fashioned. The process of European unification reinforces these traditional relations by setting specific objectives for the future of Europe that derive from the existing treaties.

1252 – The sharing by the Member States of risks and opportunities that are not capable of precise advance definition is an essential feature of the Community edifice. The effect of multiplication of potential in Europe is expected to flow from the operation of two different and sometimes contradictory impulses: that of the natural laws of economy (especially those of the free movement of goods, capital, labour and information) and that of resolute common policies (on agriculture, transport, trade, environment, health, research, education, culture, industry, etc). This cannot fail to generate dynamism, albeit unpredictably. It sometimes also generates interest on the part of foreign companies which then invest funds. (see *1154, 2281*)

1253 – Europe as a whole thus consists of relations of preference, collaboration and unification which lend a particular colour to European negotiations and also open up fresh possibilities, with the growth, for example, of multilateralism and multilingualism.

Since this type of negotiation is a priori the prerogative of the members of the Union, it creates a closed dialogue that is necessarily exclusive, and is unique in world negotiation. The agricultural market and the common currency are defined by contrast with what exists elsewhere. The adhesion of a new member of the Union is subject to a process of diplomatic negotiation that requires the agreement of every existing member. (see *2287*)

1254 – The consequences of the setting up of the Communities were not limited to the transfer of certain national competences to a higher level: they involved the definition of new competences, resulting from the existence of specific structures at Community level and the expansion of their responsibilities as an effect of negotiation among the Member States.

Despite difficult international conditions and the lack of any real coordination of national financial and economic policies, the institutional system of the Community has proved adequate to meet the current demands of Europe as a whole. But, weighed down by its ongoing commitments and paralysed by its procedures and internal division of responsibilities, it has not proved as capable of constructing a collective vision to lead it into the future. *Political initiative has reverted to summit negotiations.*

An overall reform was originally planned at Laeken in 2001 to reaffirm the personality and strategic capabilities of the Union in a single constitutive treaty that would replace all the others. This was discussed at Salonika and again in Rome in 2003, and put to a specially constituted body, the Convention on the future of Europe, which drew up a detailed text with 465 articles (the 'Constitution') that the Council then revised and put in final form. After being initially rejected in 2003, the text was adopted in Brussels in June 2004 and signed in Rome in October that year.[3] Since this instrument was in the form of a diplomatic treaty, it was subject to ratification, but was rejected by France and The Netherlands in 2005, and, according to its own terms, has not entered into force. The pre-existing treaties it was designed to replace thus remain in effect and

3 J. HABERMAS: *Après l'Etat-nation, une nouvelle constitution*, Paris, Fayard, 2000. J. M. FERRY: *La Question de l'Etat européenne*, Paris, Gallimard, 2000. M. FOUCHER: *La République européenne*, Paris, Belin, 2000. P. MAGNETTE, etc.: *La Constitution de l'Europe*, Brussels, éditions de l'Université, 2000.

continue to govern negotiation within the Union, subject to certain amendments to be introduced upon acceptance by the Member States of some of the principles set forth in the draft 'Constitution'. (see *1249, 1256, 1260, 1264, 1360, 2489*)

§1. A favoured dialogue

1255 – Established on the basis of distinct treaties, each of which obeyed its own rules of operation although since 1965 they had shared the same institutional apparatus, the Community provided a new, specific and permanent framework for European negotiation, with its own rules and system of weighted voting in which the number of votes did not depend on the size of the population. Respect for the principle of State responsibility is a further mark of its legitimacy in traditional democratic terms.

This makes for a very complex system, one that will evolve with the adhesion of new members: a Union of 27 or more States cannot be expected to function in the same way as it did with 15. There is nothing in Community principles to prevent some of its member governments agreeing on more advanced forms of cooperation: as an example, France and Germany agreed in 2004 to be jointly represented in some meetings. (see *1272*)

The Council

1256 – Composed of representatives of the Member States, each in the capacity of a member of the government, pursuant to Article 2 of the Merger Treaty of 8 April 1965, the Council is at the same time a diplomatic organ and an institution of the Community. This is the body through which the governments collectively set the direction of the entire organisation, of which it has remained the key central institution.[4] This function was confirmed in the negotiation of the Maastricht, Amsterdam and Nice Treaties, as well as during the drawing up of the draft 'Constitution' of the European Union. (see *1254, 1350, 2467*)

1257 – The Council of Ministers meets periodically, in the presence of the Commission. Its composition can vary, depending on the nature of the subjects to be discussed: ten or more different compositions have been recorded, the main one being that of the Ministers for Foreign Affairs, though the composition in which the Council meets to address economic and financial matters (known as 'ECOFIN') has taken on a character very much of its own. The Council is the basic forum for negotiation between the Member States on all the areas laid down in the founding treaties. Its fields of competence were delimited within the European Coal and Steel Community and the European Atomic Energy Community, but much less clearly defined in the case of the European Economic Community, whose objects as laid

---

4 F. A. M. ALTING von GEUSAU: 'Les missions permanentes et le contrôle des politiques nationales par les organisations internationales', in *Les Missions nationales auprès des organisations internationales*, Brussels, Bruylant, 1971–1976, 3 vols, p. 200.

down in Article 3 of the EEC Treaty were too broad in scope not to require in-depth cooperation on the part of the governments implementing them.

The composition and workings of these Councils require coordination at both Community as well as national level. This in itself is a new source of negotiations, especially as to the scope of the competences of the Council. (see *1274*)

1258 – The mission of the Council of Ministers was conceived in the context of the Community as a whole, at a time when it was envisaged to move towards a federal system. If that were to happen, the Council would not in practice restrict its role to that of ratifying agreements between the Member States, (in the case of major decisions, of all of them); it would override the national concerns that are the stuff of traditional negotiation and focus on a Community vision of the higher interests of the European entity as a whole. (see *1336*)

1259 – On this issue, the debate has been long and arduous. Nor is it over. The crisis brought about in 1965 by the stiffening of French hostility to federalism produced the 'Luxembourg Compromise', at the January 1966 conference, the effect of which at the time was to extend the Council's unanimity rule to all decisions where the major interests of one or more partners were at stake. Community negotiation has been drawn back in the direction of bargaining and compromise rather than developing into a federalist body with authority and strategic capabilities. (see *1262, 1565*)

1260 – The Heads of State and Government agreed at the Paris Conference in December 1974 to limit the practice of requiring unanimity, but without renouncing the principles decided upon in Luxembourg. However, this agreement had only a slight effect on the process of negotiation between the ministers or their permanent representatives: their mission is still to find solutions that can be adopted by all the members of the Council, respecting their mutual interests and those of the Community.

These conclusions were reaffirmed several times, particularly at the end of successive summit negotiations, but with unconvincing results. It is only rarely that national preoccupations give way before collective imperatives, which are especially strong in the fields of inter-state cooperation, namely justice, foreign affairs, defence and policing.

1261 – In 1975, at the end of the 'federalist' period, it was suggested that the European Union should have a collegial government, independent of the national governments, exercising the functions of the Council and the Commission and controlled by two assemblies, one to be elected by universal suffrage and the other chosen by the governments, as a sort of senate. But these proposals went against the interests of the States.

The Council of Ministers remains a typically intergovernmental institution following the principles of diplomatic conferences. *As the permanent framework for negotiation between the Member States where matters of European unification are concerned, the Council allows the common will of the governments to prevail when serious problems arise.* (see *1520*)

1262 – While the Community produced a true form of institutionalised legislative power, the Council's acts are in essence international proceedings: the more powerful States will not submit to a solution imposed by a coalition of the lesser ones, who in turn wish to avoid falling under the power of the former. In practice, most of the time the ministers have taken decisions unanimously, with the Commission having adapted its proposed solution to the political configuration. The need to reach agreement within a given time-frame tends to result in package deals as the outcome of marathon sessions. (see *555*)

Following various reports and conferences such as the 1985 Milan Conference, European Council negotiations have changed in the legal sense because increasing numbers of decisions are now taken by qualified majority, provided no member dissents, as at the Amsterdam and Nice summits, on the understanding that unanimity is still necessary for any decision that one of the partners considers affects its vital interests (tax and social security for the United Kingdom, for example). (see *1272*)

1263 – At all events, the relaxation of the voting requirements has not eliminated negotiation between the partners; not all problems can be resolved by achieving a qualified majority. In practice, given the diversity of the subjects addressed and the interests of the partners, the aim was to avoid placing the small countries at an advantage or a disadvantage. This has made for procedures that are complicated, unpredictable and sometimes ineffective.

There are some important negotiations where it has been difficult even to reach a majority vote: in 1982, for example, the United Kingdom disagreed on the pricing of agricultural products, and in 1983 Denmark disagreed about fishing. (see *1327*)

1264 – One good reason for the continuation of negotiation between States is the very fact that all institutional reform must be the product of diplomatic treaties. This was the case with the merger of the executive bodies under the 1965 Merger Treaty, the election of the Parliament by universal suffrage (Act of 20 September 1976), and the setting up of a Court of Auditors in 1975.

A succession of intergovernmental conferences (IGCs) was held to prepare the ground and provide the framework for the most difficult negotiations. In order to draw up a single new treaty incorporating the provisions of the existing ones, the Council, at its meetings in Salonika and Rome in 2003, entrusted the task of codification to an expanded conference. It produced a draft 'Constitution', signed in Rome in 2004 but not ratified by all Member States. (see *1254*)

1265 – As a Community institution, the Council of Ministers exercises governing powers. Aided by the Commission, it defines the common policies and directs the external relations of the Union as a whole, as well as setting its ultimate goals. Also, some of the subjects dealt with by the Member States in the course of their mutual political cooperation have been raised within the Council. This tendency has been confirmed in the deliberations in European Council summit meetings.

1266 – The Council is the basic legislature of the Union, now having powers of 'co-decision' with the Parliament. Enforceable decisions are made by agreement between these organs as well as in each of them by agreement of the States, including the many regulations and directives that each Member State must implement. *In this way a body of Community law has built up, deriving from the founding treaties, that forms part of the national laws of the members and sometimes also part of international law binding on third countries, their businesses and even their nationals, because of the spread of global commerce.* (see *298, 1596, 1644*)

1267 – Thanks to the Council, which meets as often as every month on some issues such as foreign affairs or agriculture, governments have a direct and organised form of negotiation whereby they can resolve issues relating to the institutions of the Union, such as their financing, their work and the status of their officials. They agree on mandatory spending, in other words, money spent in carrying out the treaties, which makes up most of the budget. They also decide on matters for external negotiation by the Union, which complicates and slows down the procedures since the Council is not in permanent session. This work is done in association with the Parliament by co-decision. (see *1350, 1437, 1541, 2385*)

Intergovernmental negotiation

1268 – The Council of Ministers found itself confronted with an ever-growing workload. In order to lighten its programme and ensure consistency between its deliberations in different compositions, the decision was taken to entrust the preparation of the negotiations to a committee of permanent representatives, itself subdivided according to the subject matter to be discussed. The Council and its committees have large numbers of working groups, either permanent or specially convened by the members, and a well-staffed secretariat responsible, among other things, for preparing for its meetings and debates and ensuring that its decisions are carried out. This machinery facilitates the work of the Council as well as protecting it against political risks, and the frequent meetings of experts lead to the gradual reconciliation of national positions within the Community system. These bodies, some of which meet on a frequent basis, are all chaired by delegates or representatives of the State holding the Presidency of the Council. The fact that they are so numerous tends to dissipate and protract debates within the Community, even though, in theory, the Council still holds the decision-making power. (see *1290*)

1269 – The Council takes its decisions at ministerial level, but it can do so without formal discussion in cases where the work has been done in advance, especially by the Commission. It is possible to limit the number of people entitled to attend certain meetings, or even restrict it to the ministers concerned. At the technical level, on the other hand, the number of negotiators is increasing, with some permanent representations having dozens of experts on their teams to cover all the bodies in which matters of Community policy are discussed.

1270 – It is also possible to delegate certain responsibilities to institutions better suited to carrying them out. Thus, the Council of Ministers may entrust some of the missions of the Community to the Commission: it has been suggested that this should be done more frequently, with the Council having the right to review or reopen the issues, but in practice all important decisions are negotiated in the Council.

The role of the Commission in implementing decisions of the Council was confirmed in a series of governmental negotiations, subject to respect for the principle of subsidiarity and also to certain requirements as to consultation and obtaining expert advice. (see *1311*)

1271 – The negotiation between the Member States in all these organs centred on the Council of Ministers is subject to disciplines that make the process more complicated, but at the same time, make it easier to arrive at Community-wide solutions. All regulations within the scope of the Community's remit must, according to the EC Treaty, be based on proposals from the Commission.

The difficulty in taking decisions is especially evident in the field of external relations: here, the Commission does not have sufficient room to manoeuvre to enable it to proceed without referring to the governments at every step, nor is it always unanimous in its own approach. (see *1437*)

1272 – There is constant negotiation within the Council to ensure the smooth running of the organisation. An isolated State will be urged to give way unless the issue is one of prime importance to it, and if it holds out, and no accommodation is possible, this can lead to a crisis. These compromises thus serve to make the whole system work better, with the good will shown by some States inducing their partners to assume commitments or make concessions in other areas. The whole system moves from one compromise to the next, following a process that is often slow and confused. (see *1262, 1546*)

The wider the scope of Community competences extends, the greater the degree of reserve on the part of some States: dialogue in Europe tends to be a matter of variable geometry and to progress at different speeds. The divergent paths of intra-community negotiation were illustrated by the Maastricht negotiations, which resulted in the creation of the euro and its adoption by some Member States.

The possibility was raised at the Amsterdam negotiations in 1997 that some States might move forward together to further the objectives of the Union, and this became known as 'enhanced cooperation', whereby a minimum of eight governments can, with the consent of the Council and having sought the opinion of the Parliament, develop Community initiatives except on issues having a military application or in the field of defence. The idea of a 'two-speed' or 'variable geometry' Europe was further cemented by the Schengen Agreements, the workings of the Euro zone and technical cooperation on projects such as the Airbus and Ariane. (see *1298, 1419*)

1273 – The fact remains that the difficult nature of the subjects discussed, and the requirement of unanimity on new or major issues, mean that the Council is often criticised for delay and uncertainty in its responses to the activities of pressure groups and multinational corporations, as well as to the policies of foreign States, in the face of the unpredictable environment in Europe and worldwide. Negotiation is made more difficult when States base their refusal to conform on reasons of national prerogative or sometimes on different political philosophies or economic programmes. (see *1285*)

Heads of State and Government have sought to overcome these obstacles by reserving the most important negotiations, and the political direction of the Union, to themselves. The European Council has become the highest decision-making organ of the Community and now the Union. (see *1323*)

1274 – The Council has remained the forum of choice for the ongoing, and intense, negotiation that takes place between the Member States. A variety of complex and difficult negotiations are carried on in the Council in its different compositions as well as in some of the organs attached to it, to the extent that compromise between them is sometimes necessary. This threat of 'horizontal disintegration' has made it imperative to strengthen the role of the Presidency, currently limited by its six-monthly system of rotation. The Presidency is responsible for carrying through a programme of action as well as optimising the productivity of negotiations between the States and between the institutions themselves. The fact remains that the sense of a European 'identity' is no longer as strong as it was, since it has become current practice in negotiations within the Union to accede to the lowest common denominator. (see *1033, 1204*)

1275 – The Presidency is at the same time coordinator of the works of all the governmental bodies of the Union, especially at the level of the Committee of Permanent Representatives, mediator between States when their interests are too divergent for the Commission to be able to effect a technical reconciliation and initiator of new ways of implementing Treaty objectives. Finally, it is the Union's representative vis à vis the outside world in negotiations that go beyond the scope of strictly Community matters, these latter normally falling to the Commission.

Under the authority of the Presidency, the Union is represented in matters of foreign policy and also in international organisations and conferences. (see *1321, 1457, 1462, 1567*)

§2. Institutions and rules

1276 – The founding treaties of the European Communities set up institutions with the power to create rules that the States were bound to apply: in this, they derogated from the traditional practices of diplomacy. These rules consist of a body of law, the product of negotiation and regulation, which is by nature integrationist: some of these rules are subject to reservations or negotiated temporary derogations.

1277 – Within the European Union, no State is free to shape its own rights, nor to escape its obligations by pleading another state's breach, nor take unilateral action that is not authorised by the Treaty. There is thus no place for the reciprocity typically found in diplomacy. *Sanction for breach of the rules is a matter for the institution itself.* (see *670, 1344*)

1278 – At the outset, the Commission was set up as the independent guardian of Community treaties and institutions, and in a real sense its role is that of enforcement. It can oblige States to comply with Community rules. Once it has found that there has been a breach, the Commission announces the measures to be taken to remedy the situation and bring the infraction to an end. In case of refusal to comply, the matter may be referred to the Court. Proceedings taken against Member States run into their thousands, but only a small proportion of them result in proceedings before the Court. (see *1249, 1287*)

1279 – Each government, for its part, has reciprocal remedies it can pursue before the Court of Justice, which provides a compulsory dispute resolution procedure. Sanctions for failure to comply with Community law are usual, and the Court's judgements are binding on the States and the institutions of the Union and private entities. (see *1307, 1655*)

The fact remains, however, that some of the Court's decisions have not been applied by all the States concerned. (see *1661, 1673*)

1280 – There is a tendency for the internal disciplines and the organs of the Union to become more effective, by the mere fact of their permanence, rather than because of any real desire for political federalism on the part of governments or peoples. This gives the European construct its own inherent dynamic, which certain States oppose: discussion of jointly determined policies could lead to the overall structural balance being 'renegotiated', which they would regard as unravelling the successes of integration.

1281 – Often more powerful than the governments intended, Community institutions have increased their powers by giving each other mutual support, exchanging information and best practices, respecting each others' competences and rules and developing an elaborate system of internal controls.

The Parliament can itself bring proceedings before the Court where fundamental rights are threatened in a Member State. (see *1249*)

There is even case law in which the Court has ruled on the question of mutual support and control between the institutions: it ruled in favour of the Parliament against the Council in 1985, against the acts of the Parliament in 1986, and in favour of the Commission against the Council in 2005.

1282 – The Commission was responsible for setting in motion some of the initiatives that gave an increased role to the Parliament: examples are the 1965 Hallstein initiative on the Common Agricultural Policy and also the treaties of 1970 and 1975 on budgetary powers. This desire to invest the Parliament with real prerogatives was consistent with the financial regulations, and also with the decision of 1970 defining the Community's resources. Lastly, the Commission refers to the Court where conflicts arise with the Council on questions of principle as to the delimitation of its own powers vis à vis those of the States or of the Council itself.

1283 – These initiatives caused difficulties where the governments were concerned. Among those that proved problematic were the proposals put before the

Parliament by the Commission on 31 March 1965, without having consulted the Council, on the Common Agricultural Policy. Inevitably, such an initiative provoked a reaction on the part of those wishing to confine the Commission to a technical role.

1284 – The discussions between the Council of Ministers and the Parliament that sometimes attend the adoption of the EU budget or certain key appointments show how unprepared ministers are to deal with internal crises within the functioning of the Union apparatus. The Council is the scene of intense negotiations between the partners, but in practice it is a slow-moving, heavyweight body. The Commission, the Court and the Parliament, on the other hand, benefit from the federal dynamic; the Commission is responsible to the Parliament on a collective basis, and the President of the Commission reports to it. (see *1300*)

1285 – The Council and its satellite organs have gained in importance over the years, especially vis à vis the Commission, since the signing of the Luxembourg Compromise in January1966; since then a system of mutual consultation has operated between the States where the vital interests of one of them risk being affected.

As the principal organ of negotiation between the sovereign States, the real political power lies with the Council: it has prerogatives enabling it to regulate and extend the application of the Treaties, to interpret them and use them in accordance with the governments' wishes. In relation to the Parliament, it thus has a constitutional function. (see *1298*)

1286 – As the central organ of the Community, the Council has found itself increasingly thwarted by the other institutions, which are subject neither to its authority nor to that of the member States. It is under constant pressure, mostly as a result of its own decisions in extending the scope of the Union's competences, and also of the growing recourse to joint procedures: co-decision with the Parliament involves negotiation. (see *1281, 1645*)

The Community, and latterly the Union, has been exposed to the risk of institutional dissent of the kind that can arise in managing external negotiations or budgetary procedure: these are the areas that reveal divergences between government policies and between national identities and European aspirations. (see *1493*)

The Commission

1287 – Unified under the Merger Treaty of 8 April 1965, and appointed by the governments, the Commission is a collegiate body responsible for ensuring that the Treaties are implemented. Although much changed from the days of the original Coal and Steel Authority, its composition and workings are still rooted in a federalist concept of the Community. The Commission is independent from the Member States, taking its decisions by majority and working directly with the other European institutions. (see *1275, 1524*)

At its Nice meeting, the Council drastically revised the composition of the Commission in the light of the adhesion of the countries of Central and Eastern

Europe. It gave increased authority to the President of the Commission, who is appointed with the agreement of the Parliament and consulted on the choice of Commissioners, whose respective responsibilities he allocates. In principle, since 2004, there is one Commissioner from each member State, at least until 2014. (see *1256, 1264, 1427*)

1288 – The deliberations of the Commission must serve as the basis and also the engine of European integration. The Council operates, in principle, on the basis of the Commission's proposals, which it may only accept or reject, in carrying out its legislative and regulatory functions. This system allows the Union to express its own collective, continuous and impartial vision of its interests, and it also provides a forum for mediation between the Member States in which each of them has full knowledge of the facts and circumstances.

1289 – This does not mean that the Commission is a totally integrated collegiate body: it is even likely that, in its new composition, it will be inclined to give more weight than before to national preoccupations. Within the Commission, negotiation brings with it administrative work: initiatives and compromises are drawn up, information and documents prepared, solutions sought that will be acceptable to all the members, consultations held with partners in the fields of economics and employment, and the conditions of application of intergovernmental agreements examined. The work of the various departments (of which there are more than 30) culminates at the level of the Commissioners, each of whom has a specialised quasi-ministerial 'portfolio' who then vote collectively. It is at this point that serious differences of opinion sometimes emerge.

1290 – The Commission is in a position to negotiate the acceptance of its proposals by the Council, though they are sometimes amended. The dialogue that takes place, first at the level of technical preparation and later at the political level, enables different national viewpoints to be discreetly reconciled, and the proposals to be reworked to ensure they achieve the widest possible measure of support. *The Commission's role as mediator is becoming increasingly important within the Union: these are real negotiations, especially when carried on within the hundred or more committees of national officials.* (see *466, 1268, 1553*)

The Council's practice of unanimity means that the work of the Commission often consists more of preparing the ground for discussion than of producing actual draft decisions. Its growing role as a generator of innovative ideas and producer of instruments of Community law prevent it from being reduced to the status of a secretariat.

1291 – The Commission alone has the power to put forward proposals to the Council, and to implement its decisions, and this tends to override the exercise of its own initiative. But its power is enhanced by the sheer weight of the administrative apparatus that depends on it. It is further reinforced by the Commission's responsibility to the European Parliament, the members of which are elected in each State. This makes the methods of internal deliberation and coordination in the Commission all the more important in those areas in which either the Treaties or decisions of the Council have given it competence. (see *1645*)

Under the Treaties, the Commission has its own powers: to ensure compliance with the competition laws, and draw up detailed rules for their application; to steer the work of harmonising national laws in this field, and to take technical decisions in certain areas.

1292 – Operating along the same lines as centralised national bureaucracies, the workings of the Commission, like those of its subsidiary administrations, are leading to the formation of a new legal order, not only within Europe but sometimes beyond its borders.

In practice, in issuing rules that are directly applicable to its inhabitants, the Union operates like a federal body: the administrative apparatus needed to draft and implement Community policies is growing all the time, bringing with it a proliferation of overlapping structures and regulations, increased spending and ever more officials.

1293 – The effect of this expansion on organisational negotiation among the Member States has been to increase the burden of the administrative tasks that form part of the work of the Commission. It does this work in constant consultation with the representatives of governments and the professions, for example, in the hundreds of management and consultative committees that exist for each category of agricultural products and for customs duties, in which the Council, the Commission and the professional bodies are represented so that they operate on a sort of tripartite basis. (see *1516*)

This has opened up a new way of involving the private sector in international institutional negotiations, other than through the normal channels of national diplomatic representation.

1294 – The European Union has a budget that is negotiated – often with difficulty – in the Council with the aid of the Commission, and submitted to the Parliament. It has its own sources of funding, often levied directly, such as customs duties, import levies and a proportion of value added taxes raised, and these are used to fund policies decided on by the Council. (see *1267*)

The Parliament

1295 – Set up with the aim of giving the electorate a role in the political control of the workings of the institutions of the European Union, the Assembly that chose to call itself 'the European Parliament' (a name ratified by the governments) provides a good example of how the Union has moved beyond its basic premises, closer to integration. It is, furthermore, in the nature of the institution to seek a federal direction for the Union as a whole. This tendency was apparent from the works of the so-called *ad hoc* Assembly, which, following the decision of the Council of Ministers of the Coal and Steel Community in 1952, was given the task of preparing a draft treaty that would set up a European Political Community. After the chequered history of the European Defence Community, that draft remained a dead letter, but it already included a provision for a body to be elected by universal suffrage. The same idea was taken up again by the negotiators of the Treaty of Rome.

1296 – Undoubtedly, the fact that it is elected by direct universal suffrage within each member State has reinforced the 'federal' character of the Parliament. When the States reached agreement in 1976 on the way these elections were to be conducted, this was a typical example of 'institutional' negotiation for the future. The number of members of the Parliament has in fact grown constantly since then, mainly as the result of new adhesions, and they currently number over 700. (see *2162, 2385*)

1297 – Indeed, amendments to the terms of elections to the European Parliament may never undermine the sovereign powers of the national Parliaments, or result in any extension to the powers of the European Parliament. Its competences remain limited, according to the treaties, unless the Member States unanimously decide otherwise, as they do under the 'co-decision' procedure. (see *1164, 1266*)

1298 – The Parliament seeks an increasing influence on decisions negotiated between the governments, and takes actions that extend further and further beyond the bounds of its field of competence. It raises specific questions before the Council and the Commission, and it supports certain arguments or negotiating positions, pushing back legal barriers and opening up a variety of issues to public debate, using traditional parliamentary methods. (see *1174*)

Under the 'Single Act', specific procedures were put in place between the Parliament and the Council, applicable to an increasingly broad range of subjects: the internal market, free movement, education and the budget. The Parliament has taken its place alongside the Council as the legislature of the Union. (see *1266, 1272*)

The draft 'Constitution' ratified this prerogative, which remains the current practice.

1299 – The use made by the European Parliament of its own resources has also worked in favour of federalism: it has its own internal departments, information offices and publications. It approves allocations within the Union's budget.

The same tendency can be seen from the fact that the Parliament has been granted control functions at the very heart of the Union's apparatus, including the right to vote on the budgets of joint institutions, to oppose certain appointments and to censure the Commission, which under the treaties triggers the latter's resignation. The entire Commission collectively resigned in 1999, when under threat of censure. (see *1166*)

1300 – The Council has decided to involve the European Parliament more closely in setting and implementing the foreign policy of the Union. The Presidency consults it about the basic options in this area, ensures its views are taken into consideration and keeps it regularly informed on policy developments (as indeed does the Commission). The Parliament may put questions or make recommendations to the Council and debate these matters itself. As a result, members of the Parliament are also engaged in a true form of interparliamentary diplomacy. Their debates, held in public, have an impact on negotiations between the governments which have different interests to defend. (see *1492*)

1301 – Heads of State and government have played their own part in this trend. Having noted, for instance, that the true seat of power in the Union resides in negotiation between governments, they decided that the President for the time being of the Council should present an annual report to the Parliament on the state of political cooperation between the Member States, and that twice-yearly colloquia would be held between the members of the Council and those of the political affairs committee of the Parliament.

Parliamentary debates, in their turn, generate new rounds of discussions between governments, which are anxious to reconcile the integrationist tendencies of certain strands of public opinion with the upholding of their existing prerogatives.

The Court of Justice

1302 – The Court of Justice of the European Community is a highly novel institution, with sole responsibility for giving the official and binding interpretation of the Treaties and acts done pursuant to them, and for resolving disputes arising out of their implementation. Its composite nature borrows so many of the features of national legal systems that some authors refused to recognise its 'international' jurisdiction.

The Single Act supplemented the three existing Treaties by setting up a Court of First Instance, and the Council has since then decided, in 2004, to create a European Union Civil Service Tribunal.

1303 – Clearly, through its decisions, the Court has had an impact on the law of European countries. Its influence has tended to lead in the direction of integration, as it seeks to impose a uniform and binding application of Community law, confirming its primacy over the internal laws of the Member States and giving legal backing to the Commission when that body seeks to assert its powers against the Council or the States. The Court must also take into account the principles laid down in the Charter of Fundamental Rights of the European Union, signed in Nice in 2000. (see *1343*)

1304 – Applying a true judicial policy with complete independence, the Court has moved the national legal systems in the direction of harmonisation, with results that are the more inevitable because its decisions and interpretations are applicable in domestic law, including in national courts. (see *1673*)

1305 – The judges also have the power to interpret and apply the founding Treaties, especially as to the scope and implications of the competences of the Union in negotiations with third countries. In doing so, they expand or reinforce the obligations on the member States to cooperate within the Community institutions. To take one example, by giving priority to the removal of impediments to trade over the need to organise the markets, they have forced governments to speed up their discussions on measures designed to structure production and trade.

1306 – In response to initiatives from the Commission, the Court adopted a more decisive position by retaining the power not only to interpret the Treaties so as to enlarge the scope of the Union competences but, on occasion, also to decide – in lieu of the Council – negotiated matters not yet fully concluded. This position attracted the objections of some governments for substituting its own concept of federal integration instead of the will expressed by the states in their mutual agreements. (see *1385, 1388*)

Where the Court's decisions are not applied, this is a matter for the governments – or certain governments in particular. Financial penalties may be imposed in cases of repeated breach. (see *1655, 2218*)

1307 – *In practice, where the decisions of the Court affect the higher interests of States, this can be a stage in the process of aligning their positions,* or more specifically the point of departure for a fresh negotiation leading to new settlements being reached or new rules of law applied. (see *2218*)

§3. Political cooperation

1308 – In spite of the specific nature of its laws and institutions, the existence of the European Union has not meant the end of diplomatic relations among its Member States. They still retain their international sovereignty and traditional attributes, and continue to negotiate, not only with third States but among themselves. (see *609*)

This principle is upheld in the Treaty on the European Union. *That treaty added to the existing Community competences two new areas, or 'pillars', for specific political cooperation: foreign policy, including security and even defence, on the one hand, and justice and internal affairs, in other words, policing, on the other.* The conditions for making these specific negotiations easier and more productive were laid down at various meetings of the Council, notably those in Maastricht, Amsterdam and Nice. (see *1492*)

1309 – The fact that Community institutions provide the forum for intensive negotiations between the Member States does not in any sense prevent them from reaching direct agreement on all issues not covered by the Treaties, or even in those areas that are, provided they do not breach the rules to which they have submitted. (*1474*)

1310 – In their desire to hold confidential discussions unhindered by the slow and formalistic processes of the Union, European governments have proceeded to conduct bilateral and multilateral negotiations aside from the workings of the Union itself, though this has caused concern on the part of some of the partners who fear that the major powers will reach agreements without their involvement, free from the constraints of the institution.

The increased levels of cooperation in foreign policy, security and defence, policing and justice, has given the European Council a greater role as the organ in which decisions are negotiated, usually unanimously, as envisaged by the Single Act that came into force on 1 July 1987 and as confirmed by the trend that appeared during the drafting of the 'Constitutional Treaty' in 2003.

1311 – The overlap in competences and activities of its different institutions, as well as of its Member States, is therefore one of the characteristics of the Union. In practice, on the one hand, the Treaties do not clearly define the exact areas to which they apply, but rather their ultimate object. And, on the other, the dynamics of cooperation, taken together with the impulse toward integration, have produced large number of areas of concerted action. *This has given rise to a huge amount of negotiation, and it is often difficult to determine how much of it is strictly European. Hence the wish to define the non-exclusive areas of the Union's competence, viewed as subsidiary, or in other words in which its actions complement those of the States.* This notion of 'subsidiarity' has been the subject of many negotiations, through which the States have sought to preserve their own national competences.[5] (see *1381*)

1312 – Furthermore, the existence of an area of free exchange, extended as a result of subsequent adhesions, especially in 2004, has had the effect of progressively redistributing the networks and influences that come into play in this international cooperation: political parties and cultural movements, pressure groups, employers' organisations and labour unions, all have adapted to the increasing integration of the economies within the internal European market.

Diplomatic cooperation

1313 – From the time of General de Gaulle's '*Plan Fouchet*', European leaders have argued that it would serve the interests of the member countries of the European Union to have a harmonised foreign policy in all areas of common interest. The Bonn summit in 1961 urged active collaboration between the various Foreign Ministers, by means of a programme carried out on the basis of proposals made by senior officials (the 'Davignon Committee', who began by laying the ground for the Helsinki Conference in 1970, and whose work was adopted at the Paris Conference of 1972).

1314 – From that time on, Foreign Ministers of the Member States have held periodic meetings outside the meetings of the Union, based on preparatory work done by a committee of policy directors of the various Foreign Ministries that meets on a more frequent basis and is also responsible for follow-up, as well as by working groups.

1315 – Specialist officials in the ministries and embassies are appointed to facilitate this coordination, and there is also a dedicated telecommunications system. Exchanges at this level are particularly intensive among the permanent delegations of EU countries to the United Nations, where, since the 1973 Copenhagen Conference, consultations have taken place to formulate concerted positions where the interests of the Union are involved, and special meetings can be convened if urgent matters arise. With several such meetings at different levels, common positions can be worked out that influence the attitude of third States, but in practice restrict the latitude available to certain of the Member States themselves, for example in the Security Council.

---

5 Y. GAUDEMET: 'Le principe de subsidiarité a-t-il un avenir?' in *Quelle constitution pour quelle Europe*, Paris, Sénat, 2000, p. 69.

1316 – In more recent years there has been an understanding that, as a general rule, no Member State will take a firm diplomatic position without having used this flexible process to consult its partners. *Thus the principle of the obligation to consult came into being, with each government free to propose or rule out subjects on which there must be consultation and explain their significance and implications.* (see *1494*)

1317 – The quality of this consultation has improved steadily over the years, although its results have been somewhat mitigated by the divergence of views among Member States on issues that touch on their respective fundamental values – the extent of their cooperation, for example, especially as to matters of defence and the prospects for harmonisation of their different attitudes to the United States and NATO. *The process of reaching agreement becomes more difficult with the adhesion of new members and where there is overlap with other existing negotiating frameworks.*

1318 – There are cases worthy of mentioning, however, where consultation has led to cooperation. One such instance was the efficient manner in which members of the EU worked together before, during and after the 1972 Helsinki Conference on Security and Cooperation in Europe, where the Commission, as part of the delegation of the Presidency, was able to state its position during a working session.

The subsequent crises in the former Yugoslavia and the Middle East, however, have shown the opposite tendency. (see *1329, 1492*)

1319 – Areas suitable for concerted foreign negotiation have gradually been identified, sometimes with the aid of one of the Commissioners in the event of overlap with the competences of the Union. These include the policy approach with regard to the States of Central and Eastern Europe, which were bound by cooperation agreements with the EU since 1988 and are now members, and, through the Barcelona Programme, with the Mediterranean States. (see *1406, 1409, 1415*)

The intention of the negotiators at Maastricht was to transform this coordination into a common foreign policy or at least into a set of common principles and orientations where foreign policy was concerned. This tendency was consolidated through the meetings of the Council in Berlin and Cologne in 1999, and in Nice in 2000, in order to ensure that the Union was unified at the diplomatic level on certain matters of direct concern to it. *It is possible for common strategies to be negotiated in the Council, by unanimous vote, after the Parliament has been consulted on the fundamental choices. Procedures are also available for dealing with emergencies.* (see *1328*)

1320 – The results of the consultations are made public through formal joint declarations, or via the Presidency at the time, but they are often submitted directly to the European Council for consideration. Within the United Nations, they are obvious from the frequent alignment of positions and voting among the European States. On some important occasions, such as the opening of the UN General Assembly, the President of the Council is called upon to include a jointly prepared statement in his address. (see *1300, 1330, 1462*)

1321 – Diplomatic coordination requires the positions adopted to be formulated after consultation among the partners, which often involves sensitive negotiations. The task of formulating the results of this political cooperation and representing it to the outside world falls upon the State holding the Presidency at the time. The draft 'Constitutional Treaty' of 2003 proposed the election by qualified majority of a Foreign Minister, sitting as a member of the Council and having the status of Vice President of the Commission. (see *1275*)

1322 – By making use of the embassies of the Member States, and allowing for the fact that not all of them are represented in every country, the Council has a ready-made system at its disposal that allows it to follow the diplomatic negotiations taking place outside the Union.

This political cooperation has withstood the test of time and weathered crises. It has enabled European positions within international organisations to be aligned, especially in the United Nations, where the fact that most votes or decisions are carried by consensus shows that the Member States of the Union are in agreement. It strengthened the role of the Western countries in the meetings that followed the Helsinki Conference, notably those held in Belgrade and Paris. In a general sense, it has lent added weight to the pursuit by each State of its own national diplomacy.

That said, as can be see from the divergent attitudes of the various members of the Union during the recent crises in the Near East, political cooperation has not succeeded on the scale that was hoped for.

The European Council

1323 – Cooperation at diplomatic level goes further, however: there have been major current issues to address, within the Union itself as well as outside it. The growth in such cooperation in Europe can be seen from the increase in the number of 'summit' meetings, starting from the first Conference of Heads of State and Government held in Paris in 1961. (see *2486*)

1324 – The authorities concerned made a commitment to meet each other on a regular basis. This is the function of the European Council, which since 1974 has been the forum in which the Heads of State and government come together at least twice per year, under a rotating Presidency, assisted by their ministers and usually in the presence of the Presidents of the Commission and sometimes the Council of Ministers, in order to resolve the most important issues arising out of the harmonisation of national policies within the European framework. (see *2385*)

1325 – Although it is able to act as such if the President of the Commission is present, the European Council is not, strictly speaking, an institution of the Union. Rather, it is superimposed as an additional level to unblock situations in which the Union's decision-making function is paralysed, but without depriving the existing organ of any of its competences or prerogatives. Only in those areas where the Union is competent is the Council's work subject to the formal processes laid down in the Paris and Rome Treaties: thus, it provides a channel for political cooperation untrammelled by institutional procedures.

Given the rank of its members, the strength of the Council of the EU derives from its application of the rules of unanimity, where possible, or consensus at the highest political levels. It very existence therefore lends weight to the move towards confederation. (see *1565*)

1326 – The Maastricht and Nice negotiations made the Council of Heads of State and government the central decision-making organ of the European Union. It is the scene for intensive diplomatic consultations with declarations issued after each of its meetings. The most important negotiations between Member States now take place in this forum, on a multilateral basis and at the highest levels. Frequently convened and prepared by the Foreign Ministers, it has consistently demonstrated the ability to bring the members together and produce results, thanks to its flexible workings and its independence from professional lobby groups.

1327 – The efforts of the Council and its successive Presidents not only in taking policy initiatives but in drawing up, harmonising and reconciling policies have had a major impact on the institution as a whole. They have made it possible for the Union to tackle successive crises by avoiding internal confrontations and to assume new tasks, whether in the parliamentary, monetary or other fields (the 'enhanced cooperation' envisaged by the Amsterdam and Nice meetings of the Council), as well as the enlargement of the Union. (see *1263, 1272*)

1328 – Precisely because of the freedom it has in conducting its negotiations, the Council has gradually become the principal executive organ in Europe. It was responsible for the recent progress with regard to the structure of the European entity and the greater role given to the Council. It functions in a real sense as a review body for Community matters, where initiatives and compromises are negotiated that would normally have fallen within the remit of the Council of Ministers. (see *1273, 1564*)

Its meetings have also provided the governments concerned with the opportunity and framework for holding vital deliberations in situations of international tension. *The need to respond to crises, whether they be local or global, is at the same time one of the challenges and one of the hallmarks of the European edifice.* (see *1319, 1402, 1492*)

1329 – For many years, the Council of the European Union did not resolve some of the most serious political problems: reorganisation of Community institutions, or the principles of a common policy on energy or the environment. *The Council is based on the common exercise of sovereign powers and not on their transfer, even when it acts within the sphere of Community competences.*

The hesitation shown by the Twelve, and later the Fifteen, in the face of the unfolding drama of the former Yugoslavia revealed their collective limitations. The EU, the WEU and the CSCE proved ineffective, with the crisis being progressively pushed into the hands of the Security Council and subsequently NATO. The negotiations that took place were muddled and ineffectual, at a time when military interference and grave acts of war were taking place, including bombings that did not spare the civilian population. (see *1132*)

1330 – European negotiation on matters of security and defence is at the same time the engine and the product of diplomatic cooperation. Starting with the Franco-British declaration of Saint-Malo in 1998, the year in which the crisis in Yugoslavia deteriorated, the Council became aware of the need to adopt a common approach in these areas. European security and defence policy is decided unanimously, subject to a suspensive veto and to a possible 'constructive abstention', which does not prevent a decision being adopted. This initiative coincided with the creation by NATO in 1996 of the European Defence Identity. (see *1498*)

In the fields of common foreign policy, security and defence, the President is assisted by a prominent figure of ministerial rank who has a policy committee, a military committee and a headquarters. While these bodies exists as part of the President's responsibility for international negotiation, they must work together with the Commission. (see *1402, 1492*)

1331 – The expansion in the role of the Council of the EU has highlighted the need to superimpose the agreement of the States in the exercise of their sovereignty on the will of the Union as expressed through the bodies set up under the Treaties. The improvement in the workings of this Council make it possible for debate to be opened up within it on all topics of common interest, in meetings unencumbered by administrative and legal formalities, and, provided the governments and their foreign ministries lay the groundwork carefully and with due regard for basic policy direction, this will mean that it becomes the supreme institution in the Union. (see *1492*)

The workings of the Council affect the very future of Europe. Such is the economic, diplomatic and cultural weight of Europe that the Council's role in world diplomacy will continue to expand, provided it remains unanimous and does not succumb to divisions. (see *1246, 1258*)

§4. The Community system

1332 – The Community was the first phase in the construction of a power whose legal nature is hybrid and whose workings leave a broad margin for the sovereign States to continue to pursue their own diplomatic negotiations. Within it, each State retains the sovereign right to decide on its own interests, subject to the exercise by its own parliament of its prerogatives. (see *2281*)

In practice, apart from those areas of competence that belong exclusively to the Union as part of the single market, many are shared with the governments, and some, such as fiscal matters, are matters for the States alone. Each State in its turn holds the Presidency of the Union and chairs its external negotiations.

1333 – In its own assigned areas of competence, the Union enjoys prerogatives that are binding on the Member States, and sometimes directly on its citizens. Its political and administrative structures are highly sophisticated, and its organs have the right and the ability to take enforceable decisions.

The treaties that set up and subsequently changed the shape of the Community formed the basis for a unique and unprecedented institutional construct that was neither foreseen, discussed nor approved at the outset.

1334 – However, the entire edifice rests on concordance between the Member States, the preservation of the balance between their interests and their obligations, and respect for their official languages. In reality, the governments do indeed debate the different aspects of their common policy, sometimes fiercely, and defend their claims and positions every bit as firmly as they would in traditional bilateral negotiation. (see *1648*)

It is this internal negotiation that enables the Union to adapt to a changing international environment, and ensures that it continues to grow and develop.

1335 – As the forum for free and fair exchanges, the Union provides its member countries with a framework that favours cooperation. But, as to its real legal nature, the original documents lacked clarity and the political conceptions have changed, which explains the amount of legal and political debate generated in the attempt to determine what it is. As a whole, the European system is a complex mixture of diplomacy and bureaucracy.

1336 – Already mentioned in some of the treaties, the idea of supranationality was defined by Robert Schuman as falling between State individualism and federalism.[6] The question was whether this was a stable legal condition, and if not, whether the Communities must move in the direction of integration or in the opposite direction. Some observers saw in this a 'partial federalism', or a tendency towards confederalism. Others, like General de Gaulle, wanted to counter the idea of a Union of States with that of a Union of peoples or a 'Europe of the Nations'. (see *2282*)

1337 – In any event, if relations between States were no longer based on intergovernmental practice but on a federal form of power, the legal nature of the State would radically change. Negotiation between the entities and groups that make up a federal State takes place at a subordinate level, and does not depend on the equality and sovereignty of the partners. (see *1258*)

1338 – Since the end of 1969, in other words the end of the transitional period, the system of Community institutions has operated, in practice, along the federal lines its instigators wished. It has not, however, transformed the Community into a federation or even a confederation, in the legal meaning of those terms.

1339 – The Communities – with the exception of the former Coal and Steel Community – were set up with no limit in time, and in some respects what is now the Union has progressed beyond the confederal stage because it makes and enforces law that is directly applicable in the Member States and binding on their authorities. It has its own autonomous institutions, in particular a Court of Justice that can compel the Member States to comply. (*1280*)

1340 – But the Union has not reached a federal stage. Its status, and any changes to it, depend on procedures that are, in part, diplomatic. Its internal and external competences are specific and limited. Its institutions do not have the power to determine their own competences. The States do not stand in a relationship of political

---

6 R. SCHUMAN: 'Préface' to P. REUTER, *La CECA*, Paris, LGDJ, 1953, p. 7.

subordination to them, and it is from the States that the powers of the Union flow, right down to the power of day to day management. (see *1270, 1533, 2675*)

Each State is bound to take its own constitutional structure into account; often, they do not agree collectively on the Union's exact competences in a given area.

1341 – Moreover, the experience of years of working of the Union has shown that the impulse towards federal unification diminishes as the number of Member States increases. British membership in itself has tipped the scales against supranationalism. The expansion of the Union to 25 members, soon to be 27 and with the likelihood of more in the future, and the attendant increase in the number of working languages will tend to have the same effect.

1342 – The idea of supranationalism rapidly ran into political hostility on the part of those who refused to countenance any integration of a nation into a system that deprived it of its sovereign power to negotiate. The confederal concept of the European Community gradually gained the support in practice of the States concerned, who saw the maintenance of permanent negotiation between them as the best way to safeguard their interests.

1343 – The notion of supranationality, criticised in some political circles, is now mainly illustrated by the existence of legal organs, mechanisms and powers superimposed on the national systems in defined areas. For the rest, the Community falls into the category of international organisations of a specialist regional nature, though they might have institutional attributes and be backed by especially powerful motivations of solidarity. (see *1648, 1962*)

The fact remains that European Union citizenship and the Charter of Fundamental Rights are integrationist in their effect, as is the Common Agricultural Policy. So was the introduction of the euro for those States that agreed to be bound by the disciplines of the Euro zone. The same is true of the area of free movement established under the Schengen Agreements. (see *1341, 1352, 1402*)

1344 – At the diplomatic level, the real innovation of the Community has been the institutional mechanism it has provided for achieving multilateral equilibrium between the partners: both within the Union and on its fringes, a wealth of contractual relationships are formed that promote solidarity, complementarity and unanimity. *Never has such a varied pattern of intensive and long-term negotiation flourished between European nations previously beset by centuries of conflict.* Never, too, have their agreements been implemented on such a consistent basis, with the application of the treaties and the steps taken pursuant to them conferred on Community institutions or verified by them (the Member States in this respect having a subordinate role). (see *1276, 1655*)

1345 – The prosperity generated by this intensive cooperation has proved attractive to States that held back, or were held back, from taking part in the first initiatives, and dangerous for their adversaries, who are forced in the end to accept that European cooperation, or even integration, is an objective reality.

The level of political agreement between member States on the structures of the Union has deepened with time, and gives their negotiations a particular flavour.

Different factors are weighed in the balance to ensure that it is not possible for a few powerful States to impose their will on the others, or for smaller States to form alliances that defeat the interests of the larger.

1346 – European unification is undoubtedly an expression of political innovation. It also puts a premium on diplomatic negotiation, which in this case has a structuring effect, as well as fulfilling the increasing need to give expression to economic, cultural and political *rapprochements*. This was the intention declared at the very outset by the founders of the Coal and Steel Community in the 1950s, who saw that the building of European structures would produce '*de facto* solidarity'.

1347 – This intense cooperative activity between States is not limited to regular exchanges of information or enduring efforts at mutual consultation. It involves patient negotiation of the sort that leads them to consult each other on matters of policy and adopt identical diplomatic positions. This explains how intra-community negotiation now operates in a way that, while respecting the traditional formalities of signature and ratification, itself forms part of the dynamic and the apparatus of the institutions of the internal market, affecting how initiatives are put forward, adopted in the Council in co-decision with the Parliament and interpreted by the Court. (see *1642*)

1348 – Some of the Commission's initiatives are not ratified in their entirety by the Council, however: this was the case with its programme of social action, which the Council took note of by recommending improved cooperation between the national departments concerned, and which was carried out gradually: the 1998 Social Charter, planned at the Maastricht summit, with Britain voting against, and modified in Strasbourg; the coordination of employment policies, the recognition of basic social rights and the protection of the environment and public health (Amsterdam, 1997); the European Pact on employment (Cologne, 1999), and the Charter of Fundamental Rights (Nice, 2000).

1349 – Negotiations can also cover programmes of action, devised either by harnessing together national efforts, or as part of the function of international institutions. The Conference of European Heads of State and government originated the idea of an economic and monetary union in Western Europe, and took the decision to open negotiations with a view to enlarging the Community (The Hague, 1969). The intergovernmental conference put forward two objectives: the Economic and Monetary Union and the Political Union (Rome, 1990). These were further developed (Maastricht, 1991) and set out in the Treaty of Union (Amsterdam, 1997 and Nice, 2000).

1350 – Favoured as much by proximity as by the global economic and financial crisis, negotiation within the Union works towards producing joint or harmonised policies. This is not without its problems, as can be seen from the workings of the Common Agricultural Policy, with its endless discussions about products and prices, the chequered history of the Social Fund and the Regional Fund, the failure to produce common industry and energy policies and the conceptual difficulties of a European judicial and policing area. (see *1639*)

Agriculture has dominated the European system since the 1960s and given rise to some of the most protracted and difficult debates, as well as generating more Commission drafts and regulations than any other topic, covering such things as the stabilisation and organisation of the markets, and policies on structures and financial compensation, as well as products and pricing. It was amended after tough negotiations, to keep pace at the same time with changes in agricultural practices, commitments undertaken to free up the markets, and, more recently, the adhesion of countries from Central and Eastern Europe and the Mediterranean and the association of the ACP countries. It has also produced harmonisation of national laws on foodstuffs.

1351 – The same holds true for all the so-called concerted policies. The first steps towards a European energy policy were taken when member States exchanged information on the movements of fuels, triggering a negotiation in the Council which produced regulations and directives in the 1970s. (see *2032*)

A European policy on transport has evolved over time, as one of the aspects of the liberalisation of the Common Market, with a plethora of regulations on the subject. The same is happening in other areas, where the first step in the achievement of a single market is the adoption of directives and regulations binding on the Member States. The European satellite GPS project, Galileo, approved in 2003, with the participation of China, marked a decisive step forward in European technological development.

1352 – Negotiation within Europe also tends to blur the disparities between the legislative and administrative systems of the member countries. Implementation of the Treaties calls for the exercise of complex regulatory, managerial and also legal functions requiring agreement between the States: the negotiations associated with them draw upon the services of experts, civil servants or otherwise, and they generate close technical and administrative cooperation between those involved. (see *2561*)

Under the negotiations in Maastricht, Amsterdam and Nice, the third 'pillar' of the European Union is that of cooperation between the States in the fields of justice and policing. These are intergovernmental negotiations, subject to the fact that immigration control and political asylum are national matters but also intended to be joint matters, according to the Schengen and Dublin Agreements, which will apply to the new member countries.[7] (see *1492*)

The European justice area began with reciprocal recognition of judicial decisions, and the harmonisation of the means of carrying them out, in implementation of the two Brussels Conventions of 1968 and 1998. Where police and criminal enforcement are concerned, there is increasingly active cooperation between the various Ministries of Justice and Ministries of the Interior, with Europol and Eurojust, as well as between governments themselves, especially in the

---

7 S. OCHINSKY and P. JENARD: '*L'Espace juridique et judiciaire européen*', Brussels, Bruylant, 1993. S. HOFFMANN: 'La France et l'Europe', in *Le Rôle et la place de l'Etat*, Paris, PUF, 2000, p. 28. G. BURDEAU: *L'Euro et l'évolution du droit international monétaire*, Paris, Litec, 2000, p. 473.

provision of assistance in handling crises occurring abroad, and combating major international crime, with legal coordination in the fight against terrorism and money laundering, and the introduction of the European arrest warrant. (see *1492, 2028*)

1353 – Since the Amsterdam meeting of the Council, economic and monetary union has taken more concrete shape. Those States (initially eleven, now twelve) whose policies met the five convergence criteria have adopted a common currency, the euro, freely exchangeable in the territory of each of them since 2002. A European system of central banks and a central issuing bank (the ECB) ensures that this currency is managed independently of the State authorities. But the fact that each State continues to have its own national budgetary, fiscal and social policy undermines its potential to integrate: as an institution, Europe is at the same time federal and intergovernmental. The Ministers of Finance in the countries concerned have set up a 'Euro group' under permanent chairmanship, to coordinate national policies. The Stability and Growth Pact, signed in 1997, was intended to serve as the basis for European monetary union, but several of the contracting States have departed from their obligations under it.

1354 – The partners have continued to negotiate, not only with a view to the possible enlargement of the 'Euro zone' to new members fulfilling the prescribed conditions, but also to achieve convergence among the financial and economic systems of the States concerned.

At the level of the Union as a whole, the flow of capital, goods and services should be adapted to take account of particular national factors and constraints. Also at work within Western Europe are major transnational influences such as the European Trade Union Confederation (ETU), the business leaders' group (UNICE) and the Committee of Professional Agricultural Organisations (COPA) that should not be regarded as without influence on the direction and success of European negotiation: sensible ways must be found of making them part of the unification process. (see *1901*)

1355 – Negotiation within the institution also draws upon the common ideology of its protagonists. It took only two years, and a shared vision, to prepare the 1957 Treaty of Rome. If it is to move forward, the European system must develop its own elite *cadre* and propound its own message. The powerful movement of ideas that gave birth to the European perspective has shown the importance of the phenomenon of Europe in the popular mind, as an entity with a world role that outweighs the national interests of its members and the divergences in their political and economic policies. With this in mind, the Council has attached great importance to the sustainability of European economic and development strategies, (Lisbon, 2000 and Gothenburg, 2001), though without real success to date. (see *1857, 1900, 1901*)

1356 – Negotiation between the governments has allowed the Community to adapt its bureaucracy to reflect shifts in the political context that are not always obvious to those on the inside. While the experts could not predict all the crises that have arisen as a result of international environmental factors, nor their consequences in fields such as energy, the iron and steel industry and agriculture, it is still national policy-makers who are expected to take the lead. *The transfer of powers of management and negotiation to an institution presupposes that it is capable of prompt and effective action and reaction.* (see *1319, 1520*)

1357 – Gradually, cooperative planning for the long term must take its place alongside the regulation of matters of current concern. Only when negotiation within Europe produces agreement among the partners on a coherent vision of the future will it assume the prospective dimension every diplomatic strategy must have. (see *1494*)

When mutual trust diminishes, however, this policy is reduced to a succession of partial and temporary compromises. This has been seen to happen in many negotiations within the United Nations and with the United States.

1358 – As long as there is no single unified European nation, no single political will, and no powerful or compelling influence towards federation, it is the Member States that must uphold and develop the European 'idea' through their negotiation, supported by individuals and groups dedicated to the cause, but always based on public opinion. A distinction must be drawn between matters of technical expertise and matters of administration, and those requiring the exercise of political responsibility. Despite the emergence of a body of harmonised legislation, there can be no federal system in a continent as divided as Europe. (see *1233, 1532, 2295*)

1359 – Clearly, negotiations between the States of Europe must adapt to take account of the changing place and role of their continent in a changing world. The institutional features and effects of these negotiations, economic as well as social, show that theirs is more than a traditional alliance, while at the same time the Union has expanded geographically beyond the bounds of the Brussels and Paris Treaties, whose signatories assumed an obligation of mutual military assistance. But Europe's negotiators cannot avoid the strategic choices their common future imposes: forging a deeper alliance will compensate for the limits that have been set on supranational federalism. If the whole edifice is not capable of becoming greater than the sum of its parts, it will never be able to set goals and withstand the impact of external events. (see *864, 945, 972, 1330, 1493, 1648*)

Section 2: External negotiation

1360 – Because of its very object, the Community has from the beginning been required to take part in external negotiations. On the one hand, the founding Treaties conferred competences that could only be exercised once a common policy with regard to third countries had been devised and implemented, for instance, as to trade and customs. On the other, the intensification of relations between the Member States has led them to extend their cooperation, particularly in relation to the outside world, to the point where there is talk of a Union external policy. *Lastly, the growth in negotiation between the Community and the rest of the world has, in its turn, been one of the driving forces behind its progress and has helped to cement its cohesiveness in the face of fast-changing world events.*

1361 – The progressive construction of a specific, common European system raises the question of the place it occupies in international law in terms of recognition by other powers. This is a political problem, but above all a practical one, because of the expanding scope of the technical negotiations involving the Community and the implications of multilateral agreements involving Member States. (see *614*)

1362 – Even without any real strategy, the European Union represents an economic and commercial force of worldwide importance, whose continued expansion has placed it among the leaders in external trade. It is not surprising that its creation and growth should have given rise to doubts, distrust and concern, on the part of both third States and international organisations, the more so because it has developed its own trade policy, which consists of setting up a huge internal market and a network of favoured partners. It has, in practice, helped bring about the multipolarisation of worldwide economic negotiations, while its own external negotiations serve to confirm its exclusive character. (see *1518, 1646*)

1363 – The tendency to deal with the Union as a whole typically works well where it is in the obvious interests of its interlocutors to deal only with one partner, enabling them to simplify the transaction, treat it as a single operation or limit the concessions they have to make. But at the diplomatic level, the organisation appears as a relatively closed and compact system. (see *2295*)

1364 – The recognition of the Union as an interlocutor does not mean that it is assimilated to a sovereign power. *The Union is neither a State, nor a Super-State*.[8] Usually, it cannot claim the privileges of sovereignty, and third States are right to question the capacity in which it makes commitments on the same basis as the States that comprise it: for them, when they are troubled by it, the Treaty of Rome is *res inter alios*. (see *609*)

1365 – The Soviet Union missed no opportunity to challenge the right of the European Communities to enter into valid contractual obligations on their own behalf. It changed its position after 1962, by which time commercial reality had overtaken it, though only in 1973 was the objection formally lifted.

The problem was solved when the USSR ceased to exist, and Russia became a partner of the Community in its own right in 1995. The process of normalisation of relations was marked by a joint declaration by the EEC and the former COMECON in 1988, and the following year an agreement was signed for the progressive elimination of quantitative trade restrictions. (see *1393*)

1366 – Because of contradictory trends in the application of the Treaties by the member States, external negotiation is one of the areas where there is divergence of opinion, either within the Council itself or between the institutions of the Union. This opposition should not obscure the fact that it is one of the responsibilities of the Council to define the policies common to the Member States and that this mission is a collective one; or that the Commission itself has broad technical and

---

8 R. DAHRENDORF: 'The Foreign Policy of the EEC', in *The World Today*, 1973, p. 49.

tactical potential to conduct negotiations when the governments agree to mandate it. (see *1256, 1291*)

1367 – Even though the Commission has power to take initiatives in this area, the principle of unanimity means that, in areas to which it applies, each member country can ensure that its own interests are considered before authorising any negotiation, except in emergencies. This is a matter of determining the scope of Community competences as well as of how they should be exercised. But it can also have a substantive impact, since any persistent difference between member States reduces the Union's ability, and freedom, to conduct foreign relations, whether or not the negotiations are entrusted to the Commission and whatever the subject. *Whatever is done in the name of the Union should be agreed in advance as a common position.*

§1. The capacity to negotiate

1368 – Though its nature under international law was unclear, the Court of Justice held in 1963 that the Community constituted a new legal order. The United Nations considered the European Communities as a legal entity, with legal personality conferred on them by the founding Treaties (see Opinion of the UN Legal Adviser of 24 May 1968, UN Official Journal, 1968). (see *1427, 1457*)

1369 – Controversy remains as to whether this is legal personality under international law. Where the Member States are concerned, this debate has had no practical impact, since they have interpreted and applied the Treaties as granting the Community institutions the power to negotiate and contract at international level, and also to bind the States within their respective areas of competence.

The principle

1370 – Despite the absence of any truly common system of law of intergovernmental institutions, it must be considered that, *for the Union, legal personality includes the capacity to act at international level, in addition to the legal capacity to act that it has under the internal law of each Member State.* (see *1175*)

1371 – This legal personality is not based on the traditional notion of sovereignty: it is functional in nature. In practice, in order for an international organisation to be able to intervene in the foreign relations of its Member States, it must have been granted the specific competence to do so in its founding instrument, and its actions must be directed at achieving the objectives and fulfilling the missions conferred on it by the Member States. (see *1179*)

1372 – The legal regimes governing the capacity of each of the Communities to negotiate were not uniform, with the treaties differing on this point and different needs affecting their implementation. (see *1368*)

1373 – By virtue of Article 95 of the Treaty of Paris, all matters that were not expressly reserved to the European Coal and Steel Community were to be decided by unanimous agreement of the representatives of the member States in the Council. On the other hand, it had been accepted that the external powers of the Coal and Steel Community were the same in nature as its internal powers, essentially covering the areas of foreign trade and in particular the protection of European industry.

1374 – Article 101 of the Euratom Treaty provides that the Community can negotiate and make binding commitments in the area of its nuclear competences. Article 103 limits the freedom of the Member States to enter into agreements in these areas, but has never been invoked against the governments. But when the European Court of Justice was asked to interpret these provisions, it ruled in 1978 that the negotiation by the Member States of a convention on the physical protection of nuclear material could have an influence on Community affairs, and that it therefore fell under the joint agreement procedure involving both the Council and the Commission: the Court thus gave an extensive interpretation to the power of the Community to enter into agreements in this field, and in doing so provoked a lively debate.[9]

1375 – The problem has mainly arisen in connection with Article 235 of the Treaty of Rome (now Article 308 EC), which covers situations for which there is no specific provision in the Treaty. This has been given a broad interpretation by the Court of Justice and has been frequently applied. Its implementation remains problematic, because governments tend to interpret the texts according to their own interests. (see *1391*)

1376 – Part of the mission of the EEC was to create a single economic area in Western Europe, in which trade could be carried on unimpeded and a favoured market be established. This had the effect of restricting the power of the Member States to maintain their own separate foreign relations in this field after the end of the transition period in 1969, and of conferring on the Community the capacity to act in international trade relations. (see *1370, 1383*)

1377 – The same principles that apply to the relationship between Community law and the various national legal systems also apply to acts or instruments resulting from negotiations carried on within the Community's sphere of activity. Community negotiation is thus a unique phenomenon, which explains why the governments exercise tight control over it, through the Council which represents them.

1378 – The terms of agreements entered into by the Community have direct effect in the law of the Member States, as if those States had entered into them. The States are bound to take all necessary steps to give effect to them. It is easy to understand, therefore, why the governments take care to ensure that the Community institutions do not of their own free will expand their role in this area.

---

9 J. P. PUISSOCHET: 'A propos d'une déliberation de la Cour de Justice des Communautés européennes', *AFDI*, 1978, p. 977.

1379 – The capacity to act internationally includes the capacity to negotiate and contract. While it was not part of the express intentions of the founders to grant the European Economic Community a general power to enter into international agreements (see Articles 228 and 300 EC), the Community itself gradually extended the scope of its activities, becoming in practice – as its members agreed – a major player in international negotiation in the field of trade (see for example the agreement with the Gulf Cooperation Council in 1988).[10] (see *1104, 1183*)

Scope

1380 – As the only international organisation with its own authentic power to negotiate with third States in fields that normally belong within the domain of traditional national sovereignty, the Union can bind itself, and, by direct effect, its Member States, only within the limits of those areas laid down in the founding Treaties: this could be described as an attributed or derived competence. Within these limits, the Member States have lost their national competence. However, the boundaries between these respective domains of competence are unclear, flexible and liable to change. (see *655*)

1381 – The principle of specification should prohibit institutions from supplementing or extending the basic treaties or Community organs from seeking to rely on implied powers. But the Community is a system in a constant process of internal development. Treaty clauses have been broadly interpreted by Community institutions, especially where agriculture and trade policy are concerned, as can be seen from the general reports of the Commission. Some governments have worked together to reverse this process, invoking the 'principle of subsidiarity'. (see *1311*)

The Member States often invoke the non-commercial aspects of a negotiation in order to involve themselves in it. The Commission has used the opposite reasoning to the same ends, relying on the dynamic nature of Article 113 of the Treaty of Rome, which set out the commercial policy of the Union.

1382 – A unanimous decision of the Council, based on a Commission proposal and made in co-decision with the Parliament, can authorise the Union to take, collectively, any new steps necessary to fulfil one of the objectives of the Treaty. But it is not clear whether this creative power, frequently used internally, can be extended to apply to external negotiations without an express decision of the Council.

The Court of Justice deduced from the legal personality of the Community that it had the capacity to establish contractual ties with third States on any subject within the entire scope of the objectives defined under the first part of the Treaty of Rome. (see *1304*)

1383 – The Court has held that the competence of the Community to negotiate expands along with the addition of new fields of common activity, where the Community alone is in a position to assume and implement commitments to

10 M. HARDY: 'Opinion 1/76 of the Court of Justice', *CMLR*, 1977, p. 561.

third parties. Thus, its external competences can never be narrower than its internal ones.

1384 – The Court has had occasion to extend this principle to cover all areas where the Treaties provide that the Community is competent, even if, at least in the commercial field, which is in a state of constant growth, no internal regulation exists.

1385 – The Court thus takes the view that the Treaty of Rome must be interpreted as restricting the Member States' freedom to contract in all fields which fall even partly within the Community's assigned areas of competence, so that no obligation can be entered into that might interfere with achieving the objectives of the internal market.

1386 – These principles are valid even in the case of international agreements concluded prior to the exercise by the Community of its internal competences. The Community is thus invested with the capacity to negotiate and conclude external agreements even in the absence of any express provision or deliberation by the member governments on the subject in hand, provided this is necessary to achieve the objectives of the treaty (for example, trade policy).

1387 – Foreign negotiation has thus become a means of promoting the integration of Community policies. This can be achieved in one of two ways: either rules for the Union are made first and agreements with third States under these rules concluded only later, or an international agreement is entered into, which is then used as the basis for future common rules.

1388 – Though applied on several occasions, this broad interpretation of the diplomatic role of the Union in the trade arena has been criticised. It has obvious potential for sowing confusion and uncertainty both in international relations and domestic systems, as well as leading to disputes and irresponsible action, because no single organ has exclusive powers and general responsibilities in this field under the Treaties. Nor does it take account of the ambiguities inherent in certain situations: in any negotiation about a given type of goods, there will be some Member States that are both producers and consumers.

1389 – One of the effects of this rule might have been to counteract the tendency for application of Article 235 (now 308) of the Treaty of Rome to expand the fields of activity of the Community, since some States feared losing control of an increasing share of their international negotiation if they too readily accepted the extension of the Union's internal competence.

The differences that arise between governments in certain especially sensitive discussions show how difficult it is to move forward in external negotiations without their agreement, even in the field of trade, which is essentially a Community responsibility. This has given rise to questions about the role and powers of the Commission in international negotiation.

1390 – The extension of the powers of the Community to conduct international negotiations has thus not been without its problems in areas where an issue must be resolved in order to attain the objectives of the founding Treaties, and the Treaty of Rome in particular. The breadth and vagueness of the Court's ruling complicates the relations of the member countries with third States both in bilateral diplomacy and in intergovernmental institutions, bearing in mind the numerous deliberations taking place within specialised international organisations operating at least partly in the fields of economics, trade, transport and social legislation: the ILO would be an example.

1391 – Effectiveness and responsibility are two of the essential characteristics of international negotiation: they are unlikely to be served, especially in dealings with third States, if the conditions for the Union to bind itself are complicated, or if there are problems or uncertainty surrounding the implementation of its commitments at national level, or if difficult questions arise out of the representation and participation of the Union, as such, in bodies set up under international agreements. (see *685, 1635, 2230, 2298*)

As the years have gone by, these issues have tended to be resolved, in practice, by opening up more and more areas for collective negotiation by the Union, with the agreement of the Member States. (see *1397*)

Binding commitments

1392 – The capacity to negotiate leads to the capacity to enter into binding agreements: the Community, as a legal person under international law, could be party to a treaty or convention (see the partnership agreement with Russia signed in 1995). The Union has replaced the Community for legal and diplomatic purposes.

1393 – The setting up of the European Community changed the way in which member countries can be bound by negotiation, in the Community's fields of activity. Characteristically, its negotiations now result in commitments that are not only binding upon the Community itself and its institutions, but also binding upon its members to execute, as responsible sovereign States; this sets the Union apart from other international organisations in terms of its competences. (see *1178, 1185*)

The legal effects of negotiation by the Union are broader than those of traditional diplomatic negotiations.

1394 – An agreement that is properly negotiated, concluded and published is binding on the institutions of the Union and is thus a source of Community law, which will be upheld by the Council, the Commission, following the instructions given to it, and if necessary, the Court of Justice and other Community tribunals.

1395 – Within the scope of its competence, the Union can also be bound by the acts of its member States. This mostly happens as a result of agreements signed before the European Community existed, which remain valid and effective (see Article 234, now Article 307 EC). The Union is substituted for its members, provided no third State opposes this. Member States may agree not to invoke earlier agreements that are contrary to the Treaty of Rome.

1396 – Exceptionally, it was accepted that Member States could enter into external bilateral agreements in areas reserved to the Union after the transition period: legally, these were cases where the third States involved did not accept the principle that the Union could enter into binding commitments, but in reality this derogation was based on high-level political considerations, of the sort that used to govern relations between the States of Western and Eastern Europe. Where the commitment involved the Union, it was assumed that the Member State or States in question had entered into it on the Union's behalf. (see *1319, 1435*)

1397 – The Union, like the Community before it, and its Member States, are bound by a negotiation carried on at the same time by its own organs and the representatives of the Member States: *joint agreements are those that deal with issues that fall under shared or inadequately defined competences, or that go beyond the strict purview of Community competences.* This form of negotiation, which is somewhat complicated, fulfils the need to reconcile the forward momentum of the Union with the prerogatives of the States.

In these cases, the procedures for bringing the agreement into force have to be implemented in parallel at both Union and national level. But such an agreement can only be given real legal effect by the national authorities, because part of its content is outside the competence of the Community. (see *1447, 1450*)

1398 – No agreement that is contrary to the stipulations of one of the founding Treaties can be entered into before that Treaty is amended, and the Court of Justice may be referred to on issues of compatibility.

1399 – Union negotiations can produce new legal mechanisms and specific institutions, which in their turn can themselves conduct negotiations. Notable examples are the association regime and the Barcelona programme. (see *1406, 1644*)

1400 – The Yaoundé, Lomé and Suva Conventions were the models for an international system that both resulted from negotiation and, at the same time, created a framework for new negotiation. This regime was an extrapolation of the core European system and created a new legal group of nations based on continuous and organised dialogue, with parity of representation between the States of Europe on the one hand, and nearly 80 States from Africa, the Caribbean and the Pacific (ACP) on the other. (see *2284*)

On a number of issues, however, these preferential relationships have to be reconciled with the more wide-ranging principles and obligations emerging within the framework of the WTO. (see *1102, 1742*)

§2. The areas of negotiation

1401 – The European Community exercised its own specific powers in the international arena because the original Treaty of Rome expressly conferred on it the power to negotiate in certain clearly defined areas. These were tariff agreement and treaties on trade (Article 113, now Article 133 EC), also association agreements under Article 238 (now Article 310) and certain types of relations with international organisations under Articles 229, 230 and 231 (now Articles 301, 302 and 303). (see *675*)

1402 – Within these attributed areas, the Community defines and applies its own common foreign policy, in other words, it negotiates on behalf of all its members collectively.

This kind of negotiation has been extended to areas outside the Community's competence: foreign policy and security (the second 'pillar'), and justice and policing (the third 'pillar'). The Schengen Agreement, which required the reconciliation of the principle of free movement of persons with the need to secure the European space, is an example of negotiation in both fields of competence: Community and State. (see *1328, 1343, 1492*)

Trade negotiation

1403 – First and foremost, the Community has the capacity to enter into external contractual relationships in the field of commerce, where, ever since the end of the transition period, it has had exclusive competence to deal with third countries. This refers not to general monetary or economic policy, but to those provisions that govern the exchange of goods and services.

1404 – The Community has taken part in many multilateral commercial negotiations. It has done this, however, as the need or the occasion has arisen, without the different solutions agreed upon each time following any harmonised or systematic pattern. (see *2283*)

Jointly with the Member States, it has taken part in numerous negotiations on raw materials and in implementing the resulting agreements, and this is consistent with its fundamental position with regard to commerce. (see *1636*)

1405 – Not only did the Community participate in the GATT, the framework in which it negotiated with the United States on trade and tariff matters, but it also played a decisive role from 1964 onwards in the talks leading to the dismantling of customs barriers, in spite of internal disagreements during that period between its members. It now represents the member States in the World Trade Organisation and before its Dispute Settlement Body. (see *1182, 1942, 2240*)

1406 – The Community negotiated a number of preferential trade agreements with countries mainly in Europe, the Mediterranean basin and Africa with which it had special relationships, often as an extension of existing historical or geographical links, involving either long-term cooperation on the one hand or self-imposed limitations on certain kinds of trade on the other.

The development of its policy in the Mediterranean region is especially telling in a general sense, because of the diplomatic methods employed to overcome the difficulties that arose. Negotiations with several States on the southern shores of the Mediterranean were not restricted to matters of trade, but encompassed a whole portfolio of issues such as financial, scientific, economic and industrial cooperation and various forms of aid in the form of loans and subsidies. The resulting economic and social ties have won favoured standing for the Community and encouraged cooperation at regional level between the States concerned: the Barcelona Conference in 1995 envisaged a free trade area of 27 countries, and this programme was confirmed in 2005. (see *1399*)

Within the countries with which it cooperates, the Community has gradually introduced practices to ensure that aid and loans are properly utilised and that trade agreements function efficiently. It does this through bipartite cooperation councils comprised of representatives of the country in question as well as the Council and the Commission.

1407 – These negotiations have confirmed the role of the Community, and now the Union, in the economic sphere, as well as that of the Commission in representing Member States notably vis à vis the United States, Japan, China and also States in the Middle East. They have led to the setting up of specific institutions such as cooperation commissions aimed at optimising trading relationships under the Community's agreements with individual countries or with the raw materials trade organisations. The continued liberalisation of international trade will change the nature and scope of these negotiations, which already cover a number of sectors in which there is duplication of competences.

Association agreements

1408 – The governments that founded the European Communities envisaged from the beginning the possibility of entering into association with third States, either as a preliminary to their adhesion, or as a favoured form of cooperation, and the Treaty provides for this (Article 283, now Article 310 EC).

1409 – The Treaty of Rome did not limit the Community to matters of trade, but opened the way to a new form of institutional negotiation enabling it to establish favoured relations with a number of Mediterranean or European States as well as the former colonies of its founder members, if they so wished. With British accession, the association regime was extended to include a number of developing States, and now forms a sizeable bloc of countries bound together by preferential trading relations. (see *1400*)

Association agreements were signed in 1999 with a number of Eastern and Central European as well as the Mediterranean island countries, as a prelude to their subsequent accession as full members of the Union. Albania and Turkey have their own specific agreements. (see *1221, 1416, 1417*)

1410 – The negotiation of an association agreement serves an organisational purpose that goes beyond traditional diplomatic negotiation. It involves acceptance at the same time of legal and financial obligations and the pursuit of common goals of a higher order than those of a mere trade negotiation, and it also creates lasting, structured institutions and mechanisms. For this reason, association agreements require the unanimous approval of the Council, and the negotiations must be restarted if there are amendments or additions to the draft. (see *1632, 1640*)

1411 – The association regime is the product of European cohesion, and in its turn it creates relations between the Union and the candidate State or States. (see *1966*)

Specific institutions are set up under this cooperation between associated developing countries and the Union, either within the Union structure or in parallel with its organs, such as the Council of Ministers, assisted by a committee of Ambassadors, and the consultative assembly. The Council of Ministers is competent to deal with all issues arising out of the association regime; it includes members of the Council and the Commission and one representative for each associate State. (see *1102, 1391, 1400*)

1412 – The association agreements with the ACP countries not only instituted a free trade area and a system of non-reciprocal preferential trading arrangements, but they also established mechanisms for sectoral economic cooperation with a view to stabilising export revenues on certain products and developing industry and agriculture, as well as bodies dealing with economic cooperation and financial aid. (see *1962*)

1413 – The principle governing financial aid is that aid from the Union is specifically negotiated with each State requesting it. Where the Council or the Commission gives a favourable response, this is recorded in a financing agreement. Implementation is subject to financial and accounting monitoring by the Commission.

1414 – The specific kind of negotiation the Community conducts with States that were part of former empires is a product of the internal dynamic of the European system, in which every compromise is constructed out of the initiatives and hesitations, proposals and concessions of the negotiating partners.

The strategy of association under the Treaty of Rome has extended the scope of diplomatic negotiations into new areas. (see *1983*)

1415 – This strategy might also evolve into a common European policy for developing countries.[11] In practice the debate about association is part of the discussion of the wider role of the European Union, and the extent to which it should give preference to some developing countries, whether in the form of preferential tariffs, development loans, food aid, support for specific markets or investment guarantees. It shows how the common foreign policy strategy of the Union is growing and diversifying, and how some aspects of the European organisational system are opening up to the world as a whole.

The fact remains, though, that many of the underlying principles of the WTO, in particular that of trade liberalisation, do not always favour that policy. (see *1102, 1942, 1955*)

Accession

1416 – The accession procedure is open to any European State: *the admission of new members is negotiated by the Union on the instructions of the Council, and*

---

11 C. COSGROVE-TWITCHETT: 'Towards a Community Development Policy', *Europe and the World*, London, 1976, p. 151; 'A New International Economic Order: the EC Response', *JCMS*, 1978, p. 157.

must have the unanimous approval of the member States; each one of them has to sign and ratify the accession agreement.

The procedure for such negotiations was laid down in directives formulated by the Council in 1970, and under it the Member States have one single representative, in principle the Presidency of the Council. The Commission may take part in the discussions, seek formulas for agreement and even itself represent the Union in exceptional circumstances.

Enlargement is one of the 'irreversible' features of the Union's policy, as can be seen from the summits of Lisbon (1992), Copenhagen (1993) and Gothenburg (2001). One early form of response to applications for membership was the creation, by negotiation, of the European Economic Area under the Treaty of Porto in 1992. (see *1345*)

At the Copenhagen summit in 2002, the member States decided to impose certain accession criteria on candidate countries, including those of respect for human and minority rights and an independent judiciary, as prescribed in the European Charter of Fundamental Rights.

1417 – The enlargement of the Union has brought about new obligations for the member States and, for each candidate, new issues, both internal and diplomatic, to be addressed.[12] This was already clear in 1969, when General de Gaulle laid down conditions for the accession of the United Kingdom, finally achieved in 1972 after protracted negotiations.

After that, the accession of Greece, Spain and Portugal brought the number of members to twelve, and this became fifteen when Ireland, Sweden and Finland joined. The Union was further expanded by the absorption of the former German Democratic Republic into the Federal Republic of Germany. In 2004, ten more countries joined, bringing the number to twenty-five: the Czech Republic, Poland, Slovenia, Slovakia, Hungary, Lithuania, Latvia, Estonia, Cyprus and Malta. Romania and Bulgaria are expected to accede, and others may follow.

1418 – While its continuity and fundamental content remain unaffected, enlargement of the Union forces the Member States to find a new balance, at the financial, trade and social levels. The new obligations, expenditures and risks involved in each accession require them to be approached and negotiated with caution, programmed over time and made subject to safeguards and transitional clauses. Agreement on these points between the Member States is as problematic as the negotiations with the candidate States themselves. The established '*acquis*' of the Union are not negotiable with candidates, but the timetable for their implementation in each of them can be negotiated, following the Madrid summit of 1995, depending on the degree to which each one varies from the Western model. (see *1246, 1255, 1413*)

1419 – The enlargement of the Union has presented it with a raft of institutional, organisational and relational problems. The machinery, institutions and processes

12 M. CAMPS: *Britain and the European Community (1953–1963)*, London, Oxford University Press, 1964.

designed to accommodate six members have proved difficult to adapt to much larger numbers. The single market and economic cooperation give rise to worsening practical problems. (see *1255*)

At the financial level, there is a distinction to be drawn between the structural funds allocated to the governments of new members and the collective funds intended for regional development plans fulfilling Union objectives. Separate negotiations are held with each of these countries on more than thirty issues, and funds are allocated by co-decision of the Parliament and the Council. These new members, in practice, account for around 20 per cent of the population of the Union, and only 4 per cent of its product.

The negotiation process in the Union could be amended, the regulations made more flexible and the institutions adapted in order to simplify the system. These issues have been debated in a series of meetings of the Council, and in the convention entrusted with drafting the 'Constitution'. Options might include expansion of the use of the qualified majority voting rule, increasing and redistributing the seats in the Parliament, restricting the number of Commissioners, revising the decision-making procedures and weighted voting and revising the role of the Presidency of the Union. (see *2005, 2667*)

Liaison with international organisations

1420 – In the interests of the development of multilateral and institutional negotiation, the status of the Union in international institutions and conferences needs to be clarified. These, in practice, provide the framework in which norms are drawn up, a growing number of which will be applicable to the internal market.

1421 – It is doubtful whether the European States would agree to the automatic abandonment of the advantages conferred on them by their number and their weight in favour of a uniquely collective institution. It is also doubtful whether the other members of international organisations would agree to let them do so. The real issue is that of the presence of the Union alongside its members, given that the Treaty of Rome provided for them to act collectively within the fields it covered.

1422 – The essential question is whether, within the scope of its own competences, the Union acts as the partial successor to its members. This must be true when it participates in the negotiation, conclusion and implementation of multilateral instruments in the fields of trade and customs, as well as for negotiations for the extension or amendment of the many agreements on raw materials or the functioning of the institutions set up under them.

1423 – On the Union's side, there are specific instruments that govern its participation in the work of international organisations. Broadly interpreted by the Commission, these instruments enable the Union to enter into a variety of relations with a huge range of organisations and institutions, for example, the Council of Europe and the OECD, and negotiate with them. However, under the 1966 Luxembourg Compromise, the Council must still have the opportunity to review the form and substance of the relationship contemplated, on a case-by-case basis.

1424 – The Commission has continuous working relations with these intergovernmental institutions, including exchanges of documents, participation in studies and preparatory work for treaties. These are formalised in special administrative agreements or arrangements. It has the power to conduct correspondence or enter into simplified forms of agreements, signed by its President, provided they are within its sphere of competence.

1425 – At the meetings, the Union participates through the Council and the Commission working together, either by following what is known as the 'Rome formula', or by the Commission acting as delegated spokesman, following the directives of the Council, in parallel with the national representatives, or even by occupying the presidency in a number of purely inter-state bodies. (see *1448*)

1426 – From the standpoint of the organisations concerned, these relations with the Union have required not only the agreement of their own member countries, but also governing instruments that are broadly drafted and favourably interpreted, since under the law as it stands, the Union does not have the responsibilities of a sovereign State. It has been decided that, as such, it cannot be admitted to membership of international organisations such as the United Nations, which admits only States, or the OECD, which was set up after the Treaty of Rome, where the Commission has a permanent representative. (see *1104*)

1427 – It is important for the Union to be granted official status within these international organisations both as a matter of political principle and because of its own constitutional mission. This has been slow to happen: it took years for the Community to obtain, by degrees, observer status in the UN Economic Commission for Europe. (see *1368*)

1428 – Upon the request of the Council of Ministers, observer status in the UN General Assembly was granted in 1974, which allowed the Community not only to attend General Assembly deliberations and receive documents, but also to make both oral and written interventions in its work. Though it was not granted voting rights, this regime has enabled the Community to make an active contribution, alongside that of its members, amounting to real recognition of the institution, its mission and competences. (see *1020*)

1429 – Each of these relationships is based on an agreement with the organisations concerned, or provided for in their founding instrument. Under Additional Protocol no. 1 to the OECD Convention of 14 December 1960, only States may be members of the OECD, but the Commission is allowed to take part in its work. Governments that fear the power of the Union do nothing to facilitate its participation in international institutions, but they are forced to accept this, as happened with the GATT and later the WTO. (see *1102*)

Under the Treaty of Amsterdam, the Council may, unanimously, authorise the Presidency, sometimes with the aid of the Commission, to enter into an agreement with an international organisation.

1430 – Once such agreements are concluded, the Union takes part in negotiation in the bodies and mechanisms set up under them. Whether it is assimilated to a State, with its own vote or votes as a group of Member States, it takes part in debates on issues arising under these treaties, and pleads in the case of a dispute, as in the WTO Dispute Settlement Body. (see *1652*)

1431 – The establishment of the European Community altered the relationship between its Member States and international organisations operating in fields that fall within the scope of Community competences. Its members are bound to act jointly in those international organisations whose missions, while not intended to be within the Community's competences, are of special interest for the single market. They sometimes do this by adopting a common position drawn up by the Commission and submitted to the Council, or by a mixed negotiation in which the Union and its members work in parallel.

§3. The conduct of negotiation

1432 – The founding Treaties of the European Communities did not set up any organ that could claim to have general and exclusive competence in the field of foreign relations. The Council laid down the procedure for negotiation and conclusion of Community agreements. This procedure has been clarified by subsequent practice and refined in the Treaties, especially as regards the participation of the European Parliament.

1433 – These decisions, the hybrid nature of the Union and the two-headed structure of its executive, make for a very complex regime. It has proved difficult to draw a distinction between the specific and partial attributions of the Community itself and those of its Member States – which do not regard themselves as having been relieved of their responsibilities and which third States often prefer to keep as their interlocutor of choice. Many negotiations cover subjects that occupy the borderline between Union competence and State sovereignty.

1434 – The allocation of responsibility for negotiations depends on the subject matter and the will of the other parties, without there being any absolute rules. *Where political aspects are dominant in a given negotiation, the State holding the Presidency of the Council for the time being serves as the channel of communication.*

1435 – Because the negotiation was more political than commercial, and because of the resistance of its negotiating partner to recognising the EEC, when France negotiated its economic cooperation treaty with the USSR in 1966, it did so itself. Others followed that example.

Now that those political issues have been resolved, the joint nature of these negotiations has come to prevail and it was the Community that negotiated with Russia on energy matters.

1436 – When the negotiation is technical, the Commission may have a certain amount of latitude; where it does not, perhaps because of the attitude of one negotiating partner, there is a risk that the talks will fail or become protracted, as has happened many times.

The tensions that have arisen between the Member States and even within the Commission itself in connection with trade negotiations with the United States show the difficulty of reconciling some national preoccupations with the European vision. (see *1455*)

The negotiating process

1437 – *Agreements between the Community and a third State or an international organisation are often negotiated by the Commission and entered into by the Council.* This means that responsibilities are shared on the basis of a distinction between the phase in which external commitments are discussed and the final manifestation of intention to be bound.

The workings of this procedure have been further refined through subsequent Union negotiations.

1438 – Considered by the Treaties as the initiator and executor of all European Union policy, the Commission is sometimes used as representative for the States as a whole, within the field of its competences. In that capacity, it becomes involved in the preliminaries to the negotiation, provided the constitution and customs of the particular conference allow for such a degree of flexibility. Or the States might equally agree to entrust a joint initiative to the State holding the Presidency, which is often done at ministerial and ambassadorial level, without compromising the Commission's right to intervene.

1439 – The opening of negotiations is in principle a decision for the Council, either because in the case of commercial treaties and tariff agreements, it is obliged to do so, or because of its political interest, as it is always possible for a member government or a third State to call for debate on a given matter. Within the scope of its attributed competences, the Commission can recommend that the Council begin a negotiation, sometimes based on exploratory discussions, held under the Council's guidance, which enable it to sound out third States.

National interests are taken into account at Council level, and these have implications for the powers of the Union to negotiate, as, for example, where certain Member States are opposed to agreements on raw materials.

1440 – Within those areas of competence that are strictly reserved to the Community (trade agreements, voluntary restraint agreements and association agreements), the Commission conducts the entire negotiation from start to finish. It decides for itself on what it can expect to achieve and what tactics to adopt, and pursues the negotiations to their conclusion, in a formal agreement initialled or authenticated by the Commission's representative. The exercise of this power is more flexible in the hands of the Commission than it would be for an ordinary national representative, but it is still strictly subject to the will of the Council, on whose behalf the agreement is negotiated and whose supervisory role is constantly expanding: the Commission's work is guided and monitored by committees of national officials appointed by the Council. One such committee exists for tariff and trade issues under Article 113 of the Treaty (now Article 133 EC).

1441 – This means that there is a 'dual negotiation' at work wherever the two decision-making systems cover the same ground or overlap with regard to the same subjects. *States reach agreement among themselves as the process unfolds: first, they lay the groundwork and then, negotiate with third States. There are thus two stages at which national positions an be eroded.*[13] (see *2385*)

1442 – With the exception of agreements intended to set up relations with other international organisations, the Council alone is empowered to enter into treaties negotiated by the Commission. Its representative signs the treaty, sometimes accompanied by a member of the Commission. In the case of agreements requiring a solemn procedure, signature alone is not binding if the Council decides that the agreement must be further refined before adopting it. (see *776*)

The Council decides either by unanimity or by qualified majority, depending on the subject matter. (see *1460*)

1443 – The Council approves a treaty either by decision or regulation, authorising it to be concluded and ordering its publication. Its acts, and the annexes containing the treaty text, are directly applicable as part of the laws of the Member States. Most of the time, it is the Presidency of the Council that notifies the co-contracting State that the necessary procedures have been completed for the agreement to enter into force. (see *779*)

1444 – The Council's decision is taken by agreement with the Parliament, especially in the case where a new institutional framework is being created, or in matters of accession or association. (see *1165, 1300*)

1445 – In reality, there is not so much a true sharing between the Union's institutions as a combination of different negotiating responsibilities. The Commission acts as the agent of the Council and carries on the negotiations in such a way that the Council can be informed and consulted and can participate if need be, and the Parliamentary committees can be kept directly and discreetly informed.

1446 – The Council determines the Union's position and ensures that it is observed by the member States. This first negotiation binds the participants, and at the same time it restricts their national competence to deal with third parties.

Joint negotiations

1447 – Many negotiations are carried on simultaneously by the Community itself and on behalf of each of the Member States. The power to negotiate may thus either be shared or exercised concurrently by several parties.

1448 – The 'Rome formula', so called because it was used during the international conference on wheat held in Rome in 1967, where the Council adopted it, consists

---

13 A. PLANTEY: *Prospective de l'Etat*, Paris, CNRS, 1975, p. 209.

of setting up a composite representation to take account of the fact that national and Community competences are intertwined.

1449 – The Community and the Member States take part in negotiations, each with its own delegation, but following directives jointly agreed upon using the usual procedures for cooperation and coordination, both before and during the meeting. The Union delegation will include representatives of the States, the Presidency and the Commission. The role of negotiator is allocated depending on the issues under discussion, either to the Commission representative on technical matters or to the representative of the Presidency of the Council in the capacity of single negotiator in discussions on questions of common interest that do not involve issues that must be dealt with by the Union itself.

1450 – The joint delegation formula has become increasingly widely used because of the overlap between State and Community activities, and most of the time it results in an accumulation of competences and jointly appointed delegations: this was already a feature of many major negotiations, such as those at Lomé or those that preceded the creation of the European Economic Area. (see *1397*)

1451 – On the other hand, instances can be cited where either one single delegation has represented the Community and its members, or the Community was represented by its members. Sometimes the joint delegation procedure has been used in exclusively Community matters, and on other occasions the common position has been expressed by a representative either of the Presidency if the forum so requires or if the issue is a political one, or the Commission if the governments so agree. The choice can be dictated by tactical considerations: the Multifibre Agreement was handled at Community level, but the UN Conference on the Law of the Sea, on the other hand, was dominated by considerations of national interest.

1452 – Matters that are not within the Community's competence are the subject of direct negotiations by the States concerned, conducted, within the overall negotiation, either by their representatives or by those of the Commission. National negotiators are sometimes added to the joint Community delegations.

On some occasions, by contrast, the Community has appeared as an additional partner in the negotiation, perhaps to the surprise of its interlocutors, particularly in major international conferences on topics such as the law of the sea or rules on science or technology, in which trade issues may peripherally arise. (see *1005*)

1453 – Foreign negotiation is one of the fields in which the respective strengths of the Commission and the Council can best be assessed. In refusing to give up its prerogatives, the Council merely voices the concern of the States anxious not to be deprived of their powers: depending on the importance of the issue and the rigidity of national positions, it often relegates the Commission to an executive role. That said, the Commission not infrequently seeks to force the hand of the Council, or at least of those of its members that do not endorse its position, when it considers it has obtained the best result from a negotiation. It has adopted such an attitude in various discussions, especially those with the United States on tariffs and trade, in spite of the disagreement of some Member States.

1454 – The internal logic of diplomatic negotiation applies to the Union as it does to States: the process has its own momentum that drives it towards a conclusion with each problem opening the way to a compromise. The Commission is better prepared than the Council to react flexibly to what the other parties propose, but, equally, it has also been known to go beyond the bounds set by the governments: its negotiators must understand the limits of the concessions they can make without risking rejection by the Council or the Member States.

1455 – Multilateral tariff negotiations showed that, in this critical area, States were not prepared to abandon their concerns. The Commission was entrusted with the negotiations more as the agent of the Council than as a negotiating partner in its own right. Strategy and tactics were determined at Council level, with the Commission helping the Council to reach its decisions, as well as implementing its detailed instructions, under the control of the governments.

1456 – This formula allowed the Community to defend its members' interests effectively without imposing excessive restrictions on them, and to serve as a counterweight, especially to the United States, through its astute and unified negotiating approach: as such, it was used again. However, following the problems encountered during the multilateral trade negotiations that ended in 1979, the Council delayed the final application of the agreements reached until it could verify that the implementing instruments put in place by the American authorities were in conformity with the commitments they had made. (see *1602*)

1457 – This sharing of roles sometimes works in favour of the Commission and others of the Presidency of the Council, depending on what the governments decide. In either case there can still be close coordination between the Member States and between the institutions of the Community, since the Commission will at a minimum have a part to play in informing the Council, preparing for the negotiation and implementing its results, with its status being somewhat less favourable than that of a State. The distinction between the competence itself and its exercise means that the latter can be conferred on the President – aided by officials of the Commission – where this fits better with the international system.

1458 – The fact that a negotiation is carried on by the Presidency of the Council rather than by the Commission does not change its underlying nature, which is based on agreement between the Member States; the President has no more latitude in the positions he takes than a representative of the Commission. The negotiations leading to Britain's accession, for instance, showed clearly that the outcome depended on the unanimous agreement of the original members of the Community: each time London set out its proposals, a private deliberation followed among the Six, from which a carefully worded text would emerge that laid out the mandate for the President at that time. The same happened with the accession of the Eastern European States; the Council had separated them into two groups, but even so there were ten States in the first. (see *1419*)

1459 – No external negotiation of the Union can in practice succeed without the agreement of the Member States: *the final decision-making power rests with* *the Council, in co-decision with the Parliament.* The procedures for negotiating and confirming the States' agreement are especially slow and cumbersome, since the governments still have the final choice, once their parliaments have discussed the issue, in spite of the steady erosion of their initial positions.

1460 – Hence the importance in this area of the way in which the Council functions and votes. In practice, the move towards qualified majority voting can go no faster than the States expressly wish: for many years to come, external negotiations will be considered as affecting their vital interests, and unanimity will be required on issues of principle. Unanimity is the rule in any case for association and accession. *In this as in other fields, a common position is not necessarily a Community position.*

External relations

1461 – Implementation of the common external policy of the Union is not simply a matter of spreading information about how the Union works or sending members of the Commission and officials on missions to gather information on the attitudes of third States to the Union. Rather, it involves implementing instructions agreed between the Member States, in close and constant cooperation with their local accredited diplomatic missions, as well as a flow of mutual information between the governments.

In spite of the principles decided in the Councils of Maastricht and Nice, the definition of a European external policy is highly problematic. Each of the Member States is free to decide on its own interests in world affairs and their views do not always coincide. (see *1300*)

1462 – The Council plays its role from start to finish of the negotiations, with the Commission responsible for executing the decisions taken. In this area, the Presidency of the Council acts in cooperation with the Commission. The two organs must therefore have a permanent system of coordination, either in Brussels or wherever trade negotiations take place or international organisations are located. (see *683*)

Within the European Union, the Presidency, sometimes with the help of the previous Presidency and the following one, is responsible for taking the necessary joint actions pursuant to the external policy. The Parliament and the Commission are involved in this work. (see *1275*)

1463 – In order to direct the external negotiations of the Union, the Council must be in a position to form a view of the political and economic climate in which it is operating. Most of this information comes from the diplomatic networks of the Member States, but the contribution of the Commission is becoming more and more significant, as much because of the contacts its members have with political figures as because of the existence of any paradiplomatic network.

1464 – The capacity to negotiate does not confer a right to permanent diplomatic representation. By contrast with the right to receive diplomats, provided for by the members in Article 17 of the Protocol on Privileges and Immunities, the question of permanent representation of the Union has never been systematically regulated.

1465 – Large numbers of missions have been sent to the headquarters of the European Union, both to the Council and the Commission, given the two-headed nature of the executive. Some of them have a sizeable staff, greater than those of the embassy accredited to the host country.

Under the 1966 Luxembourg Compromise, *the Council and the Commission must keep each other informed of approaches made to them by representatives of third countries.*

1466 – In principle, the head of the diplomatic mission of the State holding the Presidency of the Council is responsible for representing the Union in third countries and at major meetings of international organisations. This activity is carried out in coordination with the Commission delegation, if there is one. In the OECD and the WTO, the Commission negotiates, and the States conclude the agreements.

1467 – There must also be coordination between the ambassadors and delegations of the member States, under the aegis of the representative of the State holding the Presidency of the Council. This coordination does not prevent each mission from defending its own particular interests, but it does encourage the adoption of common positions.

The Maastricht negotiations recalled the importance of this obligation to cooperate in order to ensure that the joint positions and actions decided upon by the Council were implemented.

1468 – Responsible for applying Community policies on the authority of the Council, the Commission is represented abroad by departments operating on two different premises: in international organisations, this is a matter of prerogative, and a functional obligation; vis à vis third States, it is a simple matter of convenience.

1469 – Since the first liaison offices were set up in 1961 in the United States and at the OECD, more and more such missions have been created. There are now delegations established in many third countries, or groups of countries, which attach importance to their relations with Europe. There are also departments set up within the Union to follow the workings of international organisations such as the United Nations, the WTO and the OECD, as well as autonomous press and information offices in certain countries, delegations in countries that have signed an association agreement and special representation in areas where the Union is called upon to intervene, as in Afghanistan, Macedonia and the Middle East. (see *2644*)

1470 – As these delegations have expanded and multiplied, they have presented problems both of internal management and in terms of their relations with the authorities of the host countries. Sending its officials abroad has forced the Commission to adapt its administrative and budgetary rules. A specific legal regime has had to be devised to cover these members of staff.

1471 – The direct statutory link means that these missions fall legally and financially under the Commission, but these offices represent the Union as a whole, and are available to all its institutions, as well as its Member States: the Luxembourg Compromise laid down that the publication of information to the outside world was a matter for the Council and the Commission jointly.

1472 – In the associated ACP States, the Commission's representatives are empowered to conduct a variety of financial, administrative and technical negotiations, which makes each of them a favoured interlocutor of the host State. In addition to these tasks, however, they have others that also fall under the general development policy of the Union, such as food aid programmes and co-financing. Locally, they are recognised as having diplomatic status. (see *1411*)

1473 – There are some capitals where the Commission has established its own representation, responsible for negotiating direct with the authorities in that country, aside from the traditional role of providing information.

1474 – Each year, the Commission publishes a general report. This shows how important foreign relations have become to the Union, as well as detailing its consultations with third States, participation in the work of international organisations, and implementation of the association agreements.

§4. Union negotiation and joint negotiation

1475 – The number of negotiations carried on by the Community shows how its trade and economic policy has opened up worldwide. These negotiations are intense, but they are confined within the limits laid down by the Treaties: examples are international trade and relations with the ACP countries.

1476 – Within the scope of Community competences, *the Union's capacity to negotiate necessarily limits the competences of the member States in the diplomatic area:* even when States support a policy of progressive unification or integration, they cannot be regarded as having intended to completely withdraw from the picture. (see *610*)

1477 – Governments are clearly still concerned to retain as much of their diplomatic and political privileges as possible: this becomes important where the matters under negotiation have not been agreed between them beforehand. Thus, issues concerning the limits and methods of Community negotiation are susceptible of a variety of solutions depending on the circumstances. Here, there is no consistent pattern.

The negotiators of the Maastrict Treaty sought to resolve this problem by laying down the basic structure and direction for discussion of European Union external policy. In principle, competence lies with the Council. The Council of Ministers is responsible for implementation, assisted by the Commission, and the Parliament is consulted and kept informed. (see *1300*)

1478 – Where the Community derives its competence to negotiate from an express treaty provision, it takes over the competence of the States as their successor in the designated common areas (tariff and trade agreements) and in furtherance of policies that by definition belong to the Community. In these areas, the competence of the Community excludes that of the States: it is inconceivable for a single tariff to be set other than by common agreement. In practice, however, in implementing the commercial policy, there have been instances where competences were shared or combined.

1479 – Some States have nonetheless tried to limit as much as possible the extent of Community intervention in cases where the international negotiation was not confined to tariffs and trade, either by favouring those formulations and procedures that give the most place to national sovereignty, or by ensuring that harmonisation of foreign policies is entrusted to a body in which governments can negotiate freely together. *Member States have entered into multilateral trade negotiations jointly with the Community under the many clauses that are not exclusively commercial.*

1480 – Furthermore, devising a common external policy in areas where this could be possible is always subject to extraneous influences, among them the need for particular relations with the countries of Central and Eastern Europe, the United States and the ACP States. Governments have the capacity to assess and respect these limitations, especially in sectors that are not entirely within the internal market. They can discuss these issues among themselves in the course of their normal working relations, but do not always reach agreement.

The misunderstandings and divisions within the Union over the crises in the former Yugoslavia and in the Middle East showed that the more political the issue, the harder it is to achieve consensus. (see **1132**)

1481 – The Court has held that the Community's capacity to negotiate excludes that of the Member States (individually or collectively) where the Community has acted in implementation of a common policy laid down in one of the treaties. The legal and economic unity of the single market requires that the prerogative to negotiate and enter into commitments must lie with the party having the power to carry out the obligation, and thus Member States are prohibited from entering into obligations outside the Union's institutions that might affect Community rules. This too is broadly interpreted, since the common policies are treated as forming a coherent whole.

1482 – Except where there is specific language, as was the case with the Coal and Steel Community, there is no hard and fast rule requiring that the internal and external competences must run in parallel. In agriculture, for example, some relations between third countries and the Union have remained outside the scope of the Union's competences.

1483 – Moreover, third States and international organisations often allow the Union authorities only a limited minor role in their negotiating procedures: their presence and rights to intervene are sometimes the subject of uneasy political and diplomatic compromises, and require goodwill on the part of their interlocutors. The crisis in the former Yugoslavia was handled, for the most part, at Council level or by the Council's representatives.

1484 – Diplomatic practice allows for a distinction to be drawn between the negotiation, conclusion and execution of treaties. It can equally happen that States act to implement an obligation undertaken by the Community or that the Union has the powers necessary to carry out an agreement born of the common will of its members.

1485 – As the product of the Union's capacity to negotiate, the limitations placed on the sovereign rights of States will depend on the political concept the governments have of the Union and how they define its field of action. As long as the Union has not made the definitive move towards integration, such limitations will be strictly interpreted.

1486 – The sectoral, limited and gradual nature of European unification has left room for many joint negotiations, where Community competence and State privilege have worked in conjunction, and where the resulting commitments have at the same time bound the Community and the States collectively. *This formula, whereby each party binds itself to the full extent of its capacities, reveals at the same time the complex sharing of competences and the difficulties of the integration process.* According to some observers, sole representation by the Union's institutions in matters of common policy would be a step ahead but, especially with enlargement, this is a long way off.

1487 – Aside from strictly Community negotiations, another effect of the European Union legal system has been to restrict the freedom of the Member States to make their own decisions. The EU Treaty has precedence over treaties they enter into subsequently, thus binding them to refrain from taking any measure that could endanger the achievement of the fundamental goals of the Union.

1488 – The Member States could still not, on their own, determine the common external policy even if the entire responsibility for implementing it had not been transferred to organs of the Union. The Council must decide on policy, on the basis of the national concerns expressed within it, as it does, for example, with each new accession. (see *617*)

It is thus up to the Member States to coordinate their own negotiations in order to promote the objects of the EU Treaty, even where – as with relations with China – this is no easy matter.

1489 – The Court of Justice has preventive powers to ensure compliance with these obligations, for example, if an institution or Member State of the Union requests an opinion. But there is no legal means to annul the outcome of a negotiation, when faced with a recalcitrant member in breach of its obligations.

1490 – In 1974, the Council decided to introduce a procedure of information and consultation before Member States began negotiations on cooperation agreements with third countries. This acknowledged the fact that commercial policy is a Community matter, while negotiations on wider issues are handled at national level. *Its object was to ensure that State negotiations were compatible with Community policy and its application.*

To ensure coordination, agreements are submitted in draft so that their compatibility with Treaty obligations can be studied. This way, governments and the Commission may discuss the issues of concern to them either in a restricted committee or in a group specialising in financial coordination.

1491 – The Treaty of Rome provided that Member States would act jointly within certain international organisations on questions of particular interest to the internal market. This meant adopting a common approach within economic institutions, even on matters falling outside the scope of Community competences, whenever the issue was one that could have an impact on the activities of the Community.

It was agreed in Maastricht in 1991 that the European Union could, speaking through the Presidency, express a common position in international organisations. The delegations of the Member States work together to ensure that the common positions and actions decided on by the Council are implemented.

1492 – Faced with the need to harmonise their respective reactions to the crisis in the former Yugoslavia, the European States agreed to establish a common security policy (the common foreign and security policy or CFSP) as the second 'pillar' of the Union. Later, in Brussels in 2003, the decision was taken to extend this to include defence and work towards the establishment of a common European security and defence policy (CESDP). (see *1330, 1532, 1642*)

The European Council is thus entrusted with the mission to define the overall principles and direction of this potential common foreign and security policy, both at the level of strategy and joint action. Decisions are, in principle, taken unanimously. The Parliament is given an opportunity to debate the issues. Each Member State may take urgent measures provided it informs the others. Decisions taken as part of this intergovernmental cooperation are carried out by the President of the Council, assisted by the High Representative for Common Foreign and Security Policy. (see *1300*)

One of the first achievements of this common policy was the 1995 Stability Pact in Europe, a French initiative. (see *1242, 1692*)

The Council also decided (Helsinki, 1999) on the gradual setting up of a peacekeeping force capable of rapid intervention, to be modelled on the Franco-German Eurocorps, established in 1992 and operational since 1995, to which other countries have adhered. Armaments is another area in which European cooperation is under discussion.[14] The expenditures arising out of these decisions are a matter for negotiation between the governments.

1493 – There is nothing to prevent the Member States of the Union from cooperating to some extent in matters of foreign policy. On the contrary, the obligation to respond to crises such as that of international terrorism will provide

14 M. GUILLAUME: 'L'organisation conjointe de coopération en matière d'armement', *AFDI*, 1998, p. 283.

them with many opportunities to negotiate, often at summit level. However, if they are to have wider application, the methods and scope of such negotiations must be more clearly defined, case by case if necessary. (see *1246, 1319, 1328*)

The close proximity of nations to each other has forced Europe to rethink its attitude to the outside world. As well as Community external policy, a common approach to external relations is now emerging, through the deliberations of the Heads of State and governments in the Council. (see *1999, 2158, 2488*)

Most needed at times of crisis, this cooperation might not result in the joint defence of the Union, but has at least resulted in the setting up of an autonomous operational capability, one that could replace the Western European Union but still complies with the North Atlantic Treaty and uses NATO capabilities, as in the case of Macedonia. Another partnership followed, between Russia and NATO. (see *916, 1319, 1330, 1358, 1531*)

The meeting of the Council in Brussels in 2003 produced agreement on the distribution of tasks between the Union (responsible for Bosnia and Congo) and NATO (responsible for Kosovo). This enabled full-scale peacekeeping operations to be undertaken on behalf of the United Nations in Bosnia, Macedonia and Congo, which are in fact policing interventions.

1494 – Experience proves, though, that on the most critical issues, Member States try to reassert their freedom to negotiate and vote: they were, for instance, divided over the attitude to adopt to the draft Charter of the Economic Rights and Duties of States when it was before the UN General Assembly or when the code of conduct for maritime conferences was debated by UNCITRAL. The most telling example was their reaction to the attitude of the United States in Iraq, on which European countries, despite being members of NATO, took different policy positions.

It remains to be seen whether a European Council consisting of 25 or 27 members will be able to draw up a single defence policy.[15]

European political cooperation has produced a multitude of fora where members can exchange information and consider the issues without undue procedural constraints. The edifice of the Union is thus protected from external impact and allowed to continue with its policy-making work. Its empirical nature does, however, mean that it is not the ideal framework for joint decision-making. (see *1334, 2329*)

1495 – Cooperation within Europe has an increasingly broad impact, both on third countries and international organisations, whether or not it concerns subjects related to Community competences. This concerted action is in the interests of the Union as long as it facilitates the achievement of its goals. As yet, however, it has not succeeded in producing common strategies in the face of real international tensions, and the enlargement of the Union is bringing an increasingly wide range of interests within the European umbrella. (see *1328*)

15 F. TERPAN: *La politique étrangère et de sécurité commune de l'Union européenne*, Brussels, 2003.

It is in the field of foreign relations most of all that the Union has experienced difficulty in devising an integrated long-term policy based on the – usually short-term – views of each government. Divisive tactics and extraneous influences can paralyse unity of action, when what is needed is a system in which the members inform, consult and communicate with each other as a matter of course.

It would be appropriate to wait until the Parliament and Council have clearly defined their roles in setting and executing a true Community policy in this area, before attempting a serious assessment of the prospects this opens up for European negotiation. (see *2247, 2385, 2675*)

Chapter IV:
Organisational Negotiation

1496 – Never a day passes in the modern age without all manner of negotiations being undertaken and concluded, in the farthest-flung corners of a planet most of whose people by now have their independence. These negotiations cover an ever-growing number of countries, weaving an inextricable and complex web of bilateral and multilateral relations. (see *1091*)

1497 – The principles and practices that evolved in an era when there were no more than twenty sovereigns are no longer relevant to the two hundred or more present-day States, many of them minute and impoverished. New and varied forms of international relations are gradually taking shape, encompassing both independence and solidarity (of interests if not of sentiment).

1498 – Among the characteristics of a society today described as 'post-industrial' is the growth of activities in the services sector. Together with the opening up of countries to the outside world, this can be expected to have an effect on social relations of all kinds, especially foreign negotiation, which is one of the most durable expressions of collective power.

1499 – The needs of such a society in terms of capital, and of human capital in particular, are constantly increasing. Satisfying them will require not only preserving peace and security between nations, but also finding optimal ways, free from doctrinal preconditions, to manage all the various forms of cultural heritage. (see *1838*)

1500 – Profound technological changes bring with them tensions and uncertainties that accentuate the propensity for conflict inherent in human relations: the need to address this danger will give impetus to the search for better ways of organising relations between States. (see *1689*)

1501 – In an environment where people are brought ever closer, notwithstanding inequalities in economic and cultural development, the need of peoples to inform and communicate with each other and regulate their exchanges, and their ability to do so, will not only improve the way negotiations are conducted but make their practice more widespread. (see *1808, 1817*)

The more institutionalised the negotiation process becomes, however, the less it will have to do with reciprocity of conduct and the more open it will be to the intervention, consultation and participation of societies and groups that traditional diplomacy used to ignore. Even governments sometimes negotiate through the agencies, private bodies or, in some cases, associations that manage their public services. (see *683, 1898*)

1502 – Man's desire to intervene in the natural world and in society, coupled with a global, prospective vision of relations between peoples, points up the need for an internationally organised form of bargaining, resource allocation and participation. This need for voluntary arrangements is characteristic of the technological civilisation of an overindustrialised society. *Permanent negotiations produce institutions: these, in turn, provide both justification and support for the negotiation.* (see *55, 58, 608, 1249*)

1503 – All these reasons explain why the modern international world is in the process of organising itself, a process that is having an increasing impact on the sovereign practice of diplomacy.

The international machinery that has gradually built up is increasingly restrictive of the freedom of States to negotiate. This can be seen in its most advanced form in the European Union, especially in the way it conducts its external negotiations. (see *1360*)

1504 – Whatever else it may be, an international organisation is still a meeting of States. It remains to be seen whether these States are better disposed now than in the past to accept the disciplines of communal life, or if the advantages derived from the organisation outweigh the disadvantages of curtailment of sovereign privileges. Where there is no higher authority and no sufficient guidance, negotiation is the only way for institutions to avoid breaking up and suffering defections, and sometimes, too, it is the only way to assert internal solidarity in the face of powerful external imperatives. Negotiation by organisations is taking an increasingly prominent place in both the practice and theory of modern international relations. (see *1254, 1359, 2272*)

Section I: Organised negotiation

1505 – The functioning of international institutions and the European Union confirms that their main and primary role is to provide permanent frameworks and established procedures for negotiation between States. However, these organisations do not exist merely to respond to the desire for order and stability in relations between States but also to address the manifold real needs of the international milieu.

1506 – This complex and diverse edifice of organisations is at the same time both constructed and constructive: not only does it generate, and regulate, increasing amounts of consultation and negotiation, but it also uses them to constantly refine the rules of international life. (see *1100, 1001, 2284*)

Although international law has not evolved into an organised body, a whole series of rules relating to international instruments have emerged as a result of negotiation – on treaties, diplomatic representation, the international civil service, intergovernmental administration and arbitration. These are all fields of activity that are growing in importance every year.

The regime governing transport and communications has also assumed an international dimension, as have the law of the sea and space law.

1507 – Multilateralism in the organisational context is not to be confused with multilateral diplomacy, because it is inherently different from traditional negotiation: States do not look to it to decide their fate. It is more about means than ends: the parties are interested in convergence in limited sectors or technical areas, cooperation in response to collective needs, ongoing management and mechanisms that can be endlessly adapted. It is not so much the attitude of the participants that politicises these kinds of negotiation but the publicity they attract.

1508 – The weakening of the divide between domestic and foreign affairs, together with the growth in relations between countries in varied and technical fields, means that organisational negotiation has become the natural extension of every kind of national activity. At the same time, the methods used in negotiating have crept into the internal functioning of the State.

1509 – It could even be argued that external organisational negotiation begins at national level.[1] Public and private administrations provide the basic support for the diplomat, especially when he is dealing with specific economic, social or institutional issues. Here, no decisions are taken without careful choices being made between interests, ambitions and doctrine; as resistance to his original negotiating position erodes, the negotiator often has to refer to his capital, or his corporate headquarters, for further instructions. (see *2421*)

1510 – The number of actors involved, the complexity and diversity of the relations between them, the variety of subjects discussed and the turbulent nature of the economic and cultural environment mean that organisational diplomacy is becoming increasingly important, while at the same time, it bears less and less resemblance to the traditional practice of negotiation between States.

§1. Developing the structures

1511 – The essential characteristic of the institutional approach to negotiation is that it takes place within bodies or networks that already exist and can provide it with procedures and facilities, and sometimes even set the goal it must achieve. *Membership of an organisation implies a duty to respect its rules, unless and until these are altered by common agreement.* (see *1027, 1123, 1124*)

1512 – Organisational negotiation is not simply the end product of intense and complex discussions; it also implies that information be shared and communicated. Then, limits are set on arbitrary national positions, so that there is no systematic requirement of reciprocity of conduct, and the long-term participation of all concerned is harnessed in the collective interest. By this gradual process a new international attitude takes shape. (see *1075, 2037, 2053*)

1513 – The same factors have resulted in changes to the functions and tasks of diplomatic missions. Organisational negotiation deals with a growing number of topics of multilateral interest in which embassies are often not involved. As for the

1 A. PLANTEY: *Prospective de l'Etat*, Paris, CNRS, 1975.

permanent representations and missions of States, these are gradually being drawn into the functioning of the international organisation system.[2] (see *2467*)

1514 – The framework for organisational negotiation is sometimes defined in the discussions that lead to the setting up of multipartite conferences. Generally, though, it takes the form of an international institution or the extension of the mission of an existing body that the parties agree to use. (see *1012, 1096, 1100*)

States have many opportunities to express common views or embark on concerted manoeuvres now that international relations are becoming more and more closely interdependent. They sometimes form groupings to do precisely that.

The World Tourism Organisation, for instance, was created in this way out of a private institution, by consensus among more than one hundred countries, in order to introduce rules and ethical standards into an activity in rapid global expansion. (see *2209*)

1515 – Agreeing that a negotiation should take place in a multilateral framework means, first of all, that the protagonists must be defined, by inclusion or exclusion (the Member States of an international organisation, for example, or the States invited to a conference), even if some of the participants have no interest in the discussions. (see *753, 1129, 1728, 1991*)

But when the focus shifts from matters of diplomacy to matters of administration, and real and lasting economic, social, technical and cultural needs must be addressed, *ways will be found to enable all entities that can make a contribution to participate in the organisational negotiation, be they regions, dependent territories, administrative or private bodies.*

1516 – Joining with States in the negotiations of intergovernmental institutions are non-governmental organisations, public institutions, both national and international, private groups and local authorities. The internationalisation of institutions means that the centres of decision-making are far removed from the citizens, who therefore make themselves heard within the organisation through consultative procedures, sometimes vociferously.[3] (see *1090, 1827, 1899*)

Negotiation at European level thus produces increasing numbers of agreements of varying kinds, by bringing together public services and private persons, depending on the structure of the bodies that will facilitate the negotiation and implement its results. (see *1232, 1293, 1349*)

Some NGOs fulfil a public service mission, such as the Red Cross and the Olympic Movement. These two bodies have a stable and recognised structure, with national and international committees. The popular values they represent make them influential negotiators. This model is one that might perhaps be copied in non-profit-making activities, because it avoids the proliferation of intergovernmental offices. (see *1907*)

---

2 *Les Missions permanentes auprès des organisations internationales*, Brussels, Bruylant, Carnegie Foundation, 1971.

3 M. BETTATI et P. M. DUPUY: *Les ONG et le droit international*, Paris, Economica, 1986. Y. BEIGBEDER: *Le Rôle international des ONG*, Paris, LGDJ, 1992.

1517 – The wider the scope of an organisation's responsibilities, the less easy, or thorough, will be its negotiations. The level of cooperation achieved within the Council of Europe produces more clearly defined legal results than does the United Nations: its work in 1999 on cybercrime is an example. However, its work is only of persuasive effect, by contrast with the European Union, where much more consolidated processes exist for decision-making between States. (see *1239, 1276*)

1518 – International organisations also contribute to the stability of international relations: such was the effect, for a time, of UN Security Council resolution 242 of 22 November 1967 that laid down some of the principles for a fair and lasting peace in the Middle East. (see *1146*)

Sometimes, even before their definitive internal structures are in place, governments regard these institutions as untried systems whose strength and likely effects are not properly understood. Reluctant to have to deal with yet another different variable, States react with reserve to a development that appears to threaten their autonomy. (see *1362*)

1519 – Conversely, a properly functioning institution will grow according to its own rhythm. This was the case with the summits of Heads of State and Governments of the industrialised nations, which started out as informal, but developed their own practices and a flexible structure, first as G5, then G7, G8, and in 2005, with China, G9. (see *131, 1824, 2489*)

This structuring process is characteristic of every robust organisation. *The quest for regulation shows a natural tendency to expand and overflow into new sectors, and at the same time, the approach to problems is refined*: the creation, and expansion, of a free trade area in Western Europe generated a whole series of new negotiations, in the fields of industry, agriculture and social affairs, to name but a few. The same will happen in North America and could happen in South America. (see *1101, 1643, 1968, 2289*)

1520 – One of the advantages of an organisation is that it provides ways of dealing with novel and sometimes urgent situations without procedural preliminaries, allowing the positions of both sides to be aired as fully and objectively as possible. (see *1356, 1802, 2093*)

The effectiveness of an institution can be judged by how it responds to political, economic or other crises.[4] (see *2157*)

1521 – The more ambitious and demanding projects become in terms of technological advancement, capital investment and generosity of ideals, the greater the tendency to rely on international structures. *In reality, neither the resources available nor the regulations in force at national level are adequate to satisfy ever-growing demands, assume the burden of long-term policies or accept broad and unpredictable risks.* (see *1962*)

---

4 A. PLANTEY: *Principes de diplomatie*, Paris, Pedone, 2000, p. 421. J.-M. DUFOUR: 'Le modèle administratif français et les organisations internationales', in *L'Internationalité dans les institutions et le droit*, Paris, Pedone, 1995, p. 183. R. RUZIE: 'L'influence de droit français sur celui de la fonction publique internationale et européennes', ibid., p. 199.

The European Space Agency has made it easier to carry out international industrial and technological programmes by using its flexible decision-making process for their negotiation. New entities, set up for specific purposes, are not part of the international administration, but transact business such as selling meteorological and telecommunications services and navigation systems and launching satellites. The Agency has several hundred scientific and industrial contracting partners.

1522 – In parallel, there is an increasing tendency for governments to seek advice from experts over whom they have no direct authority, and even confer responsibility on them.

The constitution of the ILO has added another unique method of negotiation through its general conference: the national delegations comprise two government delegates, one employers' delegate and one workers' delegate, nominated by agreement with the most representative of the professional organisations. (see *1153, 1601*)

The International Law Commission, as with other similar organs created by the United Nations, draws up draft conventions, some of which are ratified by negotiation between governments.

1523 – By contrast with bodies whose purpose is negotiation and cooperation, those whose mission is to integrate States into a structured whole with its own decision-making powers are composed of persons not acting only as representatives of States but also in their own capacity. Such was the European Community, whose history illustrates the opposition between the two conceptions of international relations in Europe: diplomatic negotiation or administrative integration. (see *1332, 1640*)

1524 – In order to surmount the problem of self-centred nationalism, one suggestion was to give an international role to eminent persons who are independent of States, technically qualified and invested with legal prerogatives. In the United Nations, the proposal was made to appoint groups of '*rapporteur*-negotiators', specially chosen for their experience and competence, to facilitate certain negotiations and undertake liaison, mediation and conciliation.[5]

Relying on wise individuals who give governments the backing of their experience and prestige would not obviate the need for international negotiation: their conclusions might influence the positions taken by States, but could never be a substitute.

1525 – Organisational negotiation develops by building solidarity in progressive stages, each of which takes place in the framework most favourable to it. Choices are made at each stage which usually result in a common median position being agreed upon by most of the participants, that can later be defended in a wider forum. (see *2281*)

---

5 G. GEORGES-PICOT and M. VIRALLY: *Plan de réforme des méthodes et pratiques de l'ONU*, New York (unpublished consultative paper).

The regime of association with the European Union applies a form of bilateralism based on exactly this form of double or two-step negotiation.

1526 – This double negotiation can be used as a way of monitoring the diplomatic activity of some States or even a means of restricting their sovereignty. This method was employed by the USSR to centralise the trade negotiations of its satellite countries within what was then the COMECON. (see *1247*)

1527 – In practice, insisting on diplomatic coordination allows a government's policy line to be controlled or possibly altered, even in the domestic sphere; in addition, establishing the group of States so formed as the sole actor in negotiations ensures that the dominant power can keep its allies under control. (see *938, 946*)

Multilateralism may simply be a disguise for predominance.

1528 – The extent to which exceptions are made to national sovereignty must not be exaggerated. The General Assembly of the United Nations is a meeting of government delegations; the same is true of the governing bodies of other worldwide organisations, where, if there are any non-sovereign participants, their responsibilities are exercised through States.

1529 – Parliamentary assemblies cannot claim to superimpose electoral representation on the political expression of national sovereignty that flows from each State's own constitutional system, and – leaving aside the case of the European Union – have no power to compel governments. (see *1297*)

What has been called the 'democratic deficit' of the European Community has arisen precisely because of the distance between the decision-making process and the elected bodies, as well as the voters, in each Member State.

1530 – As for the organised core of the European Union, its leanings towards federalism have been thwarted by certain member governments who have done their utmost to minimise what has been called supranationality or technocracy, in other words, anything that would free this nascent authority from dependence on their political will. (see *1342*)

1531 – Organisational negotiation works by the will of States. It is kept alive by governments, even though there are certain international administrations, such as the European Commission, with the rank, permanence and powers to make their mark; the slow dismantling of the WEU in favour of the European Union is an example of this, though it does not affect the underlying treaties of alliance. (see *849, 1359, 1493*)

Even the Security Council often does no more than confirm or reveal the success or failure of direct, frequently bilateral, diplomatic negotiations.

States will only agree to give up part of their sovereign legal powers when it is in their interests, and almost always retain their liberty to negotiate among themselves without having to resort to an institutional framework. (see *1310, 1334*)

1532 – Even within very close-knit groups of States, such as those of Western Europe, safeguarding national interests on all issues and by all legitimate means remains the rule; in this kind of negotiation, States are developing the practice of exchanging information, consulting and cooperating and reaching compromises – in other words, they use all the methods of traditional diplomacy. It was European unification that prompted the consistent and concerted efforts to remove certain sectors from national administration: however, the gains made with respect to decision-making when the governments are in agreement do not apply to implementation, which, with very rare exceptions, remains a matter of national prerogative. (see *610*)

There are some areas, such as financial, fiscal and customs information and police and criminal proceedings, in which States insist on the guarantees offered by bilateral cooperation, which may be conducted under the auspices of an institution, for example, in the field of customs. This consideration explains how difficult it is to arrive at a unified European policy in the fight against organised crime and terrorism. (see *1492, 2040*)

1533 – Institutional procedures do not take away the difficulties of negotiation where powerful interests have to be reconciled. Sometimes the discussions can be so arduous that they cannot be brought to a conclusion without either direct pressure from outside or some more distant threat: this happened at every stage in the building of Europe. *Some meetings are the scene of veritable diplomatic battles, ending in defeats and victories, where more is at stake than questions of prestige.* (see *1340*)

1534 – Negotiation can take place between partners that are separated by profound cultural differences. The mere fact that it happens in an organised framework does not override the instinctive historic, ethnic or ideological reactions of the governments and their representatives. On the contrary, the risk of confrontation is higher, even if the conference is not public. (see *1865, 1880, 2035, 2053*)

One of the prerequisites for multilateral negotiation is to neutralise or alleviate the cultural and psychological obstacles that can paralyse or distort communication.

1535 – An organisational negotiation also has to accommodate the inequality of the actors. The unification of a system serves the interests of the dominant power because it weakens the protection available to its partners. Equality can only be reestablished if there is genuine willingness, which could manifest itself, for instance, by negotiating ground rules in advance to ensure that the parties are on an equal footing in preparing and concluding their agreements. (see *1111, 1118*)

1536 – It is understandable, then, that small nations expect the processes of organisational negotiation to provide them with the means to contain the domination of the Great Powers.[6] And, equally, that the larger States seek to ensure that their will cannot be defeated. This was, for four decades, the effect of the veto in the Security Council, because it rendered the Western alliance of the majority ineffective as long as the rivalry persisted between powers with a global strategy. (see *135, 662, 2298*)

---

6 G. de LACHARRIERE: *La Nouvelle Division internationale du travail*, Geneva, Droz, 1976.

1537 – The international organisation is criticised for its tendency to spread, fragment and proliferate just as cells multiply in a disease: indeed, the communications and negotiations going on at any one time are more and more complex and diverse.

Excessive institutionalisation of the ways and means of negotiation creates the risk of paralysis of a system that needs to be flexible in order to be politically effective. The demise of the League of Nations may well have resulted from its failure to adapt in time. If there is functioning political cooperation between the States of Western Europe, this is because it is organised on flexible lines; by contrast, it has become more and more difficult to take decisions within the European Council (see the Council of Nice, 2000). (see *1310, 1341, 2219*)

1538 – The Great Powers have difficulty in coming together in an institutional setting that deprives them of the ability to choose the timing or the subject matter, and forces them to accept partners, procedures and publicity. (see *131, 1084, 1435*)

In several organisations, 'private' diplomatic consultations take place between national representatives, without experts or international officials present and with no minutes taken. Governments often agree to negotiate on the sidelines of the UN Security Council. (see *1143*)

1539 – As a reaction against the excessive *dirigisme* of national administrations, informal practices flourish in economic, cultural and social fields in parallel with organisational work. *Formalism will be rejected in institutional negotiation, just as it is in diplomatic negotiation whenever governments want to free themselves of official constraints.* (see *1578, 1585, 1807, 2230*)

§2. Easier procedures

1540 – The methods used in organisational negotiation are not so very far removed from those of diplomatic negotiation. Many of the tactics of diplomacy are adopted, but with the addition of a logical, administrative approach to the issues. There is more emphasis on joint studies, administrative procedures, written documents and group working than on the more personal, flexible, discreet and elegant techniques of traditional diplomacy. (see *600*)

1541 – In the view of some observers, the novelty of this approach lies in the way it begins by analysing an issue on the basis of agreed priorities or an agreed order, by subject matter or in consecutive steps. When the discussions have ended, the main elements of the debate are recapitulated, in order of importance, to ensure that all those present are in agreement.[7] (see *448, 1262, 1272, 1627*)

The Council of Ministers of the European Union deliberates in different compositions, but their negotiations are not independent of each other.

1542 – There is no fundamental difference between this process and normal negotiation, where difficult and complex issues are concerned. In bilateral

---

7 G. R. WINHAM: 'Negotiation as a Management Process', *World Politics*, XXX, 1 October 1977, p. 112.

relations, too, the questions are aired, and the delegates, whose roles are coordinated by the head of the mission, conduct discussions that can either be separate, concurrent or successive. At the end, decisions are made, in the form of a package deal, on all the issues on which there is still disagreement. The effect of having multilateral negotiations, however, is that this pattern becomes enlarged and complicated to the point that the entire rhythm and atmosphere of the negotiation is altered. (see *989, 1139*)

1543 – Within each negotiation that makes up the overall effort, the skilled manoeuvrings of classical diplomacy come into play. *In an institution, the exercise remains one of balance of power, mutual concessions and the painstaking search for compromise.*

1544 – The fact remains that the negotiator's task is becoming more time consuming, ill defined and uncertain. It is difficult, if not impossible, for him to have a complete picture of the diplomatic field of play or sufficient knowledge of all the subjects to be discussed. He will be obliged to surround himself with specialists and listen to those representing various interests.

He will also have to devote time and attention to studying and applying the rules and procedures of the organisation, preparing and reading numerous lengthy documents and considering all the many possibilities for compromise opened up by the drafting work and informal approaches. (see *1271, 2451*)

1545 – Complexity of subject matter and techniques increases the uncertainty as to what information is needed for the discussions and what their outcome will be. An apparently successful agreement might prove disastrous in practice if circumstances change, and fresh negotiations might have to be started straight away as the only way of putting the process back on track. (see *425*)

Like diplomatic negotiation, in organisations negotiation is rarely over. For some States, its purpose is often to provide the means of renegotiating measures already decided, in order to prevent matters from taking an unacceptable turn. (see *800, 804, 817*)

1546 – The further diplomacy extends into every field of activity, the more types of counterpart are available to negotiators within an international organisation. In the European Union, each State or group of States may demand a concession as the condition for its acceptance of other proposals. This has been a consistent practice in the field of agriculture, where agreements are arrived at among the Member States by a process of bargaining. The same is also true of important negotiations on institutions and their procedure. (see *1272*)

The duty to conciliate

1547 – Achieving a majority within an international organisation, sometimes by demagogic techniques, will restrict even further the freedom responsible governments have to manoeuvre. (see *1778, 2284*)

This also enhances the importance of certain roles such as that of chairman of the organisation or of a particular meeting, that partake of elements of both diplomacy and organisation when they are allocated to States by turns. (see *1275, 1567*)

1548 – In organisations, the first tendency is to negotiate: in addition to the impetus provided by the collective pressure from the countries, the press and public opinion, there is the underlying logic of the very system in which contemporary diplomacy operates. Even the most uncompromising of States will feel compelled to enter into dialogue in the face of widespread fears of damage to the edifice of international relations on which the economy of nations increasingly depends. (see *1216, 1783*)

1549 – Thanks to the existence of an institutional structure, the majority of those present are able to force recalcitrant States into a defensive position. They have only limited possibilities to manoeuvre, which alters the balance of power because, if they are not quick to react, the sheer weight of procedures, structures and documents will prevent them from putting their arguments fully and in time. (see *1124, 1273*)

1550 – The slowness and complexity of this type of negotiation lead governments to change the way in which they participate, often by assigning much of the work of information gathering, preparation and conciliation to groups of experts or officials. This might explain the growing influence of the international civil service.

1551 – The anonymity of the proceedings means that considerations of vanity and repute carry less weight. 'Good offices', expressing the wish to reach unanimous agreement on legal formulations, are used in advisory or technical groups and drafting committees where the actual negotiations are diluted. (see *465*)

1552 – International organisations have injected new life into the process of conciliation between States, offering procedures and publicity that may encourage its use in the long term.[8] The early efforts of the League of Nations under the General Act of 26 September 1928 have been continued by the United Nations: the General Assembly and the Security Council set up secondary organs for this purpose. Committees were also created by other institutions (UNESCO in December 1962, and UNCTAD in December 1964, pursuant to General Assembly Resolution 1195) along with less formal procedures under the direct control of the organisations themselves. (see *470, 645*)

1553 – The insistence with which conciliation processes are pursued by international organisations can usually succeed in overcoming even the most entrenched reluctance, but they cannot overcome the absolute refusal of a Sovereign State. International institutions can follow the progress of their efforts, and if necessary lend assistance or offer helpful publicity. (see *1290*)

1554 – Collective mediation has been the subject of in-depth study in the United States, where there is a Federal department including highly qualified negotiators

---

8 A. LALL: *Modern International Negotiation: Principles and Practice*, New York, Columbia University Press, 1966.

with special training in labour relations, whom the parties may ask for help in reaching agreement, on a non-binding basis. The processes used in salary negotiations have become progressively more refined,[9] with practices observed that have come to resemble those used in international relations, as to the requirement that allegations must be proved, the prohibition on the refusal to negotiate, the principle of good faith, the tactics used by pressure groups and the methods used by the parties to approve agreements.

1555 – However, one fundamental difference will remain between labour mediation and diplomacy – the State can impose rules on its nationals but not on its peers. *No rule can govern the process of negotiation from opening to ratification, if it is not based on agreement between the governments.* (see *369, 606*)

1556 – One of the consequences of organisation at international level has been that the first attempts have been made to regulate collective bargaining, including the principles and procedures to be followed, publication of agreements and verification of implementation. *However, no one is entitled to judge the good faith of States or criticise their strategies.* (see *489, 1779, 1783*)

1557 – The methods used in organisational negotiation are growing ever closer to those used in national institutions, whether parliamentary or administrative, depending on the degree to which their proceedings are public.[10] Information gathering, drafting of documents and reports, administrative responsibilities, the division and ordering of working groups, collective deliberations, the allocation of time, the order of speaking and the importance given to minutes clearly show a definite tendency towards integration. (see *1012, 1127, 2243*)

1558 – A tacit complicity is developing between national and international bureaucracies, and the more specialised they are, the closer the relations they establish. At every level, the mutual exchange of information, best practices and officials helps to spread new forms of international dialogue. (see *2559*)

1559 – In some organisations (the European Bank for Reconstruction and Development, for example), negotiation is normally approached in stages. Technical or financial aid projects are discussed first with the beneficiary countries, then often with other international institutions or governments, then within the administration of the organisation concerned and lastly its governing body. (see *1413, 1987*)

1560 – In their desire to limit the role played by considerations of national interest, some organisations entrust their preparatory work to meetings or committees of experts chosen for their particular competence. (see *1278, 1290*)

This method promotes a better understanding of the issues of fact and law on which agreement will depend, but it does not obviate the need for the governments to work together on the proposals produced. Even when the costs of these studies

---

9 C. M. STEVENS: *Strategy and Collective Bargaining Negotiation*, New York, McGraw Hill, 1963. N. W. CHAMBERLAIN: *Collective Bargaining*, New York, McGraw Hill, 1951.
10 P. JESSUP: 'Parliamentary Diplomacy, an Examination of the Legal Quality of the Rules of Procedure of Organs of the United Nations', *RCADI*, 1956, p. 185.

and inquiries are borne by the intergovernmental organisations, national motivations still come into play. (see *1151*)

1561 – Provided their quality is good, these preparatory works can be helpful in moving ahead both the negotiation and the law. Even when its working is influenced by national, ideological or professional concerns, the greater the cultural homogeneity in a group of experts, the more searching the dialogue between them.

Effective decision-making

1562 – One of the characteristics of this type of negotiation is that it is brought to a collective conclusion, with the vote of the delegations. Rules for this differ from one organisation to another; they also vary according to the type of decision the meeting is to produce. *A negotiator will always hesitate to take the risk of public failure.*

However, in a general sense, to undertake a negotiation in any multiparty forum requires the sort of dexterity that comes only with experience.

1563 – Where decisions are legally enforceable, and important enough, it is almost always decided or understood that they must be unanimous. The usual effect of this requirement is that the spirit of internationalism gives way to rigorous protection of acquired rights; special clauses are sometimes inserted allowing a government to protect its vital interests in exceptional circumstances, as is the case in the European Union. (see *1222*)

The practice of abstention allows the institution to avoid becoming paralysed or ineffectual, without in any way supporting the position of the party abstaining. (see *1142*)

1564 – The desire to speed up the progress of international relations has led to the search for easier ways to conclude major organisational negotiations. A number of procedures have been proposed or adopted, essentially tending towards abolition of the unanimity rule. These will undoubtedly influence the negotiating process and even the nature of negotiation, but the principle itself remains intact. (see *1078, 1262, 1325, 1328*)

1565 – States sometimes agree to take decisions by majority, provided it is qualified – the UN practice, for instance, is to require two-thirds for decisions on matters of fundamental importance – which allows the Great Powers to retain their freedom of choice. But administrative, procedural or other decisions within the negotiation are easier, requiring only a majority, sometimes even a simple majority.

The trend towards international integration can be measured by the diminishing use of the requirement of unanimity in conferences.[11] The European Union is seeking to give the lead in its handling of current issues. (see *1223, 1260, 1367*)

---

11 C. W. JENKS: 'Unanimity, the Veto, Weighted Voting, Special and Simple Majorities and Consensus as Modes of Decisions in International Organizations', in *Cambridge Essays in International Law*, Cambridge, Cambridge University Press, 1965, p. 488.

Where international norms are concerned, formal signature is no longer necessary, but reservations are increasingly common and ratification is still required.

1566 – The notion of consensus is an expression of the progress made in multilateral negotiations, both organisational and prospective.[12] States wish to avoid having imprecise, albeit contradictory, notions of their interests being expressed as if they were hard and fast positions. Some do not wish to be in the minority, and others are keen to avoid confrontations interfering with their programme, thus they all agree to finish their work with a written instrument, even if not all of them can accept it in its entirety.[13]

1567 – The practice in international organisations, therefore, is that a draft is considered as adopted without being expressly put to the vote. *The chairman takes formal note that, based on the consultations he has held or the discussions that have taken place, no objection has been raised to the text, there is thus no need to put it to the vote, and it is adopted by consensus – in other words, 'he who says nothing agrees'.* (see *707, 1543*)

1568 – Despite some inconclusiveness in the terminology used, consensus is not to be confused with unanimity as it does not prevent a party from explaining, abstaining, adding a reservation, refusing to consider itself legally bound or even profoundly disagreeing, though this is not expressed. It is less indicative of the will to be bound where it relates to general principles that are neither instantly applicable nor mandatory. The results of multilateral negotiations between the main trading partners have been adopted as rules by a process of consensus.

1569 – Steering a debate towards consensus means, in practice, that great importance is attached to mutual concessions, and therefore to – often preliminary – negotiation: the concern to avoid the rigours of voting encourages compromise, though the process is often slow and arduous. *Time spent in preliminary discussions is regained in the public sittings. Consensus sometimes makes it possible to deal with emergencies.* (see *1139*)

1570 – Consensus is now widely used in plenary assemblies where voting is a slow and public process, such as the UN General Assembly. In 1964, consensus prevented a serious crisis arising out of the disagreement between the Great Powers about the financing of operations in the Congo; it became useless to threaten the withdrawal of voting rights from those countries that disputed their debt.

Consensus has also come to be used in councils with more restricted membership, such as the Economic and Social Council, and even the Security Council where certain States have the power of veto, as well as organs of a more administrative nature like the International Law Commission and the Population Commission.

---

12 E. SUY: 'The Meaning of Consensus in Multilateral Diplomacy', in *Declarations on Principles*, Liber Röling, Leiden, Sijthoff, 1977, p. 259.
13 A. -M. M'BOW: 'La pratique du consensus dans les organisations internationales', *Revue internationale des sciences sociales*, 1978, 4, p. 943.

1571 – Today, almost all international institutions and conferences follow this method in their deliberations, especially where the purpose is to produce a codified instrument. Their internal regulations sometimes prescribe consensus, as happened with the conferences on the law of the sea (which, failing consensus, required a two-thirds majority), the environment and international economic cooperation. Sometimes it is encouraged, as in the statute of the UN Special Fund or in the practice of UNCTAD. And nothing prevents its use where the instrument itself is silent.

1572 – Consensus will probably become institutionalised, following the trend towards informality and the desire for speed and flexibility. Its methods and outcomes will become gradually clearer, reducing the risk of misuses of procedure, excessive haste, unenforceable texts and bad faith. But it will continue to suffer from the absence of any mandatory legal sanction. (see *1536, 2201*)

Despite having ensured the success as well as the importance of the Helsinki Conference and laid the groundwork for the results it produced, the practice of consensus was partly responsible for the ineffectiveness of the Conference on Security and Cooperation in Europe (the CSCE, which later became the OSCE) at the time of the crisis in Yugoslavia. (see *1330*)

1573 – Consensus must express a general sentiment: as an objective, it affects the aims of the negotiation. In the first place, it encourages the formation of groups of States agreed on a common programme. Second, it leads each party to use ambiguous language and make apparent concessions in the interests of collective agreement, though few negotiators give serious thought to what actually results. *Limiting the agreement to an acceptable minimum and a passive commitment can reduce negotiation to a theoretical exercise.*

1574 – The use of consensus can serve to correct the excesses that can arise from applying the principle of equality to partners too different in terms of power: the main efforts towards conciliation and compromise are directed at those States whose agreement is indispensable. (see *661*)

This explains the reluctance of many developing States to embrace the widespread use of consensus for making decisions: to them, a vote is desirable, at least in the later stages of the process, to clarify the positions of the protagonists and their respective weight. *Moreover, no Sovereign State can accept a serious obligation imposed by the consensus of its peers*: procedural artifice can never override political realities.

Implementing the negotiation

1575 – Once they are approved, the documents, verbatim records, minutes and other assorted papers produced by international organisations are liable to be referred to in subsequent deliberations or negotiations.

Even where they have no immediate binding effect, these decisions always have some legal significance and as such contribute to international progress: the negotiation of multilateral action programmes implies that they will be implemented, even where they have been adopted following an expedited procedure.

1576 – Some of the obligations undertaken within international organisations are immediately enforceable, without further procedures. This is usually the case with financial and administrative decisions: these can result in heavy burdens, though they are either the product of very perfunctory negotiations, or are imposed by groups of States that do not have to bear the consequences, contrary to traditional principles of negotiation (see, for example, the attitude of Washington to financing the United Nations and UNESCO). (see *1968, 2232*)

1577 – International organisations and conferences must resist the temptation to dispense with the consent of their Member States. (see *1959*)

In reality, all procedures designed to avoid negotiation foundering because it is difficult if not impossible to obtain agreement between the States, are fundamentally flawed: *so strong is the hope for a settlement that it tends to be forgotten that no solid result can be achieved if the partners are subjected to excessive pressure.* The fact that a meeting is the occasion for complex and organic choices is not enough to make it productive. As to the legal effect of acclamation or abstention, it is doubtful whether either of them is binding. (see *1829, 2200, 2300*)

1578 – Efforts to find a way of reconciling the principle of State sovereignty and the practices of international institutions produce informal procedures and acts with no precise legal status. Negotiation in such cases employs the methods of voting, abstention, approvals, reservations and communiqués and other manifestations of will that are the classic tactics in multilateral conferences. It consists of a succession of monologues, usually prepared in advance and accompanied by negotiation between those attending the meeting, sometimes with the assistance of senior international officials. These acts lead, in their turn, to further discussions or negotiations. (see *94, 1286, 1539, 2199*)

1579 – The development of this diplomacy with its bias towards unanimity has had the effect of forcing numerous States to take unilateral positions that reveal which commitments each of them intends to accept and implement. The symmetry and balance of obligations, and the legal effect of treaties, are inevitably altered where States append reservations at the time of signing, adopting or ratifying them (see Vienna Convention on the Law of Treaties, Article 2) to reflect the disagreement of a minority, with the result that the effects of the negotiation are diminished.[14]

1580 – Unless there is a clause to the contrary, a State party to a convention is free in principle not to accept a reservation, and to debate it with its partners. Sometimes it might even refuse to accept the State making the reservation as a party to the agreement (see the ICJ Advisory Opinion on *Reservations to the Convention on Prevention and Punishment of the Crime of Genocide*, ICJ *Rep.* 1951, p. 21), or it may itself refuse to be bound by it.

---

14 P. H. IMBERT: *Les Réserves aux traités multilatéraux*, Paris, Pedone, 1979, p. 389.

1581 – In any event, whatever the accepted doctrine on whether reservations are unilateral or part of the agreement, they cannot be considered in isolation from the stages which led to the agreement, or indeed from the agreement itself, since they may have a bearing on what it says and how it functions. *Reservations are preceded by negotiation, accompanied by negotiation and explained by negotiation, but negotiation cannot overcome imperfections in the decision-making process.*

1582 – Reservations allow free rein to the dynamic of prospective negotiation by ensuring that a minority objection cannot paralyse the law-making function, while at the same time the body of international norms is generally considered as an indissociable whole. But it is easy to imagine the complications this practice introduces into international relations and the precautions diplomats must take against it. *Negotiators are often obliged to decide on a case by case basis when to resort to reservations, in order to avoid their excessive use. But the best way of avoiding abuse of this right is succeed in the negotiation itself.*

1583 – An exclusively legal approach may not be the fastest or most usual approach to international organisational problems: multilateral negotiation is an instrument that can be used in a variety of ways. It can serve as the basis of *rapprochement* and cooperation between partners without the need for this to be reduced to writing.

It *is interesting in this context to note how many disputes arising out of treaty implementation have been successfully referred to conciliation or arbitration.* (see 2241, 2242)

1584 – To apply a convenient, if arbitrary, classification, organisational negotiation is the same as all fast-expanding activities in the services sector. In a world that is hard to understand or evaluate, it is a slow, complex and formalistic process, and risks becoming divorced from reality. Some multilateral commercial negotiations have involved thousands of experts and gone on for years.

1585 – Some institutions have therefore tried to steer the negotiations taking place within them in the direction of greater speed and flexibility: the Nordic Council operates by exchange of views, the Council of Europe has meetings of experts and the Security Council provides a forum for sustained consultation. By exploring the subject in these ways, the problems can be better understood, and initial points of view can be formulated without any formal obligation resulting. (see *1537, 1539*)

1586 – A lasting solution to any issue depends, in the end, on negotiations carried on between governments. *Institutional negotiation does not replace diplomatic negotiation, but their practices and procedures coexist and intertwine, offering States a broader palette of actions to choose from.*

Section 2: Regulation by negotiation

1587 – Within international institutions, the deliberative function has developed to the point where there are now an absurd number of meetings and interventions.

Often, debate will dilute negotiation, making it incomplete or artificial, and debate is characterised by absenteeism and abstention. But even when they produce nothing more than recommendations, such negotiations give the appearance of an international power that has generated a wealth of literature. (see *2230*)

1588 – The dense and varied system of rules, written and unwritten, that States have approved is the product of negotiation, but, more than that, it has also become a permanent feature of the environment in which negotiation is carried on. The same is true within intergovernmental organisations and private companies. (see *1616, 1968, 2192, 2229*)

1589 – While it is a long way from constituting a world order, international law, traditionally confined to governing diplomacy, war and the sea, is gradually extending into broader and sometimes new fields: there is an increasing variety in practices and terminology as well as in the subject matter and effects of international instruments.

The sources of international law are becoming increasingly varied: as an example, the trade customs codified by the International Chamber of Commerce, a non-governmental organisation, are a source of commercial law, which means that some rules are drawn up by private entities not subject to diplomatic processes.

1590 – Not all these disciplines are either deliberate or welcome: some of the greatest and most restrictive are the increasingly strong bonds of interdependence and complementarity which grow up between States. The division of labour described by Durkheim[15] over a century ago opens up the way to functional negotiation between States and also between the groupings they form.[16] (see *1933, 2020*).

1591 – Where specialisation succeeds, it leads to monopoly. An exclusive or dominant position makes it easier to avoid having to inform and communicate, encourages the desire to consolidate the status quo, and brings with it the power to distort reciprocity. Underprivileged countries seek to mitigate the automatic effects of the balance of power, and replace them with norms that have been fairly negotiated.

1592 – In a complex, unpredictable and conflict-ridden international environment, the unexpected unilateral decision often brings risks, or even danger, for all the parties affected. *While the interests of governments do not always coincide, their main preoccupation is more or less the same: to avoid the risks of uncertainty.* (see *94*)

1593 – All thoughtful governments therefore agree on the need to control the present and future environment in which they operate; so do the managers of major corporations, who want to ensure a stable environment in which their business can adapt. (see *1545, 2074*)

---

15 E. DURKHEIM: *De la division du travail social*, Paris, Alcan, 1893.
16 G. de LACHARRIERE: *La Nouvelle Division international du travail*, Geneva, Droz, 1976.
   J.-P. BERAUDO: 'Le modèle français dans l'élaboration des conventions de droit privé', in *L'Internationalité dans les institutions et le droit*, p. 177.

1594 – Each actor must, therefore, avoid initiatives that create too much disturbance and also dissuade its partners from doing so. Each one must do its utmost to mitigate the dangerous variables that come into play, especially when these depend on the will of a third party. These principles of conduct apply equally in private business. (see *1134*)

Joint regulation therefore becomes the subject of continuous negotiation, because it is a way of resolving, or even preventing, conflict. But there is always the risk that it will fail, adding to the level of international uncertainty. (see *1133*)

§1. Normative negotiation

1595 – The negotiator knows that his achievements will only be of lasting value if voluntary agreement can be translated into a rule of law or an official institution, which are the products of negotiation between parties agreeing to be bound by the same disciplines. (see *712*)

1596 – The need for norms in international society has been recognised for centuries: it lies at the root of major doctrinal theories and settled practice. The legal disruption caused by war has thus diminished over time, preserving as much as possible of the fabric of rules resulting from multilateral and institutional negotiation, though this has not been enough to avoid the worst atrocities altogether.

1597 – This collective transcending of national interests has given modern multilateral negotiations an expanded normative role, and one that will persist, because it is rare for a legal system to remain frozen for all time. But it must go hand in hand with the sovereignty of the partners: *one of the effects of organisational negotiation is to stabilise practices, rules, contracts and decisions as long as their authors have not agreed to change them.* (see *1961*)

1598 – Closely linked to the development of negotiation by organisations, an international legislative function is growing up, in conferences and institutions whose deliberations lead to the harmonisation and codification of law or technical practices on a global or regional scale. This has happened in fields as varied as health, civil aviation, post and telecommunications, river, air and maritime navigation, among others.

1599 – A high degree of international legal integration has been achieved in whole sectors, putting them largely beyond the reach of bilateral negotiations and the prerogatives of domestic law. (see *1089*)

One of the consequences of multilateralism, however, is the reduction or dilution of the responsibility of States: an example is joint military action. In terms of effectiveness, institutional negotiation will never be a substitute for diplomatic negotiation. (see *647, 664, 977, 1785*)

1600 – This legislative mission began at the time of the League of Nations, but has expanded considerably under the United Nations,[17] within its specialised agencies,

---

17 R. HIGGINS: *The Development of International Law Through the Political Organs of the United Nations*, Oxford University Press, 1963.

and also within the European Union. As an example, a number of major instruments have been adopted on the non-proliferation of nuclear weapons (UNGA Resolution 2373 of 1 July 1968), denuclearisation of the deep sea (UNGA Resolution 2660 of 7 December 1971), the peaceful uses of space (UNGA Resolution 2221 of 19 December 1966), rescue of cosmonauts (UNGA Resolution 2345 of 19 December 1967) and liability for the acts of spacecraft (UNGA Resolution 2777 of 29 November 1971), to name but a few.

1601 – While they have been ratified only by a limited number of States and in very different ways, the more than 170 international conventions prepared by the ILO are important instruments of reference that signal the international acceptance of general principles in the field of employment law (hours of work, health and safety at work, social security and protection and collective rights and procedures). By mitigating the socially retrograde effects of fierce economic competition between States, they have undeniably played a regulatory role at least as between the industrialised nations, if not worldwide; but the fact remains that many of them have not been ratified.[18] (see *780, 1153, 1663*)

1602 – Multilateral trade negotiations have led to real international codes being drawn up to regulate customs duties, import licences, anti-dumping measures and other technical obstacles to trade and public procurement. These agreements on substance and procedure, designed for implementation by national administrations, provide for bodies to be set up to monitor their implementation and settle disputes that may arise under them. (see *1456*)

1603 – The products of institutional negotiation take many forms. Sometimes a draft agreement is submitted to a conference for adoption and then to the members for signature and ratification: this is what happens in the UN General Assembly and the Council of Europe. In other cases, once it is approved, it becomes an act of the organisation itself, as with the ILO.

The products of multilateral negotiation are not, however, always binding, and not always accompanied by legal sanctions. *International institutions have tried in vain to regulate the financial and business practices of the major multinational groups.* Only partially and progressively did the code of conduct drawn up by UNCTAD for maritime conferences become part of transport practice, or the UN convention of 6 April 1974 on the subject take effect, despite a variety of reservations: in reality, it applies only to about one-tenth of the worldwide traffic in goods.

1604 – Where an international instrument is a general rule rather than a synallagmatic contract, it is normally easier to adhere to it, even subject to reservations: the effectiveness of the rule grows along with the common willingness to understand and apply it. The relative effect of treaties does not apply to those norms that have a constitutive role in international society, however much some States might argue in favour of reciprocity. (see *611, 757*)

---

18 F. MAUPAIN: 'La France et l'action normative de l'OIT', in *L'Internationalité dans les institutions et le droit*, p. 161.

1605 – No State can invoke the benefit of a treaty when it was not party to the negotiations. But the interest in expanding the scope of new international norms to take in the greatest number of countries leads to such doctrinal and practical objections being overridden, provided none of the partners refuses.

1606 – Since it is sometimes impossible to predict with certainty which States will join them, negotiators tend to make it easy for third States to adhere to international conventions or organisations. This means that there is a good deal of vagueness surrounding the scope of norms and commitments and the degree of rigour of their implementation.

1607 – While obligations arising under conventions apply to all States that have validly agreed to be bound, certain States are subject to particular duties, among them the State designated as the depositary of the treaty, responsible for coordinating its implementation or piloting some of the multilateral activities under it: that State must keep the instrument, and any proceedings under it, up to date, record reservations, keep its partners informed and maintain a dialogue in order to lay the groundwork for fresh negotiation.[19]

1608 – For reasons of efficiency, international administrations play an increasing role in the preparation of multilateral agreements. Their Secretariats (especially those of the United Nations, the OECD and the Council of Europe) carry out factual and legal research, propose standard clauses, bring together experts, draft the texts and organise the entire procedure leading up to the approval of the instrument and its archiving. (see *1212*)

1609 – The use of experts means that many international commitments are not subject to traditional diplomatic procedures and safeguards. The reaction of governments to the resulting difficulties is inevitable. As the experience of the European Union and the Council of Europe has shown, *the more important the subject matter, the more heavily national concerns will weigh, with the result that the methods and disciplines of traditional negotiation reassert themselves.* (see *1273*)

1610 – The problem is such that some observers have been led to criticise international organisations for seizing on subjects of current interest in order to enhance their own importance, without regard for duplication of effort or for the real needs of States.

An excess of rules is not only a problem in national legal systems: the way negotiation has developed within the European Union bears this out.

1611 – Conscious of the problems and confusion arising out of the increasing number of multipartite negotiations (200 multipartite conventions in 35 years), the UN General Assembly embarked on a general study of the process of concluding multilateral treaties (see UNGA Resolutions 3248 of 8 December 1977 and 36112 of 10 December 1981). Other international organisations contributed to that inquiry. Its results show how extremely difficult it would be to introduce

19 P. H. IMBERT: *Les Réserves aux traités multilatéraux*, Paris, Pedone, 1979, p. 277.

rationalisation, so diverse are the procedures followed from inception to decision.[20] (see *2221*)

1612 – The Council of Europe included in its programme of work a study of how the traditional instruments of multilateral diplomacy might be adapted to the needs of European cooperation and development. That study covered the conditions in which the hundred or so conventions or agreements concluded under the auspices of the institution had been prepared and adopted, and it also proposed standard clauses for the entry into force of treaties.

1613 – The spread of multilateral negotiation has produced a proliferation of international regulations, under conditions that have made it imperative to reintroduce order into the entire sector. *The vagueness and variety of terminology, the accumulation of reservations, explanations and divergent interpretations, as well as problems with publication or implementation (even amounting to refusal to do either) have made international law a disparate and confused collection of rules and provisions that are uncertain, theoretical and badly understood.* The end result is that the object of the negotiation, and its outcome, are lost from view. (see *2231*)

1614 – Several organisations, including the Council of Europe, have taken a close interest in following up the negotiations that take place within them. In practice, great importance must be attached to updating and codifying those areas of law where there is particular need for harmonisation (the law of treaties and of diplomatic representation, the law of the sea, space and telecommunications, the laws on international responsibility and on literary and artistic property).

1615 – In truth, international norms are insufficiently well known, and lacunae exist in their coverage. Documents are becoming increasingly complex (there were already more than four hundred articles in the Treaty of Versailles) and they continue to multiply, as do the decisions and opinions of international tribunals. This does not mean that there is clarity as to the different combinations of obligations and mechanisms that have resulted from the instruments in force.

1616 – The complexity of the regulations is also a product of their diverse origins. International rules overlap, depending on the conditions under which they were negotiated. Thus the regime for paid migrant workers has produced, in Western Europe alone, an ILO convention, various Council of Europe recommendations and conventions on the right to establishment and social benefits, and also Community regulations and directives, as well as national laws. (see *1685, 2221*)

1617 – In many countries, public authorities are not geared for the rapid growth in international law, European law in particular. This is true at all levels, as courts will find when faced more frequently with serious problems of reconciling, or choosing between, the applicable instruments according to their scope and origin.

Legislative assemblies lose part of their legal competence to government each time matters falling within their attribution are raised in international negotiation.

---

20 *Review of the multilateral treaty-making process*, United Nations, New York, 1985.

This is likely to provoke a reaction on the part of national parliaments. (see *2235, 2385, 2520*)

1618 – The entanglement of international and domestic laws will make legal coordination especially difficult where international institutions exercise jurisdictional and executive powers that are likely to give rise to administrative or political conflicts.

The number of disparate, ambiguous, disorderly and badly drafted texts poses a serious threat to organisational negotiation: the more numerous the obligations, the less likely they are to be known and respected.

1619 – Excessive simplification of the methods by which international commitments are undertaken, coupled with the fact that there is often insufficient preparation or comparative research, means that many of the solutions currently adopted are ill suited to the needs and means of States.

Organisational diplomacy cannot be a substitute for actual negotiation.

1620 – The traditional prerogative of national representation will also come under threat in the financial area. In fact it already has, as a result of the compulsory automatic renewal of onerous obligations entered into in some international spheres, including contributions to the administration and programmes of organisations. The tendency will increase, because of the handing over to intergovernmental institutions, especially European, of funds raised from national taxpayers. (see *2169, 2232*)

1621 – There must be a return to negotiation to ensure that the dense body of rules generated by intergovernmental machinery – which rules, while they now form the legal and political backdrop of diplomacy, are far from capable of resolving all the problems arising between States – can be juxtaposed, reconciled and adapted. The threats which periodically overshadow the independence of international officials show how narrowly nationalist are the priorities of governments as soon as a crisis erupts. (see *1213*)

1622 – The standardisation of practices in the international system should lead to the progressive and steadily growing condemnation of unilateral action: the system tends to function in such a way as to avoid breaking down. But no automatic reflex will suffice to stifle the freedom of diplomatic manoeuvre of the Great Powers in particular: negotiation goes on, and as the experience of *détente* has shown, it requires constant effort. (see *94*)

1623 – Permanent structures for dialogue will emerge over time, enabling concessions to be constantly balanced and the level of achievement to improve progressively. If the United Nations has not succeeded in preventing or resolving international disputes, it has nonetheless become the preferred forum for expression of general opinion with worldwide impact – opinion that tends, both within the General Assembly and its ancillary organs, to oppose unilateral acts of pressure or force and favour cooperation between all nations. That said, the experience of the wars in Afghanistan and Iraq has shown the strength of tactics of predominance that pay no heed to collective discipline.

1624 – Theorists see in all this reason to hope that good negotiation will enable the rule of law to prevail over the traditional confrontation of forces and interests, lay the foundations of a system of collective security that is respected, provide the underprivileged with the means to progress and develop and create the institutions and norms that are essential for maintaining harmony in international relations.

Negotiation is expected to do for international society what the State administration does at national level. (see *2128, 2265*)

§2. From management to integration

1625 – In the technical and economic domain, diplomatic negotiation confronts issues of immense interest and intractable, recurring problems.[21] While the various principles that characterise diplomatic negotiation, such as balance of power and reciprocity of approach, still apply in these areas, it must be able to adapt to the methods of multilateralism, the only realistic way of approaching problems that extend beyond the capacities of the nation-state.

1626 – Trade depends on the mobility of people, goods, information and ideas. The abolition or reduction of obstacles to interaction does as much as geographical proximity to stimulate relations between States, even when their economies are in competition. The more industrialised countries become, the greater the needs and the interdependence of their economies and the more mutual relations and exchanges they will have: the members of the European Union mostly conduct more than half their foreign trade with each other. (see *1812*)

1627 – Even when its effects are mitigated by negotiation, the law of profit crushes the weak. Its mechanisms do not work in favour of justice because they favour those States best armed for competition. Its rules remain theoretical and are distorted by crises that deal them dangerous blows. The occupation of territory, the exacting of tributes and the pursuit of plunder have given way to new forms of coercion – the conquest of markets and industries, technological competition, financial controls and the upsetting of the balance and patterns of economic life. (see *389, 390*)

The delocalisation of law that flows from commercial development reinforces positions of dominance by the freedom of legal choice offered in contracts: on average, one third of international contracts involve a State entity. (see *1814, 1815, 1968*)

1628 – Peace could not exist unless economic relations were ordered in a stable and equitable manner. The crisis of 1929 and the misfortunes that followed showed how quickly and easily a local breakdown in the established order could spread outwards to the whole world.

It is normal and desirable, then, for States to seek solutions to some of their regional or global economic problems through long-term negotiation in a

---

21 R. WILLIAM: *European Technology: the Politics of Collaboration*, London, Croom Helm, 1973.

structured environment that allows information to be circulated, shocks to be absorbed, chances to be equalised and solidarity to flourish. (see *1357, 1410, 1520, 2074*).

1629 – At a practical level, international treaties have a life of their own: they give rise to disciplines and mechanisms in which the contracting States must participate. International organisations contribute to the proliferation of these obligations and the sanctions that attach to them: they create what is known in the European Union as derived law, in other words, a body of rules and institutions required to implement the founding Treaties. (see *1692*)

1630 – To answer the need to ensure long-term compatibility of national policies in a limited environment, diplomacy must not confine itself to resolving problems, but it must also seek to prevent them. This means that it will often be necessary for it to create bodies or mechanisms capable of intervening on a corrective or preventive basis. (see *2093*)

1631 – In the quest for stability and continuity, negotiation will thus generate a multitude of procedures, structures and rules that allow the interests of States to be aligned for the future. In 1979, for instance, the worldwide administrative conference on radio communications entirely revised the terms governing the future use of wavelengths and the Earth's geostationary orbit. (see *987*)

The adaptation of international programmes to diplomatic negotiation can be seen, for example, from the division into two groups of the missions of the European Space Agency, some of them fundamental and compulsory, others optional and decided only by the delegations concerned. These programmes are the subject of fierce negotiations among the main partners.

1632 – A growing number of multilateral treaties take the form of framework treaties, setting up inter-state structures. Sometimes these are boards of directors, committees or permanent secretariats, whose responsibility it is to monitor the implementation of the obligations and foster cooperation or to create new openings for future negotiations; sometimes, they are bodies with a more limited scope charged with the completion of particular technical or industrial projects. (see *1176, 1410*)

Some international activities are devolved onto hybrid groupings of semi-public or private companies set up under the national laws of one of the States involved. Arianespace, which successfully launched large numbers of satellites, is a French company with over fifty shareholders including industries from 11 countries (the French stake is 56.6 per cent).

The European radiation facility, 'Synchrotron', was set up under a diplomatic convention (the Paris Convention of December 1988) as a company under French law, but its board was composed of representatives of the interested States, and its resources came from government contributions. Various research laboratories have been set up in Europe the legal form of which differs from the classical international organisation to that of private companies or foundations.

Eutelsat is another intergovernmental body set up under a diplomatic treaty, whose original functions were both regulatory and commercial. Part of them, the commercial use of space for satellite telecommunications and broadcasting, has now been devolved to a specially created company governed by French private law, while the intergovernmental organisation continues to exercise a supervisory and regulatory function.

1633 – Bilateral cooperation is also becoming more rationalised and institutionalised, with mixed committees that can either be permanent or periodic, general or specialised, ministerial, diplomatic or technical and subdivided into working groups that can be either *ad hoc* or sectoral. These bodies are provided for in the original negotiation or created in response to needs as they arise. (see *2473*)

1634 – The sustained negotiation that results is all the more necessary because, in very many countries, cooperation at the financial, economic, technical and cultural levels is either wholly or partly a matter for the government: it is not enough simply to rely on the structures and mechanisms of trade and private enterprise.

In some cases, governmental negotiation extends to financial investment or technical cooperation between foreign businesses and State-owned companies or institutions.

The French national company, Aérospatiale, for example, became part of a European multinational group (EADS, headquartered in the Netherlands), and helicopter manufacturers then underwent a similar merger, with the setting up of Eurocoptère (a subsidiary of EADS, in France).

1635 – It will become increasingly necessary to strengthen institutional negotiation, as international conventions in all areas require an increasing amount of practical management. These operational activities are carried on in the name of governments and under their supervision, by international organisations that are more or less distinct and autonomous. The World Bank group has granted tens of billions of dollars in loans. (see *1391*)

Management decisions in any international administration are never exempt from some degree of negotiation, and governments express their agreement or disagreement on senior management hiring, the budget and programmes.

1636 – The multitude of agreements governing how products are marketed, to take just one example, requires constant administration. They are implemented by plenary or restricted-membership councils in which the interested countries negotiate, sometimes grouped into colleges of importers and exporters. These councils have regulatory and financial powers that sometimes give them the right to take concrete steps such as buying and selling or intervening on the stock exchange to limit price fluctuations; councils exist to fulfil such functions in tin, copper, rubber and coffee trades. (see *1963*)

Such is the dynamic of some of these administrations that they develop their own procedures that tend to bypass negotiation between governments. Examples are the management of industrial property and patents, in Europe especially, or the settlement of disputes in the WTO. (see *2240*)

Management negotiations are not always trouble free: there might be ill will on the part of governments or their partners, the regulatory bodies might be slow to act or incapable of acting at all, there might be illegal trafficking, parties might refuse to abide by the rules, and those rules might be of uncertain duration and subject to sanctions that are not clear. Some market organisations are weakened by competition from countries that are not members and therefore do not respect the same rules.

Diplomacy is ill-adapted to trading, market forecasting or to devising technical programmes. The development of the European space programme, with the Ariane rocket, was slowed down by a lack of long-term thinking on the part of the participant States, even though they mostly recouped their costs when it became operational.

1637 – Some international institutions have mechanisms that allow a variety of contracts to be negotiated. These include currency liquidity, financing facilities and public or private funding managed by a host of global or continental bodies (banks, funds, companies and associations) mostly run by officials under the supervision of representatives of the Member States, with a legal status that is more or less independent of State structures.

The European Bank for Reconstruction and Development is an international institution set up by diplomatic treaty between 43 countries together with two international organisations (the World Bank and the EEC). It currently has around 60 member countries. Its specific mission is to provide advice, loans, investments and guarantees to the States of Central and Eastern Europe, with 60 per cent going to businesses and 40 per cent to the public sector and infrastructure. It acts both as a commercial bank and as an investment bank, in cooperation with other banks. It is an independent institution, enjoying diplomatic privileges and immunities that guarantee the inviolability of its assets, archives, communications and premises. A Headquarters Agreement signed with the United Kingdom on 15 April 1991 guarantees its independence and allows it to function as an independent organisation under local law. (see *1186*)

1638 – Intergovernmental institutions can also provide new ways of observing and controlling the execution of bilateral treaties and multilateral agreements. They can offer monitoring, guarantees and sureties and set up bodies and mechanisms that will remain for as long as their decisions are implemented. (see *833, 1277, 1520, 2226*)

1639 – Despite various upheavals, the European Monetary System has since 1979 been the organisational response to the financial vagaries that resulted from the floating, albeit controlled, of the western currencies. In addition to the pre-existing exchange rate stabilisation measures, it brought in a body of regulations that were at the same time prospective and realistic: indicators of currency divergence, a unit of account calculated on the basis of a basket of currencies, procedures to defend currencies under attack and the setting up of an intervention fund allowing a response to any threatened breakdown of the system. (see *1352*)

It was further consolidated at the operational and legal level by the creation of a monetary cooperation fund and became an established institution: it might have served as the model for an international initiative had it not suffered as a result of the free movement of capital and the divergence between national economic policies in Europe. This system was replaced, for 12 of the States in the European

Union, by the creation of a common currency, the euro, managed by a Central Bank in liaison with the issuing institutions. A modified version of the former monetary system remained in place for the other three States, while for the 10 new Member States, a procedure has been negotiated to give them time to meet the conditions attaching to the euro. (see *1353, 1920*)

1640 – International negotiation has progressed beyond the stage of making rules and setting up institutions, superimposed on those of the States themselves. Now, it is working more towards the entry of national systems into administrative entities carrying out their own policies and with the powers and structures to do so. A number of these specialised institutions have been set up in Western Europe. (see *1241*)

Only those issues agreed by States may be the subject of integrative negotiation, as this derogates from diplomatic principles. It creates a unifying logic that is practically impossible to reverse, implying the reconciliation of national interests, the emergence of group interests and the extension of favoured areas of cooperation. (see *608, 1276, 1410, 1523, 1918*)

1641 – This type of negotiation is conducted in deliberative councils whose role and workings are different from traditional diplomatic conferences, because, here, the result of their decisions is to remove the subjects discussed from the sphere of competence of the national bodies. Integration as practised in Western Europe has thus progressed beyond the classic 'cooperation – confrontation' process that continues to characterise negotiations between States within most international and regional organisations, even in Latin America and Africa. (see *1280, 1287, 1293, 1301*)

1642 – A profound change is taking place, as a result, in the external negotiation of these new groups. Aside from working agreements that correspond to those concluded by most international institutions among themselves or with States, these integrated organisations have the power to negotiate on behalf of their Member States and in their place, and to bind them on matters within the scope of their powers. These possibilities of derogation have begun to transform the processes of international negotiation, with the result that governments have sought to reduce their impact. (see *1379, 1393, 1410*)

1643 – Sometimes, the integration of national policies is only a distant objective of diplomatic negotiations. Like the Central American common market, the recent Latin American Association was intended to have legal personality, the possibility of majority voting, and the power to conclude treaties and set up ancillary bodies and mechanisms for the purposes of cooperation. Even if these initiatives have yet to come to fruition, the intentions underlying them are important. The Andean Community, CAN, with Bolivia, Colombia, Ecuador, Peru and Venezuela as its members, was formed with the objective of using diplomatic cooperation in the service of economic integration along similar lines to the European Community. Argentina, Brazil, Paraguay and Uruguay formed their own free trade and customs zone under the Treaty of Asuncion of 26 March 1991, covering 60 per cent of

South America. The Mercosur, as it is known, signed association agreements in 1996 with Chile and Bolivia, and progressively established itself as a common market through its presidential and ministerial councils, management committees, and mechanism for resolving disputes between Member States. In 2004, the two trading blocs were formally unified under the Cuzco Declaration.

The Caribbean countries, too, are planning to set up a common market, as are those of Central America, where discussions took place in Nicaragua in 1997 on closer political union. (see *847, 1583, 1945, 2248*)

The United States set up free trade zones under a treaty of 17 December 1992, supplemented on 13 August 1993, first with Canada and then Mexico. This has effectively turned the whole of North America into one vast common market (NAFTA), for the free movement of goods, capital and, to some extent, of people.

Other free trade areas are in prospect, between the ASEAN countries and others in Asia, and also among the members of the Arab League. These areas, once defined, will facilitate and encourage the flow of trade and negotiations among businesses there. (see *1516, 1580, 1931, 1966*)

1644 – A new form of international competence appears in the principle and practice of this kind of 'integration negotiation': *the power granted to certain bodies to draw up rules that apply directly to individuals and private groups through the State apparatus, and the fact that private persons can now take their cases directly to certain international tribunals.* The European Union typifies this tendency, with the powers of its institutions, and the fact that its decision-making procedures have now become commonplace. (see *1266, 1292, 1303, 1343, 1353, 1398, 1639*)

1645 – The overall cohesion of Europe has been strengthened by its powerful and cohesive administration, increasingly driven by its own internal logic and the technical difficulty of the problems it faces to launch a variety of initiatives and improve its own resources. It also tends more and more to be perceived as a supranational constitution in the making, which appeals to those whose aim is the unification of the Member States. (see *1286, 1293*)

1646 – The integration of economic and technical projects is one of the factors that serve to strengthen international negotiation: it becomes one of the negotiating objectives. The more inward looking it becomes, the more it replaces negotiation by administrative regulations.

As integration develops, it creates systems and institutions that are more and more structured. The negotiator is trapped by these and sometimes finds himself in opposition to his own political masters. (see *1242*)

1647 – Devolving international competence onto an institution implies that this body is capable of fast and effective action, in line with the interests of its founders. It must also have the ability to prevent and resolve the differences and divergences of view that sometimes crop up among its members, so as to preserve the collective solidarity. Ideally, its bureaucracy should remain free from the failings for which national administrations are criticised: routine, delays, inconsistency and the generation of excessive paperwork and costs. (see *2519*)

Apart from situations of hegemony, unification cannot be created by negotiation unless there is some instrument capable of representing it in international dialogue.[22] (see *1527*)

1648 – In the final analysis, no international institution has any power other than the power conferred on it by States. *For each nation, the sum total of advantages has to exceed the concessions it makes. This can only be assured through continuous negotiation. Without it, each party will try to avoid those obligations it finds problematic.*[23] (see *1967, 2622*)

§3. Enforcement by negotiation

1649 – The peaceful coexistence of nations is only possible if a certain number of rules of conduct are laid down and adhered to, foremost among which, for the purposes of negotiation, is responsibility. This, however, is in decline, in the perception of public opinion as well as in the acts of international organisations themselves. The international system is constructed in such a way that, even in Europe, no sense of collective responsibility has ever established itself, either among leaders or among the peoples themselves. (see *836*)

1650 – Responsibilities do not weigh equally heavily on all nations, in terms of their freedom to manoeuvre. In a system that is only gradually taking shape, a State's obligations tends to match its capacities. *The strongest States find it less easy than before to avoid their duties because it is in their interests to promote the stability and where possible the expansion of the system as a whole: the danger of becoming the prisoner of power increases along with the power itself.*[24] (see *647, 1116*)

Aggravated by the neutralisation of nuclear power, the dependence of the Great Powers on the organised international system thus reduces their freedom to manoeuvre and increases their level of responsibility. It can also leave the field free for unilateral intervention.

1651 – Whether or not it is global, at the political level, the international organisation is conceived as a way of fostering more peaceful and harmonious relationships among its members, through its processes of consultation and sanction. This is the objective not only of the United Nations, but also of other institutions that offer procedures and bodies to settle the disputes that can arise between their Member States. (see *749, 1122, 1279, 1782*)

It is not agreements that are lacking in this area, so much as the will to implement them. Any international organisation that seeks to interfere with a nation's future is unlikely to succeed.

1652 – In practice as well as theory, a distinction is drawn between methods of settling disputes depending on whether they are legal or political. The dynamics of

---

22 J. PINDER: *Das extranationale Europe*, Bonn, Integration, 1978.
23 A. PLANTEY: 'Principes et développement du processus international de décision', in *L'Avenir des organisations internationales*, Paris, Economica, 1993, p. 25.
24 K. W. DEUTSCH: 'On the Concept of Politics and Power', in *The Theory and Practice of International Relations*, Englewood Cliffs, Prentice Hall, 1966, p. 81.

diplomatic negotiation favour the latter: *the true procedures for peaceful settlement are those produced by negotiations between States, especially between the dominant powers, taking place, for example, within or on the margins of an international institution.* The African system avowedly prefers disputes to be resolved by arbitration between Heads of State, or by commissions or delegations set up specifically for that purpose.[25] (see *533, 716, 1143, 1583*)

1653 – If a rule is to be anything other than theoretical, it must be capable of enforcement. The League of Nations Pact addressed this problem, but never resolved it. The primary characteristic of the world system is, still, that there are no real means of compelling States to comply with their undertakings and make reparation for damage, in spite of the mission conferred on the United Nations to this effect under Chapter VII of the Charter. (see *1782*)

The right of veto in the Security Council – a right that will probably come back into use in the future – has made it possible for certain States to paralyse the powers of the United Nations to prevent or punish misdeeds, to avoid being subject to them and to extend this protection to their client States.

After the invasion of Kuwait in 1990, the Security Council froze Iraq's assets abroad; in 1992, it authorised the seizure of some of those assets. Embargoes were also put in place against Libya (the aerial blockade, decided on 31 December 1992) and Yugoslavia (a financial blockade imposed on 30 May 1992, and a maritime blockade on 17 November of the same year). However important it may be to seek a balance of powers and interests within international organisations, the real instrument of world order is still concerted action by the great powers responsible for security. (see *1666, 1751*)

1654 – Some of these sanctions arise out of the application of actual disciplinary rules within the organisation itself, while others involve coercion applied to States outside the scope of the organisation. But, as long as there is no supreme and independent authority, they are all decided upon by agreement between the member States, in particular those represented in its principal councils, following the methods of organisational negotiation, in other words according to the institution's own rules of competence, procedure and voting. (see *1784*)

The comment has been made that, in the economic field, the legal and jurisdictional sanction processes are usually inadequate: except where military intervention is decided upon, as was the case in Iraq in 2003, the preferred negotiating method is to follow the practice used in trade of indirect or actual pressure. (see *1623*)

1655 – The only exception to this principle arises out of the special prerogatives granted to the Commission and Court of Justice of the European Union, which have the power by treaty to find States in breach of Community rules and impose sanctions, as well as adopting specific regulations to bind them to respect their obligations. (see *1278, 1305*)

That said, not all of the Court's decisions are complied with. (see *1307*)

---

25 M. BEDJAOUI: 'Le règlement pacifique des différends africains', *AFDI*, 1972, p. 85.

1656 – If ways of verifying the implementation of international commitments can be found and can establish themselves, this will enable obligations to be enforced, and open the way to future negotiation. *But international organisations are not equipped to concern themselves directly with whether the negotiations among their members are put into practice, except where States confer on them the task and the means to do so. Even where they do, the powers generally stop short of coercion, but depend on relationships between the States.* (see *832, 833, 1227, 1307, 1741*).

1657 – As can be seen from the European Union system, international society is gradually building legal mechanisms that will make it possible to ensure that its fundamental norms do not remain a dead letter. This could take the form of a jurisdictional function with its own procedures and institutions, in other words, an organisation of States.

The process of giving concepts and structure to international law is mostly the result of the work of courts: the International Court of Justice operates on a system of successive 'precedents'. Sometimes, a court will formulate a rule of customary law before it is codified, as with the law of the sea. European Community law has been built up in a similar manner, on the basis of treaties.

1658 – Devised as a way of depoliticising international relations and resolving disputes by peaceful means, international courts have in practice been at the centre of a huge web of international negotiation, throughout their existence. The creation of the PCIJ and its successor the ICJ, as well as their jurisdiction, depended on agreement between governments (see *Mavrommatis Concessions* case, PCIJ Reports, 1924, p. 15) and this often implies direct or indirect negotiations being pursued in parallel with the proceedings before them. Negotiators sometimes receive instructions to favour arbitration clauses over clauses conferring jurisdiction on the Court.

1659 – Even where States have bound themselves to bring their disputes before a court (for example, under the Brussels Treaty of 17 March 1948 and the Paris Treaty of 23 October 1954, Article VII), they do not consider this as an obligation, and leave all but the precise points of law involved in the dispute for their diplomats to deal with. *The general tendency of governments is to avoid all procedures that paralyse their foreign negotiations.*

Where major interests are at stake, this can even induce some governments to refuse to submit to the legal processes they had previously accepted; thus, the United States refused to plead on the merits of the *Nicaragua* case before the ICJ in 1985–1986, just as in 1983 it had ignored the United Nations' condemnation of its behaviour over Grenada. Furthermore, ever since 1946 the acceptance by the United States of the jurisdiction of the Court has been subject to wide-ranging reservations. (see *2218*)

1660 – States are generally disinclined to have recourse to judges, and this tendency is becoming more apparent both at international and continental level. *With the exception of disputes in the European Union, the more bitter and decisive a conflict, the more likely it is to escape judicial resolution and become the subject instead of negotiation or even confrontation.* (see *462*)

1661 – The regard in which legal settlement of international disputes is held is further undermined by the fact that the means do not exist at this level to enforce judicial decisions, even where they are binding, or reparation for damage, even when proved.[26] An international judicial decision becomes, in its turn, part of the diplomatic process: sometimes it offers a compromise solution, while at others it provides a line of argument that can be used in negotiations that are still ongoing. It is through diplomacy that it will be implemented, wholly or in part, assuming there is no State to interfere in the proceedings of the international institution or hold up the negotiations. (see *834*)

In the absence of legal means of enforcement against States, the only way of ensuring that international law is implemented in practice is through international negotiation. (see *90, 729, 1665, 1673, 2218*)

1662 – The main purpose of negotiation in organisations is to lay down rules. However, the fact that norms are established by external procedures or authorities poses problems for their transposition and implementation in the domestic legal system, which is done either because the State has made a reciprocal commitment, or because it is in its interests. While they are subject to agreement, the rules that apply in this regard are different for each State. (see *2230*)

1663 – International influence varies in strength from one sector to another, but as soon as several States appear to be in agreement, it becomes possible, at continental or even global level, to discuss principles with a view to harmonising and sometimes unifying the different national laws.

The deliberations of the International Labour Organisation have this effect, with new and consistent core legal principles emerging on some topics to serve as the basis for future national laws and regulations: that organisation has been responsible for the production of 176 conventions and 160 recommendations in every area of economic and social activity. (see *1601*)

1664 – The problem is that neither parliaments nor perhaps governments will be able to analyse the entire output of these international bodies, so many and varied are they, even in those fields where the instruments in question have legal or regulatory force. (see *2233*)

The changes in the law of treaties produced by the growth in multipartite negotiation in international conferences and organisations, and the development of European Community law, give rise to internal legal problems in many countries. Courts are required to give effect to an increasing number of documents that do not emanate from the national constitutional authorities, and sometimes to give them primacy over domestic law. This places a very heavy legal burden on the negotiators. Every year, it is estimated that between 300 and 400 international agreements and documents, of varying degrees of importance, come into force in France, only a tenth of them after ratification was authorised by the parliament.[27]

---

26 W. FRIEDMANN: *De l'efficacité des institutions internationales*, Paris, Colin, 1970.
27 French Conseil d'Etat: *La Pénétration du droit communautaire dans le droit français*, Paris, 1981. *La Pénétration dans le droit français des dispositions de conventions internationales*, Paris, 1985.

1665 – International procedures are already being devised to verify whether national authorities are complying with their duly ratified commitments, and with decisions taken pursuant to treaty provisions setting up intergovernmental bodies. States are more or less sensitive to this pressure, but the effect of diplomatic reciprocity is that none of them can go on refusing to submit to limitations on their autonomy in the long term. (see *2036*)

The need to negotiate remains so strong, however, for governments as for private groups, that it vitiates the enforceability of court or arbitral decisions, as can be seen from the weighty and interminable disputes referred to the WTO. And governments are the first to agree on how to adapt their obligations, even when they are known to the public – the attitude to the conditions for admission to the euro zone is a case in point. (see *2218*)

1666 – Rather than continuing to produce more legal instruments, all international organisations are today engaged in a constant process of verifying whether those already in existence are being implemented. It is not enough for them to suggest standard implementation clauses in conventions, as the respective Secretaries General of the United Nations and the Council of Europe have done. *They must encourage governments to keep themselves and each other informed about how decisions negotiated in organisations are being applied in practice.*

In several instances, especially for verification of the implementation of conventions concerning certain types of weapon, the Secretary General of the United Nations has been granted powers of investigation. He can only exercise these powers, however, with the cooperation of the States concerned, and this has to be negotiated.

1667 – One method is to publish the numbers of signatures and ratifications and the status of implementation; specialist committees can be set up to report on the status, as do the main committees of the Council of Europe, and investigative procedures devised to help in the process.

Another way is to invite governments to present a report on their ratification and implementation of conventions, either to their national parliaments or to an international organisation or assembly. In the International Labour Organisation, it is possible to file a complaint against governments that breach conventions they have ratified. There are some institutions that can be assigned the task of verifying the implementation of particular agreements, as the International Atomic Energy Agency does with regard to compliance with certain treaties by the partners of the United States, or with certain decisions of the UN Security Council. (see *645*)

Many treaties expressly lay down the methods to be used in monitoring compliance: these include on-site inspections, the possibility of making a formal complaint, and periodic reporting. Examples are the treaties signed on 10 April 1972 and 1 June 1990 on the prohibition of biological and chemical weapons. The OECD Convention on Combating the Bribery of Foreign Public Officials in International Business Transactions, signed in 1997, provides for monitoring by peer review, which is carried out in two stages. A similar model was adopted by the Financial Action Task Force (FATF) with respect to its recommendations on the prevention of money laundering. (see *1766*)

1668 – The best method is to reopen the negotiation, provided certain States are prepared to do so, in order to ensure that international conventions are properly implemented, in such a way as to provide a level playing field for economic and social functioning. (see *816*)

The UN Security Council set up a system for compensating the victims of Iraq's actions during the Gulf War: that Commission, representing the members of the Security Council, has negotiated a number of awards. (see *1638, 1653*)

1669 – The desire to ensure that their negotiations are backed by sanctions sometimes leads governments to accept substantial limitations on their privileges as Sovereign States.

Some international conventions govern the relations of a State with its own citizens, giving them rights vis à vis the national authorities, and guaranteeing that the obligations they impose will be respected and enforced. *The definition of human rights and certain collective freedoms has contributed to the emergence of the individual in international relations. The transformation of international society that results from these innovations will be both irresistible and revolutionary.* (see *1645*)

1670 – Examples can be cited that show this tendency at work. The International Labour Organisation produces annual reports on the implementation of its conventions by the countries that have approved them. These can provoke complaints from other signatory States, or claims by professional organisations, triggering an adversarial disputes procedure in which national authorities can become directly involved if there is a commission of inquiry. These procedures cannot overcome all the difficulties that arise, but they confirm the advantages of continued negotiation, and other institutions have copied them.

In 2000, for the first time, the Administrative Council of the ILO pronounced sanctions under Article 33 of its founding instrument against Myanmar, where forced labour was being practised.

In 1998 the ILO adopted a declaration on the principles of fundamental rights, designed for the protection of workers.

1671 – The European Convention on Human Rights sanctions the violation of its provisions by means of complex procedures whereby national authorities are brought before a Court that exercises its jurisdiction for the benefit of the nationals of 40 member countries of the Council of Europe, and whose judges are elected by the Assembly for a six-year term. Execution of its judgements, of which there have been several hundred, is a matter for the national authorities of the State concerned, under the control of the Committee of Ministers.

1672 – The response of the European Union on this question has been innovative: its actions benefit or affect private individuals as well as companies, whether through regulations, the consultations of the Economic and Social Council or of the numerous different committees (where professionals are able to play a part in drawing up the rules of the Common Agricultural Policy, for example), or the judgements handed down by the Court of Justice.

Admittedly, by contrast with other international institutions, the EU was set up to achieve its own particular goals, which are also binding on its Member States. (see *1246, 1254, 1333*)

1673 – Unlike the International Court of Justice, The Court of Justice of the European Union can be seized of cases not only by States but also by private enterprises seeking enforcement of treaty obligations and the measures taken to implement them. Its function is not that of a court of appeal from decisions of the national courts, but it has the independent power to decide and interpret, which is progressively asserting itself over the national legislatures and judiciaries, as well as in the public consciousness, in all fields of Community law. (see *1304*)

The fact remains that the ability to impose an obligation on a Member State that fails to implement a decision of the Court of Justice does not mean that there is any way of compelling that State to comply. (see *2218*)

It should also be remembered that the somewhat praetorian attitude the Court has adopted to its role within the institutional system of the European Union has been criticised.

Part III
Prospective Negotiation

1674 – Negotiation has developed to a level where it has become one of the main specific activities of the modern State, both in its domestic affairs and in its relations with the outside world. *As such, the practice of negotiation adapts itself, as indeed it must, to the contemporary climate of profound and irreversible upheaval.* It evolves in ways that are both qualitative and quantitative, whenever new influences arise to render obsolete some of the traditional reflexes of State superiority.

1675 – Diplomacy as originally conceived was limited to Europe, but it has since had to adapt to the extension of international relations across the whole world. The First and Second World Wars, and the achievement of independence by developing nations, opened up the field of diplomacy so broadly that the role of the Old Continent has been correspondingly reduced.

Despite the burdens of bureaucracy, negotiation today encompasses the vast fields of economics and finance as well as cultural relations. Increasingly, there is a blurring of distinctions between the actors of diplomacy and those of civil society and the media. Most of the methods honed by centuries of practice for use in diplomatic negotiation can also now be applied to negotiations between private sector companies, many of which are often more active and dynamic than governments.[1] (see *403, 1807, 1932*)

1676 – For centuries, diplomacy concerned itself with safeguarding established positions and balances of power, some of them extremely fragile. However, present-day economic expansion, technological advances and the communication of ideas have produced worldwide mobility that brings it own anxieties. The pace of growth in agriculture and industry has become a positive influence for peace, while at the same time exposing the world to risks of unprecedented gravity. These affect not only the outcome of negotiations but also the spirit in which they are conducted, and the level of understanding between nations.[2]

Disorder is now appearing in areas such as thought and religion, which were traditionally safe from it. Not even culture has escaped the revolutionary changes going on worldwide. Strategic and economic issues of indescribable complexity present a more or less frontal challenge to diplomacy, while traditional liberal

---

1 C. A. MICHALET: 'Les métamorphoses de la mondialisation', in *La Mondialisation du droit*, Paris, Litec, 2001, p. 88.

2 T. de MONTBRIAL: 'Le monde au tournant du siècle', *RAMSES 2000*, p. 13.

methods are unacceptable to those who practise totalitarian fundamentalism, imperial expansionism or aggressive forms of anarchy. (see *75*)

The breakdown of Communism as a system of government, if not a system of thought, showed how anachronistic this rigid diplomacy had become. Soviet dogma gave way to a climate of unpredictability, all the more to be feared because there were no known ways of managing it. New structures must take account of the immutable facts of geography and national history. The thorny issues of State succession must be addressed and the existence of new powers recognised, as well as the fragmentation of the political environment.

1677 – As with any complex society, the international world is especially sensitive to disruption and destabilisation. Responses can be found in the intertwining manoeuvres of all the actors on the international stage – governments, private sector companies, and a variety of institutions and associations.[3] (see *221, 1648, 1698, 1702, 1806, 2028, 2239, 2597*)

Increased use of the media has aggravated the impact of threats, attacks and aggression, as a result of which overt force has reappeared in its most cynical form, in relations between nation States and private groupings alike. As Frederick II remarked, the world would be a better place if negotiation were the only means available for maintaining justice and establishing peace and harmony between nations. (see *114, 1771*)

In the present century, the challenge confronting mankind is that of a global society having neither structures nor points of reference, and neither higher authority nor ethical standards. (see *77, 334*)

1678 – International society may be insufficiently organised, but people are increasingly unwilling to accept disorder and violence in relations between States. While not aspiring to the structural unification of human society, they look to their governments to agree upon a more effective system of rules than those currently in existence (see Article 33 of the UN Charter). (see *1624, 1899*)

As the activities of international networks operating in fields such as corruption, drugs, financial and human trafficking and terrorism take place in the territories of States, their national authorities face a correspondingly increased burden, even in the private sector. New areas are opening up to international cooperation. (see *1813, 1881, 1914, 1961, 2306*)

1679 – The irreversible changes the technological age has wrought in traditional relations between States make negotiation more necessary than ever, not only between those States already in a position of power, but also those that believe they can hold to their own policy line. In diplomatic relations, methods are changing, and so are the subjects addressed.[4] (see *84, 1498, 2189*)

However, just as progress exacerbates the inequalities between States, the fear is that the disciplines of the future will be imposed rather than negotiated, by those

3 M. BONNEFOUS: 'Anciens et nouveaux désordres internationaux', *Revue de Défense nationale*, October 2001, p. 167.
4 P. CHAIGNEAU, etc: *La Gestion des risques internationaux*, Paris, Economica, 2001.

powers with the capacity to observe, analyse and address the challenges of civilisation.

Even the United Nations often does no more than ratify the decisions taken by the great powers (as with the resolutions passed in 2003 and 2004 on the future of Iraq).

1680 – In a changing international environment rendered fragile by constant disturbance, the sheer number of negotiations taking place is a factor for stability and even order. Only by negotiation will it be possible to reconcile the need for greater organisation with the historic, cultural and ethnic diversity between nations: so great is the suspicion between States that even trust is still a matter of aspiration.[5] (see *1802*)

The market, in terms of both time and place, balances the supply and demand in products, funds and services. It evolves in accordance with the technical and social features of a changing world. Negotiation will diversify its methods, and spread its effects, into the marketplace.

Major global business transactions and financing operations will, over time, spawn a wealth of new instruments designed to facilitate them, such as information and decision-making tools, legal and financial guarantees, forms of partnership and joint enterprise, as well as procedures for enforcement or arbitration.[6] (*817, 1968, 2607*)

Progress in relations between States can only be achieved by successive stages. International negotiation can, by a process of empirical adaptation, assist States themselves to progressively limit their sovereignty, foster the participation of private sector companies and entities, and open the way to long-term change in international society.

---

5 R. BADIE: *Un monde sans souveraineté. Les Etats entre ruse et responsabilité*, Paris, Fayard, 1999. F. GERE: *La Guerre psychologique*, Paris, Economica, 1987.
6 J.-Y. DEZELAY: *Marchands de droit*, Paris, Fayard, 1992.

Chapter I:
The Aggravation of Threats

1681 – While the traditional methods of diplomacy, with its limited and well-known themes, can be applied to any subject, the diplomacy used by the great powers to express their strategies has changed so completely in the twentieth century that the course of history has irretrievably altered.

1682 – After Hiroshima, the world entered a different era.[7] Even without understanding its scientific basis or military aspects, mankind has felt this change, at some deep level: this vague sense is at the root of the constant anxiety that conflict might break out between powers, cultures and even religions. People's living conditions may alter and even improve, but it takes a very long time to change their mentality. (see *1932*)

1683 – Certain governments are investing massively in the research, development and production of weapons whose power of destruction bears no comparison with those that existed before. Alongside these carefully maintained and constantly updated arsenals, the arms trade supplies even the most impoverished States, and this has resulted in a kind of parallel system of clandestine diplomacy on a global scale (the developing world is said to spend twice as much on arms purchases as it receives in public development aid). (see *87, 1727*)

1684 – The sheer violence and range of new weapons and their delivery systems, and the speed with which they can be deployed, have radically altered strategy, and with it diplomacy. With the advent of the concept of total war, all forms of national military and civil activity were already subordinated to the need to fight and win. The march of technology compounds this by making responses urgent and their consequences unpredictable, with the risk that nascent quarrels will escalate irreversibly. (see *82, 1802*)

1685 – The problem has taken on a global and spatial dimension, in which no country can claim to be safe from the military effects, the diplomatic implications or the nuclear, chemical or biological fallout from a modern war waged using the new ballistic and electronic technology.

   War throws up the issue of environmental degradation in an increasingly acute form, because of the massive effects of the weapons and the threat of devastation out of all proportion to what is strategically necessary. Lawyers and scientists

---

7 L. B. PEARSON: *Diplomacy in the Nuclear Age*, Toronto, Saunders, 1959. R. ARON: *Le Grand Débat, initiation à la stratégie atomique*, Paris, Calmann-Lévy, 1963; *Penser la guerre, Clausewitz*, II, *L'Age planétaire*, Paris, Gallimard, 1976.

working under the United Nations Development Programme have agreed that the obligation to avoid any unnecessary damage to the environment is part of the customary laws of war. Governments, however, have proved to be deeply divided in their acceptance of the need for new rules and the possibility that sanctions might be imposed for failure to apply them. They see the issue as one of preserving the right to use their military potential, and, at best, complying only with law that is precise in form, but limited in content. (see *1797*)

1686 – The second half of the twentieth century was characterised by the rivalry between two great powers that were at odds in every way: their political regimes and ideologies, their economic and social systems, and their desire for power. There are clear lessons to be learned from the Cold War. The conflict was fundamentally geopolitical in nature, and resulted from differing concepts of civilisation itself. Polarities of this kind contain within them the seeds of conflict and also its justification, and they can flare up at any moment.

A new phase of contemporary history began in 1989–1990. The disappearance of the Berlin Wall, which symbolised the division of Europe and also the world, altered the strategic picture. This change was limited: nuclear weapons did not go away – on the contrary, they have become more widespread. And the situation has become even more complicated. Not only has strategy become multi-polar, but the globalised economy and the accelerating speed of communications have meant that security has become a real and universal concern. International crime, illegal trafficking, speculation and bribery, terrorist-related crime, extremist movements, fanaticism and panic are all producing changes, that may or may not be visible, in the balances of power on which international stability is founded. (see *1867, 1995*)

1687 – All these dangers have accumulated in the twenty-first century, including some of natural origin (demographic imbalance, environmental degradation, the spread of endemic disease) and, in an environment of intense and interactive communication, they drive the negotiating stakes ever higher. The reappearance of fundamentalism with worldwide ambitions, and the spread of cultures, are challenging the already fragile balance of international society and thus aggravating all its power struggles.

The increasing unpredictability of the tactics used makes hegemonic strategies more dangerous than ever.

Section I: The polarisation of hegemonies

1688 – For centuries, peace has suffered from the rise to power of princes, peoples and empires, whose desire for hegemony has rendered their foreign relations and negotiations fraught with sometimes unbearable tensions.[8] One need only recall the extent to which Hitler speculated on violence to force the western democracies to abandon their allies, and how Stalin triggered a whole variety of crises to achieve his objectives in Europe. (see *79*)

---

8 R. ARON: *Paix et guerre entre les nations*, Paris, Calmann-Lévy, 1962.

It is most unlikely that these antagonistic tendencies will disappear in the future. On the contrary, they seem almost fated to resurface each time social evolution reaches another milestone, and the centre of gravity shifts.

1689 – New technologies in all their forms, not only in weapons, have upset the traditional power ranking among States, setting some nations dramatically apart from others. The numbers of people and armies that can be mobilised have been replaced as indicators of strength by factors such as technical potential based on economic prosperity, scientific innovation and espionage. (see *82*)

These balances of power are not immutable: new players will appear that possess different means of coercion or destruction.

1690 – It would have been surprising if the wealth and capacity of certain countries did not sooner or later lead them to arm themselves with appropriate military capabilities. What is known as the 'nuclear club' already extends beyond the five permanent members of the Security Council.

Control of the nuclear threat should not in any sense mean that the level of international risk is any less: there will always be recourse to the strategies of conventional warfare, subversion and terrorism.

In the absence of reliable verification and of real trust, measures of prohibition or limitation of the potential for aggression are of no avail against the most resolute States: the UN Security Council could do no more than deplore the nuclear testing carried out by India and Pakistan in 1998.

Few States are willing and able to take the risk of disarmament and put their trust in peace.

1691 – Progress in the maritime, aerospace and ballistic fields will continue to push diplomacy into increasingly far-reaching areas. So will the use by the major private sector corporations of technical refinements and telecommunications technology. (see *1704, 1714, 1834*)

This has opened up a gulf between States that is difficult to bridge, and is even growing. Inequalities in military power open the way to hegemonic tendencies, that smaller States find extremely difficult to resist when forced by circumstances to seek support, or which may even turn them into pawns in a wider dispute. Their best hope would lie in joining forces, if it were not so easy for the great powers to prevent them making common cause. (see *845*)

1692 – The game of strategy is merciless. It turns the will and ambitions of each of the protagonists into forces capable of subduing or at least rivalling those of its potential adversaries. *In reality, it is not interest that prompts powers to make mutual concessions, but fear.* (see *863, 1849, 1864*)

Where escalation in weapons and technology does not reveal one party's superiority in combat, it must lead to negotiation. After Stalin's death in 1953, the confrontation between the superpowers began to take the form of indirect diplomatic strategies, as evidenced by the Cuban missile crisis of 1962. Such an approach was all the more necessary because, by definition, the use of deterrence, even as a warning, is not compatible with discussion, concession or hesitation. (see *1694*)

Each great actor seeks to preserve and exploit its own strategic autonomy.
Thus, for the purposes of its own interventions, the United States has successively
invoked the authority of the Security Council (in the Gulf War), made use of the
Atlantic alliance (in the former Yugoslavia) and exploited bilateral cooperation (in
the Afghan crisis), while at the same time strengthening its ties with the Shanghai
Group, or proceeded to form a traditional military coalition (as in the Iraq war of
2003). (see *856, 2157*)

These concerns explain, at least in part, the waning influence of the UN as seen
in the crises in Kosovo, Afghanistan, Africa and the Near East. (see *1710, 2163*)

1693 – Meanwhile, however, the very foundations of strategy have become more
complex. Competition between powers has been overlaid by a general concern for
security, in every area of national life.

In reality, it is war that has changed, or rather diversified, abandoning the old
concepts of fronts and frontiers, territory and nation. This insidious change, which
applies also to terrorism, is spawning dangerous attitudes of frustration, anxiety
and sometimes hatred among peoples.[9]

*Diplomacy has a role in carefully working to defuse the effects of surprise and
presumption, of error and despair.* This is no more or less, in fact, than a new form
of deterrence. (see *96*)

§1. Managing deterrence

1694 – *It is not procedures or institutions that prevent war, but the fear of what
will result.* (see *115*)
Deterrence has a long history. In the past, sovereigns would put their
adversaries on guard by moving their headquarters, armies or gunboats:
convenience and discretion meant that the navy was always an effective instrument
of diplomacy, either by its presence or the mere threat of it. There is, however, no
single absolute notion of deterrence, either in men's minds or in terms of the
weapons they might use.

The final act of deterrence is the firing of a warning shot. (see *266*)

1695 – As between powers with armed operational capability, deterrence as a
method of diplomacy is based on there being a sufficient probability of reprisals
out of all proportion to the object of the initial attack. If the result is that a certain
form of conflict becomes unlikely, this is because the threat is credible, in other
words because the effectiveness of the weapons, and the presumed readiness of
the holder to use them, make such a response possible.[10] This explains the efforts
of a number of countries to acquire weapons they might have no occasion to use.
(see *111*)

*Military deterrence leads the protagonists to favour a verdict based on
negotiation or diplomacy over one resulting from war.* It confirms the adage: *si vis
pacem* ...

9 D. DAVID: 'Violence internationale, une scénographie nouvelle', *RAMSES 2000*, p. 79.
10 H. A. KISSINGER: *Nuclear Weapons and Foreign Policy*, New York, Harper Row, 1957.

1696 – Having started from notions of massive and indiscriminate reprisals and intolerable destruction, military thinking has moved in the direction of milder responses and a more tailored approach. Today a response may be measured and selective, the tactics employed can be local and small-scale, and the target might be indiscriminate, industrial or specifically military. These doctrines have been the subject of intensive analysis and discussion within alliances.

New weapons encourage political debate as much because of the effort they call for and the environment they require, as because of the risks associated with their use.

The collapse of the Soviet totalitarian model is not enough, by itself, to obviate the need to devote serious attention to security in Europe. The former satellite States, that are concerned to obtain the collective guarantee only the West can give them, and proclaimed their attachment to the Atlantic alliance before their adhesion to the European Union, have understood this very well. (see *916, 946, 1691, 1699, 1762*)

1697 – Strategic negotiation is dominated by the very concept of modern warfare. Clearly, this is dependent on the overall potential of the nation concerned, but also on the ever-growing range of possibilities offered by its weapons and logistics. It is a function of the use to which these weapons can be put, in other words the nature and level of the attack or response. These concepts have been re-evaluated as the potential for destruction has increased, and also in line with the changing policy concerns of the protagonists, which are not necessarily mutually consistent and may not even be rational. (see *323*)

1698 – The international world of the twenty-first century is wealthy and active, though many of its people still live in marginal conditions; it is proof neither against power struggles nor against the hand of misfortune. All strategies are possible, including the most aggressive. And the movements against the proliferation of nuclear weapons are themselves not necessarily pacifist.[11]

1699 – Worried by the dispersal of risks and the unpredictability of the threat, American strategists have moved away from the doctrine of deterrence in the direction of control of all kinds of extraterritorial space: the sea, the air and space, cyberspace and the realms of ideology. The weakening of the nation State, even in Europe, and the globalisation of all forms of exchange, have led these strategists to envisage and negotiate global forms of policing, with the aid of several partners chosen for their responsible attitude and because they are expected to be able to influence the 'rogue States'. This willingness to intervene for political reasons in fact amounts to a new form of deterrence. (see *111, 334, 345, 946, 1692, 2607*)

Russia, on its side, still bases its strategic doctrine on deterrence accompanied by rapid intervention in areas of major interest to it: its 'foreign neighbours'. There is also the Chinese strategy, based on the discreet accumulation of powers over the long term. (see *1714*)

---

11 L. POIRIER and F. GERE: *La Réserve et l'Attente*, Paris, Economica, 2000, p. 71, 255 and 272.

Thus differing responses to a single international phenomenon can be seen, depending on the ambitions and the means of each protagonist. The dramatic rise in terrorism has thrown these strategies into a new perspective. (see *1692, 1713*)

1700 – Since the Second World War, negotiation in Europe has been dominated by the quest for stability and security, with the Budapest negotiation (1969), the Helsinki Act (1975), the Paris Charter (1990), the Moscow Conference (1991), the creation of the common European foreign and security policy (Maastricht, 1991 and Cologne, 1999), the Stability Pact (1995), the Budapest Conference (1997), and so on. Created in response to these concerns, the Conference for Security and Cooperation in Europe (CSCE, now the OSCE) has made hesitant attempts to tackle crises as far afield as the Caucasus, in Georgia, Chechnya and Ngorny Karabackh among others.[12] (see *76, 217, 1004, 1793, 1884, 2010*)

One reality underlies all this negotiation: the guarantee that a great power alone can bring, one that is accepted as such by the others. (see *1733*).

1701 – The range of available tactical and strategic ripostes resulting from the lowering of the threshold at which recourse might be had to weapons of mass destruction means that negotiation is still possible even after hostilities have broken out. In spite of the fact that the former Soviet capability is in disarray, and because it is now widely dispersed, the possibility of escalation means that it is still worth keeping weapons in reserve for deterrent purposes, and still desirable to seek diplomatic ways to neutralise them. (see *226*)

The same strategic concepts hold good for States newly empowered with nuclear, chemical or biological weapons, despite their deep-seated historic or ideological rivalries. (see *1852, 2732*)

1702 – It should also be borne in mind that each nation has its own political and military preoccupations. The modern tactic is to deter a potential adversary by creating a climate of uncertainty. However, a more suitable approach from the standpoint of maintaining world security would be to use negotiation as a way of anticipating the dangers that can result when the main strategic players make errors or disagree in interpreting a given situation. (see *2093*)

In practice, in an environment so unpredictable and fraught with tension, unilateral interventions will inevitably trigger concerns, anxieties and reactions. States that consider themselves threatened by others tend to align themselves. Thus, when an alliance is formed that stretches like a continuous entity from North America to Central Asia, the resulting restructuring of the space for strategic manoeuvre takes on a provocative aspect. (see *929, 946, 1718*)

1703 – The terrible destruction that threatens both individuals and society is such that the very existence of these new weapons should be a sufficient deterrent, without the need for them to be deployed. But, the neutralisation of strategic power does not mean that negotiation itself is neutralised. On the contrary, it will raise the threshold beyond which States might decide to choose war rather than

12 V. E. GHEBALI: *L'OSCE dans l'Europe postcommuniste (1990–1996)*, Brussels, Bruylant, 1996.

negotiation. As Henry Kissinger wrote, power has never been so great, but nor has it ever been so useless.[13] (see *130*)

The more dangerous the world becomes, the more essential it will be for governments to communicate effectively with each other. (see *1705*)

This kind of dialogue is all the more vital given the risk that weapons will escape the control of responsible governments and be used for terrorist aggression. (see *182, 1802*)

1704 – Throughout the whole period of Soviet-American confrontation, the development of global strategy was dominated by negotiation seen as a function of military potential, with each of the protagonists endeavouring to acquire new ways of raising the stakes and enhancing its own bargaining position. This led to innovations and proliferation in weapons. These weapons, in turn, gave rise to new dangers and a renewed obligation to negotiate. There is no reason why some similar pattern should not reappear in the future.

1705 –The nuclear danger is not the only one. Irrespective of prohibitions, States are pursuing their research into other types of highly effective offensive and defensive weaponry such as toxins and biological weapons, rays, explosives, ballistic missiles and satellites, hundreds, if not thousands, of which have military uses. (see *1714*)

As long as the military applications of scientific progress are not entirely subject to negotiation between the States concerned, the world will become ever more dangerous: *the threat of spectacular disaster casts a shadow over the future of modern civilisation.*

1706 – In a world that is shrinking, all great strategies must involve the projection of power, in other words the ability to call upon a number of technical means: transport, communications, interception, and surveillance.[14]

Strategic thinking has come to focus on missiles, because of the remarkable technical strides that have been made in this field, and also their wide marketability. They can be divided into several categories, depending on their range, and they can carry all kinds of weapons, sometimes across continents. (see *1740, 1797*)

The convention on delivery systems of guaranteed mutual destruction, the Anti-Ballistic Missile Treaty of 1972, marked the beginning of strategic negotiations between the United States and the USSR, and its successors Russia, Byelorussia, Ukraine and Kazakhstan. It was denounced by the United States in 2001. The agreement remained in place without however having any decisive effect, given the progress being made in this field by various emerging States and the threat presented by ballistic missiles, especially from the standpoint of Western governments. (see *457, 837, 1732, 1749, 1768*)

1707 – The degree of determination of each protagonist depends on the values that underlie its strategy: where there is a danger of destruction, those values must be either simple or very elevated. Deterrence cannot function where there are

---

13 H. A. KISSINGER: *The Troubled Partnership*, New York, McGraw Hill, 1965.
14 H. CURIEN: 'La conquête de l'espace,' *RAMSES 2000*, Paris, p. 153. P. JURGENSEN: *L'Erreur de l'Occident face à la mondialisation*, Paris, O. Jacob, 2004.

unclear or contested responsibilities, or where the objectives are too complex or disputed; deterrence requires thinking that is clear and overriding. The American proposal to create a multilateral strike force within NATO failed because it proved impossible to decide who was to have the power to deploy it. (see *2337*)

This explains the observable fact that, in spite of widespread globalisation, arms, and especially nuclear weapons, tend to reinforce the nation as an entity. Nuclear armament will, as such, function as a stimulus to diplomacy especially in its preventive function, aided by the progress being made in analysing and predicting human behaviour. (see *913, 2321*)

The information civilisation encourages defensive positions characterised by watchfulness, forbearance and reasoning.

1708 – Diplomatic moves and discussions are used by the parties to explore or clarify their strategic intentions, assess the potential for conflict and the degree of willingness to fight, and show the adversary the limitations of its manoeuvres. At the same time, they must draw whatever advantage from the use of threats that the state of political and technological development will allow. In this sense, diplomacy serves to uphold and validate deterrence. (see *424*)

The consequences that flowed from Ronald Reagan's Strategic Defence Initiative showed how a statement of credible intentions backed by sufficient means can alter the diplomatic landscape and lend new impetus to prospective negotiation. The United States hope to achieve the same results with their programme of interception of ballistic missiles, a 'shield' not, this time, directed against Russia, but one that might even benefit Russia by protecting it against irresponsible acts. (see *335, 1711, 1768*)

1709 – Beyond a certain threshold, every weapon becomes a means of coercion that no responsible State wants, or can allow itself, to be the first to use. Thus negotiation comes back into play, its role more vital than ever, and with it the usual means of persuasion, pressure or domination. Its objects are the same: forestalling the unpredictable and ensuring the balance of power, even if only partially, reducing localised tensions and conflicts and ensuring they do not spread. (see *150*)

The Gulf crisis of 1991 would have unfolded differently if Iraq had possessed the operational potential for mass destruction. The object in fact was to prevent this coming about, though, ten years later, it was still being claimed that Iraq did possess such a weapon.

The strategic danger of ideology is that it furnishes motives that often defy political and military reason, and are not susceptible to the usual preventive effects of deterrence. This observation is still true in an era of globalisation of economic and cultural exchange. (see *1750, 1753, 1802, 1869*)

1710 – Whether deterrence is effective, and negotiation possible, depends on the overall vulnerability of the adversary, or, more precisely, the balance between the vulnerabilities of the protagonists, which calls for finely tuned psychological appraisal. (see *263*)

No one can predict what will be the attitude of a nation, a government or a leader when faced with the threat of open conflict, either in the course of negotiations or after a war.[15] The fact that the use of even tactical nuclear weapons depends on political decisions increases both the scope for diplomacy and the amount of effort this requires.

With the development of the media, this principle applies with equal force to other weapons systems, as soon as public opinion becomes aware of the dangers they pose.

The crisis and campaigns that followed the terrorist attacks of 11 September 2001 in New York and Washington revealed the existence of latent worldwide solidarities: among the industrialised nations, focused on the United States; among the nuclear powers, including Russia and China; and among those States with military or ideological leaders. In the face of such powerful interest groupings, the United Nations has found itself playing a secondary role (in some of the African countries, for example, and also in Cambodia, where a high price has been paid for three years of intervention). This role is by no means negligible, however, because the UN offers governments a stable and neutral forum for them to meet and negotiate. (see *1692, 1786*)

1711 – There has never been such uncertainty as there is today about what the results will be of acts of duress, force or war, because no-one can precisely or definitively assess the implications or the consequences of using these destructive weapons, the conditions under which they will be used, or the range of their geographical or biological effects. This uncertainty is the key to deterrence and to negotiation. (see *70, 111*)

In this sense, nuclear weapons have for several decades played a stabilising role in world politics.

As long as the expectation of final gain is too unpredictable, the possessor of the weapon will only take the initiative to use it in the absolutely last resort. It leaves disputes in which it has no real interest to be resolved instead by small-scale hostilities or traditional forms of bargaining. (see *1678*)

1712 – As always, the value of the deterrence results from the credibility of the threat. This is not simply a matter of maintaining a hypothetical superiority in terms of forces, as well as systems of observation, transmission and processing of data. The adversary must also be left in no doubt that these means will be used, with speed and determination, if circumstances require, this last being a matter of discretion. Yet again, the diplomat comes to the aid of the soldier. (see *100*)

On the other hand, the strategist must take into account the extreme mobility, flexibility and speed of his partners or adversaries, who are not always confined by structures or bound by law, like States: in a fluid and unpredictable global environment, in which there are neither territories nor fronts, he must be resolute, patient, and constantly on his guard.

1713 – *Deterrence is worthless if it is not accompanied by diplomatic explanations to ensure the message gets across.*

---

15 O. R. HOLSTI and A. L. GEORGE: 'The Effects of Stress on the Performance of Foreign Policy-Makers', *Political Science Annual*, 1975, p. 255.

Prevention can never be taken for granted, not only because of developments in military technology, but mostly for reasons of political psychology. Because he cannot be certain of the real intentions of his adversaries, or even who they are, the statesman can never be sure that he has succeeded in dissuading them in the long term from hostile action. He must remain constantly alert. (see *2093, 2793, 2807*)

1714 – As soon as it is clear that the protagonists have the ability to destroy each other, or cause irreparable damage, deterrence turns into a kind of mutual guarantee. This was the conclusion reached by both American and Soviet leaders during the 1970s. Each strategist aimed to use negotiation to neutralise any factors of risk and uncertainty in his own as well as the opposing camp.[16] (see *825, 2131*)

However, the assumption that every national space could be turned into a sanctuary was swept aside by far-reaching indirect strategies, international terrorism and civil wars. (see *221*)

In their own way, militants project both their solidarity and their aggression across frontiers, unimpeded by the principle of non-interference. The fact that the concept of deterrence might become obsolete caused concern among the great powers that led to the meeting of the American, Chinese and Russian Heads of State in 2001, and has increased the role of preventive action and policing. (see *225, 1649, 1699, 1705, 1753, 1758, 1792*)

1715 – Strategic strength is not the strength of traditional combat: capability does not have to be superior to the other forces on the battlefield. It can be used in ways that have nothing to do with strictly military imperatives. The possessor of nuclear, chemical, radioactive or bacteriological weapons and of ballistic means may only use them in a political context, and must thus be open to negotiation. The more powerful nuclear weapons become, the less likely it is that they will be freely used for aggressive purposes, and the more inclined responsible holders will be to accept or impose strategic debate.

The proliferation of all kinds of weapons encourages enhanced levels of diplomatic cooperation among States interested in international stability. As a tactic, negotiation is then aided by the possession of non-strategic weapons. (see *1702, 1768*)

1716 – Deterrence benefits all those who possess a disproportionate power of destruction.[17] It is not the monopoly of the great powers. (see *111*)

However, the multipolarisation of deterrence makes negotiation more complex as well as more necessary. Each protagonist is fearful of alliances with others, and seeks to protect the autonomy of its own diplomacy. (see *1732, 1735*)

Smaller weapons and more precise ballistics mean an increased tendency towards tactical diversity.

1717 – To maintain peace, it is normal to look first to those powers capable of provoking conflict. The pursuit of strategic negotiation, however, implies that each

16 H. A. KISSINGER: *The White House Years*, Boston, Little, Brown & Co., 1979, 1.
17 P. GALLOIS: *La Grande Berne*, Paris, Plon, 1976; *Géopolitique: Les voies de la puissance*, Paris, Plon, 1990.

protagonist must be willing and able to prevent another State causing major hostilities, and especially to keep its own allies in line. The broader a coalition becomes, the less unanimous will be its obligations and objectives. (see *229, 899, 2043*)

A deterrent strategy might be the expression of a will to impose hegemony; even so, its objective is still the avoidance of overt conflict. *The threat always depends on the political, psychological and moral credibility of its author, meaning his capacity for making speedy decisions.* Thus, while not ruling out preliminary consultation, deterrence leaves no time for discussion with allies when urgent action is required.

1718 – Strategic negotiation must extend its scope ever further. Not only is there no moratorium on technological advance, but the partners are increasingly exposed to the initiatives of other States, which can even be encouraged where the capability to strike is neutralised on both sides. (see *1705*)

The increase in the number of nuclear powers has reaffirmed the importance of traditional means of intervention, for example by conventional forces, and with it the freedom for secondary powers to play their role on the international scene.

1719 – *Despite the risks, the temptations of challenge and risk still live on in the human mind.* The consequences of the use of powers of swift and massive destruction are as impossible to verify as they are horrific. These two contrary considerations combine to incite some politicians to push their manoeuvres to the very brink of danger without regard for legal prohibitions or ethical constraints.

That, at any rate, is the impression given by the turbulent state of international life, with vast areas still torn by strife and bloodshed widespread and dangerous enough to endanger the balance of power as well as the fate of civilisations. (see *1932*)

1720 – In the traditional pairing of war and diplomacy, the role of the latter is still extremely important.

Where there is no way of preventing conflict from breaking out, it is only by negotiation, even including third parties, that the issues can be identified, the stakes limited and the course of the dispute kept in check to prevent the situation from spiralling out of control. (see *224*)

Strategic decisions and negotiations demand the rarest qualities of courage, resolve and intelligence, as can be seen from the success of Kennedy's challenge to Kruschev in the Cuban missile crisis. (see *2328, 2536*)

§2. Strategic challenges

1721 – For decades, weapons arsenals have grown in strength and sophistication, giving States a destructive potential that greatly exceeds the needs of even the most radical conflict. The power and precision of ballistic systems have also increased, along with techniques for observation and detection, and for transmitting and processing data.

Through negotiating, antagonists have gradually come to realise that they are facing danger together: in their turn, newcomers to the diplomatic scene must understand that solidarity is a response to the threat of collective destruction. (see *157, 1731*)

1722 – This is how diplomacy was applied to the issue of the limitation, and later the reduction, of strategic weapons, an issue that is always topical because, with each new stride in technology, the governments concerned must renew their efforts at mutual understanding.

Since nuclear strategy took on a global dimension, negotiation has done the same. This global dimension is used, by the United States and others, to justify putting in place measures of control, prevention and even worldwide intervention, sometimes amounting to interference. Nations united in their opposition to 'colonialism' have no hesitation in imposing their own modern forms of dominance. (see *946, 1647, 1708, 2607*)

1723 – The purpose of present-day strategies is to ensure that no one State can achieve a position of superiority that upsets the balance of power; as a result, they have favoured the maintenance of ongoing relations and continued discussions, not only between the great powers but also between each of these and third parties. (see *64, 158*)

Themselves the product of a techno-military balance, these negotiations are now needed in order to give it shape.

1724 – One basic question is to decide what factors should be taken into account when determining the balance of power. The limiting of meetings to strategic issues does not prevent other destabilising factors from being brought into the equation: these might include conventional weapons, naval and air forces, traditional armies, observation systems, civil defence and allied forces, as well as the financial, economic and technical factors that influence them (this is the mission of the National Economic Council of the President of the United States). (see *126*)

1725 – While, initially, strategic exchanges were by their nature typically bilateral, their wider implications made it necessary to exceed these bounds and introduce secondary powers into the equation, though without the result always being capable of enforcement. These secondary powers, by contrast, only kept their own powers of deterrence by maintaining their independence of political decision-making.

The disappearance of East-West tensions has not diminished the use of this tactic by governments on every continent wishing to play on their independence. *It may almost be presumed that, where States are not actually allies, or united in the face of a common danger, their strategies will diverge.*

1726 – By the very nature of the threat, the future of nuclear negotiation has been poised between two approaches: the one direct and sometimes secret, and the other multipartite and therefore open. In the present state of world affairs, both these diplomatic methods were equally necessary. However, the fact that both approaches are possible often creates difficulties, anxieties and illusions, mostly on the part of other States.

In any major crisis, nations must be circumspect when great powers are in confrontation or in negotiation.

1727 – On numerous occasions, multilateral conferences have been charged with this kind of negotiation. But the composition of these bodies, initially limited to countries with real responsibility, has been extended, under pressure voiced within the United Nations, to include other countries whose participation has proved either useless or obstructive. Not one of these conferences, as a result, has produced a definitive outcome. It is easy to see how, despite the amendments made in 1978 to the composition and functioning of the UN structures working towards a negotiated disarmament, US-Soviet collusion reared its head as soon as a specific issue was put forward. (see *1515, 1517*)

Yet again, this proved that negotiation is strongly linked to responsibility. (see *647*)

1728 – In so sensitive and at the same time so vital a sphere, the decision had to come from those directly responsible for technological and strategic development: they had no choice but to negotiate face to face in spite of the disquiet this engendered in third parties. The United States were forced to do this after the point was reached when the Soviet Union had advanced so much that their own nuclear predominance was no longer certain, either in research or application. The USSR, on its side, had nothing to lose from entering into direct contact with those really responsible for forming western strategy.

1729 – Only contacts such as these could produce results, most of all after 1963, when they were made easier by the opening up of a direct line of communication between the two capitals. (see *2029*)

In this way, agreement was reached to prohibit certain kinds of atmospheric, space and maritime testing, in the Moscow Treaty of 5 August 1963, to which over a hundred States have adhered, and later, also, land-based tests under the Treaty of 3 July 1974, and certain types of civil explosions under the Treaty of 28 May 1976. The Treaty on the Non-Proliferation of Nuclear Weapons ('NPT') of 1 July 1968 was ratified by over one hundred States (including Iran, in 1971), and extended indefinitely in 1995. These joint US-Soviet initiatives were supported by Great Britain, but not at the time by either France or China, though France indicated that it would abide by them. (see *1749, 1765, 1790*)

1730 – At each stage, however, it was necessary to involve other States and obtain their adhesion to the resulting agreement, which mainly covered the non-proliferation and thus the control of nuclear weapons. Despite a major effort at persuasion on the part of the United Nations, with the 1991 and 1994 Conventions on Nuclear Safety, this was only partially successful. (see *1799*)

Those who refused to participate pointed out that this was not true disarmament. In fact, almost all of them wanted to keep a free hand in case their own national technology progressed to the point where they could have their own 'bomb'. India and Pakistan fell into this category, and so did other so-called 'threshold' States: Israel, Iraq and North Korea, and also, at the time, South Africa, Argentina and Brazil. (see *237, 1718*)

1731 – In the privacy of their major meetings, meanwhile, the United States and the Soviet Union sought to agree on the limitation of certain kinds of launchers and certain weapons in order to preserve, as far as possible, a hypothetical balance between the means of destruction and of response, sometimes using different routes to reach their goals. Discussions about strategic arms limitation led, after years of debate, to successive agreements on limiting 'strategic weapons' (and especially their means of delivery, under the SALT Agreements I and II of 1972 and 1979), and then on limiting their numbers (the START I and II Agreements of 1991 and 1993, extended in 1997.)

One of the best-known negotiations was in 1987, about 'Euromissiles' (meaning mid-range missiles that threatened Western Europe). It seems that these commitments were broadly speaking respected by the two Great Powers. As a result, nuclear arsenals diminished by several thousand warheads, though this did not mean their destructive power was any less. Direct discussions between the respective Heads of State led to agreement in November 2001 to reduce their nuclear weapons by two thirds within a given time-frame. (see *1747*)

This whole legal apparatus is threatened with obsolescence, not only as a result of recent American initiatives, but most of all because of the widespread progress that has been made in ballistic technology. (see *1712, 1714, 1715*)

1732 – Between States, as elsewhere, those who hold power also have prerogatives. This can be seen from the agreement between Moscow and Washington to prevent all nuclear war or all situations arising that could lead to it, not only resulting from their own acts but also from initiatives of other States that were not signatories to the 22 June 1973 Treaty. (see *129, 1724*)

While multilateral debates on disarmament were going on, the two capitals were conducting their own secret discussions with a view to limiting the potential risks arising from certain dangerous activities, in the nuclear field as well as from the movements and actions of conventional forces. By the agreements of Washington (15 September 1987) and Moscow (12 June 1989), they reserved to themselves the information necessary for handling such crises. (see *1740*)

1733 – The ways and means of strategic negotiation are not really very different from those used in traditional diplomacy. Detailed bargaining is key, and progress is achieved by successive, balanced concessions. But the fact remains that offers and commitments are sometimes made on the basis of unilateral hypotheses and assessments carrying a high degree of risk. (see *423, 708*)

In the private sector, too, long-term thinking produces strategies that are often aggressive. (see *1812, 1823, 1829*)

1734 – None of the protagonists would willingly give up the means at its disposal or its development programme, or the right to control the deployment of its forces or the secrecy that protects it, or the right to interpret for itself the behaviour and the potential of its adversary. However, the tendency to place discussions on strategy within the general context of competition between the powers concerned could have the effect of enlarging the scope of the negotiation and raising the level of international tension.

1735 – *The distinguishing characteristic of this type of negotiation was mainly the speculative and hypothetical nature of its subject.* Concessions were based on ceilings that often were never reached, and types of weapons and launchers that could never be made. It is a characteristic of these techniques that they require enormous investment and long years of research and development, but their content is known in advance, and this can be made subject to agreements on authorisation, limitation or prohibition of weapons and technology. (see *2093, 2189*)

1736 – *When dealing with matters so far in the future, there is a great deal of uncertainty as to what will in practice be the effect of such compromises, as the parties are not in a position to make any precise or measurable comparisons.* This has lent the negotiations a particularly abstract air, especially as inequality of potential meant inequality of commitments. It also explains why there were such long and detailed discussions about the classification of weapons, factual comparisons and interpretation of different situations: distrust has been the order of the day. (see *709, 2054*)

Considerations of this kind could apply equally to other types of weapons technology and financing, as well as to other States.

1737 – *Those negotiations also showed the development of preventive diplomacy.* The first US-Soviet agreement on strategic arms limitation (the SALT I Treaty of 26 May 1968, amended on 3 July 1974), contained restrictions on the anti-missile defence systems of the two great powers in order to enhance the deterrent effect of offensive weapons. The United States, France and Great Britain signed treaties with the USSR in 1971, 1976 and 1977, designed to prevent nuclear accidents, so as to avoid one of the powers making an incorrect interpretation of the facts. The United States and the USSR also signed an agreement, the Washington treaty of 22 June 1973, whereby they committed to consult each other at once in the event of risk of nuclear war, and, on 31 May 1988, an agreement on the launch of ballistic missiles. (see *335*)

The Washington (15 September 1987) and Moscow (12 June 1989) agreements were signed in response to the desire to prevent major nuclear and military incidents. Also, in 2001, the Council of the European Union reached agreement, in Gothenburg, on a programme for the prevention of violent conflict. (see *1733, 1741, 1789, 2076*)

In modern society, any form of insecurity challenges the power of States.

1738 – A further characteristic of this approach is that it applies to the potential and uses of weapons technology and delivery systems, and is constantly being refreshed and renewed as developments progress. It is the ambition of some States to succeed in forging a role for themselves in these fields. (see *1765*)

Whatever may happen to their formal agreements, ratified or not, the result is that the strategic powers are forced to continue to communicate through talks, messages and signals: the stakes are so high that each of them must plan for the future. (see *512*)

1739 – Because this type of negotiation seeks to impose flexible future ceilings on weapons, it has taken a step forward each time a breakthrough in research has produced new technologies and methods. Each shift in strategic emphasis or the balance of power has heralded new discussions destined, directly or indirectly, to maintain the balance in relations between the powers and their respective camps, against a background of increasing technical complexity.

Also covered are weapons delivery systems, some of which have a range exceeding 10,000 kilometres, ground installations, mobile and otherwise, long-range submarines, bombers and support aircraft, as well as all electronic simulation, communications and verification equipment (see for example the 1998 agreement between the United States and Russia on the sharing of information on the launch of ballistic missiles). (see *1768*)

1740 – The development of 'anti-proliferation' diplomacy poses the problem of how to verify the implementation of commitments concerning a technology that is rigorous but also secret and changing, a problem complicated by the fact that no government wants another to know much about the finer details of its own techniques and installations. This question has been addressed by deploying finely tuned instruments of detection, identification and measurement, while observation satellites are now capable of giving very accurate and detailed information about measures that have been taken on the ground. (see *812, 2027*)

The effectiveness of negotiated solutions is reinforced by the widespread use of on-site verification procedures, either by the experts of the parties to the treaty, or via the involvement of observer missions. For a long time the great powers refused to accept this, mainly because they alone possessed the means of electronic surveillance enabling them to uncover the adversary's secrets, as provided in some treaties (Moscow, 26 May 1972).

1741 – However, under the Washington Agreement of 8 December 1987 on the elimination of mid-range 'Euromissiles', the United States and the USSR provided for methods of inspection on their respective territories and on those of certain of their allies. From that time on, a fresh negotiation became possible: that of the objectives and terms of monitoring of the implementation of the treaty. In practice, this type of verification was reproduced in later agreements, such as the START I Treaty in 1991. (see *1765, 1732*)

On the other hand, though endorsed by the G8 in 2002, as well as by other States, and by the Security Council in 2004, and entrusted to an international organisation, the IAEA, verification of compliance with the Non-Proliferation Treaty (NPT) is in fact exceptionally difficult. This became clear from the adjournment of the UN conference in May 2005 on the effective application of the Treaty. (see *1762*)

1742 – The collapse of the Soviet Union and the Warsaw Pact caused a radical shift in the balance of power in Europe and, as a result, throughout the world. Its effect was not to eliminate the potential for conflict, but rather to disperse the risk by making it impossible to control. It also gave rise to uncertainty as to whether the successor States were capable of assuming the commitments undertaken by the Soviet Union in a field as sensitive as nuclear arms control and disarmament. (see *652*)

Now that the traditional desire for superiority on the ground has given way to the quest for faster and more precisely-targeted means of destruction, fuelled by the development of space-borne observation and weaponry, the scope and vision of strategic negotiation must expand accordingly. As can be seen from the conduct of the great powers, the positioning and deployment of the necessary means for implementation of major strategies are now the subject of negotiation.

1743 – The peace-keeping mechanisms set up under the UN Charter were never developed to the full because of the lasting conflict between the strategic powers from 1950 to 1990. Once this antagonism was over, they were put to much broader use, in negotiating and verifying disarmament and setting up intervention or peace-keeping forces, as well as in discussions about the conditions for collective security and the procedure for intervening in the internal affairs of countries in crisis. (see *1132, 2052*)

1744 – The United Nations has consistently thrown its weight behind the creation of multilateral mechanisms for controlling disarmament. The fact remains, however, that the mechanisms designed to monitor the prohibition on nuclear testing, including some 400 detection posts, have proved very difficult to implement. (see *839, 1745, 2230*)

Over fifty States have ratified the Nuclear Test Ban Treaty of 24 March 1996. Despite the conclusions of the Vienna Conference of October 1998, it will probably not come into force. Not only has the United States Senate refused to ratify it, but other signatory States, notably China, Russia, Iran, Algeria and Israel, have adopted the same position, while some States (North Korea, India and Pakistan) have not signed at all. France, for its part, has implemented it since conducting its last tests in the Pacific.

1745 – The UN Secretary General appointed a High-Level Panel to examine 'Threats, Challenges and Change'. The Panel's report, '*A more secure world: Our shared responsibility*' was published in 2004. In it, the members enumerated a number of dangers, notably the proliferation of weapons and all forms of arms trafficking. The 2005 General Assembly did not reach any conclusions on the basis of this report, which went so far as to propose punitive measures. Insecurity has become a real international obsession. It must be a matter for the collective responsibility of States, because any unilateral approach to the problem is likely to prove excessive, inappropriate, provocative and counterproductive.

Collective security is a difficult task, one that the Charter entrusts to the Security Council as the basic organ of the United Nations (see the report of the Secretary General, '*In Larger Freedom*', 2005). (see *1777, 1782*)

Section 2: The spreading risks

1746 – The freedom to choose defensive and diplomatic goals, and also to choose which means are necessary to preserve this very prerogative, is among the essential attributes of sovereignty claimed as of right by all States, even the youngest and smallest. (see *2319, 2325*)

Any nation that has some sort of advantage, military or otherwise, will ultimately make use of it in its relations with others: none will ever give up an advantage. It might seek to impose its will by intimidating its rival or attacking it head-on. It might equally confine itself to thwarting any hostile pressures designed to paralyse its political manoeuvres vis à vis third States. (see *79*)

1747 – Today, it is difficult to tell whether the strengthening of international relations will make war more difficult or, on the contrary, more frequent: over a hundred cases of open conflict have been recorded since the Second World War. One thing is certain, though: for centuries, hostilities erupted mostly between neighbouring States, but the problem has now assumed a global dimension. Even internal, localised wars provide third countries with a pretext to intervene. (see *2255, 2260*)

When their principal source of capability is neutralised, powerful States will find an intermediary through which to act.

1748 – The issue is more critical than ever. *Nuclear, chemical, electronic and bacterial weapons are capable of inflicting damage on a scale that would make victory meaningless in human terms for those that survived.* The threat of escalating destruction has become a major theme of diplomacy, displacing the traditional role of war in regulating relations between States. (see *80, 223*)

1749 – At the highest levels, there is no distinction between military responsibility and diplomatic responsibility. (see *229, 239, 2325*)

War is no longer a matter of which side wins in open combat: instead it takes the form of a whole range of economic, ideological and political confrontations that the techniques of international negotiation could define and resolve.

Thus there is general agreement that measures taken regularly and officially pursuant to Chapter VII of the UN Charter ('Peace-keeping') are not regarded as acts of war, even where they involve the overt use of force and actual fighting. (see *1784*)

In reality, the Security Council has experienced difficulty in fulfilling its legal role, even since the antagonism between the Great Powers ceased to exist. With neither real military force, nor any means of disciplining States, it has been used to confer legitimacy on the military interventions of some States: it allows certain powers to do what it cannot do itself. (see *1782*)

1750 – *The all-encompassing strategies of the great powers must extend to conflicts that are limited in scope but nonetheless represent a danger to them.* (see *1757*)

In practice, States that are excluded from the normal course of interaction by reason of poverty or ideology are tempted to use their tactical autonomy in order to provoke, destabilise and disturb an order to which they consider they do not belong. (see *1931, 1978*)

On the other hand, often unwisely, powerful States either damp down local conflicts or stoke them up, depending on their interests. But interests can differ and change, and conflict is contagious. *Thus, responsible players will in future negotiate not about how to exploit a risk but how to avoid and contain it.* (see *1678, 1705, 1715*)

Such is the fear of deep-rooted crises and conflicts that global diplomatic agreement can be reached to engage in undisguised tactics of policing and intervention, though the effects of such actions can prove impossible to control by subsequent negotiation.[18] (see *12, 665, 1132, 1785, 1802, 1933*)

1751 – The challenge presented by these endless tensions calls for responses. Governments will need to agree on disciplines that bind private sector entities as well as States. Intergovernmental organisations are working on international rules for the prevention, sharing and coverage of risks. The United Nations is addressing the issue of terrorist financing, and the ICAO is responsible for new safety standards in civil aviation; the European Union will have its own Security and Defence Policy and is working to strengthen police and judicial cooperation. Disputes will have to be resolved that far outweigh those dealt with by the WTO, some of them involving fundamental strategic interests. (see *1532, 1967*)

1752 – The growth in conventional weapons and the increasing diversification of weapons of mass destruction, with more and more States in a position to use them, must be a factor in these negotiations, both in evaluating the risks and deciding which direction alliances should take, as well as in the use of deterrence.

As an example, the Gulf War of 1991 gave rise to the notion of the ongoing use of military means starting from the outbreak of serious tensions and continuing until the consequences of a war have been dealt with, even after the war itself is over. Hence the series of sanctions imposed on Iraq: the exclusion zones, the disputed inspections, the embargo and the bombings carried out in 2000 and 2001, at a time when Chapter VII of the Charter no longer applied; the review of the 'Oil for Food' programme in 2002, and the various references to the Security Council culminating in the war of 2003–2004. (see *1237, 1709*)

§1. Tactical autonomy

1753 – Considerations that for the major powers are matters of tactics have strategic implications for weaker States. For the former, the entire vast field of diplomacy is open to them: they can trade assurances and promises from one theatre to another, and third States can do very little about it.

To those who subscribe to fundamentalist ideologies, openness, discussion and negotiation are mere temporary tactics, but never strategies for peace.

1754 – Despite the existence of so-called 'anti-hegemony' clauses, coalitions form around those States with the power of last resort in a second level of interdependence. Here, too, negotiation remains a powerful and versatile tool: it is possible for a secondary power to influence the foreign policy of the lead State so that it exceeds its own original goal. (see *852, 972*).

1755 – Faced with the ultimate challenge, however, no matter how solid each alliance and despite the need to call up reinforcements, only a single centralised authority can decide to deploy the overwhelming power of modern weapons. It alone makes the strategic choices, including in negotiations. (see *2320*)

---

18 F. PAGANI: 'L'administration européenne de Mostar', *AFDI*, 1996, p. 224. F. LAGRANGE: 'La mission intérimaire des Nations unies au Kosovo', *AFDI*, 1999, p. 375.

This principle can work to the advantage of States whose leaders are capable, responsible, act in good faith and remain long enough in office.

1756 – Sustained by advances in science and technology, the threat of mass destruction means that no promise of military support can be treated as certain. Governments will be less inclined than ever to face risks on behalf of others that they would not accept themselves. The unwise or the speculative might be satisfied for a while by appearances to the contrary, but statesmen are not deceived by them: this uncertainty makes reasoning by diplomacy more hazardous than ever, and requires the negotiator to have a constant mastery of the changing situation. (see *908, 2027*)

1757 – A climate of risk and fear generates new opportunities for negotiation, as it does for war. Never have threats been so widely used, or crises – even economic and financial crises – so cynically exploited by governments. The options opened up by this new strategy are broad enough to include acts of small-scale and covert belligerence. (see *902, 1711, 1801*)

1758 – Resort to outright force as a means of settling disputes will never disappear, as long as States cannot reach agreement on ways to prevent crises and resolve their differences.

Threats are not the exclusive prerogative of the front-line powers: certain other States are also to be feared because of their long-range missile capabilities. Terrorism, too, can have a deterrent effect. National strategies can no longer ignore these unpredictable risk factors. *Distance is no longer an obstacle to aggression, and this has altered the traditional patterns not only of warfare, but also of diplomacy.*

1759 – Since weapons of mass destruction first appeared, the means available for use in war and in diplomacy no longer always obey the same rules as before. Part of the forces that could come into play are neutralised, as long as the great States remain firm in their publicly-declared resolve: having responsibility for heavy weapons obliges each of them to avoid certain kinds of confrontation, partially depriving them of their freedom to intervene and the means of doing so, and opens up the field to other nations, and sometimes even private firms.

1760 – Never have small and mid-sized States enjoyed such freedom to manoeuvre, ranging from the use of threats to open hostilities. The successive challenges they face as they grow in power continue to manifest themselves in the form of overt crises.[19] (see *172*)

The first step of the strategist must therefore be to ensure the safety of his own camp: negotiation with outsiders is, for him, a way of measuring their respective strengths and understanding which of them pose a threat, direct or otherwise. (see *972*)

1761 – That same willingness not to be exposed to the use of strategic power can create real solidarity among the main protagonists, and a duty to negotiate about any

19 H. A. KISSINGER: *Nuclear Weapons and Foreign Policy*, New York, Harper Row, 1957.

problem that might lead their respective camps down the path of conflict. It is in the interests of each of them to maintain the predominant position of the other, minimise any element of uncertainty or irresponsibility at the international level, and resolve disputes directly on a bilateral basis: the Cuban missile crisis in 1962 was resolved without the Cubans playing any part in the settlement. (see *64, 226, 229*)

1762 – States go to considerable lengths to obtain their own weapons of mass destruction, nuclear weapons in particular. This is a question of time as well as money. It also requires the taking of a decision, one that implies assuming a heavy burden of long-term constraints that might not be justified by developments in strategic threats. (see *877*)

1763 – The holding of a strategic weapon and the necessary ballistic missiles can mean not only that a State has a potential for reprisals sufficient to ensure that it cannot be drawn into disputes, but also that it has the ability to lead the dominant powers into dangerous conflict: its effect should be to extend the margins of negotiation both within and outside alliances. (see *879, 902*)

1764 – The financial and technical effort and the political and biological risks involved in becoming a military power, even a minor one, are only justified if there is a strategy. The nations understand this need very well, and will not support any such enterprise that is not based on a clear vision of their role. On the other hand, they are prepared to accept and finance even nuclear armament where, as in the case of France, it is an expression of their independence. (see *321*)

The 1968 Non-Proliferation Treaty confirms the powerful in their prerogatives. (see *1829*)

1765 – Those second-line powers that have not signed the Non-Proliferation Treaty, and, *a fortiori*, those that have acquired nuclear weapons, or are conducting scientific experiments in this field, are unwilling to be deprived of the diplomatic possibilities this position affords them, unless they are given specific security guarantees. (see *1741*)

1766 – Armament increases diplomatic inequality, not only because of the differences in military potential, but for the simple reason that the supplier always has control over the buyer. (see *856*)

In spite of the climate of uncertainty created by technological advances, the phenomenon of military diplomacy is starting to develop, on the margins of traditional negotiation. It has its own goals, limitations and methods; the purely commercial nature of the supply relationship is undermined by considerations of prestige and sovereignty.

Military negotiation has great tactical importance.

1767 – Concern for preventing the spread of nuclear weapons is present in the clauses used in the sale of fissile materials and equipment designed to prevent or prohibit their use for military ends (see the 1977 'London Directives'). But the same concern is not visible in the case of weapons arbitrarily classified as conventional. The 38 members of the 'London Club' were the only States prepared to control sales of military materiel.

Ever since 1972, debates have taken place within the United Nations about the prohibition of the manufacture of biological weapons and the destruction of stocks, under international control. The Convention of 1 June 1990, drawn up under the auspices of the Geneva Disarmament Conference, provides for the complete prohibition and elimination of chemical weapons and includes verification mechanisms. It was followed by the Paris Convention of 15 January 1993. The 'Australia Club' consists of States wanting controls on the sale of chemical and bacterial technology. However, the progress of scientific research and the secrecy surrounding it, coupled with the possibility that pathogenic substances are being covertly stocked and the extreme difficulty of putting effective controls in place, will require continuing negotiations accompanied by verification techniques.

1768 – Such was the proliferation of guided weapons and ballistic missiles that some thirty governments came together to negotiate joint guidelines with a view to controlling the use of that technology. These included the G7 initiative, the negotiation and publication by 32 States in 1987 of 'guidelines' on the sale of missiles and launch technology, the 1998 agreement between the US and Russia on information-sharing, and, since 2001, the cooperation between Europe and Russia via NATO. (see *1730*)

These negotiations met with very limited success, which partly explains the new strategic thinking of the United States, Russia, and, more recently, France. (see *1708*).

1769 – The arms trade has become one of the hallmarks of political presence on the world stage. It involves the installation of experts and officers, and sometimes also machinery for aid and intervention. But, more than that, cooperation in weapons research, development, production and sale has spawned a whole raft of institutions, mechanisms and industries which serve as the vehicles for preferential diplomatic relations and alliances.

The illegal traffic in light weapons is a major source of profit, and led the United Nations to issue its embargo in 1998 on arms sales to Africa. Notwithstanding this, tens of billions of dollars are spent each year on buying arms.

1770 – Many States, even in the developing world, that are anxious to exploit their industrial potential protect the viability of their national military output by negotiating arms exports of ever-increasing value, unhindered in practice by any embargo. In various parts of the world, arsenals are being amassed that contain the most sophisticated varieties of modern technology, ready to be used in support of new or unexpected strategies. Traditional weapons technology, like that of nuclear weapons, satellites and delivery systems, is constantly improving, and with it the potential for threats and the exertion of pressure.

1771 – In a very fluid and uncertain international environment, every secondary conflict, whatever its potential, prompts each protagonist to enhance its capabilities. It also creates heightened tensions, which can be used for provocative ends, resulting in increased recourse to diplomacy. The role of negotiation is enhanced, while at the same time hostilities are limited to acts that will not upset the strategy of one of the dominant powers, or, by implication, of the others.

Arms control, already unpredictable as between the great powers, has been rendered impossible by the present state of world disruption.

1772 – Under the 'balance of fear', every country, however small, sometimes enjoys greater freedom than the major powers: the small can get out of trouble with ease where the large cannot, as La Fontaine put it.[20] *Mindful of their past historic exploits, States are once again starting to follow their own policy, each seeking to foster its interests and increase its influence, sometimes by taking risks that are too great for itself and its allies.* (see *369, 608*)

This was the calculation made by Iraq in invading Kuwait in 1990.

1773 – Where more than two parties are involved, the uncertainty increases. The more perilous the behaviour of second-line players, the greater the obligation on major leaders to agree on a minimum level of order: in turn they become responsible for guaranteeing it, each on its own terms, and while still remaining in competition.

They share a common fear of the international collusion of terrorist movements and the contagion of internal strife. The concept of 'legitimate defence' against these threats has been invoked to justify preventive operations, even those carried out without the backing of organised international processes (as in 2003 in Iraq). This has become a new theme of negotiation, the subject of angry debate in both the Security Council and the European Union, as well as of the recent report of the High Level Panel of the UN. (see *1722, 1800, 1807*)

1774 – In a world so dangerously unbalanced, matters will not be decided ultimately by victory or by military supremacy: fewer and fewer problems will be settled by armed force. The role played by war must be kept in check by the swift and extensive use of the powers of diplomacy.

In the present climate of international relations, there can be no resolution of major problems, even in the United Nations, without the approval and support of States, which, in the end, they will have to negotiate.

1775 – Where no other solution can be found, negotiation is not the same as peace: it becomes, instead, the most decisive and difficult phase of the conflict.[21] (see *225*)

Driven by the threat of wars of unprecedented horror, States are rediscovering the meaning and the role of negotiation. But few of them have completely mastered it, and few statesmen have the ability to exploit its true potential. (see *2538*)

§2. Conflict prevention

1776 – The more it builds, the more sensitive international society becomes to any threat to alter its balance by force. This risk is exacerbated by the arms race, both in qualitative and quantitative terms. There are some years when the total spending

---

20 'Les petits en toute affaire esquivent fort aisément; les grands ne le peuvent faire': J de la FONTAINE: *Le combat des rats et des belettes* (The fight between the rats and the weasels).
21 A. PLANTEY: 'Stratégie et negotiation diplomatique', *Revue africaine de stratégie*, 1979, 2, p. 17.

on weapons worldwide exceeds the gross national product of sizeable States, and the march of technology and its applications means that competition between States is continually stepped up. (see *1678*)

1777 – States endeavour to use international negotiation to ward off conflicts between them. In so doing, they are developing the organisational and prospective aspects of negotiating procedure as well as making progress in the field of disarmament. (see *716, 1745, 2091*)

In pursuit of this goal, the concept of arms control has driven modern negotiation in three directions: the use of observation, information and communications techniques to prevent 'accidental' wars; the prohibition or regulation of experiments in, as well as the dissemination and use of, weapons in order to restrict their availability; and, lastly, the path of careful and progressive disarmament. (see *2093*)

Implicit in the concept of effective security, negotiation provides a continuous, effective and lasting approach to every international issue, not only military, but also terrorism, trafficking, drugs and their financing, under the aegis of the UN Security Council (see the report of the Secretary General, March 2005).

Collective procedures

1778 – Ways and means can be devised of stabilising relations between States and keeping them peaceful. Therefore, international society must develop its capacities in terms of information, order and security. Investigative procedures and objective fact-finding techniques could be widely used. Tensions must be reduced and situations of potential conflict defused. The use of armed force must be prohibited, and hostilities nipped in the bud; arms control is necessary, and so, too, is institutionalised negotiation to eliminate the abuse of force. (see *1548, 1653*)

History reveals how little these initiatives have produced, and how unpredictable are their results. For example, even today, no institution, either at worldwide or regional level, has proved capable of preventing the appalling wars in Africa and the Middle East. (see *1784*)

1779 – After the First World War, some political doctrines saw collective international security as the answer to the recurring problem of war between nations. Article 10 of the League of Nations Pact set up a mutual guarantee of territorial integrity and political independence between all the signatories. (see *216, 1552*)

It was said at the time that, assuming a viable objective definition of foreign aggression could be found, this could lead to a universal sense of discipline that would force the protagonists to the negotiating table. (see *716*)

1780 – However, aside from what could be achieved by treaties of alliance, the duty to assist remained a dead letter, since there was no means either of determining how it should be implemented by deciding which party was the aggressor, or of setting out the objectives of an eventual mutual commitment. The League of Nations proved powerless to prevent attacks on China and, later, Ethiopia.

To this day, the vagueness and relativity of the concept of aggression mean there are no precise criteria for defining legitimate defence or collective security. (see *118, 1773*)

1781 – The failure of collective security, confirmed by the events that led up to the Second World War, showed how difficult, if not impossible, it was to draw nations that were not directly concerned into a bloody conflict, except where they were acting out of respect – never guaranteed – for alliances concluded for that precise purpose. Any deterrent effect of that system of diplomacy was bound to fail. (see *369*)

1782 – The United Nations continued to debate the subject of international conflict prevention and the collectivisation of security guarantees, with first the Security Council and then the General Assembly being granted powers, in 1950, to keep warring factions apart. In fact, though, maintaining and re-establishing peace both depend on the good will of the States concerned, and neither coercion nor condemnation will have any impact on those States once they have formed alliances and split into mutually hostile spheres of influence. (see *1654, 1748*)

When the matter or Iraq was first discussed in the Security Council in 1990, no veto was used. However, the recent war in Iraq has confirmed that the UN system can do nothing against the will of a great power determined to show its strength.

1783 – It might be thought that once local conflicts were absorbed into a wider perspective, they would be overtaken by the emergence of more complex balances of power and peace-making initiatives. But the aim to create global peace-keeping systems was defeated by divisive national strategies, either in the form of the pursuit of alliances, or attempts at regional organisations for peace in Europe, Africa and the Americas, or the consolidation of nuclear power. In reality, international organisations were not created to confront major risks. (see *858*)

At no time has the level of world harmony been adequate to replace diplomacy based on the balance of power and interests. (see *1553*)

1784 – As an essential part of international policing, the sending of observers or contingents itself depends on delicate negotiation, whether this takes place at the level of the member States of the United Nations, or whether it is done with the consent of the host State as to the objectives, terms and duration of the operation contemplated: successive interventions by the United Nations have shown the limits of peacemaking in a highly charged conflict situation.

Since the thaw in East-West relations, *the Security Council has pursued a general policy of intervention in the internal affairs of certain countries in crisis, thus relieving the major powers of the need to act.* The objectives are varied: interposition, policing of borders, providing humanitarian aid, re-establishing public order and administration of justice, enforcing a cease-fire or intervention by military contingents, often multinational. This was the case with Somalia in 1992, Haiti in 1994, the French 'Turquoise' operation in Rwanda in 1994, the Australian-led 'Interfit' mission in East Timor in 1999, and the interventions in Kosovo and Macedonia in the same year. (see *729, 745, 839, 1132, 1732, 1946*)

In 2005, intervention forces deployed worldwide under the aegis of the Security Council numbered about 70,000, drawn from 100 different countries.

Such are the risks associated with these operations that they must be accompanied by continuous negotiation, especially if they are to stay within the bounds that distinguish them from open warfare. (see *1750*)

Following the events in Afghanistan, the Security Council decided, in 2001, to send a military assistance force of 17 nationalities to Kabul (the ISAF) and, subsequently, extended the freezing of various funds and bank accounts to apply in UN member States with the possibility of referring to the Sanctions Committee.

The members of the Security Council, or the majority of them, have attempted to implement its resolutions imposing sanctions on trade with Iraq and Libya, among others, but the results of Security Council interventions have not met with universal approval. (see *1692*)

1785 – The example of the Kosovo crisis, in the former Yugoslavia, showed how difficult it is to set up negotiations in these situations. In practice, there have been two conflicting approaches: diplomatic and military. Many interventions were carried out under the United Nations flag by the great powers or their organisations: these included the EU, the WEU, the OSCE and NATO, a defensive alliance that has been a 'partner' of the EU since 1994. (see *1132, 1599*)

In 1999, the Security Council conferred responsibility for re-establishing peace and maintaining order in Kosovo on the multinational military units of KFOR, which at the time had 35,000 personnel drawn from some 30 countries, including 4,000 French. These units had the support of NATO, logistical support form Macedonia, and diplomatic support in the form of NATO agreements with Albania, Macedonia and finally Slovenia. They operated under the NATO Rules of Engagement, a system of rules governing military engagement and conduct.

The civil administration of the territory was put in the hands of the UNMIK Commission, managed by a special representative of the United Nations Secretary-General, with legislative and regulatory powers and a 3,000 strong police force, UNCIVPOL. The overlap between these two organisations compelled them to negotiate a Joint Declaration on power-sharing, issued on 17 August 2000. KFOR entered into logistical agreements with Yugoslavia-Serbia, and later with Slovenia.[22]

Both Yugoslav and international law are applicable in Kosovo, a territory with substantial autonomy according to Resolution 1244, but the laws of the intervening powers may also be invoked (thus, French law would apply to damage caused or sustained by French military detachments). Apart from the courts set up by UNMIK, the jurisdiction of the International Criminal Court has been recognised.

In this way, by a process of implicit negotiation, the United States and Russia have legitimised their military presence in the Balkans. (see *17, 695, 946, 1171, 1786, 1894, 2229*)

1786 – Powers both large and small deal with each other direct, international institutions having neither the credibility to bring peace nor the strength to enforce it.

22 S. SUR: 'L'affaire du Kosovo et le droit international', *AFDI*, 1999, p. 280. E. LAGRANGE: 'La mission intérimaire des Nations unies au Kosovo', ibid., p. 335.

This principle should inform nuclear diplomacy, a field where the risk of destruction is greater, and could arise in the territory of any country on earth. (see *1661*)

A collective security agreement was drawn up at the Tashkent Conference in May 1992, under the Community of Independent States that succeeded the Soviet Union, but it was never entirely clear which were the parties to it. (see *987*)

In Africa, groups of States have undertaken peacemaking or peacekeeping operations, without much success, despite the intervention having the agreement of the governments concerned and a limited degree of support from the Security Council. Within the African Union, a proposal has been made to set up a Council for Peace and Security, which would in theory have the power to sanction unconstitutional changes within the member States.

Organised procedures have thus not supplanted direct negotiation, even on those issues within the statutory competence of the institutions, or where the reason for intervening is the preservation of peace or the protection of human rights.

The only role that remains for these processes is to provide a sort of preliminary round or context for confrontation, by allowing third parties to intervene to keep the peace: in other words, they open up another field for negotiation.

Disarmament

1787 – The issue of arms limitation was first raised, unsuccessfully as it turned out, about a century ago. The work of the Hague Conferences of 1899 and 1907 was taken up by the League of Nations, whose Pact provided for arms limitation but whose successive initiatives were to fail. The intentions set out in the Atlantic Charter of 1941 were later enshrined in the UN Charter. A procession of commissions, committees, conferences and assemblies followed, all of them devoted to the subject, some of them under the auspices of the United Nations and some outside it, along with studies and plans for general disarmament or the demilitarisation of certain zones. These efforts fell foul of national ambitions and ideologies, interests and entrenched habits. (see *150*)

1788 – It is not acceptable from the standpoint of diplomacy for détente and cooperation between the great powers to depend entirely on the fact that stocks of nuclear weapons have reached the level where war becomes impossible, or that other countries, too, are moving unchecked in the direction of over-armament with its potential to aggravate the pervasive instability of the modern world.

1789 – Multilateral negotiation must thus extend beyond the scope of bilateral discussions and point the way to agreements enabling regulation of the sale and production of weapons, of transfers of military technology and the military applications of science.

Regulation of arms sales can only partly be achieved by conventions on the laws of war. Account must also be taken of advances in the fields of science and technology.

1790 – The spread of weapons of all kinds is set to become one of the major themes of international negotiation: ways must be found to limit the misappropriation of resources that are required to satisfy the normal daily needs of mankind, and thereby limit the potential of States for aggression. As an example, the implementation of the Non-Proliferation Treaty is subject to periodic review by international conferences. (see *1729, 1741*)

Disarmament can only be negotiated if the fundamental principle of the balance of power is respected. (see *147, 150, 154*)

1791 – Spending on weapons breeds confrontation, not only because it provides even developing countries with the means of waging war, but because it consumes vital resources, both human and material.

If these expenses could be successfully reduced or limited through multilateral negotiation, it would free up considerable sums to be channelled into economic and social progress, especially in the developing world. France proposed, without success, that a Disarmament Fund for Development be set up, to use the money saved from arms programmes.

1792 – The goals and methods of negotiation must therefore be adapted to suit the dimensions of the problem. Negotiation must be constant and widespread, and this requires an institutional framework. The United Nations could probably fulfil this need, though its financial and technical capacities might sometimes prove inadequate to the task.

Article 26 of the Charter provides for a system of arms regulation, and the theme of disarmament has been the subject of several debates in the General Assembly. The Disarmament Conference has become the main, if not the only, venue for multilateral negotiation on the subject. The fact remains, though, that most of the progress made in this area has been dependent on the prior agreement of the great powers. The 'Agenda for Peace' proposed by the UN Secretary General has had no impact. (see *1728*)

As for the prohibition of anti-personnel mines (Ottawa, 2 December 1997), 121 countries voted in its favour, but others, including the United States, Russia or China, did not: it has had no effect whatever.

1793 – Second-line States inevitably seek to circumvent the dialogue between the major powers: they want the benefit of the security guarantees they claim as of right, even when the major powers are more interested in preserving their own freedom to manoeuvre. (see *146*)

In Europe, there have been initiatives aimed at reducing the risks resulting from the accumulation of weapons. Various discussions were held in Vienna in 1973 and again in 1989 between alliances on the reduction in conventional forces, but nothing came of them. These negotiations were later brought under the auspices of the CSCE. Under this mandate, an agreement on the reduction and balance of conventional armed forces in Europe was signed in Paris by 23 countries on 19 November 1990, after almost two years of negotiation, and amended on 23 July 1997 at the request of Russia, bringing the number of signatories up to 30. It issues precise figures for the maximum levels of arms for every State between the Atlantic and the Urals.[23] (see *175*)

---

23 J. CHARPENTIER: 'Le pacte de stabilité en Europe', *AFDI*, 1995, p. 199.

1794 – There will be no arms limitation until there are procedures whereby tensions and disputes between States can be reliably defused, taking account of geographic, economic and cultural reality: these negotiations are mutually dependent. For this reason, it was a positive step to use diplomacy (as was done at the 1986 Stockholm Conference) to adopt measures aimed at ensuring greater transparency and confidence in military decisions and operations. (see *1799*)

1795 – A succession of initiatives followed, such as the plan presented by France to the United Nations in 1971, to hand over the monitoring of implementation of disarmament agreements to an international satellite agency whose mission would be to use intelligence made available by States, in the first instance, and later by observation satellites funded by governments that were members of the agency or used its services. By making this international, it should be possible to preserve the independence of the agency's intelligence-gathering function, and hence its judgment, thus promoting the levels of trust necessary for long-term security. It remains to be seen whether satellites are capable of supplying images of a sufficiently high quality to enable miniature, hidden or mobile weapons and instruments to be detected and counted.

Follow-up mechanisms will appear, along the lines contemplated in the European treaties on conventional weapons, to ensure all parties are heard when disarmament measures are taken, particularly with regard to transparency, verifications and inspections. The effect of this will be to prolong the negotiating process. (see *946, 1735, 1880, 1884*)

1796 – There has been a movement to exclude certain definable zones from military and nuclear competition: the deep seabed (Treaties of 11 February 1971), outer space (Treaty of 27 January 1967),[24] celestial bodies (Treaty of 18 December 1979), Antarctica (Treaty of Washington, 1 December 1959), Latin America (Treaty of Tlatelolco, 14 November 1967), the Indian Ocean (UNGA Resolution 2832 of 16 December 1971, confirmed in 2000), the South Pacific (Treaty of Rarotonga, 6 August 1985), South-East Asia (Treaty of Bangkok, 15 December 1995), Africa (Treaty of Palindabe, 19 April 1996), and also Poland, Hungary and the Czech Republic (1996).[25]

1797 – Strategic negotiation will be needed, too, to set limits on other types of high-technology activity, as soon as their military applications begin to pose too great a threat. This has already happened in the case of biological weapons: 148 States are parties to the Treaty of 10 April 1972, which updated the system set up under the 1925 Geneva Convention. As to chemical weapons, Russia and the United States signed an agreement on 1 June 1990, the UN General Assembly passed a resolution on 30 November 1992, and 130 States signed the Paris Convention of 15 January 1993. Discussions are ongoing with regard to certain types of satellites and delivery systems, since the signing of the European Declaration against the Proliferation of Ballistic Missiles in Gothenburg in 2001. (see *1706*)

---

24 T. GARCIN: *Les Enjeux stratégiques de l'espace*, Brussels, Bruylant, 2001.
25 S. SUR, etc: *Le Droit international des armes nucléaires*, Paris, Pedone, 1998.

The elimination of certain types of weapons, in particular nuclear, poses extremely difficult financial, industrial and technical issues, not only because of waste but also because of the cost of converting missiles, bombs, mines and miscellaneous other items into harmless or re-usable material. (see *1685*)

1798 – In future, negotiation will be used in the service of a new discipline: the publication by governments of information on the presence of forces for the purposes of allowing control by public opinion and elected representatives. This will have the added benefit of reducing the level of anxiety on the part of the protagonists, one factor in the escalation of conflict.

By making their intentions known before their interests are threatened, governments will also be helping to reduce the distrust born out of fear of the unknown. (see *2030*)

1799 – Ways must be found for States to acquire military and strategic intelligence about each other, aside from secret verifications the results of which can rarely be used: other possible ways could be opened up by negotiation, including voluntary, even-handed and multilateral exchanges of information on budgets, forces and command structures, as well as future military movements and exercises (see the Treaty of Helsinki of 24 March 1992). (see *2210, 2028, 2239*)

The Western European Union has drawn up voluntary procedures for the verification of the type and numbers of weapons. (see *925*)

Set up in 1958, the International Atomic Energy Agency (IAEA) serves as the instrument for monitoring compliance with nuclear non-proliferation obligations (see the 1997 Protocol on application of the NPT), thanks to its permanent powers of inspection. Use of these powers is sometimes the subject of subsequent negotiation, as was the case both in Iraq and Iran (2003–2005).[26] (see *1729, 1741*)

In 2005, after seven years of negotiation, the United Nations General Assembly unanimously adopted a Convention for the Suppression of Acts of Nuclear Terrorism.

Published in 2004, the report '*A more secure world: Our shared responsibility*' prepared by the UN High-Level Panel on Threats, Challenges and Change, appointed by the Secretary General, contained about a hundred proposals and recommendations on these subjects. It concluded that, in practice, the unilateral use of force cannot be condemned in cases of imminent threat, but that in other cases the Security Council would have the deterrent power and capability to intervene in the interests of collective security. In implementation of one proposal, a Peace-Building Commission was set up in December 2005, as a subsidiary organ of the Security Council but with a broader composition, with the aim of preventing countries relapsing into conflict.

In reality, what States expect from the United Nations is that it will confer legitimacy on them and support their actions.

1800 – The international strategic complex is characterised by two concomitant phenomena: the increasing exclusiveness of certain technology, and the

26 J. CLERCKX: *La Vérification de l'élimination de l'arme chimique*, LGDJ, 2001.

uncontrolled accumulation of weapons. These phenomena are in contradiction, since the first tends to contribute to balance, while the second does not. But their combined effect is to make the idea of a complete moratorium an illusion in the short term, and to divert effort from the necessary development of numerous countries.

1801 – There is a risk that the same could happen with any negotiation on traditional disarmament. Aside from programmes and proposals, the real purpose of such negotiation will emerge – multilateral legislative cooperation to impose rules and limits concerning weapons and conditions for their use. *It is not the place of negotiation to prohibit technological progress, but to enable its effects to be discussed.*

The suggestion was made in the G8 that the way to eliminate vast stockpiles of weapons, disarm and withdraw nuclear submarines and combat illegal and dangerous arms trafficking was by partnership. Responding to these concerns has a price, especially in terms of the precautions and safeguards involved – insurance, for example – for governments as well as the private sector. Negotiations on security are set to become more and more difficult. (see *1757*)

1802 – It will never be possible to eliminate intolerable situations or conflicts, but new means of prevention and regulation must be found that will allow them to run their course without leading to destruction. A proposal has been made within the OSCE for a code of conduct for States to be drawn up, including all the norms necessary for mutual trust and collective security.

However, as a result of the slow and sometimes unseen progression of ideologies, new threats are appearing that use the basic stuff of everyday life such as air, water, transport and the internet to foment the risk of nuclear, chemical, biological or technological damage on a scale that will render national frontiers obsolete. New dialectics that leave no room for traditional strategy, and new logistics based on networks and the propaganda of terrorism, require States to negotiate together about the disciplines of administration and policing, and require their justice, finance and technical functions to organise joint governmental responses, including private support. (see *335, 345, 1693*)

New types of crises, conflicts and balances of power can be expected to appear. Goals, as well as the means of attaining them, must be decided by diplomatic manoeuvres, more sophisticated than anything seen before: these negotiations must be conducted without delay, and their effects must be durable. (see *2091*)

Science will not only provide new tools and methods for resolving these crises, but also generate new subjects and goals for negotiation. (see *2093*)

Chapter II:
The Increasing Complexity of International Relations

1803 – If a global system of international relations indeed exists, any attempt to define it would exceed the capacities of the human imagination. *On the other hand, it is clear that the great challenges civilisation now faces are worldwide in their impact, and the social and economic environment carries great weight in State strategy.* States see their freedom of movement diminishing, while the main issues of the day call for a greater degree of mutual cooperation, even in areas where they may be capable of self-sufficiency.

In 2000, the Heads of State and government and members and the United Nations met for the Millennium Summit, with the stated aim of working for a decade to combat poverty, disease and injustice. When they met again after four years it was apparent that very little had been achieved. (see *401, 2255, 2302, 2328*)

1804 – Signs of a change in the world economy were already present in the oil crisis of 1973, but could have been predicted as long ago as the end of the Second World War, with its upheavals in production, trade and currencies and also in the persistent financial and technological disparities between nations, some of them newly independent. Each government responded with solutions geared to the immediate problem, but on a scale that was inadequate to address the dangers.

In a shrinking world, more fields are opening up to negotiation: States can no longer take refuge behind their frontiers. Military, monetary and language barriers are being eroded, and numerous practices becoming standardised or codified. As a proportion of national resources, trade is growing faster than production.

1805 – Competition in the fields of economy and technology is sharpened by ideological and political conflicts, thus sovereignty is, to some degree, at stake in all negotiations. Too often, both the thoughts and actions of leaders and negotiators are characterised by fear or cunning, doubt or mistrust. Too often, also, negotiations degenerate into barter, in the absence of any stable common values. (see *383, 483, 1921*)

The need for trade in products, services and human resources has made competition, and its corollary, negotiation, overriding themes in modern life. The search for investments, the cost and the power of science and innovation and the profit-making imperative weigh heavily on society, businesses and States alike.[1]

The United Nations has acknowledged the importance of civil society in international life. It encourages the participation of non-government entities in

---

1 C. BARTLETT and S. GHOSHAL: *Managing Across Borders, the Transnational Solution*, London, 1989.

international relations. The UN Global Compact was adopted in Davos in 1999, to promote corporate citizenship in the world economy, and its first summit took place in New York in 2004. (see *1826*)

1806 – The uncertainties resulting from financial expansion and the increase in transnational criminality undermine the trust, stability and openness that are the essential preconditions for all diplomatic negotiation. Technological progress is another destabilising factor.

Faced with a radical redistribution of economic power and international trade, so far-reaching that it will alter the existing balance between the continents, the world needs not only constant dialogue between States, but also institutions, rules and procedures that are capable of responding to the collective challenges.

Freedom of exchange is the way of the future, but it presupposes security: this depends on the collective power of States, provided it is exercised effectively and responsibly. (see *1706, 2704*)

1807 – International negotiation must address the major issues of national fragility and future security, amid increasing global turbulence. It is easy to see why developments in negotiation are driven by circumstance and marked by informality, with the main emphasis on commitments as to future conduct, projects and forward-looking collective initiatives. International economic law, the product of these negotiations, has been defined as conditional, voluntary law. The same would hold for international cultural norms. (see *1539, 1959*)

The weakening of international frontiers, the role of new information and communication technologies, the growing proportion of trade that is unlawful or even criminal and the power of transnational influences make it more complicated to know where the decision-making power lies, with the result that it tends to be concentrated in a few countries, or even in a few hands.[2] At the same time, these very factors make it more and more vital for States to agree on new disciplines where they can, particularly in fields where national sovereignty has to give way, such as the sea, space, telecommunications and the environment. (see *1914*)

The coalescence of economies and technologies worldwide serves as a counterweight to military dislocation; this explains the importance of the WTO negotiations. However, it has to be said that, since the end of the Uruguay Round in 1993, attempts at dialogue have been frustrated by different cultural approaches.

Section 1: Transnational factors

1808 – Mankind is starting to become aware of the fact that the worldwide biological environment is fragile and finite: some observers are even forecasting catastrophe. Protecting the natural environment has become a matter of international concern: the dimensions and the severity of the problem are such that it has passed beyond the reach of any government to resolve. (see *2260*)

---

2 M. HARDT and A. NEGRI: *Empire*, Paris, Exils, 2000. R. GILPIN: *Political Economy of International Relations*, New York, Princeton University Press, 1987.

1809 – This has given a vigorous new perspective to multilateral negotiations, but brought no immediate success. The Stockholm Conference in June 1972, under the aegis of the United Nations, produced 106 recommendations; the ministerial level meeting of the Environmental Committee of the OECD in November 1974 produced an overall recommendation, supplemented in May 1976, and in Helsinki in 1975, the Conference on Security and Cooperation in Europe devoted a special section of its final Act of 1 August 1975 to the subject. Hundreds of participants attended the 'Earth summit' conference in 1992 in Rio, and there followed conferences on climate change in Kyoto and subsequently in Buenos Aires, The Hague, Marrakech, Johannesburg and Hong Kong. (see *2193*)

1810 – The economic system, too, is becoming more consistent year by year, as technical advances lead national systems to integrate into larger ones. International negotiation is needed to ensure that this process goes forward with due regard for the requirements of national sovereignty and the need for balance between States. This is especially true as experience shows the extent to which economic instability can bring about political risks and diplomatic changes: so severe were the effects of the Great Depression in 1929 that it can even be held responsible for the rise in totalitarianism and, in part, for the Second World War.

Globalisation manifests itself especially in the breadth and speed of large-scale speculation and the contagious effect of financial and economic crises. It works in favour of modern economies based on flexibility and diversification of services.

1811 – The eruption of new information and communications technology has overtaken the traditional practice of diplomacy. Changes in the diplomatic environment show up in the cultural and social fields, where some of the upheavals or crises originate that alter the balance of power and the future of nations, especially where the media are concerned. Science, too, is a universal phenomenon, and its effects know no borders: the teams and technologies at the leading edge in all manner of fields are international. The United Nations has tried to address this new social dimension in its Millennium Goals.

However, the increasing unification of the global economy has not diminished the profound cultural diversities between nations; on the contrary, it aggravates local or latent conflicts.[3] (see *1750, 2249*)

§1. The multinational economy

1812 – One clear sign of how cohesive the global environment has become is the extent to which the economy has become multinational, a phenomenon well known today by the somewhat exaggerated name of 'globalisation'. By design as well as by effect, it operates to bring States together either to minimise or eliminate commercial frontiers, or in associations of countries that are economically, geographically or culturally interdependent. Examples are the European Union, the NAFTA in North America, the Cuzco Conference in South America, the ASEAN in Asia and NEPAD in Africa. (see *1449, 2279*)

3 J. -M. LUSTIGER: 'Ethique et mondialisation', *Politique étrangère*, 1999, 4, p. 99.

Private and public sector entities such as oil companies also play a role in long-term strategies as well as in tactical competitiveness: national policy uses them in ways that include financing, forming alliances and partnerships, investment, mergers and bringing companies under State control. (see *1829, 2302, 2307*)

1813 – For businesses that are able to do so, having centres of activity in several countries can, depending on their knowledge of the people and the place, the guarantees they are offered locally, their use of local resources, the extent of their business and financial networks and the tax incentives offered by the governments concerned, form part of a strategy that uses all the advantages the international environment can offer to drive their financial, industrial and technological expansion.[4] (see *55*)

The mobility and delocalisation of services, leading to the denationalisation of private and even public capitalism, have major implications for international negotiation. They favour the redistribution of investment, markets and responsibilities. But they can also serve as an umbrella for trafficking and interference, even in sports, thus forcing governments to negotiate ways of controlling them, where possible. (see *390, 1626, 1678, 1826, 1932*)

1814 – Although this global dynamism is of ancient origin, it has generated a rich variety of contemporary writing. Some movements hold it responsible for many of the worst malaises of modern society, viewing it as an extreme and appalling manifestation of large-scale capitalism. On another analysis, transnationalism is one factor in an economic strategy that might allow nations to integrate peacefully into a future international environment. (see *387, 403, 1862, 1885, 2303*)

1815 – Some of these corporations occupy a place among the leading world powers, by virtue of their turnover, subsidiaries, information networks, financial and technological potential and the quality of their management: there are States whose authority seems feeble and outdated by comparison. Their flexibility in responding to the changing environment, their capacity to adapt to restrictive or excessive national demands and their ability to mobilise massive resources in terms of funds, techniques and knowledge to undertake their own projects, means that no one State can hope to control either them or their profits for long. (see *1680*)

In addition, the location of its headquarters allows each business to choose the legal regime that will govern it, as well as the courts to which it will be subject. These can be decisive factors in a negotiation. Similarly, the choice of where to establish its business will be made on the basis of a cost-benefit analysis that the corporation may avoid discussing with the national authorities.[5] It is a well-known fact, too, that there are some sixty tax havens – territories and islands where innumerable companies are registered with the agreement of the government – of which around a dozen are in Europe. (see *1627, 1819*)

1816 – Among the effects of this 'multinationalisation' of the economy are the increasing complexity of trade flows, the delocalisation of businesses and their

---

4 N. BOUKHARINE: *L'Economie mondiale et l'impérialisme*, Moscow, 1917; Paris, 1971.
5 *Rapport moral sur l'argent dans le monde*, Association d'économie financière, Paris, 2005.

finances and the law that applies to them, the externalisation of services and the general availability of information, meaning that high-value activities are no longer at the service of national goals or disciplines. It is easy to see, then, how difficult it is for such a complex and mutant phenomenon to be integrated into the framework of international negotiation. (see *2029*)

On the government side, their inability to deal collectively with issues as serious and wide-ranging as energy, the environment, the trafficking in organs, drugs, medicines and even human beings, as well as that of human migration, is a potential source of major risks and conflicts. (see *1824*)

1817 – Because of their means, large corporations and public agencies hold in their hands the beginnings of the power of global regulation. Their natural propensity is to bargain, sometimes secretly, in their own interests. They influence relations between States without needing to pass through national diplomatic channels, while the States themselves, anxious to keep control of their own strategy, no longer agree to be bound by such manoeuvres even when they include certain companies in their plans for national expansion.

The majority of development projects are now international, bringing together suppliers, engineers, bankers, insurers and clients from a variety of countries. Governments cannot remain indifferent to their success, nor to the disputes that can arise, which, if badly managed, can draw the States in so that each one considers itself the defender and champion of its own nationals, as if it were the agent of public opinion where important matters are at stake.

1818 – Responsible for over half the world's financial and trading transactions, multinational corporations are usually organised in complex networks, often disguised, around the centres of decision-making, most often located in their country of origin: many negotiations are carried on under this umbrella.[6] The increasing value of service industries, the mobility of higher levels of management, distance-working and the free flow of capital and information all serve to accelerate this trend to internationalisation, which inhibits the strategic and decision-making capabilities of States.

The temptations of hegemony are no longer confined to the military sphere.[7]

With establishments in several countries, these corporations are able to intervene in more or less clandestine ways, especially in government foreign policy. Ever since the time of the East India Companies, they have pursued their objectives by whatever means they think fit, independent of national policy directives, manoeuvring to promote their own interests. Cases of corruption have arisen that have had significant political and diplomatic ramifications.

---

6 P. JACQUET: 'Nouvelle économie, du virtuel au réel', *RAMSES 2001*. S. KUBRIN: 'The Architecture of Globalisation', in *Government, Globalisation and International Business*, Oxford, 1997.

7 R. KEHANC: *After Hegemony, Cooperation and Discord in the World Political Economy*, Princeton, 1984. *La mondialisation entre illusion et utopie*, Dalloz, Paris, 2003. P. JURGENSEN: *L'Erreur de l'Occident, face à la mondialisation*, Paris, O. Jacob, 2004.

1819 – The weakening of certain States, whose frontiers operate as restrictions on their own power but not on that of others, reinforces dominance from outside. Multinational corporations play a decisive role in international trade, because they control the market in many of the major sources of industrial production in mining, oil, mechanical engineering, chemicals, pharmaceuticals, foodstuffs and also in the cultural field; they account for almost half of the exports of the countries of the South. Whether intentionally or not, in practice they contribute to the dominance of certain States. Some three hundred corporations are responsible for one quarter of the entire production of Western countries, but there are thousands of others, including some mid-size concerns. The amount of speculative financing involved is beyond calculation: there are thousands of funds managing billions of dollars, most of it placed on the New York markets. (see *375, 382, 386, 1932*)

1820 – Because these corporations have business activities in a number of different countries, a major proportion of technical, financial and commercial transactions is conducted outside the realms of international negotiation: perhaps as much as one-third of all world trade. (It has also been estimated that one-tenth of gross product worldwide comes from unlawful international trade.) Corporations wish to retain complete control of these exchanges, which are not only vital components of their strategy, but generators of major profits.

1821 – The networks created by multinational corporations by their frequent contacts, open or otherwise, are not limited to the sphere of economics, finance and technology: they allow data to be discreetly transferred to centres for storage and processing outside any governmental control, and beyond the reach of international conventions on property or moral rights such as patents and trade marks or national copyright laws. Flows of information occur that would be of enormous benefit to the negotiator having access to them; *they generate poles of decision-making and activity that can sometimes upset the balance of diplomatic negotiation.* (see *2029*)

1822 – Some partners in the private sector are more powerful, entrepreneurial and interesting as interlocutors than official representatives: governments sometimes have to deal with foreign companies almost on the same footing as they do with independent States. While the contracts they enter into do not have the legal force of diplomatic treaties,[8] they can sometimes create interdependence that affects every aspect of a country's diplomacy. The way they are managed, and the disputes that can arise, sometimes brings the will of the contracting parties into conflict with the sovereign wishes of the State. This happened, for instance, with the many disputes over oil.

As for high finance, it long ago freed itself from accountability to State power or diplomacy, and often from any requirements of transparency. (see *1828, 2307*)

1823 – By making use of private companies, dominant powers can secure for themselves sources of information, energy and raw materials, leading-edge

---

8 NGUYEN QUOC DINH, P. DAILLER and A. PELLET: *Droit international public*, Paris, LGDJ, 1992, p. 116.

technology, supplies and weaponry, the control of which serves to deprive many other governments of a large part of their diplomatic autonomy.[9] (see *373, 2031*)

On the other hand, the presence, in their territory, of major foreign companies has enhanced the resources as well as the potential influence and negotiating power of a number of countries with growing economies in Asia and the Americas.

1824 – Anxious to face up to the dangers that can result from the interference of transnational corporations, all States, even the most powerful, will have to agree on the disciplines to be imposed on these businesses, and give assurances that they will respect each others' political sovereignty.

This will be no easy task, since many governments are in competition rather than negotiation with each other when faced with the power wielded by industrial or financial groups, a situation that suits the tactics of many private sector companies.

The FATF (Financial Action Task Force) has drawn up a series of standards and specific recommendations to assist in the fight against money laundering, unlawful trading and terrorism. The French agency TRACFIN, set up following a G7 meeting in 1983 in Paris, implements these, in close coordination with agencies in other countries. (see *1049, 1519, 1819*)

1825 – One of the tasks confronting international negotiation, then, will be the difficult one of bringing entities under control whose very raison d'être is to avoid it. This might involve renegotiating trade, tax or financial agreements, or the redistribution of activities around the world based on criteria other than the imperatives of short-term profit. Precautions must be put in place to discourage certain practices that arise in the course of inter-State relations: discriminatory practices, the transfer of funds, data, technology and manpower, currency manipulation, tax exemptions, misappropriation of funds, financial violations, counterfeiting, speculative manoeuvres and political racketeering.

1826 – Laying down the general outline of a definition and form for multinational corporations is proving a difficult task, since the interests of States can be very different in this regard. After difficult negotiations the OECD Council adopted guidelines in 1976 for use in the context of the market economy; these are very general in nature, but the organisation has updated them and monitors how they are implemented through the national laws and administrations of its member States. (see *2210*)

In Davos in 1999, a Global Economic Forum of heads of major companies, with the participation of certain political and media figures, adopted the Global Compact, later endorsed by the United Nations, with the aim of enforcing respect for human rights, applying international labour conventions, respecting the environment and (an addition in 2004) condemning corruption. This commitment was restated in New York in 2004 and Paris in 2005. (see *1804*)

1827 – For their part, many multinational entities seek to influence the research, debates and programmes of the major international organisations, fearing the adoption of positions unfavourable to them. (see *1516, 2285*)

9 R. ARON: *République impériale. Les Etats-Unis dans le monde*, Paris, Calmann-Lévy, 1973.

Other multinationals lend their support to separatist movements, anarchist groups or fundamentalists in the course of building their networks. (see *1678*)

1828 – The phenomenon of multinationalisation continues to spread, with a variety of consequences that contribute towards global integration. These include the development of emerging systems of business law, increasingly delocalised and self-determined, a growing coordination in the attitude of trade unions, the worldwide dissemination of economic information through the media, the spread of products and technology, the standardisation of rules and languages, the formation of public opinion and the international perspective of communication and negotiation. Increased freedom of the press can be used to advantage in revealing the existence of underhandedness or corruption against the wishes of those involved, and this can have a deterrent effect.[10] (see *1821*)

1829 – Inequalities in the growth and speed of economic and technical development are opening the way to a new geography of power in the world. Markets, resources and activities are changing radically, in themselves and among countries, thus exacerbating the gulf between developed and developing nations and the others. (see *1978*)

As they take the measure of the competitive expansion of major corporations, emerging and developing countries are becoming more cohesive in their criticism of the growing liberalisation of trade under the WTO programme: forthcoming negotiations in this area risk turning into serious confrontations, if the disputes surrounding some pharmaceutical products are a reliable indication. (see *1102, 1627, 1931, 1955, 1969, 1979*)

Globalisation itself is the source of acute contention. (see *385, 1812, 1969, 1976*)

1830 – Though they may reject the idea, consideration should be given to involving major multinational corporations in government negotiations. They can produce information and arguments that will enhance the chances of success, in addition to their present and prospective contacts. They would also be implicated in executing whatever may be agreed: the multilateral commercial negotiations leading to the lifting of customs restrictions showed this to be the case. The Great Powers understood this very well.

1831 – Now that they are *de facto* players on the international scene, it is up to multinational corporations to abide by the rules and assume the responsibilities of the difficult game they have entered. The increase in illicit trade will inevitably force them to do. (see *1814, 1824, 1961*)

As a result of the development of international commercial arbitration, many of the disputes between such entities can be resolved without becoming enmeshed in intergovernmental rivalries.[11]

---

10 F. FLANNAGAN, A. R. WEBER, etc. *Bargaining without Boundaries*, Illinois, Chicago University Press, 1974.
11 A. PLANTEY: 'L'arbitrage dans le commerce international', *AFDI*, 1990, p. 307.

§2. *Cultural* rapprochement

1832 – Culture and ideology are not bounded by the legal or economic frontiers between States: they are expressions of the inner life and motivation of human groupings, with a direct impact on the individual and the masses alike. Improved communications facilities serve to increase their influence, despite the measures taken by some States to protect themselves. Among the forces that permeate the internal life of nations more or less deeply, as well as the conduct of their mutual relations, are religious ecumenism, the widespread recourse to ecological or humanitarian principles and international political, labour or cultural movements. (see *1680, 2213*)

1833 – Negotiating parties are thus obliged to take account of these influences, even where they have their the origins or centre in other countries. Their effects are felt over a broad span of different territories and peoples, giving rise to new forms of interdependence and joint action.[12]

The treatment of national minorities, while a source of dreadful conflict, can serve as a powerful stimulant to negotiations between neighbouring States. This is evident from the agreements concluded between some of the States of Central Europe, such as the treaty of cooperation between Hungary and Romania signed in 1995, the joint German-Czech declaration of 1997, and the border negotiation between Russia and Estonia in 2005. (see *76*)

1834 – On the other hand, the field of diplomacy is strewn with information and signals that influence, directly or otherwise, how negotiations are prepared, conducted and concluded. The current view is that any entity or even individual whose message crosses borders, or has a significant impact, even if only at the internal level, becomes an actor in international relations. (see *16*)

The extraordinary advances in telecommunications, in terms of both speed and quality, and the widespread use of the Internet, have had the effect of increasing the level of cohesion in the international environment. So, too, has the influence of certain models, signs or conduct which the negotiator must factor in, while ensuring that the fundamental cultural underpinnings of his work are not forgotten or neglected as events succeed each other under the media spotlight.

1835 – In practice, international negotiation can only flourish if it respects the basic values of civilisation.[13] (see *2048*)

Some international institutions such as UNESCO were created precisely with a view to satisfying the universal need for cultural exchange and development.

1836 – In negotiation, the culture of each country must be respected insofar as it contains a system of human relations, norms, values, signs and unspoken

---

12 J. W. FELD: *Non-Governmental Forces and World Politics*, New York, Praeger, 1972. J. NYE and R. KEOHANE: *Transnational Relations and World Politics*, Cambridge, MA, Harvard University Press, 1972. S. MACBRIDE, etc. *Many Voices, One World*, UNESCO, 1980.
13 A. PLANTEY: 'Pour une approche culturelle de la négociation internationale', *Revue internationale des sciences sociales*, UNESCO, 1981.

language.[14] The necessary communication between groups and individuals can only be effective where these factors are correctly interpreted. (see *508*)

Such is the force of cultural differences, prejudices included, that they can override economic and technical cooperation between States.

It is by contrast with others that each civilisation affirms its own identity. Communication is not, by definition, a peaceful affair.[15]

1837 – Negotiation is also the vehicle by which civilisations advance in all their diversity, and it has been thus since the earliest times: the roots of Greek artistic influence in Germany can be traced back to the marriage of Emperor Otto II to the Byzantine Princess Theophania, in 972. *The cultural and ideological dynamic, enhanced by increased access to information, can inject new vigour into the practice of negotiation.* (see *2644*)

1838 – With the multiplication of dealings between nations, negotiation serves not only as a means of giving expression to cultures in all their diversity, but also to ensure that they are not harmed by conflict or destroyed, which would damage the wealth of civilisations and the stability of relations between the different groups.

A worldwide market in cultures is taking shape, involving events and tourism, art and literature, *objets d'art*, artistic productions, images and personalities, in which nations compete in promoting their ethnic, cultural and linguistic identities through a variety of lucrative businesses.[16]

1839 – The extension of negotiation, including ever more diverse partners, alters its traditional formal conventions by requiring the cohabitation and reconciliation of widely different value systems, which often are ignorant of, or hostile to, each other, but all of which deserve respect and protection. (see *2054*)

1840 – Despite the ease of communication between countries, their respective mentalities are still very different. Or perhaps it is rather because of communications that these differences play an increasing role and can turn into opposition or rivalry.

Many are the conflicts that have been triggered or exacerbated by the lack of a common language between the protagonists. (see *2049*)

The globalised international environment shows how easy it is to disseminate the ideas, images and irrational fears that hamper negotiations.

1841 – Collective perceptions have implications for politics and diplomacy. Western civilisations place a high value on reason and expression, while others emphasise feeling and impressions. Some function by allusion and implicit communication, others by feats of oratory. (see *511*)

1842 – When moral forces and ideological imperatives come together they can enlighten the negotiation and strengthen the agreement. Where they are

---

14 E. T. HALL: *The Silent Language*, New York, New York University Press, 1959.
15 D. SCHNAPPER: *La Relation à l'Autre au coeur de la pensée sociologique*, Paris, Gallimard, 1998.
16 C. TAYLOR: *Multiculturalism*, Paris, Flammarion, 1997. G. LECLERC: *La Mondialisation culturelle*, Paris, PUF, 2000.

incompatible, the resulting agreements can be unpredictable, uncertain and fraught with risk. The more distant the relations, the greater the danger. With the collapse of totalitarian regimes, cultural antagonisms have appeared – or resurfaced – that have complicated, if not paralysed, the establishment of harmonious diplomatic relations between certain States.

1843 – The exercise of diplomacy is neither one of philosophy nor morals: its goals and methods reflect the interplay of the predispositions of nations and leaders.[17]

Everything in the negotiating process, from the choice of terminology to the contents of the agreement, is determined by the underlying cultural diversity or affinity of the parties. (see *2051*)

1844 – Negotiation can only be meaningful or worthwhile where the nations and individuals concerned are not so far removed from each other or so antagonistic that no understanding is possible between them. This makes it part of the duties of the diplomat to pay due attention to the cultural environment of the host country. (see *511*)

International movements in civil society can serve either to assist or hinder a negotiation, depending on the image they convey of a nation or an ideology. (see *2167*)

1845 – The negotiator must also be mindful of customs and impressions. Where one makes statements that are brief and direct, others might take this as a sign of lack of intelligence or tact. Cutting short a discussion could be interpreted by some as a gesture of arrogance and contempt, or as a sign that one is too easily satisfied.

1846 – Refusal to make a commitment for the future is not always a sign of disagreement, reservation or underhandedness. It can simply be a mark of respect and fear of divine will. (see *513*)

1847 – It is easy to see why negotiation is made considerably easier where strong ties exist between the nations involved, whether they consist of a common language, the presence of immigrant populations or elites, common sensibilities, ideology or religion, or particular relations between their dominant political structures. (see *860, 2049*)

1848 – Knowledge of different civilisations is a precondition for the harmonisation of national laws undertaken by international organisations with a view to facilitating trade and standardising regulations. The entire legal edifice of the European Union rests on a shared legal history, and the same tendency can be seen in South America. (see *2007*)

1849 – There can be no lasting union between peoples unless their cultures are in harmony. Age-old conflicts or dealings between certain nations have progressively forged links that provide the foundation on which they can safely build new relations in different spheres. This is evident from the experiences of Europe, the

---

17 W. C. OLSON: 'Democratic Approach to Diplomacy', in *The Theory and Practice of International Relations*, Englewood Cliffs, Prentice Hall, 1966, p. 256.

Arab world and also Africa and the Americas, despite the vicissitudes that beset them. A spirit of humanism and generosity can only serve to promote *rapprochement* between States and make it easier for them to reconcile their interests. (see *1236, 2054*)

1850 – This is what lies at the root of the new theme of international negotiation: the free circulation of information and ideas (known as the 'third basket' during the Helsinki debates), a precondition for any genuine understanding between States whose political philosophies are different if not in opposition to each other. (see *2048*)

The development of telecommunications on an international scale gives signals, messages and information greater diplomatic significance against a background of global competition. Within this broad field of information, a distinction should be drawn between those types of negotiation addressing substantive issues such as freedom, confidentiality, intellectual and industrial property rights and the other – usually multilateral – negotiations that govern means of communication (air, sea and space networks, satellites and so forth). (see *1007, 1821, 1834*)

1851 – Communication between nations raises the issue of how to preserve the distinctive and defining characteristics of each one. In practice some civilisations carry such weight, and convey their message so forcefully, or have such economic sophistication or military presence, that they achieve a position of cultural, psychological and moral domination whether they seek to or not. This is nonetheless a form of predominance and interference that provokes others to react either by asserting their own identity or closing themselves off. (see *133*)

1852 – Political and cultural pluralism can be maintained only if ways are found of containing the kind of dominance that tends to assimilate others and deprive them of their identity: negotiation must be harnessed to this end if deep-rooted popular reactions are to be avoided that upset treaties, alliances and even institutions. (see *674*)

1853 – A network of communication and exchanges has grown up within certain scientific, artistic and political circles characterised by their openness to new ideas and approaches.

In many countries, the different elites have merged over time: high public office, banking and the management of major enterprises. The next phase will be for these to merge at international level: this has already started to happen.[18]

1854 – Outside these institutions, or at their margins, the members of these 'invisible colleges'[19] communicate and negotiate directly, exchanging information and devising projects. These are the living seedbeds for fresh thinking on international goals and regulation, unchecked by considerations of national preconceptions, diplomatic process or sometimes even ethical 'bias'. (see *1897, 2659*)

---

18 L. S. SENGHOR: 'Une communauté organique pour le développement des échanges culturels', *Revue juridique et politique, Indépendance et Coopération*, 1980, p. 648.

19 D. CRANE: *The Invisible College*, Chicago, University of Chicago Press, 1972.

The International Socialist movement dates back to 1889. Christian Democrat parties have moved progressively closer together. As to the unifying ambitions of Communism, they were blighted by the cultural totalitarianism of the movement. For the rest, the experience of the European parliamentary assemblies shows how difficult it is to realign political parties around a common theme.

1855 – This phenomenon is particularly present in Western societies, thanks to informal meetings, joint projects and the mobility of prominent people, especially business leaders. The flow of information, opposition of ideas and knowledge of each other make it easier for elites to move closer together, thus promoting better mutual understanding between nations and more effective diplomacy between States. (see *2048*)

1856 – Some of these meetings take place at frequent intervals and on a more or less institutional basis, with the backing of private foundations or international organisations. Their conclusions or reports are published, a notable one being the 'Interfutures' report produced under the auspices of the OECD.[20] Others lay down the principles for a course of action, such as the Trilateral Commission set up on the initiative of the United States. The Rome Club was another such 'thinktank', but the conclusions it produced were so daring as to undermine its credibility. UNESCO, too, was responsible for one report that was much acclaimed.[21] The Global Compact, if applied, could provide a useful framework for negotiation. (see *1826*, *2267*)

1857 – Understanding between States can be facilitated where their political or economic programmes coincide, as was the case when the first Western European negotiations took place between statesmen from France, Germany and Italy, some of whom belonged to the Christian Democrat school and others of whom were socialists. The 1950 Schuman Plan, held to be the archetype for long-term diplomatic operations, was able to mobilise the support of a broad sector of European public opinion. (see *1355*)

The Maastricht Treaty recognised the role of political parties in forming the European conscience and expressing the wishes of the people. In this respect it drew on the lessons of the European Community, in particular of the European Parliament. The European Charter on Fundamental Rights, drawn up in 2000 at Nice, was a further step in that direction.

1858 – Conferences and assemblies that bring together parliamentarians from different States help to give new direction to international debates, especially when the participants align themselves not according to their nationality but according to their political views and leanings. (see *1154*, *2053*, *2569*)

1859 – The sheer diversity of types of government is one of the main obstacles to the achievement of international consensus.[22] *In the face of all the factors that oppose it or dilute its effects, international negotiation thrives in a cohesive*

20 OECD: *Interfutures* Report, Paris, 1979.
21 S. MACBRIDE, etc: *Many Voices, One World*, UNESCO, 1980
22 H. A. KISSINGER: A World Restored, Boston, Houghton Mifflin, 1957.

political and cultural environment, and also where there is a common awareness of the issues. (see *2052*)

1860 – The personal relationships that frequently develop between leaders is reminiscent of the role formerly played by the great reigning dynasties in promoting international cooperation through their family ties as well as their shared education.

The question remains, even more so now than in the past, what relevance this kind of elite diplomacy has to people's actual aspirations.

1861 – A distinction should be drawn, in practice, between the acts of groups united for particular political or professional reasons and those of the major ideological movements. 'Militant' opinion can be active and produce results, but unless there is mass awareness of the issue, it remains the preserve of the minority. This does not mean that it has no influence on negotiation, as can be seen from the process of European unification, as well as the vocal and violent organised demonstrations against globalisation at important meetings of world leaders. (see *1829, 1877, 1892*)

1862 – When specific objectives are united with popular sentiment, this is the sign that international public opinion is forming. The reaction of the public to the main issues of the day lends legitimacy to some of the statements made, and contributes to the success or failure of negotiations.[23] *The practice of diplomacy increasingly requires access to information, the signals sent, the channels used and the logistics available.* (see *725, 2612*)

§3. The expansion of ideologies

1863 – By contrast with public opinion, which is changeable and emotive, religions and ideologies are characterised by stability. True, some die out and others appear, but these movements reflect the human mentality at its most profound, and their life-span must therefore be considered in terms of generations. This means that they often act as a brake on innovation, especially where diplomacy is concerned. They also inspire solidarity: certain countries are allies because the same major themes dominate their policies.

1864 – Major ideological upheavals are responsible for the most serious policy reassessments and the greatest diplomatic and military anxieties. They produce the most daring and lasting achievements as well as the most violent assaults on the established order. It is only natural that politicians have sought, often successfully, to harness this force in the service of their strategies. (see *1692*)

1865 – Nor has the advance of rationality eliminated this perennial phenomenon: *communalities or rivalries between ideals and sentiments that cross national boundaries in the professional, cultural, humanitarian and religious spheres remain*

---

23 H. A. KISSINGER: 'The Viet-Nam negotiations', *Foreign Affairs*, 1969, 47, p. 219.

active influences. Their political effects are further magnified by the growth in communications. (see *1534, 2273*)

Through negotiation, it is possible to define and promulgate new norms and ideas, and also rights. It gives expression to views held in common, both at regional and worldwide level. The various declarations on human rights, even though differently formulated, have produced effects not only in Europe, but also in the Americas and elsewhere. The same holds true in fields such as the environment, sport and dispute resolution.

1866 – The negotiator must take ideologies into consideration, as their strength lies in their ability to generate certainty. Global strategy owes much to some of these rather oversimplified concepts, which have enough evocative power to convince and mobilise people on a wholesale and lasting basis.

When the irrational rears its head in negotiation, it is the more dangerous for being less and less bound by national structures or logic. (see *618, 1876*)

1867 – *No temperament is more opposed to that of the negotiator than that of the mystic or the militant*: in reality, passion is more inclined to give way to force than to reason, as Aristotle wrote. And diplomacy is an art founded on prudence and wisdom, in which all doctrinal excesses, as well as all traces of bias, are to be avoided. (see *93, 1697, 2438*)

1868 – Traditional negotiation uses the methods of discussion and compromise: doctrinal certainties and imperatives will paralyse it. At the same time as he was predicting the downfall of the capitalist system, Stalin managed to reconcile the Leninist worldview with a pragmatic and effective vision of his own country's interests, but he in his turn was to underestimate the political and diplomatic power of democracy and of religions.

The cold and calculating mentality of the trader is hostile to ideals and their message, and impervious to their influence.

1869 – As a result of ideological intransigence, the rejection of flexibility, adaptation and innovation can cause a diplomatic initiative to fail, but in the end political realism generally triumphs when the interests of States have to be reconciled, and an objective assessment made of the balance of power between them. (see *369*)

1870 – A philosophy based on universal brotherhood and man's natural goodness can be a source of weakness in negotiation, where it is accompanied by a failure to grasp the realities of a world in which there is a constant struggle for wealth and power. (see *22, 174*)

Ideology must be exceptionally powerful if it is to overcome the barriers erected against it by national interests and prejudices. Where it succeeds, negotiation no longer has any raison d'être.

1871 – Political and ideological dogmatism rejects certain changes and concessions that are necessary if negotiation is to succeed. But it also encourages and consolidates both interdependence and domination between States. Soviet foreign policy showed no hesitation in discriminating between its partners on the basis of their doctrinal allegiances; relations between the 'Socialist countries' followed their own closed pattern, including periodic meetings, which gave their discussions the appearance of unanimity. (see *2278*)

1872 – For a great many States, religious faith remains a political imperative and a thriving cultural bond; it has an appreciable bearing on how they conduct their mutual relations, and thence on the workings of the international system as a whole. The names of many negotiators come to mind who were wise and forbearing men of faith.

It has become apparent that, in a number of countries, religious dogma is incompatible with negotiation in any form. (see *1692*)

1873 – The motivational power of orchestrated religious fervour should not be underestimated, especially where other nations sustain it by following suit. Rational motives will never have the same force, nor will they carry as far. In this way, phenomena arise that are difficult to control because of their spread: international terrorism is effective and dangerous precisely because it is often the expression of ideological movements that break their silence in order to strike dramatically and unpredictably.

1874 – The more the world's dominant ideologies make use of modern propaganda techniques in pursuit of their expansionist goals, the more effective they become. We are now in the age of computers and satellite telecommunication. *Advances in the means of communication and dissemination of thought have meant that elements emerge, sometimes violently, onto the international scene that would previously have been confined within their own national spheres.* (see *2645, 2651*)

1875 – Since information, comment and commands are all spread directly and rapidly through these channels, statesmen would do well to consider the implications these networks have for the confidentiality of their undertakings as well as the formation of public opinion. (see *2654*)

1876 – The expansion of ideologies turns them into rival forces that are far from peaceful or peace making. The situation in the Middle East, to take one example, must be looked at in the light of sociology and history.

As soon as motives come into play that go to the very heart of how mankind views its future, negotiation is powerless to reconcile antagonisms or deal with the manifestations of fanaticism.

1877 – Struggles between religions or peoples can never be resolved by compromise as long as religion or ethnicity are held to be absolute values. Because of the diversity of their origins, it is difficult to determine to which ethnic group many peoples belong. Culture, history and religious faith, on the other hand, are all the more potent and inflexible as marks of human identity in a world where they are threatened or offended. (see *423*)

1878 – Within multipartite conferences and organisations, too, ideology and culture can have a major impact: often, they explain differences in the way delegations behave and governments react. Specialists in this type of negotiation must learn to give them due consideration. (see *1076, 1534, 2053, 2173*)

1879 – When it comes to relations between States, even the most dogmatic and monolithic worldview is open to negotiation on the many issues of mutual interest. The benefits of peaceful resolution can sometimes have the effect of moderating intransigence on matters of doctrine.

However, the use of force, in the form of aggression, attack or war, whether overt or not, is difficult to deflect or avoid by traditional diplomatic means. Dialogue takes place at the political level, in the hope that it will succeed by persuasion. (see *1879*)

1880 – Sometimes, ideologies emerge from negotiations strengthened and recognised; the regimes concerned take advantage of this to confirm their own individual identity and enhance their credibility, especially among their own people. (see *681*)

After 1975, the Conference on Security and Cooperation in Europe threw its weight behind the doctrine of human rights, particularly in the face of certain regimes that underestimated its motivational force. This became for many years a major theme of diplomatic negotiation and wrought radical changes in Europe.

1881 – Inevitably, militant tendencies come into direct opposition to the interests of States. Experience shows that it is often difficult for their proponents to act in an organised fashion: the Komintern, for example, was dissolved in 1943 and the Kominform in 1956, despite the expansionist power of international Communism. That said, international negotiation does not make cultural affiliations disappear: on the contrary, these provide the motivating force and the framework for unlawful collusion that can even amount to terrorism. (see *1678, 1994*)

1882 – The dynamics of the major systems of thought that exist outside the national framework lead them to cause divisions within States, as already happened at the time of the Wars of Religion in Europe. Conflict among different ideas and beliefs will ultimately influence even the most authoritarian of regimes. The proliferation of sects not only causes nations to divide,[24] but also brings with it new kinds of international solidarity and, sometimes, extreme forms of terrorism. (see *1814, 2311, 2250*)

1883 – No doctrine, however generous, has succeeded in bringing about harmony between peoples. Neither appeals for solidarity among workers or intellectuals, or for peaceful coexistence between nations, have stood in the way of powerful States arming themselves and fighting each other. And neither Christianity nor Islam has prevented conflict from breaking out among its followers. (see *2250*)

The reawakening of nationalist tendencies in Europe has by no means been a peaceful affair, especially after the collapse of Soviet totalitarianism. Nor is it any more so in other parts of the world.

1884 – One of the achievements of the Helsinki Conference on Security and Cooperation in Europe was to formulate rules for European diplomatic exchanges that allow different political and ideological systems to coexist, as the Treaties of Westphalia had done in the seventeenth century. (see *1122*)

---

24 A. TOFFLER: *Future Shock*, New York, Random House, 1970.

The 1995 Stability Pact in Europe, under which 52 States adhered to the OSCE, was followed by the conclusion of a number of arrangements between neighbouring States regulating their coexistence. (see *76, 1330, 1692, 1793, 1880*)

1885 – The upsurge in federalist thinking, both in Europe and worldwide, produced movements that achieved short-lived fame, particularly at the time when the concept of a supranational Europe was largely accepted. (see *1336*)

1886 – In an indirect, but nonetheless powerful, way, these ideologies have influenced diplomatic negotiations in Europe, often in a way that was the opposite of what the governments wished to achieve. One such instance was the unilateral drafting by the German Bundestag of the preamble to the Franco-German Treaty of Friendship of 1963, which went against the intentions of the Treaty's negotiators, General de Gaulle and Chancellor Adenauer.

1887 – The question arises whether the modern world is in reality witnessing the decline of nationalism. The emergence of international public awareness would undoubtedly be welcomed by all those who support attempts at world order, especially in the field of peace and security. Instead of being confined to the theoretical, technocratic and bureaucratic level, this could create real political solidarity. (see *5*)

However, the discovery of unexploited resources generates, or aggravates, disparities more than it creates new forms of solidarity among the nations concerned.

1888 – As soon as it is realised that the problems nations face are connected or identical, or people become aware that higher interests and shared risks are involved, governments – and often opinion – start to respond in a similar way. Currents of opinion are already forming in the capitals at a similar speed and along similar lines, that influence foreign policy in the name of new, common, spiritual values. In the eighteenth century, a similar phenomenon occurred, that began with the elite classes and spread, after 1789, to the public as a whole, though it remained confined to Western Europe. Today it has become more widespread, while still having its most powerful impact within groups of nations whose opinions are forged out of the same traditions, beliefs and language.

1889 – The awareness of joint interests is progressively reinforcing the general principles underlying international relations. (see *2613*)

Even if, in the final analysis, it is only through national authorities and their official channels that the main strands of thought can influence foreign policy, the fact that these 'forces of opinion' tend in the same direction acts as a stimulus to negotiation and makes it easier for the partners to reach agreement. (see *2614*)

1890 – Ideology can be used in the service of diplomatic ends. One example was the expansion of the French Revolution into Europe; another was the expansion of orthodox and Tsarist Russia before 1914. As a fundamental political theme, the expansionist philosophy of socialism increased the pressure brought to bear by Soviet negotiators on their partners in Eastern Europe; their explanation of imperialism as capitalism in its most extreme form helped to speed up the process of decolonisation. (see *2512, 2612*)

1891 – Some forms of domination are based on solid doctrines. The so-called Monroe doctrine, for example, was initially devised as a way of achieving commercial expansion, but its effect was to close the New World to European political expansion, and give birth to a form of Pan-Americanism under the control of Washington. It led to a specific round of negotiation in which the different powers on that continent variously subjected each other to coercion or showed each other favour. (see *636*)

1892 – Modern diplomacy shows signs of an attempt to establish an international order based on ideologies common to the entire human species: humanitarian law, economic and cultural development, respect for human rights and protection of nature, are all themes that open the way to a new approach to relations between States, and to a growing number of agreed standards. (see *2173*)

This tendency runs directly counter to vested interests: the series of conferences on the environment and development, beginning in Rio in 1992, brought together thousands of participants, among them numerous Heads of State, but this did not prevent them from becoming the setting for serious confrontation.

Some of these movements, more or less representative and often bearing the hallmarks of anarchy, show their opposition to negotiations between industrialised nations by staging massive, violent demonstrations attracting blanket media coverage, focused on the rejection of 'globalisation', despite being themselves the products of this phenomenon and depending on it to live. Such protests were seen in Seattle, at the 1999 meeting of the WTO; in Washington and Prague in 2000, this time directed against the IMF and the IBRD; against the EU Council in Nice and Gothenburg in 2000–2001; at G8 meetings in Genoa, at Porto Alegre and Bombay in 2002, 2003 and 2004; and against the liberal-globalising tendencies of the Davos-New York Club and the negotiating programme that was accepted by the WTO in Doha, though the negotiations continued at its meetings in Cancun, Genoa and Hong Kong. (see *1829, 1910, 2489*)

1893 – The desire for each human being to enjoy fundamental freedoms is among the ideals for which Western democracies argue in their negotiations with other States, often underestimating both the differences that affect how these rights are defined, and the difficulty of ensuring they are understood and applied by people living in deprivation or belonging to other civilisations. (see *508*)

The more comprehensive and detailed the conventions and recommendations, the more difficult, if not impossible, they are to implement.

1894 – Sanctioning the violation of human rights can involve interference by foreign authorities and interest groups in a State's internal affairs, passing judgement on the actions of its national leaders, and can even call into question the ethnic, religious or cultural balance of countries where the population is mixed.

The UN Security Council has practised various forms of sanctions depending on what its members have negotiated.[25] Its debates on East Timor were very revealing

---

25 J. LEPRETTE: 'Le rôle de la France au Conseil de sécurité comme organe de décision juridique', in *L'internationalité dans les institutions et le droit*, p. 127.

in this respect, as were the interventions by NGOs in support of human rights in that country, between 1994 and 1999. (see *1146, 1784, 1907, 2173, 2784*)

The fear is that this ideal, like the defence of the natural environment, will merely become a means for vested interests to exert negotiating pressure or a technique used to spread disunity in the opposite camp. *Exporting freedom often implies interfering in the affairs of other countries.*

1895 – The negotiator must take care not to create the impression that he is using a humanitarian doctrine for the purposes of a political intervention or to exert pressure: this would be a travesty of the doctrine, depriving it of its power to rally support, if not indeed provoking an opposite reaction. He should remember that the best way to show virtue is by example, which is worth more than any praise or criticism.

Any hopes that the deliberations of international organisations might forestall unnecessary conflict and produce universally applicable programmes of action have not been borne out by the experience of global trade negotiations, or at the worldwide conference in Rio, where all the specific issues were avoided.

§4. Internationalism in professions and cultures

1896 – An objective approach to the realities of human life is necessary in order to understand how negotiation is carried on between States in the modern world and what role it plays.

The main features of the international social environment should be made the subject of research, to enable the relations between the players on the world stage and the constraints under which they operate, to be better understood and managed.

1897 – Transnational forces already exercise a growing influence over the foreign policy of even the largest States, either through discreet pressure or because of an instinctive urge to imitate. Added to this are the effects of increased travel and tourism. The result is enormous confusion in terms of policy and even terminology, with new actors emerging on the international scene, too many and varied to be properly identified, still less regulated. (see *1874, 1932, 2048*)

1898 – Hundreds of movements have arisen, and will continue to arise, with the specific aim of influencing international negotiations and bodies to promote their interests or views by means of petitions, lobbying, demonstrations, even strikes and boycotts. They use all available means of media communication, including the press and publishing, in making their appeal to public opinion, political leaders and the business community. (see *1892, 2640*)

1899 – These associations, trade unions, religious institutions, humanitarian groups, professional bodies and secret societies influence the debates in international institutions and conferences, as well as the course and outcome of diplomatic negotiations, in directions that often have nothing to do with national interests. No government or major business can remain aloof from their activities, such is the flexibility and speed with which they act and the political, economic and social power they exert. (see *1516, 2213*)

1900 – There is a further aspect of the activities of these organisations that the diplomat needs to bear in mind: the quiet but constant negotiations that take place within them between nations whose interests do not necessarily coincide. No government can afford to ignore the fact that an international pressure group may have fallen under the influence of some tendency or other, or is taking a particular position in a matter on which it is engaged.

1901 – New forms of solidarity have grown up within the European Union, centred on the joint activities of national groups and movements: these express their views through associations or unions that have achieved continental proportions, and hold discussions with European institutions over the heads of the national authorities. (see *1355*)

1902 – Created in 1951 by the International Confederation of Free Trade Unions (ICFTU) under the European Coal and Steel Community, the trade union advisory committee became the European Confederation of Free Trade Unions from which, in 1973, the European Trade Union Confederation emerged. The influence of this Confederation has grown constantly since that time. It now includes more than thirty trade union federations throughout Europe. At its Congresses, the main issues of common interest to its member organisations are discussed, in spite of the ideological differences that separate them.

1903 – The growth of the European Union has brought with it realignment and dialogue between professional organisations in countries with a strong interest in agriculture and industry, through the Committee of Professional Agricultural Organisations (COPA) and the Union of Industrial and Employers Confederations in Europe (UNICE). These allow the main economic issues arising at European level to be jointly studied and debated and the interests of producers to be represented in the institutions of the Union. These professional bodies are granted a number of seats on the advisory committees for the Common Agricultural Policy. (see *2285*)

1904 – At the international level, pressure groups, too, have multiplied: political parties, workers' or employers' unions and chambers of commerce, as well as humanitarian, cultural and religious institutions and secret societies, are all active, while representing different collective interests.[26] There are also international 'clubs' of business leaders some of whose meetings are held in public, as with the Global Economic Forum in Davos. (see *1137, 1899, 2137*)

1905 – The hard-fought and detailed tariff negotiations between the United States and the European Community had the effect in Europe of bringing together the professional organisations in the fields concerned, and, in America, of reinforcing the pressure brought by private groups already well represented in political circles and adept at using the media.

1906 – As for the labour unions, depending on their doctrinal leanings and ties, they hold discussions mainly within well-known worldwide federations. They still

26 A. LARCAN: 'Aide humanitaire et Etat', in *Le Rôle et la place de l'Etat*, p. 263.

suffer from ideological divisions, in spite of the work of the International Labour Organisation to reinforce their role.[27]

In addition, faced with multinational corporations, unions have sought to coordinate their activities sector-by-sector at international and European level, in the hope of achieving collective bargaining in certain areas: however, the difficulty of reconciling immediate professional interests with joint aims that are foreign or more distant means that these groups have often been unable to act effectively in major negotiations.

Non-governmental organisations

1907 – The term international non-governmental organisations (NGOs) is used to describe non-profit-making groups set up by private individuals or associations with no regard for national borders, sometimes even as a reaction to the compartmentalisation imposed by State frontiers.

1908 – Irrespective of their legal nature or their aims and scope, these organisations have the merit of bringing together and sustaining on an institutional basis a variety of cultural, social, religious and humanitarian initiatives that have sprung up at national level, opening international debate to them and allowing them to play a part in bringing different nations together.

It is impossible to estimate the extent of the network of relations that develop between all these international associations.[28]

1909 – Private organisations often provide the most favourable environment for promoting an international mindset. They serve as the incubator for many major projects that later receive State endorsement, and often lead to the setting up of official institutions. They provide a forum for intensive negotiations between partners who, while they may not have any official function, are nonetheless credible, representative and motivated. (see *1133, 1137, 1894*)

1910 – The vitality of these voluntary movements at the international level is obvious. Some of these groups, of which there are more than two thousand, have millions of members and substantial amounts of money. The causes they represent ensure that they have the attention of sovereign States, even if, in practice, it is not easy for them to muster public support where the political powers are opposed to them. They have contacts, often amounting to active dialogue, with intergovernmental organisations, which agree to the presence of their observers (whose numbers can run into hundreds, as at the WTO, or thousands, as at the 2001 Durban Conference). (see *1892*)

Hundreds of them have a recognised advisory role, either at United Nations level or within the European framework: more than four hundred are recognised by the Council of Europe.

---

27 L. ULMAN: *Multinational Unionism: Incentives, Barriers and Alternatives*, Berkeley, California, 1975.

28 A. TOFFLER: *The Third Wave*, New York, Bantam, 1980.

1911 – The main feature of these non-governmental organisations is the fact that each has a specialised mission. The causes they represent can be special interests, or competing ideals. None of them can claim to be universal, ideologically, politically or geographically. Some of them defend the interests of States or groups of States, often taking the role that States would otherwise play. Others show themselves hostile to international negotiation and inspire fear in governments, though at the same time there is no means of verifying who they represent and where their money comes from. (see *1892, 2173*)

1912 – The growth in international awareness of the issues of the day can only lead to an increase in the numbers of such representative or pressure groups and a greater role for them, especially in the areas of economic, cultural and technical negotiation. The more this tendency develops, the more bilateral and multilateral negotiations will, at least in part, reflect the balance of these influences, which are active and sustained, even when covert or indirect, and sometimes themselves tainted by the violence that is causing such upheaval in the international environment.

Section 2: The birth of a global vision

1913 – As the principal actor in both national and international affairs, the State negotiates in two theatres at the same time. Even for those governments that insist on independence as a fundamental principle, it is difficult to draw an absolute distinction between the play of internal and external factors; national frontiers have become porous and permeable to all kinds of exchanges in both directions. (see *632*)

1914 – Each State provides a framework that is subject to interference from international variables – interference that it strives to control. *Negotiation is one of the ways every responsible government has of ordering, predicting and measuring the external pressures to which it is subject and the relations of its national administration with the outside world.* Only by negotiation can it obtain the external assistance it needs to implement its national plans or prerogatives. Negotiation alone makes it possible to contain and punish the cross-border criminality exacerbated by the free movement of persons, capital and goods. In several Western countries, for instance, all financial intermediaries are subject to a general obligation to provide information to their governments, enabling them to identify those individuals, companies and regions that are 'at risk'. (see *1678, 1807, 2322*)

1915 – Every State plays multiple roles in international systems, networks and mechanisms, involving many powers and institutions. Negotiation is one of the means by which these systems are regulated, as well as one of the factors for balance and change, and one of the types of interdependent relationship they necessarily involve. As a communication technique, it allows them to overcome the limitations of national policy. (see *1745, 1850, 2049*)

Zones of preferential negotiation have been set up. Aside from the European Union, these include the APEC countries bordering the Pacific, as well as the

NAFTA, the various fora in South America and the South–East Asian States that make up ASEAN. (see *845, 847, 1949*)

1916 – The diplomatic approach to trading and financial exchanges oscillates between bilateralism, reciprocity and even most-favoured nation agreements on the one hand, and institutional multilateralism tending towards a universal free trade model on the other. Both approaches stimulate political interaction between States, without ever having succeeded in resolving the disarray and imbalance in international relations. (see *373, 1007, 1968, 2250*)

Ever more complex, the legal underpinnings of major investment projects and major commercial agreements bring with them new types of long-term State and private activity, carried on by sustained negotiation. (see *1816*)

1917 – A global 'strategy' is slowly emerging, aiming to guarantee nations a higher level of security, more harmonious growth and a better sharing of available resources and to offer guarantees to investors. This allows diplomacy a chance to rise above its traditional national goals.

Defining these objectives and the means of achieving them will inevitably be one of the major negotiating themes of the present century, provided the development can transcend ideological confrontation. (see *1807*)

§1. International competition or integration

1918 – It will be evident to any observer that contemporary phenomena now operate on a much more widespread and complex scale, coalescing into worldwide movements in which certain powers are achieving dominance.

But negotiation has a variety of responses to the problems resulting from inequalities in global integration, depending on what is the dominant political model: this might be based on the law of the market and the need for order, it might favour the preservation of established positions or challenge them or it might promote nations individually or as groups. It also depends on whether its ideals are dynamic or in decline. Some of these negotiations are almost unprecedented in their toughness. The old East–West rivalry has disappeared, giving way to the North–South divide.

1919 – Global integration is especially visible in the economic and technical fields, because of the expansion of trade during the past few decades. Trade has grown by more than 7 per cent in particularly prosperous years, and in some countries the volume of exports has been growing faster than gross domestic product. In some countries, too, imports pose a threat to domestic production.

The increasing complementarity of national economies creates mutual dependencies between countries, and thus renders States vulnerable; this should act as a stimulus to their negotiations and give them a more precise and substantial range of objectives, one recent example being the effort to reduce tariff barriers.

1920 – The same tendency dominates the growth of the currency and financial markets, which are even further forward in terms of integration than trade, where currency arbitrages and collection of funds take place directly, and where interest rates and time limits are set that have an impact on national economies. (see *382, 1813, 1820*)

Governments are concerned about the unpredictability of finance and also of criminality, resulting from the new freedom of movement of capital and the fact that transactions on the currency markets daily run into hundreds of billions of dollars. Accounting standards are becoming more uniform, with the United States taking the lead.

1921 – States are witnessing the dismantling of their traditional economic and monetary privileges without being able to properly protect themselves against the attendant risks they face both individually and collectively, in every area. The existence of offshore legal and tax havens has made it so easy to speculate, conceal assets and misappropriate funds that financial, police or judicial control is completely undermined. The anonymous nature of this disorder increases the burden on governments to assume their responsibilities and cooperate. (see *1815, 1914*)

Some governments have readily espoused the competition-based approach and implemented deregulation and privatisation programmes that sometimes affect their public services. Others, however, are not prepared to follow this line.

1922 – The tendency for the global economy to become increasingly interdependent does not favour all States equally. Access to the financial, commercial, technological and cultural markets, even to multilateral negotiation, is not open to all countries and companies on the same terms. In a changing world landscape, the vicissitudes of nature and circumstance work to the advantage of some States and the disadvantage of others, not by any means the same ones every time. (see *1823, 1994*)

In a world where States are involving themselves in markets with no clear limits and where leading edge technologies in economics and banking are spreading internationally, dominant currencies appear around which zones of stability and influence are forming; their respective rates fluctuate in accordance with market developments and the prevailing political circumstances.[29] (see *1964*)

Many currencies are protected by the negotiation of mutual systems of preference: this type of regulation binds together a number of West or Central African States as members of the former French franc area, or many of the countries of Western Europe in the Euro zone. (see *1639*)

1923 – The extent of government duties and prerogatives in diplomacy, economics and finance differs as between countries with a private capitalist system and those where capital is State-owned, despite the fact that both have tended to develop along convergent lines in technological or sociological terms: State trade is the product of official negotiations which often have a contagious effect on countries with a liberal economy. (see *384*)

Furthermore, by direct contrast with those countries whose economies can function without government support, developing States are obliged to include the

---

29 C. GAVALDA: 'L'internationalisation du droit bancaire', in *L'Internationalité dans les institutions et le droit*, Paris, Pedone, 1995, p. 273.

protection and promotion of all their activities, even private ones, as part of their diplomatic negotiations.

1924 – Political responses to changing circumstances are very different; this clearly has implications for relations between States. It impacts the whole range of diplomatic activity, no matter how close the ideologies concerned or how complementary the countries' interests: monetary instability provides a good example.

1925 – Competitiveness, openness to dialogue and diplomatic latitude vary in content, not only between countries but also within countries, depending on the sector or even the enterprise. These factors are linked to the political regime and the sturdiness of its power base, as well as its ability to master international trade and to find solutions to the raft of problems that trade brings with it. (see *392*)

Thus, with the market economy working in their favour, the United States have resolutely opposed the *dirigiste* tendencies found in the development programmes and strategies of the 'new economic order'. (see *1959*)

1926 – Quite naturally, every State strives to bring all its forces to bear on these competitive challenges. If some States claim the right to freely dispose of their natural resources, by nationalisation if necessary, the aim is not necessarily to use these within their own economy, but to trade them against resources or assistance they need. They seek to replace the mechanisms of direct and private initiatives with those of government negotiation. (see *402, 1825*)

To the extent that negotiation between governments concerns international markets, the reason is almost always to direct or regulate them. (see *1971*)

1927 – Claims for fair and guaranteed prices, the desire to process their own raw materials and the emerging solidarity between producers, are responses to the need for greater trading power for the many States which between them account for about three quarters of the world's population. Inequalities in the global economy have become so severe that these States sometimes introduce political conditions into their economic negotiations. (see *1204*)

1928 – It is difficult for some developing countries to participate fully in worldwide economic negotiation because there are not enough experts capable of negotiating on their behalf. To remedy this, international institutions offer various services to these States as part of their aid programmes, including training experts, setting out the rules for negotiation, drafting standard forms of agreement, drawing up codes of conduct, providing information about the main international markets and multinational corporations and compensating for the inadequacies of the national diplomatic service.

Private companies and even governments in developed countries must be on their guard to ensure that commercial and financial negotiations do not work against their interests in a globalised world. (see *2021, 2397*)

1929 – There are some States whose competitiveness is dwindling: unwilling to submit to the internal disciplines needed to enable them to develop policies, they find that foreign negotiation serves only to increase their dependency, and sometimes seek refuge in a show of exaggerated sovereign intransigence. Other, so-called 'emerging' countries have succeeded in entering the international arena and ensuring that their interests are respected: China, India and Brazil are examples, along with the other States that make up the G20 created in Beijing in 2005. The experience of Japan shows how aspiration to power can act as the driving force for negotiation.

1930 – The severity of world competition is such that it is sometimes difficult to achieve the desired result through negotiation. While, generally speaking, the majority of States suffering from the difficulties of world trade look to negotiation as a means of achieving stability and expansion, there are many attempts to reach agreement that fail, showing that the methods and objectives of some of the protagonists are mutually incompatible. (see **2224**)

It is dangerous, however, for States to hold themselves aloof from international discussion: others will be strongly tempted to disturb them. *Dialogue between nations should always remain open.* (see *1081, 1757*)

1931 – Contrary to the theories of 'globalisation', the market is not in practice a mere matter of making the supply fit the demand, even at international level. It is distorted by private agreements and influenced by governments, and it is also prey to the value systems of different nations. Most of all, though, it is influenced by power games. (see *761, 1266, 1829, 1923*)

In this way, the economic might of certain States allows them to impose their domestic legislation in trade negotiations, whether presented as a *fait accompli* or raised in the form of a threat. Notable examples include Section 301 of the United States Trade and Tariff Act and the federal law on export tax credits.

By stimulating competition between countries, as well as between private companies, economic integration, whether worldwide or regional, tends to have the effect of harmonising conditions for production and trade, but it favours those who offer the best price. (see *1693*)

Globalisation should not be confused with democratisation.

1932 – *Predominance can be involuntary: it comes about when values, norms and rules, techniques and production, sometimes even credit and prices, fall into line with those of the dominant countries.*

The negotiator will sometimes accept facts, quite unwittingly, which are not negotiable but nonetheless determine the outcome of the agreement. (see *911, 1897*)

The 30 members of the OECD are together responsible for three-quarters of world trade, though they represent less than a quarter of the global population. It is quite clear that this inequality of wealth and potential is one of the causes of tension in international affairs. The globalisation of the media and the free circulation of ideas favour negotiation; it allows passions to creep in, however, that render the process more complicated by exposing the growing gulf in development between different nations and exacerbating the sense of injustice felt by their elites. These tensions come to the surface not only at international conferences but also in the demands of non-governmental organisations, some of which are not themselves immune to fundamentalism.

1933 – The modern instruments of domination are economic and ideological. *But, when the predominance of some States becomes structural, the frustrations this brings in its wake can produce aggressive reactions.* The function of negotiation between governments is to provide ways to prevent and resolve these crises. Many ideologies are, in reality, the expression of a need, or will, to dominate. (see *1675, 1822*)

From protection to cooperation

1934 – Governments alone have the right to grant freedoms, allocate public aid, make concessions to foreign States, organise their police service, and enact and enforce laws. They alone have the means to provide regulation and financing, security and sanctions, all of them necessary conditions for international peace and good order. It is, therefore, in their interests to confer on these matters.

In certain multipartite negotiations, agreement between States is the only way forward: the agreements in the textile sector are an example.

1935 – However, whether in spite of the growing interdependence between States or because of it, the hardening of competition and the increasing climate of uncertainty lead many States to take action, either unilaterally or in concert, to limit the constraints imposed on them from outside. (see *93, 384, 445*)

In reality, most emerging and developing countries are not prepared to submit to disciplines – in the fields of environmental or employment protection, for example – that might hold back their progress.

Equally, there are nations for whom certain specific imperatives, such as the need for water or energy, or access to the sea, are the cause of latent disputes, if not overt conflict.

1936 – The tendency for the apparatus of modern industrial and cultural life to become concentrated in the hands of certain powers and societies has given nationalism a new lease of life. In practice, in developing or 'emerging' countries, hostility towards global liberalism is spreading, sometimes forcing governments to take extreme action: control of their territories, dependencies and their natural resources or measures to limit international capitalism and its 'stranglehold' over the principal sources of information, media and technology. Such a policy leads them to reject or neglect negotiation, or even comparison, with the outside world. (see *403*)

1937 – At all events, while the weakening of frontiers gives increasingly free rein to political confrontation, economic competition and social comparison, national authorities still try to keep control as long as possible over the interplay of those factors that are still in their hands. The strongest resistance to the integration of the State into a broader system is to be found in the field of foreign relations: *each State endeavours to protect its freedom to exercise all its domestic prerogatives.* (see *851*)

1938 – International harmonisation normally starts in the technical field: in appearance at least, it is easier to make sovereign choices in political, military and diplomatic matters, even for those governments that have little real power. (see *1089*)

Agriculture, despite its profound links to territory, is now becoming an issue in foreign relations.

1939 – Some States try to exempt themselves from the effects of competition by setting up an economic autarchy that is in reality a projection of their political doctrine. Others distort the laws of the marketplace by resorting to protections that are more or less covert but often based on ancient custom. Lastly, there are some such practices that are broadly accepted by public opinion: this is true of the State direction and protectionism widely practised in developing countries. (see *1215, 1920*)

The collapse of the planned system (COMECON or CAEM) constructed for political reasons around the former Soviet Union has left the economies of the countries of Central Europe in disarray, while competition in world trade is stronger than ever. The accession of these States to the European Union has opened up to them a worldwide field of trade and political negotiation.

1940 – Reference has been made to a return to national or collective protectionism. Seen from the perspective of international negotiation, the effect of such a policy is to inhibit the free play of the market by making it subject to the diplomatic process. This opens the way to trade-offs, adjustments and retaliation, and it raises the question whether the State is capable of assuming the responsibility of negotiating increasingly complex rules both at national and international level and of applying them.

External tension breathes new life into affirmations of sovereignty, as with the Arab countries that made the Amman Declaration in 2001. It does the same for protectionism, to the extent that this allows some governments to muster the necessary trade-offs in order to safeguard their interests.

Such a reaction, however, rarely lasts long: little by little, most States are losing absolute control of their means of independence. (see *2189*)

1941 – Far from remaining isolated and protecting themselves, however, some States have chosen to prepare themselves for fair and effective competition, starting by regulating their administrative structures so as to ensure that they do nothing to hold back this competitive potential. In some instances, there are voluntary agreements restricting trade, often entered into between private sector companies, making it possible for governments to preserve the general structure of a free trade system.

1942 – In the course of a few years, the number of countries adhering to the GATT increased threefold, thus extending the reach of its activities in structuring and promoting free trade. This grouping, intended as temporary, grew into a thriving permanent centre for tariff negotiations, and also provided the framework for the creation of the World Trade Organisation under the Marrakech Agreement of 1994. That institution, part of the United Nations system, has broad responsibility for mediation, conciliation and arbitration among its members, but many developing countries regard it as an unsuitable negotiating framework because it is the embodiment of the 'globalisation' that they believe works to their detriment.[30] Recent meetings of the WTO (Cancùn, 2001 and Hong Kong, 2005) have revealed the difficulty of reconciling the different approaches within it, but China's economic success confirms its viability. (see *1102, 1400, 1406, 1651, 1828, 1926, 1956, 2240*)

1943 – It is not enough for negotiation to be limited to those exchanges dictated by increased specialisation, or to the financial and cultural assistance needed to speed the pace of development: it must also embrace issues vital to the future of the planet such as security, expansion and justice. *It remains to be seen whether agreement between governments will in fact strengthen the international fabric and make it somewhat less fragile.* (see *1708*)

1944 – This kind of negotiation implies choosing between different trading, financial, technological and cultural models that are often in confusion if not actual opposition. Trade deficits and surpluses are not mutually compensatory. The movement of persons does not go hand in hand with transfers of funds and know-how. The starting point is to seek mutual understanding and to exchange information, proceeding the coordination of activities depending on the common interests and concerns of the parties, and finally progressing to the stage of bilateral or multilateral action.

1945 – There will be new opportunities for diplomacy, thanks to discussions and agreements which, while often a matter of bargaining, are nonetheless important because they go beyond narrow, short-term national interests and address the needs and viewpoints of the wider groups to which States belong. Examples include the cooperation between South American countries to promote the development of their vast territories bordering the Amazon; also the Senegal River development project, involving African States and lenders including a number of governments, which will take almost half a century to complete.

The free trade zone is sometimes used because States face common political issues rather than because their economies and trade policies complement each other. These divergences sometimes prove to be too great. (see *1643*)

1946 – Conservation and exploitation of natural resources, currency relationships and trade balances, the development of material and human investments, market-sharing, mutually complementary production, improving communications and reducing all kinds of discrimination – all these are at the same time subjects of discussion and factors limiting each partner's diplomatic autonomy.

It should be understood, however, that poor countries do not approach these negotiations in the same way as rich ones: their basic impulse is to reject an established order they regard as unjust and wish to destroy, while the so-called 'emerging' nations wish to take their place within it. (see *1935*)

1947 – The more widespread injustice and disorder become, the more obvious it will be that cooperation is a necessary condition for collective progress. The cost

---

30 H. RUIZ-FABRI: 'La contribution de l'OMC à la gestion de l'espace juridique mondiale', in *La Mondialisation du droit*, 2000, p. 347.

of measures designed to prevent pollution, ensure security, protect the biological and social balance and defend the 'common heritage of mankind', to use the language of the United Nations, will be so high that every government will have to subscribe to these disciplines and share these costs in order to avoid unfair competition. (see *402, 2193, 2232*)

1948 – Aware that it is in their interest to join forces to face these worsening problems, governments are endeavouring to agree upon international or regional structures more conducive to cooperative growth, progress based on stability, mutual well being, a greater level of harmonious interaction, generous development aid and support for the great multilateral institutions. But these notions still reflect work-in-progress rather than substantive achievements. More and more, States must exercise their privileges with moderation, and conform to the disciplines of international cooperation of their own accord.

Towards collective strategies

1949 – Never before has each nation's prosperity depended so much on external factors. Nations that are aware of this seek out others in order to find ways of surmounting, together, the problems that beset them.

1950 – Meetings between political leaders, sometimes at the highest levels, have become increasingly frequent, enabling them to study the international scene together and decide on concerted action to address their common or related concerns. In 1977, the heads of government who met in London went so far as to issue a declaration that the world economy must be considered as a whole. In 1980 in Venice, and again in 2002 in Monterrey, they suggested the adoption of a 'global strategy' to deal with the world's energy and development needs. (see *2044, 2490*)

The creation of the International Energy Agency within the framework of the OECD was intended to stave off crises in oil supply. The IEA has put forward a variety of proposals for future changes, at both the technical and economic levels, in the way energy is used.

1951 – Through negotiation, it has been possible for national leaders to move ahead in a greater knowledge of the problems that confront each of them and with a better understanding of the benefits of adopting a joint approach. The liberal economy States agreed in this way on a joint commitment to reduce their oil consumption; likewise, developing countries were able to use the UNCTAD umbrella to meet in order to reconcile their respective programmes, and the oil-producing States in OPEC, whose number has risen from five to eleven, have attempted to use their organisation to similar effect. (see *2033*)

1952 – The word 'strategy' has been much overused, but it gives a good indication of how international negotiation looks to the future in its search for common goals and the means to attain them. Worldwide conferences organised by the major institutions such as UNCTAD and the WTO seem almost to be competing with each other to provide a periodic platform for debate and confrontation. (see *2074*)

1953 – In 1963, the UN General Assembly requested the Advisory Committee on Science and Technology for Development to draw up an overall plan for developing countries. These high-level experts, assisted by teams of specialists, produced the outline for global cooperation programmes in a wide range of areas: agriculture, industry, energy and information technology, communications, transfer of technology, research and resources, natural disasters, the environment and demography.

The UN Conference on Science and Technology showed that these proposals, albeit often still at the theoretical stage, could give rise to widespread conflict, but these are all subjects that it has been possible to address though international negotiation.[31]

1954 – The United Nations Industrial Development Organisation put forward an industrialisation programme for the developing countries along with the regulatory and financial means to put it into effect, provided the developed States were prepared to commit to it.

As regards developing countries, the attitude of the United States, as the predominant economic power, to the idea of collective negotiation has been reserved if not altogether negative: the 1974 Declaration on the Rights and Duties of States has remained a dead letter, the global North–South dialogue came to an end in Cancùn in 1981, and, in spite of its having been ratified by Russia, implementation of the 1997 Kyoto Protocol on climate change remains problematic, even after the London meeting of 2005. (see *1809*)

1955 – Multilateral trade negotiations have led to the creation of a real framework designed to stimulate, facilitate and spread international commerce. (see *1602*)

Work under the successive cycles of GATT negotiation (the Dillon Round of 1961–1962, the Kennedy Round of 1963–1967, the Tokyo Round of 1973–1979 and the Uruguay Round of 1986–1993), was directed towards the reduction of tariffs and obstacles to world trade. These negotiations were characterised by the lively, sometimes ill-tempered competition between the United States and the European Union, or some of its members. The will for economic domination has accompanied the extension of these talks into new sectors.

Following the Marrakech Conference of 1994, the decision was taken to pursue these negotiations within the framework of the WTO. Environment, agriculture, services and industrial property are all fields in which the breaking down of legal and commercial barriers is at the same time contentious and unequal, and can only progress slowly and painfully from one compromise to the next.[32] (see *756, 1102, 1652, 1829, 1942, 2221*)

1956 – However their results might be judged, the characteristic feature of these strategies is that they adopt an overall perspective, whether this be worldwide as in the case of universal institutions such as those belonging to the United Nations, or simply regional, as with the European Union.

---

31 UN: *Sciences, Technology and Global Problems*, New York, Pergamon Press, 1979.
32 T. FLORY: *L'OMC*, Brussels, Bruylant, 1999.

Often acting against their own interests or addressing issues that are beyond their own capabilities, States adopt an increasingly broad perspective, whether to their own security needs, their mutual rights and obligations or how their activities fit into the natural, economic and political environment to which they all belong. (see *1007, 1829*)

1957 – In a world under construction, organisational negotiation leads on to negotiation for the future.

The work done by international organisations and conferences, and the recommendations in which they set common or shared objectives, contribute to a greater willingness to manage the planet's resources in a sustainable manner. (see *2190*)

The same trend can be seen in the growth of non-governmental organisations, some of which have achieved worldwide power through their wealth, leaders, experts and communications, enabling them to exert an influence on intergovernmental negotiation.

The growth of the United Nations system has confirmed its universalist tendencies: the abandoning of the Communist ideology and economy has resulted in a great increase in the number of its members.

The International Monetary Fund has over 180 members, including Switzerland and the 15 States formerly part of the USSR. Its function in monitoring financial and budgetary policies is one that generates the most intensive negotiations within the Fund or involving it, though this did not prevent it being criticised for lack of foresight during, for example, the financial crises in Asia and, later, Argentina. (see *2161*)

1958 – These negotiations prepare the ground for shifts in the international balance of economic power. The emerging economies of Asia and Latin America will require various negotiations about technology transfer, price stabilisation, cooperation for development and control of multinational corporations through collaboration between the various countries.

The European edifice appears from this perspective as an advanced example of a concerted effort to negotiate beyond the bounds imposed by national goals.

1959 – International economic negotiation might develop in the direction of a new kind of *dirigisme*, resulting either from intergovernmental agreements, decisions taken at the headquarters of international organisations, or the acts of autonomous intergovernmental establishments. Certain aspects of the work of the European Community raise this prospect, which could come about either through its existing achievements and regulatory systems, such as the Common Agricultural Policy or the euro, or its future goals, such as the common regional or industrial policy, or its relations with developing countries, with plans for an 'integrated policy' including all aspects of development: economy, human rights, environment, public services and democracy. (see *1349, 1981, 2511*)

As for the World Bank (IBRD), following the Prague Conference, where there were demonstrations by a variety of non-governmental associations and organisations, it plans to extend its involvement in matters of worldwide public interest especially to developing countries: major infrastructure and social projects, the fight against AIDS, the Internet, all of them long-term initiatives that will require the support of wealthier countries. However, its financial means, like those of the IMF, are dwarfed by the investment capital available in the private sector.

1960 – Governments, like major industry, undoubtedly have the stature to defend themselves against bureaucratic intrusion, even – indeed, especially – where it is international in origin. Trade unions, political and professional organisations also have an interest in ensuring that the real seat of democratic responsibility, in other words, the decision-making power, remains at national level.

The United States make no secret of their refusal to submit to any international rule that would have an unfavourable effect on their economy. (see *1925, 1973, 2193*)

1961 – That said, despite the informal and prospective appearance of economic negotiation, one of the logical consequences of European unification and international globalisation has been the emergence and growth of new normative powers produced by cooperation between governments.

In the environmental field, toxic industrial waste, and especially radioactive waste, has become a matter of global concern, the subject of negotiations both within the United Nations framework and elsewhere, particularly with a view to prohibiting dumping in the ocean and regulating its transport and storage. Article 39 of the Lomé Convention of 15 December 1989 prohibits the export of these substances. The UN World Charter for Nature of 28 October 1982 and the Action Plan for the 21st Century, unveiled in Rio in 1992, cover a very broad range of such topics, some of them disputed, as evidenced by the conference in The Hague in 2000, but all of them forward-looking, as can be seen from the Bonn meeting in 2000, the report of the intergovernmental group on climate change presented in Marrakech in 2001, and the UN Millennium Development Goals. Preservation of the environment is among the principles of the Global Compact. (see *1797, 1803, 1804*)

1962 – The tendency in Europe – and it is now among the major trends in modern diplomacy – is for economic factors to make negotiation increasingly institutionalised. Also, as between the European Community and the ACP States, there are indications that negotiation is becoming more 'administrative': development funding and exchange rate stabilisation funds reinforce the interventionism of State and international bureaucracies. The integrationist character of the European organisational system is extending beyond the original confines of trade, with initiatives being announced in areas as varied as agriculture, public health, social standards, the environment and cultural diversity. The Member States will have less room to manoeuvre as they are regulated by rules and disciplines they have not always themselves negotiated. (see *1410*)

1963 – The same trend can be seen at work at global level. Market regulation in major raw materials and oil, price adjustment mechanisms, the building up of stocks designed as a hedge against variations in supply and demand and the financing necessary for all this machinery all involve proposals or decisions of an interventionist kind, the effect of which will be to bring economies together under rigid administrative structures where even the negotiating role of the State is regulated. (see *1636, 1931*)

This cooperation is by nature different from anything that existed before. The fight against criminality, bribery or counterfeiting requires common established goals and common administrative methods. (see *1241, 1596, 1807, 1830*)

1964 – The attitude of States in this regard is sometimes contradictory. Some forms of liberalisation come about as a result of their hard-won agreements: the reduction in customs duties on manufactured goods was the result of long and painstaking negotiations that began in 1914. On the other hand, state initiatives often create cartels of producers, as in the oil business: this is due to the predominance of certain products in their export markets. All this fundamentally changes the spirit in which States negotiate with each other, since their concern now is to influence the market away from direct negotiation between their partners. (see *1919*)

The same is true of the progressive division of the world into huge zones of preference in which negotiation becomes the preserve of favoured nations: in the European Union, for instance, or NAFTA or between the States of South America, the Caribbean or the Asia-Pacific region. *The world's zones fragment and re-form depending on which is the dominant economic power.* The result is that negotiations and exchanges are said to be polarised. (see *1519, 1643, 1922*)

1965 – Among the major issues facing modern diplomacy is the question whether the nation State remains substantial enough to undertake major responsibilities. At the economic level this is open to doubt, except for those States with vast territories and unexploited resources: very many States depend on the outside world for a major part of their economy. It is doubtful, too, in matters of the environment, leading-edge science and space, all areas of global interest in which States cannot act alone.

The actions of some international institutions tend to favour the grouping of countries into broader economic collectives, as is the case in Africa, where financial and technical aid has triggered the negotiation of regional programmes between the governments.

1966 – It is easy to understand, then, that one of the main themes of Western European diplomacy has been to maximise the economic benefits of the European Union. This goes beyond the goals of normal multilateral negotiation, because it involves a new legal entity with its own dynamic and the power to define its own objectives and regulations. The system has progressed beyond the areas of trade into those of agriculture and transport, and thence into new areas such as policy coordination, security and foreign relations. (see *1348, 1411, 1519, 1644, 1980*)

The European programme of aid to developing countries, particularly in Africa, is accompanied by multi-faceted policy initiatives. Free trade zones tend to have the same objectives in terms of complementary economies and trade, but their legal underpinnings are very different. This can be seen from the 1992 and 1993 NAFTA treaties, the 1991 Mercosur treaty, the 1993 treaty between the Baltic States and the 2001 ASEAN–China treaty. (see *1583, 1643*)

1967 – All rigid international systems presuppose a fair and harmonious basis, while at the same time, there is no common authority to issue and enforce their rules: there can be no question of placing huge bureaucracies in charge of the essential interests of mankind.

The future for negotiation must lie in the direction of collective management of global interests, at least in the short term: all States should play a role in this cooperative enterprise, but the major powers will seek to keep it under their own control.[33]

§2. Negotiating a world order

1968 – The international environment is a vast market, or rather several vast markets, for capital, products, services and information, in which relations are either bilateral or multilateral, depending on the autonomy of choice of the participants. The most usual form these relations take, in almost every field, is contract. The greater the level of cooperation, the easier it becomes to adjust the supply to fit the demand, and the advent of the Internet means this can be done almost in real time, with the State either not involved or not wishing to be. This tendency will spread to every field of international relations.[34] (see *393, 1813, 1816, 1984, 2205*)

Negotiation covers the whole area of development and cooperation between nations. Its very nature can be expected to change, both in terms of how it is conducted and the results it produces, because it will usually appear as only one stage in the continuous cooperative process of building a community. Often, it operates on two levels. Where it results in the formulation of general rules, these are the product of voluntary agreement between States, or of major conferences or institutions, whether public or private: one example is the arbitration of disputes. Here, its only effect is the relative one of producing stipulations as between two or more parties, and in general, as in the WTO, what emerges is more likely to take the form of general terms and conditions of trade (the 'rules of the game') than substantive law. But where negotiation forms the basis for the relations between two or more parties to a contract, it will sometimes bind them to very detailed terms, even going as far as to exclude any system of national law; on the other hand, it cannot bind third parties.[35] (see *761, 831, 1007, 1863, 1916, 1937, 2623*)

1969 – Most States are conscious of the need to make choices between national interests and international needs, thus reconciling sovereignty with independence, but in doing so they remain free to decide what is in their own interest and look for the least sacrifice and the greatest possible advantage, as the European Union experience has shown. (see *1931, 1988*)

In reality, the world economy is heading in the direction of increasing numbers of disputes. States and businesses alike find themselves in competition because of

---

33 OECD: *Interfutures Report*, Paris, 1979, p. 82.
34 S. MACBRIDE: *Many Voices, One World*, UNESCO, 1980.
35 P. KAHN: 'L'Internationalisation de la vente', in *L'Internationalité dans les institutions et le droit*, p. 297.

their huge financial needs, while those with capital make their choices based on what will be profitable. Competition reigns, too, in the markets for goods, services and information. One of the main activities of the WTO is to provide a system of resolution for disputes arising from the liberalisation of trade, which has a different meaning in different countries and sectors. Transatlantic trade has already proved to be a rich source of conflict, thus ensuring that the organisation's Dispute Resolution Body is known about, even if its rulings are not always respected: it has, for example, condemned the US tax incentives for exports. (see *1922, 1955, 1963, 2039, 2040*)

1970 – Public opinion in the West was disappointed in its hopes in 1945 that the United Nations would succeed where the League of Nations had failed in creating a new world order. (see *215*)

Later, under the influence of worldwide demands, it was hoped that international negotiation would come to address a subject that was at the same time global, strategic and prospective: the new world economic order, generously defined by the United Nations in 1974 as being based on interdependence between nations, equitable trading conditions, a just and equitable relationship between the prices of raw materials imported and exported and increased investment and assistance for developing countries. It was given expression in 1974 in the Charter of the Economic Rights and Duties of States.

1971 – However, this notion of a world order represented a moral and political goal rather than an identifiable reality,[36] its underlying ethos was one of restructuring the world economy through dialogue rather than by pressure or confrontation. In spite of differing interpretations and recurring competition and discord, the notion has begun to gain some credence, and public opinion has become sensitised to the issue, despite the fact that in reality, where information is concerned, there is no such thing as a world order.

Even if assuming a new world order were achievable, it could never be imposed by decree, not even by the United Nations itself. *Any such order must be negotiated, not only between States but also with the cooperation of private enterprise, having regard to prevalent ideological trends.* (see *1828, 2190*)

1972 – This perspective is one of sustained and continuous negotiation, the novelty of which lies not only in its goals but also in its methods.[37] Some governments prefer, for tactical reasons, to conduct their diplomacy on a case by case basis. What they now wish to achieve, however, is nothing less than an overhaul of the entire system of movement of funds, goods, people and knowledge, in written as well as customary law, based on a new form of negotiation that is intense but comprehensive, of which the North–South conference on international economic cooperation was a short-lived example. (see *674, 1675*)

---

36 M. BEDJAOUI: *Pour un nouvel ordre économique international*, Paris, UNESCO, 1978.
37 B. MENON: *Global Dialogue: the New International Economic Order*, Oxford, Pergamon Press, 1971. S. COLE: *Global Models and the International Economic Order*, New York, UNITAR, 1977. P. JUILLARD: 'Existe-t-il des principes généraux de droit international économique?', in *L'Internationalité dans les institutions et le droit*, p. 243.

1973 – The many international meetings held for this purpose showed up the conflicts inherent in such an approach. Between the industrialised democracies and the Group of 77 developing countries (which now numbers 133), mutual understanding and common ground proved difficult to find: the adoption of an integrated programme was possible only by consensus and subject to reservations, which meant that it remained a creature of diplomatic theory. (see *1067, 1960*)

The pre-negotiations held on different trading products show how vulnerable cooperation can be to distrust and misunderstandings between negotiators: *pragmatic realism is easily submerged by the use of obscure and incriminatory language*, as at the Durban Conference on racism in 2001.

1974 – The sheer inequality of resources and opportunities between States can colour international negotiation in an alarming way. *Any issue can be used as a source of conflict between States depending on how rich and powerful they are.* This is why, during the efforts to draw up a law of the sea, less-favoured countries attempted to reestablish the balance of power by limiting the field and means of action of the most powerful nations in terms of freedom of navigation, the extended exclusive economic zone, rights of access to the sea and the legal regime of the deep seabed.

1975 – Bilateral and multilateral negotiation can play a role in the resolution of specific problems, as one of the ways to integrate national actions more closely into those taken at continental or global level. But achievement of this goal demands far-sightedness, broad vision and patience on the part of the political powers, as well as competence and hard work on the part of the negotiator. (see *1646*)

The growth in international dialogue is not linear: it is affected by political upheavals as well as cultural or religious onslaughts such as the attacks on 11 September 2001.

Any uncertainty or risk has a price that must be negotiated in its turn, whether this is political or financial. There exists a market in risk, only partly under the control of States, and highly profitable for those operating in it.

1976 – Negotiation is the only way to address the problems caused by persistent and deteriorating economic and monetary instability, that pose a threat not only to many States in their struggle for development but also to the sustainable collective expansion of the industrial economies. Lack of discipline in this regard undermines the credibility of liberal democracy. Here again, internal phenomena, often due to the transient personal influence of political or financial leaders, can be seen to spill over into global relations. (see *369*)

1977 – Whether as a result of accidents of history or more structural factors, the ever-widening gulf in development creates tensions that manifest themselves in a worldwide climate of threat and disorder. While their very prosperity blinds industrialised nations to the dangers that are building up, negotiation offers a peaceful, collective and rational way of bridging the gap that is appearing between States, working within their different capabilities and respecting their dignity. (see *1757*)

The law of globalisation must not become the law of the jungle: instead it must represent the fusion of a huge diversity of interests and ambitions.

1978 – The negotiating programme of the emerging and developing countries has gradually taken shape: on the agenda are reorganisation of trade and communications circuits, review of bilateral and multilateral diplomatic treaties, re-examination of established economic and cultural positions, the drawing up of new bodies of rules to ensure a better worldwide balance of resources and opportunities and the systematic use of the possibilities opened up by international organisations. (see *2181*)

1979 – The only way to avoid a return to aggressive and violent nationalism is the sustained use of what is termed 'positive sum negotiation'. Where trade between certain countries produces excessive surpluses and profits, these should be diverted to the sectors where they are needed. *Here, negotiation can be viewed as a procedure for the redistribution of surpluses and employment, especially with regard to those countries whose population is growing faster than their national product and which have the greatest potential to erupt.*

The fact remains that any uncontrolled deregulation of the flow of goods and capital opens the way to those who wield economic and financial power. (see *1828*)

1980 – In the light of this, development aid has become a major theme in international debate: here, traditional diplomacy been overtaken by concrete negotiations in an organisational framework, focused on the future, and reflecting the first tentative steps towards an integrated international environment. However, whether the discussions are bilateral or multilateral, cooperation in the form of aid will only be welcome or productive if the recipient States are allowed a voice at the negotiating table. (see *1637, 1966*)

The notion of a right to development has never progressed beyond the realms of theory, in spite of the efforts of the United Nations and the attention it has received in the academic literature.[38]

1981 – Most of the economic formulas currently being negotiated or examined fall outside the ambit of the liberal principles of which the WTO is the guardian: examples are guaranteed export receipts, price stabilisation mechanisms and solutions for storing products, technology transfer, relocation of manufacturing plants, protection of salaried and other workers, the use of taxes to fund State aid, the proposed setting up of a worldwide public exchequer fed by international taxes, the diversification of the media and protection of cultural and artistic integrity. (see *1959, 2226*)

1982 – Except for humanitarian aid, international aid is not an end in itself: it is simply one way of laying the foundations for a more equal balance between States, and as such it must be a concern of governments. Where it is badly negotiated, it can be counterproductive: it can, for example, help to perpetuate structures that are unfair or outmoded or encourage prevarication or channel the efforts of the recipient States in the wrong direction.

---

38 M. BEDJAOUI: 'Le droit au développement', in *Droit international. Bilan et perspectives*, Paris, Pedone, 1991.

1983 – The wealthiest States – which are not for all that the most generous or peace-loving[39] – as well as the most dynamic private sector enterprises, have discovered that it is in their interests to deal with developing countries because they see in them the potential to become valuable future allies or partners, likely to give a sufficient 'return' on the money invested in aiding them. (see *1414*)

It might be hoped that they will show more conviction in this regard: aid amounts to only a small proportion of the gross domestic product of these countries, and in some cases, is declining, by contrast with spending on weapons.

1984 – However, it is inappropriate to expect nations having received external assistance to keep any promises or express gratitude. They often regard such assistance as their due, and profitable to the donors.

The cancellation of part of the public debt of the poorest countries by the richest is an example of a well-intentioned decision the effects of which might be the opposite of what was hoped for, if relaxing internal and external financial disciplines stifles national initiatives, commercial opportunities and the search for new lending.

1985 – Affirmations of cooperation and solidarity between nations do not exclude specific and sometimes onerous trade-offs or even military allegiances being negotiated in exchange for cooperation.

Without going as far as certain powerful States that have used the contributions they make to fuel their own national expansion, all governments will come to realise that, at the political level, *international aid is not neutral. Sometimes it can be the scene of bitter struggles for influence.*

Non-governmental organisations, some of which have enormous financial resources, are not immune from these problems.

1986 – International aid must be looked at from the perspective of the future. How it is negotiated depends on the end in view. In this spirit, the UN General Assembly formulated the aspiration – reiterated at the Rio Conference but never actually achieved – that spending on aid should reach 0.7 per cent of the gross domestic product of the industrialised nations. As for agreements on financing and expert assistance, most of them are signed in connection with specific projects, and renewed subject to the progress or prospects of these projects.

1987 – Technical and financial aid and cultural assistance will only flourish if States take full responsibility for programmes, staffing, funding, guarantees and, therefore, negotiation. The responsible national authorities in this area will learn to cooperate with each other, or with the major international organisations, using empirical methods to carry out specific operations. (see *1194, 1559*)

One of the objectives of negotiation within an organisation is to help States, if not compel them, to put their economies in order. This may involve transferring control of major activities out of the country, as happened with the resolution of financial crises in Asia and Latin America. (see *1957, 2232*)

---

39 H. MORGENTHAU: 'A Political Theory of Foreign Aid', in *The Theory and Practice of International Relations*, Englewood Cliffs, Prentice Hall, 1966, p. 304.

1988 – Negotiated cooperation, whether multilateral or bilateral, must take account of governmental priorities, because the authorities will be using it as a way to resolve a number of issues within their general policy framework: the provision of financing via donations or loans on special terms; the concern to balance their foreign trade accounts; the need to take precautions and insure against the various risks faced by private investors; protection of expatriates and their property; and the channelling of interventions by international organisations. These and other specific issues lend a political dimension to even the most technical of negotiations. *If State competences are to be respected, diplomatic channels must normally be used.*

1989 – The pursuit of worldwide economic balance has resulted in marked changes in the way negotiations are conducted. *Newcomers to the international scene tend in practice to object to some of the conventional and customary acquired rights on which the edifice of international relations has been constructed and wish instead to change the traditional rules of the diplomatic game.* (see *652*)

As for the major private sector operators, they impose their own conditions and guarantees on the international markets in capital, products and services, through negotiations in which they often prove harsher to deal with than governments. They often compete with each other. (see *1931, 1968, 1969*)

1990 – In a more open society, whose members are numerous and diverse, negotiation must innovate. Its dialectic develops hand in hand with the search for a new order that places a higher value on the equalisation of opportunities between States than on their equality before the law, and on preferential treatment or the abandonment of discrimination than on reciprocity of concessions. The most-favoured nation clause, so characteristic of the GATT, is giving way to the practice of preferential tariffs in favour of developing countries. Negotiators must look at the economic and social realities behind the legal forms and appearances. (see *666*)

Logic is not the rule in negotiation between States: their main interests can be clouded by ideologies that lead them to take extreme positions. Depending on the issue under discussion, they can find themselves upholding contradictory arguments, sometimes in the same forum such as the WTO.

1991 – As soon as numbers become more important than power, it is only natural for negotiators to pay close attention to the framework in which majorities can emerge. Whether the expected result is achieved depends on the States that are involved in drawing up this framework, its working procedures and voting conditions for the passing of resolutions. Developing States have, because of this, made no secret of their reservations with regard to some of the great world financial institutions.

1992 – Colloquia, conferences and organisations exist to enable the arena of debate to be extended, programmes to be devised and arguments developed, all of which serve to nourish and direct the actual negotiations when they happen: in this way, the UNCTAD has been able to serve as a test bed for the airing of a variety of cultural and political issues that helped to strengthen the negotiating hand of the developing countries, as was seen in Sao Paulo in 2002, where 183 States participated.

In practice, though, the experience of negotiating programmes within the WTO (for example, at Cancùn in 2003) has shown the difficulty of achieving compromise between the different groups of partners, especially where they wish to avoid any clear commitment.

1993 – The scepticism that surrounds what can be achieved in international conferences and organisations will be dispelled once they have shown themselves able to stimulate positive debate on specific, clearly defined and well-chosen issues, while at the same time anchoring these negotiations in a collective mindset that responds to the principal needs of tomorrow's world. (see **2242**)

As an example, the entire activity of the European Space Agency is geared to focusing and stimulating negotiation among European States on long-term research and development programmes and on contracts to be performed by private enterprises in exchange for a fair return on their investment.

1994 – Opposition, both ideological and specific, often results in national viewpoints being reinforced and vindicated, thus making them more coherent and consistent as bargaining positions. It would be a mistake to fall into the erroneous belief that international relations can be reduced to mere doctrinal constructs. In reality, competition is tempered by nationalism, alliances evolve and capitalism reinvents itself in new forms. As for the issues that matter most to States, the same preoccupations recur constantly. *The use of international institutions as a means of ordering international relations will thus lead to national, and therefore political, considerations interfering more and more in legal, technical and financial negotiations.* (see **1228, 1881**)

Chapter III:
The Prospects For Negotiation

1995 – Diplomatic relations between States rest on traditional principles and methods. But where security, economics and technology are concerned, everything has changed.

Timescales are very different now: deadlines are shorter, the process of bargaining has speeded up, the medium term grows ever closer and threats are swift to appear. (see *520*)

Distances are shrinking, too, as networks develop, with greater openness to communications and competition through the media, professional bodies, interest groups, benevolent organisations and political movements, and States are now working together.[1] This fluidity affects not only the processes, but also the actors themselves: the model of the structured and responsible State is no longer universally applicable. The climate of unpredictability and uncertainty undermines even the strongest of diplomatic traditions. (see *1706, 1821*)

1996 – The rapid pace of modern life affects the practice of diplomacy as much as other forms of activity. Computer technology enables information to be obtained and transmitted and calculations made in milliseconds.

As a result, the human being is required to think and decide more quickly, and, if not to actually forestall events, then at least to act and react with a degree of speed that is sometimes alarming and often allows no opportunity for prior review.

1997 – All progress, and each wave of social, technical or cultural innovation, extend the possibilities for collective action, and thus for competition, cooperation or even solidarity, between nations, societies and individuals.

Mankind's most recent conquests, whether in atomic physics, outer space or the ocean floor, and its most spectacular achievements in Internet technology or biogenetics, serve either to further complicate competition and even conflicts between States, or to open up new areas of possible cooperation to them.

1998 – Not only is daily life increasingly hurried, but there is also a desire to look further ahead: issues are debated well in advance, on the basis of more and more information, and there is real concern about the future and the interdependence it will inevitably bring. Constant adjustment is needed to meet new needs, and this confirms the unsuitability of traditional structures and methods, especially in relations between States.

---

1 M. BONNEFOUS: 'Logique de réseau, logique de territoire', *Revue de Défense nationale*, July 2001, p. 134.

As an example, the needs of the world population for water mean that rights to water will have to be negotiated. Negotiations on the laws of water must inevitably follow, in a climate more strained than ever.

1999 – It is not surprising, then, that at international as well as national level, new disciplines of thought and action are taking shape that use the possibilities opened up by technology. Both because of their magnitude and the risks they involve, major investments will be planned, structured and implemented through long-term negotiations between capital investors, banks, international agencies and companies in the private sector, as will the attendant guarantees and insurance.

It is extremely difficult to have knowledge of the countless negotiations involved in present-day international life; however, this should not paralyse the study of the ways in which negotiation responds to this growth in activity, nor detract from the effort to understand how these negotiations are part of a coherent whole. In the United States and elsewhere, this is one of the major tasks facing the centres of strategic planning.

2000 – The risks confronting mankind make it imperative to plan for the future with the utmost care. This was the objective of the United Nations in formulating its Millennium Development Goals, which started with a summit in 1991 and culminated in a meeting of Heads of State in 2003. The goals include the eradication of extreme poverty and hunger and the reduction of endemic diseases and child mortality, with a view to securing greater equality between nations and environmental sustainability.

Negotiating for the future means forecasting, planning and anticipation. It encompasses the future, the possible and even the hypothetical; it follows new approaches, uses new methods, and obeys new rules. This kind of negotiation requires a political and intellectual effort that draws on both considered reflection and imagination. But it is the only process to offer a way to address the common global problems of a rapidly changing world, in need of regulation as well as of hope.

Section 1: Refining the methods

2001 – Clearly, a government's capacity to negotiate is influenced by its data storage, the range of its telecommunications, its simulation and forecasting capabilities, and the quality of its officials. (see *1046*)

2002 – However powerful it may be, no State can afford to ignore the new dimension of the problems it must face, the forces in play, and the threats that can arise. If it wishes to take part in decision-making at international level, it must prepare itself, with facts, materiel and manpower. These will enable it to make its presence felt on the diplomatic scene, and depending on its ambitions, even at global level.

Although the traditional State apparatus was not designed to deal with such phenomena, the modern State must be mindful in its negotiations of the challenges posed by a global society without discipline or ethics, in which goods worth hundreds of billions of euros are counterfeited, funds embezzled, endemic diseases recur on a large scale, cyber-crime and terrorism are rife, public opinion is manipulated and entire populations migrate.

2003 – The view whereby the public authorities can harness new technologies to work for their benefit is seductive, and new techniques do indeed serve to introduce an element of order and reason into the business of understanding, explaining and predicting human behaviour.

Also, the livelier than ever competition between industrialised nations will result in faster improvements, bringing the methods and instruments of diplomacy up to date.

The same will happen through the international activities of major businesses, which now find themselves involved, actively or passively, in foreign negotiations and even takeovers. And, as currencies become increasingly dematerialised, this process will gather momentum. (see *1812, 1968*)

2004 – International negotiation can benefit from advances in information technology. Enhancements to tools and procedures will allow negotiators to refine their approach to issues before and during the discussions, to explore the consequences of their hypotheses, and research those of their interlocutors. This will also mean the reorganisation of many administrative, communications and distribution systems. Computer technology has proved indispensable in the continuous evaluation of the possible outcomes of each proposal put forward in financial and trade negotiations, for example in the GATT and now the World Trade Organization. (see *1046*)

The major television and media channels broadcast information in real time across the world, and negotiators often misjudge their effectiveness as strategic networks.

2005 – That said, in international relations, there is no single theory or formula capable of digesting all the factual complexities, empirical methods, pragmatic results and imprecise terminology: the way actions are decided on and carried out still depends on the circumstances.

This is why prudence is called for when using definitions and categories in attempting to describe and evaluate activities as sensitive as politics and negotiation. (see *264*)

2006 – *Far from leading to greater consistency in behaviour, modern methods of information, communication and decision-making place a premium on the power of the State and the personal skills of the negotiators.* (see *2389*)

§1. Information

2007 – International negotiation is a great consumer of information of all types and from all sources. The efficiency of the diplomatic machine depends on the proper circulation of information. The same is true for the world of international organisations in general, as well as trade, finance and the media. Power relationships determine what techniques and what information are available. The reverse is also true: information can destabilise a business or even a government.

Information has become one of the subjects of negotiation between States; the way it is used, which includes knowing the facts and also distorting them, is part of the negotiator's art. (see *1834, 2597, 2644, 2651*)

Information and negotiation

2008 – It is a bad negotiator who neglects to obtain the information that could be helpful, if not vital, to his task. Not only can the enterprise not hope to succeed unless he is properly informed about the circumstances of the negotiations, the environment in which they will take place, the reasons for them and the goal, but, worse, he will be unable to understand his interlocutors if he does not know their culture and approach, and if possible, their language. (see *346, 440, 506, 1847*)

2009 – Fashions exist in politics and diplomacy as elsewhere: nineteenth century attitudes were coloured by the idealised portraits of each of the nations of Europe produced by the great writers of the time. The shock of the First World War was all the more rude because of them. Wise and impartial minds know how to avoid the clichés and look to the ethnic, geographic and strategic realities rather than at commonly held stereotypes.

2010 – In this sense, negotiation has become even more difficult today, because the nations becoming drawn into international dialogue are separated by profound differences in their language, thought and civilisation. Ignorance and lack of understanding make contacts difficult and agreement unpredictable, especially when the multiplication of bureaucracy places even more barriers in the way of the negotiator. (see *2450*)

The media traffic in information, now a commodity that is paid for, has magnified the role culture plays. Communication today is effective as never before. The extension of conflicts into the cultural arena raises questions about the accuracy and purpose of information, both for the public and for those in political power. In reality, there is no common understanding of international action and intervention: information is simply one of their instruments. But leaders have learned how it can be used to provoke or defuse tensions, and also to understand the role of journalists, especially in their choice of news and images to broadcast. (see *524, 2608*)

2011 – All realistic diplomacy rests on the sound collection and astute exploitation of intelligence. The methods themselves are centuries old,[2] but progress in telecommunications now makes it possible to intercept communications and process the information.

Organising the handling of intelligence does not mean using only one source, or exercising so much supervision over the sources that it undermines their

2 F. de CALLIERES: *De la manière de négocier avec les souverains*, Paris, 1716. C. W. THAYLER: *Diplomat*, New York, Harper Row, 1959.

independence, and thus their value. On the contrary, the greatest available number of sources of information should be drawn upon, and the most varied contacts. *Modern negotiation attaches greater importance to the rational use of 'open' intelligence: the smallest clue, or the slightest indiscretion, can prove useful.* (see *296, 2603*)

It is no longer possible to ignore the potential of the Internet, while still bearing in mind that its underlying concepts, networks and even system of nomenclature are all American, which means that it is not a neutral resource.

2012 – As well as the traditional need to know about the other negotiating party, multilateral negotiating procedures now impose their own requirements, more complex in terms of content as well as approach: the negotiator must formulate his proposals, demands, responses, and concessions using judgment based on a vast and varied pool of available intelligence. He should set his policy direction at the outset, in order to guide the collection and selection of the data he needs. *Intelligence must serve the needs of strategy.* (see *2053, 2619*)

2013 – The great powers understood the importance of information. From the time of Lenin, the USSR attached considerable importance to gathering all available data on the outside world. In the social sciences field, this work was mainly done by the Academy of Sciences, whose Institutes (in particular the Institute for World Economy and International Affairs) conducted in-depth studies on all the major issues of foreign policy, within the former Soviet bloc as well as outside it. Russia inherited its work.

2014 – It is in the United States, however, that the greatest amount of work has been done, by the administration itself, the universities and major corporations: more than two thirds of the largest databases are located there, including increasing amounts of international research material. In 1973, the State Department set up a central mechanism for processing information from its foreign posts and other available sources. It also stores information on certain sensitive negotiations when it wishes to keep a record or look again at the methods used.[3] (see *2607*)

2015 – For the purposes of negotiations being conducted by themselves or their nationals, governments will be forced to find, collate and store increasingly specific, detailed and current information on foreign affairs. The proliferation of foreign information is already apparent in major Western countries, where computer technology not only permits more comprehensive and orderly research, but also allows for a logical approach in place of intuitive and disparate assessments.

2016 – This research material, the inevitable product of increased competition in all spheres of activity, cannot all be retrieved and processed. *Private sector companies, universities and public bodies, as well as the Internet, offer all negotiators*

---

3 B. BERKOWITZ and A. GOODMAN: *Best Truth: Intelligence in the Information Age*, New Haven, Yale University Press, 2000.

permanent sources of information and links, on payment of the fee for the service: the US Federal Administration has already entered into contracts on these lines.

2017 – In Moscow, in the field of foreign policy, research was mostly entrusted to the specialised Institutes whose approach to the issues was geographic, systematic and multidisciplinary. These bodies had thousands of staff drawn from all disciplines (diplomats, soldiers, scientists, linguists and sociologists) to undertake in-depth studies.

2018 – Technology has done much to advance this cause. It prompts the question whether, given the hardening of international competition, liberal regimes might set limits on the use of these new technologies in order to preserve the freedom of their citizens, without running the risk that their less scrupulous adversaries will be able to use them to the full in the service of their own diplomatic ends.

2019 – It is also to be expected that the use of telecommunications technology will increase the volume of international contacts, producing faster results and also more competition and imitation. The accumulation of data will highlight the similarities between countries if not actually tending to bring their laws and practices into alignment, and will in its turn lead to increasing interchange of research materials. (see *1590*)

Another factor is the number of 'evaluations' and 'ratings' of the economies of various countries or corporations, broadcast worldwide by agencies whose business this is.

2020 – In more than one respect, the systematically increased use of intelligence and automation is not an unmixed blessing for negotiation. Often, the more people know, the more fearful they will become and the less inclined to initiative or action. (see *2651*)

2021 – Intergovernmental organisations are responsible for gathering the maximum available amount of data and harmonising research in their respective fields, using their own resources and the help of their member States. They will make growing use of new information and automation technologies and their influence will increase accordingly.

This is already the case with the European Union, which has computerised all the research materials relating to Community law, including treaties, agreements, regulations, decisions, directives and recommendations, as well as the national implementing measures – regulations, case law and academic writings.

The European Space Agency is an example of one that has set up a database containing, amongst other things, the staff rules of large numbers of international organisations.

2022 – The Council of Europe has computerised the work of drafting and monitoring the conventions it draws up: drafts and amendments to them, signatures, reservations and updates can all be looked up where needed during negotiation or implementation.

The UN Secretariat General has done the same for the registration of treaties of which it is the depositary (see Article 102 of the UN Charter and Resolution GA 32/144 of 1977).

2023 – As intelligence becomes systematised, databases and funds of research material will be rapidly available from decentralised sources, but the end result will be saturation. It is easy to see how systematic access to a database containing all the relevant provisions of treaties and conventions can lend impetus to negotiations; it is equally easy to see how the quantification of all this information will add to the workload.

2024 – Centres for the archiving and processing of the documentation needed for negotiation are taking on a strategic importance. Especially rigorous rules and practices will be required, since these documents are only of use if scrupulously archived and constantly kept up to date. Outdated information is worse than useless: it can be dangerous. (see *2607*)

The possible uses of all this information have already developed to the point of outstripping the capacities of the human mind, both in terms of speed and power.[4]

2025 – This intelligence should be available to all national representatives depending on their mission and the level of confidentiality: this would enable the public authorities to set up departments for the research, dissemination, summarising and consultation of information relevant to foreign negotiation. (see *1706, 2605, 2607*)

Control of this information will bring about new working methods at every level.

2026 – Negotiators must do what is necessary to gather, prepare and transmit an ever-increasing quantity of intelligence to their contacts. Diplomatic representations will have a role to play here, not only with respect to the information needed to prepare for particular negotiations, but also in terms of understanding the underlying public opinion of the countries in question in order to anticipate their attitudes and responses.[5] (see *2084*)

2027 – Another factor in the progressive shrinkage of the domain of national secrecy is the refinement in techniques of space surveillance. Remote sensing, an extension of the techniques used in aerial photography, means that satellites in regular orbit can provide close-up, detailed and constantly updated views across the frontiers of the planet, and these are available for use in negotiation. The development of strategic installations has been the subject of observation, as well as movements on land and sea, in the air and in space: this is how national resources and activities will be monitored in the future (see the 1992 Treaty of Helsinki). (see *1741, 1756, 2258*)

Satellites have played an important part in preventing and managing a variety of international crises. They facilitated direct communications between the crisis reduction centres provided for in the Washington Agreement of 1987. They aided the rapid military deployment in the Gulf War in 1991, in Afghanistan in 2001–2002, and again in Iraq in 2003. And, as the achievements of China have shown, they are an indicator of power and, as such, command respect.

---

4 A. PLANTEY: *Prospective de l'Etat*, Paris, CNRS, 1975.
5 M. MEAD: 'The Importance of National Culture', in *International Communication and the New Diplomacy*, Indiana University Press, 1968.

Nor should the role played by aviation be ignored: it has been the cause of a number of notorious diplomatic incidents.

2028 – The strategic arms limitation talks have highlighted the role of verification of information. At the outset, each partner rejected the idea of direct verification by the other, and devoted considerable resources to controlling the monitoring processes necessary for implementing the treaties. (see *2607*)

It is to be expected that the prevention of terrorist plots and accidental wars will come to rest entirely on a single rapid and objective information system, and this very fact opens the way to negotiation, whether diplomatic or within organisations. (see *1799*)

In an environment under threat of insecurity, intelligence has assumed great importance. But it is worth nothing unless it is protected. It can only be handled by bilateral negotiation and mutual concessions.

2029 – Certain powerful States, sometimes with the help of multinational corporations, are using intelligence to gain an increasing foothold in the internal sovereignty of smaller States, correspondingly limiting their freedom to manoeuvre. (see *1816, 2259, 2607*)

Set up in 1963 and the subject of a number of subsequent refinements, the direct communications link between Washington and Moscow has been used during every major world crisis since: the Arab-Israeli conflict, the Indo-Pakistan and Cyprus confrontations, the invasion of Afghanistan, the Gulf crisis, and the wars in the Balkans. Used in parallel with traditional diplomatic channels and backed by direct satellite links between risk management centres under the Washington Agreement of 1987 and the Moscow Agreement of 1989, these modern techniques have helped in the containment of international tensions.

2030 – Governments are faced with a conflict between the concern to preserve their sovereignty and the urge to play their part in promoting the circulation of goods and ideas. This is essential for achieving progress though healthy international competition.[6] Whether or not to gather intelligence about every one of the parties to an international negotiation is a matter for each one to decide. But governments will find it difficult to invoke, against each other, rights of ownership in the data concerning them, especially now that domestic laws are moving in favour of the citizen – though such disciplines will take a long time to reach the international level. (see *2654*)

2031 – On the other hand, it is conceivable that States will be able, by judiciously amassing certain types of information and carefully protecting them, to force others to negotiate with them in order to obtain and use this data. This will open up new possibilities for exerting predominance.[7]

---

6 K. W. DEUTSCH: *Political Community at the International Level*, New York, Doubleday, 1954, 1970. J.W. BURTON: *Conflict and Communication*, London, MacMillan, 1969.

7 A. PLANTEY: 'Informatique et rupture des équilibres politiques', *Revue africaine de stratégie*, 1979, p. 17.

Information is expensive in terms of investment, research and management, but it fast becomes obsolete: it is destined to become a further source of inequality between States and societies.

The negotiation of information

2032 – The usefulness, necessity and cost of major bodies of documentary research material will lead to terms being negotiated enabling them to be used internationally, especially where they do not include confidential data. *Either on a reciprocal basis or on payment of a service fee, States will have the use of this information, as well as the assistance of private sector companies that devise or operate user programmes*; we are still a long way, however, from a worldwide bank or system of data management.[8] (see *2607*)

The negotiation of measures of protection against the dispersal of radioactive waste necessitated the harmonisation of the technical definitions to be used, in other words agreement between the governments on the basic conditions for their international cooperation.

2033 – The study of conflicts and ways of preventing, containing or resolving them, confirms how important it is to determine and correctly characterise the underlying facts.[9] Procedures for the peaceful settlement of disputes depend on the availability of objective information, and resolution of labour disputes under domestic legal systems has shown how vital it is to seek out the facts, the more so because many crises are accidental in origin or accidentally aggravated. (see *1700*)

The Moscow Agreement of 1989 on the prevention of dangerous military activities requires the partners to agree on determining the human and material factors that produce crises, given the threats created by modern technology and the incidents that can result from third party intervention, not to mention chance or error: the document thus begins with a series of definitions.

The notification of significant military activities arose as a response to the need to use a diplomatic approach to crisis prevention (see the 1989 Moscow Agreement on military accidents, and the conclusions of the 1984–1986 Stockholm Conference on measures of trust and security in Europe).

2034 – The international fact-finding investigation is one of the most convenient ways of understanding and defining a given situation: one of the signs of progress in the international community has been that it is now easier for the parties to prepare the ground for such investigations. The methodology for carrying out such investigations has been progressively clarified, as well as the conditions for its success and the goals of such a negotiation. (see *464*)

An investigation involves two main steps. First, the facts must be established using methods that are beyond dispute, continuously valid, and binding on the governments, and this means laying down procedures for inspection, evaluation

8 A. TOFFLER: *Future Shock*, New York, Random House, 1970.
9 W. L. SHORE: *Fact-finding in the Maintenance of International Peace*, New York, Oceana, 1970.

and reporting. Then comes the difficult task of interpreting and defining the facts thus established from the legal, diplomatic and political standpoints.

2035 – What has emerged is that, in this field, multilateral procedures produce better results: the participation of third parties can help facilitate the resolution of a dispute. Investigation thus tends now to be included as an indispensable component of an organised system of dispute resolution: the negotiation of investigative procedures is both encouraged and regulated, for example within the WTO or the Mercosul, each of which has its own formal adversarial procedure. (see *207*)

These types of intervention are likely to remain indirect for some time to come. In practice, except in cases of military coercion, any investigation carried on in the territory of a State presupposes that it has given its consent, either under a treaty or at the time the verification was requested. What often complicates the negotiation of such an intervention is the presumption that it is prompted by suspicion, or by an intention to interfere. It would thus be helpful if investigations came to be seen in certain sectors as routine procedures rather than as police or military functions. Respect for sovereignty still requires that the competent authorities be given notice, though this must be short, to avoid the risk that facts will be concealed or falsified. (see *836, 1666*)

2036 – The negotiation of international investigations is among the normal activities of institutions such as the United Nations, in particular the Security Council and the General Assembly, the European Union or the WTO. The proposal was once made in the UN to set up a special international investigative body, but it was not adopted.

On the other hand, the implementation of the Non-Proliferation Treaty by its almost 200 signatories will involve verification exercises, the results of which will be submitted to the United Nations for review every five years. In order to be acceptable and legitimate, any such investigation will require the prior agreement of the States concerned. (see *1741, 1745, 1765*)

2037 – The interest of international inquiries goes beyond the realms of dispute resolution, since fact-finding answers a growing need for full, rapid and impartial information, obtained with the involvement of both sides if possible, in a wide variety of situations. Its negotiation calls for conditions of objectivity, seriousness and efficiency which will be all the more detailed as this technique comes to form part of public, or at any rate institutional, proceedings, whether the bodies involved are political or technical, global or regional, legal, governmental or other. (see *834, 1098*)

2038 – Ordinary administrative investigations are usually conducted by bodies that are part of an existing institution. Where its nature is political, the States concerned reserve the right to agree on a bilateral basis on its scope and methods, but, little by little, the international system is starting to impose multilateral procedures with which States can no longer refuse to cooperate. This issue is one of current interest in the UN Security Council, which for instance set up an inquiry into the assassination in 2005 of the Lebanese Prime Minister. (see *1548*)

2039 – The problems governments face with regard to protecting the confidentiality of certain information are not new: in former times, the seafaring powers refused to make public the maps needed for navigation. Today, however, advances in the gathering, processing and use of intelligence brought about by computerisation raise questions of a different order: the transfer, central storage and summarising of this data are often controlled by the dominant political or financial powers. Their monopoly over certain types of knowledge creates inequality in negotiating capabilities. (see *2600*)

2040 – Ever since diplomatic consultations became commonplace, and now more than ever, information has been the subject of negotiation, so important is it for political decision-making, the efficiency of public services, the success of private business and the progress of science and technology. (see *2654*)

Negotiation about information requires reciprocity between the partners, and such negotiations are, for this reason, often bilateral. (see *1532*)

The first step, and essential precondition, for international cooperation is the sharing of the information on which the discussions will be based: in the EU, the European Commission does the necessary research, to the extent that it is competent, to enable the national policies of the member States to be coordinated.

2041 – The means of analysing and using information are being refined and developed, as these are necessary for forecasting as well as action: errors of judgment are more often the result of misuse of intelligence than of lack of it. Here, too, competition between States is likely to increase.

The judicious use of information enables astute and effective ways to be deployed of searching for more.

2042 – Diplomacy uses all forms of knowledge relevant to negotiation: science has uses in intelligence, direction setting, cooperation, selecting priorities and foreign expansion, both for industrialised and less-developed countries.

The United Nations has come to recognise this, especially in the field of development aid.

2043 – One of the traditional tasks of the negotiator is that of finding out what information his interlocutors have available to them: what is new is that this is now a matter of dialogue. In a complex, changeable situation with disparate kinds of information, parties wishing to come to an agreement have an interest in ensuring that their respective analyses, whether bilateral or multilateral, will lead in the same direction. (see *1712, 1719, 2159*)

2044 – It is thus not unusual, in a negotiation, for the discussions to begin with an attempt to find a common understanding of the environment, and a common agreement on the group objectives: this is done by an exchange of basic intelligence and ensuring that the underlying concepts are in accord. Having the same information generates strong factual links between States, and reinforces the obligations they have mutually undertaken.

2045 – Additionally, gathering, uncovering and compiling data, as well as handling and processing the facts that emerge, allow detailed quantitative estimates to be made of the negotiating potential of States, and thus create inequalities in their ability to manoeuvre. (see *2063*)

Information becomes a major economic and cultural object of negotiation because of the influence it offers and the possibility for action it opens up.

2046 – Obviously, the question will always be asked whether every State is really bound to play an honest and effective part in international programmes that restrict its own freedom of action. The more a State agrees to exchange information, update its planning or realign its approach with those of others, the more political problems are likely to arise when it finds itself bound by increasingly restrictive obligations, imposed by mechanisms it has not agreed to, especially when these are the product of institutions set up and working without its consent. (see *2319*)

2047 – Whatever reservations governments might entertain about the strategic and technical threats it poses, the spread of information is a growing phenomenon in our society, one to which politicians and civil servants alike will have to devote close attention. *The habit of collecting, handling and processing information will impose on negotiators disciplines of thinking and working that will have to be taught.* (see *2643*)

§2. Communication

2048 – A community is made up of persons and groups who are able to communicate with each other and know how to do so. This is not merely a question of trust, persuasion or habit, but also of networks and agreements. These principles are as valid for national diplomacy as they are for trade between nations.[10] (see *1849, 1915, 2262, 2629*)

2049 – The exercise of diplomacy involves the exchange of signals that are sometimes difficult to perceive. *The rules of the game are a communications code that may be shared only by a few partners: so are the procedures and language used to conduct and conclude a negotiation.* The European Union is a good example of the intensity of relations of this type that can develop between States. (see *229, 393, 511, 1841, 1855*)

New techniques for dialogue might appear that facilitate diplomatic contacts. By stimulating public opinion, advances in communication can force States to negotiate, even outside the traditional processes.[11] (see *2243, 2333*)

2050 – The nervous system of any alliance depends on the communications between its members. Experience shows that this is not simply a matter of consultations between capitals, but can involve taking actual operational command: in readiness for potential crises, it was decided in the 1960s that all transatlantic communications should pass through a single agency. (see *859*)

10 K. W. DEUTSCH: *Nationalism and Social Communication*, Cambridge, MIT Press, 1966.
11 H. A. KISSINGER: *White House Years*, Boston, Little, Brown, 1979.

2051 – Negotiation depends entirely on good communications between the protagonists, which means that negotiators must be chosen with care.[12] This is also the role of the chair in multipartite meetings. In a general sense, the greater the exchange of information, the higher the chances of achieving agreement and cooperation.[13] (see *1897*)

Emmanuel Kant, in his essay on 'Perpetual Peace', advised acting first and justifying oneself afterwards: *the good negotiator always has justification ready to pass on.*

2052 – The recourse to third party techniques such as conciliation and mediation confirms the importance of communication: what these mainly do is place the parties in a situation that makes it easier for them to reach agreement by facilitating relations between them, smoothing out problems of contact and comprehension, and suggesting approaches and compromises that are more likely to be accepted because they are not based on the proposals of either of the protagonists. (see *451, 1854*)

Assessing a sensitive situation or conflict is the first step in negotiating its resolution. The interpretation of gestures, words, attitudes and signs is part of the discipline of negotiation, and among its challenges.

2053 – International organisations are opening up increasing numbers of institutionalised channels of communication between States, whether between governmental or parliamentary delegations, or within conferences and councils. The traditional diplomatic route is no longer the only one used for official contacts. (see *1099, 1858, 1880*)

This modification and multiplication of the channels of information makes its exchange much more flexible: one element in the tactics of persuasion or argument is the choice of forum, depending on the effectiveness of its communication, and sometimes on the publicity it attracts.

2054 – The number of actors involved in international negotiation makes problems of communication more complicated: *languages, thought processes and concepts are not the same from one nation to another. Clashes of culture are one expression of these differences.* Administrative barriers exacerbate them. However, agreements between States such as those signed in the OECD and the Council of Europe free up the flow of information, and offer protection to individuals in the use of computerised data. (see *508, 1834, 2190, 2597*)

2055 – Often, one of the first tasks of negotiators nowadays is to agree on the terminology, its use and meaning, in order to translate accurately and comprehensibly notions that are difficult to grasp because of their technical nature and complexity. For instance, the achievement of arms limitation and the regulation of outer space presuppose that the protagonists have agreed on the definitions to be given to the new devices. (see *804*)

---

12 T. C. SCHELLING: *The Strategy of Conflict*, Harvard University Press, 1963, p. 57.
13 J. FRANKEL: *International Politics: Conflict and Harmony*, London, Harmondsworth, 1973.

All practices that make it easier for negotiators to communicate are good: in this respect, there is no substitute for the role played by diplomatic missions.[14] (see *526, 1737*)

2056 – The conflict between the purism of translators and the pragmatism of interpreters itself symbolises the problem with diplomatic terminology, especially in international organisations. Multilateral negotiation can only go forward if an effort is made to study the content of legal, economic and political concepts and the way they are used.

The fact remains, however, that often the most delicately nuanced – and thus the most important – expressions in statements are not capable of being translated into another language.

2057 – As with any field of human activity, negotiation has been affected by the use of new means of communication. First it adapted to telegraph and rail, and then to radio and the aeroplane. Now, though, the effects of the truly major advances are being felt: computerisation, satellite transmission, the widespread use of the Internet, remote conferencing, smaller equipment, interconnection to a variety of networks, and mobile terminals. (see *1006*)

2058 – The ability to transmit information in a fraction of a second to the other ends of the earth, and have it encrypted, processed and stored, makes it possible to use it both instantly and in the longer term, and thus increases the value of the information itself.

Telecommunications are now the true nervous system of diplomacy, whose administrative and technical networks must be adapted to keep up with technological progress. The necessary means must be available to enable complete, continuous and effective negotiation, without however exposing it to the vulnerabilities of over-elaborate systems. More and more diplomatic missions will have their own direct means of access to centralised databases, provided the systems are secure and the confidentiality of messages can be guaranteed. (see *1834*)

So important is the transmission of information that governments seek to retain authority or control over the means, despite the increasing internationalisation of the technology, markets, financing and know-how.

2059 – This is not simply a matter of upgrading to more powerful systems, such as the hotlines that provide secure and direct links between capitals for purposes of information, warnings and ultimately negotiation. (see *2159*)

The lessons of progress must also be applied to staff training and qualifications, and also their working methods. By facilitating and speeding up the ways in which information is coordinated and feedback given, how decisions are made and messages transmitted, telecommunications have changed the way ambassadors and negotiators carry out their missions, as well as the very role of Heads of State.

14 S. HOFFMANN, etc: *International Communication and the New Diplomacy*, Bloomington, Indiana University Press, 1968.

Technology will not make people think or behave in similar ways, but it will bring them increased capabilities and knowledge. It will have the effect of accentuating the inequalities between nations, communities and intellectual elites.

2060 – The statesman can take with him everywhere he goes the experts and instruments needed to keep him in constant contact with central intelligence sources, so that he can react speedily to any eventuality. Without going to the same extremes of refinement, every negotiator must find ways of remaining in discreet and constant contact with the capital or headquarters.

2061 – The speed and variety of means by which messages can be sent serves to reinforce the unity of command. In times when travel was slow and difficult, the general instructions given to plenipotentiaries allowed for a certain liberty as to how they were applied. Today, objectives can easily be reviewed while the discussions are ongoing, and the negotiator is left with no discretion over anything that can be decided by the central bureaucracy. (see *2419*)

2062 – As can be seen from political cooperation in Europe, the communication of information makes it easier for countries to consult together and coordinate their diplomatic positions, while they are not required to give an automatic and identical response as they would in the case of a formal alliance. (see *2050*)

2063 – The march of information, telecommunications and space technologies explains one phenomenon that is truly of our time: the trend towards homogeneity and globalisation of information. Communications can now range over ever widening areas. Some can be deployed over entire continents, making investments more profitable, thus giving large countries an advantage and forcing the smallest into a form of technological annexation. Satellite surveillance and broadcasting are planetary in their scope. The necessary technical and administrative regulations are themselves the product of international negotiation.

2064 – The costs of investment and operation of these networks and systems means they must serve multiple purposes, and that signs and language must be encoded. The Internet is developing in the direction of sophisticated multifunctional networks, used for education, messaging, defence, policing, and trade, which makes interception, fraud, threats and aggression difficult to prevent. After the attacks on New York and Washington of 11 September 2001, messages crossing the Atlantic were counted in hundreds of thousands.

2065 – The negotiator will have to take account of the increasing extent to which computer networks are linked, both in terms of the enhanced services they can offer and of the threats they pose, because they are dependent on major multinational corporations or dominant powers whose state of scientific and technological advancement thus has an indirect bearing on the user's freedom of manoeuvre.

2066 – The widespread sharing of production, information and messaging networks can also be the result of cooperation between certain States on a preferential basis. Here, too, this leads naturally over time to a reduction in diplomatic and military freedom to manoeuvre. Such a system feeds on its own technological and financial success, leading governments, administrations and societies to try to find new areas of agreement.

2067 – These advances open up new possibilities and fresh opportunities for foreign policy, while emphasising its traditional problems. At the same time, though, it makes transnational cooperation, both public and private, a matter of necessity: the more refined and demanding a technique, the greater the cooperation it requires from a variety of sources. For example, negotiation is taking place between States on the joint building and use of satellites for use in the GPS and also the Galileo positioning and telecommunications systems. (see *414*)

2068 – In order to be effective, communications must be easy, free and continuous: it is the function of negotiation to ensure that they are.

Unless international rules exist, States will tend to protect the confidentiality, use and security of important intelligence, by seeking, despite the extension of the Internet, to control the transfer of public or private data across their borders in order to be able to regulate the effects these movements and influences have both on their independence and on legitimate international trade. (see *1816, 1824, 1961*)

2069 – The free movement of information is also a factor in creating mutual understanding, and thus a factor for peace. This problem was central to the discussions on security and cooperation on Europe, where a real division appeared between those political regimes that accepted the free spread of information in its various forms, and those that did not. The resulting tensions lasted until the breakdown of the totalitarian regimes of Central and Eastern Europe.

So great is the efficiency of the media that some negotiations are almost conducted informally and publicly, between interlocutors or groups some of whom may not even be identified at the time: the Afghan crisis in 2001 and the situation in the Middle East provide examples. (see *1844, 2173, 2199*)

2070 – The concept of world society as a global system depends on the internationalisation of the communications, languages and conventions it uses, not only between States but also the other actors in diplomacy, some of whom are private. (see *2258, 2597*)

Commercial operations conducted via the Internet are many and varied. Whether or not political and diplomatic negotiations could ever be conducted via a medium that is so public, unreliable and unpredictable remains open to question, though there are secured networks that enable communications between certain Heads of State or government. Videoconferencing can be used to lay the groundwork for some types of discussion, but only rarely to pursue them to a legal conclusion.

2071 – In practice, international cooperation will always work in favour of some of the participants, for commercial, cultural and sometimes political reasons: the movement will develop of its own accord, even extending to the setting of goals and directions in a wide variety of fields, and to the legislative and budgetary work of national parliaments.

2072 – The result will be that new forms of power sharing spring up between States, depending on their potential in communications: some of them have the human resources, knowledge and capacity to garner information and act on it that no amount of sovereignty can defeat. *Those enterprises with capital, investment capability, technology and research capacity seem difficult to overtake*: two thirds of the worldwide flow of information and communications appear to be controlled from the United States.

2073 – Many States and private businesses will react against the concentration of communications in the hands of certain powers with access to advanced technology. This attitude – already seen among the emerging countries of Asia and South America – will be apparent in their foreign negotiations: they will assert their national individuality more strongly than ever, and refuse all forms of financial, cultural and technical dependency. They will devise their own policies concerning information and the means of transmitting it, and seek to monitor the transfer of information – none of them tactics that are guaranteed to succeed, given the speed of change.

2074 – The mission of international organisations will expand for as long as they can provide all governments, on equal terms, with communications networks based on increasingly complete data storage. The United Nations and some of its specialised agencies, as well as the European institutions, have worked in a common cause to build up computerised research and data transmission systems.

2075 – Thanks to the globalisation of data transmission, intelligence that might have seemed of secondary or even no importance at national level assumes great significance at the international level when it is sufficiently consistent to allow a malaise to be diagnosed, or the dominant players in future negotiation to be identified. (see *1638*)

§3. Forecasting

2076 – Diplomacy is based on the weighing up of probabilities at national level: this will continue for as long as States are centres of autonomous decision-making.[15] As Cardinal de Richelieu wrote, foresight is a necessary part of governing a State.[16]

The reduction in nuclear risks was the subject of detailed and searching negotiations between Moscow and Washington: each of the two powers set up a centre for the purpose and, under the 1987 Washington Agreement, direct, secret links were established between these bodies using meetings and the transmission of information. The Moscow Agreement in 1989 extended these discussions to cover other dangerous military activities, and a whole series of precautionary measures were put in place to prevent them, including a joint military commission to monitor their implementation. The changes that followed in the former USSR aggravated these problems without providing a solution. (see *1733*)

15 R. ARON: *Paix et guerre entre les nations*, Paris, Calmann-Lévy, 1962, p. 22.
16 'La prévoyance est nécessaire au gouvernement d'un Etat', *Testament politique*.

2077 – Anticipation is a way of reacting to uncertainties and countering doubts. It must be practised by the modern negotiator all the more carefully because he is taking quicker decisions in a broad, complex and changing environment, in which the sheer numbers of actors and messages can result in events moving faster, information overload, and sudden upheavals and political shifts.

Forecasting is essential for trust and credibility, and therefore for negotiation.

2078 – Behavioural studies recommended by some researchers take a maximum number of possible variables into account when applied to diplomacy, including such factors as the attitude of the principal players in a negotiation.

Negotiation has the effect of reducing the number of unknown quantities in the political or financial equation, thus limiting those areas not susceptible to reason or forecasting.

2079 – The diplomatic arena worldwide can be seen as a single whole, given the permeability of national frontiers and the emergence of transnational influences. (see *2252*)

Such a vision is a response to the increasing burden of international relations and their economic and social background. It puts a premium on the gathering and use of data, activities still too often underrated by public administrations.

2080 – States are often unprepared to adapt effectively to international realities, whether in terms of their readiness to negotiate, or the conduct of the negotiations themselves. *Ad hoc* decision-making is still too common in the public as well as the private domain, while technical progress adds to the uncertainty, fierce competition is widespread, and, even within Europe, criminality thrives on the permeability of borders. (see *810, 1777*)

2081 – Neither States nor businesses are any better prepared in terms of their responses. It is not enough to know in advance what factors will influence a decision: what matters is to be able to respond fast and effectively to events, especially crisis situations. Here, too, there is room for improvement in diplomacy, with refinements to be made in the uses it makes of human resources as well as tools.[17] (see *2157*)

2082 – Any government must be capable of a sufficiently detailed analysis of the factors that will influence its decision at any given moment, and be able to deal with the consequences as events unfold. A liberal regime must know how to forecast if it wishes to overcome the problems and contradictions of the world around, without resorting to authoritarian forms of planning.[18]

2083 – Advances in the sciences of communications and forecasting have made enormous improvements possible in both the public and private domains, especially in the field of international negotiation. Their approach to these issues combines the gathering of information and the application of sociological analyses in order

---

17 H. A. SIMON: *The New Science of Management Decision*, Englewood Cliffs, Prentice Hall, 1977.
18 A. PLANTEY: *Prospective de l'Etat*, Paris, CNRS, 1975.

to gain a better understanding of the factors and trends in the situations governments have to face.[19]

2084 – The first step is detailed, accessible, complete and up-to-date research, followed by interpretation, constantly refined, of the intelligence acquired. These operations, when carried out in a careful and controlled manner, will provide the negotiator with the means to forecast political, economic and military developments and to decide accordingly on plans for the short or even medium term. This means that new working disciplines must be respected, affecting the use of intelligence and the direction of research, the quality of the data, the speed at which information is transmitted, the need for open-mindedness, the use of aids to decision-making, and the systematic monitoring of the way decisions and agreements are implemented. (see *2020, 2026*)

2085 – The development of new, scientific techniques for analysing international events improves the quality of preparation by making it easier to calculate probabilities, target the operational research and build a better 'game-plan', applying multiple types of reasoning to any given situation or chosen objective. These processes are used in the private sector and can also be applied in diplomacy.[20] (see *558*)

2086 – Professional specialisation and the refinement of methodologies are responses to growing needs and new possibilities. On the one hand, decisions about action must be based on a better quality analysis of events, one that projects further into the future. On the other, it can be tactically useful to publish forecasts that are likely to be fulfilled, and which support the intention to act. (see *558*)

2087 – There are models, often secret, that enable all the factors in a choice to be identified, their influence calculated depending on their respective strengths, and the consequences of certain events simulated. By using them, a diagrammatic representation can be created to explain and predict certain behaviours and the likely outcomes of international negotiation.[21] (see *1777, 2270*)

Situational modelling is current practice, mainly in areas where the data is quantifiable, such as finance, economics, arms and statistics. In the United States, it is often contracted out to private or academic institutions or service companies. (see *2125*)

2088 – Some of the reactions of leaders, as well as of public opinion, can therefore be forecast even before a given diplomatic move is made. Psychological analysis of the major political leaders has been undertaken by certain institutions based on a variety of information, and predictions of collective behaviour refined by the study

---

19 D. DOBROW: *International Relations, New Approaches*, New York, Free Press, 1968.
   N. CHOUCRI and T. W. ROBINSON, etc: *Forecasting in International Relations*, San Francisco, Freeman, 1978.
20 M. SHUBIK, etc: *Game Theory and Related Approaches to Social Behaviour*, New York, Riley, 1964. G. D. BREWER: 'Gaming, Prospective for Forecasting', in *Forecasting in International Relations*, 1978, p. 208.
21 D. DOBROW: *International Relations, New Approaches*, New York, Free Press, 1968.

of each individual nation and the image it has of others. These indicators can sometimes be helpful in guiding negotiation.[22] (see *558*)

2089 – Thanks to research material, improving in quality as well as quantity, and to the ever more refined software available, it is now possible to attempt predictions of events such as shortages and violence. This enables new situations to be evaluated and the risks calculated, and responses suggested knowing their likely consequences. *The preparation and conduct of a negotiation are part of a dialectic with strategic objectives, each of whose steps can, at least according to some researchers, be mathematically calculated with precision.*[23] (see *2667*)

2090 – This opens up a very broad field of inquiry, as these methods allow a tighter grip to be kept on reality, especially where they provide a better understanding of the factors at work within a State's domestic politics, along with a corresponding reduction in the uncertainties that make foreign negotiation difficult.

Chance is the product of a whole range of factors whose influence, or very existence, it is not possible to comprehend: the science of forecasting offers a way of limiting its inherent risks. (see *1630, 1777*)

2091 – Anticipation also requires imagination: the search for information will be guided by the search for hypotheses, and both negotiator and policy will be informed by exploring the future in this way. Forecasting is thus determined by will, and conditioned by strategy. It benefits from the exchange of data and results, and this in its turn makes it a subject of diplomatic negotiation.

2092 – It is doubtful whether negotiators will ever be sufficiently well informed to foresee every eventuality in a changeable international environment. This will not stop governments from trying: many uncertainties pose risks to them, making it more difficult to prevent open conflict. (see *716, 1630, 1700, 1736, 1777*)

International observers failed to predict the swift and total collapse of the Soviet system, so powerful and cohesive did the Communist system seem. However, those events transformed the diplomatic landscape, allowing nationalist and other movements to spring back to life after a period of suppression.

2093 – Constant reassessment of the international environment and national needs should act as a spur to initiative and point the way to diplomatic moves. Sound information is essential for any form of constructive action against unpredictable risk, that might be pursued though diplomatic, commercial or institutional negotiation. The preventive function of such negotiation can only increase in importance as modern societies seek to maintain their security. (see *231, 1706, 1802*)

The century's great strategists will be statesmen and businessmen who can commit the unpredictable, break out of the constraints of conventional logic, and create new models for the future.

22 D. DOBROW: 'International Interactions: Survey and Computers', in *Computers and the Policy-Making Community*, Englewood Cliffs, Prentice Hall, 1966, p. 81. O. HOLSTI: 'Content Analysis in Political Research', ibid., p. 111.
23 D. DOBROW, J. L. SCHWARTS, etc.: *Computers and the Policy-Making Community*, 1966.

2094 – Strategic, economic and financial negotiations bring particularly interesting prospective elements into play: since these are focused on the prevention of crises and conflicts, their pursuit will give opportunities to further refine the methods used in calculation, forecasting and verification. As to strategic arms limitation talks and trade liberalisation agreements, these could even be said, given their difficult and complex nature, the importance of the interests at stake and the amount of effort expended, to have marked a sort of revolution in diplomatic methodology. They have been the subject of in-depth studies, the results of which are mostly confidential. (see *1777, 2157*)

2095 – International discussion will increase among certain States that favour this method, with the harmonisation of the goals and practices of economic intervention as its focus. This can be seen in the European Union, where the governments agree on their interpretation of events, consult each other on the principles of common policies, and often agree on collective or even unified action. There have been proposals to connect and harmonise the respective national planning systems: matters of negotiation are becoming matters of administration. (see *1520*)

2096 – Technical progress has confronted negotiators with some unusually difficult problems, for which skill and imagination will no longer be adequate. If negotiation is to be backed by solid preparatory and decision-making processes, it needs the help of powerful and effective political and administrative institutions.

Keeping information up to date, and unpredictable variables in check, as well as predicting the environmental constraints and the reactions of other parties, are among the duties on which governments must be prepared to expend the necessary money and effort.

2097 – International forecasting is becoming a mainstream activity, with its own experts, tools and specific methods. *Specialist bodies are being set up wherever a need is perceived to gather, process and use information in strategic decision-making.*[24]

2098 – Departments responsible for international forecasting have become a common feature of modern States. In the United States, for example, the President has the National Security Council,[25] the State Department has the Policy Planning Staff, the Defence Department has International Security Affairs and the CIA has the Office of National Estimates.

2099 – There are several bodies of this type in different countries. In the French administration, these include the Prime Minister's strategic analysis council, a forecasting and analysis centre, which is part of the Ministry for Foreign Affairs, and a permanent group for the analysis of international crises at the Defence Ministry, in addition to various other departments not exclusively dedicated to international forecasting.

---

24 K. W. DEUTSCH: *The Nerves of Government: Models of Political Communication and Control*, New York, Free Press, 1963.
25 H. A. KISSINGER: *The National Security Council*, Washington, US government, 1970.

2100 – Since no regulation is possible without forecasting, international organisations, too, are engaged in examining the future. In the UN, studies have been undertaken into disarmament, especially since the setting up of a specialist institute for research in the field, UNIDIR. There is also an advisory committee for the application of science and technology to development.

Among the responsibilities of UNIDIR is to conduct long-term research into disarmament, the problems it poses and the negotiations that will be required in the interests of international security. Its works are published in Geneva.

2101 – Forecasting centres can do a variety of work to support diplomatic negotiation, including background studies, analysis of topics suggested in advance, bringing a multidisciplinary approach to the issues, both horizontal and vertical, offering training and bringing together different administrations and prominent people from all fields.

2102 – The Soviet Union was the first State to try to plan its foreign policy. Based on studies that were primarily economic, and proposals put forward by scientific bodies such as the institute for international relations, plans were drawn up by the Moscow government that were designed to set short and medium term diplomatic goals, as well as annual programmes of work. The main feature of these deliberations was that there was no public representation involved: the Central Committee of the Communist Party set the policy direction.

2103 – If a negotiation is too well planned, however, this can stifle its spirit of initiative, flexibility and adaptability. It can deprive the negotiator of the chance to seize whatever opportunities may arise to bring about agreement, even on matters of substance. Time limits can result in difficult issues being postponed, disputes left unresolved, and entire negotiations having to be restarted at a time when they should already have been over. (see *521*)

2104 – Neither forecasting nor planning, however good they are, can prevail over the vicissitudes of national life, the sudden and powerful rise in ideological movements, the tricks of circumstance or the unpredictability of statesmen: *international affairs are not determined by reason, especially at times of crisis.* (see *2157*)

2105 – Methodological research has its own natural limits. It is impossible to quantify all the factors and circumstances in a negotiation, if only because of the difficulty in isolating and calculating some of the variables, the passion of human reactions, and the unsettling effects of scientific innovation.[26] That said, certain factors, economic, financial and military for example, lend themselves more easily to calculation than others.

2106 – A distinction must be drawn between forecasting and prevention: the exercise of operational responsibilities, or even the prospect of it, is enough to undermine the independence and authority of a prediction. In practice, *the more*

---

26 F. W. HOOLE and D. A. ZINNES: *Quantitative International Politics*, New York, Praeger, 1976.

uncertain and disturbing the future seems, the more the statesman will be inclined to move from forecasting to decisive action.

2107 – New negotiating approaches will be found to international conflict, so that it can not only be resolved but prevented. Though they lack powers of compulsion, international organisations can help maintain relations between the parties, and even compel them to attend conferences under threat of sanction: they can force adversaries to negotiate, perhaps by imposing onerous provisional measures such as an embargo on supplies or a ban on flights. They can also order and set up investigations and record any facts that might aggravate a dispute. Measures of this type can only be ordered with the consent or approval of the major powers, in this case acting under the guise of an institution such as the Security Council. (see *1132*)

2108 – It might be thought that the attentive study of how crises develop will allow the focuses and areas of confrontation to be pinpointed more accurately, thus allowing for better-targeted diplomatic intervention to resolve incompatibilities and conflicts. The very limitations of prediction and simulation show how vital negotiation still is in preventing risks, both national and international. For this reason alone, deterrence is likely to remain a part of the negotiating repertoire.

§4. Decision-making

2109 – The international political scene will always be pluralist, changeable and impossible to control. But the more intensive relations between States become, the greater will be their interdependence in political attitudes, and the more difficult it will be to take separate diplomatic initiatives.[27] In negotiation especially, decision-making will have to be ever better informed and prepared.

2110 – The practice of negotiation is becoming ever more nuanced and complex, with increasing numbers of players, some of them dependent on each other, thus multiplying the scope for change and risk. At the same time, the more countries can be associated with the resolution of a dispute, even one in which they are not directly involved, or the creation of an institution, the more stable and secure will be the outcome of the negotiation. (see *2337*)

This has been one of the considerations underlying the periodic meetings of the WTO, such as the Doha Round, despite the lack of unanimity in Hong Kong in 2005.

2111 – In such an environment, negotiation appears as a complex balance between dependencies assumed and constraints accepted. Negotiation works by a constant process of comparison, and the course it takes depends on how the different factors interact, and especially on how power is exercised within every national decision-making system.[28]

---

27 T. C. SCHELLING: *The Strategy of Conflict*, Cambridge, Harvard University Press, 1963.
28 A. ETZIONI: 'Reciprocal Influence', in *The Theory and Practice of International Relations*, Englewood Cliffs, Prentice Hall, 1966, p. 231. G. KAUFMAN: *Il sistema globale: immagini e modelli*, Udine, 1974.

Internal constraints are rarely understood in the outside world.[29] (see **2549**)

2112 – Effort has been made to apply more scientific methods to negotiation, both in the preparatory phase and in its actual conduct. This work has improved the conditions under which decisions are made, but its effects should not be exaggerated. *Experience shows that rationality is limited and at the same time multiple: it is based on pre-existing values and on insufficient information, and governed by the will, which in its turn is subject to prejudice, ambition, ill-defined goals and intuitive responses.*

One way to preserve secrecy is to create unpredictability.

2113 – The goal will not always be rational. Where it is, the means used to attain it will be rational too – coherent and appropriate. But rationality only applies to intermediate goals, as strategy is dominated by subjective considerations, both individual and collective. *The drawback of a rational approach when applied to diplomatic decision-making is that it underestimates the effect of dysfunctionalities and disruptions: foreign policy is often founded on risk, compromise, cowardice and inconsistency.*[30]

The rational negotiator is instinctively inclined to assume that his opponent follows the same rational approach.

2114 – The rational is not purely linear, especially in negotiation. There can be a number of different, contradictory or successive solutions that are reasonable, depending on the choice of political objective, the external or opposing constraints, and the reliability of the information available. The stronger and clearer the ideals, the harder they are to reconcile.

The growth in international organisations and the expansion of the competences conferred on intergovernmental or European institutions make rational choices more difficult because they deprive national decision-makers of a great deal of their negotiating powers and responsibilities. (see **2682**)

2115 – It is impossible to quantify what is at stake in diplomacy. Only when the results are put to the test can an assessment be made of the quality of the judgment or intuition that guided the negotiations. Analysing a given situation means knowing everything about it, including both rational and emotional aspects. (see **276, 367**)

Preparing to negotiate

2116 – Experimental work carried out mainly in the United States, based on the study of major domestic and international events, has enabled a better analysis of the process of preparation for negotiation. These studies emphasise the combination of pressures exerted by forces at play within each State. (see **203, 278, 441**)

---

29 G. T. ALLISON and M. H. HALPERIN: 'Bureaucratic Politics, a Paradigm and Some Policy Implications', in *Theory and Policy in International Relations*, Princeton University Press, 1972.

30 H. A. KISSINGER, *White House Years*, Boston, Little, Brown, 1979. N. HOWARD: *Paradoxes of Rationality: Theory of Metagames and Political Behavior*, Cambridge, Mass., MIT, 1971.

2117 – There are different theories that make it easier to understand and describe situations of conflict, how they arise and the form they take. One of these is game theory, based on the premise of rational decisions and consistent behaviour; this has proved doctrinally important but of limited practical use in cases where the actors were not principally motivated by gain but by other factors such as prestige.[31]

2118 – Studying foreign policy with the benefit of hindsight has also contributed to teaching and research in this promising field. It has generated a wealth of literature in the United States, with some commentators claiming that there is much to learn from the US in terms of method.[32]

2119 – When applied to an ever-changing process like negotiation, modelling presents enormous problems due to the extreme unpredictability of the circumstances and of the methods used. This is true for internal matters and all the more so for relations between States.

Some of the major financial institutions have constructed partial models of emerging markets, in other words the production and consumption capacities of developing countries. They reveal a high potential for change, with continued growth, subject to exceptions based on political reasons, a sound balance of payments, increased integration into world markets, especially among developing countries, and a more active role in international trade and finance negotiations. The developing country 'model' is one that has worked extremely well for some States, especially in Asia, the Near East and South America. (see *1919*)

2120 – That said, there could never be a general model valid for all diplomatic actions, no matter how much effort was made to rationalise, calculate and simplify. There are, moreover, many different ways of approaching an issue, as well as variations in the information available and the political assumptions. The very fact that negotiations break down shows that any attempt to predict human behaviour is uncertain.

2121 – It is, on the other hand, possible to create simulations of elements of the individual technical, economic or military issue under negotiation, where the information available is complete, valid, and properly processed and verified.

The serious consequences of the lack of information, or of mistakes in using it, prompts the conclusion that several persons should be involved: up to a point, the more experts there are, the easier it is to verify the facts. This formula is applied in the private sector.

2122 – Building a model rarely suggests the answers to the issues to be negotiated: if it were otherwise, problems could be resolved without the political powers ever becoming involved. Also, in a multipartite environment, the sources of information and the play of reciprocal concessions become extremely complicated.

---

31 J. von NEUMANN and O. MORGENSTERN: *Theory of Games and Economic Behavior*, Princeton, 1944 and 1953.
32 R. TANTER: *Modelling and Managing International Conflicts, the Berlin Crisis*, London, 1974.

Use of the Internet has spread the practice of games, challenges and combats whose tactics, though not their rhythm, often resemble those of diplomatic negotiation.

2123 – There are, nonetheless, cases where governments reach agreement on the basis of purely technical work, such as the definition of a frontier or the projection of a trend by applying mathematical procedures, using criteria agreed between the parties or imposed on them: the United States has been known to do this in its diplomacy.

2124 – The principal merit of constructing models is that it identifies the information needed and the parameters to be used, and also how these interact. It permits a first inventory of the facts and variables to be drawn up, and a preliminary review of the issues before discussions open.[33] (see *2087*)

2125 – By applying the disciplines of systems analysis to the limited number of possible diplomatic or financial configurations, models can serve as a catalyst and stimulant to decision-making.[34]

Often, these simulations provide the negotiator with a very sophisticated framework providing much information about the players and the factors in the discussion, thus enabling him to weigh up their interactions from the standpoint of his own concerns. Each camp can thus decide on its own behaviour as a function of the goals and constraints. These methods will become progressively more refined.

2126 – When preparing to negotiate it must be recalled that human behaviour is partly irrational, especially since the essence of strategic reasoning is that it depends on unpredictable extraneous factors the effects of which it tries to assess and control: no social system can be entirely regulated, fixed or controlled in advance.[35] Situational models that draw on earlier methods now exist, enabling characters and incidents to be factored into the forecast and their effect calculated in scenarios based on different patterns of behaviour, action and reaction, even including breakdown.

2127 – Studies based on scenarios must allow for chance as well as reason: they are becoming more adept at isolating those factors that produce risk and uncertainty, and calibrating their impact. Their use is not confined to strategic threats and military conflict. Diplomatic negotiation, too, whatever it is about, should have the benefit of the latest techniques in forecasting, analysis and reasoning.

Governments must be ready to entrust these strategic or pre-strategic studies to institutions or private businesses specialising in the analysis and evaluation of international events, based on information that is often difficult to gather.

---

33 F. EDMEAD: 'Analysis and Prediction in International Mediation', in *Dispute Settlement through the United Nations*, 1971, p. 221.

34 S. COLE: *Global Models and the International Economic Order*, New York, UNITAR, 1977.

35 J. FRANKEL: *Making of Foreign Policy*, London, Oxford University Press, 1963.

2128 – The devising and use of full-scale scenarios will create *rapprochement* between the international scientific and administrative communities that use them: by changing the spirit in which negotiation is approached, they will improve its quality.[36]

2129 – Mathematics, information technology and scientific experiment are all resources that can be used to gather facts and set the criteria for the necessary choices in command and decision-making: statesmen can be expected to use them intelligently, which will enhance the potential for them to express their own talent. (see **2616**)

2130 – These methods keep the negotiators better informed, and better able to choose the best approach to complex discussions. They also allow adjustments to be made to that approach as the negotiations go forward, depending on the results produced, thanks to retroactive techniques of correction or simulation.[37] This keeps in check the feelings of superiority and the passionate reactions that create the danger of a diplomatic process that is over-personalised.

2131 – Aids to decision-making do not remove the obligation to decide or the responsibility that goes with it. The factors taken into consideration are subject to interpretation; not all the risks can be calculated. *Goals are part of tactics and also of strategy: the more important and confidential the issue, the more policy will be influenced by personality.*

2132 – The intensive analyses carried out in recent years of the way government policy is drawn up can help a better understanding of how events abroad are shaped and the reactions they produce.[38] They show the great and varied impact of underlying preconceptions, including the role of the irrational in decision-making[39] and the effects of conformism in stifling imagination and willingness to adapt.[40]

2133 – The fact that the limitations on international negotiation can be explained by the interplay of various political, administrative, professional or cultural forces is not enough to justify or dictate the course it follows. Even within the most highly-structured bureaucracies, decision-making will be affected by individual, psychological and sociological factors such as patterns of behaviour, speed of work, temperament, responsiveness, personal experience and place in the hierarchy.[41]

---

36 K. W. DEUTSCH: *The Nerves of Government, Models of Political Communication and Control*, London, Free Press, 1966.
37 R. J. RUMMEL: 'International Pattern and Nations Profile Delineation', in *Computers and the Policy-Making Community*, p. 159.
38 M. HALPERIN and P. CLAPP: *Bureaucratic Politics and Foreign Policy*, Washington, Brookings Institution Press, 1974.
39 R. C. SNYDER, H. W. BRUCK and B. SAPIN: *Foreign Policy Decision Making*, New York, Free Press, 1962.
40 S. T. POSSONY: *Foreign Policy and Rationality*, Philadelphia, Orbis, 1968, p. 132.
41 M. HALPERIN and P. CLAPP: *Bureaucratic Politics and Foreign Policy*, Washington, Brookings Institution Press, 1974. H. RAIFFA: *The Art and Science of Negotiation*, Harvard University Press, 1982.

2134 – Even the idea of the national interest can be viewed in different ways, depending not only on the political opinions and cultural ties of the decision-makers, but also on the information they have available, their particular fields of responsibility, the preoccupations of the domestic administration, the influence of ethical and ideological solidarity, and their awareness of the consequences of failure.[42] (see **597, 2360**)

2135 – The trend to internationalisation affects the decision-making powers of national authorities in a variety of ways, especially where foreign negotiation is concerned. *Reactions to the pressures of the environment are not always the same: the notion of independence does not have the same meaning or carry the same weight from one nation to another.* (see **2310**)

2136 – Within the great continental powers, whose security and prosperity do not depend to any great degree on what happens outside their borders, the diplomatic aspect of these issues can often even be of quite secondary importance, which explains how the negotiator can run up against the inflexibilities of his national system when concessions need to be made. (see **2551**)

2137 – Starting with the exchange and use of intelligence, negotiation will focus increasingly on the search for agreement between the partners on how to analyse the facts of a given situation, exercise their powers of decision, and prevent the crises that could arise. Major multinational companies, too, make a contribution to this process where they have an interest in a stable and predictable business environment. (see **2157**)

Negotiators will learn not to overestimate how much freedom of manoeuvre the other parties have.[43] (see **2040**)

2138 – Depending on the subject-matter under discussion, where there are convergent interests or programmes in place, there is much fruitful cross-border collaboration of this kind between professionals, government officials and technical experts.[44]

2139 – There is a further complication to be factored in when preparing for major negotiations, namely the sheer number of technical issues to be discussed. During the negotiations for the lifting of customs barriers, the products discussed ran into thousands. *Sometimes this presents such problems that it is only when negotiations are already under way that certain issues come to light, and central government can be asked to issue instructions to its representatives.*

2140 – Added to this is the number of States involved, and the degree of variation in their administrative and legislative practices. It is no easy matter to arrive at a national position on all these issues, especially where, as in the case

---

42 J. FRANKEL: *National Interest*, London, Pall Mall, 1970.

43 H. A. KISSINGER: 'The Viet-Nam Negotiations', *Foreign Affairs*, 1969, 2, p. 217.

44 J. W. FIELD: Non Governmental Forces and World Politics: a Study of Business, Labor and Political Groups, New York, Praeger, 1972; *International Relations, a Transnational Policy Approach*, Sherman Oaks, Alfred, 1979.

of the European Union, it must be a position common to several countries. (see *1267, 1442*)

The process of negotiation

2141 – Commentators have been right to emphasise the limited role of rationality in the choices that guide foreign policy.[45] On the other hand, the course of the negotiation is in turn limited by the dialectic of bargaining, whether bilateral or conducted within the procedural framework of an international institution, and this makes it susceptible to study based on logical analysis.

2142 – Irrationality does not always lead to empiricism, but, on the contrary, it does lead to continuous improvement in working methods. Studies published in the United States have been able to define the main characteristics of the major types of negotiation[46] and of negotiators.[47]

The overall study of negotiation from the scientific, psychological, sociological and historical perspectives enables a picture to be built up of the dynamics of relations between States and how they can be constantly adapted. Such analyses proceed from the basic themes of bilateral negotiation to address the most complex and unstable patterns of multipolar debate.

2143 – Prudence is called for here, though: however useful it may be to have diagrams based on past experience, such is the variety of situations and strategies that every new negotiation is different.

2144 – The actual process of negotiation has been the subject of comprehensive theoretical studies by the proponents of different schools of thought, each focused on their specific themes. Much was published in this field in the United States following the growth in collective labour negotiations and arbitration. (see *202*)

2145 – Any negotiation of importance will be the subject of forecasting and planning all the time it is going on. This might involve the use of diagrams, calculations, sequential processes and simulations. The methods used might be more or less refined, from simple decision trees to the application of the latest techniques of selection, cybernetics or operational research.[48]

2146 – The unfolding of a negotiation consists of a succession of more or less clearly-defined alternatives, the choice between which depends on tactics or strategy. These choices, in turn, affect the course of the discussions. In a bilateral negotiation, information can be kept up to date by computer and detailed preparations made, and these advantages will also be felt before long in

---

45 S. T. POSSONY: *Foreign Policy and Rationality*, Philadelphia, Orbis, 1968, p. 132.
46 M. A. KAPLAN: *System and Process in International Politics*, New York, Wiley, 1957.
47 M. SCHERIF: *Group Conflict and Cooperation: their Social Psychology*, London, Routledge, 1966. H. TOUZARD: *La Médiation et la résolution des conflits*, Paris, PUF, 1977, p. 223.
48 K. W. DEUTSCH: *The Nerves of Government, Models of Political Communication and Control*, New York, Free Press, 1963.

multilateral procedures. This scientific approach often leads to the rediscovery of old formulas that have been used for centuries.

2147 – Science may not be able to eliminate the unpredictable from human behaviour, but it can limit its effects. No computer can trace the course of a negotiation in the same way as it would a road-map, but, depending on its memory and programming, it can narrow down the unexpected and evaluate the hypotheses before it.

2148 – *It is often when the subject matter is broken down logically and chronologically during a negotiation that solutions take shape, stage by stage and sector by sector.* Scientific methods have the merit of evaluating the phenomenon of self-regulation within each camp in order to make the best use of the results of successive negotiations. (see *264, 329, 520, 586*)

The architecture of a negotiation is gradually revealed, not as a sequence but a complex pattern, made up of processes that are concomitant, concurrent and simultaneous, as well as impulses and reactions, reserves and projections. This architecture can be approached systematically and mathematically tested.[49] (see *422*)

2149 – For every question there is a range of possible initiatives or answers. Within each logical or chronological whole there are sub-sets that are themselves worthy of minute and careful study.

2150 – Psychologists and psycho-sociologists, too, have studied the ways and means of negotiation, in other words the behaviour and relationships of the parties, their motives and goals, how they arrive at their hypotheses and make their choices, the framework and level of the discussions, the tactics of compromise and opposition, how conflicts unfold and how joint decisions are taken.[50]

2151 – The variables, both individual and collective, internal and external, that come into play can be studied in the same way as any conflictual process can be studied, by looking at its components and taking it as a whole.

For this reason, it is vital to clarify the parties' motives: where they complement each other, the negotiations will go faster and, likewise, competition is fiercer between protagonists pursuing the same objective.

2152 – Obviously, any logical approach to negotiation must begin at the beginning: from that moment, the setting of the objectives gives the exercise its definition, and imparts its particular political and intellectual nature.[51]

According to many theorists, the highest gains often come from exaggerating the original demands and proposals: the British experience in the framework of the European Community proved that firmness pays. *The hardest tactic is the most*

49 K. E. KNORR and J. ROSENAU: *Contending Approaches to International Politics*, Princeton University Press, 1969. O. YOUNG, etc.: *Bargaining, Formal Theories of Negotiation*, Chicago, University of Illinois Press, 1975.

50 I. W. ZARTMAN, etc.: *The Negotiation Process*, London, 1978.

51 M. DEUTSCH: *The Resolution of Conflict*, New Haven, Yale University Press, 1973.

profitable. But, in most cases, the pressure of time overcomes intransigence. (see *304, 444, 557*)

2153 – Firmness does not mean that there can be no concessions, but it is difficult to choose the most effective course of conduct. Negotiations in which one party's hands are tied from the outset will give the impression of a *fait accompli*, and induce the others to go further than they had intended, free from unacceptable constraints. In this way, negotiation creates its own field of manoeuvre. (see *95*)

2154 – It sometimes happens that the goal of a negotiation only becomes clear as the discussions progress: the parties work together stage by stage to find the solution to the problem.[52] Where the environment is uncertain and difficult, the negotiation will tend towards cooperation, starting with the search for agreement on how the situation should be analysed.[53] (see *329, 422*)

2155 – The use of ratification, coupled with a degree of distrust, often leads politicians to withhold from the negotiators themselves the right to decide what concessions should be made in order to reach an agreement. Except where it is impossible for practical reasons, the maker of concessions is looked to when instructions need to be changed. (see *449*)

For an international negotiation to have strategic significance, the responsibility for each successive choice must lie with those whose vision extends beyond the particular discussion in hand. (see *2334*)

2156 – The successive moves a negotiator can make depend on his mandate. The same is true for all the protagonists. This is well known in diplomatic circles, and this fact alone is often enough to neutralise any tendency for the discussion to become personalised, and to head off confrontation. (see *557*)

It is the very absence of serious constraint, or the fact that it is very vague, that creates the greatest risk of conflict in summit negotiations, where the opposing interests and ideas of governments can take on the appearance of personal quarrels. (see *2492*)

Crisis negotiation

2157 – Decisions are not taken under the same conditions if there is a crisis as they are under normal circumstances: when the situation is serious, choice becomes urgent, and there is a risk that the first satisfactory solution will be adopted. New methods of forecasting and preventing conflict should make it easier to handle urgent situations.[54] (see *715, 2094, 2105, 2108, 2113*)

---

52 D. STEINBRUNER: *The Cybernetic Theory of Decision: New Dimension of Political Analysis*, Princeton University Press, 1974.
53 I. W. ZARTMAN: 'Negotiation: Theory and Reality', *Journal of International Affairs*, 1975, XXIX, p. 69.
54 C. F. HERMANN, etc: *International Crisis: Insights for Behavioural Research*, New York, Free Press, 1972. T. DUNGWORTH: *The Structure of International Conflict*, Michigan State University, 1971.

In an environment where interests coagulate, both open conflict and latent tensions are capable of spreading rapidly, with severe consequences in all areas – security, finance, trade, culture and religion. (see *1492, 1493, 2079*)

2158 – Analysis of the concept of international crisis also shows that negotiation is the best response. What causes crises in practice is incompatibility between the goals of the international actors, the will of one or more of those actors to achieve its goals by unilateral means – against the will of the others if necessary – and the inability of the existing machinery to head off the conflict.[55] (see *55, 228*)

Within alliances, international crises are useful and necessary tests.

2159 – The search for a solution thus implies a concerted process that examines motives, revises objectives, prevents the use of force, seeks the *rapprochement* of the different sensitivities, holds back manoeuvres and puts in place the machinery for intervention, in order to maintain or re-establish strategic balances. These are complex, detailed and promising areas of work, involving painstaking and careful research. (see *1520, 1679, 2043*)

The increasing numbers of cases of emergency humanitarian intervention have been made possible by the Security Council's interpretation of the prescriptions in Chapter VII of the Charter: this means that there can be intervention in the domestic affairs of States when a decision is taken in the Security Council within its remit under the Charter with no permanent member objecting, and without the need for any new diplomatic instrument. There has been talk of a 'right to interfere', but the fact remains that no State has the right to enter the territory of another without its consent. Use of force in this context might at any moment generate political opposition that would plunge the UN back into the state of inaction that prevailed between 1950 and 1980. (see *645, 729, 823, 1667, 2785*)

2160 – Within the best organised governments, crisis units often exist whose function is not only to keep the authorities informed, but to take whatever diplomatic or military measures may be called for. In case of emergency, international negotiation is still one of the ways to prevent risks becoming aggravated and to re-establish the balance. (see *266, 1503, 2093*)

Aside from the Balkans, certain trouble spots are starting to appear, especially in Africa and Asia, now in the grip of the arms race. *Crisis negotiation will therefore take its place as a discipline in its own right.* (see *1692, 1892*)

2161 – While it is possible to speak of 'conflict management', it would be flying in the face of logic and good sense to suggest that acts of negotiation were anonymous or automatic: they remain marked to a very high degree by the personality of their authors and actors.[56] (see *2105, 2538*)

---

55 C. F. HERMANN: *Crisis in Foreign Policy*, Indianapolis, Bobby Merril, 1969.
   D. DOBROW: *International Relations, New Approaches*, New York, Free Press, 1968, p. 37.
56 A. PLANTEY: 'Crise et pouvoir', *Revue stratégique*, 1982. 'Quelques réflexions sur le traitement des crises', *Revue stratégique*, 1984; 'La psychologie de crise', *Revue de Défense nationale*, 1988; *Actualité des conflits internationaux*, Paris, Pedone, 1993.

By giving structure to the confrontation and sometimes the conjunction of two or more wills, the communication process reduces the role of chance in how crises unfold. It is also true that diplomatic moves can sometimes provoke the tension needed to drive a negotiation forward. (see *2091, 2108, 2189*)

International institutions are ill-prepared to assume the risks and responsibilities that ensue, as was seen from the duplication of effort between the UN and NATO at the time of the crisis in the former Yugoslavia. (see *1132, 1692, 2221*)

Section 2: Anticipation and hypotheses

2162 – All manner of disparate goals and aspirations, economic, political and ideological, national and private, come into play at the international level. This gives a new dimension to international negotiation: it is no longer enough for States to agree at the purely tactical level, but they must also agree on their respective policy directions in order to have any prospect of dealing with unexpected eventualities. (see *733*)

2163 – Harold Nicolson observed many years ago that international relations were no longer a matter of the expression of national policies through rival and opposing diplomatic services: the need for a common order required international cooperation. Negotiation should be harnessed in the general interest.[57]

2164 – Diplomacy will be more necessary than ever for the social entity whose aspirations it expresses. At a time when the lives of people as well as businesses are directly exposed to international influences, governments would do well to work together when setting their national goals, harnessing the common, complementary or similar interests of States.[58]

2165 – The interests and ambitions of States can converge or diverge, depending on the circumstances. A forward-looking approach to negotiation is required if international society is to adapt: the politics of Western Europe and the American continent show this to be so. Negotiation for the future also makes possible the sometimes rapid forward momentum of international society, providing the only peaceful means for States to consolidate their rights and carve themselves an international role while respecting the dignity of others.

The United States have led the way in showing how national strategies can change and adapt to the various generalised and unpredictable threats in a deeply conflicted environment, lacking in any moral authority. (see *1699*)

2166 – States could negotiate endlessly about future prospects and programmes of action. The goals of the European movement are constantly being debated in a changing world: the Common Market was variously regarded as an end in itself, a stage towards a goal, or as having already gone too far. The same could be said of military objectives and the new economic order, as well as the law applicable to space and cyberspace. (see *1350*)

---

57 H. NICOLSON: *Diplomacy*, Oxford, Oxford University Press, 1945, III, 1.
58 F. C. IKLE: *How Nations Negotiate*, New York, Harper Row, 1964.

In order to reconcile future strategies, it is first necessary to negotiate their underlying assumptions. (see *2329*)

§1. The negotiation of ideas

2167 – Negotiation is an exercise of will. As such, it not only provides the means of maintaining harmonious relations between States, and making their interests converge, but its development also amounts to a process of social change. By allowing the exchange of conflicting ideas, it enables actual confrontation to be avoided. This has been true of all the great negotiations in history, whose geopolitical effects have been felt down the decades. It is true today of the work of major multilateral conferences, whose dynamic expression of their participants' vision of the future rests on the hope of a more peaceful world order.

Public opinion has been stirred by a number of ecological incidents and disasters. *The attitude of States might be lukewarm, but the international community has shown itself sensitive to major ethical problems by the gradual setting of standards in the fields of environment and humanitarian aid.* This development has led to an increasing willingness to interfere in the internal affairs of States based on principles that have assumed the character of customary norms, and are legally defined even if not clearly binding. (see *2213*)

2168 – Many national and international institutions are engaged in reflection about the future, or encouraging it by devising topics for research based on detected needs, and by providing the information, contacts, exchange of ideas and circulation of works on the subject. There are a number of intergovernmental organisations and 'think-tanks' such as UNITAR, engaged in defining new issues, giving shape to ideas that are forming, and putting forward programmes of action, all of which provide a rich seam of material for diplomatic discussion.[59]

2169 – A growing proportion of the debates in the UN General Assembly betray the concern to build a new vision of the future of mankind. Its committees work for long periods on drawing up proposals, declarations and conventions, which means that the groundwork for the exercise by the organisation of its 'pre-normative' role has already largely been negotiated.[60] The political effects of the debates and declarations on the issue of self-determination were to last more than a decade.

In UNCITRAL, some of the proposals made took years to bear fruit, and generalised tariff preferences, rejected by the United Nations in 1964, were accepted in 1970 and adopted by the European Community in 1971. The fight against racism, based on the Charter, was the subject of major international meetings in 1978 and 1989, and also a conference held in Durban in 2001 on Racism, Racial Discrimination, Xenophobia and Related Intolerance.

---

59 UN: *Science, Technology and Global Problems*, Office for Science and Technology, Pergamon Press, 1979.
60 H. BOKOR-SZEGO: 'The United Nations' Role in Treaty Making', in *Questions of International Law*, Budapest and Leiden, Sijthoff, 1977, p. 9.

2170 – The negotiation of ideas starts with psychological and ideological preparation: the idea is to provoke the strongest possible reaction, in order to generate awareness of the issue and set in motion a multilateral debate. It is this search for a solid basis of shared conviction that will affect the way nations behave. Even language has a role here: the tendency is towards the use of sweeping concepts that, once accepted, will drive forward the international debate.

Ambitious methods and ambitious terminology are used to stimulate the work of international institutions as well as those of Europe: vast areas are opening up to them where State sovereignty has hitherto not been subject to outside interference. In calling basic values into question and challenging political and cultural absolutes, such negotiations open up a huge range of possibilities.

2171 – Human rights is one area covered by the UN Charter (see Articles 1.3, 62 and 76) that has been developed through the work of the organisation. The Covenants on Civil and Political Rights and on Economic, Social and Cultural Rights were signed in 1966; the Global Compact was drawn up in Davos in 1999 and adopted by the United Nations the following year. (see *1948, 1979, 1989, 1990*)

The European Convention on Human Rights, signed in Rome in 1950 in the framework of the Council of Europe, sparked an upsurge in diplomatic negotiation in this area. That Convention was ratified by Russia in 1995. At the time of its 2005 summit in Warsaw, the Council of Europe had 48 members. Similar instruments have followed, involving growing numbers of partners, in Europe as elsewhere. The OSCE Conference in Copenhagen in 1990 made reference to its rules. The European Charter of Fundamental Rights was signed in Nice in 2001: its principles should form part of the body of European law alongside the 1950 Convention. The Inter-American Human Rights Commission, founded in 1960, is based on the same broad principles. (see *1249, 1393, 1671*)

Humanitarian aid is another area in which the entire international community is interested and in which new ideas might be expected to develop.

The OSCE, for its part, has made a specialisation of observing elections, particularly in the countries of the former Soviet bloc, a fact that has been criticised by Russia. (see *1700*)

2172 – In spite of the time it consumes, a general debate marks the beginnings of collective consideration of the issues, and sets the scene for negotiation: starting with the mutual exchange of information, it progressively brings out conflicts over programmes and symbols. The legal nature of the oral debates means that the process sometimes comes to resemble a parliament, with the same risks of overload.

The struggle for ideas is not always peaceful, or even conducive to peace. (see *1866*)

2173 – These developments show the spectacular success of a number of concepts that modern society has embraced – not always coherently – and which are coming to be widely accepted as the major themes of the day. Thus, human rights, self-determination, non-aggression, development, technical assistance, international justice, environmental protection and ethical dealing have established themselves as modern imperatives. The developing world has succeeded in ensuring that its chosen formulations are used throughout the entire United Nations system, as in the Global Compact. (see *1218*)

Non-governmental organisations and other unofficial movements, whether they serve as the vehicle for major trends in thought or simply as pressure groups, have a role to play in these areas: they see to it that their voice is heard wherever world leaders gather. There were some 20,000 participants at the World Social Forum in Porto Alegre in 2001, and 120,000 in 2004. (see *1516, 1892, 1907, 1911, 2489*)

There is a constant two-way flow of national laws and international ideals going on within these negotiations, which helps to give them their forward-looking quality.

2174 – The systematic exaggeration of doctrinal starting positions does not prevent negotiation from moving forward. On the contrary, it brings faster awareness of what some of the issues are, and sometimes allows quite bold convictions to gain widespread currency, as can be seen from the annual and ten-yearly programmes the United Nations devotes to forward-looking themes. With time, attitudes change, ideologies spread, and the protagonists adjust their positions through meeting each other.

Though they do not have binding legal force, the recommendations, resolutions and declarations drawn up at these international conferences, both official and private, form the high point, at least for the time being, in what are often difficult multilateral negotiations. Each time, this represents another milestone in the process of developing international rules and standards.

2175 – Because its goals are moral or social in nature, this kind of negotiation does not produce the traditional types of outcome: it is more likely to result in agreements on general strategy in language that is evocative but sometimes badly-drafted, than it is to produce legally enforceable instruments. Antithetical notions come to be reconciled over time, such as peaceful coexistence and détente, sovereign equality and 'protective inequality', reciprocity and compensation for delays in development.

In a negotiation about ideas, the parties often find common ground on the objectives, and equally often diverge as to the means if achieving them. The United States have taken part in the adoption of inter-American instruments on human rights ever since the Bogotà Declaration in 1948, but have never recognised them as binding, and refused to ratify the Pact of San José in 1969. (see *2171*)

2176 – When the new economic order appeared on the agenda of world organisations, this was the result of a broad movement of ideas that went beyond the routine negotiation of financial aid, technical assistance and technology transfer. As early as 1970, the possibility was raised in the United Nations of an international strategy on development, then on creativity, an idea suggestive of targeted global effort. The notion of development has been progressively refined ever since the first meeting of UNCITRAL in Geneva in 1964.

2177 – The collective effort that followed, one of information-gathering, critical reflection and generous anticipation, gave a new direction to international negotiation by forcing it, through persuasion or moral conviction, to adopt new objectives. This process was pursued with tenacity, and international relations advanced through several stages in legal, diplomatic and ethical terms as a result. Its product, the Charter of the Economic Rights and Duties of States, served in its turn as the basis for further progress in the broader areas of socio-cultural, technological and legal development. Also involved in these efforts are the specialised agencies, each of them promoting international cooperation within its own sphere of competence.

2178 – The concern that international relations should be based on negotiation rather than imposed from above has led governments to cooperate in every possible area, even against the wishes of the most powerful States. Here, again, the driving forces of ideology can be seen at work. (see *1953*)

2179 – Some governments rely on general theories to strengthen their negotiating position. The use of human rights as a tool of diplomacy might influence the freedom of certain States to manoeuvre, without necessarily having any concrete effect on how they conduct their internal affairs: the conference in Vienna in 1993 on the subject produced only an unenthusiastic consensus. (see *1893*)

A community-based approach allows moral and financial obligations to be laid at the door of the richest.

2180 – Negotiation can have innovation as its goal: the most striking examples are the Treaties of Paris and Rome that set up the European Communities.[61] The guiding brains behind them were wagering on the future: they anticipated a dawning of collective awareness, as happened later with the law of the sea and the environment, where initiatives sparked by the United Nations triggered government action and legislation in countless countries. (see *1333, 1970*)

2181 – The introduction into the diplomatic debate of conflicting ideas, of irrational claims, moral considerations, expressions of condemnation and exhortation, the scientific and the prophetic, has altered its methods and spirit. The quest for a 'new economic order' imposes goals that are different from those of traditional diplomacy. Among the innovations for which States now seek the sanction of negotiation are attempts at global restructuring and affirmative action, the recognition of majority rights and the special responsibilities of the richest States, regulation of information and markets, and the sharing of benefits. (see *666, 1279, 1981*)

2182 – International law is as much the product of situations that consolidate, and customs consistently applied over time, as of diplomatic negotiation in the strict sense of the term. It is understandable that the effects of time or repetition could be the same for principles of recent origin, that arise out of the acceptance of new trends or new obligations in policy, economics or ideology. *It is safe to predict that much of the business left unfinished by negotiation will still spark unexpected legal*

61 F. C. IKLE: *How Nations Negotiate*, New York, Harper Row, 1964, p. 35.

*advances, where they coincide with the current state of practice and convictions
and once they have the consent of most States if not all.*

2183 – Statesman should pay careful attention to the political programmes of
emerging and developing countries, which carry the immense persuasive force of
large and underprivileged populations. Even if it is not possible to accommodate
all their wishes, they influence the course of negotiations in the direction of
adopting new norms that are not yet clearly defined, but already partly recognised
by those countries whose wealth and power they restrict.

The Cuzco Conference, which brought together the twelve States of South
America, showed how strong were their hopes of alliance and collective action, as
well as the practical difficulties in the way of achieving them.

2184 – The resulting shift can be seen both in the means of diplomacy and its ends.
On the one hand, it means that a whole range of arguments or approaches that
used to be routinely deployed in political manoeuvres cannot now be used, as they
are regarded as evil or cynical. On the other, rules of international ethics are
creeping in as sources of positive law, and progressively gaining acceptance.

The balance of power between States has changed so much that, even with
nuclear deterrence, whole new areas are still opening up to political initiatives and
diplomatic negotiation.

2185 – The negotiation of future goals thus colours even traditional bilateral
relations between States: agreements are drafted that include forward-looking
declarations of principle intended to govern relations between States sometimes for
decades in advance. A large proportion of negotiation within the European Union
is prospective in nature, as with the Treaties of Maastricht and Nice: so, too, was
the spirit in which the draft constitutional treaty was put forward.

Some of the old traditions of diplomacy are thus now reappearing: a promise
expresses a tactic rather than a strategy. The changing attitude of the United States
towards Panama is an example: the 1977 treaty provided for sovereignty to be
restored to Panama and the Canal zone jointly managed until 1989, but a further
treaty, signed in 1978, imposed an obligation to guarantee the neutrality of
the Canal.

§2. The normative dynamic

2186 – Negotiations normally deal with the future. Today, negotiation is often
approached in very new ways, with the parties accepting from the outset that
renegotiation or challenge is possible, or by anticipating future developments.
(see *1545*)

*No progress is continuous or definitive. Freedom is among the risks that
negotiation can be used to limit.*

2187 – Within an organisation, negotiation aims to attract the greatest possible
number of adherents. It becomes exposed to ambiguity, criticism or opposition
once it extends beyond the traditional concerns of diplomacy and admits

obligations based on the sorts of broad collective notions to which all parties can bring their own motives and preconceptions. Concepts like supranationality, economic integration, the reparation of injustice, solidarity in the fight against under-development, and the common heritage of mankind have yet to be precisely defined. (see *2220*)

2188 – Where it is not possible to transform an ideology immediately into an executory norm, countries or groups seek ways to open up discussion on it, or put it into practice. This innovative dynamic is much in evidence in Europe, and also in many emerging and developing countries that have their own different ways of interpreting international law. During the two World Wars, there was already sufficient solidarity of democratic opinion against aggression to provide the basis for the negotiation that created the League of Nations and later the United Nations.
Using a concept makes it clearer and more credible.

2189 – These characteristics have been identified and written about in relation to the right to development. However, this is not the only field of international negotiation in which they can be found.
Prospective diplomacy expresses the wish of States to address the changes and uncertainties that affect them: the discussions on arms limitation, for example, were not at the outset directed so much towards reducing military potential, as to securing voluntary control over its growth for the foreseeable future. Negotiation of this kind, with a potentially much wider impact, is a response to the need to predict and limit the effect of variables that concern States all the more because science has progressed to the point where they can no longer control them. At the same time, it leaves open the possibility of innovation: some commitments are made for a limited time only, with each opposing party counting on events to alter the situation in its favour. (see *1736, 1741*)

2190 – Traditional international law has been defined as a system of norms with a given geographical bias (it was a European system), a given ethico-religious basis (it was law founded on Christian principles), economic underpinnings (it was a mercantile system) and political designs (it was the law of imperialism).[62] Challenges to it have raised large-scale debate and caused many negotiations to be reopened.
To give a different example, the Chinese interpretation of the main principles of law emphasises sovereign prerogatives over human rights, reciprocity of exchanges over humanitarian intervention, and future calculation over short-term commitment.
The collective re-examination of the principles that govern friendly relations between States, advocated by proponents of the non-aligned ideology, would have offered an opportunity for reassessment and reaffirmation of the basic concepts in the UN Charter.

2191 – Law has always been, at least in part, the vehicle and the expression of cultural and ideological values. To the extent that international organisations have a role in creating it, they bring to bear the influence of ideas that have been

---

62 M. BEDJAOUI: *Pour un nouvel ordre économique mondial*, Paris, UNESCO, 1978, p. 51.

negotiated. The issuing of resolutions, recommendations or drafts that have no binding force can be a step towards achievement of a particular European or international policy, or an end in itself. (see *721, 2054, 2171*)

The entire process of constructing the European Community has been dominated by the will to harmonise or integrate, with the partners often divided about these objectives. (see *1957, 1966*)

2192 – International legal negotiation must take account of changes in the balance of power, the appearance of new cultural values and the need of peoples for development and justice. Coexistence should give way to participation, sovereignty to solidarity, the minority to the majority, and bilateral concessions to collective projects. (see *48, 1816*)

Within the international system, a distinction must be drawn between law with material content and law that is instrumental. The development of international instruments is characteristic of a period of structural growth, even though the actual content of the discussion remains confidential, as is the case with arbitration or diplomatic agreements. This is how diplomatic and consular law develops, and also international administrative law, treaty law, investigative procedures and arbitration.[63] There is also an increasing tendency for certain intergovernmental entities, such as those in the fields of telecommunications, television, space and meteorology, to be managed on a private commercial basis. (see *1588*)

2193 – The deliberations of most major international conferences and assemblies are affected by the rapid pace of change in the modern world, and by the need to plan ahead and predict events. The work of the UN General Assembly illustrates how international negotiation is tending more and more towards the formulation of future principles of law and governance: the Universal Declaration of Human Rights, for instance, has had an appreciable influence on contemporary civilisation and on some political regimes.

When the Earth Charter was drawn up in Rio in June 1992, it contained an entire programme for the protection of the environment in the twenty-first century, adopted amid great fanfare by the thousands of participants to mark the twentieth anniversary of the Stockholm Conference.

At the Kyoto Conference in 1997, when 159 States took part, 38 industrialised countries made a commitment to reduce carbon dioxide emissions before 2012 by 5.2 per cent from average 1990 levels. The United States did not consider themselves bound, though Russia ratified the agreement in 2004. The negotiations to implement the Protocol have shown how far removed good intentions are from political reality. The Bonn Conference in 2000 laid down the terms of application of the Protocol, and in Marrakech in 2001 a fund was set up to enable developing countries to make the necessary adaptations. (see *1804, 2213, 2225, 2275*)

2194 – The methods and achievements of the major European and global organisations show the importance of initiatives by groups of States and

---

63 I. BARRIERE-BROUSSE: 'La création normative des Etats, point de vue privatiste', in *La Mondialisation du droit*, 2000, p. 133. M. COSNARD: 'La création normative des Etats, point de vue publiciste', ibid., p. 142.

secretariats in anticipating events, drawing up medium and long-term programmes of action, and, in a general sense, in all forms of negotiation geared towards the future. When the worldwide administrative conference on radio communications was held in 1979, for example, it marked an advance in the role of the developing countries, which succeeded in obtaining substantial changes to the future allocation of space frequencies. There is also a long-term programme in preparation by the European Commission to protect the continent's water resources. (see *1604*)

2195 – Governments on occasion take unilateral steps to implement certain negotiations even before the final instruments are drawn up, bypassing the procedural formalities. This happened in the case of some of the drafts produced at the UN Conference on the Law of the Sea, which the participating States were using as texts of reference even before they had voted on them or signed them. The same is true of the Kyoto Protocol against the 'greenhouse effect'. (see *1738, 1739, 2213*)

2196 – It is true that the decisions of the UN General Assembly, whether taken by vote or by consensus, are only theoretical or symbolic, be they in the form of recommendations, resolutions or declarations. However, they may have legal effects, not only as universal norms whose value in treaty interpretation is recognised by courts, but also as powerful indicators of customary law in the making, acknowledged not only by the International Court of Justice but also by the Court of Justice of the European Community.[64]

2197 – Institutional negotiation has thus brought forth a new form of social rule, more ethical than legal, rich in sensibility, open to growth, and facing towards the future. The many forms of subtle psychological pressure will gradually turn this 'rule of recommendations' into binding law. This tendency is evident in interparliamentary assemblies: scientific bodies already create objective regulations in their own fields, such as biology, genetics and technology. (see *1154, 1578, 2542*)

2198 – Negotiation is the expression of a voluntarist and generalised view of international relations, and as such it feeds upon itself. The building of the international system has acquired its own dynamic. Declarations of the UN General Assembly, such as Resolution 1962 of 13 December 1963 on space law, are turned into treaties. (see *1600*)

In 1990, ten years after the adoption of the Declaration on the Rights of the Child, the United Nations drew up a Convention that achieved very broad ratification, the effects of which were prospective in the sense that it was designed to change laws and customs worldwide. This was followed by work towards an international regime on adoption and special protection for children before the courts.

2199 – Once a negotiation has matured, its main lines of thinking emerge, and the chairman and secretariat of the meetings usually seek to encapsulate these in words, sometimes aided by the delegations themselves. (see *1564*)

---

64 E. SUY: 'Innovations in International Law Making Process', in *The International Law and Policy of Human Welfare*, Leiden, Sijthoff, 1978.

The resulting documents, which are sometimes unduly long, take a wide variety of forms, ranging from declarations to diplomatic treaties. Often, they fail to be formally adopted, and do not enter into force in accordance with the traditional rules of international law. (see *736, 777*)

Alongside formal proclamations, the role of the informal must also be acknowledged: many of the disciplines States apply are not contained in a diplomatic document, but are a matter of implicit common acceptance, whether through reciprocal commitments, the discreet consensual workings of groups like the Paris Club that deals with international debt repayment, professional custom, protocol or simple convenience. The same is true in private business. This practice can be of benefit to international society.[65] (see *97, 131, 514, 1519, 1569, 1578, 1855*)

2200 – Consensus does not amount to the creation of a rule of law: the absence of opposition to an instrument is not enough to make it binding on sovereign States, except where expressly provided. The resulting norm is thus more of a political, cultural or moral directive than a traditional legal instrument. Moreover, it often lacks the necessary clarity and precision, and is accompanied by explanations, reservations or commentaries that undermine its effect. (see *1577*)

2201 – This expanding use of consensus is typical of a world that is working towards new values that are, at present, ill defined and not yet established. Already, though, decisions of major importance are taken using this summary form of procedure: this was how the UN General Assembly adopted the definition of aggression. The Security Council has dealt with certain disputes by consensus.

In multipartite meetings, consensus can mean that opposing strategies have been reconciled in the interests of making progress in the future.

This was one of the goals of the Final Act of Helsinki in 1975, and also of the work of the CSCE (now the OSCE), whose successive meetings facilitated the negotiations on the limitation of conventional weapons in Europe. (see *1752*)

2202 – Consensus appears to be one of the stages in the process of negotiating ideas that goes on in international institutions and conferences. *Such is the desire to reach a conclusion that sometimes it is clear that a consensus is forming that should be noted by the chair: this is what is known as 'emerging consensus'.* This procedure offers a number of advantages for the negotiator venturing into relatively uncharted areas.

2203 – Whatever is or has been the importance of international custom, as the product of general usage and at the same time of spontaneous consent, in the progressive development of the main principles of international law, it does not have the precision, authority or sanctions to override written law. What it can do, thanks to multilateral negotiations, is accelerate the process by which such law is built up, extend the scope and term of agreements, even tacit, and serve as the basis and the point of reference for national initiatives. (see *599, 720*)

---

65 A. d'AMATO: *International Law and Political Reality*, The Hague, Kluwer, 1995.

2204 – This ongoing questioning of the law will mean that many negotiations have to be repeated, either to change the outcome, even where this is settled, or to introduce new partners into the process. (see *752, 1515, 1517*)

2205 – Among these forms of prospective negotiation, some are designed to influence States so that they apply new principles of their own accord. The International Labour Organisation, for example, has produced 176 conventions, all of them subject to national ratification. Sometimes, States are left to themselves to carry the international dialogue forward at the political, legislative and administrative levels; there are other occasions when their lack of enthusiasm or interest, and the inadequacies of their internal systems, must be countered by keeping them involved in negotiations on future themes.[66] (see *603, 674*)

Market forces are another source of the norms and standards required by business, affecting information, employee relations and best practices, but they are not necessarily mutually compatible, especially as between freedom of exchange and workers' protection. (see *1968, 2226*)

2206 – The spirit of anticipation is not only present in the terminology used, for instance in Europe where the 'technocratic imperative' is now common parlance. It covers all eventualities, even breach of contract: certain treaties contain safeguard clauses to provide for cases where States refuse to comply with them, in the absence of any powers of compulsion.

2207 – This means that a huge variety of subjects is now covered by prospective negotiation: solar energy, interstellar space and its uses, the earth's atmosphere and the biosphere, the preservation of life forms and water resources, animal and plant species, the prevention of certain kinds of accidents or natural disasters, and humanitarian aid. Odd as it may seem, the UN General Assembly drew up an agreement as long ago as 1979 on the status of the moon and other celestial bodies: the object was to prohibit their use for military purposes and regulate the scientific and economic activities that could be carried on there. (see *2217*)

The International Atomic Energy Agency adopted a code of best practices in 1990 designed to govern international transactions concerning radioactive waste. These guidelines were adopted by consensus, and are not binding. The issue was taken up again at the 1992 Rio Conference on the environment and development in order to bring national policies voluntarily into line. (see *2229*)

2208 – Prospective negotiation is gradually producing new principles that, without achieving general diplomatic acceptance, still exert a considerable influence over the way States conduct themselves. *This unperfected law and developing ethic is often expressed in the form of 'codes of conduct' addressed to the authorities in the industrialised countries and the major corporations in the expectation that they will comply.*

---

66 T. NARDIN and D. MAPEL: *Traditions of International Ethics*, Cambridge, Cambridge University Press, 1992.

2209 – Thanks to meetings of experts and then government representatives, the practice has developed in the UN of devising codes to promote technology transfer, restrict the movement of dangerous goods, govern multinational corporations and dismantle barriers to international trade. By contrast, marine navigation has avoided regulation by the shipowners and instead observes a different draft code of conduct under the 1974 Convention, though this was subject to reservations by the European Community.

2210 – The concept of the code of conduct is still unclear, however: on one view, any such body of principles and rules should be binding (as are some of the rules imposed by the IMF), while for others, they are merely voluntary. Even if there is no legal resolution to this question and no possibility of setting up an authority to monitor application of these texts, the formulation of these international principles has a major impact on negotiation because it creates a body of doctrine that unifies and reinforces the position of those who adopt it, slowly and persistently forcing the other parties to comply. (see *1807, 1826*)

Within the OSCE a code of conduct for States was proposed that would set out all the norms necessary for collective security and trust between governments. The practice is encouraged of giving prior notification of operations likely to create military or political risks, and of impartial monitoring, in other words institutionalised ways of verifying whether States are complying with their obligations (see the Treaty of Helsinki, 1992). (see *1799, 2239*)

2211 – Developing countries are no longer alone in using these techniques. They are also practised in the United States, in the context of enforcing the laws against corruption by multinational corporations, and in implementing the doctrine of non-proliferation of nuclear materials and technologies. This is not a matter of allowing custom to develop over time, but rather of deliberately pursuing new norms.

Among the missions of the World Tourism Organization is to draw up a worldwide code of ethics laying down rules for the profession that will reconcile market freedom with the responsibilities of the players in a field prone to disputes, most of them of a commercial nature. (see *1314*)

In the OECD, a convention was signed in 1997 to prevent the corruption of foreign public officials, the product of a consensus built up through a series of earlier, non-binding, instruments. The European Community drew up rules on arms sales in 1998, and on the prevention of violence in 2001. Within the WTO, the concept of 'fair trade' underlies the efforts to ensure developing countries receive a fair price for their exports.

2212 – It is an established fact that *the trend in international conferences towards majority voting, consensus or tacit approval and away from formal procedures and signature makes it easier to bind States to measures they do not support, even against their will.*

The same tendency can often be seen within the Council of Europe. By contrast, the Organisation on Security and Cooperation in Europe has used its flexible consensual decision-making process and pragmatic approach to good effect in its successive meetings since 1975: that said, the crisis in the former Yugoslavia proved that the effects of deep-seated cultural antagonisms are impossible to regulate. (see *1004, 1132*)

2213 – This is not only a public law phenomenon. While international law as that term is traditionally understood does not govern activities in the private sector, new rules are developing in that area and gaining wide acceptance. Governments will be faced with the need to agree on ways to defend themselves against multinational pressure groups, and force these to abide by negotiated systems of rules. There are hundreds of organised groups with a permanent presence in Brussels, and thousands of communications professionals whose role is to lobby the different organs of the Union. Organisations are springing up whose activities cross national boundaries and are proving more and more difficult to regulate by means of domestic law: this is already the case with religious, social and cultural structures. (see *1899, 2285*)

Academic writings have emphasised the forward-looking nature of these norms, as a body of 'soft law' that often has no organised sanctions to back it, but that brings together custom, common strands in judicial and arbitral decisions, major principles that have achieved widespread acceptance and national legislative measures. The high water mark of this prospective phenomenon has been the invention in the 1997 Kyoto Protocol of the 'emissions quota', the implementation of which is dependent on a number of technical hypotheses. (see *2193, 2232*)

2214 – In future, governments will agree to set up new institutions or mechanisms where necessary to overcome lacunae or contradictions in rules of law, procedural, jurisdictional, fiscal or social problems: the European Legal Area and the proposed statutes of the European Company might have been viewed as forerunners. Another such initiative was the setting up under the Treaty of Port-Louis in 1993 of OHADA, an organisation whose objective is the harmonisation of the business laws of the different countries of Africa, with its own joint court of arbitration.

Domestic legal systems will digest the presence of these new structures and make a place for them as part of their traditional systems, with all the implications this may have for the social, economic and political institutions of each country.

2215 – In law as in any other area of human activity, example is contagious. Countries facing similar problems compare their legal experiences, taking the opportunities offered by high-level international conferences. The tendency is for solutions to be chosen that are harmonised, or that align or converge: this can be seen in corporate law, tax, employees' rights, food safety and authors' rights. Some institutions or conferences have as their declared objective the adoption by States of parallel laws or regulations. In the field of competition law, there are decisions emanating from the Court of Justice of the European Communities and also the US Federal Trade Commission.

Social and technological similarities reinforce this trend, as does the fall in the levels of legal and commercial protectionism in the industrialised nations. Institutional impetus comes from bodies such as Unidroit, which has issued conventions on the international sale of goods and on stolen or illegally exported cultural objects.

2216 – The pressures of reality are decisive in negotiations, as is the tendency simply to imitate the best-drafted or most clearly expressed law, or to accede to coercion by a dominant economic power. Governments should be aware of this phenomenon, and take particular care to negotiate international codifications rather than simply allowing unfamiliar practices to be transformed into legal obligations because they are used by the world banking system or multinational corporations, or because of the hegemonic designs of a particular economic power.

2217 – There is also an undeniable tendency for States to seek to outbid each other in their claims, as notably happened with the development of the law of the sea: even before the law had been definitively codified, States were putting forward a variety of competing claims to different maritime zones.

Though the United Nations has sought (as did the League of Nations before it) to control and suppress the illicit traffic in drugs and narcotics through its 1971 and 1988 conventions, and despite the programmes and the institutional and financial resources committed for this purpose in cooperation with the World Health Organisation, it has been unable to halt the rampant growth in the drugs trade, its diversification into new products, or the laundering of hundreds of billions of euros and dollars that fund it.

2218 – Even where the national authorities have the power to refuse to apply regulations originating from outside, or do so subject to reservations, in practice it will become more difficult for them to avoid complying with disciplines agreed upon by others in the mutual interest. The constraints of coexistence and reciprocity and the need for universal norms will serve to increase compliance with rules that are drawn up and adopted as the result of international negotiation. (see *1665*)

Where governments are concerned, negotiation will be required to achieve this, as with questions of execution of the decisions of national and international courts, since there is no enforcement procedure binding on States. Negotiations will be necessary, too, with the major players in the private sector. (see *1307, 1969*)

§3. The risk of unintended consequences

2219 – No legal instrument is guaranteed to do exactly what its author intended and nothing more: negotiation, like any other form of social activity, can produce unintended and perverse consequences where there is no logical connection between the decision itself and the results that flow from it. The terrible massacres perpetrated in parts of the former Yugoslavia and Africa at a time when they were under the protection of peacekeeping forces, serve as examples. (see *61*)

2220 – Diplomacy offers the temptation to employ means whose effects can prove to be the opposite of the desired objective. This is true of traditional negotiation, where bad faith, coercion, bluff and blackmail can all appear. As for negotiation within institutions, the greatest threat lies in the verbosity of their assemblies, and the routines of their international bureaucracies, which threaten the role of negotiation. (see *713, 798, 1537, 1984*)

2221 – It is at the strategic level, though, that this concern is most real. The risk of conflict will remain as long as the partners have contradictory political objectives. It will multiply as more players continue to appear on the international scene, and more intergovernmental bodies are set up whose activities are overlapping if not in opposition. (see *350, 1131, 1231, 1391, 2226, 2385*)

The crises that followed the collapse of the former Yugoslavia showed the degree of risk associated with this dispersal of responsibilities, and also the difficulties it creates for negotiation. In the case of Bosnia and Herzegovina, the negotiations were concluded not in Europe, but in Dayton, under the auspices of the United States administration.

Events in Darfur have been examined by the UN, the African Union, NATO and also the European Union: here, too, the same risks exist of duplication of effort and action. (see *2229*)

The aim of negotiations in the WTO are very different from those of the ILO conferences on employee protection, or of the European Union in concluding association agreements with the ACP countries.

As for dispute resolution, there is a degree of overlap between the competence of the institutions of the WTO and the UN Tribunal on the Law of the Sea. (see *2240*)

In the field of biological research and bioethics, too, a variety of organisations are involved, including the UN, UNESCO, the WHO, the European Union and the Council of Europe, whose approaches risk overlapping if not in fact competing.

2222 – Modern science has shown how difficult it is to blend several strands of knowledge. At one end of the spectrum is the unique and random historical event, and at the other the long term that far exceeds the potential of human vision. *A negotiation will be viewed differently depending on whether it is considered as a self-contained act of diplomacy or as one step in a long process.* (see *2264, 2477*)

2223 – The greatest care is needed when evaluating the conclusions of a negotiation. Often, gains in terms of reach translate into losses in terms of content or value. Even though public opinion may only have a vague grasp of what a diplomatic commitment really means, the statesman should still give it his fullest attention. Treaty provisions unwisely entered into have been the cause of the most serious crises, including war. (see *1584*)

2224 – To take an example, official negotiations often have the result of giving structure to a conflict. Anything vague that is disputed becomes clear and precise, and anything dubious is proclaimed and thereby justified: discussion clarifies ideas and inflates claims, and as soon as they become public, they crystallise. This happened during the discussions on a new world economic order, especially within the United Nations.

Tacit negotiation and implicit arrangements have the opposite effect, though their contribution to international security is no greater. (see *717*)

2225 – It can happen that a negotiation reawakens or aggravates a conflict the parties would have preferred to avoid. Sometimes, it removes factors that could moderate potential hostilities, and sometimes it opens up the field for third parties to intervene, sooner or later, and aggravate the problem. (see *1230*)

A solution that is beyond the capacity of a State to implement undermines the effectiveness of its negotiation.

2226 – Where it leads to the setting up of a powerful organisation, international cooperation provokes reactions of concern or antagonism from the outside world, as happened with the emergence of the European Community as a powerful and compact trading bloc. Within the institution itself, cooperation between States tends to be supplanted by administrative bureaucracy. (see *713, 2227, 1220, 1518*)

The increasing numbers of participants in international decision-making (at the European level, for instance) results in overlapping and overburdened negotiations and dilution of responsibilities.

2227 – Even when it is not a total failure, the immediate result of a negotiation can be to confirm or provoke the abandonment of other projects. *This is a classic manoeuvre: States and leaders wishing to sabotage the grand designs of their partners find ways of burying them in the slow-moving procedures of an international conference.* (see *1539*)

A party wishing to destabilise an adversary or undermine its reputation will engage it in a negotiation that is doomed to fail.

2228 – When hopes are disappointed, whether because the negotiation breaks down, is postponed or simply proves fruitless, the resulting feelings of frustration quickly turn to hostility, because the malaise has its origins not in the need itself but in the perception of the need, which will have been sharpened by the dispute. (see *1067, 1228, 1913*)

Discussions of the future should remain focused on those issues that are ripe for negotiation, and avoid creating illusions or concerns by the use of intemperate language.

2229 – The sheer volume of international negotiations will increase this danger of secondary and contrary effects. The impact of so much free interaction is spreading, with negotiations generating the risk, especially for third parties, of contradiction, frustration and escalating demands. This risk increases each time the result is a compromise in which each party does not clearly gain something its public opinion can understand. (see *323, 2519*)

Neither the great powers nor the Secretariat General of the UN were able to measure with accuracy the legal, and hence political, complexity of the situation produced by their interventions, direct or otherwise, in Kosovo. (see *1132, 1332*)

In its desire to ensure that modern sources of energy are available to aid countries in their development, the IAEA did not foresee the risk that this technology could be put to military uses.

2230 – The fact is that the international system is subject to a serious but age-old threat: the lack of effect of its regulations and conventions, in other words insecurity in all its guises, including cases where there is a vacuum and where words are used that have no real and concrete meaning. (see *354, 1230, 1539, 1587, 1599, 1662*)

In order to be complete, a legal system must include a third party responsible for weighing the facts, stating the applicable law and impartially resolving disputes. It must also include measures of coercion to ensure that the judgments are properly enforced, such as the daily fines under the Maastricht Treaty. An edifice of international rules implies negotiation to make it effective vis à vis the States. *Even jurisdiction is negotiated.*

The function of the International Court of Justice is to decide disputes between States: it derives its legitimacy from the agreement of the States that set up the institution, when its mission, jurisdiction, and the execution of its judgments were decided, and of others that have subsequently accepted its jurisdiction. It needs the trust of those who are subject to its justice: this is why its work is characterised by a tension between prudence and expectation.

2231 – In the absence of a higher authority, or even of any diplomatic coordination, it is only to be expected that the sheer number of international negotiations and conventions will result in contradictory provisions. The 1969 Vienna Convention laid down the principles for resolving such contradictions, namely by combining, amending or suspending various clauses. The fact remains that, at a political level, the resolution of this kind of problem depends on the means each partner has available to ensure that others respect its rights, whether by political or military strength, moral force, finance or alliances. (see *1610, 1613, 1638*)

2232 – Patently, the intensification of negotiation at organisational level, reaching into ever deeper areas, has growing implications for the law and finances of States, especially when it introduces rules and obligations of external origin the reasons for which are not immediately obvious. (see *1576, 1673, 2576*)

Some of the rules of sound financial discipline emanating from the IMF have been vigorously contested, and it has proved difficult to apply the sanctions for non-compliance. Programmes of structural adjustment, designed to restore order in the economy and finances of certain States, have often led to great social upheaval.

The economic cost of the disciplines required by the Kyoto Protocol, now in force, was not evaluated in detail at the time of its negotiation. The problem was discussed at the Bonn Conference in 2000, but the cost of compliance (reafforestation, 'eco-taxes', etc) will inevitably increase the financial burden on those States and businesses that apply the agreement, even in part. (see *1232, 1576, 1947, 2193*)

The costs of international administration can also be considerable, particularly when they have to cover large-scale operations such as the peacekeeping missions ordered by the Security Council in Cambodia and Kosovo, or development projects. Concessions often have to be made as part of the quest for financing: no less than 42 countries, including the Scandinavian States, contribute to the Inter-American Bank's development subsidiary. (see *1784*)

The problem of resources becomes worse when one of the major powers stops contributing to the costs of a particular organisation: this calls for negotiation, often in politically difficult conditions.

2233 – For reasons either of government reluctance or legislative procedure, the outcome of many a diplomatic negotiation is not transposed into domestic law in a timely, correct or complete manner. From the legal and administrative standpoint, practices need to become more certain and consistent, especially between nations with the same levels of economic and social development. This opens up a new field of negotiation, which will have a greater role to play in many questions of implementation that would previously have been regarded as matters of domestic law. (see *1664, 2518*)

2234 – The newer generation of specialists in international law sees the need for radical change. No longer can it remain a body of intangible principles, consolidating acquired rights and advantages, and crystallising political and economic relations. Instead it must express the ways in which society is transforming, and serve as the instrument of this transformation through negotiation. It should stimulate negotiation and validate the progress it achieves, whether towards regional integration or global development. (see *2190*)

The fact that international norms are flexible sometimes permits negotiations to be concluded and implemented effectively. However, the right methods must be chosen for interpreting treaties, on the one hand, and actions on the other. It is important to know whether a text can be modified or explained by reference to intentions alone, or whether a treaty can be avoided or supplemented by reference to the spirit in which it was concluded. Since 1980, the Vienna Convention of 1969 has been interpreted as consolidating the pre-existing practices and solutions based on the notions of good faith and the ordinary meaning of the terminology.

2235 – This can however only happen with the will and agreement of the States themselves, in other words through diplomatic negotiation: even those political leaders who are best disposed towards international integration will not agree to be bound by provisions they have not had sufficient time to deliberate. *Governments themselves are torn between their desire to benefit from the regulations they have negotiated, and their reluctance to accept some of the implications for their freedom of action and for national public opinion.* (see *777, 1619*)

This explains the reaction of some States to the creation of international criminal tribunals, following the example of the Nuremburg and Tokyo Tribunals that were set up to punish war crimes in 1945. The International Criminal Tribunal for the former Yugoslavia was set up in The Hague in 1993 pursuant to a resolution of the Security Council; in the first 12 years of its existence it issued some 120 indictments and handed down more than 30 decisions. The Rwanda Tribunal, with its seat in Arusha, Tanzania, followed, and has sentenced over twenty people.

After extremely difficult negotiations within the UN, the International Criminal Court, also in The Hague, was set up under the Rome Convention of 18 July 1998. This came into force after obtaining 60 ratifications, including that of France in 1999, though not of the United States. The Court's mandate is to punish behaviour characterised as 'war crimes'. Contrary to the general principles of criminal law, that term was not defined in advance, because it is a political notion.[67] (see *645, 2335*)

There is also the Special Tribunal for War Crimes Committed in Sierra Leone, set up in Freetown under an agreement with the United Nations in 2002. (see *645, 723, 728*)

2236 – The risks are aggravated by the fact that many negotiations and agreements remain secret: this has been the case always and everywhere, including in those regimes whose diplomacy is subject to the influence of public opinion. The same is true when it is agreed in a negotiation to defer important matters for later discussion, without setting the principles governing their resolution or the time limit.

The right to officially rectify information,[68] and the duty to give reasons for actions taken, could serve to mitigate these effects.

The Yalta Conference, and the Declaration of 11 February 1945, were archetypal examples of this type of negotiation because there was never any agreement between the three Allies on questions as serious as the frontiers, and indeed the freedom, of the Danube and Balkan States, over which the USSR was quick to seize control, having refused them free elections, at the same time as it renewed its annexation of the three Baltic States. Coming within only a few weeks of victory, this silence on the fate of several nations of Eastern Europe, on the shared occupation of Germany and on the Montreux Convention on the Bosphorus Straits, revealed how unprepared certain of Stalin's partners had been.

2237 – Another source of instability is that, often, powers will accept a combined diplomatic solution as a temporary stopgap, intending to reverse it at the earliest opportunity, which they then have no difficulty in creating: this, undeniably, was Hitler's approach both before and after the Munich agreements in 1938, but his contemporaries had neither the courage nor the lucidity to grasp its implications at the time.

2238 – *Except during times of great religious fervour, statesmen have always found the idea of keeping their word a problematic one, whether the promise was their own or someone else's.* What country has never abandoned an ally, or failed to abide by a solemn agreement? Machiavelli knew that where there was a risk that a treaty would not be kept, the solution was not a wise one. (see *646*)

Procedures for monitoring the implementation of treaties will continue to be hampered by the difficulty in obtaining accurate and properly analysed information. Aside from inspections that take place outside the area of national sovereignty (on the deep seabed or in space, for example), their results largely depend on the good will of the governments concerned, which will often be

---

67 J. P. BALELAIRE and T. CRETIN: *La Justice pénale internationale*, Paris, PUF, 2000. J. F. DELABELLE: 'La convention de Rome portant statut de la Cour pénale internationale', AFDI, 1998, p. 356; *Reflections on the International Criminal Court*, The Hague, Asser, 1999.
68 S. MACBRIDE, etc.: *Many Voices, One World*, UNESCO, 1980.

restrictive in their interpretation and reticent in their approach. However, the mere threat of verification will be enough to have a deterrent effect, except where – as in the case of the 1972 agreement on biological weapons – the mechanism is clearly inadequate. There is scope in the future to refine the practice of rapid and objective international investigations, and it will become increasingly difficult to avoid having to negotiate them. The Helsinki Treaty of 24 March 1992 gave signatory States the right of overflight in order to observe military installations: this 'open skies' regime is different from the practice under civil aviation agreements. (see *1665, 2024*)

2239 – It is rare for disputes between States not to be susceptible of a political solution, just as it is a rare dispute between companies that cannot be solved by money. In international society, the law is not an end in itself, but an instrument in the hands of a good negotiator, even if the case he has to work with is unpromising.

No major negotiation should be concluded without the parties having agreed on how to resolve disputes arising from the interpretation or execution of their treaties, instruments or contracts, even if this is only a preventive measure. (see *2214*)

2240 – Article 33 of the UN Charter obliges States to settle their disputes peacefully, but the ways and means for such resolution remain to be laid down. More and more treaties, decisions and contracts provide for the means whereby disputes are to be resolved, whether these disputes are official or private. The Free Trade Agreement between the United States and Canada provided for resolution by binational groups. The NAFTA treaties of 1992 and 1993 envisage mediation, conciliation and arbitration.

The WTO has groups of expert arbitrators to resolve disputes, with an investigation followed by an adversarial proceeding. There is an appeals body to rule on questions of law. Governmental delegations may still decide, by consensus, not to abide by the decisions of the Dispute Settlement Body. Dozens of claims have resulted in proceedings being commenced and also in fresh negotiations between the parties. These have sometimes succeeded in restoring diplomatic calm. (see *1643, 1969*)

In Mercosul, there is a permanent dispute settlement function to which individuals can have access through the national sections of each State. It consists of negotiated arbitration in keeping with Latin American legal traditions. The arbitral awards are enforceable, on pain of compensatory measures. Under the Ouro Preto Protocol of 1994, all of these institutions are intergovernmental. (see *1583*)

The World Bank set up a specialist centre, ICSID, under the 1965 Washington convention, to arbitrate disputes between States and private companies.

The International Tribunal on the Law of the Sea applies the 1982 Convention on the Law of the Sea that entered into force in 1992, when it is seized of disputes under it.

2241 – Treaties often carry within themselves the germs of disputes. This is true, firstly, because there is no international situation in which the risk of misunderstandings can be completely avoided, even in the closest of alliances: it is the business of the diplomat to prepare for this, and be ready in particular for differences of interpretation. *Every State must beware that its partners have not and do not contract other commitments, voluntary or otherwise, that make it impossible to perform the agreements entered into with it.* (see *357*)

Those diplomats who, following the example of Mazarin, excel at building into agreements the grounds for dispute, pretexts for breach and excuses for intervention are every bit as dangerous as the ones who insist, sometimes unwisely, on setting out their terms in excessive detail.

2242 – Many governments attempt to revisit at the implementation phase what they conceded in principle. The ideas-based negotiation practised in the major international conferences makes this easier to do, both because of its methods and the goals it pursues. (see *1993*)

In future, intergovernmental institutions will have to distinguish more clearly between what is general debate and what is conclusive negotiation in the strict sense.

2243 – The international negotiators of the future must have regard to the long term and secondary consequences of what they are doing: scientific methods can help to analyse these better. A forward-looking approach is needed to give direction to negotiation and seize the benefit from its results, and most of all to evaluate the short and long-term consequences that will ensue if governments fail to cooperate. (see *1679*)

The experience of the European Union shows how important it is to have systems in place for communication and mediation that, however slow and costly, ensure a steady two-way flow of information, consultation and debate between States and improve the quality of the negotiation that is being carried on by specialist teams of moderator-conciliators. In North America, too, the NAFTA free trade zone, which has taken 15 years to create, is a major step in the progressive economic, financial and cultural integration of the continent. (see *462, 1524, 1583, 1643*)

Part IV:
Negotiation: A Political Art

2244 – The transition from bilateral, multilateral or institutional diplomatic relations to the concept of mankind as a worldwide collective entity is not a matter of extending the scope of political manoeuvre, but of progressively altering its fundamental nature.

2245 – The general network of international relations is becoming more and more dense. There are a number of theories that seek to describe and explain them, from the various standpoints of communication, forecasting, group relations and behavioural sciences. Others refer to the lessons of history, the geopolitical constants and the main ideological movements.

2246 – Diplomacy can seem a very different exercise depending on the perspective from which it is viewed.[1] Some theories regard it as the product of dominant forces, while others focus instead on the deliberate human choices, motives and expectations: analyses vary according to the prejudices, assumptions and preferences of their authors.

Depending on the interpretation, negotiation is either a meeting of accidental contingencies or of historic destinies. Its study can be technical, economic or military, or it can combine these different viewpoints.

2247 – The truth is that, both from the individual as well as the collective angle, negotiation is essentially a political art, as it tends to establish a new human and societal order. It is the product of the creative will of those who have ideas and put them into practice, and it is likewise the product of their talent and responsibility. As Aristotle observed, there is no art in the effects of necessity, nor in the products of nature. (see *59, 648*)

2248 – Negotiation is one of those fields of activity that consist of directing individuals and groups. Its exercise is difficult and unpredictable, because human behaviour is still dictated by factors in which reason plays a lesser part than passions and instincts, imagination and sentiment, bias and ambition.[2] (see *2166*)

The successive treaties of the European Communities, and their evolution into the Union, are good examples of the importance of political will.

1 S. HOFFMANN: *Contemporary Theory in International Relations*, Englewood Cliffs, Prentice Hall, 1960.
2 J. MORIZET: 'La France et la négociation internationale', in *L'Internationalité dans les institutions et le droit*, Paris, Pedone, 1995, p. 145.

In a society still in the grip of contagious and unpredictable disorder, negotiation becomes one of the ways by which nations govern themselves, since it is at the same time the means by which peoples express their will, a means of regulating relations between nations, and a way of guiding societies as they develop. (see **1677**)

Chapter I:
System and Strategy

2249 – There are two main reasons why the world today seems dangerous. The first is that, taken as a whole, it does not add up to an organised system; its growing economic cohesion does not override the diversity among nations, each of which seeks to further its own prosperity and security, even to the detriment of the others. Second, it is made up of sub-groups that are themselves ill-controlled, fragile and often insecure: political multipolarity is in itself no guarantee of overall stability.[3] (see *369, 606*)

2250 – Furthermore, it is only possible for groups to adapt peacefully to change if they are cohesive enough to resist the antagonisms they provoke. The state of internal disorder, if not actual civil war, of many nations is cause for anxiety if not alarm.

Where they are not resolved, the uncertainties and contradictions of international society carry over into the domestic affairs of States and generate discord, upheaval and subversion sometimes severe enough to jeopardise their very existence.

Now more than ever, internal crises, and the retaliation they provoke, fulfil the traditional functions of warfare. In resolving them, one camp or the other achieves dominance in the competition between nations. (see *1882*)

2251 – In a world where vast spheres of influence are a fact of life, control over the diplomacy of weaker States has taken the place of ancient disputes over distant territories, as the stakes in the struggle between major powers. (see *30, 125, 240, 636, 2312*)

The collapse of the Soviet system has not invalidated this observation.

2252 – At the same time, increased awareness of global constraints is changing the character of the entire international system: pollution, economic disorder, accelerating population growth, scarcity of resources, the power of doctrines and beliefs and the threat of nuclear war have become matters of worldwide concern for which negotiated responses are sought. (see *2166*)

2253 – The challenges facing negotiation are dramatic indeed, where the only alternative to rampant and uncontrolled growth is poverty, famine and debt, the only restraint on the self-satisfaction of a society founded on material consumption is the fear of nuclear apocalypse, and the only response to social anarchy, political

---

3 H. A. KISSINGER: 'The End of Bipolarity', in *The Theory and Practice of International Relations*, Englewood Cliffs, Prentice Hall, 1966, p. 50.

terrorism and religious hatred is to accept the constriction of space, contacts and competition.

2254 – The normal role of diplomacy is to prevent this environment from degenerating into unpredictability and chaos, and to offer ways and means to peaceful progress. *On a global view of international relations, negotiation plays a pre-eminent role in offering order and system, but the fact remains that it is ultimately based on strategy, in other words the devising and carrying out of political manoeuvres.* (see *605, 1502*)

Section I: International and national systems

2255 – The notion of distance – whether seen from the point of view of the human being as an isolated biological unit, or from that of a group occupying a territory – is in reality different now from how it has been understood for centuries.

2256 – There is more to this than the obvious effects of the speed and frequency of travel, or the fact that objects, messages and even persons can now be projected into space. The means available for transmitting information, orders and influences have brought the world – and States – closer, especially where diplomacy is concerned: the days when emissaries crossed countries on horseback belong to the recent past, but they have gone for good.

2257 – Science knows no impenetrable frontiers. Neither does technology, or the cultural influences it transmits. (see *1748*)

These advances are eroding the natural protections of States as well as their political autonomy. The various uses of satellites and telecommunications and the freer circulation of people and ideas will accelerate and also accentuate this tendency. (see *1803*)

2258 – The internationalisation of information, messaging, production, pressures and influences is evident in every field of human activity. It increases the weight of the dominant cultures and the prevailing financial and strategic powers. While the phenomenon of the State remains robust, policies on currency and investment, energy sources, raw materials, defence, public health and research are no longer made in isolation. (see *2027, 2030, 2048*)

As the instruments of international negotiation, even languages are changing, especially the ones most widely used: they are becoming less precise and borrowing more heavily from advertising and ideology.

2259 – The frictions caused by differences in conduct and mentality between States, coupled with the similarity of the situations they face, their interests, needs and intentions, mean that any strategic conception of international negotiation must take the maximum number of factors into account, and integrate them into a logically structured approach.[4] Great negotiators must have a global vision of the diplomatic playing field. (see *310, 2325*)

---

4 H. A. KISSINGER: *The White House Years*, Boston, Little, Brown & Co., 1979, I.

2260 – At the same time, there is a tendency for disagreements to become dramatised.[5] Faced with some kinds of danger, there is no longer room for neutrality, indifference, or even political reserve. (see *1685, 1748, 1808*)

The prospects for international relations thus pose an acute problem: how to distinguish between the development of the whole and that of its constituent parts, in order to understand and anticipate possible structural change.

2261 – The worsening gulf of technological, economic and social inequality, the crisis in energy and raw materials, the collapse of certain monetary systems, and the widespread and sometimes violent challenge to old political values, give the impression that humanity is headed for chaos.[6]

2262 – Set against this are the pressures exerted by the major powers when they agree, even implicitly, the growing number of international organisations, the development of transnational business and other influences, and the freer circulation of people, goods and ideas. The growing awareness of basic human needs and those of the natural environment works in favour of reconstruction and order, and is a potential source of broad-based solidarity. (see *55, 2279*)

2263 – The profound transformations taking place in the international environment, coupled with the rise in general levels of use of technology, are increasing peoples' needs. And, the more people need, the more they will trade and communicate.[7]

There is a correlation between the progress of civilisation and the volume of international negotiation.

2264 – Against this background, every assessment of the future of international negotiation depends on a certain point of view.

If international relations are viewed as a whole, the foreign policy of the State is one of several variables that must be controlled in the interests of the overall system, sometimes at the expense of the individual nation's political regime and public opinion. If, on the other hand, the traditional model is favoured, the international system is merely the environment in which the principal diplomatic, economic and cultural players operate. (see *2302*)

2265 – The fact that there is no global regulator at the international level makes the first hypothesis completely theoretical. *In reality, however desirable it might be to view world affairs from a global perspective, it has to be said that this offers no substitute for negotiation between States, whether this is regarded as a relational or a decisional procedure.* (see *1624*)

The broader the scope and the more flexible the methods of diplomacy, the more weight attaches to the choices freely made at national level, the more effective the expression of the values of civilisations, and the clearer the mission and ranking of the State, which is the main actor and the only one with real responsibility in the international arena. (see *2321*)

---

5 G. BOUTHOUL and R. CARRERE: *Le Défi de la Guerre*, Paris, PUF, 1976.
6 H. KAHN and A. WEINER: *The Year 2000*, New York, Hudson Institute, 1967.
7 C. de VISSCHER: *Théories et réalités en droit international public*, Paris, Pedone, 1970, p. 488.

§1. The system

2266 – With the aid of advances in mathematics and technology, recent research has invested the notion of the system with dimensions hitherto unimagined, in other words the idea of reality as an ordered whole, with its own organisational dynamic, forming more than merely the sum of its parts.[8] This general approach has been applied in social and political sciences among others.[9]

This study of systems was prompted both by the increasingly penetrating analyses of certain decision-making processes, and also by the extraordinary and irreversible growth of the Internet, with its networks and memories.

2267 – The same logic has, by contagion, led to the whole world being viewed as one single system, or a single system in the making, a melting-pot with its own interdependencies and rules. This macroscopic approach, dating from around the time the Massachusetts Institute of Technology published its report in 1971 on the limits to growth, attempts a general diagnostic of the needs and resources of mankind as a whole, and also of the risks it faces in the foreseeable future.

That vision gave rise to the audacious hope that the worldwide system of States would function by self-regulation, with negotiation between its sub-systems being only one form of this.[10]

2268 – Functionalist theory saw the concrete development of specific activities and operational structures as the best way to override the limits of the State without offending against sovereignty.[11] Based on European doctrines of supranationality and the experience of the European Community, the doctrine of integration is one of functionalism with political institutions.[12]

2269 – As for the theory of communication, this is based on the development of preferential relations between certain States: the effects of communication can prefigure political communities, but without destroying independence.[13] It was supplemented by an attempt at logical explanation based on the notion of the network, which does not share the rigidity, structures, demarcations, coherence or centralisation of the notion of the system.[14] (see *2049*)

---

8 L. von BERTALANFFY: *Théorie générale des systèmes: physique, biologie, sociologie, philosophie*, Paris, Dunod, 1973.

9 D. EASTON: *A System Analysis in Political Life*, New York, Willey, 1965; *Analyse du système politique*, Paris, Colin, 1974.

10 D. C. McCLELLAND: *Theory and the International System*, New York, MacMillan, 1966. M.A. KAPLAN: *System and Process in International Politics*, New York, Wiley, 1957.

11 D. MITRANY: *The Functional Theory of Politics*, New York, St. Martin's Press, 1976; *A Working Peace System*, London, 1966.

12 E. HAAS: *Beyond the Nation-State, Functionalism and International Organization*, Denver, Stanford University Press, 1964. J. W. FELD: *International Relations, a Transnational Policy Approach*, Sherman Oaks, Alfred, 1979.

13 K. DEUTSCH: *Nationalism and Social Communication*, Cambridge, EU, 1966.

14 A. JUDGE: 'International Organisation Networks: a Complementary Perspective', in *International Organization*, New York, 1978, p. 381.

2270 – It has been suggested that it should be possible to establish objective indicators of State power,[15] and scientifically study the factors that produce closeness and solidarity between States,[16] especially within a coherent structured framework. Another exercise often repeated is the simulation of a future scenario, as pessimistic as possible, based on a world development model including a number of quantified relationships and factors, using a simplified theoretical approach to the issues, and offering a better prospect of overcoming and transcending national interests.[17] (see *2085*)

2271 – Even though they are in large measure artificial, these researches contribute to a multidisciplinary knowledge of the forces at play that the negotiator must factor into his work, and also to a dynamic vision of international relations that starts from researching and studying all the hypotheses, but can still produce results surprising to those working in the field.

2272 – This work is all the more useful given the increasing scope, complexity and importance of multilateral negotiation, which not only expresses, but also creates, interdependencies that cannot be regulated by using the traditional diplomatic approach, but require an analysis of the system itself, especially where a market economy is involved. *A rational analysis of these international relations might allow their similarities to be objectively exploited and developed.* (see *1502, 1680, 1787*)

2273 – Any attempt to formulate an all-encompassing conceptual description of international society, however, must acknowledge that it is fundamentally heterogeneous,[18] and that the patterns and practices of political, military, economic and other relations between modern States are extremely diverse.[19] Where these coincide, they have spawned a multitude of diplomatic and legal concepts, based on analyses and descriptions without any common overall vision: cooperation, coordination, harmonisation, organisation, association, parallelism, confederalism, integration, supranationality, federalism and 'globalisation'.[20] *The truth is that the international environment is deeply diverse and thus difficult, if not impossible, to regulate, describe or even understand as a whole, even within Europe.*[21] (see *1812, 2280*)

2274 – It is also true that the uncontrolled, disordered and conflict-ridden nature of international society makes it impossible to view the modern world as one single

---

15 R. COX and H. JACOBSON: *The Anatomy of Influence: Decision-Making in International Organization*, Yale University Press, 1973.
16 R. COBB and C. ELDER: *International Community. A Regional and Global Study*, New York, Holt, Rinehard and Winston, 1972.
17 J. N. ROSENAU: *The Scientific Study of Foreign Policy*, New York, Free Press, 1969.
18 S. HOFFMANN: 'The International System Today', in *The Theory and Practice of International Relations*, Englewood Cliffs, Prentice Hall, 1966, p. 54.
19 J. N.ROSENAU: *Linkage Politics: Essays on the Convergence of National and International Systems*, New York, Free Press, 1969.
20 J. N. ROSENAU: *International Organizations, a Conceptual Approach*, New York, Frances Pinter, 1978.
21 R. ARON: *Paix et guerre entre les nations*, Paris, Calmann-Lévy, 1962, p. 108.

coherent system, or a rational collection of systems having stable rules, rhythms and structures to allow negotiation to develop.[22] Some authors have therefore limited their concept of systems to those elements that are capable of action: States clearly fulfil this test, and must be included in any calculation of power. Others have demonstrated how systems have different levels of integration, with conflicts between nations confirming that a worldwide system is still in the embryonic stage.[23] (see *1790, 2053, 2252*)

2275 – The specific nature of relations between States has not altogether disappeared. It is not safe to attempt a general analysis on the basis of the bureaucratic principles applicable to large modern States. The fact that States are increasingly engaged in non-diplomatic negotiations does not deprive these relations of their international character.

2276 – The more variables a system includes, the more fragile it will be. Multilateral and organisational negotiation can only produce lasting effects where it gives control over the maximum possible number of parameters: monetary agreements are merely theoretical where economic policies diverge, in the fields of credit, exchange and inflation, for example. This is the challenge the euro was created to face, with the governments concerned seeking to address it in the Eurogroup by parallel meetings of their central banks. (see *1553*)

2277 – A highly evolved society, in which tasks are specialised, internal processes complex, great needs and dispersed resources, is a vulnerable society. In an increasingly interdependent world, every tension that arises produces effects that spread without regard for borders. In practice, the prevention of international conflict is in its infancy, and does not in any way depend on the existence of an independent or organised decision process. (see *2093*)

2278 – A homogeneous international system would also presuppose the abandonment of revolutionary doctrines and expansionist ideologies and ambitions, whereas in fact human society still contains huge potential to erupt. When there is no outlet for the tensions that build up, the results may be good for progress but they are damaging to overall cohesion.

The assumptions on which negotiation rests are thus mostly negative: competition, bad faith, confrontation, crisis, terrorism and war are all forms of present danger.

There are so many points of weakness and rivalry to be found within the community of nations that its existence as a concrete reality might very well be questioned. (see *1864, 1871*)

---

22 R. TANTER, R. V. ULLMANN, etc: *Theory and Policy in International Relations*, Princeton University Press, 1972.
23 J. W. BURTON: *Systems, States, Diplomacy and Rules*, New York, Cambridge University Press, 1968. R. COX: 'A prospective view', in *International Organization, World Politics*, London, MacMillan, 1969, p. 295.

2279 – Some debates at international level are worldwide in scope, especially when they raise new and forward-looking concepts such as the common heritage of mankind, the natural environment and even nuclear security. Others, like multilateral trade negotiations or strategic discussions, reflect a worldwide vision of sectoral issues. But none of this activity amounts to a concept, let alone the construction, of a universal system.

The first real efforts at collective negotiation for the future have been the responses to the danger of climate change. However, the attempts to draw up a phased programme of precautions and disciplines under the Kyoto Protocol have generated heated debate between States and met with resistance on the part of some of them. (see *1809, 2193, 2225*)

2280 – Globalisation, as it is called, is a cluster of major trends affecting the higher levels of modern society and their leading edge activities. In practice it is evident from the real cohesion within the international system in matters of information, patents, trademarks and banking, not only in periods of growth but also in times of crisis and recession. (see *1803, 1822*)

In truth, though, the main forms of human solidarity will continue to be less abstract for some time to come, being groups limited by geography or sector of activity. These will progressively become part of networks that will limit their freedom of manoeuvre without removing it entirely, and within which negotiation will remain the principal source of governance.

There exists no overall concept of international society that provides a central, harmonious, unified theme for negotiation between States or major private enterprises. (see *1577*)

§2. Sub-groups

2281 – International systems can be analysed at a number of levels, depending on the types of autonomous entities and the particular rules they include.[24] An alliance, with its obligations of consultation and assistance, can be analysed according to this method, as it limits and structures the freedom of negotiation of its component parts; the same is true, for example, of a customs union. *These groups are designed to function coherently; they are all the more powerful and compact because their internal balance is determined by negotiation.* (see *921, 929, 1026, 1252*)

2282 – These groupings are extremely varied, depending on the types of entities that they include or the relations between them: they might be military, financial, economic or ideological, regional or global.

There is still research and study to be done while these mechanisms and networks are developing. Largely because of the rules of procedure and voting, they are creating a new international dynamic, in which well-balanced groups,

---

24 J. D. SINGER: 'A Cybernetic Interpretation of International Conflict', in *Unity through Diversity*, New York, Gordon and Breach, 1973, p. 1105. J. FRANKEL: *International Politics, Conflict and Harmony*, London, Penguin, 1973.

assembled or integrated, operate to limit the random effects of external pressures on their members.[25] (see *922, 1026, 1506, 1507, 1547*)

2283 – The creation of international organisations and groups is the result of political empiricism and not of any historical or sociological predetermination. Their survival thus depends on the quality of the relationships generated between their members and the speed of their interaction. Those that resist a variety of hazards and survive, become more coherent and structured, and devise their own systems of rules. (see *1102, 1106*)

2284 – These sub-groups are effective not only because they offer a favoured framework for dialogue, but because the group has the same objectives. The more pressing the objective, the more intense and productive is the internal negotiation. (see *844, 1358, 1359*)

Both in the relations between their members and in the competition that arises between the various preferences at work, the vigour of these systems depends on the strategy underlying them. (see *1233, 1410*)

2285 – Some international groupings are the product of the predominance of a few States. They have the effect of polarising negotiation by gathering neighbouring or allied States around them:[26] the sphere of influence is an age-old factor in diplomacy. Other forms of relations between States have become institutionalised, either at global level in pursuit of specific objectives, or as a function of continental or 'regional' solidarity. (see *898*)

The European Union represents a particularly highly developed form of international construction, given the continuous cooperation not only between the Member States themselves, but between the different interest groups within it.[27] (see *1253, 1336*)

Community negotiations thus take place under the influence of hundreds of pressure groups or professional bodies in Brussels that represent high-level sectional interests within Europe. (see *1903, 2213*)

2286 – These groups have a natural tendency to define themselves by reference to the environment in which they operate: they seek to restrict the benefits of unity to their members alone. The greater their degree of internal integration, the more different they are from the outside world. There are some types of preferential treatment that the European Union does not wish to see become widespread, but it will have great difficulty in maintaining its special relationships within the framework of the rules of the WTO. (see *1253, 1655*)

2287 – Organisations are gradually building up cohesive networks based on mutual support. Some, for instance, make arrangements whereby each of them

25 J. W. BURTON: *International Relations, A General Theory*, Cambridge, Cambridge University Press, 1965.
26 R. ARON: *République impériale. Les Etats-Unis dans le monde (1945–1972)*, Paris, Calmann-Lévy, 1973.
27 G. KAUFMAN: *Il sistema globale: immagini e modelli*, Udine, 1974.

may be represented in the meetings of the others' decision-making bodies, and conduct a number of joint operations. (see *1182, 1186, 1424*)

The fact that some of these organisations have the same members makes it easier for them to work closely together, or even unify: this happened with the European Communities, whose institutions merged in 1965. (see *1368*)

2288 – Between systems based on a different underlying logic, relations grow out of competition or negotiation, sometimes driven by States that belong to a variety of organisations at the same time and apply their respective rules, such as the United Nations, the European Union, and specific alliances. (see *930, 1427*)

A study of these relations between sub-systems would contribute to a better understanding of the realities of international life.

Evidently, in the eyes of the US administration, where Western Europe is concerned, NATO is more of a political reality than the European Union; there are some States in Eastern Europe that take the same view.

2289 – Successful institutional negotiation not only strengthens international relations, but prompts the adoption of the same pattern. The European Community system had a great influence on the European Free Trade Association, also on Mercosul and the former Soviet COMECON. There is also a proliferation of specialised agencies of the United Nations, all based on the same main common principles. (see *1345, 1363, 1400, 1518*)

2290 – A systematic approach to the environment produces a better understanding of how negotiations can be made to work within international groupings. It shows how these groupings determine the course of a negotiation more often than it changes them, and how intermediate levels of solidarity can help nations achieve greater maturity in their conduct. (see *1518*)

However, in order to be effective, any grouping presupposes that the entities of which it is made up are duly, correctly and viably constituted and have the capacity to enter into normal mutual relations. (see *1097*)

2291 – With few exceptions, no inter-state system is itself in a position either to set the conditions for membership, or to verify them: such normative and regulatory processes as exist are at too early a stage of worldwide development.

It suffices to note that the recognition and admission to the United Nations of the States that emerged from the former Yugoslavia took place without precaution or guarantee, even where the delimitation of their borders was concerned.

All international organisations are built on postulates that give their deliberations an artificial character.

2292 – The society of nations has, in fact, become considerably younger. *Many countries are making their first forays into international negotiation, even before all of them have achieved cohesion and stability, although older States, too, sometimes lack these qualities.* This produces a risk of international disorder, which is increasing despite the apparent crystallisation of frontiers. The concept of the State is thus often weakened in terms of its political and cultural content, if not its geographical and economic meaning and legal credibility.

2293 – There has never been such heterogeneity or inequality between the actors on the international scene.[28] While the powerful seek to restrict the number of decision makers, this diversity is necessary as it enhances wealth and choice. But it makes any joint strategy difficult, if not impossible, in global conferences and institutions and even in smaller-scale organisations.

No international system, however perfect, can prevent States from failing; it can only contain the effects.

2294 – On the other hand, no international grouping, even one that is very localised, has yet succeeded in taking control of its component entities. The European Common Market, for example, despite its aim to become a complete system with rules and institutions, lacks the power to regulate because of the sheer range of negotiations individually undertaken by its Member States. The powerful transnational forces within it have no autonomous political counterpart capable of responding to, or controlling, them. (see *976, 1352, 1356*)

2295 – What is more, a system can only equip itself with effective mechanisms if it is sufficiently watertight and coherent in the way it reacts to attacks from outside. Even the European Union does not entirely satisfy these conditions: internal and external negotiations still play a very important role because it has neither a joint strategy, nor autonomy of decision making, nor automatic regulation, but requires such frequent and difficult adjustments that the whole edifice has at times appeared ungovernable, hence the notion of a 'two-speed Europe'. (see *1044, 1252, 1358, 1359, 1363, 1391*)

2296 – The disorder or incoherence of certain international sub-groupings can give rise to upheavals that produce anxiety throughout the international world: the lack of discipline on the part of some of the oil-producing States has prompted nostalgia for the days when OPEC coordinated them effectively. *The politicisation of debates on technical questions diverts and dilutes the efforts of the specialised international organisations.* (see *1228*)

2297 – Where alliances are concerned, it is clear merely from the conditions in which they define their strategies that even in times of crisis – or perhaps especially at such times – national goals predominate. (see *977*)

It is the lack of clear, common, strategic thinking that has long made collective external negotiation by the European countries ineffectual or impossible: the Yugoslav tragedy is a case in point. (see *1319, 1330, 1359, 1492*)

2298 – From the moment there is imbalance between the sacrifices agreed to, or exacted, on both sides, group conflicts will naturally surface. But, in the international arena, the power configurations that result are especially fluid and unstable. (see *1391, 1535*)

States have a strong tendency to negotiate the setting up of cohesive or homogeneous structures where they have shared interests: it is rare, however, for

---

28 S. HOFFMANN: 'The International System Today', in *The Theory and Practice of International Relations*, Englewood Cliffs, Prentice Hall, 1966, p. 54.

them to give up their right to negotiate; the European Union is the clearest example of this, being both localised and partial. (see *611*)

2299 – National temperaments have a constant bearing on negotiation, where deep-seated historical or ethnic reflexes are very quick to resurface. Governments thus attempt to justify the demands they make on their populations by appealing to their national pride, often inflated by the media. The tendency to disputes is therefore far from likely to disappear, especially where religious sensibilities – the factors behind the longest and cruellest conflicts – become involved.

2300 – Although international negotiation benefits from the growth of groupings and networks that favour mutual influences, exchanges and alliances between the members of international society, this does not mean that international society is becoming totally integrated. Instead, it shows all the signs of a disordered proliferation of communication, institutions and rules.

§3. The State

2301 – The institutions and mechanisms of the politics of war, trade and finance tend to transcend the boundaries of the State. Science and technology, like major economic forces and ideological movements, can no longer be confined within the narrow framework of national sovereignty that, in France, is the legacy of the Revolution. (see *3, 603*)

2302 – This means that the concept of the nation State, the product of centuries of European civilisation, can now seem an outdated and devalued notion, as can the patriotism from which it draws its emotional support. The question now is what place nations have in a world living with the nuclear menace. (see *6, 1814*)

There is no denying that the internationalisation of trade, capital, networks and risks has relativised and weakened the power of the State, including the great powers. (see *19*)

2303 – There are many who would hold the nation State responsible for all the evils of the modern world, or at least for aggravating them: the overpopulation of certain regions, the wasting of natural resources, the deterioration of the environment, excessive spending on unproductive items such as weapons, as well as discord and war, are blamed, at least in part, on the lack of foresight of the power-obsessed leaders of nation States and their cynical quarrelling in the face of events and competition.

2304 – It is enough, however, to observe how peoples react to any form of dependency, even if these are more direct and insidious than before. Not only has the traditional State framework not been swept aside, but the sociological factors it expresses and encompasses are still founded on a categorical affirmation of national identity[29] that is as strong as ever, even in Western Europe.[30] (see *1887*)

---

29 M. ALBERTINI, S. HOFFMANN, etc: 'L'idée de nation', *Annales de philosophie politique*, 8, 1969.

30 S. HOFFMANN: 'Le sort de la nation dans l'Europe occidentale de l'après-guerre', in *L'idée de nation*, Paris, PUF, 1069, p. 139.

The State remains the unit for making the economic, social or cultural choices of which modern collective life mostly consists, and for bearing political responsibility for the exercise of these prerogatives. (see *1805, 1913, 2265*)

2305 – In modern States, where the tendency is to obey nothing but one's own personal reason, national motivation has come to be prized more than ever because it transcends materialism and selfishness: the doctrine of patriotism invests negotiating tactics with a just and noble purpose. Nationalism was never more present in Europe than it has been since Communism was overthrown, as for example, in the former Yugoslavia, the former Czechoslovakia and in Russia.

Although it is an imprecise and ambiguous concept, the national interest is still the basis of diplomatic strategy. (see *369, 1693, 2335*)

2306 – In an ever more intense and hurried world, where everything happens faster, solidarities, oppositions, complementarities and rivalries are forming between individuals and groups in which the State is sometimes the actor and sometimes the author, sometimes the instrument and sometimes the object.

Now more than ever, government authorities are called upon in crises involving exceptional international risks. (see *1678, 1687, 1691*)

2307 – Whatever a country's political regime, this extension of the external role of the State has domestic implications that are all the greater because they affect all strands of the economy, technology and even culture, and because, in many countries, the modern industrial system is part of the State.[31]

In order to negotiate under optimum conditions, governments are forced to support a growing number of activities, which tendency has further eroded the separation of public and private affairs. (see *1913, 1968*)

2308 – On the other hand, there are many projects that, for financial, technical or commercial reasons, can only be realised with the involvement of several governments. For them, international cooperation becomes the generator or the means of internal growth. This phenomenon moreover extends into the private sector: high finance with its increasing ambitions has broken down frontiers; so have the media. (see *337, 1822, 2302*)

2309 – Periods of heightened international tensions or competition coincide with a sudden and marked increase in the role and powers of the State, in which the collective will and means of the people come together: this has been especially true of the major wars and crises of modern times, as the history of contemporary Europe shows. (see *1225, 2135*)

2310 – Political power, especially in a democracy, makes the State the natural and necessary guardian of the security and interests of its nationals. Some of the commitments required by expansion and competition are so onerous that only a State is able to guarantee or assume them. It is to the State that people look in the race for progress. It is to the State, as well, that they turn for protection against the commercial or technological expansion of foreign economies. (see *8*)

31 J. K. GALBRAITH: *The New Industrial State*, 1967.

2311 – Even within the most efficient alliance or the most solid organisation, the State remains the judge of what is best for it. As the arbiter and defender of the interests of the group and of its own mission, it is the protector of its security and inheritance and its authentic character, as well as guardian of its national values and freedoms. (see *866, 894*)

2312 – It is within the State that most of the political and moral forces that express a nation's sentiments and ideals develop and operate. It is when the will of the State is enfeebled, or where it is undermined or collapses, that the greatest threat arises to order and peace between nations. (see *628, 643, 1225, 1711, 1882*)

Inadequacy or failings in a State's apparatus are often enough by themselves to threaten the effectiveness of systems of governance or other cooperative activities in which it is involved. (see *124, 636, 2250*)

2313 – By keeping the greatest dangers at bay, foreign negotiation can offer a degree of respite to national systems that are ill-adapted to international competition; it cannot, however, save them when they are put to the test, or undermine the process of natural selection.

The most effective way for an opponent or competitor to avoid its commitments, breach its alliances and upset the international balance is by provoking or facilitating the break-up of a State.

2314 – However developed and complex it may be, the international system does not yet, even in Europe, have processes enabling it to verify the wisdom and legitimacy of choices made at national level – the level at which the goals, priorities and means to be used in a negotiation are set – even in areas with the highest degree of business globalisation or European integration. Such control as already exists is limited to the execution of certain validly negotiated obligations. (see *369*)

2315 – International organisations cannot set or achieve their objectives without the cooperation of their Member States: not only do decisions about missions and goals depend on them, but also the execution of obligations negotiated within the organisations themselves. In practice, in relations between States, the exercise of negotiation replaces that of authority.

2316 – In addition, there are some States that reject any compulsory or binding procedure, and invoke the principles of sovereignty (which they regard as legitimacy) and non-intervention in their internal affairs. The good offices of neighbouring or allied States often prove more effective than large formal meetings: the African experience is instructive in this regard.

2317 – However, the respective weight of States in a negotiation is the product of a combination of factors that may appear unconnected: an expanding population can for example sometimes aggravate the effects of lack of development. A State's power does not simply depend on its resources, the extent of its territory or the number of its inhabitants: its history, culture and institutions are part of a heritage that is often underestimated, but still remains a vital and indivisible force. (see *2134*)

2318 – More than in its material wealth, a nation's real capacity to protect its existence and independence and play a part in negotiation resides in its moral force and unity, which are the foundations of its cohesion as a State. Without them, it cannot withstand the tensions of modern life for long, but becomes the subject of rivalry and the generator of anarchy. (see *14, 2250*)

A wise negotiator will ensure that the States negotiating have the real capacity to respect the commitments they undertake. (see *82*)

2319 – Even where its autonomy is reduced, its public and private affairs are no longer a strictly national matter, the State is still the basic component of any international system because it is the only entity whose existence and substance are not negotiable, and also because it is at State level that active solidarities and strong loyalties are formed, and strategies devised. (see *230, 647, 1775, 1981*)

2320 – While all institutional forms of international relations, even the European Union, apply only derived policies and, at best, react to the changing environment, only at the level of State policy and negotiation between States are diplomatic intentions devised and expressed that are based on a strategic conception and backed by effective responsibility. (see *239, 1746, 2325, 2334*)

2321 – The future of the international system thus depends on the capacity of the State to continue to serve as its solid foundation, while avoiding becoming the source of uncertainty and injustice for others. *The society of nations will not be achieved by stifling the State, but by using it to govern human society through negotiation, of which it is at the same time the only author as well as the only true actor.*[32] (see *647, 2356*)

2322 – But, at a time when new global forces are springing up, when those States that are active, prolific and determined are coming to the fore and many others, old-established and valiant, are reduced to a defensive role, the only nations that can exercise worldwide influence are those that can offer a successful social model. The only ones able to conduct fruitful negotiations and attract profitable alliances will be those capable of creating and offering not only wealth and security, but also generous cultural values.

2323 – *There is no prestige without the will to merit it.* With the blurring of distinctions between what is internal and external in public affairs, it is the stable and pacific character of the State that enables it to negotiate towards an international society able to contain conflict.[33] (see *2336, 2511, 2696*)

Section 2: Negotiation and acts of State

2324 – Cardinal de Richelieu wrote that a State must conduct itself according to the rule of reason. The multiplicity of communications, meetings and discussions

---

32 R. H. BATES: *Prosperity and Violence*, New York, Norton, 2001.
33 R. E. JONES: *Principles of Foreign Policy: the Civil State and its World Setting*, Oxford, Martin Robertson, 1979.

in the international life of a State must only appear to be improvised or unprepared, since no State can afford to waver or to be inconsistent or contradictory without seriously jeopardising its own interests and the needs of mankind as a whole. (see *347*)

A rational policy, unified in space and time, is still one of the essential principles for the government of a State. Clarity of thinking is necessary for any negotiating strategy.[34]

§1. Diplomatic strategy

2325 – Politics, war and diplomacy are all parts of the art of human government as a whole, and they come together and complement each other at the level of strategic planning. Policy lines must be sure and coherent, and decided at the highest levels of the State whose future and security they may determine. (see *225, 320, 323, 1693, 2320, 2350*)

It is the role of politicians to explain and apply these decisions. *Every strategy that is judged to be legitimate will in its turn have a legitimising function.* (see *325, 1693*)

Strategy itself is freely conceived, and it is no substitute for the trials and rigours of tactics.[35] (see *256, 336*)

Strategy sets priorities, and at the same time determines the ways in which they will be applied. But, the evolution of civilisation has brought increasingly sensitive, indirect and abstract subjects within its scope: the stakes are very different, depending, for example, on whether the object is the conquest of territory or the control of the flow of finance and culture. (see *288, 1710, 2134, 2297*)

2326 – Everything in politics is subject to negotiation, except strategy itself, which is considered as a body of imperatives: a strategy derives from a philosophy, while negotiation chooses its methods and compromises in the service of purposes that are beyond its control.

At the highest levels, abstractness, uncertainty and contradiction in doctrines and plans of action are serious failings. (see *352, 2054, 2632*)

2327 – Despite the difficulty of the exercise, it is always advantageous to deal with men of principle, resolute governments and countries that are sure of themselves. *Hesitation gives encouragement to an adversary while an ally is disturbed by versatility.* (see *821, 837, 2356*)

However, too many States do not know how to conceive and apply a diplomatic strategy: they confine themselves to reacting to events, and fail to realise how they can protect themselves by adopting a waiting posture.[36] (see *329, 336, 637*)

2328 – Strategy is the projection of thinking and the product of character, but it must surpass and outlive those who happen to be its authors. When it expresses the fundamental strengths and aspirations of a nation, it becomes a lasting principle.

---

34 H. A. KISSINGER: *The White House Years*, Boston, Little, Brown & Co., 1979, vol. I.
35 R. ARON: *Penser la guerre, Clausewitz*, Paris, Gallimard, 1976, vol. 1, p. 85.
36 L. POIRIER and F. GERE: *La Réserve et l'Attente*, Paris, Economica, 2000, p. 34.

Underlying English negotiations throughout the eighteenth and nineteenth centuries were that country's ambitions in seafaring and trade. The motive that dominated the policy of the Bourbons, and later of the revolutionaries, was the urge of France to achieve primacy over the continent, even after the sovereign freedom of peoples had emerged as a theme. (see *289, 326, 338*)

2329 – For centuries, such strategies as existed were national. They have a broader span now, within alliances, conferences and institutions where collective or global programmes are drawn up. The external negotiation of the European Union is an example of this development, as well as being a sign of a new worldwide economic order. (see *1360, 1971*)

Even in Europe, however, as long as power remains the dominant objective of negotiation, collective strategies will take second place to those of States: in much the same way, national security is incompatible with international largesse. (see *372, 637, 2166*)

Taking part in international policing operations or humanitarian intervention does not amount to a national defence policy. (see *1329, 1492*)

2330 – At a time when competition between nations is more severe than ever, any failure of strategic power is bound to have extremely serious consequences, if only because it leaves the management of public affairs in unqualified hands. Centuries ago, in 1250, the death of Barbarossa's grandson, Frederick II Hohenstaufen, left the German Empire in a difficult interregnum, at the mercy of violent and anarchic competing claims, until the first Habsburg, Rudolph, a nobleman from the Rhineland, was elected in 1273.

It is dangerous for a government to have a national strategy that depends on an external negotiation.[37]

2331 – International society in its present form is still incapable of addressing the real problems facing mankind, nor could it possibly do so. The doctrine of political realism rightly maintains that where the future of nations is concerned, the State's interest is the dominant consideration in the choices it makes. (see *78, 337, 2297*)

The greater the constraints on a negotiation, the greater the need for a new and creative strategy.

2332 – The State is the institutional expression of the primacy of the interests and security of the nation: the *salus populi* is the highest law.[38] (see *606*)

However, the acts of a State are not necessarily the expression of an unjust, immoral or brutal will. They are as likely to be motivated by wisdom and effectiveness as force and trickery. In diplomacy, the State is sufficient unto itself: no sovereign power is obliged to justify itself to another. (see *590*)

2333 – The acts of a State are self-moderating: when the strategist agrees to reconcile his policy with others, the duty to negotiate overcomes the arbitrary. (see *369, 597, 637*)

37 H. A. KISSINGER: *The White House Years*, Boston, Little, Brown & Co., 1979, vol. I.
38 T. HOBBES, *Leviathan*, London, 1651: 'Salus populi suprema lex'.

The more weight a State has in a negotiation, the greater its duty to adopt a strategy of moderation and continuity.

2334 – A decision taken at high level is based on a simple overall design. Only at the implementation stage do circumstances make the picture more nuanced and complicated. It is the same with negotiation, where the art of execution depends on a strategic directive. The fundamental issues are not always the most complex, but the entire balance of the negotiation depends on their being resolved. (see *321, 330, 356, 1710*)

2335 – In its desire to give a manoeuvre the best chances of success, there is nothing to prevent a State from conducting several negotiations in different fora, which is made easy by the proliferation of international conferences and meetings.[39] This approach may provide the information necessary to make choices and sometimes decide on a strategy. (see *312, 328, 2367*)

The fact that a strategy is applied incidentally in a particular negotiation must not detract from the logic and coherence of the overall plan of action. (see *931, 2259, 2325*)

2336 – The most serious political failures are the ones that lie at the heart of the system, the central strategic theme. The very principle of the negotiation can be turned against its author, and the enterprise can damage those who planned it. The Kings of France acquired many territories by negotiating marriages, but Eleanor of Aquitaine transferred her provinces from French to English hands by changing husbands. The ageing Emperor of Germany, Charles V, himself divided between his successors the empire he had built up through marriage, inheritance and conquests. Much later, it was a series of errors of strategic judgement that brought about the final downfall of the USSR in 1990–1991. (see *323, 329, 342*)

2337 – It is not enough to decide in advance that a certain event shall or shall not take place: what is needed is to prepare the ground so that it does or does not happen. (see *281*)

Where independent forces, separate interests and converging efforts are brought to bear on a negotiation, this contributes to the success and stability of the policy.

2338 – Negotiation, however, is not always the easiest solution, because it obliges the negotiator to come to terms with competitors or enemies. For a government, conflict and war can also be sources of stability, autonomy and prestige, and for a nation, they can bring cohesion.[40] (see *260, 2110*)

2339 – Political choices always involve an element of imagination or arbitrariness. The list is long of the tactics princes have used to serve their passions or interests, or to secure their own domination or glory: for centuries, the peace of their peoples as well as their neighbours depended on the initiatives they took. This is still true.

39 R. ARON: *République impériale. Les Etats-Unis dans le monde (1945–1972)*, Paris, Calmann-Lévy, 1973.
40 M. McLUHAN: *War and Peace in the Global Village*, New York, Bantam, 1968.

Innovation is a quality indispensable in strategy: in order to reign, one must dare. (see *184*)

2340 – The freedom of strategic choice does not obviate the need for perseverance on the part of its author, or for sustained effort. On the contrary, it involves challenges: one of the priorities of the statesman must be to find out the strategies of the protagonists, and one of his wishes will be that these strategies are reliable and proof against surprises.

2341 – Continuity is a precondition for security and credibility. In international even more than national negotiation, attitudes are evaluated in terms of their political durability. Generally speaking, it is a characteristic of diplomatic manoeuvres that they unfold slowly and with prudence. (see *328*)

2342 – In the international environment more than any other, given its complexity, the will to act must transform inspiration into clear ideas, and these must proceed from a broad and historically informed vision of relations between nations. Forecasts must be projected as far into the future as possible, overcoming the prudence and pessimism of the intelligence services and the routine reluctance of the administration, as, once it is set in motion, the diplomatic process has a way of following its own logic.[41]

2343 – Skill and authority should allow the statesman to steer the negotiation in accordance with the higher interests of his country, free from the immediate constraints of public opinion and the bias of its leaders. In order to fight the powerful rival house of Habsburg, François 1, King of France, made an alliance with Suleiman the Magnificent, and his successors joined forces with the Lutheran princes of Germany against the Catholics. (see *330*)

Sooner or later, a government will be judged, not on its faithfulness to its promises, but on its ability to resolve the problems presented to it.

2344 – At a time when powerful movements exist beyond the State's control, it takes very particular skills to analyse the diplomatic situation. (see *345*)

The better a statesman understands the major issues of his day and perceives the consequences of his decisions, the better qualified he is for his mission. Metternich, who for forty years was responsible for Austria's foreign policy, was masterly in his direction of European diplomacy for as long as it followed the traditional model; as soon as its political underpinnings were swept aside in 1848 by a renewed tide of national sentiment, he failed. (see *2155*)

2345 – Political leaders alone have the ability and the impetus to overturn the status quo and exceed the narrow limits of negotiation. They are different from diplomats in this respect. *The professional negotiator does not find it easy to innovate: he is inclined to prefer secrecy and follow the established routine when faced with colleagues who are doing the same.* The role of certain Western statesman, such as Robert Schuman, Konrad Adenauer and Alcide de Gasperi at the birth of the European Communities, is proof of the exceptional effect political

41 P. GALLOIS: *Géopolitique, les voies de la puissance*, Paris, Plon, 1990.

initiatives can have when their authors have enough support to make them succeed. (see *325, 2492*)

2346 – When it is based on real strength, moral, military or otherwise, prestige can increase levels of attention and respect; this makes negotiation easier. In reality, this type of attitude is more often used to serve the cult of a personality than the interests of his country. (see *2616*)

Strategy is at its most valuable in the service of a nation when it is conceived, formulated and applied by persons who are worthy to represent it: the positive images of France and the United States projected by Charles de Gaulle and John F. Kennedy were of lasting value to the diplomacy of their countries.[42]

2347 – Deprived of any higher moral or political authority, and in search of balance and security, international society cannot fail to submit to diplomatic strategies: some of them bring stability, some uncertainty and even risks.

2348 – Considered as the art of conducting relations between States, diplomacy is certainly one of the fields in which the qualities of the strategist can be exercised most freely. He must not, however, lay the blame for his own failings at the door of the soldiers or negotiators: the pursuit by France, and later the United States, of military interventions in Vietnam was not the product of inadvertence but of fundamental errors of political judgement.[43]

2349 – It is diplomatic strategy that makes the statesman. (see *320*)

Much has been written about Bonaparte, as the young general of the Italian campaign. But nor should the negotiator of Loeben and Campoformio be forgotten, who at less than thirty years of age was negotiating with the seasoned plenipotentiaries of the Austrian Emperor, and who exceeded his mandate by committing France to a new foreign policy. The dominant force of his personality was already in evidence then, in war as in diplomacy: after years of battles, peace won him as much popularity in France as his victories. (see *431*)

2350 – The typology of the statesman is a matter for political, psychological and historical study. It can be applied to foreign negotiation, and shows how important it is to know how to move beyond the immediate next step to the main goal: mastering the sometimes inextricable complexities of the international configuration of the time requires a great effort of reflection, innovation and will.

All great strategists have, by their imagination and their actions, brought new themes to diplomacy. (see *2335*)

§2. Negotiation as an instrument of policy

2351 – In a State, the ultimate choices depend on political power. No authority within a nation, other than the political, could exercise such a prerogative, as it

---

42 A. WOLFERS: 'The Actors in International Politics', in *The Theory and Practice of International Relations*, Englewood Cliffs, Prentice Hall, 1966, p. 13.
43 R. ARON: *République impériale. Les Etats-Unis dans le monde (1945–1972)*, Paris, Calmann-Lévy, 1973, p. 121.

alone can make an overall assessment of the forces in play and, most of all, decide on the order of priority of social objectives and assume responsibility for them. (see *2254*)

2352 – The groundwork for a negotiation is laid on the basis of policy. Policy determines when the negotiation shall start and what shall be its object and purpose; it steers the negotiation and gives it direction. Policy determines the relationship between diplomacy and war, depending on what the contest is meant to achieve: attack or defence, prevention, destruction or conquest. Policy also determines the nation's networks of friendship and necessity; adversaries and allies are chosen according to what is perceived to be in the interests of the State. (see *914*)

2353 – At the highest level of a State's concerns, all that really matters is the political benefit to be derived from a given activity. *Negotiation is an instrument of policy, as Clausewitz wrote of war. In this sense, it is, like combat, a subordinate activity. It means nothing in itself, but counts only because of the results it can produce.*

2354 – In relations between States, no subject is exclusively technical in nature. No negotiation, however trivial, is without its place is in the overall perspective or without possible consequences in the long term.

So diverse is the subject matter of international negotiation that a view of the total picture is needed if coherent action is to be taken. But this requires a constant series of choices between the nation's domestic needs and its foreign potential. (see *2545*)

2355 – Negotiation derives its principal characteristics from policy. When used in the service of a clear and firm design, it can be exercised with strength and forbearance. It is difficult to find words for the lack of perspicacity or of any sense of reality or determination shown by the French and British leaders in the face of Hitler's cynical audacity from 1936 onwards.

Power must be secured before it can be exercised.

2356 – A State whose unity is insecure, whose power is wavering or that lacks a coherent policy introduces an element of unpredictability and danger into international relations. It becomes a pawn in the competition between other powers, and can no longer play a meaningful part in international life: this was the position of Turkey during the fall of the Ottoman Empire. The statesman who hesitates or procrastinates, refuses to commit, or is unclear as to his goals and intentions, will find that his negotiators take no risks in the moves or the judgements they make.

A diplomat caught between doctrine and empiricism will take contradictory positions.

2357 – It takes time for the international environment to absorb changes that have taken place within States, either in terms of political power or public opinion. (see *685, 1618*)

Sooner or later, though, States' regimes, their constitutional and decision-making systems and the balance between their internal political forces will have an effect on international dialogue. Capacity and a solid power-base are among the preconditions for international competitiveness. Sterile internal debates about policy and ideology undermine a State's potential to negotiate.

2358 – The degree to which a State's domestic politics influences the international negotiation of other States depends on whether it is in a dominant position or whether its support is needed, for example within an alliance.[44] The less powerful and independent the State, the more its room for diplomatic manoeuvre will depend on extraneous factors. Its tactics will thus be to minimise or conceal the fact of its subordination. As La Rochefoucauld said, it is difficult for the weak to be sincere. (see *133, 136*)

2359 – The negotiator's tactics are dictated by the political regime of his country. A totalitarian regime will necessarily have a different approach to diplomacy and its methods from that of a democracy, where political pluralism makes contradiction and compromise a fact of life.

The style of their foreign negotiations is one of the defining characteristics that set liberal societies apart from the rest: style is largely determined in practice by how legal, moral and cultural codes are understood and applied in the country concerned, and the effect they have on those in power and on public opinion.[45] An aggressive or duplicitous negotiating style is often the mark of a tyrannical regime. (see *392, 2135, 2597*)

2360 – In many States, the internal negotiating environment is made simpler by the political system. The sole or dominant party holds the reins of the political, administrative, cultural and economic apparatus, constituting a force that makes up for the absence of public opinion. But even in the presence of such a monolith, identifiable groups such as the army or big business, or ethnic or religious communities can still act, and historic prejudices survive. (see *2512, 2549*)

2361 – The search for, and preservation of, a political majority, characteristic of Western democratic regimes, must obey the same principles as negotiation: moderation in expression, discretion in negotiation, prudence in judgement, absence of political bias, openness to mutual concessions and the rejection of doctrinal imperatives. (see *2675*)

2362 – *It is difficult to hold to a diplomatic line in a democracy: the effects of passion and sentiment can intrude upon and cloud a realistic vision. That said, the changing moods of leaders are more to be feared than shifts in public opinion.* (see *2512*)

It is of little use to reflect in depth on international strategy unless the workings of the internal political system have been mastered.

2363 – The means available to plenipotentiaries to persuade or fight are those their leaders give them, since it is the leaders who choose whether to engage, based on their judgement of the circumstances and the forces in play. Similarly, where a negotiation is well conducted, it contributes in its turn to the State's power and

44 R. NEUSTADT: *Alliance Politics*, New York, Columbia University Press, 1970.
F. SCHURMANN: *The Logic of World Power*, New York, Pantheon Books, 1974.
45 N. J. HOLSTI: *International Politics: a Framework for Analysis*, Englewood Cliffs, Prentice Hall, 1977.

prosperity, by enhancing its resources, confirming its influence and legitimising its claims, stabilising its power, and attracting partners to its side that have an interest in preserving the status quo.[46] (see *1803*)

2364 – In States that are open to external influences, and even in others, it is increasingly difficult to distinguish what belongs to the exclusive realms of foreign policy. The play of domestic forces determines a country's diplomatic strategy and sets its limits.

It is the need for internal stability that leads powers to reach agreement on ways to control shared economic crises.

2365 – Negotiation is thus shaped by circumstances within the country as much as by the strategic line. From 1936 onwards, when the country faced grave and mounting threats, France's military and diplomatic positions in the face of German rearmament were steadily weakened by the economic crisis. In the 1970s, a similar economic blight affected almost all the States of Western Europe.

2366 – A country should adapt its negotiation to suit its internal means. In this respect, the political starting position is decisive. The initial plan can succeed or fail depending on whether it is good or bad. In the seventeenth century, the deteriorating Spanish economy combined with that country's depopulation and the impoverishment of the Madrid branch of the Habsburgs, forced them to abandon their ambitions in France and beyond: the Pyrenees Treaty of 1659 enabled them to save face, but it allowed the Bourbons in France to supplant them as the predominant dynasty in Western Europe.

2367 – Nor should a country's position be weakened by disunity, excesses or contradictions on its diplomatic front, as happened with the Austro-Hungarian Empire: the number of conflicts in which it was embroiled, and the variety of political approaches this demanded, left it so vulnerable that it ultimately disintegrated and left Europe at war.

2368 – The same problem has always beset powers with far-flung possessions, diverse interests and multiple commitments. Unless they refuse to assume their role, as the United States did when it disowned the League of Nations Pact negotiated by President Woodrow Wilson, all powers that are open on several fronts must overcome centrifugal forces and impose unity on contradictory policies.

Only by winning this battle did the Roman Empire survive, like that of Charlemagne. The collapse of these empires, like that of the Habsburg monarchy and later of the USSR, unleashed new and powerful forces that transformed international relations, forcing other States to adapt to these new disruptive influences. Today, as before, the major States must engage in unceasing efforts to fulfil the competing, if not contradictory, responsibilities imposed by their rank, their wealth and their own interests. (see *133*)

2369 – The best of agreements is useless in the face of reality. In spite of the resolve they showed in reaching three successive compromises, the European powers that

---

46 H. A. KISSINGER: *A World Restored*, Boston, Houghton Mifflin, 1957.

had divided Poland among themselves in the eighteenth century never succeeded in annihilating it completely. As for the Peace Treaties of 1919, the frontiers they delimited in Eastern Europe proved inadequate to resolve centuries-old disputes, as is still evident today. (see *339*)

2370 – *State policy, war and diplomacy offer no certainties, either in how they judge the past, how they interpret the present, or what they predict for the future.* In all of them, issues are resolved not on their merits, but according to the inclinations of the actor, depending on what he thinks is timely, what he wants and sometimes even what pleases him. The action unfolds in accordance with the leader's own assessment of the situation and the options available, and he alone bears the responsibility. (see *2537*)

2371 – Depending on the countries, characters and circumstances involved, a tension exists between those who would stand firm and those who are willing to change; those who are tenacious and those who are flexible; those who seize the moment and those whose approach is logical.[47] But a diplomat always does well to adapt his tactics to the internal climate in his country: where there are financial, economic or other problems, he will obviously adopt a cautious and considered approach and slow the pace of the negotiations. He may have to make unexpected concessions: in 1924, the fall in value of the franc forced France to promise to evacuate the Ruhr in order to obtain foreign facilities.

2372 – In any initiative or negotiation, or any tactic in general, variable factors come into play. *Negotiation is a combination of simple ideas and calculated manoeuvres. Its success largely depends on the timeliness of the initiatives and how tenaciously they are pursued, as well as on the ability to innovate, take the adversary by surprise, and make the best use of men and situations. It is an art that requires skill and talent.*

2373 – Every political position is liable to change, either on its own or in relation to its context: the wise negotiator is quick to take advantage of circumstances that favour him. (see *268*)

Every advantage is transitory, and all freedom is relative; the strategy does not exist that does not contain the source of its own weakness and limitations. (see *2340*)

2374 – The essence of political activity is to adapt to the facts and the means available.[48] Diplomatic tactics are a mixture of reactions to the prevailing realities and contingencies of the external environment, and decisions emanating from the internal political hierarchy.[49] (see *293*)

While negotiation is one of the natural instruments of policy, the statesman will not expect too much from it; he will measure his commitments and limitations against the forces at his disposal, and can thereby succeed in using diplomacy to defend, uphold or alter the factual or legal picture. (see *60*)

---

47 P. RENOUVIN: *Le Traité de Versailles*, Paris, Flammarion, 1969.
48 C. von CLAUSEWITZ: *On War*, Berlin, Dümmlers Verlag, 1832, VIII.
49 H. A. KISSINGER: 'Domestic structure and foreign policy', in *Daedalus*, Spring edition, 1966, p. 503.

2375 – Once the policy line is decided, even though the diplomat might be inclined to concede or compromise, the political leader must hold firm if his policy is to succeed. A firm position is readily accepted, and sometimes actually welcomed, by a negotiator prepared to compromise. The negotiators of the treaties of Westphalia are praised for their pragmatism, and their flexibility in leaving the way open for the nations of Europe to develop in different directions, but in fact this tactic was based on a very clear principle laid down by Richelieu and upheld by Mazarin: in refraining from making increased demands for territory, France was aiming above all to prevent Germany becoming unified under a powerful dynasty or a single dominant religion.

2376 – The aim of politics is success, and this depends as much on the astute use of opportunities as on skilful advance planning. The interplay of these varied and unpredictable factors means that there is no place for preconceived abstract principles. Frederick the Great of Prussia, and others after him, have made an outward show of moral uprightness and philosophical wisdom, but this has not stopped them from using deceit, brutality and cynicism.

2377 – It is a long way from intentions and proposals to action and reality: *events conspire to deflect even the best-laid plans.* For this reason, the results of a negotiation should not be judged simply on the basis of initial diplomatic intentions. (see *354*)

2378 – When setting out to achieve international goals, a certain sense is needed of how diplomacy is best approached. Only as discussions unfold can new baselines be set, one stage at a time, depending on the successes or failures to date, and also new limits acknowledged as to its aim. The art of negotiation can thus serve as a fitting complement to the art of politics.

2379 – Foreign policy, in its turn, exercises an influence over domestic policy, which is not indifferent to the success of a negotiation. There are some statesmen who rely on peace as the basis of their influence. Others owe their fame and power to a successful foreign enterprise: the Franco-British capitulation at the Munich meetings in 1938 did much to strengthen the power of both Hitler and Mussolini. And the place of the United Kingdom in the European Union is still a recurring theme of internal political debate in Britain.

2380 – International negotiation sometimes has the effect of giving structure to domestic political life: the strategic issues it raises serve to emphasise the divisions among those in government and sometimes also in public opinion. France provides some striking examples: in 1954, Mendès France secured his election as President of the Council by giving a commitment to conclude a peace agreement in Indochina before the summer. In the same year, the parliamentary debate on the ratification of the treaty setting up the European Defence Community revealed the major divisions in French political opinion.

Refusal to take part in certain debates or certain treaties can reveal political intentions: this is true for nuclear proliferation and also financial cooperation.

2381 – Some treaties produce a real solidarity of interests and ideology among the governments concerned: regimes consolidate each other, to the benefit of those in power, both civilian and military.

The development of economic and cultural negotiation contributes to the political effects of diplomacy: the common market in agriculture benefited from the electoral stability of the countries of the European Communities. Negotiation should therefore be viewed in terms of how it relates to public opinion. (see *2613*)

2382 – When properly conducted, negotiation can defuse any number of tensions, especially in internal politics.[50] More is expected of it today: needs and activities flow across frontiers, giving impetus to trade between nations and urging inward-looking regimes to make peaceful overtures to the outside world.

2383 – It is a general principle that no international negotiation can alter or breach a Constitution. However, there are cases where it has had an impact on a State's institutions. When Norway became independent in 1905 as a result of the dissolution of the union with Sweden, it chose to elect a new King in order to facilitate its contacts with the main European monarchies at the time. More recently, in 1975, the referendum made its appearance as part of the British political system as a result of the renegotiation of the terms of entry of the United Kingdom into the European Union.

In France, there have been occasions when the results of negotiations were contrary to the Constitution. Several revisions have been made to the basic text, on the holding of referenda to ratify Community treaties and regulations, and for the implementation of the 1998 Treaty of Rome on the International Criminal Court. (see *723, 1249, 2235*)

2384 – External negotiation sometimes serves to reinforce and centralise the State apparatus, even in federal systems: competition from outside strengthens them and makes them more unified and coherent. The USSR took this centralisation to extremes, but used it to great advantage in its international dealings because it was the sole interlocutor for Western interests riven by competitive divisions. The collapse of that totalitarian structure opened the way to various negotiations, some of them unpredictable, especially with Western Europe and the United States.

2385 – Negotiating in institutions forces the political powers to incline to new disciplines, by diluting or substituting their right to make concessions and conclude agreements. This first erosion of national positions readies them for negotiation in a wider forum that will involve them in a second wave of compromises. This process can cause the re-examination of government responsibilities. (see *1441, 1617*)

The course of development of the European Community is a good example. Despite the sophistication of its institutional machinery, the daily management by the Councils and their working groups is carried on by intergovernmental negotiation; Heads of State and government must decide on their positions in the Council. This method works well in practice, provided the Member States agree that their differing national strategies are subordinate to the interests of the Union. The democracy of this approach, however, depends not only on the skills and

---

50 C. von CLAUSEWITZ: *On War*, I.

authority of each national Parliament, but even more on national public opinion being in fundamental agreement as to the primacy of Europe. (see *1257*)

2386 – The multiplicity of rules and institutions arising out of international agreements can, in some cases, have an anaesthetic effect on the political, legal and financial milieux. *Sometimes it can take sudden shocks or crises to alert legislators and public opinion to commitments that have been made without their knowledge.* When worldwide or regional organisations function according to their own logic, by means of successive adaptations, it is governments and their officials that will be held responsible, in their parliaments or by public opinion, for concessions they did not make and negotiations over which they had only partial control (see *2229*)

2387 – The outcomes of foreign policy provide arguments that can be used to serve all manner of purposes: international negotiation has become part of the stakes in the struggle for power, as well as a determinant of success or failure. Negotiation can be turned against itself, to serve the publicity or propaganda purposes of ambitious or visionary personalities, whose appearance on the diplomatic scene spells danger for the stability and harmony of international relations.

Chapter II:
The Skills of the Negotiator

2388 – In war, apart from some essential principles, there is no universal system, only circumstances and personalities.[1] The same is true in diplomacy. Negotiation cannot be reduced to a set of theoretical rules, because it is based on observation, deduction, analysis and the ability to see things as a whole, in which personal experience, intuition and improvisation are as important as knowledge of law, customs and history. (see *59, 449*)

2389 – The practice of this art is all the more difficult because its rituals sometimes appear theatrical or even dramatic. *The personality of the actor affects the way the role is played. An official approach can work best when seeking to formalise the outcome of a negotiation, while oblique and secretive methods are sometimes better for steering the talks towards the desired result.*

2390 – There can be no game without rules – which, when generally accepted, should give all parties a fair chance of success – or without methods to provide rational, orderly and usual ways of achieving the goal. (see *2397*)
   The negotiator takes risks, knowing that this is a way of increasing the potential gains.

2391 – In the art of negotiation, as in war or trade, there are formulas and customs: this is why diplomats, like soldiers and financiers, understand each other so well. Each of these disciplines has its own kind of reasoning, communication and vocabulary, though the real talent lies in knowing when to break with routine and preconceptions in order to innovate and surprise.[2] (see *2425*)
   Little by little, and particularly since 1815, a kind of international code has taken shape which, though largely a matter of custom, governs the practice and profession of diplomacy.

2392 – It can happen, though, that this order is overtaken by irrationality or violence. The goals of negotiation concern the future of States, not of their envoys: how can diplomats be expected to abide by the accepted rules when the dangers for the country are so great that they cannot risk failure?
   Such is, and will always be, the case in confrontation between individuals, societies and States that have no common system of values. (see *271, 508*)

---

1 C. de GAULLE: *La Discorde chez l'ennemi*, First published by Berger-Levrault, Paris, 1924; subsequent edition Paris, Plon, 1971.
2 R. REICH: *The Work of Nations*, New York, Knopf, 1991; *L'Economie mondialisée*, Paris, Denoël, 1993, p. 163.

2393 – New technologies for gathering and processing information will bring out the qualities of the individual negotiator and the particular nature of his task. Education, judgement and courage will prove irreplaceable, as on these depends the ability to combine and deploy all available means in the fight. (see *2006*)

2394 – Even after a successful result, the negotiator rarely reaps the rewards, since this is a discipline of discretion and restraint, not of prestige or glory. *That said, the statesman is still called upon to devote all his talents and energy to the mission, and this, at critical moments, can be an all-consuming commitment.* (see *2630*)

Section 1: The role of personality

2395 – Despite the anonymity of modern society, in diplomacy, the role of each person is decisive for the course of events: *savoir-faire* is indispensable to the success of the enterprise.

Hence the importance of choosing those who are to conduct international talks, whether they are official or unofficial envoys: a change of negotiator usually alters the negotiation.

2396 – For centuries, diplomacy was the preserve of dignitaries, whether secular or clerical, who were often appointed for reasons that had nothing to do with the discussions themselves. The Italians of the Renaissance were the first to use professionals, chosen for their talents rather than their affiliations. Starting in the time of Richelieu, the French monarchy created a staff of diplomats who already had a kind of career.

2397 – From the seventeenth century, it became the accepted practice in chanceries if not in political circles to call on specialist negotiators.

This profession has become progressively 'nationalised' because of its association with the exercise of sovereignty, but it will become more and more usual for States to employ professional negotiators, irrespective of nationality, to prepare for or even conduct diplomatic transactions. This is a field in which expert assistance has a role to play, with service companies being formed to assist States with the preparation and conduct of negotiations. (see *1522, 1928*)

2398 – The transfer of major international decisions to the highest levels of authority, and the growing number of political meetings, has enhanced the diplomatic dimension of the activities of politicians confident of their own personal abilities and eager to impress public opinion. The importance of a treaty can be gauged from the rank of its signatories. (see *2485, 2534*)

Government members frequently develop a taste for international missions, duplicating or neutralising the efforts of their diplomatic representatives. (see *2402, 2431*)

2399 – At the same time, diplomacy is adopting the methods of direct administration, drawn from its involvement in the procedures and workings of international organisations and in European institutions. (see *1176, 1521*)

Negotiation in organisations fosters solidarity among envoys, to the point of complicity among groups of specialists whose objective is sometimes to reach agreement among themselves without political intrusion.

§1. The choice of envoy

2400 – History shows that it is often the most difficult negotiations that bring out the talents of a statesman, in other words the qualities that enable him to withstand great pressure: intelligence, skill, patience and resolution. King Louis XI of France demonstrated these qualities when Charles the Bold of Burgundy sought to humiliate him during their encounter in Péronne, northern France, in 1468.

2401 – It is rare for political leaders to have the qualities of a negotiator, especially those who are democratically elected: *winning an election is evidence of competitive political skills and powers of persuasion, but not of the ability to mediate or compromise.* The problem can even arise at governmental level: irrespective of professional background, a Foreign Minister must know how to negotiate. (see *2437*)

2402 – Oratorical skills can benefit from the practice of diplomacy, as well as complementing it, provided the orator is able to learn from experience. He must go against his natural leanings and learn when to keep silent, speaking only on the issue in hand, to rein in his imagination and consider only what is likely, to restrain his generous impulses and make no promises or concessions that are not reciprocated – in short, to commit to as little as possible, whatever his personal opinions or loyalties. Winston Churchill's temperament led him to alternate between detailed discussions and calculated flights of enthusiastic oratory, and this made him a unique and convincing negotiator. *A good negotiator knows how to make the maximum personal impact, especially on the international scene.*

2403 – A strategist who wants his plan to succeed must commit to it completely, not only personally but through the envoys he chooses for the purpose. It takes wisdom and moderation to decide, but vigour and energy to implement. He must secure the collaboration not only of capable experts, but also of advisers who are well versed in all the intrigues and pitfalls of diplomacy, At every stage, he must ensure that their actions remain consistent with the policy line. (see *2487*)

2404 – It goes without saying that a plenipotentiary must have the full confidence of those who appoint him. In 1801, when he was new to power, Napoleon sent his brother Lucien as ambassador to Madrid to reach agreement with the Bourbons, and entrusted his brother Joseph with the conclusion of peace treaties with Austria and later with England. Even so, he was betrayed some years later, by Talleyrand.
   The choice of plenipotentiary is an indicator of the importance of the negotiation: not all the ambassadors of the Soviet Union were members of the party Politburo.

2405 – A negotiator must have sufficient credibility in his own country to be able to represent it validly. This is a precondition for his interlocutor to take what he says and does seriously, and agree to make binding commitments. By insisting that the request for the 1918 Armistice must come from the representatives of the German people in order to humiliate the Prussian army, Woodrow Wilson allowed that army to keep its national prestige intact. (see *688, 2633*)

2406 – Mindful of the special difficulties of negotiation, the political leader cannot and must not neglect to keep a close eye on the manner in which the diplomat carries out his instructions: nothing is more likely to force him to intervene at an inappropriate level and at what may be an inopportune moment than inertia, ineptitude or faint-heartedness on the part of his representative. (see *269*)

Having chosen the right envoy, the statesman must ensure that he obtains the desired result, while leaving him free to choose his methods: the skill and resolve of the envoy will protect his masters' freedom to manoeuvre.

2407 – It makes no sense to entrust a tough negotiation to an ambassador better suited to ceremonial duties. On the other hand, a sensitive mission calls for someone with astute observation and sound judgement, able to interpret any situation, having both an awareness of the intrigues of diplomacy and a taste for strategy. (see *450*)

2408 – The choice of negotiator will also be influenced by other, non-personal factors. It might depend, for example, on who the interlocutors will be. As a general rule, unless the object is to stir up tension or confrontation, a mismatch between the envoy and the country is not advisable: the success of the venture will depend to a great extent on the relationships established, and especially the degree of mutual trust.[3] (see *505*)

2409 – A government in a difficult position is well advised not to issue rigid instructions, but rather to entrust its interests to plenipotentiaries who, by virtue of their character, loyalty and experience, will have a sufficient understanding of the other side's position to bring about an agreement while still maintaining the right degree of distance. Prince Orlov did this at the Paris Conference in 1856, when he was able to use his personal relationships and talents to serve the cause of Russia. (see *2420*)

Those with a common language or background work well together. This is also true of those with a shared adversary, in the same way that there is mutual understanding among sailors, in the face of the sea. (see *507*)

2410 – Even if he is uncompromising and distrustful, the best interlocutor is one whose firmness and vigilance make it possible to analyse his strategy. He does not express his own opinions lightly, and the messages he is given are correctly understood and passed on. (see *2327*)

2411 – Care and precautions are also needed when choosing a national representative for negotiations at a conference or within an international institution, since these require the qualities of a parliamentarian as well as a

3 M. de MAULDE LA CLAVIERE: *La Diplomatie du temps de Machiavel*, Paris, Leroux, 1892.
A. de WICQUEFORT: *L'Ambassadeur et ses fonctions*, Cologne, Pierre Marteau, 1715, I, 13.
F. de CALLIERES: *De la manière de négocier avec les souverains*, Paris, 1716, ed., XXII.

diplomat, including the ability to direct teams of experts and lawyers, and follow the technical work done in meetings and committees right through to the stage when documents are drafted and debated.

2412 – It is important to be able to recognise those individuals with credibility, both within delegations and on their margins. A delegate's role, title and position are often transient: they are decided for the purposes of the particular exercise, to ensure an equal or superior footing vis à vis the other party. This results in international negotiators being accorded increasingly exaggerated ranks. (see 688)

A person's rank in terms of protocol does not always reflect his actual influence.

2413 – In this regard, especially now that problems are becoming more and more technical, a distinction must be made between representation and negotiation. Some exchanges, or preliminaries, not intended to have formal binding effect, are not strictly diplomatic, and are conducted without accredited envoys present.

Not every ambassador negotiates, and not every negotiator is an ambassador. (see 691)

2414 – There are many instances where governments have used intermediaries with no official status, or even foreigners, acting away from the capital: the proposals they make do not bind the government in question, nor do the ones they receive.

It is helpful to be able to disown or ignore an envoy.

2415 – Prominent people who are not diplomats can prove ideal for making contacts, either in a foreign capital or at a major meeting. Richelieu, Mazarin and their successors used this method frequently; at the end of the reign of Louis XIV, it was a tradesman from Rouen who served successively as envoy in The Hague and intermediary in London, where he signed the preliminary peace agreement, thus skilfully paving the way for the Treaty of Utrecht. Later, in 1801, it was a native of Bad in Germany who went to England on Bonaparte's behalf to draw up the document that became the Treaty of Amiens. (see 440, 695, 696)

2416 – Sometimes the same person is charged by both parties with securing agreement between them, or is accepted by them both. Then, the government that has the closest relationship with the emissary stands to do best in the negotiation. It is easy to understand why Napoleon rejected Metternich's offers in 1813, suspecting him of bad faith, despite the trust he placed in his own father-in-law, the Austrian Emperor. (see 462)

2417 – This reasoning does not apply, however, to the disinterested peacemaking mission, of which historical examples are rare: one was that of Nordling, the Swedish Consul General in Paris, who negotiated a truce in August 1944 between the leaders of the French Resistance and the German military authorities, and thus helped to save the capital.

A mediator must not negotiate on behalf of one of the parties.

2418 – There used to be a practice, especially in pre-revolutionary France, of sending a number of negotiators on the same mission, sometimes with differing instructions and without full knowledge of the situation. These agents reported back directly on what they did, and also on the activities of the ministers they were watching. This method might possibly have enabled major settlements to be reached, but it was certainly responsible for some major diplomatic problems and grave political errors. (see *2599*)

The instructions

2419 – Sovereigns have sometimes allowed their own chosen representatives great freedom of action. Since classical times, however, the usual practice has been to determine the object and scope of the negotiation in advance, sometimes in carefully revised documents, and also set out the expected outcome. (see *700, 1050, 2061, 2409*)

2420 – These instructions, drawn up in conformity with general policy, remain valid as long as their authors do not amend them. Some of them are mandatory and must be carried out to the letter, which does not mean that they cannot be changed.[4] When these instructions are very detailed, dealing for example with technical matters, they take away part or all of a diplomat's initiative and freedom of manoeuvre; on the other hand, the more flexible they are, the greater the ultimate responsibility of the plenipotentiary.

From the seventeenth century, French diplomacy has attached great importance and devoted great care to the lasting written instructions issued to negotiators departing on mission.[5] The invention first of telegraphy and then of modern communication technology, led to an increase in the number, as well as the detail, of directives issued while the negotiations are actually taking place. (see *1509, 2477, 2546*)

2421 – When flexibility seems necessary to achieve the desired result, the true diplomat must be able to free himself of the constraints imposed by an invasive bureaucracy. Based on an astute judgement of what is in his country's interests, he must exercise his discretion depending on the state of the negotiation or the circumstances, especially when there is no time to consult his political masters. (see *2056*)

The envoy must often begin the negotiating process while still in his own capital, in order to obtain instructions that will allow him sufficient room to manoeuvre.

2422 – In any event, despite being bound by the orders he has received, the arguments a diplomat makes will play a decisive role if they succeed in convincing the adversary, especially if they present him with an alternative. As Callières

---

4 F. de CALLIERES: *De la manière de négocier avec les souverains*, Paris, 1750 ed., II, p. 47.
 M. de MAULDE LA CLAVIERE: *La Diplomatie du temps de Machiavel*, Paris, Leroux, 1892, II, p. 124.
5 *Recueil des instructions données aux ambassadeurs et ministres de France, depuis les Traités de Westphalie*, Paris, CNRS. H. NICOLSON: *The Evolution of Diplomatic Methods*, London, MacMillan, 1954.

pointed out, dexterity in negotiation lies in knowing how to find the easiest paths to a solution, the best one being to convince the other party and make him feel that he is understood. (see *1845*)

2423 – Where he feels he does not have the full support of his capital, the diplomat will preserve his freedom of action for as long as possible, but without ignoring any occasion for a profitable tactical agreement. Sheltered to some extent from the negotiation, he will mask his intentions, keep his positions vague, not commit himself, and commit his principals only rarely, late, and cautiously. (see *2404*)

Deficiencies in strategy usually manifest themselves by the absence of clear, firm instructions.

2424 – Sun Tse taught that where prompt action was needed, the envoy should not wait for orders from above. Nor should he hesitate to act fearlessly against the orders received, if the occasion demands.[6] Obedience does not imply servility or weakness of will.

In negotiation, compelling external pressures can moderate respect for the hierarchical order.

The qualities of the negotiator

2425 – While a real diplomatic milieu exists in which customs, traditions and characters are formed, each negotiator has his own ambitions, fears and loathings, temperament and habits.[7] (see *441, 2391*)

2426 – Many authors have described in detail what makes a good negotiator. Apart from suitable professional training, the personal qualities required are varied and often contradictory. His behaviour must at the same time be firm and flexible, courageous and prudent, and with no trace of timidity, pride or vanity. Other qualities include presence of mind, warmth of expression, intelligence, discernment, tact, *sang-froid*, patience and accuracy. All this, however, is a matter of judgement: nobody can tell when perseverance shades into obstinacy, or sincerity becomes apologetic, or how much importance should be attached to the ability to learn by imitation. (see *263, 478*)

2427 – In classical antiquity, ambassadors began as orators: the primary attribute required of them was the ability to sway or persuade public opinion, however deep the gulf that turned out to separate their actions from their words. Remarkably, centuries later, diplomacy is returning to its roots, with negotiation again taking place to some degree in the public eye, especially in the major international political assemblies.

2428 – This is not to suggest that the art of negotiation is that of the *prima donna*: flying visits, well-turned phrases and photographs have more to do with

---

6 SUN TSE: *The Thirteen Articles* Fifth century BC.
7 H. A. KISSINGER: *A World Restored*, Boston, Houghton Mifflin, 1957. E. C. IKLE: *How Nations Negotiate*, New York, Harper Row, 1964, p. 143.

entertainment than with government. *Where public affairs are concerned, negotiation is an important, serious and difficult matter, requiring character as much as intelligence.* (see **481**)

A major negotiation must be carefully thought through. (see **441**)

2429 – Bismarck was originally called on to defuse an internal political crisis in Prussia, but stayed in power for twenty-eight years. His implacable will to dominate, audacious personality and imagination, and his instinct for judging forces and men secured him a unique place in the history of his country. But his role was not simply confined to building a unified Germany through victory in war. The Iron Chancellor also masterminded the diplomacy of the Kingdom of the Hohenzollerns, and later the German Empire, at a decisive period in the history of Europe. He was both firm and astute in his use of negotiation, which earned him a position of authority unchallenged abroad.

2430 – The true negotiator is a man of action, one who rounds off his assessment of a situation by taking action to move it forward. *Diplomacy, like politics and war, is about acting on people, through people, against other people.* (see **263, 481, 2247**)

The diplomat learns the trade by following the great negotiators and pitting himself against them.

2431 – Technological progress has altered, and often reduced, the role of embassies, but it has the advantage of allowing diplomats to focus once again on their primary and essential mission, which is to negotiate.

It is advisable for a diplomat to have been in office long enough to have acquired broad and solid experience. It is unwise for States to neglect specific training in all aspects of foreign negotiation. (see **449**)

2432 – The envoy is well advised, too, to cultivate a certain individual style of behaviour, since this is part of the diplomat's art. By contrast with the bad example set by Talleyrand, he must remain a man of probity, resistant to the many temptations placed in his way in the course of his functions.

2433 – In order to command attention, the envoy must be respected – in other words, feared. The reputation that precedes him, and the first impression he gives, are decisive in this regard. He may well inject a certain sense of the theatrical into his mission if it is important enough – as Nikita Kruschev did when he banged his shoe on the table at the UN General Assembly – but this should not be overdone: grandiose displays might seize the popular imagination and the government's, but they are no guarantee of success, and can exacerbate differences that arise. (see **450**)

2434 – The diplomat should not be concerned merely to make his own personal mark, especially with his adversaries and competitors, but also to stage-manage events so that they unfold in such a way as to offer good prospects for a solution. De Gaulle knew the value of a well-orchestrated scenario with many minor twists of plot, in which the suspense is maintained until the final dénouement. (see **492**)

2435 – Long-serving diplomats who have never reached the front line tend to exaggerate their own importance and set so much store by appearances that they start to make mistakes. Occasional negotiators, on the other hand, too often lack not only experience and knowledge, but also the necessary combination of sound judgement, patience and restraint.

2436 – It is a mistake to believe that difficulties can be overcome with elegant scepticism and superficial ease. Every negotiation involves some degree of political judgement. It also implies a great deal of work, starting with knowing the files. Nor must the most sensitive issues be glossed over, even those likely to provoke anxiety or irritation, if hopes are not to be disappointed, or disputes not to arise later. (see *441, 810, 1867*)

2437 – Political leaders view the end as more important than the means. It is for the diplomats to offer them a tactical approach that leaves aside considerations of passion and ideology by using tried and tested methods of gathering information and acting upon it. (see *575, 2501*)

2438 – Negotiators bring a unique approach and unique gifts to what they do. (see *442, 449, 481, 567*)

They derive satisfaction from bringing together different points of view, using all normal methods of communication. Using good sense and patience, they know that there must be give and take in any negotiation, and that the process must be approached and conducted in a spirit of good faith, with no place for cynicism or mediocrity. Their long-term vision allows them to rise above devious practices, selfish interests and short-term gain. (see *489, 536, 573*)

2439 – The range of possible ways of presenting a case extends from persuasion to intimidation. Hence it is good for the negotiator to put himself in the other party's place, to guess his tactics and understand what will be the consequences of his own. There is no reason why he should not give the appearance of indifference to the other side's argument, provides he follows all its turns and understands what it is aiming to achieve: in order to stay in control of the case he must take note, not necessarily in writing, of all the points that might affect the outcome. (see *688*)

2440 – Without risking reproach for a too elastic interpretation of his instructions, *the negotiator will carefully weigh up the effect his tactics will have, and how his words and gestures will be interpreted. He will refrain from offering an opinion unless strictly necessary, will go no further than is needed, and will never do anything to offend his adversary's self-esteem.* (see *576*)

2441 – The wise diplomat is never quick to answer to questions that have not been asked, or even those that have. Problems are always better avoided. Problems for the other side, however, are always worth creating, where there is something to be gained from embarrassing, disorienting or harassing an interlocutor. But the diplomat should never allow himself to be carried away by the heat of the debate, as Napoleon did, perhaps intentionally, with Pope Pius VII in 1802. (see *284, 544*)

2442 – A discussion must be approached prudently, with neither presumption nor indifference. Refraining from making assumptions or appearing proud or self-important does not mean a lack of self-confidence or of readiness for the combat. (see *442, 551, 2067*)

2443 – Reopening a clearly formulated proposal gives the impression that it was not properly thought through, or that its intention was to abuse the good faith of the interlocutor. It is unwise to make too many demands or approaches. The real skill may lie in giving the impression of being uninterested in the thing one really wants.

2444 – Armed with a full knowledge of the context of the case, the negotiator will not be taken in by the occasional discussions, digressions or overtures all of which are intended to cause him to miss a favourable opportunity. Nor will he be distracted by snubs, delays and unreasonable proposals designed to give the impression that he is responsible for the failure of the negotiation. (see *571*)

2445 – Unless he is in a position to make demands, a negotiator with nothing to offer cannot ask for anything in return: he will be faced with a straightforward and damaging refusal, or with conditions that he cannot accept.

The less pressure he can exert and the fewer bargaining counters he has available, the more the negotiator will have to use his persuasive talents to convince the other party.

2446 – It is here that remarkable skills can be deployed: the negotiator plants the seeds of problems in the opposing camp, acts in pursuit of several goals at once, lays the groundwork for a future policy, and presents his concessions in the most favourable light. He knows how to attract partners without binding himself, induce another party to suggest something he himself wants, exploit convergent interests and similar weaknesses, paralyse a potentially harmful alliance, force the reluctant to intervene and cast doubt on the good faith or credibility of a too skilful adversary. This is indeed an art.

2447 – It takes a mind constantly on the alert, that disregards nothing and finds a use for everything, to deploy these multiple, parallel tactics. One such man was Cavour, to whom modern Italy owes its unity: so swift and perspicacious was his judgement, and so finely tuned and timely his negotiation that he was able to exploit and discard assistance first from France and then from Britain.

2448 – Sensitive to nuances and alive to events, the good negotiator must be able to weigh up instinctively where the power lies and also the chances of success of a given manoeuvre, so as to be the first to seize any advantage. Subtly and effectively, he composes a picture out of all the strengths and weaknesses that make up his particular diplomatic environment – geographical constants, historic legacies and economic and financial imperatives – and makes the best use of them that the circumstances and the interlocutor will allow. (see *427*)

It was Britain's good fortune, in the nineteenth century, to be represented by remarkable ministers during the negotiations that were to change the shape of Europe: for fifty years Castlereagh and after him Palmerston, left their particular stamp on the outcome of all the great negotiations.

2449 – The negotiator must know and use all the devices of his art as well as having a good deal of savoir-faire. Some individuals are more inclined towards observation and others to negotiation, just as there are those who will never possess the tactician's instinct, either through awkwardness or hesitancy, obduracy or refusal to compromise. *The qualities of the diplomat are not always those of the soldier: a talent for dialogue is not the same as a talent for combat. But a combination of intuition and reason, an ability to seize opportunities, and acute judgement of people and situations, are among the attributes essential to success.* (see *256*)

2450 – It has to be acknowledged that old-style diplomacy left negotiators much more freedom to practise their art than they have now, with ease of travel and communications subjecting them to a degree of political and administrative supervision that is often limiting. The best of them, however, still manage to find a place for art in the practise of their profession. Even in relatively technical negotiations, there is a political dimension to be found.

§2. Collective efficiency

2451 – International negotiation is becoming a more and more complex exercise, in which a variety of particular factors come into play. In different fora and at different levels, it involves the interplay of meetings, information, argument and concessions, each of which must be identified, placed in its context and exploited to achieve the desired ends. It cannot function unless assumptions are continuously and methodically challenged, up to the time agreement is reached. (see *2547*)

2452 – This explains the current practice whereby the negotiator is attended by experts and colleagues that he should be able to choose himself where the stakes are high, depending on how many the nature of the negotiation, conference or organisation requires.

The good negotiator knows how to have the negotiating done by others, and sometimes prefers this approach.

2453 – In addition, unless it is a matter of pure routine, it is unwise to embark alone on a negotiation. Both principal and envoy must realise that this amounts to making what might be a long and difficult enterprise depend on the health and availability of one man. It also makes assumptions about that individual's capacities, however gifted he may be.

2454 – The negotiator must also provide for the possibility that he will be replaced, or leave, or that something will happen to interrupt his mission. He is responsible for keeping a record that will show, at any given time, the state of advancement of his mission.

2455 – Sometimes, on an exceptional basis and where the discussions concern issues of principle, those with full powers of representation, who might be Heads of State, hold talks in secret: they alone are privileged to be able to bind their countries or the authorities that sent them. (see *691, 1269, 2487*)

2456 – There is a natural temptation for each party to try to gain some superiority over the other by increasing the numbers of its representatives and experts. It can therefore be helpful for this question to be agreed in advance, based on the principle of reciprocity. Provided it is not excessive, a fully staffed delegation on each side enables them both to maintain discreet contact throughout the negotiation, and resolve the numerous organisational and procedural questions outside the formal debates. (see *1048*)

2457 – Among the most compelling reasons for the changes that have come about in diplomatic practice is the increasing role of commercial, military and technical considerations.[8] Especially within embassies, negotiations are handled by experts drawn from the various sectors of State administration.

2458 – Furthermore, there are numerous financial, economic or technical negotiations in which individuals represent and bind their governments, either on an occasional basis or over long periods, who do not belong to the diplomatic or official hierarchy: modern States can draw on a number of negotiators, capable of dealing with a wide variety of subjects. Sometimes these are foreign nationals. (see *1928*)

2459 – So diverse and specialised is the work of the major international conferences and institutions that governments are often obliged to entrust responsibility for their interests to large composite delegations specially constituted for the purpose. (see *1544*)

2460 – Even where it is made up of members from different parts of the administration, who take part in the work of subsidiary bodies, a national delegation representing a State at a designated conference must form a united whole, though there may be rivalries within it between individuals and groups with different ambitions or interests. (see *587*)

2461 – A delegation should be under the authority of a head of mission invested with overall responsibility for the project, since problems might arise, for example between political leaders and officials, diplomats and experts. *The head of delegation is not only responsible for directing and coordinating his team and ensuring it works efficiently: although tasks are shared among the delegates, he alone has the power to bind his government.* (see *691*)

2462 – The degree of harmony within any working unit made up of a team of negotiators depends on the effort invested by the leader or his deputy. *Like a play, a negotiation is a whole, in which several actors take part, and which is assembled, and reassembled, from the roles played by each of them.*

2463 – These choices will require all the more competence and resolve where there is a wide range of factors to be taken into account, which is the case today with most major negotiations, either because the subject matter is of interest to several government departments or because the forum of discussion is enlarged.

---

8 H. NICOLSON: *Diplomacy*, Oxford, Oxford University Press, 1945, VII.

2464 – Relations between diplomats and experts are not always easy: their criteria for decision are not the same, nor is their approach to the negotiation itself. Having the support of technical experts can provide helpful details for concluding and implementing an agreement, but it can also have the opposite effect of interfering with the political will to agree. *Competence is not synonymous with skill.*

2465 – The head of delegation must bring his team together, not only to gather information from them and give them instructions, but also to solicit their open views, to help him choose the best tactic and apply it in a coherent and disciplined manner. The efficiency of the team can be measured by the gathering and flow of information necessary for the negotiation to succeed.

2466 – It serves the interests of the head of delegation to use his collaborators to obtain information on his adversary's tactics and intentions, or to alter the pace or the level of the discussions if tension is mounting or the talks threaten to become stalled.

There are some roles that should not be performed by a plenipotentiary. There are often more modest ways of transmitting a message, provided it reaches the person intended. *An ambassador must be alive to every approach, to each new item of information, and to every sign, even indirect.* (see *297*)

2467 – The Member States of an institution, and they alone, are entitled to send a permanent delegation. They include whomever they choose, subject to the organisational rules of the conference. (see *1269*)

These representations tend to differ from traditional diplomatic missions in their composition, functions and working methods: on the one hand, they keep their capitals regularly informed, negotiating on their behalf and following their instructions, but on the other they are bound by particular duties and rules by virtue of their involvement in the life of the organisation. Their indispensable freedom of manoeuvre depends on the credibility of their head with his government; he can, among other things, obtain consent for arrangements made necessary by the practices of the international administration, at every level where this is needed. (see *1189*)

2468 – In practice these representations are often part of a process of institutionalisation: it is often through their meetings that intergovernmental organisations are run, with advisers meeting at different levels and different intervals to agree on the fundamental direction of the work of the international administration. (see *1035*, *1267*)

2469 – Contrary to popular belief, directing a negotiation is becoming increasingly complex, requiring a broad knowledge of facts and law, and the coordination of effort from many sources.

Studies carried out mainly in the United States have tried to define what effect the size of a group has on its cohesiveness, its internal relations and its effectiveness in negotiations.[9]

---

9 K. E. KNORR and J. ROSENAU: *Contending Approaches to International Politics*, New Jersey, Princeton University Press, 1969.

2470 – The degree of integration of groups of negotiators varies according to the circumstances. The higher the rank and the decision-making power of the delegates, the more reluctant they are to fall into line; the more numerous they are, the less disciplined. This means that a constant process of adjustment is necessary within national delegations, particularly when they include representatives of the major administrative entities with an interest in the outcome of the negotiations: *the head of delegation often needs to work hard to ensure the entire team is following the same line, and must concentrate his energies on the task in hand.*

2471 – The pressure of events and of the international climate weighs upon teams set up to address issues that are often highly technical, required to conclude their work in a fixed timeframe. The negotiation takes shape at lower levels, where contacts and friendships are formed between delegations. (see *1349*)

2472 – As to personal qualities, there is no guarantee now, any more than there ever was, that the delegates will always possess those needed for a harmonious negotiation. This might become a matter for concern, to the extent that debates in international organisations offer tactical freedom, and also an outside audience, that were unknown in traditional bilateral negotiations.

2473 – In an organised system, or one in the course of integration, negotiators are no longer expected to have the skill to overcome problems or even deceive their opponents. On the contrary, they are now expected to propose lasting collective solutions. *Between specialists, there sometimes exists a level of communication, understanding and even connivance that facilitates their common work more than the divisions between the camps impede it.* The difficult nature of the subject matter and the pressure of outside factors forces the parties to reach agreement in order to provide practical answers to common issues. (see *1628, 1633*)

2474 – At the same time, though, negotiators must be alive to the diversity within their own camp: they must be mindful, throughout their mission, of the interests and ambitions of dominant personalities, administrative bodies, pressure groups, and political or cultural movements. In tariff negotiations, the representatives of the United States have to account for their activities to numerous domestic committees defending private interests, including hundreds of specialists.[10]

2475 –These internal complexities are perfectly visible from one camp to the other, and can open the way to some productive manoeuvres. The most skilful negotiator is the one who successfully conceals the contradictions and hesitations on his own side while at the same time weighing up and exploiting any potential divisions among his adversaries. Within any one delegation, divergences can be found between technical and financial experts, diplomats and military specialists: the skill lies in emphasising the interventions of those interlocutors who are likely to prove the most favourable, and giving them greater weight in the debate.

---

10 G. R. WINHAM: 'Negotiation as a Management Process', *World Politics*, 30, October 1977, p. 87.

2476 – In an institutional or procedural setting, the initiative and talent of the diplomat do not always have free rein in a negotiation: wit and charm count for little where there are difficult problems of a financial, technical or military nature to be addressed. However, a practitioner well versed in confidential moves, skilled in tactics and prudent by nature, will still look very closely at the complex indirect and incidental consequences of the commitments proposed. When it comes to negotiation, the private sector, too, demands high intellectual and scientific standards. (see *1499*)

2477 – The difficulty and variety of the subjects dealt with have meant that negotiation within organisations has become depersonalised, with only rare individuals having the professional capacity to grasp the whole issue in all its detail. At every stage of the negotiation, it may be necessary to refer back to the central administration. Once concluded, the agreement is verified all the more painstakingly because it is not merely a question of drafting a settlement, but laying down rules that must not only be applicable but applied: here, technical experts come into conflict with politicians, both on the ground and in their country. (see *1598*)

2478 – More and more people are negotiating internationally, at every level and in every field, from distinguished statesmen to highly specialised experts, and also businessmen. Those whose primary mission is diplomacy have never had a monopoly over it, but it is slipping out of their control. It has become almost impossible to be familiar with all the various correspondence, talks and interventions taking place, or to know all the commitments made and promises given.

2479 – However, if wasted or conflicting efforts are to be avoided, each camp must have one single authority that is central to the entire negotiation, whose role it is to ensure that there is a balance between counterpart and concession, not only vis à vis the opponent or between allies, but within his own camp. He must not lose sight either of the goal, or of the tactics to follow to be in the best position at the critical moment.

2480 – Another factor that swells the delegations is the need to include their own interpreters: these persons will be privy to thoughts, intentions and tactics, and therefore their choice cannot be left to others.

2481 – It is easy to see why international negotiation is becoming increasingly costly for States. However, governments are ill advised to weaken the capacities of their envoys to work and to have influence, by cutting back on the means they need, be it staff, funding, vehicles or encrypted codes. Obviously, though, spending is proportionate to what is at stake.

2482 – In all modern States, these developments have not made things any easier for the department in charge of foreign affairs. Faced with the difficulty of following all its external negotiations, the central bureaucracy pays more attention to the ones it can control. Directing foreign policy is all the more complicated by the fact that, at national as well as international level, coordination is a difficult and thankless task, requiring endless attempts.

2483 – However one may judge this ever more marked trend, there is no denying it, as it is symptomatic of the increasing interdependence between States. *Governments should therefore take steps to find and train representatives who not only have the particular knowledge needed for each negotiation, but also the qualities and experience required for traditional diplomacy. The same will be true in the private sector.*

2484 – It is abundantly clear, given these considerations, that the various internal administrations will have to look to practices in the private sector and open themselves up to the methods and pressures of foreign negotiation. This is particularly evident within the European Union, where extensive and continuous negotiation takes place. But it is equally true for all countries wishing to assert their individuality and protect their interests in an ever more confined and difficult world. (see *2397*)

Section 2: Summit negotiation

2485 – Foreign negotiation serves to strengthen the prerogatives of the authority responsible for its conduct. When carried on at the highest level, it becomes the expression of the strategies that confront each other. History shows how difficult the great conferences often were, and in particular, how much more important personal factors were than institutional ones.[11] (see *2506, 2529*)

2486 – Leaders motivated by strategy generally find it hard to resist the temptation to resolve for themselves the issues closest to their hearts, and agree to meet and talk, even when their countries are not bound by any alliance.[12] Encounters between political leaders are as old as diplomacy itself, but ease of travel has made them more frequent and wide-ranging, to the point that they now occur on a regular basis, in the form of series of meetings, successive visits, formal gatherings or international conferences. (see *694, 1001*)

Frequent contact makes for political complicity, and can increase the credibility of a leader in terms of domestic public opinion.

2487 – Machiavelli wrote that a prince who does not wish to live in a continuous state of alert must march in person at the head of all his expeditions. (see *2400*)

The leader embarking on a diplomatic manoeuvre needs to travel in order to form a personal judgement about the chances of success and the best routes to follow. Bismarck formed his personal views of Napoleon III through contacts with him, and they provided the basis for his policy towards France. And, in 1938, Neville Chamberlain believed he was working towards peace when he met with Hitler, but he was deceived.

2488 – The fact that, today, Heads of State or government are subject to a greater burden of risk that compels them to hold discussions, where possible without

---

11 K. EUBANK: *The Summit Conferences, 1919–1960*, Oklahoma, Oklahoma University Press, 1966. D. ACHESON: *Meetings at the Summit: a Study in Diplomatic Method*, Durham, New Hampshire, 1958.
12 H. A. KISSINGER: *The White House Years*, Boston, Little, Brown & Co., 1979, I.

intermediaries, especially in times of crisis. The serious nature of the decisions needed to pursue and resolve the two world wars of 1914 and 1939 required many meetings between those in the highest political office in the main nations involved, or their personal envoys. (see *2539*)

Since then, summit meetings have become common practice,[13] whether as an expression of the personalisation of power, or as the instrument of multilateral strategy. They can also be a manifestation of solidarity in a particular field, such as the summits of French and Spanish-speaking countries; summits of the Americas have also been held regularly since 1994. (see *1001, 1519*)

These different strands can be seen at work in Europe, where the European Council takes major political decisions, including the decision to have the European Parliament elected by universal suffrage, and also to proceed with the Union. (see *1324*)

To the extent that these summits take place during major conferences, they can be taken, sometimes wrongly, as evidence of the 'new diplomacy'. (see *1001, 1519, 1850*)

2489 – Since 1973, the Heads of State and government of the major industrialised nations have found it necessary to meet periodically, initially on financial and monetary issues and later on political matters as well. The original four (the United States, France, Germany and the United Kingdom) were later joined by Canada, Italy and Japan, and Russia followed in 1994 though only for political issues: the G7 thus became the G8, and, with China, the G9. These meetings, planned in advance and chaired by the host country, have given a real impetus to negotiations on a wide variety of subjects, such as human rights, AIDS, the environment, drugs, employment and international debt.

As such, they have stirred public opinion, and recent summits have been attended by sometimes violent demonstrations. These summits have gradually been expanded to include ministers and experts. It suits the interests of the protagonists to have a certain amount of media attention, but this in turn has an effect on their discussions. (see *1892, 1910*)

2490 – Official visits between Heads of State and political leaders are not merely matters of protocol: they are the only real way of knowing a partner and often prove to be the decisive phase in some negotiations. Even when negotiated in advance, they can still turn out differently from what was originally contemplated, depending on those taking part and on the circumstances, sometimes with dozens or even hundreds of officials in attendance and millions of viewers watching on television.

2491 – These meetings involve lavish precautions and also publicity, since one of their objects is to make it easier for the outcome of the negotiations to be accepted in national political circles and by public opinion. These are not always enough to ensure that the participants themselves understand or agree among themselves,

13 E. PLISCHKE: *International Conferencing and the Summit: Macro-Analysis of Presidential Participation*, Orbis, 1970, p. 673.

bound as they are by precautions and appearances, and obliged to engage in ceremonial before an increasingly indifferent or sceptical public. History relates the serious political consequences that flowed from the personal antagonism between Metternich and Palmerston.

Summit negotiations require a higher level of precautions than any other. (see *2665*)

2492 – Whether they are bipartite or multipartite, these political meetings are often designed to avoid institutional procedures and administrative routine. The negotiator at a summit is the author of his own mandate. Thus, the most important political issues are discussed outside the confines of the traditional diplomatic process, and influenced by new factors, often imponderable or unforeseeable, like the quality of the contact between the leaders of different countries. The same could be said of meetings between businessmen. (see *2056, 2346*)

Summit negotiations depend on the direct responsibility of the protagonists. But they cannot be allowed to depend on their illusions or excesses. (see *2414, 2431*)

2493 – More than any other, a summit negotiation draws on the fundamental principles of diplomatic strategy: the resolution of major crises depends on this, as there is no-one more likely to understand a strategist's thinking than his counterpart. During the Cuban Missile Crisis, Nikita Kruschev was quick to realise that John F. Kennedy had decided to play the card of nuclear deterrence and reacted accordingly, with no meeting being necessary: much of that negotiation was implicit. (see *2157, 2161, 2538*)

Dialogue of this kind can be useful in informing the parties and mediating between them, and can also sometimes offer a last chance to appeal to reason.

2494 – The advantages of such encounters, like those between Chancellor Adenauer and General de Gaulle, who in the course of fifteen meetings resolved the differences between France and Germany and turned them into an alliance, or between Presidents Kennedy and Kruschev, who set their countries on the path to *détente*, should not mask the risks they involved: with a summit, whether the outcome is good or bad, there is often no recourse, but there is usually publicity.

2495 – When matters are dealt with at a very high level, with no recourse, by leaders who may not necessarily be accustomed to handling such issues, and whose personalities may be too strong to be compatible, they should understand that, when a country's highest interests are at stake, negotiation must be based on caution, calculation and reciprocity: inexperience leads some politicians to look for quick success, fall victim to vanity or put their own personal advantage above that of the nation.

Negotiations at the informal summits of the seven or eight industrialised nations range over a wide variety of topics, but have not so far produced a coherent diplomatic strategy with which to face the challenges of the new millennium. (see *131, 1950, 2489*)

2496 – Summit negotiation is bound up with the personalisation of power, and thus works in favour of stable regimes and seasoned politicians. But the burden of responsibility it places on Heads of State and government is becoming more and more onerous. (see *2537*)

Some of the inconvenience can be avoided by the judicious use of advanced telecommunications technology such as videoconferencing.

2497 – Many commentators have expressed reservations about the sort of itinerant diplomacy summit negotiations involve. It is self evident that these conferences can only succeed if careful thought is given to them in advance and they form part of a longer-term diplomatic plan. Historians have expressed surprise at the lack of coordinated preparation by the Allies for the Yalta conference, despite the seriousness and difficulty of the issues.

It can sometimes happen that the outcome of a meeting is determined before it even takes place, if there is a common will to reach agreement or thanks to the efforts at conciliation of a particular statesman. Often, though, as one French commentator put it, the conference runs its course like the final days of a patient on life support.[14]

2498 – Established procedure comes into its own at this point. It is the ambassadors who are called upon to identify the issues on which agreement will or will not be possible, and to propose ways of reaching these goals. They, too, are responsible for setting the expectations of their interlocutors and preparing public opinion, sometimes by indirect means. And it is the ambassadors who are asked to give an accurate reading of the attitudes and proposals of the other party, or a correct interpretation of previous acts or agreements: in the absence of witnesses, a *tête à tête* is subject to different, if not opposite, explanations.

Preparations for these meetings often become progressively more difficult and formal, even when they take place at predetermined intervals.

2499 – *Ill-timed and badly prepared conferences can lead to results that are the opposite of what was intended: the discussions become stalled or broken off altogether.* They can aggravate the general political situation rather than clarifying it. The irretrievable breakdown in relations between Napoleon and Tsar Alexander can be traced to the failure of their meeting in Erfurt in 1808, despite the fact that their meeting one year earlier, in Tilsit, had proved fruitful.

On the other hand, the tendency of some governments to try to institutionalise such meetings may underestimate the political merits of informality. (see *1539*)

2500 – It is only natural for a negotiation to be deeply influenced by the temperament of the politicians directing or sometimes conducting it, but this is not necessarily an advantage. Woodrow Wilson's reservations in negotiating the peace in 1919 were due to his sense of moral superiority, his conviction that he was in the right, his contempt for the political scheming commonly practised in Europe and his failure to grasp the facts of the situation.

As for Stalin, the circumstances in which he was able to come to power, and stay there, had a profound effect on both his attitude and the diplomatic methods

---

14 J. de BOURBON-BUSSET: *La Grande Conférence*, Paris, Gallimard, 1963, p. 124.

he used. A suspicious and patient mind, coupled with a cynical realism and a way of seeking tangible gains under the cloak of ideological orthodoxy, made him a devious, merciless and overbearing negotiator.

2501 – For the politician used to time pressures, negotiation is too slow and formal. He forgets, though, that discretion and process can help reduce the risks, avoid humiliations, upset exaggerated claims, make concessions look less like defeats and prevent positions and arguments being superficially exploited and publicly criticised.[15] (see *763*)

The path leading to a successful summit is winding, even where the meeting itself is brief and informal.

2502 – Negotiation often embarrasses leaders, who find it hard to accept that it involves them in making concessions and commitments, or brings these to light. Compromise appears futile and dangerous to a leader who considers himself the more powerful, and who would therefore prefer to act on his own decisions and surprise his adversary. (see *23, 93*).

Summit discussions therefore tend to involve the giving of personal guarantees along with formal commitments, which can undermine the solidarity between the different countries' bureaucracies and technical experts. (see *1356, 1494*)

2503 – It is always a matter of regret when statesmen ignore or disregard the opportunities negotiation offers them. Victorious at Marignan, François I of France proved so disconcerting a prospect to the German princes that they rejected his claims to the Empire in favour of Charles V: François could have avoided handing power to his rival if, instead of pressing his cause, he had negotiated a compromise, perhaps by conferring his patronage on a third candidate who inspired no fear.

2504 – These reservations are not general: many statesmen prove to be excellent diplomats at their own high level, sometimes keener and more skilful than the specialists. That said, they must still keep in mind the very principle of negotiation, which is the exchange of concessions and advantages on a mutual basis. In this regard, any fixed position, whether ideological or personal, will expose them to the risk of making serious errors of judgement. *Arbitrarily oversimplifying the facts of a particular negotiation can cause it to fail just as much as an excess of ambition.* (see *767*)

The highest stakes in this kind of dialogue are largely in the future: most of the time, they are difficult to predict, measure or verify.

2505 – Meetings between strategists do not necessarily make for harmony between strategies. (see *2338*)

The first condition for peace is compatibility between the countries at the level of their political goals. But these goals might be chosen by statesmen whose ambition leads them to seek confrontation, and who disapprove of wars only when offended or damaged by them. (see *75*)

---

15 H. A. KISSINGER: *The White House Years*, Boston, Little, Brown & Co., 1979, I.

2506 – The choice of national leaders is therefore important for negotiation. There is a risk that the political selection process will bring to power only the most ruthless, duplicitous and cynical, to whom the sincerity, generosity and human warmth necessary for cooperation and agreement do not come easily. If negotiations are entrusted to those who are less than wise or lucid, it is hardly to be expected that the results will be satisfactory and lasting.

At all events, human diversity being what it is, summit negotiations are more suitable as a vehicle for resolving crises than for addressing the major issues facing civilisation.

Chapter III:
Negotiation and State Power

2507 – It is in the nature of the political leader to be more sensitive and better attuned than others to the rhythms of national life and the preoccupations of the people. But he is also motivated by a fierce sense of competition and a desire for power. *Once he has imposed himself and his choices within his own group, the strategist naturally seeks to do the same outside it.*

2508 – Except for certain extraordinary occasions, diplomatic negotiation has always been a privilege reserved to the 'prince', the sovereign who is entitled to executive power. One of the consequences of the development of international relations has been the confirmation of this role as part of the apparatus of the modern State. (see *685, 806, 2486*)

In practice, governments alone have the means to draw up and implement national foreign policy. The techniques of negotiation, and also its strategy, give them a favoured position compared with the other organs of State. (see *1266*)

2509 – However, diplomacy also raises the question of national commitment: leaving aside ethical considerations, the extent of the powers of leaders to take initiatives and decisions must be defined. History abounds with examples of alliances and confrontations that the people did not want.

2510 – In this field as in others, no government, however authoritarian, should underestimate the power of public opinion to support or undermine it. On the other hand, no government, however democratic, should be unaware of the limits of public support for foreign policy or the conditions attached to it.

2511 – When examining the qualities of a democracy, however, the French writer Alexis de Tocqueville found that they had virtually no place in foreign policy. Because of the way this type of government managed its foreign interests, he regarded it as inferior in principle to others. Coordination of a major enterprise is difficult in a democracy, as is deciding on a plan and following it in spite of obstacles.[1] (see *264*)

Anatole France took the view that the lack of secrecy and follow-up made it impossible for a democratic republic to engage in international affairs.

2512 – In practice, experience has shown that popular diplomacy spills over quickly into excess, as it is no longer restrained by reason in moments of crisis when the dangers are greatest; too often, it ends in confrontation. This is the lesson of the great revolutions, when ideological generosity causes political frontiers to be

---

1 A. de TOCQUEVILLE: *De la démocratie en Amérique*, Paris, Lafond, 1835, II, p. 8.

ignored in favour of the spread of new ideas and sometimes of military expansion. (see *2362*)

2513 – States in which power is firm, concentrated and secret have an advantage over those where diplomacy is influenced by political and cultural diversity, or even ideas from outside. (see *2360*)

Where authority is divided, changeable or weakened, it is difficult to protect international negotiation from partisan or deeply felt influences, pressure from interested parties or even violence. (see *1898*)

2514 – The people's natural concerns and attitudes do not make it easy to conduct long-term diplomatic enterprises. Popular opinion is never ready for them, lacking a complete picture of the interests that have to be considered; it reacts too late and dislikes being asked to make sacrifices. *It is easier to judge the past than to decide on the future.*

Depending on the stability of the regime or group in power, time does not run at the same speed in politics.

2515 – The question arises today whether nations are ready to understand all the implications of the radical changes taking place in worldwide political and economic relationships, and whether even their elites appreciate the need for international negotiation that is at the same time open to new influences and aware of the climate of heightened competition.

Inability to handle international competition is as fatal for any political regime as it is for any major private sector enterprise. (see *2213*)

Section 1: The mission of government

2516 – The identification of the nation with the State is still powerful today, especially vis à vis the outside world: the gravity of military, ideological and economic threats is a factor. *Notwithstanding this, the margin of freedom and responsibility of national authorities is shrinking all the time.* This is especially evident in Western Europe.

2517 – International negotiation has such sweeping consequences for a State's domestic powers that they can affect the balance and effectiveness of constitutional power. The problem is thus no longer technical but becomes political. (see *1619*)

2518 – The extension of the methods of foreign negotiation substitutes anonymous collective procedures for governmental authority and responsibility. A State's authority can be seriously undermined in the eyes of public opinion by interminable international discussions that give rise to uncertainty, impatience or concern. (see *1647*)

2519 – National administrations will find themselves forced to negotiate with international agencies whose interventions are ever more frequent and whose means are expanding, while governments will seek to protect from internationalisation those parts of their structure necessary for their independence in decision making and negotiating. (see *1199, 1619*)

2520 – The multiplicity of rules emanating from international negotiations or conferences will be a source of frustration to legislators, who might take the view that they are not automatically bound by legal or financial commitments made in an irregular or summary fashion, subject to reservations or hidden in budgetary or technical documents. (see *1617*)

2521 – Within its own territory, a State traditionally exercises its sovereign prerogatives to the exclusion of all foreign entities. Its internal system often prescribes in detail the conditions for the drawing up and implementation of political, economic and legal decisions, in terms of the hierarchy, conformity, formal presentation and binding effect of laws, regulations and various other legal instruments. These principles, essential to the rule of law, can be thrown into question by international negotiation.

2522 – In many countries, treaties that are duly signed, ratified and published take precedence over domestic law. Not only must the courts and administrative authorities know and apply them, despite their daunting proliferation, but individuals can often invoke their provisions, sometimes against the national authorities. European law, which grows ever stronger and has profound effects on the fabric of national legislation, is provoking increasing confusion between national and Community rules. (see *1632, 2232*)

The negotiator must be alive to the effects of his actions on the stability of organised legal systems that are indispensable to communal life, the protection of freedoms and the smooth functioning of government. (see *2234*)

§1. Government prerogative

2523 – The personal nature of their power in former times led sovereigns to handle their negotiations in person: in 843, the three sons of Louis the Pious of France divided up the empire of Charlemagne among themselves. Negotiations of this kind went on during the whole of the feudal era until the Renaissance, sometimes accompanied by lavish ceremonial and the exchange of gifts: one need only recall the Field of the Cloth of Gold, where François I of France met Henry VIII of England in 1520. These encounters were characterised by distrust and hedged about with precautions: examples are cited of meetings that took place on islands, in the middle of bridges or some other place where protecting oneself was easy.[2]

2524 – Starting in the seventeenth century onwards, politics became a more complicated affair. Sovereigns no longer negotiated in person, but still acted as their own Foreign Ministers, or even their own ambassadors, especially within their own family circle. The English Queen Victoria continued to bring great moral authority to this role in the nineteenth century. They often drafted or verified their own correspondence, chose and instructed their envoys, decided upon negotiations and organised them.

---

2 H. NICOLSON: *The Evolution of Diplomatic Methods*, London, MacMillan, 1954.

2525 – During the first years of the French Revolution, the Assembly condemned the allegedly secretive and cynical methods employed by sovereigns and sought to remove the conduct of the nation's foreign affairs from the King's control. As early as 1790, however, Mirabeau risked his own popularity by defending the special suitability of the executive to deal with foreign States. He was already questioning the capacity of national representatives to control negotiations carried on in the name of the sovereign people, the only valid commitment vis à vis other nations. (see *2598*)

2526 – With the disappearance of absolute power, the calculated and secretive diplomacy of the French court gave way to that of the people – spontaneous, changeable and powerful, until order was restored: even before the advent of Napoleon, negotiation had reverted to being an activity conducted with prudence and discretion.

2527 – Using, once he became Emperor, the same methods that had served him well in negotiations at Leoben and Campo Formio, Napoleon was the first nineteenth century Head of State to always negotiate in person, whether with sovereigns, like the Pope and Tsar Alexander I, or with ministers such as Metternich. From that time onwards, Europe's political leaders have held frequent meetings, either in congress, when the solidarity between them has to be organised and put to use, as with the Holy Alliance set up at the Tsar's suggestion, or in a closed circle, to deal with a chosen partner, as Napoleon III was later to do, and afterwards Bismarck.

2528 – The institution of parliamentary regimes took away the sovereigns' real authority in this field and gave it to elected representatives, who were subject to censure by the people. If a monarch occasionally sought to deviate from this new regime, it was only ever in exceptional circumstances of short duration: one diplomatic initiative taken by Leopold III, King of the Belgians, without his government and outside all official channels, almost resulted in the entry of British and French troops into Belgium in January 1940.[3]

2529 – In constitutions as well as contemporary political practice, it is the dominant power in the executive that sets the policy for all foreign negotiation. Depending on the political system, this might be the Head of State or government in person, or the collective leadership of a single political party. The principle whereby treaties are negotiated and ratified by the Head of State bears different meanings depending on the particular constitutions.

2530 – In countries where the Head of State has no political responsibility, the decision falls on the government and its head: in Britain, it is the Prime Minister who heads both the executive and the majority party in Parliament. By contrast, in the United States, the prerogative of the President is fundamental in foreign negotiation, subject to the roles attributed to the Senate and the administration.[4]

---

3 P. H. SPAAK: *Combats inachevés*, Paris, Fayard, 1969, I, p. 68.
4 E. PLISCHKE: *Conduct of American Diplomacy*, New York, Van Nostrand, 1967.
  R. E. NEUSTADT: *Presidential Power*, New York, Wiley, 1960.

When the USSR was still in existence, major diplomatic decisions were made by the Politburo or the party's Central Committee, with the help of its secretariat. This was the case with the talks held between Presidents Nixon and Brezshnev in March 1974. (see *2485*)

2531 – The current system in France is a hybrid, as can be seen from the 1958 Constitution. The President of the Republic is responsible for directing, and sometimes conducting, major foreign negotiations; others are carried on under his direct authority. Thus it was General de Gaulle himself who set his country's new approach to the Atlantic alliance and Great Powers such as Germany, the United States and the USSR, and who directed the resulting negotiations.

France is represented in the European Council by its President, as well as at bilateral or multilateral summits. During periods of political disagreement, the Prime Minister insists on accompanying or preceding him. This latter is responsible for securing the binding commitment of his government, but rarely does so on questions of foreign policy. Parliament was informed in 1991 and 2001 of the situations in the Gulf and Afghanistan, respectively, but not of the Kosovo crisis in 1999. On the other hand, under the Constitution, which is restrictively interpreted, Parliamentary authorisation is required for a declaration of war.[5] (see *2489*)

2532 – Most of the time, foreign negotiation escapes prior public scrutiny. The workings of the competent parts of the administration are protected by secrecy; whether this is the Foreign Ministry or a central advisory organ, public opinion has no control over them. Even in the United States, the Supreme Court has recognised that the President has the right not to communicate diplomatic information to Congress, although under the Freedom of Information Act, the executive is obliged to prove that secrecy is necessary. (see *2600*)

2533 – Strategy in foreign affairs requires ever more careful, complete and confidential preparation. This explains the important role of the advisory committees operating at the highest levels within a State: for example, the President of the United States has the National Security Council, and the French President has the *Conseil de Défense*. These bodies are highly restricted, but multidisciplinary; they play a crucial role in deciding on military and diplomatic strategy.[6] (see *2098*)

The execution of any major strategy requires coordination, involving the development of operational systems and installations.

2534 – Nuclear policy is decided at the highest levels, requiring in particular a reconciliation of the views of the heads of the armed and diplomatic services, and the line to be pursued in other major negotiations flows from that. These are also conducted at a very high level: this explains both the slow-moving procedure, especially in countries with a planned economy, and the fact that progress is suspended in Western democracies each time there is an election.

---

5 G. ZOLLER: *Droit des relations internationales*, Paris, PUF, 1992, p. 169 and 256.
6 H. A. KISSINGER: *The National Security Council*, Washington, US Government, 1970.

2535 – The tendency for power to be concentrated also applies to negotiation. *In many countries, the effect of centralisation and personalisation of the regime is that many negotiations are conducted at the level of the Head of State or the head of the dominant party;* in some of them, presidential approval is needed for the most trivial foreign negotiation. In the 1970s, the Soviet leader would receive a visit from each of his allies once a year, and set his diplomatic strategy accordingly.

2536 – Nuclear weapons have reinforced the dominance of the leaders of the great nations. Not only does possession of nuclear weapons change the nature of the presidential function, but the whole of a country's foreign policy will revolve around it where the nation's future is at stake. *The conditions for the use of nuclear weapons, and the attendant risks, are such that only the holder of the highest political office can assume such responsibility with the necessary speed and authority.* (see *1711, 1721, 2534*)

2537 – The head of the executive thus becomes the final arbiter, responsible in the last resort for decisive external negotiations, on which he leaves the imprint of his personality and for which he must be personally held to account. (see *2496, 2607*)

2538 – This strategic prerogative comes to the fore in times of crisis, when psychological factors assume great importance because each protagonist is attempting to influence the other's will by messages, signals and questioning that involve a mixture of threat, offer, deterrence and promise, seeking out its weak points, testing its resolve and preparing the ground for victory. (see *253, 1775, 2157, 2493*)

2539 – The involvement of the supreme powers is also justified by the growing confusion between the domestic and international aspects of all the issues discussed at a summit: it is for the leaders to simplify, decide and command. Individual temperament comes into play here: some are interested only in the overall direction, some concern themselves with carrying on the negotiations and others will centralise or delegate depending on the subject matter.

2540 – The Soviet system provided an example of collegially determined diplomacy. In practice, it was the central committee of the Communist Party, two sections of which (the international section and the section dealing with relations with allied parties) had particular competence in this field, that set the line to be followed in negotiations, depending on the political or military elements within it. This structure has disappeared, and Russia has reverted to a more traditional regime.

2541 – These findings confirm the usefulness of a serious and objective study of the factors at play in negotiation, in order to appreciate the complex nature of the work done within governments or by diplomats and the effect the power structure has on the conduct of foreign policy.[7] The same principles apply in the private sector.

---

7 H. A. KISSINGER: 'The End of Bipolarity', in *The Theory and Practice of International Relations*, Englewood Cliffs, Prentice Hall, 1966, p. 50. J. N. ROSENAU: *The Scientific Study of Foreign Policy*, New York, Free Press, 1969.

2542 – Within each State, provided there are enough issues to be discussed, the work of analysing and monitoring them is shared between various institutions, some official and others private. Each of these entities sees itself as having its own mission, seeks to impose its own goals and expects the negotiation to address its concerns.[8]

Leaders often have less freedom to negotiate at the international level than it seems.[9] (see *784*)

§2. Bureaucratic structures

2543 – Prior to the negotiation, and later during the actual procedure if necessary, the State machinery will make internal choices and compromises, which depend on factors not all of which relate to foreign policy, and some of which will be a matter of personal prestige, social class, electoral necessity and professional or financial interest.

The same choices and compromises are made, and the same factors encountered, in the private sector.

2544 – In highly integrated systems such as single-party regimes, difficulties often arise at the governmental and administrative level due to strategic choices made, of necessity, prior to the negotiation. Rather than expressing themselves publicly, cultural trends and pressure groups operate at the very seat of power: sometimes it is only when an adjustment to the diplomatic line is announced that the outside world learns of changes within the group in power.

2545 – In sum, every important international negotiation is preceded and accompanied by an internal negotiation, sometimes demanding an equal amount of time and effort, or even involving the resolution of real conflicts of which the adversary might be aware.[10] This was the case during the negotiations between the United States and the Soviet Union on strategic arms limitation.[11] (see *2132*)

2546 – The difficulty of making internal decisions sometimes produces rigid bureaucratic positions that are unhelpful to international negotiation, which demands adaptability and flexibility. *A carefully refined strategy can leave the negotiators with a mandate that is so detailed as to be restrictive, which in turn increases the risk that the talks will slow down or break down.* (see *2354*)

No bureaucracies share the same ideas about the methods and goals of foreign negotiation, which fact in itself complicates international relations.

2547 – Major negotiations are reserved to the higher political echelons: behind every statesman there is a whole operational network. The increased burden on the

---

8 R. C. SNYDER and J. A. ROBINSON: *National and International Decision Making*, New York, Free Press, 1966.

9 G. ALLISON: *Essence of Decision: Explaining the Cuban Missile Crisis*, Boston, Little, Brown & Co.,1971.

10 H. A. KISSINGER: *The White House Years*, Boston, Little, Brown & Co., 1979, I.

11 J. NEWHOUSE: *Cold Dawn, the Story of SALT*, New York, Holt, Rinehart and Winston, 1973.

offices of Heads of State and party chiefs has led them to expand to the point of becoming veritable superstructures, especially in the fields of diplomacy and defence, their privileged domains.

2548 – These institutions allow the government, or even the Head of State, to make its own choices between different, and sometimes opposing, doctrines, interests and sentiments: the solutions adopted will thus form part of a coherent policy line, binding on the administration and its representatives.[12]

2549 – There are other factors that explain the bureaucratisation of diplomatic negotiation. Facility and speed of communications make it possible for civil servants to prepare for negotiations and track their progress, adapting the instructions to the delegates and ensuring they are followed. On the other hand, the technical nature of the work requires the assistance of experts, often chosen from the seat of the administration or the headquarters of private sector companies: such specialists operate only with the approval and cooperation of their own hierarchies. (see *2450*)

2550 – It is no exaggeration to state that, in the administrations of the future, all or almost all public services will have to maintain direct relations with their external counterparts, both at national and international levels. This will considerably complicate the overall design of the State apparatus, with each authority seeking to retain responsibility for the outcome of negotiations. At European level,[13] the ministries of the member countries almost all have a direct interest in Community negotiations. (see *1558)*

2551 – This development will be reinforced by the practices of the international institutions themselves. Their rules provide for, and sometimes require, the direct cooperation of the national authorities and organs in the field, usually for reasons of efficiency. The composite delegations attached to these organisations are more administrative than diplomatic in nature. (see *1349)*

2552 – The incremental growth in international activity adds to the burden on those departments whose role is to prepare, steer and monitor foreign negotiations in line with government policy. Only those departments responsible for foreign policy are capable of explaining the negotiating environment and coordinating the work accordingly. They imprint on it their well-established national and cultural traditions.

In new States, such departments are often set up even before the government has decided its foreign policy.

2553 – Some countries have laws and regulations that enshrine, and govern, the competence of the Foreign Ministry to conduct external relations and negotiations: in France, for example, the earliest of these date back to Napoleon, in 1810. The main exception concerns the ILO, which requires a direct relationship with the competent ministry for labour.

---

12 H. A. KISSINGER and B. BRODIE: *Bureaucracy, Politics and Strategy*, Los Angeles, University of California, 1968.
13 F. E. ROURKE: *Bureaucracy and Foreign Policy*, Baltimore, Johns Hopkins University Press, 1972.

2554 – The extraordinary proliferation of multilateral negotiations is gradually causing activities to be shared between Foreign Ministries and other ministries, whose technical competences are called upon to deal with the subject matter of international negotiations.[14] This is especially true for defence, finance, foreign trade and labour issues.

2555 – Many foreign contacts take place without the involvement of diplomats, by virtue of their technical nature and because specialised government departments negotiate directly.

While, in the diplomatic world, the powers of senior officials are limited to dealing with administrative arrangements, in economic and other fields, negotiations on matters of great importance are often entrusted to members of independent institutions such as banks, chambers of commerce, public bodies and State trading entities.

The indispensable work of coordination can as well be done in the capital, within the Foreign Ministry, as in each diplomatic mission or permanent representation. In France, an ambassador, negotiating on behalf of the State, receives instructions from each different minister, in principle through the single channel of the Minister for Foreign Affairs.

2556 – All these factors raise the question of the mission of ministries in charge of foreign affairs in international negotiation, and of the means available to them. Since it is neither desirable to allow the country's foreign relations and commitments to become fragmented, nor possible to reserve them to diplomats alone, coordination of these attributed responsibilities will be necessary. Within the European Union, this process of harmonisation has already proved so complex and difficult that some countries have specialised departments with this as their primary function.

2557 – By virtue of its rigid routines, and because it is stable and anonymous, government administration can impose filters on the ebb and flow of politics: it decants and sorts information, defuses dramatic situations, absorbs shocks and ensures a uniform response, delays reactions and ensures they are consistent. This has its advantages: administrative regulation brings an element of continuity and objectivity to political initiatives, as well as the investment of effort, and it also provides the necessary means – all of them prerequisites for a successful negotiation. *Only a dramatic or revolutionary turn of events can interrupt the bureaucratic domination that is so characteristic of industrial and post-industrial society.*[15] (see **2157**)

2558 – Despite the inertia that characterises much State activity, negotiation will bring fresh stimulus and new methods and structures to the public services. Governments will have to devote more means and greater effort to agreeing and

---

14 G. T. ALLISON and M. H. HALPERIN: 'Bureaucratic Politics: a Paradigm and Some Policy Implications', in *Theory and Policy in International Relations*, Englewood Cliffs, Prentice Hall, 1966.
15 H. A. SIMON: *Administrative Behaviour: a Study of Decision Making Processes in Administrative Organization*, New York, Free Press, 1966.

carrying out foreign commitments, and also to building up national competitiveness in all areas. International dialogue will bring new obligations, new experiences and fresh progress.

2559 – International negotiation is one of the essential prerogatives of the executive. National administrations, as well as private sector enterprises, will view foreign negotiation as a natural extension of their particular domestic activities and will reorganise accordingly.

2560 – As major economic and technical projects are successfully presented, analysed and carried out, a degree of international cooperation will follow. The need for financial and technical returns, and for the dispersal of risk, will be met by increased computerisation and levels of investment. Even now, joint programmes are negotiated irrespective of frontiers, taking a number of legal forms. Communications, telephony, air travel, the press and the broadcast media now function across borders, along with exchanges in culture, trade and industry. (see *1349*)

2561 – Organisational negotiation has expanded and diversified beyond the material and human capacities of States, especially the smaller ones, and also of the international institutions created to facilitate it.[16] However good the preparatory work for codification done by advisory organs such as the International Law Commission, governmental and intergovernmental administrations are overburdened with tasks that multiply with every stage of a negotiation: gathering information, preparing for and holding meetings, drafting of legal instruments, circulation of the resulting documents and monitoring. (see *1522*)

2562 – One can see why foreign negotiations are dominated from the outset by the working system of the State. This limits the freedom of action of those responsible for the negotiation, and instead works in favour of the varied and complex structures and paths of the public administration or political party concerned. Even where the teams in question include leaders of a dominant party, they do not have the support of the people or its elites.[17]

2563 – However powerful it may be, it is not for the bureaucracy to set strategy or drive initiatives. Often, the prominent people in the government are actually civil servants with little political power, although they enjoy a great deal of administrative influence.

Lack of coordination, communication and command between the government administrations will result in contradictory negotiations, carried on in different fields by an assortment of departments and envoys.

2564 – Many international or European institutions are producing drafts or texts of a legislative nature that reassign whole segments of activity from parliaments to

16 E. SUY: 'Innovations in International Law Making Process', in *The International Law and Policy of Human Welfare*, Leiden, Sijthoff, 1978.
17 R. E. NEUSTADT: *Presidential Power*, New York, Wiley, 1960. W. R. SCHILLING: 'Scientists, Foreign Policy and Politics', in *Bureaucratic Power in National Politics*, Boston, Little, Brown & Co., 1978.

governments: the greater the powers assigned to international organisations, the more they will serve to consolidate the role of the administration in the machinery of State. (see *1266, 1617*)

§3. The role of the legislature

2565 – Democracy has led to a profound transformation in the spirit in which diplomacy is conducted, as well as in its methods, because assemblies are influenced by public opinion in a structured and continuous manner, providing checks and balances on government action, especially when questions are put to ministers, budgets are voted and major treaties fall to be ratified.

2566 – However, there is no country today, with the exception of the United States, where the elected assemblies play an essential role in the choice and conduct of foreign negotiations. The decision whether or not to proceed with a given negotiation, or whether its outcome is acceptable, is in practice left almost entirely to the discretion of the government, or the ruling party in certain regimes. There are even instances where ministers do not deem it necessary to inform parliament of the outcome of extremely important negotiations.

2567 – The executive can use parliamentary procedures to orchestrate a manoeuvre, to test an idea or communicate a message, but there will always be a barrier separating those who decide and act from those who deliberate, correct, control or censure.[18] While relations between the administration and the elected assembly are often difficult, it is incumbent on the executive to ensure that the constitutional prerogatives of the legislature are respected and foreign policy is understood by the public.

Foresight and negotiation work better than demands and compulsion, in domestic politics as well.

2568 – This is no easy task, because of the way representative institutions work, debate and vote. Elected representatives often have no interest in foreign policy and no taste for it. Their analysis is coloured by electoral considerations.

Since their mandate is for a limited period, subject to renewal, they usually have neither the time nor the opportunity to familiarise themselves with diplomatic negotiations, although there is a widespread practice of including elected representatives in government delegations, as national delegates or advisers: members of the United States Senate and House of Representatives were thus able to take part in, or attend, the discussions on strategic arms limitation.

2569 – It is therefore understandable that elected representatives are generally only interested in those aspects of international negotiation having direct and short-term repercussions on the internal political scene: this is true even within the European Union. Suffice it to say that parliamentary control in this area is neither general nor systematic. (see *1161*)

18 E. B. HAAS and A. G. WHITING: *Dynamics of International Relations*, New York, McGraw Hill, 1956.

2570 – Nor is that control in any sense complete. The elected assemblies might have voted on treaties under examination, or on government policy in general, but it is only rarely that all the aspects and implications of a foreign negotiation can be brought into the public arena.

2571 – Moreover, a large body of elected representatives is rarely in a position to take diplomatic initiatives: its approach will almost always be passive and divided, reflecting the political plurality of the nation. It plays only a secondary role in the negotiating process, and cannot easily influence the outcome as long as the government does not inform it of its plans, even in outline, or where the process is already too far advanced in the direction of agreement or failure.

2572 – Obligations deriving from international conventions are many and onerous, especially in the field of finance. Elected representatives complain that they have not been sufficiently involved in discussion of the legislative, budgetary and regulatory consequences, which they see as the erosion of their powers in favour of the technocrats. (see *1632, 2212, 2232*)

National administrations can and do use international negotiation to override votes hostile to their plans: the investigative powers of many parliaments are no longer adequate in such cases. (see *1619, 1620*)

2573 – Tension in relations between the public authorities can be aggravated by the intervention of international organisations. As expressions of government negotiation, and using its administrative channels, these bodies take decisions that escape the normal processes of parliamentary scrutiny, but still have the effect of limiting the sovereign prerogatives of the legislature. While legislators are sometimes invited to send representatives to the meetings of international assemblies, these merely replicate the procedures and practices of national parliaments – their sessions, committees, political groups, reports, questions and votes – but without having the same powers in relation to the executive.

2574 – The ratification procedure is, par excellence, the instrument of democratic control of the product of negotiation.[19] It allows the elected representatives, or even the electorate itself where referenda are held, to approve the outcome of major diplomatic negotiations, in other words, those with an impact on the institutions and territory of the State, its laws, public policy and budget and matters of war and peace. (see *780, 2383*)

The decision to hold a referendum in France in 1972 on the enlargement of the Common Market was made on the basis that the treaty would affect the functioning of State institutions. The same was done with the Maastricht Treaty in 1992, and in 2005 for the draft 'Constitution', which was rejected. (see *1254*)

2575 – Where it is required by law or custom, the obligation to consult the legislature prior to ratifying the most important diplomatic treaties is unevenly observed depending on the countries and the subject matter: often, military pacts are kept secret, economic or cultural matters are dealt with by simplified forms of

19 H. NICOLSON: *Diplomacy*, Oxford University Press, 1945, IV, p. 2.

agreement and operational arrangements are decided between the administrations directly.

The Supreme Soviet had no such power, which resided with the Presidium: the periodic speeches made to it by the minister allowed the government and the Party to emphasise certain negotiations and inform the public of them. (see *2233, 2587*)

2576 – The rare debates on ratification that occur in Western Europe do not amount to an effective way of directing or controlling negotiation. This is a cumbersome and often vague procedure, leaving no room for initiative and, in particular, no amendments. The fact that it is often delayed reduces still further the possibility of exerting parliamentary influence: it is for the government to decide when to begin the process. Some diplomatic treaties are implemented before they are submitted to parliament.

2577 – Governments try to restrict intervention by parliaments as much as possible where treaties are concerned. Parliaments have other ways of controlling the diplomatic activities of the executive, either in plenary session, or by written questions, or through committees, whose role largely depends on the person chairing them.

2578 – The United States is a good example of the problems that arise where there are concurrent competences. In interpreting the letter of the Constitution, American political practice complicates the relationship between the President and Congress, in particular the Senate, in foreign relations.[20] There is an ill-defined border between executive prerogative and legislative control, which varies according to the character and the force of personality of the President, the Secretary of State and the senators. Periods of smooth collaboration are followed by outbreaks of tension and crises, especially when the subjects under discussion involve fundamental principles of national security, human rights or Pan-Americanism.[21]

2579 – The Senate exercises a great deal of its power by using its prerogatives in diplomacy. Under the United States Constitution, it must approve treaties by a two-thirds majority: it refuses to allow the President to present it with a *fait accompli*, and requires him to explain the negotiations he has led. It sometimes makes adjustments or amendments, proposes reservations[22] and puts forward interpretations to the texts before it or it quite simply rejects them. Some observers take the view that the demands it makes can distort the functioning of the federal institutions in the diplomatic arena, especially when it introduces new conditions into a negotiation or forces the result to be renegotiated.[23] (see *618, 785, 2652*)

20 E. BRIGGS: *Anatomy of Diplomacy: the Origin and Execution of American Foreign Policy*, New York, McKay, 1968.
21 B. M. SAPIN: *The Making of United States Foreign Policy*, Washington, The Brookings Institution, 1966. R. E. NEUSTADT: *Presidential Power*, New York, Wiley, 1960. E. PLISCHKE: *Conduct of American Diplomacy*, New York, Van Nostrand, 1967.
22 P. H. IMBERT: *Les Réserves aux traités multilatéraux*, Paris, Pedone, 1979, p. 395.
23 R. HAAS: *Congressional Power: Implications for American Security Policy*, London, Adelphi Papers, 1979.

2580 – The US Constitution thus sets out a true system of power sharing for the negotiation and conclusion of treaties: in this field, the President acts on the advice and with the approval of the Senate, whose approval is also required for certain major appointments (including ambassadors). This Constitutional clause is interpreted as suspending the entry into force of diplomatic treaties until they are examined by the Senate, which allows it to formulate mandatory advice to the President before or during certain important negotiations, to demand to be consulted before certain treaties are denounced or even to summon the representative of a foreign power to appear before it.

2581 – The weight of these procedures has led to the frequent resort to simplified forms of diplomatic arrangement, made in the name of the President, or the administration, on the condition that the Senate does not raise any objection while the negotiations are going on. Thousands of these executive agreements have been signed and simply communicated to both Houses or their committees, within two months of coming into force, sometimes on a confidential basis.[24] In this way, the General Agreement on Tariffs and Trade (GATT) was substituted for the draft proposal to set up an international trade organisation, ratification of which would at the time have been refused.

Congress thus intervenes frequently in votes on the budgets or contributions to international organisations: the attendant publicity is a factor in the formation of American public opinion on global issues.

2582 – Relations in the United States between the executive and the legislature have been so problematic that political observers agree that they need to be revised, especially in the area of foreign policy. Congress has put forward a series of proposals designed to increase the information it has on foreign affairs and its role in decision making, even in the conduct of negotiations. On the other hand, the administration has tried, sometimes unsuccessfully, to protect certain sensitive types of negotiation from legislative scrutiny.

2583 – The House and Senate committees have large permanent staffs; they have access to all non-confidential documents of the administration under the Freedom of Information Act, and they can hold public or closed hearings and obtain detailed reports from the executive on negotiations of interest to them. Nor do they hesitate to summon the officials in charge of certain foreign negotiations, at any time, for questioning.[25]

2584 – The United States Congress has effective ways of monitoring the President's foreign negotiations. Its research departments, working in liaison with the Library of Congress, continue to grow, to the point that there can sometimes seem to be too much information and too many constraints. It is becoming increasingly difficult to preserve confidentiality because of the publicity surrounding the work of the Houses,

---

24 L. HENKIN: *Foreign Affairs and the Constitution*, New York, Norton, 1972.
25 'Congress and Foreign Policy', *Report of the Special Subcommittee on Investigations of the Committee on International Relations*, House of Representatives, Washington, USGPO, 1977.

their committees and departments.[26] Congressional procedures and interventions can sometimes force the executive to reveal its intentions while the negotiation is under way or still at the preparatory stage: in 1963, the Senate demanded reassurance that the United States would retain the right to pursue its nuclear tests, despite the fact that discussions were taking place with the Soviet Union on that question.

2585 – In Europe, the development of institutional negotiation has triggered a reaction on the part of national Parliaments threatened with the loss of their prerogatives, especially following the increase in obligations and regulations emanating from the Community, some of them excessively detailed. (see *1377, 1379*)

In practice, within the Community legal system, many rules and decisions are directly incorporated into national law or require the national authorities to make sometimes minute adjustments to existing legislation.

2586 – The sheer quantity of obligations contracted within the European Community has aroused the vigilance of the Parliaments in the Member States. Their concern has been to ensure that they are better informed about negotiations that might result in obligations in the fields of legislation, finance and policy. They also wish to be in a position to exercise the parliamentary control to which they are entitled under their respective Constitutions.

The break in the organic link between national Parliaments and the European Parliament, now that the latter is directly elected by universal suffrage, will make it even more vital for the executive and the legislature to maintain constant liaison in all fields of Community negotiation.

2587 – The reaction of each Parliament against the predominant role of the executive in this area has manifested itself in the creation of organs specialising in European affairs. These generally take the form of parliamentary committees or commissions with limited membership, as in Belgium, Denmark, Greece, Ireland, Italy, Luxembourg, The Netherlands and Spain.

In France, two delegations were set up, in the *Assemblée nationale* and the *Sénat*, whose role it is to bring certain aspects of European negotiations to the attention of the relevant parliamentary committees.

In Germany, the government has to respect the normal working procedures of the two Houses, with each of the *Bundesrat* and the *Bundestag* having their own committees for Community issues.

2588 – Control of negotiations conducted by the government takes place before and after deliberations in the European Council in Germany, Italy and the United Kingdom. In Belgium, Ireland and Luxembourg, Parliament is mostly informed after the Community negotiation. In Denmark, even the mandate of the negotiators is the subject of deliberations in Parliamentary committee.

2589 – The referral of the matter to Parliament is mandatory in Denmark, where there is direct ongoing control of the negotiation by Parliament, and also in

26 R. HAAS: *Congressional Power: Implications for American Security Policy*, London, Adelphi Papers, 1979.

Germany and The Netherlands. In all Member States, this is done by transmitting to it documents drafted by the organs of the Community, or draft legal instruments put before the European Council.

In France, the Constitution was amended in 1992 and again in 1999 to introduce new control mechanisms allowing a greater degree of preliminary scrutiny of draft legislative instruments and an increased role for Parliament on policy issues. (see *2383*)

2590 – In many cases, European drafts are discussed in public session. In the United Kingdom, the relevant committees filter them and submit the important ones to Parliament: the government may be asked, by a vote, to revise its position. In both Germany and Italy, there can be a full parliamentary debate before the draft instruments are examined by the European Council, based on the report of the competent commissions or committees, and the government pays close heed to the outcome of these sessions. In France, each parliamentary delegation files its opinion with its parliamentary chamber, and these opinions are published.

2591 – While not creating the same mass of legal instruments that has resulted from the process of European unification, the increasing burden of new provisions of international law will eventually pose problems of the same magnitude for all States. Parliaments will complain that they are being stripped of some of their prerogatives, and often presented with the results of a negotiation as a *fait accompli*. Governments might regard any increase in these powers of scrutiny as intrusive, but they could have the advantage of strengthening the government's position in a negotiation.

2592 – The rise in the number of direct contacts between the leaders of different countries is helping to form a new style of negotiation, combining the practices of diplomacy with those of politics.

This explains the entry of members of Parliaments onto the international scene, and the interest of institutions in allowing this influence to spread, which is a unique feature of the cooperation among the States of Europe: precisely because elected representatives bear no direct responsibility for the negotiation, their freedom of speech and imagination allow them to offer suggestions and criticisms that can be useful when negotiations threaten to stall or are going in the wrong direction. (see *1154, 1167*)

2593 – A political discussion is difficult to limit and stabilise: negotiation, on the other hand, must be both limited and stable. A Parliament cannot easily restrict its own debates, which have a natural tendency to overflow the bounds of its competences; furthermore, by their very nature, what is said in its debates can be contested and revised. By contrast, the object and purpose of a negotiation must be firm and precise: its intended result is an agreement that, once in definitive form, is deemed to be binding on the parties. (see *1161*)

Section 2: Public opinion and negotiation

2594 – To govern, as the French President Georges Pompidou explained, is to lead people collectively on a path and towards goals that are neither natural to them, nor clearly perceptible, nor in line with their immediate aspirations.[27] As a political exercise, diplomatic negotiation is subject to the same uncertainties.

2595 – Having for centuries been an expression of the will of the few, the strength and direction of national government now derives from the choices made by each of its citizens, in other words, their judgement of what is good or bad for themselves, their families and perhaps the nation.

When faced with the question whether a State should conduct its external affairs in accordance with the national sentiment, the democrat would answer in the affirmative, while the lessons of international history indicate the opposite:[28] A diplomatic strategy cannot be constructed out of petty preoccupations. (see *2512*)

2596 – In a democracy, as in all regimes that rely on public opinion for the choices they make and the means at their disposal, decisions cannot be taken as fast or as secretly as in other regimes that have much more tactical flexibility, because those others can alter, or even reverse, their positions without having to justify themselves, even against their established doctrine.[29] This is what Stalin did before the Second World War, when he skilfully negotiated with the West on one side and Germany on the other, the results of which only came to light with the signing of the Germano-Soviet Pact in August 1939.

2597 – Authoritarian powers need not concern themselves with public opinion except where they shape it themselves, by manipulating information and directing propaganda: they can thus absorb a great number of problems on the foreign front without needing to fear pressure and criticism from the electorate. In negotiation, therefore, they are freer both with their concessions and their demands. (see *2359*)

Democratic regimes become more vulnerable as the amount of published information increases. There is confusion in the public mind between the process of negotiation and its outcome. Openness to the ideas of others can weaken the resolve. (see *1678, 2054*)

§1. Diplomatic secrecy

2598 – Leaders like to keep their negotiations hidden: failure can be concealed, and when success comes, it is unexpected. The negotiator must have the freedom to make overtures and respond to them, when his adversary is free to do so. This was why King Louis XV of France set up a secret service, '*le Secret du Roi*', an idea that spread from one chancery to another in spite of the dangers it presented for coherent diplomacy. (see *2418*)

2599 – There are practical considerations to support these policy reasons. Discussion of a sensitive matter, or the reconciling of different claims, requires patience and moderation, and has to be handled unobtrusively. Disagreements do not degenerate into conflict if they are kept hidden, and concessions do not breed

---

27 G. POMPIDOU: *Le Noeud gordien*, Paris, Plon, 1974, p. 58.
28 H. NICOLSON: *Diplomacy*, Oxford, Oxford University Press, 1945.
29 H. NICOLSON: *The Evolution of Diplomatic Methods*, London, MacMillan, 1954.

humiliation. At summit level especially, revealing or confirming a secret is a form of threat or provocation. (see *1072, 2532, 2643*)

Audacious manoeuvres can benefit from the element of surprise. According to Callières, most major issues were resolved by sending secret envoys, and this is, on the whole, still true. (see *331*)

2600 – In diplomacy, contrary to appearances, reticence or reservations serve the cause of integrity. The truth, even the truth of the moment, is difficult to know and express, especially in politics. It is often hidden for reasons of convenience, respect for the hierarchy or conformity with received ideas. It will also be undermined by any disparity between thoughts and actions, between what the negotiator wants and what he will concede. (see *602*)

2601 – Especially in times of war or tension, diplomats must beware of indiscretion. Neither negotiators nor the public will accept negotiations in which the stakes are falsified, except where they are faced with a *fait accompli*. (see *296, 872*)

2602 – A government that wishes to defeat its rivals prefers not to reveal its political and diplomatic objectives or interests, unless forced to do so. If it chooses to reveal anything significant, this will be for purposes of deterrence.

In international negotiation, protecting the secrecy of a State's strategic designs is a precondition for its tactical success. (see *2678*)

2603 – As between negotiators, secrecy is accepted, even if it goes hand in hand with duplicity. But it is hardly ever total, or lasting. Calculated indiscretion is part of the diplomat's tactics. Berlin abandoned the treaty of mutual guarantee secretly negotiated by Bismarck with Russia in 1887 because it feared Austria would learn of its existence. (see *494*)

2604 – In 1918, attributing the ills of the nations to the underhand machinations of their leaders, and endorsing the condemnation of the covert manoeuvres made by the Soviets in 1917, President Wilson expressed the view that secret agreements between States should be condemned, and diplomacy should proceed in the open, in full view of the world: the publicity given to foreign relations would lead governments to appeal to the moral values of the people and refrain from lies and aggression. But, only a few months after having set out his 'fourteen points', he was forced to renounce them in negotiating the Treaty of Versailles, and his successors have had to follow suit.

2605 – There is more: in many modern States, the centralisation of government has gone hand in hand with secrecy about the conditions in which the most important decisions are taken, especially where defence and foreign policy are concerned. *Even for the negotiator, it is often difficult to know at what level, on the basis of what advice and after what consultations the principles were decided of the enterprise for which he is responsible.*

2606 – The problem has undergone a further evolution: the secrets to be protected are no longer the same. In a society based on the growing use of the media and technology, the field of knowledge necessary for diplomatic negotiation has shifted: regular intelligence about the other party's intentions and capabilities must be supplemented by a scientific approach to the economic and technical aspects of the international environment. (see *2023, 2039*)

2607 – In the present day, secrecy relates less to procedures than to facts, with information being the essential precondition for continuous and effective decision-making. *While it is the privilege of the leader to make policy, in order to exercise this prerogative he must have, and maintain, access to complete and constantly updated information.* (see *2025, 2537*)

The installation in the United States, Canada, the United Kingdom, Australia and New Zealand of a powerful system capable of monitoring telecommunications worldwide, coupled with the interception of messages on the Internet, provides the American authorities with secret intelligence that is useful not only in national strategy and diplomacy, but also for businesses in which there is a national interest. All this information is sorted and anything useful is stored. (see *1697, 1699, 1706, 2014, 2027*)

China, Russia and certain European countries are now beginning to use satellites designed to capture information.

2608 – It is becoming ever more difficult to protect the secrecy of negotiation against deductions or investigations by journalists, some of them specially chosen and accredited. Multilateral negotiating practices and the intervention of international organisations help to spread information about ongoing negotiations. (see *2010, 2532*)

2609 – The erosion of the boundary between domestic and foreign affairs, the instant broadcasting of news and the confused fears that disorder induces, all lead people to take a greater interest in external negotiations, especially during election campaigns. (see *2634*)

2610 – In societies experiencing growing anxiety, confrontation, impatience and demands, diplomatic negotiations will require to be justified. While diplomacy used to be protected by the secrecy of government, new developments in negotiation, as well as its outcomes, must now be explained and weighed against the fears and expectations of the many who turn to the State for help and protection and are critical of everything. It is rare for a political negotiation to satisfy everyone at once. (see *2629, 2661*)

2611 – The evocative powers of diplomatic negotiation are magnified by the speed and range of news broadcasting. This is not limited to those with special interests, such as the farmers of Europe reacting to decisions taken under the Common Agricultural Policy. The Helsinki Conference in 1975 generated considerable interest: a welter of testimony and positions were later expressed throughout Central and Eastern Europe on the basis of that treaty, to ensure that it would be applied to areas as broad as public freedom, cultural and religious identity and working and living conditions. (see *795, 2382*)

The fall of the Iron Curtain was not unconnected with the results produced by that seemingly anodyne negotiation.

2612 – Public opinion will be subject to the broadening influence of movements that are international, if not global, in scope. The facility and spread of means of communication will be one factor, as will the creation of groupings whose aim is to intervene in the internal affairs of States and activate their citizens to influence their policies. This assault on national sovereignty is inevitable where everyone is free to take a view on everything, but its effect on negotiation depends on how open the regime in question is to outside influences. (see *1888*)

2613 – Taken together, these considerations explain why, even though public opinion is not as lively and quick to react everywhere as it is in the Western world, nor always as able to obtain information and express itself as freely, negotiation must, after centuries of prudence and secrecy, be practised today with popular movements in mind, irrespective of whether they are spontaneous or organised, justified, timely, or neither. Even the most rigid and controlling policy can no longer obviate the need for leaders to be conscious of this. (see *1815*)

2614 – When offended or ill informed, public opinion can weaken a country's competitive position, by forcing it into negotiations at an unfavourable moment or into making damaging or pointless concessions. Some tacticians miss no opportunity to obtain intelligence about the other government's position and use it against their interlocutors. (see *1881*)

2615 – The availability of information about foreign negotiation has the advantage that it helps to forestall public concern, discontent and panic and brings many leaders together in the cause of the country's competitiveness. (see *100*)

2616 – The demand for more transparency in diplomacy is also a reaction against excessive personal influence in the choice of leaders, who decide to hold and conclude negotiations without any explanation. *The more secret the negotiation, the greater the risk that those involved will be removed from profound shifts in public opinion, and their efforts might lead nowhere.* (see *2331*)

2617 – The discreet methods of traditional diplomacy have undergone radical change, with the development of negotiations in conferences and institutions where large numbers of parties are usually represented. There is now a whole spectrum of possible tactics and approaches, from the absolute secrecy of political talks to the publicity of parliaments. (see *1043, 2012*)

2618 – Consultation and cooperation between the members of international organisations is devoted to subjects that are of real and direct concern to their populations. While a better-informed public opinion is useful in ensuring the outcome of a negotiation is understood and implemented, it means, on the other hand, that currents of opinion, national or international, must be borne in mind when negotiating. (see *1133*)

2619 – Obviously, the way in which parties approach the issues, advance their positions and make and rebut their arguments is not the same in multilateral meetings as in diplomatic talks. With rare exceptions, when debates take place, they are, if not always open to the public, then at least published in the media and used by the information departments, which can be decisive where the subject is one that is easily understood. *The political problems that arise in negotiations within an organisation are very often due to their openness to public opinion.* (see *1042, 1228*)

2620 – It is easy to provoke a confrontation, or simply trigger a discussion, in a large assembly, which is more susceptible to eloquence than a gathering of seasoned negotiators. This produces pressure on the delegates, particularly when their nations are anxious, or suffering injustice. Those who refuse to engage in debate, or even to make certain concessions, risk finding themselves in a difficult position, not only in the eyes of public opinion but also by virtue of the workings of the institution in which they sit. They are sometimes reduced to defending or justifying themselves or offering expressions of regret. (see *1063*)

2621 – Even when they have no power of autonomous decision making, and exercise no real control over governments, international assemblies and interparliamentary meetings use movements in public opinion to validate or condemn certain positions and to weaken or isolate certain protagonists.

2622 – Political leaders and diplomats are past masters at using the possibilities offered by major conferences, not only with an eye to the public opinion that follows their workings but also at the level of negotiating tactics. In doing so, they force their interlocutors to take account of political factors that may have nothing to do with the matter in hand: the general public reaction, the ideological colour of the arguments and the turns taken by the debates undermine or reinforce the positions of the different parties, pushing them towards intransigence or reconciliation, and determine the course of the negotiations. (see *1895*)

Although they have no primary legitimacy, international organisations can create systems of values on which diplomacy can draw. (see *654*)

2623 – While professional negotiators agree easily on the disciplines of their art, it is difficult for them to agree to hold secret discussions with an interlocutor who does not apply their methods or in whom they have insufficient confidence. *In order not to be overtaken by events, and to retain public support, each party is tempted to disclose, or allow the disclosure of, certain arguments, conclusions or versions of events. In case of doubt, it is preferable for the parties to agree in advance on contacts with the media, press conferences and communiqués, and what departures are permitted from the usual rule of discretion.* (see *761*)

§2. The support of public opinion

2624 – Every negotiation involving effort and risk will be more than ever dependent on the support of the nation, even if the public is not really in a position to understand the usefulness of diplomatic negotiations and procedures. This is especially true where the results of the negotiation have to be put to the test or are expected to stand the test of time. (see *326*)

2625 – For anyone negotiating on behalf of a State, the support of the people is indispensable, especially where the situation is serious. Such support might be difficult to measure, but it represents a force to be reckoned with within strategy: some negotiations have even been imposed by the will of the people. In Europe, ever since 1848, nationalism has triggered a rise in public awareness that has had lasting effects on diplomacy. (see 8)

On the contrary, where public opinion is instinctively hostile, this can completely undermine agreements negotiated in secret. (see 2325)

2626 – Those who can afford not to take notice of adverse reactions to their plans are strong. Stronger still are those who have the solid backing of informed public opinion, either in their own country or even in their adversary's, even where this advantage is offset by a reduction in their room to manoeuvre.

2627 – Bureaucratic and diplomatic routines do not need popular support, whereas the deep-seated commitment of the nation is fundamental to success in politics. *Lively and informed public opinion can prove so helpful to a government's position that it is sometimes tempted to provoke an open display.* In 1709, Louis XIV appealed to his subjects to protest against the conditions his adversaries were seeking to impose for peace, and the people responded.

2628 – Concern for public opinion can guide the choice of the mode of negotiation. A concession that would have been viewed as a betrayal will be accepted if it is recommended by a mediator. On the contrary, clumsy intervention by a third party can look like interference and may derail the negotiation. (see 454)

2629 – The negotiator can rarely count on public support for his undertaking. Certain past dangers or advantages linger on in the public perception; on the other hand, an apparently innocuous negotiation can harbour the seeds of risk. It is even more difficult to keep these things in perspective when the gains from the negotiation may be threatened by disclosure of certain factors, favourable or unfavourable.[30]

2630 – Safeguarding a country's independence and defending its interests require a combative spirit, resolve and discretion: these often expose the negotiator to the risk of unpopularity against which he cannot publicly defend himself. It is difficult in practice to make the general public understand a subtle course of action, or developments in an external context of which they know nothing. It is easier for the citizen to grasp issues of principle than the mechanics of negotiation and to understand political slogans than manoeuvres.

2631 – Public opinion is dominated by superficial and instinctive perceptions, and does not comprehend the exact hierarchy of external dangers and pressures. Its sudden and unconsidered reactions can interfere with a discussion or agreement.[31]

The same masses can applaud and then reject the same man with no regard for logic or justice: in 1938, the French and British negotiators returning from Munich were somewhat troubled and ashamed by the welcome they received in their capitals.

30 H. A. KISSINGER: 'The Viet-Nam negotiation', *Foreign Affairs*, 1969, 2, p. 211.
31 H. A. KISSINGER: *The White House Years*, Boston, Little, Brown & Co., 1979, I.

2632 – Sudden and contradictory reactions are bad for the smooth progress of a negotiation, and diplomacy can only function properly if it follows the policy line imposed by those in power. Where it does, all the internal political forces of a democratic nation will have their effect on diplomacy.

In industrialised countries where the distinctions between internal and foreign affairs and between public and private matters are breaking down, international negotiation can be a factor in undermining the authority of political power when there is no guiding strategy.

2633 – The representation of interests abroad and the pursuit of foreign negotiation do not easily withstand the crises that periodically affect governments, whatever the country's regime, but least of all in a democracy. *An envoy will be received with reservation where his government's position seems insecure*: when signing a treaty it is advisable to verify the other party's standing. (see *2405*)

2634 – While all the time keeping in mind the highest demands of national interest, the political leader must always have an eye to the wishes of public opinion, or at any rate to what it might accept, either in specific instances – where, for example, it wants to see an end to a dispute that has grown tiresome – or at a more fundamental level, where it is dominated by deep-seated tendencies such as insularity or isolationism. In 1918, the Allies were practically forced into peace by spontaneous expressions of popular opinion, from the moment the Americans revealed that the Germans had requested armistice negotiations. Today, too, the needs and wants of the people can force the great powers into dialogue. (see *890*)

2635 – Appealing to public opinion is one of the tactics that can be used to overcome an obstacle in a negotiation.

Making plausible accusations is a way to discredit, isolate or exasperate one's opponent. Forcing him into a denial often obliges him to show his hand, or give up an argument or claim. All the negotiations carried on by Hitler prior to 1939 were subject to pressure, or rather threats, from an overexcited and aggressive German public opinion.

2636 – There are some negotiations whose entire interest resides in opening up a new psychological process. Among these are disarmament proposals, which are generally favourably received by popular opinion even though they have little practical effect. In this respect, propaganda, or use of the media, can facilitate diplomatic initiatives.

2637 – It can be useful for the politician to provoke or exploit the general sentiment, to the extent that this will increase his influence, his strength and his success both within and beyond national borders. When embarking on a sensitive negotiation, he must therefore know how to get public opinion on his side, especially where it has an influence on his adversary: an uneasy conscience makes for vulnerability.

2638 – It is easy to understand how some negotiators have proceeded to use the weight of public opinion to strengthen their camp and weaken that of the adversary, especially within his own borders, to force him to accept certain conditions or make certain concessions, or even on occasion to bring him to the negotiating table. Credibility can affect the psychological impact of public support for a negotiation: the influence of the press and other media cannot be ignored.

2639 – This reliance on popular sentiment can also serve to cement a treaty and extend its effects, as was the case with the Moscow agreements on non-proliferation of nuclear weapons, the formal signature of which came to be exploited as an argument by world opinion. (see *1745*)

Appealing to a sense of national responsibility can have its uses, in the sense that, by contrast with monarchs who regarded it as a matter of honour to keep their word, democracies pay little heed to their international reputation and are ill equipped to resist pressure from groups undeterred by legal or moral scruples.

2640 – Mass opinion is slow to decide, but sometimes more lucid than its leaders: the French revolutionary leader Saint Just said that the people make fewer mistakes than statesmen.

Public opinion can have a stabilising effect on negotiation to the extent that it makes contradictory arguments, ill-advised initiatives, about-turns and blackmail difficult: logic argues in favour of continuity.

2641 – It is a mistake to criticise a population for being indecisive or sometimes fickle. Not every citizen formulates views on the basis of broad principles: sometimes it is more a matter of instinctive reaction to questions of war and peace, independence and alliance. Napoleon's position in France began to weaken when the foreign powers made it known that they agreed to negotiate with him on the basis that they would leave France the natural borders of the Pyrenees, the Alps and the Rhine that it had before 1789. Later, the French and German governments succeeded, invoked by the sensitivities of public opinion, in cutting short the stationing of occupying troops in their respective countries after the great wars of the nineteenth and twentieth centuries.

2642 – On the fundamental issues, the public response in all countries shows a deep sense of cohesion and a remarkable continuity, whence its strength and character. The splendid isolation of the British is one example. Another dates from 1526, when François I of France, held prisoner in Madrid, was forced to cede Burgundy to the Emperor Charles V. That province – both the people and the ruling bodies – rose up against the treaty, declared the clause null and void and gave a decisive boost to the King's policies.

It is not surprising that public opinion takes an interest in the provisions of major treaties and that its reactions to those it finds unacceptable can be violent and lasting. One need only look at the consequences of the annexation of Alsace and Lorraine by the German Empire after the war with France of 1870–1871: it was decades before any *rapprochement* was possible between the two countries.

2643 – Because it lacks discretion when laying the groundwork for a negotiation, democracy often deprives itself of major tactical advantages. (see *426*)

The likely effect of any declaration must be weighed in the balance. The political stakes might be such as to justify a refusal to make information available, if this might endanger, disclose or paralyse the diplomatic operation. But the fact remains that the only way to counter indifference or passivity on the part of the public, and avoid making them anxious or rebellious, is to give them as much information as possible about the main negotiations conducted in their name. *To boast of a negotiation is to become its prisoner in the eyes of the public.*

2644 – The press and broadcast media have increased the influence of popular opinion on public affairs, especially foreign policy. Not only is it the intermediary between opinion and governments, but also sometimes between governments themselves, serving as the channel for messages, proposals, explanations and protests. Adverse propaganda can be enough on its own to substantially weaken a government's power to negotiate.[32] (see *525*)

Likewise, the role of public opinion has strengthened that of the media: the thirst for information is growing, especially in diplomatic circles. (see *1837*)

2645 – While information can help to shed light on diplomacy and bring it public support, it can also have the opposite effect. The press can bring a negotiation to a halt or cause it to fail, either by publishing attacks against one of the parties, or spreading tendentious or ill-timed information, or more generally by presenting a particular negotiator or his position in an unfavourable light.[33]

The rejection of a diplomatic initiative only becomes insulting if the public is aware of it: publicity is what makes an affront serious. (see *1881*)

2646 – Governments, like international institutions, experience an ever greater need to maintain links with the media. Their information offices are growing and their publications increasing in number. There are hundreds of journalists accredited to European institutions; the Parliament and the Commission have substantial budgets for the publication of information and studies about the activities of the Community. Within diplomatic missions, too, there are numerous officials responsible for following the local press, circulating documents and maintaining relations with important media circles. (see *1469*)

2647 – The excessive weight of some of the major press agencies has concentrated the global media in the hands, if not of governments, since these agencies are independent, then of those responsible for the main strands of cultural influence. An international debate is taking place, at the instigation of developing and emerging countries, about the real meaning of notions such as liberty and pluralism in this field, and whether professional cooperation and concrete policies are possible between States wanting a new world order in information.[34]

2648 – Appealing to the public has become an effective weapon in diplomacy, in spite of the counter-measures taken by certain governments to stifle news from abroad and to prevent free or even clandestine publication within the country itself.

---

32 R. JERVIS: *The Logic of Images in International Relations*, Princeton, Princeton University Press, 1970.
33 H. A. KISSINGER: *The White House Years*, Boston, Little, Brown & Co., 1979.
   H. NICOLSON: *Diplomacy*, Oxford University Press, 1945.
34 S. MACBRIDE, etc: *Many Voices, One World*, UNESCO, 1980.

Some governments use the press to make known their intention to negotiate and the conditions on which they will do so, without the need for an official announcement and without risking a refusal.

2649 – According to Harold Nicolson,[35] Richelieu was the first statesman to have understood how helpful explanation could be to the success of a foreign policy. Today, the use of the media for propaganda purposes has become widespread, whether to point out intransigence or goodwill. There is no place in negotiation, however, for attitudes that distort or aggravate the conflict it is intended to resolve.

2650 – It may be easier for a policy to succeed if it adopts the methods of commercial advertising. It was thanks to the services of an advertising agency, and later by calling on the press, that Chancellor Adenauer persuaded the United States to acknowledge his efforts to improve the status of Germany.

2651 – The growth in information available to the public, and especially to those directly concerned, will inevitably have repercussions for diplomacy. In part at least, it was the mass availability of transistor radios that originally triggered the resurgence in Pan-Arab and Pan-Islamic sentiment. Television has since taken over.

The uncontrolled broadcasting of information can add to the degree of risk in international society. Public opinion is made up of a succession of contradictory reactions, sometimes transient, often tendentious, and at times violent. The rise in multinational pressure groups has aggravated the problem. The publicity given to the political crises in Europe after 1919 was certainly not conducive to an atmosphere of peace.

2652 – With the public now better informed, particularly through live broadcasting and real-time Internet communication, the influence of negotiations on public opinion is growing. Anything relating to the initial discussion of the European Common Agricultural Policy, for example, or the way it presently functions, can be directly evaluated by the interested parties. Governments and their administrations will be aware of how difficult it is becoming to keep their foreign negotiations secret.

In the United States, for example, revelations of diplomatic concessions have provoked an impassioned response from public opinion. (see *2275*)

2653 – For some observers, the 'global society' begins with the globalisation of information. Advances in the sending and receiving of messages are certainly having an effect on the collective mentality. There is less individuality and originality as dominant patterns of communication expand; culture is becoming standardised, while at the same time ideologies confront each other in violent opposition.[36] (see *2046*)

Freedom of the media has a beneficial effect on international communication: the decision-making process is influenced by national or worldwide trends in

35 H. NICOLSON: *The Evolution of Diplomatic Methods*, London, MacMillan, 1954.
36 A. LALL: *Modern International Negotiation: Principles and Practice*, New York, Columbia University Press, 1966.

opinion, some of which bring into the realms of negotiation matters of public concern that would otherwise be alien to the bureaucratic mindset.

2654 – The political leader must refrain from treating public opinion as binding or taking it as a moral reference. The best way, in the long term, to secure the support of public opinion is to take decisions based not on the expected popular reactions but on what is in the nation's interests, and make the public understand this.

Section 3: Democracy and negotiation

2655 – The principles of democracy and those of international negotiation are far from coinciding. To avoid this contradiction, a distinction must be made between foreign policy in general, and negotiation in the true sense, which is its instrument. While a country's interests may often conflict with public opinion, which is more instinctive than rational, the people should nonetheless be aware of the main aspects of national policy. By contrast, it is neither necessary nor possible for them to judge the implementation of this policy. (see *2137*)

2656 – It has often been claimed that no negotiation is possible without secrecy. This is true, up to the point when the parties reach agreement. In practice, where the agreement involves issues on which the security and the future of the nation might depend, it is desirable and usual for it to know about the commitment, even if it is unlikely to grasp its full significance at once.

2657 – The citizen, on the other hand, does not have to understand the elements of procedure and tactics in a negotiation, the success of which often depends on swift, secret and delicate moves. Moreover, contrary to what might have been expected, since the end of the First World War and in spite of the views of President Wilson, the paths of diplomacy are sometimes more covert now than they were before.

2658 – Even if, in the long term, public opinion always has some effect on the success of a negotiation, its impact on tactics should never be exaggerated: in politics, there is often only one path open. *Whatever may be the results of elections or polls, a negotiation unfolds according to its own logic over which public opinion has little influence in reality: it is the outcome that will be judged when it is made public.*

2659 – It is natural for a political regime based on the influence of public opinion to take an interest in the reaction of its citizens in all areas, especially foreign policy, while those same citizens do not always understand the principles on which this consultation is based.

Populations perceive international threats in a vague but alarmist way, and their fear restricts their leaders' freedom of movement. In France, the 1992 referendum on the ratification of the Maastricht Treaty weakened the government's intentions in Europe because it showed a high degree of reluctance on the part of the public. This effect was exacerbated in 2005 when the people voted against the draft 'Constitution' in the referendum.

2660 – That said, it would be too sweeping a judgement to say that the general public is incapable of a reasoned assessment of major negotiations: on this as on other issues, any criticism of the democratic system must be qualified.

In fact, any power that seeks the support and cooperation of public opinion must lead it progressively to take external factors into account. Democracy gives the people an increased role in future choices, and it must accordingly inform them about their international aspects. (see *2511*)

2661 – By involving in the preparation of a negotiation those who have the most interest in its outcome, democracy contributes to the success of its major foreign policy undertakings, more effectively than if it presented the public with a *fait accompli*. This may sometimes justify the intervention of a sizeable number of pressure groups representing particular interests, as well as underlying forces affected by the negotiation. (see *1898, 2627*)

2662 – A democracy is inclined to favour material and cultural prosperity, and therefore peace, which is its precondition: it must be more attentive than any other regime to the principles of its foreign policy.

Amid the great mass of the indifferent, an active minority made up of the leaders of parties, movements, unions and businesses and also the media, will stand out, following their respective tendencies and affiliations.[37] Where such pluralism exists, it should be preserved, as it can be a source of alternative strategies. It does not make negotiation any simpler, however, especially when the divisions are reflected at government level or the government is obliged to do battle simultaneously on two fronts, in order to bring the people's aspirations into line with what diplomacy can be expected to achieve. (see *1854, 1897*)

2663 – Since their foreign policy depends on the results of elections and sometimes on the media, modern democratic States often find the thrust and parry of diplomacy very difficult. But, when a choice has to be made, the strategist will know how to put the interests of his country above the popularity that comes from satisfying public opinion. (see *2537, 2630, 2678*)

2664 – In regimes that are viewed as representative because the will of the nation is expressed through elections, the citizen usually has only an indirect influence on negotiation. Changes in public life, however, have meant that there is now a much more direct relationship between public opinion and diplomacy. The manner in which this mutual interaction is handled is a matter of great importance in most modern States, especially in Europe, where foreign policy and defence are regarded as the main attributes of international sovereignty.

Given that the fundamental choices available to different national electorates are not the same either in terms of content or timing, there can be uncertainty or distortion in the programmes of intergovernmental institutions.

---

37 J. N. ROSENAU: *The Attentive Public and Foreign Policy*, Princeton, Princeton University Press, 1968.

2665 – The threat of popular reaction, abroad as well as at home, can expose the diplomat to the risk of being misunderstood or disowned. These risks are particularly great for those representing democratic countries, who may find that their backing is withdrawn at the very moment they are required to give the most solemn pledges, thus depriving their commitments of credibility. From the 1919 Paris Conference onwards, it was feared that, despite the legitimacy of his position, President Wilson would not have his country behind him: this is exactly what transpired, as his predecessor Theodore Roosevelt had predicted. More recently, the meetings of the G8 have showed how difficult it is to carry on diplomacy in the face of violent demonstrations. (see *2489*)

2666 – Because of the difficulty of reconciling the principles of democratic control with the techniques of negotiation, ways must be found for the nation – in other words, its elected representatives – to participate in making the choices that will govern the conduct of its diplomacy.

The art of politics lies in capturing and expressing the mood of the citizens in order to give them what they want: however, where this perception is based on intuition, it must be substantiated.

2667 – There are various ways of gaining the support of public opinion. Many statesmen have made appeals to the public in their own way, but rarely on matters of foreign policy. General de Gaulle held a referendum to secure the ratification by universal suffrage of the results of his Algerian negotiations; President Pompidou and Prime Minister Harold Wilson did the same for the enlargement of the European Community.

2668 – Only in vary rare cases do legislation or principles of law make it mandatory to consult the people, as the French Constitution does for treaties that transfer sovereignty or cede territory. It is a matter for the statesman's judgement whether he refers to the peoples' representatives, or even the people themselves.

2669 – The most obvious way to ascertain and respect the will of the public is to ask them to express it when electing those who will be charged with controlling the government's actions, particularly in the field of foreign policy.

Where foreign policy is concerned, all elections show is the relative strength of the different tendencies represented by the parties and individuals elected. (see *2531*)

2670 – Voters do not always have the same taste for public affairs, the same capacity for collective action or the same judgement of what is in the common interest. Generally, they are not much interested in foreign negotiations, which seem remote and complex, nor do they fully understand their repercussions on daily life. It is rare to be able to base an electoral campaign on diplomatic issues alone: even the elections to the European Parliament were marked in most member countries by an emphasis on internal political debates.

2671 – The modern practice of opinion polls offers a more scientific way of ascertaining public opinion. Carried out using predetermined criteria and individuals chosen to form a representative sample of the electorate, these surveys are common practice in all sorts of fields, especially in industrialised countries. Although they can be an aid to forecasting, they should be treated with caution especially when they relate to foreign policy issues.

No opinion poll can amount to a mandate or confer the power to negotiate. (see *2089*)

2672 – This is not only because the issue must be formulated in a way that is at the same time neutral, intelligible and precise, which is no easy matter in diplomacy. The responses must then be interpreted in a changing context, especially where foreign policy is concerned.

Extrapolating information gathered in this way is all the more dangerous because the publicity surrounding the exercise is not always reliable.

Foreign powers should never attribute any legal or official value to these exercises, even if they appear to reveal trends in opinion.

2673 – Whatever the power of the ballot-box and however sincere the voters' intentions, international authority is not founded on domestic elections alone. *It is not enough for a nation to speak: it must have the power to assert its interests, and its leaders must have the capacity to represent it successfully in negotiations.*

2674 – Founded on trust in the judgement of the electorate, the strength of public opinion and the advisability of consulting it, democracy assumes that governments accept peoples' freedom and regulate how it is exercised, especially in the field of diplomacy, and that they would risk unpopularity rather than conceal danger or failure.

But the methods used to consult the electorate, and the results they produce, are out of step with international needs, and therein lies one of the principle difficulties of negotiation in democracies.

2675 – The question is whether Western democracy is capable of addressing the major problems of the modern world instead of simply exporting its own crises and difficulties, and whether it can subordinate its national goals to imperatives agreed upon in negotiation with other countries, that might sometimes be at variance with its own immediate interests. A further question is whether it can override the choices dictated by its own elections each time it is faced with the harsh realities of confrontation. (see *2361*)

2676 – International society will only be governable if every nation agrees to make real sacrifices, and it is incumbent on their internal political leaders to explain what these are and justify them. Democratic governments will have to devote ever more attention to ensuring that both leaders and people are properly informed about foreign negotiation, competition and cooperation. Furthermore, since States are likely to lose the exclusive privilege of expressing the general will, in the face of other major forces with the means of exerting pressure, they need domestic public opinion to be better informed about national values and international structures in order to support their negotiations. (see *1199*)

2677 – The debate about democracy in foreign negotiation is today central to the fundamental problem of constitutional regimes. *To expect the public to have the imagination, or the resolve, to succeed in a major undertaking is an act of faith in the capacities of the people; to bring out these qualities is the mark of an outstanding and exemplary political leader.*

2678 –Bound by the need to discuss and justify, hampered by the succession of new leaders, and threatened by the abuse of freedoms and powers, the only way for democracy to succeed against totalitarian and technocratic regimes in international negotiation is by fresh initiatives, flexibility of response, and the quality of its leaders. The protection of its interests and its existence depends on its strategists' capacity for innovation and dynamism, assuming they are able to win the nation's deep and lasting support.

2679 – Every negotiation, diplomatic as well as private, is subordinate to strategy. It expresses values, but does not create them. However skilfully it is handled, it offers neither future choices, nor justification for excesses, nor reasons for sacrifice. It is vain to expect it to provide theoretically rigorous solutions: its conduct and outcome may be fair, but they might not be just.

2680 – In public life, no negotiation can have legitimacy unless it is backed by political leaders responsible to the people. Thus, international negotiation is a part of the national power in any democracy. Even within the European Union, negotiation is essential for the Member States to enhance their cooperation while maintaining their national identity.

International negotiation today, both in diplomacy and within the private sector, serves strategic purposes. It demands capability, effectiveness and commitment, not only on the part of the negotiator but also at the level of leadership, especially in a democracy.

2861 – International negotiation cannot provide answers to the great issues of the time. What leader, conscious of the lessons of history and of present-day realities, would take the terrible risk of dismissing any possibility of a return to serious open conflict or consider for an instant that the era of great conquerors and great revolutionaries is finally over? Diplomacy must address these unrelenting, ever-present dangers and it must do so unfailingly if it is to respond to the overwhelming needs of so many nations for harmony, development and peace.

2862 – There can be no international peace between nations that do not enjoy internal peace. Likewise there can be no international order between states that do not enjoy internal order and are unwilling to submit themselves to the principles of international order.

Printed in the United States
109999LV00001B/39/A